DATE DUE

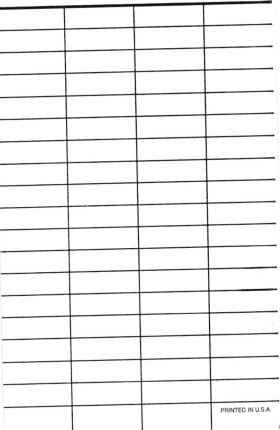

PRINTED IN U.S.A.

When Lions Roar

When Lions Roar

~

THE CHURCHILLS

AND THE

KENNEDYS

~

Thomas Maier

CROWN PUBLISHERS
New York

Published in the United States by Crown Publishers, an imprint of the
Crown Publishing Group, a division of Random House LLC, a Penguin
Random House Company, New York.
www.crownpublishing.com

CROWN and the Crown colophon are registered trademarks of Random
House LLC.

Library of Congress Cataloging-in-Publication Data
Maier, Thomas, 1956–
    When lions roar : the Churchills and the Kennedys / Thomas Maier. —
First edition.
    Includes bibliographical references and index.
    1. Churchill, Winston, 1874–1965—Friends and associates. 2. Kennedy,
John F. (John Fitzgerald), 1917–1963—Friends and associates. 3. Churchill,
Winston, 1874–1965—Family. 4. Kennedy, John F. (John Fitzgerald),
1917–1963—Family. 5. Great Britain—Relations—United States.
6. United States—Relations—Great Britain. 7. Great Britain—Politics and
government—20th century. 8. United States—Politics and government—
20th century. 9. Churchill family. 10. Kennedy family. I. Title. II. Title:
Churchills and the Kennedys.
    DA566.9.C5M235 2014
    941.084092'2—dc23   2014007201

ISBN 978-0-307-95679-8
eBook ISBN 978-0-307-95681-1

PRINTED IN THE UNITED STATES OF AMERICA

Jacket photographs: (front) Keystone/Stringer/Hutton Archive/Getty; (back,
top) JFK Library, (back, bottom) Library of Congress
Author photograph: Joyce P. McGurrin

Frontispiece photographs: (left) The Imperial War Museums;
(right) The John F. Kennedy Presidential Library

10 9 8 7 6 5 4 3 2 1

FIRST EDITION

For my father and sons,

James

and

Andrew, Taylor, and Reade

*Winston at Chartwell. Churchill's magnificent home south of London
vivified his many talents as a writer, politician, raconteur, artist,
landscaper, and even bricklayer.* TIME & LIFE PICTURES/GETTY

"Have I not in my time heard lions roar?"

—WILLIAM SHAKESPEARE, *The Taming of the Shrew*

"Some people pretend to regard me as the British Lion.
But I am not the Lion. I am simply the Roar of the Lion."

—WINSTON CHURCHILL

Contents

Cast of Characters

THE CHURCHILLS

SIR WINSTON CHURCHILL, *prime minister of the United Kingdom (1940–45, 1951–55)*

CLEMENTINE CHURCHILL, *Winston's wife*

RANDOLPH CHURCHILL, *Winston's son*

DIANA CHURCHILL SANDYS, *Winston's daughter*

SARAH CHURCHILL, *Winston's daughter*

MARY CHURCHILL SOAMES, *Winston's daughter*

PAMELA CHURCHILL HARRIMAN, *Randolph's first wife*

JUNE OSBORNE CHURCHILL, *Randolph's second wife*

WINSTON CHURCHILL, *son of Pamela and Randolph*

LORD RANDOLPH CHURCHILL, *Winston's father*

LADY JENNIE CHURCHILL, *Winston's mother*

JACK CHURCHILL, *Winston's brother*

LADY SARAH SPENCER-CHURCHILL, *Winston's cousin*

JOHN CHURCHILL, *First Duke of Marlborough and subject of Winston's biography*

THE KENNEDYS

JOHN FITZGERALD KENNEDY, *thirty-fifth president of the United States (1961–November 22, 1963)*

JACQUELINE BOUVIER KENNEDY, *JFK's wife*

JOSEPH P. KENNEDY, *JFK's father*

ROSE FITZGERALD KENNEDY, *JFK's mother*

JOSEPH P. KENNEDY JR., *JFK's brother*

ROSEMARY KENNEDY, *JFK's sister*

KATHLEEN KENNEDY, *JFK's sister*

EUNICE KENNEDY SHRIVER, *JFK's sister*

PATRICIA KENNEDY LAWFORD, *JFK's sister*

ROBERT F. KENNEDY, *JFK's brother*

JEAN KENNEDY SMITH, *JFK's sister*

EDWARD M. KENNEDY, *JFK's brother*

CAROLINE KENNEDY, *JFK's daughter*

JOHN F. KENNEDY JR., *JFK's son*

JOHN F. "HONEY FITZ" FITZGERALD, *JFK's grandfather*

MUTUAL FRIENDS AND OTHER MAJOR FIGURES

LADY NANCY ASTOR, *Member of Parliament, Kennedy friend and Winston critic*

BERNARD BARUCH, *American businessman, friend of Winston and Joe Kennedy*

LORD BEAVERBROOK, *Max Aitken, British press magnate, friend of Winston and Joe Kennedy*

SEYMOUR BERRY, *son of newspaper owner Lord Camrose, best man at Randolph's wedding, Kathleen Kennedy friend*

LORD BIRKENHEAD, *F. E. Smith, Winston's friend and Conservative Party politician*

SECOND EARL OF BIRKENHEAD, *Frederick "Freddie" Smith, friend of Randolph Churchill and Evelyn Waugh, son of Lord Birkenhead*

BRENDAN BRACKEN, *Winston's top aide, friend of Kennedys*

MARIA CALLAS, *opera singer, Onassis intimate*

LADY JEANNE CAMPBELL, *writer and Beaverbrook granddaughter, Randolph friend and JFK intimate*

DEBORAH CAVENDISH, *Duchess of Devonshire, Kathleen Kennedy sister-in-law, one of six Mitford sisters friendly with Churchills*

WILLIAM CAVENDISH, *Marquess of Hartington, husband of Kathleen Kennedy*

ÉAMON DE VALERA, *Irish leader, critic of Winston, friend of Kennedys*

ANTHONY EDEN, *prime minister of the United Kingdom (1955–57), close aide to Winston, friend of Kennedys*

PETER FITZWILLIAM, *wealthy earl, friend of Randolph and lover of Kathleen Kennedy*

COUNT ENRICO GALEAZZI, *Vatican administrator, friend of Kennedys*

LORD HALIFAX, *British diplomat and politician, Winston rival and friend of Kennedys*

KAY HALLE, *writer-socialite, friend of Churchills and Kennedys*

AVERELL HARRIMAN, *American diplomat, friend of Churchills (later married Pamela Churchill), JFK aide*

HARRY HOPKINS, *FDR aide, friend of Churchills, critic of Joe Kennedy*

TYLER KENT, *U.S. aide convicted of stealing secret Churchill-Roosevelt papers in Ambassador Kennedy's embassy*

HAROLD LASKI, *British economics professor, Labour politician critical of Winston, friend of Kennedys*

CLARE BOOTHE LUCE, *American writer-politician, friend of Kennedys and Churchills*

HENRY LUCE, *publisher, friend of both Kennedys and Churchills*

HAROLD MACMILLAN, *prime minister of United Kingdom (1957–63), Churchill ally, Kennedy distant in-law*

EDWARD R. MURROW, *American broadcaster, friend of Churchills, critic of Joe Kennedy, JFK administration official*

ARISTOTLE ONASSIS, *shipping tycoon, friend of Churchills, married Jacqueline Kennedy*

DAVID ORMSBY-GORE (LATER LORD HARLECH), *British ambassador to the United States, JFK friend*

FRANKLIN D. ROOSEVELT, *U.S. president who sent Joe Kennedy to London as U.S. ambassador, worked with Churchill during World War II*

JAMES ROOSEVELT, *president's son, friend of Kennedys, visited Churchill home in 1933*

ARTHUR M. SCHLESINGER JR., *JFK aide and historian, friend of Randolph Churchill*

EVELYN WAUGH, *novelist, friend of Randolph Churchill and Kathleen Kennedy*

Part I

DYNASTY AND EMPIRE

〜

"All men dream, but not equally. Those who dream by night in the dusty recesses of their minds, wake in the day to find that it was vanity: but the dreamers of the day are dangerous men, for they may act on their dreams with open eyes, to make them possible."
—T. E. LAWRENCE

"Public life is regarded as the crown of a career, and to young men it is the worthiest ambition. Politics is still the greatest and most honorable adventure."
—JOHN BUCHAN, *Pilgrim's Way*

1

Overture: "The Special Relationship"

On the distant hill before them, greatness awaited. Rose Kennedy could feel it in her bones. Her family's long journey from America to England culminated at Chartwell Manor, the magisterial home of Winston Churchill, a celebrated British statesman-writer better known to Americans than the king, George V.

From their approaching automobile, the Kennedys could see the old Tudor-style building made of red brick perched high above a meadow, water gardens, and surrounding beech trees. As their car drove up the winding gravel road of the wooded eighty-acre estate, a large, imposing gate swung open to let them in.

As if by some gravitational pull or providential design, these two dynastic families—one American, one British—seemed fated to meet, their fortunes soon intertwined forever.

"At last the coveted invitation arrived to visit Mr. and Mrs. Winston Churchill at their home in the country outside of London," Rose recalled years later. "We were very excited and delighted at the prospect of meeting him *en famille* as we motored through the lovely English countryside on a typical English rainy day and arrived at the simple comfortable country house for lunch."

Some historians contend that the first meeting between the Kennedys and Churchills took place in October 1935, though there is much to suggest this initial encounter occurred two years earlier, at Chartwell. As the oft-repeated story goes, Winston Churchill and Joseph P. Kennedy, the family patriarchs, began a visceral dislike for each other almost immediately, one that would devolve into rancor and several fateful differences leading up to World War II. "Winston *despised* him," the American diplomat W. Averell Harriman, an intimate of both families, emphatically told historian Arthur M. Schlesinger Jr. four decades later.

But the reality between these two families was far more complicated, as life tends to be, both personally and in public.

When the Kennedys arrived at Chartwell, Rose remembered a most convivial greeting. Churchill's wife, Clementine, came to the door dressed in tweeds and a rose-colored sweater that enhanced her "pink fresh coloring and soft grey hair." Rose took note of Clementine's refined features. "She is one of the most attractive women I have ever met," observed Rose, herself a stylish, thin woman who appeared no worse the wear for having borne nine children. She found Clementine "keen on politics and well-informed" just like her. Winston delighted in shaking their hands. "Mr. Churchill with his puckish face was clad also in tweeds and looked more like a country squire than an English statesman," wrote Rose. "We found him charming, amiable and very frank in his discussion of events."

Like most women of her era, Rose Fitzgerald Kennedy—the daughter of Boston's former mayor and wife of a multimillionaire who aspired to the White House—found herself relegated to the position of an observer, rather than a participant, in the exchanges between powerful men. On both sides of the Atlantic, the world in the early twentieth century was still ruled by fathers and their sons. Yet in Rose's political judgment, savvier than most, Churchill was "one of the great men of the generation." Meeting him at Chartwell merely confirmed her belief.

Undoubtedly, John Fitzgerald Kennedy, her second-oldest son, agreed about Churchill. While recuperating in America from his constant illnesses, young Jack had read many of Winston's accounts of manly heroics, faraway adventures, and bloody battles. Churchill's words captivated young Kennedy, illuminating a world that the often sickly and painfully thin schoolboy could only dream of sharing one day. Within Churchill's sprawling histories, Jack found a piece of himself. He gobbled up the masterful biography *Marlborough*, about John Churchill, the First Duke of Marlborough, an ancient ancestor of Winston's who helped save the British monarchy. (As president years later, Kennedy called *Marlborough* one of his favorite books, along with John Buchan's *Pilgrim's Way*.) In his writings, Churchill offered fascinating lessons in high politics and wartime strategies, combined with moments of personal danger and exemplary acts of courage. Each journey brought a new story of derring-do and near-death escapades told with his trademark wit. "Although always prepared for martyrdom, I preferred that it should be postponed," Churchill explained.

After a rocky start as a student, Winston emerged as a self-made man. He extolled the virtues of the British Empire as one who had seen the world in all its blood and glory and lived to tell about it. As a war correspondent in the Sudan, he witnessed the royal army's last cavalry charge against the frenzied swordsmen called "Whirling Dervishes"— swarming down a hillside with bloodthirsty zeal, "the sun glinting on many thousand hostile spearpoints." In India, Winston avoided death and eluded the onslaught of Pathan tribesmen along the Afghan border, who chased him with their guns ablazing. And in South Africa, Churchill was taken prisoner while covering the Boer War, only to escape and travel secretly on a freight train to freedom while the Boers advertised a bounty for his head. How could any red-blooded American boy like Jack Kennedy not be enthralled by the never-say-die spirit of a British gentleman at war like Winston Churchill?

"In one respect a cavalry charge is very much like ordinary life," Churchill advised. "So long as you are all right, firmly in your saddle, your horse in hand, and well armed, lots of enemies will give you wide berth. But as soon as you have lost a stirrup, have a rein cut, have dropped your weapon, are wounded, then is the moment when from all quarters enemies rush upon you." With a vicarious thrill, Kennedy admired Churchill's eloquence and pluck, the joie de vivre of a man who, after nearly being killed by gunfire, could declare with glee, "Nothing in life is so exhilarating as to be shot at without result."

Most Americans, like the Kennedys, shared a similar heroic image of Churchill. The press portrayed him as a Renaissance man born of the Victorian age yet very much a product of his modern era. Chartwell reflected Churchill's vision of himself as a soldier, writer, essayist, journalist, orator, and statesman. Evidence abounded there of a man who enjoyed being a polo player, huntsman, painter, and even bricklayer. His home was incorporated into the legacy Winston planned for his only son, Randolph, a golden-haired lad who was a more naturally gifted orator than his father. "Chartwell is to be our home," Winston wrote to his wife, Clementine, when they bought the place a decade earlier. "We must endeavour to live there for many years & hand it on to Randolph afterwards."

Life to Winston was part of a family continuum, connected to the history of Great Britain and to all English-speaking peoples. In his own distinctive way, he sometimes acted more like an artist or a historian than a calculating politician. As the *New York Times* observed in 1931, those familiar with Churchill were "astonished by his versatility, and rather bewildered—as if there were something odd about a man who, in addition to having held almost every post in the Cabinet except that of prime minister, can paint pictures that people are proud to hang on their walls, write books that are called masterpieces, build brick houses with his own hands, and make speeches, classic in structure, in quality bold, vivacious, epigrammatic."

The memorable first encounter between the Churchills and the Kennedys came at a nadir in both their lives. By the time the Kennedys arrived at his door, Winston was well into what biographers later called his "wilderness years." During this time, Churchill lost a fortune in the stock market and the heavy expenses of running Chartwell were almost overwhelming him. He suffered a near-fatal accident when a car struck him while he was visiting New York. His bouts with depression—what he called "the black dog"—sometimes got the best of his ebullient spirits. Perhaps most disheartening, the long ascendant arc of Churchill's life in the public arena seemed over. He had switched parties repeatedly, from Conservative to Liberal and back again. "Anyone can rat," he quipped, "but it takes a certain amount of ingenuity to re-rat."

Now at an age when most men thought of retirement, Churchill found himself out of power. He'd alienated enough parliamentary colleagues to wonder if his dream of becoming prime minister would ever come true. He considered leaving politics altogether until longtime friend American financier Bernard Baruch told him he "would be hopeless as a businessman": "Here I am, discarded, cast away, marooned, rejected and disliked," Churchill lamented, as if a lion in winter, a relic from the past.

The future of young Jack Kennedy also seemed much in doubt as he joined his parents on their trip to England in 1935. Jack intended to enroll at the London School of Economics, while "Kick," as nearly everyone called his sister Kathleen, who accompanied them, would study at a convent school in France. Once again, the family's second-oldest son would follow the path set by his older brother, Joseph Jr., a gregarious young man who was his father's favorite. In contrast, Jack had earned the scorn of his parents for his pranks and listless attitude. His tomfool-ery nearly got him tossed from Choate, a top New England preparatory school, where Joe Jr. had been a star football player graduating at the top of his class. In a letter comparing his two older sons, Joe Kennedy Sr. admitted to Choate's headmaster that "the happy-go-lucky manner with a degree of indifference that he [Jack] shows towards the things that he has no interest in does not portend well for his future develop-ment."

Exasperated with his son, Joe Kennedy first tried reasoning with him. "Now Jack, I don't want to give the impression that I am a nagger, for goodness knows I think that is the worse [*sic*] thing any parent can be, and I also feel that you know if I didn't really feel you had the goods I would be most charitable in my attitude towards your failings," wrote his father in December 1934. "After long experience in sizing up people I definitely know you have the goods and you can go a long way. Now aren't you foolish not to get all there is out of what God has given you and what you can do with it yourself."

A few months later, after a French teacher complained about Jack's lack of success in class, Joe let his second son know he'd had quite enough. "Don't let me lose confidence in you again, because it will be pretty nearly an impossible task to restore it—I am sure it will be a loss to you and distinct loss to me," Joe Sr. warned. "The mere trying to do a good job is not enough—real honest-to-goodness effort is what I expect."

Going to London offered a second chance for Jack Kennedy, a way to redeem and redefine himself in the eyes of his father.

The senior Kennedy also hoped for a new beginning. His own politi-cal future appeared uncertain, if not finished, as he claimed. He'd left the administration of President Franklin D. Roosevelt after a short but remarkably successful stint as the first chairman of the U.S. Securities and Exchange Commission. In appointing Kennedy, a wily Wall Street speculator who had managed to keep his fortune amid the stock market crash of 1929, FDR joked that he'd "set a thief to catch a thief." To the surprise of many, Joe Kennedy proved a tough-minded administrator and a pioneering regulator against Wall Street abuses. Before leaving for London in 1935, Kennedy wrote a letter of thanks to the publisher of the *New York Times* for praising his SEC stewardship in an editorial. "I am leaving public life today for good," Kennedy avowed, "but before I go I want to express my appreciation to you for all the courtesies paid to me."

Despite what he said, Joe Kennedy's pals knew he'd soon be back in the political limelight. Baruch, a business associate to both Kennedy and Churchill, recognized that Joe longed for a bigger prize: to become the first Irish Catholic elected president, even if such a chance was a laughable long shot. Before Kennedy departed New York, Baruch had sent a cable to Winston Churchill reminding him of Kennedy's growing prominence.

SUGGEST YOUR WIRING HIM MAKING APPOINTMENT TO SEE HIM AS HE IS IMPORTANT AND GOOD RELATIONSHIP BETWEEN YOU TWO MIGHT HAVE FAR REACHING RESULTS, read Baruch's note arriving at Chartwell.

Baruch also sent an affectionate note to Kennedy: BON VOYAGE TO THE TOP CHAIRMAN AND AFFECTIONATE GOOD WISHES TO HIS FAMILY.

Soon, aboard the massive *Normandie,* a French ocean liner with splendid Art Deco interiors, the Kennedys received a cable from Winston Churchill: TRUST I MAY HAVE PLEASURE OF MEETING YOU OVER HERE PLEASE CABLE YOUR MOVEMENTS.

Surely a pleasant social visit between the Kennedys and the Churchills would pay dividends down the road—even if Winston's and Joe's political careers were indeed over, and even if they never reached, respectively, 10 Downing Street and 1600 Pennsylvania Avenue, as they aspired. In this friendly exchange, there was always the next generation to consider, the lasting legacy. Perhaps the "far reaching results" from such a Chartwell meeting would someday be recalled fondly by the two family members with, quite arguably, the brightest political futures of all: Randolph Churchill and Joe Kennedy Jr.

During lunch at Chartwell, Rose remembered, Winston envisioned "a special relationship," as he later called it, between Great Britain and its former backwoods colony, the United States of America. He argued for a strong navy, developed together, that "would dominate the world and police it and keep the other nations in their present status quo." Churchill conceded that his plan was "impractical" because of opposition from American isolationists, especially in places such as Boston. "Too many Irish haters of England, too many people that would prefer to remain outside England's sphere," Churchill complained. Well ahead of his time, he worried about "the rising Nazi strength" and how an Anglo-American force could stop it. Rose's written recollection, now contained in the John F. Kennedy Presidential Library, doesn't mention what her husband might have said in reply, if anything. Although archivists contend it pertains to a 1935 meeting, this typewritten note by the usually fastidious Rose specifically states that this first meeting took place in 1933, when the Kennedys did indeed visit London for a very important and secret business reason. The mystery surrounding the year underlines the overall misunderstandings about the origins of the "special relationship" between the two great families.

When they finished eating, Rose recalled, the Churchills walked leisurely with their guests over to Winston's painting studio. Colorful pictures of flowers, vegetables, and other still lifes were displayed all over. Rose noticed each in various stages of completion. She marveled at Churchill's sensibilities. Back home, politicians known to Rose were usually found in saloons, not their own salon. "I cannot pretend to be impartial about the colours," Winston once observed of his artwork. "I rejoice with the brilliant ones, and am genuinely sorry for the poor browns."

As for the rest of the residence, Winston had carefully supervised Chartwell's reconstruction, pouring in nearly more money than he possessed, until the place became as vibrant as the man himself. Inside its study, Winston composed countless books, articles, speeches, and correspondence, enough so his literary voice reached the most distant audience. All around the manor, Churchill allowed beloved dogs, cats, white and black swans, fish, and rare horses to roam, thus creating his own world. In a butterfly house, he collected the white-veined variety of flying insects. Occasionally, he'd release them into the English countryside, where such beautiful creatures were otherwise extinct. Even farm animals became part of the family. He could wax poetic on the nobility of the pig. "You carve him, Clemmie," he said of one goose about to be eaten. "He was a friend of mine."

By the time of the Kennedy visit, Winston was in his sixth decade of a life now seemingly in repose. His pale, almost alabaster face was puffier than ever with the exaction of age. No longer was he a youthful warrior. His light red hair crestfallen from his brow, the sagging muscles of his chest, and the droop of his middle belied his reputation as a man of action. All that he still possessed, it seemed, were his lively eyes, the swaggering curl of his lip, and his cocksure smile. In the comfort of his beloved Chartwell, Churchill greeted guests wearing an open-throated white silk shirt or a dressing gown, and slippers embroidered with Oriental dragons, rather than his usual parliamentary three-piece suit with a polka-dot bow tie and carrying a gold-headed cane. He intermingled visitors between games of bezique and backgammon, his sipping of Scotch whiskey and champagne, his two baths a day and an after-lunch nap. "My tastes are simple," he'd proclaim. "I like only the best."

Eventually the Kennedys strolled with their host past the brick wall Winston had built surrounding the main house. Block by block, squeezed with mortar, Churchill had pieced together the wall with his own hands while an expensive cigar dangled from his mouth. In the 1930s he oversaw the construction of two cottages, water gardens and an elaborate man-made falls with golden carp swimming in them, and a heated swimming pool for the human guests to enjoy. (Ever mindful of their family's burdensome expenses, Clementine made sure to turn off the electric motors as soon as everyone left the water.) Rose Kennedy marveled at the redbrick wall built by this great figure. "It seemed a queer avocation for a man to have, a man of letters, a man who had been brought up to shoot, to ride, to fish like all other Englishmen," she wrote, "but there was his hobby and there was the wall to bear mute testimony." During their chat together, Clementine asked Rose whether America's current First Lady, Eleanor Roosevelt, was "an exhibitionist and was using her husband's high office to court publicity for herself." Rose assured her this wasn't so. "I tried to convince her that I thought Mrs. Roosevelt was sincere," Rose recalled. "Gradually people would become accustomed to her unconventional approaches." This exchange further suggests that their first meeting took place in the fall of 1933, when the public controversy surrounding the new outspoken First Lady was in full fury in the newspapers.

There is no doubt, however, about an October 1935 meeting at Chartwell between the two families. Soon after that later visit, Joe Kennedy Sr. sent a telegram to Bernard Baruch telling him that all had gone well with their friend in Great Britain, wording it as if they had been there before. The (unpunctuated) cable read: ROSE AND I HAD MOST PLEASANT TIME WE HAVE EVER HAD AT CHURCHILLS THANK YOU APPRECIATE IT MORE THAN I CAN TELL YOU BACK HERE IN A COUPLE OF WEEKS SEEING HIM AGAIN. But a planned follow-up meeting with Churchill was postponed indefinitely. Jack contracted hepatitis shortly after arriving in London, forcing both father and son to change plans. Poor health had plagued young Kennedy for years, requiring him to be hospitalized several times, including at the Mayo Clinic. Jack's condition was a constant concern for his parents, even seemingly trivial matters. "Jack's blood count was checked yesterday and it is back to normal," Joe noted to Rose a year earlier. "His eyes were checked and they have taken away his glasses. He needs only light ones."

Prior to leaving America for the 1935 visit, the Kennedy patriarch had let Jack's instructors at Choate know that he planned for his second son to "meet the high officials of three or four countries" before starting at the London School of Economics. But the sudden deterioration in Jack's health alarmed his father enough to bring him back immediately to the United States, where he would be treated by specialists who feared he might have leukemia. "Jack is far from being a well boy," Joe informed Robert Worth Bingham, the U.S. ambassador in London, shortly after his family's trip, "and as a result I am afraid my time for the next six months will be devoted to trying to help him regain his health with little or no time for business and politics."

When he heard about young Kennedy's failing health, Winston sent a sympathetic note to Joe, as one father to another: "I am deeply grieved at your anxiety about your son and earnestly trust it will soon be relieved." The question was not whether John F. Kennedy would become a great man, but whether he would live at all.

This thoughtful letter sparked another interchange between the Kennedys and the Churchills, part of a complex relationship over the ensuing decades. They would meet many times again, in both triumph and tragedy, often against the backdrop of splendid façades or wartime destruction. Their overlapping circles of friends, lovers, and political associates would help define these two extraordinary families as historians traced their public actions. But few knew how much of their personal lives and interests had crossed already, well before this exchange, and defined the drama to come.

2

A Troublesome Boy

"Malborough s'en va-t-en guerre. Dieu sait quand reviendra." ("Marlborough has gone off to war, God knows when he'll return.")

—LEO TOLSTOY, *War and Peace*

Mark Twain, the longtime bard of the Mississippi, introduced Winston Churchill to a crowd of wealthy Americans packed inside New York's Waldorf Astoria hotel ballroom in December 1900—one of those rare meetings of historic figures that occurred so often in Churchill's life. "I was thrilled by this famous companion of my youth," Winston recalled of Twain, a literary inspiration. "He was now very old and snow-white, and combined with a noble air a most delightful style of conversation."

Winston expected to be lionized by Twain but instead had his tail tweaked. The twenty-six-year-old celebrated British war correspondent was on a lecture tour, picking up handsome fees to talk about his bloody adventures and headline-grabbing writings on imperial conflicts around the globe. By contrast, Twain, at age sixty-five, loathed the chest-beating of war—especially the jingoistic, romanticized accounts of farm boys ground up and left for dead on the battlefield. Twain feared his nation might someday become an empire like Great Britain. The night's verbal swordplay between the old American and the young

Englishman reflected so many differences between the Crown and its former colony.

Within no time, Twain whittled Churchill down a peg or two. Although his friendly introduction wasn't a tar-and-feathering, Twain made plain how wrongheaded Churchill had been about the British Empire pestering those poor indigent people in places like India and South Africa. Churchill "knew all about war and nothing about peace," Twain told the standing-room-only audience, many of whom seemed to agree with him. As an account of the evening by the *New York Times* explained, "War might be very interesting to persons who like that sort of entertainment, but he [Twain] never enjoyed it himself."

Graciously, Twain ended this battle of wits by proclaiming he'd always favored good relations between England and the United States. He even touted the night's guest speaker as a product of such amity. "Mister Churchill by his father is an Englishman, by his mother he is an American—no doubt a blend that makes a perfect match," Twain declared. "England and America, we are kin. And now that we are also kin in sin, there is nothing more to be desired."

It was a closing line by the old master intended to bring a hearty laugh by all.

Churchill's encounter with Mark Twain appears in the former's 1930 autobiography, *My Early Life*, certainly one of his most revealing books. On display in it are the conflicting themes of Winston's life: his tortured relationship with his famous father, whose legacy he strove to exceed; his sense of being half-American despite an unswerving loyalty to the British Crown; and his fascination with war, both as an adventurer-writer and a statesman-politician who deeply understood the power of words.

While war and peace provided a backdrop for his 1900 lecture tour, commerce remained Churchill's frontline concern. He had been elected recently to Parliament, but without a steady source of income. A seat in the House of Commons then didn't pay any salary, and Churchill depended on his writing assignments for a living. An agent convinced him he could earn a tidy sum by lecturing in America. "I have so much need for money and we cannot afford to throw away a single shilling," he confided to his mother.

America always held a special affinity for Churchill. Five years earlier, he had visited his mother's New York cousins and been mightily impressed by the young nation's restless energy. "Picture to yourself the American people as a great lusty youth—who treads on all your sensibilities and perpetrates every possible horror of ill manner—whom neither age nor just tradition inspire with reverence—but who moves about his affairs with a good hearted freshness which may well be the envy of older nations of the earth," Churchill described to his brother in a note echoing Alexis de Tocqueville. In New York, he met Congressman William Bourke Cockran, an Irish American friend of his mother's and a riveting public speaker, upon whom Winston modeled his own rhetoric. "You are indeed an orator," Churchill told Cockran. "And of all the gifts there is none so rare and precious as that." Winston learned to argue convincingly rather than divisively, to persuade rather than condemn. Although British at heart, he described himself as "a child of both worlds." Friends such as Violet Bonham Carter (whose father, Henry H. Asquith, became prime minister) thought of Winston as half-American—both "an aristocrat and yet our greatest Commoner." Driven more by an innate power than any belief in the divine, Winston seemed destined to find a place in history. "We are all worms," he told Bonham Carter. "But I do believe that I am a glow worm."

This potent cross-Atlantic combination of genes seemed a key to Churchill's compelling personality, what the British historian A. L. Rowse called "the strength of the two natures mixed in him—the self-willed English aristocrat and the equally self-willed primitive American—each with a hundred-horsepower capacity for getting his way." Winston was amused by those who traced his American roots to the Iroquois or to America's 1776 Revolutionary leader against the British. "It certainly is inspiring to see so great a name as George Washington upon the list," Winston said of one published genealogy. "I understand, however, that if you go back far enough everyone is related to everyone else, and we end up in Adam."

In recounting Churchill's early years, more Freudian-minded historians suggest the chaotic marriage of his brilliant, erratic, and possibly syphilitic father, Lord Randolph Churchill, and his beautiful, promiscuous, and social-climbing mother, the former Jennie Jerome, created an emotional ache that Winston sought to remedy his entire life. "She shone for me like the Evening Star," Winston recalled of his Brooklyn-born mother. "I loved her dearly—but at a distance."

Jennie grew up the multi-talented daughter of Leonard Jerome, a Wall Street speculator and racetrack operator (his initial fortune made in Rochester, New York, publishing the newspaper house organ for the anti-immigrant Know-Nothing Party). In describing the aggressive tycoon Jerome, Churchill biographer Roy Jenkins later said "there was a touch of Joseph P. Kennedy about him." Jennie wed Lord Randolph in Paris after an abrupt romance that produced Winston's premature arrival eight months later, on November 30, 1874.

Like his father, Winston Leonard Spencer Churchill was born at Blenheim Palace, his family's ancestral home and the most celebrated residence in England next to Buckingham Palace. Blenheim, a sprawling Gothic castle on two thousand acres, had been a gift to John Churchill, the First Duke of Marlborough, by a grateful nation for masterfully defeating the French in 1704. (Marlborough's reputation was such that his name was invoked in Tolstoy's *War and Peace*.) Though born half-American, Winston never wavered in his allegiance to king and queen. He dedicated his life to defending the far-flung British Empire where the sun never set. At the turn of the century, Australia, British East Africa, Canada, Egypt, Hong Kong, India, Iraq, Ireland, Pakistan, and South Africa were part of the colonies and imperial interests spread gloriously around the world, like jewels in a crown. "I was a child of the Victoria era," Churchill explained, "when the structure of our country seemed firmly set, when its position in trade and on the seas was unrivalled, and when the realisation of our Empire and of our duty to preserve it was ever growing stronger."

Winston's childhood, at least the first "wavering lights and shadows of dawning consciousness," began in the most unlikely of places: Eire. "My earliest memories are Ireland," he explained in his autobiography. "I can recall scenes and events in Ireland quite well, and sometimes dimly, even people." The Churchills wound up there when Randolph gained an appointment to serve as private secretary to his father, the Seventh Duke of Marlborough, named Lord Lieutenant of Ireland in a predominantly Catholic land then yearning for its independence. Randolph found this haven after a quarrel back home involving the Prince of Wales prompted his temporary banishment.

In Ireland, Winston quickly learned about violence, and that not all imperial inhabitants appreciated British rule. The stabbing of Lord Frederick Cavendish, the chief secretary for Ireland, by four knife-wielding Irish extremists, who butchered Cavendish in Dublin's Phoenix Park, became part of Churchill lore. (A visiting former Boston mayor, John F. "Honey Fitz" Fitzgerald, on a 1908 trip with his young daughter Rose, called the murder spot "a Catholic monument.") Lord Randolph Churchill told reporters that he felt "confident it was the work of Fenians." The adult most responsible for Winston's parenting, his beloved nurse, Mrs. Elizabeth Everett, detested these Irish-Catholic upstarts and their religion. "Mrs. Everett was very much against the

Pope," Winston recalled. "If the truth were known, she said, he was behind the Fenians." Naturally, Mrs. Everett's view "prejudiced me strongly against that personage and all religious practices supposed to be associated with him."

As a Member of Parliament, Lord Randolph, never a stalwart of consistency, blew hot and cold about the Irish question, as he did on most everything. At first he seemed to favor the home rule measures proposed by Irish Republican Charles Parnell. Then he changed his mind, deciding to "play the Orange card." He supported the Ulster Protestants in Northern Ireland, who didn't want any part of a government run by the Catholic majority to the south. "Ulster will fight, and Ulster will be *right*," he railed.

Lord Randolph emerged as an outspoken leader of the Conservative Party, formulating his own brand of "tory democracy" that critics derided as nothing more than sheer opportunism. With his dark, glaring eyes and thick handlebar mustache, he proved himself a mesmerizing orator, enjoying a rapid ascension in government. At his career pinnacle in 1886, Lord Randolph became the Chancellor of the Exchequer, responsible for all money matters in Britain. But this proved a momentary post after he wound up quitting in a huff. He never recovered politically. Increasingly, Lord Randolph's excessive behavior—wild drinking sprees and carousing with women—seemed to take a toll on his mental well-being. "No man is so entirely alone and solitary as I am," he bemoaned.

Alarmed at her husband's deteriorating health, Jennie hoped to revive his spirits by accompanying him on a tour around the globe. Randolph only became worse, dying in 1895 at the age of forty-five. "A veil of the incalculable shrouded the workings of his complex nature," Winston later wrote of his father's last days. "No one could tell what he would do, or by what motive, lofty or trivial, of conviction or caprice, of irritation or self-sacrifice, he would be governed." Most family members, including then-twenty-year-old Winston, believed Randolph died of syphilis, though the true cause, like the man himself, remained a mystery.

Lord Randolph Churchill's death ended an agonizing relationship with his older son, though never completely enough to heal Winston's wounded feelings. Admittedly, Winston could be "a troublesome boy," a red-haired ruffian who didn't think twice about "cocking a snook at anyone who got in his way." Throughout Winston's adolescence, his father berated him as a poor student destined for uninspiring mundanity, or even worse, as someone to be purposely ignored. At age ten, while away at a prep school near Brighton, Winston read in the local newspaper that Lord Randolph had given a speech in town; though his father never stopped by to visit him. "I cannot think why you did not come to see me, while you were in Brighton," Winston beseeched his father. "I was very busy but I suppose you were too busy to come."

Winston struggled mightily to overcome a speech impediment, a lisp that slurred each sibilant he uttered. His father deemed him inadequate for Eton or for a life in the law. So off Winston went instead to Harrow, boarding school, and then he was admitted, on the third try, to the Royal Military Academy at Sandhurst. In a cold, distant tone, Randolph performed his fatherly duty by chastising his wayward son for his transgressions. His lashing in words surely stung. "I am certain that if you cannot prevent yourself from leading the idle useless unprofitable life you have had during your schooldays & later months, you will become a mere social wastrel one of the hundreds of the public school failures," he admonished, "and you will degenerate into shabby unhappy & futile existence." Whatever hope Winston had for closeness with his father was firmly rebuffed. "If ever I began to show the slightest idea of comradeship, he was immediately offended," Winston recalled of his futile search for approval.

Jennie Churchill's remoteness also wounded her son. Too busy with social affairs in royal circles, she didn't even bother writing much to him while he was away. "You must be happy without me, no screams from Jack or complaints," Winston chastised, after he and his younger brother, Jack, left home following a Christmas visit. "It must be heaven on earth." As Winston grew older, he undoubtedly learned of his mother's numerous affairs—before and after his hapless father died—and the effect of her vivaciousness on men. One of her intimates, Lord D'Abernon, described Lady Churchill's beauty with deepest appreciation: "A diamond star in her hair, her favourite ornament—its lustre dimmed by the flashing glory of her eyes. More of the panther than of the woman in her look, but with a cultivated intelligence unknown to the jungle." Five years after Lord Randolph's death, Jennie married a much younger man, the same age as Winston. When she took on yet a third husband, in 1918, following a divorce, she told friends, "He has a future and I have a past, so we should be all right." Only when Winston emerged as a prominent adult did his mother seem to notice. Jennie became her son's ambitious adviser, though never an adoring maternal figure as Mrs. Everett, his nanny, had been to him. Though Winston would acknowledge of Jennie, "in my interest she left no wire unpulled, no stone unturned, no cutlet uncooked," he was "now in the main the master of my fortunes."

Lord Randolph's tragic, scandalous demise continued to haunt Winston. He sought a public exoneration from Lord Randolph's critics, somehow to relieve his own hurt. After his father's death, Winston vowed, "The dunce of the family will take revenge on the whole pack of curs and traitors." Years later, in his first speech in the House of Commons, he mentioned "a certain splendid memory" of his father—probably the only one in the hall who shared it. Most wondered if Lord

Churchill's son might suffer the same fate. In 1904, when Winston forgot his words and had to abandon a speech in the House of Commons, some suggested that he, too, was going mad, "possessed by the spirit of his father." Winston insisted that his father had been a great man, grossly misunderstood, and vowed to resurrect Lord Randolph's image from disgrace. He pretended they had planned to fight for a common cause someday in the House of Commons. "All my dreams of comradeship with him, of entering Parliament at his side and in his support, were ended," he wrote decades after his father's death. "There remained for me only to pursue his aims and vindicate his memory."

As a way of rewriting history, Winston turned to words to express his feelings about his father. After a handful of successful books about his own war experiences, his first major biography appeared in 1906, the two-volume *Lord Randolph Churchill*, a literary work far worthier than the real life it depicted. The American president, Theodore Roosevelt, called it "a clever, forceful, rather cheap and vulgar life of that clever, forceful, rather cheap and vulgar egotist." The *New York Times* reviewer, however, said that Winston's book "has rendered good service to his father's memory." In England, one editorialist, like others at home who knew father and son more closely, concluded that Winston was "in fact, a more stable and less meteoric but in many respects an equally brilliant edition of his father."

Stability in life, never a constant for Winston, emerged with his marriage to Clementine Hozier in 1908. Like Winston, Clementine came from an influential family wracked by infidelity, enough that her actual biological father remains in dispute. In her own life, Clementine was determined to have a faithful union. Winston, tired of the sexual intrigue among his own parents, admired Clementine for her sincere character as well as considerable beauty. "For what can be more glorious than to be united with a being incapable of an ignoble thought?" he rejoiced, placing Clementine on an idealized pedestal where she'd remain for the next half century. Tall and statuesque, Clementine resembled a Greek goddess found on a pedestal or an ancient coin, with wide expressive eyes, a long neck, and wavy brown hair wrapped above her head. She possessed both intelligence and moral clarity, and came to understand Winston's grand intentions as no other. Single-mindedly devoted to his cause, she became his tireless advocate in trying political times and an honest broker when he needed a dose of reality. "My business and my toys have made me a poor companion," he confessed to her. "I will never love any woman in the world but you," he said, expressing his gratitude "for so much happiness in a world of accident and storm." Together they brought five children into the world: Diana, Randolph (named for Winston's father), Sarah, Mary, and Marigold, who died of illness as an infant.

Winston's career remained center stage, however, as his headstrong ascent to power paralleled his late father's path. Like Lord Randolph, he was described as a "young man in a hurry," convinced of his future greatness. Winston's proficiency with words, recapturing heroic moments and analyzing epic wars, would help turn his personal fame from writing into political capital. In particular, he became a national celebrity after the details became known of his 1899 exploits covering the Boer War, the armed independence fight by Dutch settlers and local farmers against the British Empire in southern Africa.

Aboard an armored British Army train, Winston acted bravely to free the engine when the attacking Boers suddenly derailed the rest of the locomotive. Under heavy enemy gunfire, four British soldiers were killed and thirty more wounded. With bullets whistling past his head, Winston helped carry those hit by gunfire into the engine's cab and coal car, and ordered the driver to take off for safety. Most remarkably, Winston then headed back to the disabled train cars to aid the other soldiers. Unarmed, he was captured by the Boers. For weeks he remained a prisoner. He argued that his credentials as a foreign press correspondent should allow him to be freed, but laudatory newspaper accounts of his heroic actions in freeing the train engine convinced the Dutch-speaking local government officials to keep him jailed.

One night, Winston managed to escape. He hitched a ride on a supply train traveling through the night. Before daylight, he jumped off the train and hid for days in an underground mine. Meanwhile, the Boer government issued a twenty-five-pound reward for his capture, dead or alive. Perhaps most cruelly, in its description of him, the Wanted poster mentioned his lisp, saying he "cannot pronounce the letter 's.'" Winston fled in another train, hidden among bales of wool, until he arrived in Portuguese East Africa, where the British consulate immediately announced his freedom. He remained in Africa for a time, but by 1900 he had returned home, where he was elected to Parliament on the fame from his adventures.

"I believe I am to be preserved for future things," Winston wrote to his mother about his Boer War experience. With his photo in newspapers and his heroism celebrated around the world (including the New York audience with Mark Twain), many believed Churchill was headed for greatness.

Unlike his father's meteoric political career, which swiftly disintegrated, Winston's public trajectory proved more up and down—a long, tumultuous ride in which he bumped his head more than once. In 1911, as part of the Liberal government of Prime Minister H. H. Asquith, Winston became the First Lord of the Admiralty, one of the most important jobs in the Cabinet. As World War I approached, he threw himself into the task of defending England and its far-flung dominion—from learning how to fly a fighter plane to masterminding large-scale military attacks. He did so with the utmost faith in the British Empire and his destiny as a Churchill to lead it.

"The Great War" humbled Winston, however. This four-year global conflagration starting in 1914 left him feeling unprepared despite his lessons at the military academy, his historical study of war, and a lifetime of serving with the Fourth Queen's Own Hussars and other cavalry regiments. The romance of a courageous warrior charging on horseback had given way to the sooty horsepower of the faceless tank—dismissed by the British as "a pretty mechanical toy" until Winston came along. Churchill had first recognized the impact of machines in battle two decades earlier, while witnessing the slaughter of the ill-equipped Dervishes in the Sudan. "These were as brave men as ever walked the earth . . . destroyed, not conquered, by machinery," Winston wrote in his second book, *The River War.*

In the twentieth century, modern warfare among nations taught him of technology's decisive killing power. With armies stuck in deadly trench warfare, grinding up thousands of soldiers, Churchill championed the production of tanks that could leap across the enemy front in impressive strides. He also favored gigantic railway guns, heavy trench mortars, and other military equipment that could provide the needed edge for victory. As First Lord of the Admiralty, he pressed for funds to build new submarines and update all battleships in his command, convinced that these armored vessels were vital to the Crown. Facing sophisticated attacks by the Germans in 1916, Churchill bristled at British commanders who suggested his reforms threatened the Royal Navy's storied traditions. "And what are they?" he demanded, with utter contempt before storming out of one strategy meeting. "They are rum, sodomy and the lash—Good morning, gentlemen!"

In war, Churchill learned that diplomacy could be another weapon, though implemented more subtly, especially with allies. He forged an alliance of fleets with the usually prickly French. He overcame difficulties with the Russians, though never his revulsion for communism and their Bolshevik Revolution. Churchill recognized America's neutrality until 1917 as a reflection of that country's isolationist history and its wariness of foreign entanglements, even if it frustrated his own British colleagues. "It was natural that the Allies, burning with indignation against Germany, breathless and bleeding in the struggle, face to face with mortal dangers, should stand amazed at the cool, critical, detached attitude of the great Power across the Atlantic," he explained. Not all his dealings with Americans were amiable. In 1918, he managed to alienate a young Franklin D. Roosevelt, then U.S. assistant secretary of the navy, who had traveled to London for a strategy session. "He acted like a stinker at a dinner I attended, lording it over all of us," Roosevelt later told Joe Kennedy. The war's most lasting American friendship for Churchill was with Bernard Baruch, the wealthy businessman appointed by President Woodrow Wilson to oversee U.S. munitions. Unfortunately, this alliance didn't come along in time to save Churchill from the most embarrassing calamity of his early career.

As First Lord of the Admiralty, Churchill promoted an ambitious naval plan for the Allies to free up the Dardanelles Straits—the vital but treacherous waterway leading from the Mediterranean to the Russian ports in the Black Sea. If successful, this bold strategy, Winston believed, could end the brutal stalemate of trench warfare along the Western Front and help his nation win the war—a move just as daring as Marlborough's at Blenheim a century before. But the pivotal 1915 fight along the Gallipoli peninsula in Turkey proved disastrous. More than forty thousand British and French soldiers died in the bloody, poorly executed campaign. "He came, he saw, he capitulated," Winston complained of one general's evacuation plan at Gallipoli. The massive loss of life and the collapse of his own once-bright career personally devastated Winston. The political fallout led to his exclusion from a newly formed coalition Cabinet, leaving him in exile on Parliament's backbench. "I had long hours of utterly unwanted leisure in which to contemplate the frightful unfolding of war," he later confided.

Eventually, as if to atone for the Gallipoli disaster, he joined the fighting at the front, gaining command of an infantry battalion. Under fire in Belgium, he characteristically wore his French helmet and led his Scottish soldiers into the fray without flinching. "It's no damn use ducking," he advised one comrade after some artillery fire, "the bullet has gone a long way past you by now." Once again, at age forty-one, he faced the no-man's land of battle, wondering in letters whether he'd survive. Clementine, at home with their toddlers, assured him, "When it is all over we shall be proud that you were a soldier & not a politician for the greater part of the war." Many known to Churchill didn't survive, including the prime minister's son Raymond Asquith, killed in combat. "The War which found the measure of so many never got to the bottom of him," Churchill wrote of young Asquith, a passage Jack Kennedy later memorized; ". . . he went to his fate cool, poised, resolute, matter-of-fact, debonair." Family legacy remained uppermost in Winston's mind. While fighting with the frontline troops during the war, he wrote to Clementine, "If anything should happen to me, Randolph will carry the torch."

By mid-1917, Churchill returned to London and became minister of munitions, dealing often with Baruch, who held a similar job in America. Both agreed that the outcome of this war, in which some fighting men still rode on horseback, would be decided by industrial supremacy rather than methods of yesterday. "Nature has made you and Winston Churchill for each other and it does you both great good to meet," Brendan Bracken, one of Winston's closest political associates, assured Baruch. Working together, Baruch and Churchill ensured that the flow of nitrates from Chile (a key ingredient for explosives, located in only a few sources in the world) remained in Allied rather than German hands. Though Churchill's appointment as minister of munitions had been motivated by diplomatic reasons, he seized the opportunity as his political rebirth. "I now became the Nitrate King," he enthused, "the greatest there will ever be."

After victory in the Great War, America retreated to a postwar "Roaring Twenties" isolation. Winston Churchill returned home to compose his best-selling book about the conflict, called *The World Crisis*. When the first volume appeared in 1923, former prime minister Arthur Balfour labeled it "Winston's brilliant autobiography, disguised as a history of the universe." The four-volume work helped rehabilitate Churchill's political image with the British people and reinforced his international renown. "Politics are almost as exciting as war, and quite as dangerous," he observed. "In war, you can only be killed once, but in politics many times."

Churchill's fidelity to the British Empire remained undaunted, even if the imperialism of its past might be fading. Appointed as the British secretary of state for war in 1919 and then for the colonies, Churchill relied on advisers such as the white-robed T. E. Lawrence, popularly known as "Lawrence of Arabia," to exert a powerful interest in the Middle East. "He [Lawrence] looked what he was, one of Nature's greatest princes," declared Churchill, who knew a master showman when he saw one. In carving up the old Ottoman Empire after World War I, Churchill helped create the modern state of Iraq, defended Egypt's Suez Canal, and maintained Britain's lucrative oil interests in the Gulf region. Prophetically, he warned that the armistice terms that ended World War I would only invite another war. "The causes of war have been in no way removed," he cautioned, with "the soul of Germany smoldering with dreams of a war of liberation or revenge."

Ireland galvanized Winston's attention again in the early 1920s. Despite his father's old opposition, Churchill cosigned the Anglo-Irish

Treaty creating a self-governing Irish Free State in the south. He made sure Britain kept control of three important deepwater ports at Berehaven, Cobh, and Lough Swilly, which had been important in battling German U-boats. He also approved the methods of the much-hated Black and Tans (royal constables) in thwarting Irish Republican Army activities, which he likened to the Chicago or New York police battling armed gangs. Though he admired Michael Collins, an Irish leader who negotiated the treaty, Churchill grew to loathe Irish president Éamon de Valera, who opposed the agreement, as a murdering extremist. During this drama, Scotland Yard picked up an IRA irregular carrying an assassination list of prominent Englishmen, Winston's name at the top. Undoubtedly, it reminded Churchill of the Fenian stabbing of Lord Cavendish a generation earlier in Dublin's Phoenix Park. "I've had a number of threatening letters each week, some telling me the actual time and method of my death—and I don't like it," Churchill deplored. That these nationalists might be patriots didn't occur to Winston, even though Clementine reminded him that, if born Irish, he'd probably have been with the Fenians, too.

Eventually, Churchill's dissatisfaction with the Liberal Party prompted his return to the Conservative Party, after he was appointed Chancellor of the Exchequer. With this new round of party switching, "Winston was very unpopular," remembered his friend and biographer Lady Violet Bonham Carter, a sister to Raymond Asquith. "The Liberals regarded him as an *arriviste* and a thruster—and the Conservatives as a deserter, a rat and a traitor to his class." As head of the Treasury, Winston initially gained praise and advocated England's return to the gold standard. But unlike King Midas, Churchill saw his economic moves soon turn to mud, and cause deflation, strikes, and unemployment.

His political fortunes fell swiftly. In 1929 the Conservatives lost in the general election, and many in the party, including Neville Chamberlain, privately criticized Winston for his self-centered behavior and out-of-date notions, such as denying independence to India. Lady Astor, another Conservative in Parliament, called him a warmonger. When they returned to power, the Tories kept Churchill out of the Cabinet. He seemed permanently exiled—lost in "the wilderness," the term he would use to describe this era in his life.

At age fifty-five, a decade longer than his father had lived, Winston thought his political career might be over, his dream of becoming prime minister never realized. "I have made up my mind that if N[eville] Ch[amberlain] is made leader of the CP or anyone else of that kind, I clear out of politics & see if I cannot make you and the kittens a little more comfortable before I die," he vowed to Clementine.

For the time being, Churchill would try to make money the only way he knew how: with words.

3

Speaking Engagements

At a Hollywood reception in 1929, Randolph Churchill glowed like a movie star. The handsome eighteen-year-old Oxford student, dressed in a dark suit and white shirt and tie, with his wavy blond hair neatly combed, gazed at all the famous faces around him. Inside the MGM ballroom in Culver City, they had gathered to honor his father. Nearby on the dais, the multimillionaire newspaper tycoon William Randolph Hearst and movie mogul Louis B. Mayer smiled royally, like kings of Tinseltown. Their guest of honor, Winston Churchill, sat between them.

Surrounded by British and American flags, Winston promised the Hollywood crowd that the "peace of the world can be best assured by the cooperation of the two great English-speaking democracies." Even Randolph, who feigned a superior air, couldn't help but be impressed with this glittering assemblage, which included actor Douglas Fairbanks Jr. and Hearst's mistress, actress Marion Davies. "There were about 200 people at the lunch—mostly film stars and producers," Randolph recalled in his diary. "I thought Marion Davies was the most attractive."

Throughout that late summer, Churchill toured North America

with Randolph; his brother, Jack; and his nephew Johnnie, on a quest to make money but mostly to relax and enjoy himself. With the Conservatives out of power, Winston remained in Parliament, though no longer in office as Chancellor of the Exchequer overseeing Great Britain's finances. During this father-son journey, lasting four months in Canada and the United States, Churchill began piecing together his massive biography of the Duke of Marlborough. He also gained a lucrative deal to write for Hearst's newspaper syndicate, despite their political disagreements. The tycoon's money could be found all over Hollywood, a sunny, warm land peculiarly American. Hearst, a big man with the face of a cigar store Indian, was a major investor in Mayer's MGM studio (and even talked with Joe Kennedy about producing films together). The weekend before this Hollywood luncheon, the Churchill party stayed as guests at San Simeon, Hearst's fabled mansion, which later inspired Xanadu in *Citizen Kane*, the film loosely based on him. Exquisite paintings, white marble statues, Renaissance tapestries, ancient artifacts, ceilings covered in gold, silver Tiffany lamps, and indoor swimming pools filled this larger-than-life castle. Just as everyone in Hollywood wanted a piece of him, Hearst had taken an artifact from everywhere around the world for himself. "I got to like him [Hearst]—a grave simple child—with no doubt a nasty temper—playing with the most costly toys," Winston described to Clementine, back home in England. "A vast income always overspent: Ceaseless building & collecting not v[er]y discriminatingly works of art: two magnificent establishments, two charming wives; complete indifference to public opinion, a strong liberal & democratic outlook, a 15 million daily circulation, oriental hospitalities, extreme personal courtesy (to us at any rate) & the appearance of a Quaker elder—or perhaps better Mormon elder."

While Hearst's wife, Millicent, served as their hostess at San Simeon, the Churchills, after their much-publicized Hollywood luncheon, stayed at the Malibu beach house built by Hearst for Davies. This Shangri-La by the sea, the Churchill men noted, featured black marble bathrooms and a huge heated swimming pool between the house and the beach.

"Draw up a list of all the film stars you would like to meet and I'll get them to come along for a banquet," Hearst told Randolph and his cousin. True to his word, Hearst hosted a fabulous party in which Charlie Chaplin and Marion Davies performed. Charlie impersonated "Sarah Bernhardt & Lillian Gish, and then he did Napoleon, Uriah Heep, Henry Irving, John Barrymore as Hamlet and many others," Randolph relished. "He is absolutely superb and enchanted everyone." Chaplin blended both American and British sensibilities as the Little Tramp of the cinema. He'd become a Churchill favorite, later visiting the family at Chartwell. When Winston asked about his next film role, Chaplin impishly replied, "Jesus Christ." Not to be outdone, Winston paused and replied, "Have you cleared the rights?"

On this North American trip, Randolph grew up quickly, learning the forbidden secrets of adulthood. Crossing the border from Canada, he carried his father's bottles of liquor in his own luggage, avoiding detection by the dry detectives still active during America's Prohibition era. At the Hollywood luncheon, Hearst's duplicity "amused me," Randolph noted, when the obviously philandering tycoon suggested Randolph's father was having too much fun without his wife, Clementine. "He said that Papa had been anxious that there should not be too much speaking 'like the man who did not take his wife abroad as he was going for pleasure,'" Randolph recalled. "Considering that he had just left Mrs. Hearst [at San Simeon] and was in Los Angeles with his mistress—Marion Davies—it seemed to me rather good value!" At San Simeon, young Randolph—who hadn't had much exposure to the opposite sex at Eton, his elite all-boys school in England—tried to seduce a married woman named Anita, without luck. But he did succeed with Tilly Losch, the Hungarian belly dancer staying there. "With her—a lovely green-eyed faun—he trod paths which were much talked of but not actually explained in detail at Eton," wrote another cousin, Anita Leslie, in whom Randolph later confided.

In Winston's eyes, Randolph could do no wrong. Whatever the young man's transgression—enough sometimes to draw the wrath of his mother, Clementine, or his masters at school—it didn't faze his father, who seemed to find in his son a better version of himself. A few years earlier, Randolph had traveled with his father to Italy, gaining a private audience with the Pope. Though Vatican visitors usually genuflected toward His Holiness, Winston politely declined—"as a Minister of a Protestant country," Randolph later recalled. Instead Winston bowed three times to the Pope as he would a prince. "It is a pleasure to me to show the world to Randolph," Winston wrote to Clementine from Malta. "He is v[er]y well, v[er]y good mannered & seems to take things in."

Randolph's quick mind and impetuous tongue were signs of brilliance, his father believed, and saw his son as a formidable prodigy who would ripen with time. "The logical strength of his mind, the courage of his thought, & the brutal & sometimes repulsive character of his rejoinders impressed me very forcibly," Winston told Clemmie. "He is far more advanced than I was at his age, & quite out of the common—for good or ill." Winston, once a rather disinterested schoolboy, didn't seem bothered by warnings from educational bureaucrats blind to his son's gifts. "This is most unfair," he objected to a history teacher who criticized one of his son's papers. "He's going to be a great man."

With all the lessons that travel can teach, Winston felt sure this 1929 voyage would help mold his son's character and cement their friendship as father and son. During this trip, they went fishing together in the Pacific. When the spool on his son's rod suddenly broke, letting his catch get away, Winston commented merrily, " 'Tis better to have hooked and lost, than never hooked at all." After only a few weeks of travel, Winston told his wife in August that their teenage son "is growing into a v[er]y strong man" and that "he speaks so well. So dexterous, cool &

finished . . . He sleeps ten & sometimes 12 hours a day—deep oblivion. I suppose it is his mind & body growing at the same time. I love him v[er]y much."

Winston's view of his son's potential remained ever optimistic, quite the opposite of how Lord Randolph had treated him. Instead of offering withering criticism mixed with overall indifference, Winston indulged his son whenever his demanding work schedule allowed them time together. By age seven, Randolph was asked by his father to recite poems for his polite friends, an early showcase before some of the leading men of their day. " 'The meteor flag of England shall yet terrific burn; till danger's troubled night depart and the star of peace return,' " intoned little Randolph, standing on a stool. During the Great War, Randolph and his siblings received their father's letters from the front. Winston kept the demands of wartime heroism simple and understandable for his children. "Soon we are going to go close up to the Germans and then we shall shoot back at them and try to kill them," he wrote. "This is because they have done wrong and caused this war and sorrow." Like most children, Randolph knew when he had been naughty but liked testing limits, even when there were none. "We must have been horrible children," he reflected years later. "Very few nannies or nursery maids stayed very long. The departures of those we disliked were serenaded by bumping their bags down the stairs shrilly crying, 'Nanny's going, Nanny's going. Hurrah! Hurrah!' "

In retrospect, Randolph admitted he "could never brook authority or discipline." He learned that having a powerful father could inure him from the wrath of others. "Your father murdered my father!" once screamed another schoolboy, whose father had been killed in the Dardanelles. Young Churchill—ever adamant and unquestioning of his father's public positions—allowed no measure of sympathy for this protest. "I am sorry to say it made me feel immensely proud," he recalled of this other boy's bloodcurdling accusation, "for I realized my father was a boss man who could order other fathers about." At age ten, when

Randolph was molested by a young assistant master at his school, Winston traveled there immediately in anger, only to learn that the teacher had been already fired for another reason. "My father said to me, 'Never let anyone do that to you again,'" Randolph remembered. "This was the only homosexual experience I ever encountered."

Family members, including Clementine, knew of Winston's indulgence with Randolph when he didn't behave, but there was little reform they could effect. "It would have been difficult for any son to call Winston father, but much of Randolph's egotism has to be blamed on a great man's tendency to pander to his beautiful only son," wrote cousin Anita Leslie. "Winston could not resist holding up his famous cigar for silence at the dinner table whenever Randolph held forth. It may seem difficult to imagine Winston listening enraptured to the views of a mere boy, but so it was, and Randolph's ease of delivery and his extraordinary memory increased his father's pleasure."

During their 1929 trip, Randolph confirmed his father's adoration with a bravura public performance. In September, before they reached California, the elder Churchill appeared at a large Canadian Club luncheon in Vancouver, giving an hour-long talk before being peppered with questions by the dean—"a foolish cleric with socialist leanings," Winston recalled in a letter to Clementine. To the crowd's discomfort, this inquisitor went on and on, stuffing his own haughty views into "a number of cheeky questions." Instead of entertaining him with answers, however, Churchill deferred to his son, who seemed as surprised as anyone to be allowed into the fray. Randolph proved more than up to the task. Off the top of his head, the teenager gave a number of witty responses. "His performance not only showed his curious facility for spinning words but gave proof of great poise, judgement and tact," Winston wrote to Clementine. "He knew exactly how far to go and how to win and help the sympathies of this audience. I could not have done it so neatly myself."

His son's performance confirmed Winston's outsize expectations.

The senior Churchill had spent years practicing his own delivery, over-coming the imperfections of his speech impediment. Before appear-ing in public, he'd write out each speech, then arduously memorize it until he eventually learned to speak publicly with an even flow. Yet here, his son glided naturally over the rough waters of debate, without the promptings or cues that aided a lesser talent. As Randolph later re-called, the impromptu speech "proceeded to very mildly twit the dean, and answer the asinine questions as humorously as possible." The pub-lic jousting filled Winston with pride.

"Papa was delighted," Randolph recalled. At that very moment, young Churchill later realized, he "achieved the greatest success I have ever had."

"The Churchill Troupe," as Winston called them, soon left Cali-fornia. They traveled back to the East Coast on a private railroad car provided by steel magnate Charles M. Schwab. Like Baruch, Hearst, and other powerful American businessmen, Schwab counted both Joe Kennedy and Winston Churchill separately among his legion of con-tacts. Winston readily accepted the largesse of such men as a courtesy among friends.

Upon his return to England, Randolph Churchill was expected to resume his studies at Oxford. Clementine feared her son had neglected his education. In a cable to Winston, she mentioned that "Prof [Profes-sor Frederick Lindemann, an Oxford professor who became Winston's key science adviser] seems anxious about Randolph's Oxford career if he does not return in time for term." As usual, Clementine's instinct was correct. Randolph's promise to come back didn't seem to matter. His North American tour—peering down everything from Niagara Falls to the plunging necklines of Hollywood starlets—had embold-ened young Churchill more than any university degree might have.

He didn't want to study life in the abstract after witnessing it in the flesh. Although his father was delighted by his admission to Oxford, Randolph hadn't been a stellar performer. Now he didn't want to show up for classes at all. He preferred getting his lessons at the local pubs or supper clubs, from young Oxford dons and fellow students. "It was far less laborious than getting up early in the morning and going to lectures," he later explained of his absences. "At the luncheons, one met the cleverest, witty dons on level terms and learnt a great deal which was later to prove serviceable in the battle of life."

Upon hearing of his son's dereliction at Oxford, Winston felt betrayed. He took a hard stance and resolved to be firm. "Your idle & lazy life is v[er]y offensive to me," he wrote four days after Christmas 1929. "You appear to be leading a perfectly useless existence." If Randolph didn't reverse his shameful approach, his father vowed, this would be his last term at Oxford. Churchill's disappointment in his son, whom he'd encouraged all summer during their North American travels together, was palpable in his letter. "I have tried to—perhaps prematurely—to add to our natural ties those of companionship & comradeship . . . You give nothing in return for the many privileges and favours you have hitherto received. I must therefore adopt a different attitude toward you for y[ou]r own good." This scathing letter bore a striking similarity to a chastisement sent many years earlier by Lord Randolph to Winston, when he was a similar age to Randolph. Winston's indulgence and his kindhearted attempts to be more of a friend to his son, more than a distant figurehead like Lord Randolph, now mocked him.

While his academic fortunes soured, Randolph kept up his keen interest in public debate. His sharp forensic skills were amply displayed at the Oxford Union, the century-old debating society, whose speakers once included former prime minister William Gladstone and his own father. In this arena, Randolph Churchill could prove himself a man with a golden tongue, the rightful heir to a political dynasty, born to lead and give inspiring speeches. His maiden lecture in February 1930 drew raves. "A fair-haired handsome youth, 18 years of age, electrified the audience at the Oxford Union debate tonight by launching a smashing attack on the proposed Anglo-Egyptian treaty, for which he used all the colorful rhetoric and manners of Winston Churchill," rhapsodized the *New York Times* in a generous notice. "Except that he was more restrained in his speech than his impetuous father, the young Mr. Churchill showed conclusively he was a chip off the old block."

If he didn't fail out of Oxford—and even if he did—Randolph Churchill looked like he might someday be prime minister, the lofty political trophy that appeared to have eluded Winston. "As the students left for their rooms," reported the *Times,* "it was freely predicted that young Mr. Churchill should have a brilliant career in the Conservative party and would perhaps leave his mark on British politics."

The flattering press coverage caught the attention of an agent for a New York speakers' bureau, who dangled before Randolph a then-princely sum of $12,000 (about $150,000 today) for an American tour. This offer sounded too good for Winston's teenage son to turn down, even though he'd have to leave Oxford permanently, to nearly everyone's horror. In particular, his mother, Clementine, objected, aggravating tensions between them that had existed since he was age nine. Back then at boarding school, Randolph's antics caused his mother to scold him unmercifully during what should have been a friendly visit. "She slapped my face in front of the other boys," Randolph recalled. "That was the moment I knew she hated me."

Despite her devotion to Winston, Clementine realized that her husband's skill at overseeing England's finances or military didn't apply to regulating the behavior of their children. Difficulties with Randolph—or his troublesome sisters, Diana and Sarah—were handled by Clementine, by family nannies, or often not at all. If the Chartwell household became too chaotic, with her husband too indifferent or busy, Clemmie simply left, as a way of getting across her appeal to Winston for help. "It was very effective," she'd later explain. "I would just take off and go and stay in a hotel for two or three days. And not let him know where I was. And when I returned, everything was fine again."

Clementine feared Randolph's soapbox tour in the States would ruin any chance he had for a quality education, the kind he'd genuinely need in the future if he assumed the Churchill mantle from his father. Typically, Winston didn't put up much of a fight with his son. "Everyone, except Winston, thought the scheme a harebrained venture," recalled their youngest daughter, Mary, who never caused much of a fuss for her parents. "Clementine feared it would, in fact, mean the end of his studies at Oxford, and that he would never get his degree. In this she was proved right. Randolph was of course aware once more of his mother's opposition to his wishes and intentions, which were, as on so many other occasions, encouraged by his father."

Randolph liked the idea of standing on his own, even if his father didn't approve. "Papa is amused & rather outraged at the idea of me going to America without him!" he said. "But I think I should prefer to go alone & not as the appendage of a distinguished man!"

Unable to stop Randolph, the elder Churchill relented. To puzzled friends, Winston expressed "high hopes" for the success of his son's tour. Perhaps such an experience, even if a failure, might be enlightening. Rather than let his son, whom he still adored, leave England angry, Winston threw a party for him at Claridge's, the swankiest hotel in London. Then, after a short jaunt to Venice, Randolph headed to America as a guest lecturer on his own.

"I thought it was more blessed to teach than to be taught," Randolph later remarked. "Everybody except my father thought I was crazy."

4

Love and Friendships

Blonde and tantalizing, Kay Halle first caught Randolph Churchill's attention at a wedding reception, the day before the impulsive young Englishman would give a speech in Cleveland, Ohio. Mingling among these midwestern guests, Randolph spotted Halle, a daughter of the city's wealthy department store owner. He insisted the host introduce them. Both Kay and Randolph were immediately smitten.

At age nineteen, Randolph, with his piercing blue eyes, finely chiseled jaw, and high cheekbones, appeared as "a young Apollo, golden haired," Halle recalled, alluding to a line from a favorite poem. Young Churchill was a man "of striking, classic Greek beauty," she said, left "dazzled by Randolph's skills with words, his logic and his ability to speak on unpinioned wing."

Halle wasn't a natural beauty, though her long hair, dancer's body, and vivacious spirit attracted many men. In life, Kay never married, but she'd enjoy flings and love affairs with famous men, such as composer George Gershwin (who supposedly wrote "Summertime" on her piano), diplomat Averell Harriman, columnist Walter Lippmann, and eventually Joseph P. Kennedy. During World War II, she worked abroad as a journalist and for the Office of Strategic Services, the spy agency.

Eventually Kay became a Washington society hostess, with a coterie of famous friends in politics, media, and other high places—more than she ever dreamed. But at this wedding reception in 1930, Kay Halle's world still revolved around Cleveland and her family at home. "Randolph inspired me," she later recalled, "to look above the hedgerows of my young life and explore the world."

Randolph's speech before the local branch of the English-Speaking Union in Cleveland proved a big hit, just like his talks in New York and around America. In observing him in October 1930, the *New York Times* noted Randolph's similarities to his father and "his share of the fiery temperament and eloquence of his grandfather, Lord Randolph Churchill." During his presentation, this brash visitor took America to task for "the barbaric, unlawful Negro lynching in your South." When asked about his opposition to India's independence, Randolph countered by mentioning "the outrageous treatment of your Red Indians whom you almost decimated while our Indians multiplied under benevolent British rule." Yet he didn't hesitate to criticize his own country. "The government of Britain and her empire has for some peculiar reason been entrusted to the weakest invertebrates in the country," he charged. The farther Randolph traveled from England, the sharper his attacks grew. He alleged the British government was run by "a crowd of doddering incompetents," calling the Cabinet "a gang of political charlatans." Watching this heir to the Churchill legacy, many assumed he might someday be prime minister, with the *Times* noting that Randolph was "looking forward to entering Parliament in 1932, when he becomes of age." When he reached California, Randolph was "creating a sensation wherever he speaks," reported another newspaper. "Notwithstanding his mild appearance, he has the vigor and personality of the Churchills and the fiery eloquence all his own."

Bernard Baruch, Winston's friend in New York, kept Churchill informed of the public's reaction to his son's talks, "all of which seemed to have been great successes," he reported. Privately, Baruch cautioned

Randolph about "being too critical in this country of those to whom he was opposed in England." As Baruch explained to Winston about his son, "I tried to impress upon him that as a young man he ought to be restrained in his criticisms." Randolph didn't heed the advice, however. His head seemed turned by the public acclaim and the sizable speaking fees he was pocketing. "I do not think he is making quite the stir he thought he would," Baruch wrote to Winston, "but at the same time it is wonderful experience for him."

Randolph's courtship of Kay Halle escalated, with hopes of marriage to this "half-Irish, half-American" woman eight years older than himself. He decided to extend his speaking tour for another three months, traveling back and forth to Cleveland from wherever he was commissioned to speak. When this romance became known at Chartwell, Clementine decided, at Randolph's reluctant invitation, to visit America and meet this special girl in her son's heart.

"He intends to marry her if he can persuade her to do so," Clementine wrote in February 1931 to Winston, back in England. "He has already asked her several times & been put off, but last week she became more favourable to the idea & said that if she liked me & I like her & she liked you, & you liked her, she might consider the question." Clementine mentioned Baruch's "secret enquiries" that found the Halles to be "a solid respectable family & that the children had been well brought up." In a blunt assessment, she described Kay as "tall with a *beautiful* figure, a sensible intelligent face, *not* pretty." This twenty-seven-year-old woman from Cleveland, she added, was "not cosmopolitan" but rather "earnest in her outlook & a little provincial."

Unlike their combative relationship at home, Randolph acted like "a darling" to Clementine in America, with an engaging manner that "has captivated me," she rejoiced. "I am enjoying myself enormously—it is quite like a honeymoon." Joining "a crowded and thrilled audience" in New York, she attended one of her son's lectures. "There are some extremely funny and even witty things in it, & he has a most fascinating manner & delivery & the audience seemed spellbound," she explained to Winston. Still, Clementine gave her son's audacious presentation an overall mixed grade. Randolph hadn't prepared well, she determined, and didn't seem to try very hard. The Churchill standard seemed much higher than that of the public, which was duly impressed by this nineteen-year-old with his own international speaking engagement. "Frankly it was not at all good," Clementine wrote with her trademark soberness, attributing the crowd reaction to "his looks & his colossal cheek."

In private with her son, Clementine had several long conversations about Kay Halle. Randolph claimed he wanted a wife much like his mother. "He said a younger woman would bore him & that he felt the need of a wife who would not allow him to bully her and overbear her," Clementine relayed to her husband. Randolph admitted he was "lonely" and needed a companion like Kay to satisfy his manly needs. "He said that he couldn't live without women in his life, that he objected to prostitutes, that affairs with married women might land him in the Divorce Court & that affairs with young girls might land him on the altar steps with the wrong one," Clementine wrote matter-of-factly. If Randolph could "wear down Miss Halle's objections," he hoped they would marry in October. Despite his lucrative speaking tour, Randolph was burning through money in America. He expressed confidence he could earn enough eventually to support a wife. In the meantime, he hoped to keep getting an allowance from his father, and that the wealthy Halle family might chip in, too.

Deeply concerned with his own finances, Winston worried that an early marriage for his son—no matter how stabilizing for Randolph, and how fine a young lady Kay might be—would place too much pressure on their family. By 1931, Winston's debts totaled 9,500 pounds, an enormous sum during the Depression. At first, he joked with his son about it. "Come home, dear Randolph," he wrote. "We all await you— all except the fatted calf." But when Clementine's note underlined their son's intent to marry soon, Winston's opposition couldn't be plainer. In April 1931, he warned that an early marriage could bring Randolph financial and political ruin. "It will be an intense grief to me to see the hopes & interests I had founded upon you, my only son, jeopardized, if not indeed extinguished; & to feel that we shall not be able to work together in the political arena, wh[ich] is once again becoming filled with lions and gladiators," the senior Churchill cautioned.

The determining factor rested with Kay Halle and none of the Churchills, however. From the very start, she felt an attraction to Randolph and loved his "utter honesty and a breathtaking directness; a passion for truth, and an almost blind courage." But Randolph's erratic behavior proved too much for her to consider marriage. Sometimes he listened to her advice, such as after an early disappointing lecture at Princeton, when Kay suggested he speak slower the next time. On other occasions, his actions were too impulsive even for Kay, a free spirit. During one of his visits to the Halle family home in Cleveland, Kay fell asleep in the living room. She awoke to find Randolph standing over her with a pair of scissors. He had cut off her long, beautiful blonde hair, from waist level to shoulder length. How could he have done such a thing? she angrily demanded like a newly shorn Rapunzel. He uttered some reply, his voice slurred, apparently by alcohol, about how she looked better this way. He never apologized. "She would be Randolph's greatest friend for life, but to tie herself to this willful, sparkling, undisciplined boy—that she feared to do," wrote Churchill cousin Anita Leslie. "She could not see herself as another Clemmie, ready to wear herself out looking after a demanding, exciting husband." Even Clementine sensed Kay's reluctance. "She is I think very fond of Randolph but rather flustered and worried," his mother concluded.

Kay may have sensed that Randolph's impulsive behavior included other women. In a March 1931 letter marked "Private," Clementine sketched out her suspicions about their son to Winston back home in England. She warned that his rich friend Bernard Baruch might be jealous enough of Randolph (aptly nicknamed "the Rabbit") to launch his own undercover investigation. "I think there *is* a froideur on Mr. Baruch's part towards Randolph, caused I imagine by the Rabbit having a flirtation with a lady whom Mr. Baruch considers as his property," Clementine surmised. "Randolph thinks Mr. Baruch had them followed!!"

At the heart of this romantic triangle was Clare Boothe. A smart, strikingly attractive divorcee at age twenty-eight, Clare worked in New York as a top editor at *Vanity Fair* magazine. Her sharp, funny comments were already the talk of the town. Randolph seconded photographer Cecil Beaton's observation that Clare was "drenchingly beautiful," her rapturous eyes able to devour powerful men in her gaze. "A man has only one escape from his old self: to see a different self—in the mirror of some woman's eyes," she'd later write. Eventually, Boothe, one of the most fascinating American women of her time, would meet and marry Henry Luce, the owner of the Time-Life empire. But in 1931, it was Bernie Baruch, the famous New York financier, who squired Clare around New York. With his thick mane of white hair, dark eyebrows, penetrating stare, and six-foot-three-inch frame, Baruch had become well known working as an adviser to President Woodrow Wilson. During World War I, he headed the War Industries Board, and dealt with the likes of Churchill. But now Baruch was a sixty-year-old married man with grown children, a millionaire many times over. His wife spent most of her time at their South Carolina estate, an arrangement that allowed Baruch a great deal of liberties in Manhattan.

This odd romantic triangle, created by Randolph's dalliance with Clare, would play out for much longer than Baruch anticipated. Several months later, in England, when all three—Clare, Randolph, and Baruch—happened to be staying at Chartwell, Clare went to bed alone, only to hear someone trip over the coal scuttle in her darkened room in the middle of the night. "It was Bernie Baruch," she'd recall years later.

"But I was expecting Randolph!" Young Churchill later followed Clare to Paris, where they stayed at the Ritz.

Winston had no idea of his son's affair with Clare—or how it might affect his relationship with Baruch—until he received Clementine's letter. To be sure, there was something unseemly about a powerful older man running after a much younger woman, but also something distressing in his mistress's willingness to reveal their intimate secrets to Randolph. "She had been very indiscreet, not to say disloyal, & described in minute detail all her transactions physical & financial with Mr. B.," Clementine wrote to her husband. "I will tell you the rest when we meet, meanwhile please burn this portion of the letter & please do not, unless the Rabbit confides in you, tell him that I have told you."

Despite his own investigation, Baruch never showed any telltale signs to Randolph or his mother about this affair. "He never shewed the flicker of an eyelid," Clementine explained, "but he complained to the Lady [Clare Boothe,] who reported the matter to Randolph."

To his mother, Randolph called Baruch "a cagey old Bird," using Yankee slang he'd picked up in the States. Because of his spendthrift ways, however, Randolph had to borrow two thousand dollars from Baruch before he left the United States following his tour. Clementine became convinced of Baruch's unhappiness with Randolph when he promised to meet them as they traveled through Washington, DC, yet failed to show up. "He rather let us down," she told Winston. "He is a curious old Boy rather revengeful."

Winston could ill afford to offend Baruch. For years, Bernie had been his best friend in America, a valued source of financial assistance and political gossip. During the Churchill family's trip to America in 1929, Baruch played the perfect host, meeting them in Chicago as they traveled in his private rail car from California to New York. He covered their expenses at the Plaza Hotel, on Fifth Avenue, and picked up the tab for Winston's brandy, cigars, and other amenities. "It is really a pleasure for me to know that people I like are enjoying the things which I have," explained Baruch, who earned his first million dollars before age thirty. Baruch greatly impressed Churchill's son, who declared, "Baruch is the greatest speculator there has ever been." His father no doubt agreed.

In handling Wall Street investments, Churchill depended on his American friend's advice. Although once in charge of Great Britain's Treasury, Winston seemed a neophyte with his own finances. His gambling impulse took over with stocks, landing him in trouble when he was on his own. "He knew nothing of what he was doing: to him it was like playing roulette at Monte Carlo," described John "Jock" Colville, who served as Churchill's private secretary before becoming a merchant banker. Arriving in New York just in time for the 1929 Wall Street crash, Churchill placed big bets on stocks that plummeted, sweeping away all his writing fees and much of his bank account. He realized he'd have to sell his beloved Chartwell and told Baruch he was "ruined." Bernie, a master of manipulation, organized a scheme of back-and-forth stock swaps so that Churchill recovered. "Presumably Baruch paid the commissions," Colville wrote of this near-death experience. "Churchill never forgot the debt he owed."

By late 1931, Winston decided again to return to America, seeking more lecture fees to relieve his debts, as well as a chance to meet Randolph's sweetheart, Kay Halle, and her family. His lecture tour (nineteen cities over three weeks) would earn him more than a British prime minister's salary. By then, the crushing expenses of Chartwell, and his mounting stock losses, had forced Churchill to dust-sheet his dream house, closing down everything except the study where he worked. The Churchill family had moved into the small cottage on the grounds, a sign of their diminished fortunes. Austerity, though, didn't prevent

Winston from buying champagne (a vintage year of his favorite Pol Roger) to sip regularly, or from smoking Romeo y Julieta cigars from Havana. "I believe that, if I did not have to spend so much time earning money by writing, I could one day become Prime Minister," Churchill declared. When his lecture tour stopped in Cleveland, the Halle family invited him for dinner and to stay that night as their guest. Before she headed back to England, Clementine had also visited the Halles along with Randolph. "Of course you will understand that there will be no question of our children marrying—Randolph is far too young," Clementine insisted. Sam Halle, the department store magnate and one of Cleveland's richest men, immediately agreed.

Kay remained nervous about meeting Randolph's famous father, worried what he might think of her. "I sensed his way he had of looking at and through you," she recalled years later of Winston. "It was scary. It was sort of like what we now call the laser beam." Kay let her mother know that Mr. Churchill liked to retire with a bottle of Scotch on his night table. Rather than a lecture about Prohibition, Mrs. Halle did her best to make her daughter's guest feel content.

Soon after dinner finished, Winston announced he'd retire to bed. Mrs. Halle, who obtained her whiskey through a local bootlegger, offered it to him. At first Churchill refrained. "My dear Mrs. Halle, what makes you think I would want to take a bottle of Scotch to bed?" he asked.

Kay's mother didn't flinch. "Mr. Churchill, we offer this to all our house guests," she replied, a statement quite untrue but appropriate under the circumstances.

"In that case, I'll take it," Winston said, before marching upstairs to sleep.

Winston Churchill's American lecture tour appeared a great success, as many enjoyed this visiting Englishman's wit and speaking style.

"Some of his epigrams, so it is wickedly asserted by his enemies, are carefully prepared in advance, and even practiced before a mirror," declared a *New York Times* editorialist. "But their sting and point are nonetheless delightful." On December 13, 1931, though, the Churchill bandwagon came to a screeching halt. That evening, Winston planned to go to bed early at the Waldorf Astoria, his Manhattan hotel. Instead, at nine o'clock he received a telephone call from Bernard Baruch, inviting him to his home on Fifth Avenue to meet with two mutual friends. Into the night, Churchill took a taxicab. Along the way, he realized he didn't have Baruch's precise home address, only a general idea of its location from an earlier visit. At one point, Churchill bounded out of the cab toward the sidewalk. He looked left but not to the right. When he turned, he saw "a long dark car rushing forward at full speed." The driver hit the brakes, but too late. In a lingering split second, Churchill, then fifty-seven, thought to himself, *I am going to be run down and probably killed.* He fortunately wasn't—another near miss in a life lucky enough to rival any cat's. His heavy fur-lined coat seemed to cushion some of the blow. But the automobile took its toll, smacking Churchill's head to the pavement with "an impact, a shock, a concussion indescribably violent," and dragging him for several yards. "I do not understand why I was not broken like an eggshell," he later observed. In the middle of Fifth Avenue, a boulevard of American ambition, Churchill lay prostrate, bleeding and in pain, as police and a crowd rushed to his aid.

"A man has been killed!" someone cried.

While being picked up and carried away by rescuers, this fallen stranger was asked for his name.

"I am Winston Churchill, a British statesman," he moaned.

By the time he arrived at Lenox Hill Hospital, Churchill felt sharp pain yet realized he would survive. Baruch and Clementine soon stood at his bedside. "Tell me, Baruch, when all is said and done, what *is* the number of your house?" he uttered, a sure sign he'd get well and that his quick wit never needed a crutch.

This almost-deadly car crash derailed Churchill's lecture tour, which he needed most urgently to pay his bills at home. Instead, he spent the next several weeks mending, and mulling over his future. "You will find me, I am afraid, a much weaker man than the one you welcomed on December 11," he wrote to Randolph, back in England. Clementine conceded to her son that Winston had suffered "three very heavy blows" in recent years, leaving him without either political power in Parliament or much of his personal savings on Wall Street. "The loss of all that money in the crash, then the loss of his political position in the Conservative Party, and now this terrible injury—He said he did not think he would ever recover completely from the three events," Clementine wrote. The prospect of a diminished life seemed more unbearable to Winston than if he had been killed on the street. It marked the darkest period in his "wilderness years," an agonizing time when he felt pushed aside from his countrymen and good fortune.

By February, Churchill had recovered enough to travel and fulfill most of his speaking engagements in the United States. His loyal circle of friends and patrons rallied to his cause, deciding to buy him a Rolls-Royce "to celebrate his recovery" and deliverance from oblivion. "We think there is a certain appropriateness in the presentation of a motor car to a man who has been knocked down by a taxi-cab!" wrote Brendan Bracken to Baruch. Though his career seemed over in England, Churchill's popularity among Americans stayed intact. Some in the press pondered if Winston, born to an American mother, would ever consider running for president. "I have been treated so splendidly in the United States that I should be disposed, if you can amend the Constitution, seriously to consider the matter," he joked.

Near the end of his American adventure, Churchill returned to New York and received a tour of the Empire State Building, a sky-scraping symbol of America's power in the twentieth century. He was escorted up the newly built tower by the recently deconstructed governor of New York Al Smith, a friend of Baruch's, who now served as a glorified guide around the building. Smith, a giant in his time, had shriveled after his devastating loss in the 1928 presidential race, where his Catholicism was an overwhelming issue, even more so than his proposed repeal of Prohibition. "Really, there is only one issue—and that is religion," Baruch said to Churchill bluntly in 1928 of Smith's ill-fated Democratic candidacy. Baruch planned to support Smith for president again in 1932, instead of fellow Democrat Franklin Roosevelt, who replaced Smith as governor. Roosevelt's only supporter among conservative businessmen seemed to be Joe Kennedy, a friend and business associate of Baruch's.

Up in the eighty-sixth-floor observation deck of the Empire State Building, Churchill, carrying a cane, looked upon the surrounding metropolis. His face filled with childlike glee atop this newest of life's wonders. He had cheated death down on the streets below and lived to write a story about it, "My New York Adventure," for a handsome fee.

"It's the highest I've ever been," said Winston, as recorded by the newsreel cameramen touting his recovery.

Smith, wearing his trademark derby and bow tie, smiled ironically. "Probably the highest I'll ever be," this son of Tammany Hall replied.

5

A Man on the Make

An exciting mood of anticipation—the rousing, almost palpable feel
of victory—filled the Ritz-Carlton hotel suite of Democratic presidential candidate Franklin D. Roosevelt during the final days of the 1932
campaign, when the New York governor came to Massachusetts for a
rally at the famed Boston Garden. Inside the Ritz, FDR's brain trust
gathered to ensure their Election Day plans would lead to the White
House. A certain frenetic energy—shouts across the room, ringing telephones, people clutching papers, impassioned arguments as campaign
workers moved from one table to the next—made this impromptu campaign headquarters fascinating to watch.

Kay Halle gained a front-row seat to this last-minute politicking
because of her friendship with Betsey Roosevelt, the daughter-in-law
of the future president. The young women had known each other at
school, and had family ties to Cleveland. Betsey and her husband,
James Roosevelt, arrived at the Ritz-Carlton to help out with the campaign and invited Kay to join them. In this busy suite of people, as Kay
recalled, she noticed a handsome man with light reddish hair sitting
quietly in the corner.

"Who is it that you brought with you? You haven't introduced him," she asked of Felix Frankfurter, a trusted Roosevelt supporter, who was then a Harvard law professor and later appointed to the U.S. Supreme Court. Kay had spotted Frankfurter walking into the suite with this unknown man.

"Joe, tell them who you are," Frankfurter urged.

"I'm Joe Kennedy," the stranger replied. That fall, Kennedy had served as both an advance man for some FDR campaign appearances and a behind-the-scenes financial rainmaker in obtaining contributions. To Kay Halle and her friends, though, Kennedy simply said he'd given some money to the Roosevelt campaign. "I've been interested in all sorts of businesses in Boston and California—in films and banking, and though 'Honey' Fitzgerald, Mayor of Boston, is my father-in-law, I've never had the thrill of being part of a presidential campaign," Kennedy explained. "I'd like to go along with you all and take part in the fun."

Halle surely didn't mind. From the very moment she observed Kennedy, she felt him to be "a very attractive Irishman," she recalled. "He was unmistakably Irish, with copper colored hair, and a beaming smile that exposed his shining teeth." Energetic and dynamic, Joe had an "apricot" hue to his skin that "seemed to give him a permanently suntanned look." His rimmed glasses magnified his blue eyes. At Roosevelt campaign headquarters in Boston, Joe displayed a "quick intelligence, tremendous Irish charm and teasing wit [that] recharged the room," she observed. Kennedy's engaging manner won over both Halle and the young Roosevelts. "From then on he attached himself to us in a charming way," Kay remembered.

Sometime later, Halle joined Betsey and Betsey's sister Mary Cushing as they left the Ritz to visit their father, Dr. Harvey Cushing, at the Peter Bent Brigham Hospital, where he was a renowned brain surgeon. (The two sisters, along with another nicknamed Babe, would soon be known as the "fabulous Cushing sisters," grabbing glamorous Depression-era headlines for their high-society exploits and marrying into power and money.) Before departing the Roosevelt suite, Kennedy asked Kay a favor. "He wanted me to go with him to see one of his sons who was in the same hospital," Halle recalled. "After visiting Dr. Cushing, Joe took me to his son Jack's room."

Lying flat on his back in a hospital bed, young Jack Kennedy was encircled by piles of biographies and history books, the only companions of a sickly boy alone. Joe provided a vague answer about the reasons for his son's hospitalization—part of the family's decades-long obfuscation surrounding Jack's ill health. "He had some football accident and had developed what they thought was a sort of an anemia and Joe was a bit worried about it," Kay remembered for an oral history. A thin and gaunt youngster, Jack didn't look his age of fifteen, she recalled. "He couldn't have been more than twelve or thirteen," Kay estimated while gazing at Kennedy's son. She remembered the young Kennedy's face as "very pale which highlighted the freckles across his nose." Since age three, when he suffered scarlet fever, Jack had been in and out of hospitals with infections. "We used to laugh about the great risk a mosquito took in biting Jack Kennedy—with some of his blood the mosquito was almost sure to die," his brother Bobby later recalled.

Most memorably, Halle saw Jack sick in bed with Winston Churchill's *The World Crisis*, the book about which she knew so much from Randolph and his father, the famous statesman and author. That a young boy would be reading Churchill's adventurous, sprawling account of the Great War while lying on a hospital mattress like some literary raft, greatly impressed Halle, an image that remained in her mind decades later. These demanding books were evidence of "Joe's iron will and vaulting ambition for his brood," Halle said. "Joe once told me, paraphrasing the German poet Goethe, that you are bound to succeed if you want something hard enough. But the great thing was to be sure of what you wanted as you were certain to attain it."

While in Boston, Kay continued accompanying Joe on his daily hospital visits to see his son. "He saw to it that his teenage Jack pursued his studies even in the hospital," she recalled. Before long, the department store heiress began an intimate relationship with the Kennedy family patriarch. A 1997 *New York Times* obituary would say those closest to Halle were "certain that she had been Joseph Kennedy's favorite mistress." Though few details exist about her involvement with Kennedy, her own words suggest a strong attraction. Halle, who didn't need Joe's money, was bowled over by his energy. "Every word Joe uttered oozed horsepower," she marveled.

Joe carried on his politically risky behavior with Kay Halle without regard for what the Roosevelts might think. Nor did he seem particularly bothered that his philandering might be detected in the same city where his wife's father, John F. "Honey Fitz" Fitzgerald, had once served as mayor and still had plenty of friends. With Kay, Joe acted just as he had with actress Gloria Swanson in the 1920s, when they had an affair while producing movies together in Hollywood. Without acknowledging the obvious, Joe treated his paramours as if members of the Kennedys' extended family—and he expected his wife, Rose, to act none the wiser. Like Swanson, Kay Halle was later introduced to Rose by Joe, who encouraged them to socialize together as if sorority sisters. Swanson couldn't figure out if Rose was "a fool . . . or a saint? Or just a better actress than I was." Most likely, Rose sensed her husband's infidelities with Kay Halle but chose to ignore them for a higher purpose—in the interests of what she once called the Kennedy "family enterprise."

The marriage of Joe and Rose Kennedy wasn't always so duplicitous. It began two decades earlier, after a great romance, when Joe courted Rose, the mayor's beautiful and witty daughter, with the same fervor as he'd pursued his first million. The mayor wasn't pleased with Rose's choice—no man seemed good enough for his daughter. Only after enough prodding did Honey Fitz eventually relent, a slight Joe would never forget. Rose, the product of Catholic academies for girls, was filled with notions that "your heart should rule your head," she explained decades later. "I was very romantic and there were no two ways about it." They wed in the private chapel of Boston's future cardinal. Rose discovered herself pregnant soon after their honeymoon. Although her affection for her partner never completely faded, the succession of nine children, the demands of Joe's hard-driving career, and eventually his infidelities with women like Kay Halle and many others hardened Rose's heart and averted her eyes from the obvious. Whatever Joe did in Boston with this willowy blonde single woman appeared of little relevance to Rose living with their brood two hundred miles away in Bronxville, a New York City suburb. By then, their love found its greatest expression in their proud collection of children and the running of a family, with its everyday trappings and demands, rather than in the passion of their youth.

Earlier that year, 1932, Rose gave birth to their ninth child, Edward Moore Kennedy, a chubby, amiable boy whom the family called Teddy. ("Can I be Godfather to the baby?" Jack asked his mother.) Rose, weary and seriously ill from childbirth at age forty-two, was confined to bed for several weeks until she recovered. Rather than run the risk of another pregnancy, and unwilling to violate her Catholic Church's teachings about birth control, she came to an accord with her husband that essentially ended sex between them but didn't stop Joe from pursuing affairs with other women. The animal spirits of this master capitalist would not permit such capitulation. While Rose looked the other way, Joe's sons eventually learned about their father's wandering eye and need for "dates" with other women. Later, in the 1950s, Halle, by then a Washington society matron, was asked by Jack and Bobby about helping with preparations for their father's upcoming DC visit. They apparently felt Halle understood their father's needs. "The gist of the conversation from the boys was the fact that their father was going to be in Washington for a few days and needed female companionship," Halle recalled. "They wondered whom I would suggest, and they were absolutely serious."

Inside the Roosevelt presidential campaign, Joe Kennedy's importance revolved around money. His business contacts provided a huge financial advantage for FDR in this 1932 race, with one of the lowest overall amounts spent in years because of the Depression. Kennedy personally gave fifteen thousand dollars to the Democrats and loaned the party another fifty thousand. Meanwhile, JPK's business associate Bernard Baruch provided the campaign's single biggest donation, of forty-five thousand dollars. Another Kennedy business ally, National Distillers Products head Seton Porter, offered five thousand dollars, perhaps tasting the impending end of Prohibition. Most significantly, publisher William Randolph Hearst gave twenty-five thousand dollars and arguably the support of an entire state. At that summer's Democratic Convention, Kennedy helped convince Hearst to swing the California delegation for Roosevelt. Hearst valued Kennedy's judgment ever since their involvement together in Hollywood films during the 1920s. Before the convention, Joe visited Hearst at San Simeon, arguing that FDR would stabilize the nation's economy and political pulse more than other Democratic possibilities. Without Kennedy's intervention, Roosevelt ran the risk of a deadlock among the delegates and not gaining the nomination on the fourth ballot.

Historically, Kennedy would prove pivotal in financing two winning presidential campaigns in the twentieth century: the 1932 race with FDR and his own son's winning campaign in 1960. In both, Joe Kennedy was a dynamic force, the hidden hand pulling political levers and twisting arms for cash, just as Baruch had been in earlier Democratic campaigns. Joe convinced Baruch, who initially favored 1928 nominee Al Smith, to support Roosevelt instead in 1932. "You drew to the purpose you were serving many men who, dubious of the candidate, were willing to have your conviction imposed upon theirs—I was one of them," admitted Baruch's friend and close aide Herbert Bayard Swope. In 1932, the *Boston Globe* described Kennedy as a "man of mystery," quoting one Westerner who asked aloud, "Is he the Barney Baruch of the Roosevelt campaign?" Even when Joe was in his hometown, he kept his father-in-law, Boston's former mayor, seemingly in the dark. "Joe is always in the background, you know," explained Honey Fitz. "He keeps tabs on things independently of the official party. I think he moves around in his own car."

Kennedy, who traveled thousands of miles during the campaign, portrayed his efforts for Roosevelt as purely altruistic. "There is nothing I want," he avowed to the press. "There is no public office that would interest me."

Joe Kennedy's fortune, one of the largest in America, would derive from several sources, some quite respectable and others balanced on the edge of illegality. For instance, his 1946 purchase of the gargantuan Merchandise Mart in Chicago proved a miraculous business deal that, if not divinely inspired, was certainly traceable to the Roman Catholic Church: a real estate broker for New York's archdiocese, run by Cardinal Francis J. Spellman (a close family friend for years), had suggested the buy, which would become Joe's biggest moneymaker. Earlier, on Wall Street, Joe had made millions in complex trades based on inside information. He relied on sharp-minded associates such as Baruch and Swope, and jumped into speculative "pools" with shady partners such as Henry Mason Day, who had gone to jail in the Teapot Dome scandal. Yet with exquisite timing, Joe knew when to exit a deal. He cashed out of the market just before the 1929 Wall Street crash. In any deal, Joe possessed a "unique instinct for the right time to go ahead or back out," observed James Fayne, one of his closest aides. With the merger of RKO studios and other ventures in Hollywood, Kennedy showed that financial engineering could be as important and lucrative to filmmaking as plot construction and smiling close-ups. His adventures in the liquor trade prompted unproven rumors of bootlegging during Prohibition and more than a nodding acquaintance with organized crime figures, including at least one later in his employ.

There was no denying Kennedy's genius. He was a financial whiz with the Midas touch, building on each new pot of gold. When other spendthrift family members were scolded for wasting funds, his son Jack joked that the "only solution is for Dad to work harder." By pulling out of the stock market just before the 1929 crash, Joe protected his fortune and family from the ravages of the Great Depression, the worldwide economic collapse that left one in four Americans unemployed. "I have no first hand knowledge of the Depression," Jack Kennedy admitted thirty years later. "My family had one of the great fortunes of the world and it was worth more than ever then. We had bigger houses, more servants, we traveled more. About the only thing that I saw directly was when my father hired some extra gardeners just to give them a job so they could eat. I really did not learn about the Depression until I read about it at Harvard."

For Joe Kennedy, politics was the secret ingredient in moneymaking. His father, Patrick J. Kennedy, known to all as P.J., was one of Boston's top legislators and a ward boss. Like many Irish Catholics who'd landed in Boston, P.J. emerged from the hardscrabble life of his immigrant father, Patrick, who left County Wexford in 1847, during the height of Ireland's famine. The elder Patrick Kennedy arrived in America as a migrant worker in East Boston and died of cholera after only a few years. With help from his widowed mother, P.J. became a successful tavern owner in East Boston and relied on politics to get ahead. He secured for his only son, Joseph, a job as a state bank examiner shortly after the young man's Harvard graduation. At Harvard, which then accepted few Irish Catholics, Joe had gotten his snoot full of the stratified class divisions between the "Brahmins," the wealthy white Anglo-Saxon Protestant majority, and the emerging Catholic immigrant population, typified by the Irish and Italians, vying for power. Joe's sense of resentment, rooted in the Irish-Catholic experience on both sides of the Atlantic, would fuel his ambitions and last a lifetime. With skills burnished in his state examiner position, he engineered the takeover of Columbia Trust, a local bank in which P.J. and friends had a minority stake. This bold gambit enabled Joe Kennedy to call himself, at age twenty-five, the nation's youngest bank president. True or not, this claim carried enough prestige to impress his future bride, Rose Fitzgerald, and her father, Honey Fitz, the city's former mayor and a U.S. congressman. The young couple's 1914 marriage arose from this fertile hotbed of politics. Honey Fitz and P. J. Kennedy were friendly clubhouse allies whose family vacations together in Old Orchard Beach, Maine, set the stage for this permanent union of the Fitzgerald and Kennedy clans.

Politics played a hand in Joe Kennedy's next move, which brought him into the realm of Winston Churchill. As America entered World War I in 1917, Honey Fitz's influence convinced Charles M. Schwab, the owner of Bethlehem Steel, to hire Kennedy as assistant general manager to run the firm's Fore River shipbuilding yard in Quincy, Massachusetts. This cushy, well-paying job allowed Kennedy, unlike his Harvard classmates, to avoid the draft and gain the trust of Schwab, one of the nation's wealthiest men. That same year, the Kennedys' second child, John Fitzgerald Kennedy, was born.

At Fore River, Schwab had ramped up production of battleships under a lucrative British Navy deal organized by Churchill as Lord of the Admiralty. Although the United States had yet to enter World War I, Schwab's shipyard was soon producing boat and submarine parts at a record-setting pace. Schwab shipped these parts to Montreal for completion in order not to violate U.S. neutrality law barring direct sale of ships and submarines to bellicose nations. When Kennedy arrived,

Fore River was a sprawling boomtown-like shipyard cloaked in secrecy. Keep Out signs warded off visitors. Schwab's aggressiveness in pursuing the British Navy deal with Churchill eventually put him in an advantageous position when the United States declared war in April 1917. The following year, while Kennedy was working for him, Schwab's success at Fore River earned him a federal appointment as director general of the Emergency Fleet Corporation, an agency overseeing the U.S. manufacture of naval battleships and submarines during the war. In a cable quoted in the *New York Times,* a "delighted" Churchill applauded Schwab's appointment, though American officials later had their regrets. After the war, a U.S. lawsuit accused Bethlehem Steel of overcharging the government for those warships and Schwab of abusing his government role to give an edge to his company. Nevertheless, Schwab's friendly relationship with Churchill remained undaunted, with the iron maker later paying Winston's travel expenses when he came to America in 1931. "We got on very well," Winston said of Schwab. "He risked his life to carry out his contract."

While overseeing Fore River during the Great War, Kennedy never directly met Churchill, the shipyard's British benefactor, with whom he'd have extensive dealings in years to come. But he did have a confrontation with then–U.S. Assistant Secretary of the Navy Franklin D. Roosevelt. When Kennedy refused to turn over new vessels at Fore River until they'd been paid for, FDR sent combat-ready marines to fetch them. "Roosevelt was the hardest trader I'd ever run up against," recalled Joe Kennedy. "I was so disappointed I broke down and cried."

Soon after the war, Kennedy again relied on Honey Fitz's help, this time in joining a local brokerage firm, where Fitzgerald steered some government work. Joe's gregarious father-in-law also provided an introduction to Bernard Baruch, the rich Wall Street speculator. One afternoon, Fitzgerald telephoned Baruch and talked for several minutes about a possible investment, and then told him to hang on for a young man he should get to know. Honey Fitz handed the receiver to his son-in-law. Although a generation apart, Baruch and Kennedy soon became friends, a complicated relationship that would last decades. Baruch had become rich by playing his gut instincts on Wall Street and seemed even more concerned with gaining social respectability than Kennedy. "Modern usage has made the term 'speculator' a synonym for gambler and plunger," Baruch explained in an otherwise unrevealing 1957 autobiography. "Actually the word comes from the Latin *speculari*, which means to spy out and observe. I have defined a speculator as a man who observes the future and acts before it occurs." In politics as in Wall Street, both Kennedy and his friend Baruch were master capitalists motivated by opportunities rather than ideals. "Old Joe succeeded in the Great Bull Market of the '20s and magnificently survived the crash because he possessed a passion for facts, a complete lack of sentiment and a marvelous sense of timing," a friend told *Time* magazine.

During Roosevelt's 1932 campaign, Kennedy and Baruch remained behind-the-scenes players, mainly because their ethnic and religious backgrounds kept them from seeking center stage. Kennedy had moved to New York partly because of restrictions placed on the Irish by Boston's Brahmins in areas such as banking. Nationally, Joe and Rose had been stunned by the anti-Catholic bigotry faced by Al Smith in his 1928 bid. Smith's defeat seemed to set back the dream of any Catholic running for president by at least another generation. For his part, Baruch, a Jew who'd graduated from New York's City College, certainly talked as if he wanted to be president, but he artfully renounced any such plans. "I never had the least ambition to be Alderman, let alone President," Baruch claimed. "Such ambition, of course, is essential to the game of politics. Consequently, Presidential dreams never disturbed my slumber."

As conservative Democrats, Joe Kennedy and Baruch worked vigorously for FDR's success, especially in rounding up support within the business community. In Roosevelt, both men saw a vehicle for their own ambitions, and sought a place within his administration. In a memo to FDR, Kennedy suggested Baruch for secretary of state and alluded to the latter's friendship with figures such as Churchill. "He has foreign friends and associations, but these might be beneficial and I have never heard them described as discredible [*sic*]," Kennedy advocated. He dissuaded Roosevelt from considering Al Smith for the secretary of treasury post, a prize Joe himself coveted. "He is believed to have boarded the band-wagon merely to save face," Joe wrote about Smith. "Furthermore, he will always be a candidate for president and he never has been loyal and never will be."

The Kennedys saw something special in Roosevelt, the ability to win, that many Democrats didn't perceive at first, which allowed Joe and his politically astute wife to avoid the clannish devotion to an Irish-Catholic candidate like Smith. After meeting Roosevelt, Rose Kennedy thought he possessed "more charm than any man I have ever met." She admired Franklin's moral courage as a cripple who hadn't let polio, contracted as an adult, stop his political career. On one occasion, she watched as Roosevelt boarded a yacht and maneuvered himself around while wearing heavy metal supports on his legs. "For a fleeting second, I caught a glimpse of him sinking exhausted into a chair saying 'For God's sake let's take off these darn braces,'" she recalled. That willpower seemed enough to turn around America in the depths of a depression.

During the 1932 campaign, Baruch attended the Democrats' convention in Chicago with *Vanity Fair* editor Clare Boothe on his arm, the same beautiful divorcée Randolph Churchill had courted recently. "The impact which she made on men of that type had the effect, approximately, of a queen cobra on a field mouse," observed Frank

Crowninshield, her *Vanity Fair* boss. If Baruch's wife wasn't aware of this affair, certainly the future president noticed. "You know she was Barney Baruch's girl," Roosevelt later recalled. "Yes, he educated her, gave her a yacht, sent her to finishing school, she was his girl."

Throughout that campaign year, Baruch stayed in contact with Churchill, keeping him informed about Roosevelt's challenge to Republican incumbent Herbert Hoover. In reply to Baruch, Churchill's trusted aide Brendan Bracken—still smarting from the parliamentary struggles in England that had left Winston in "the wilderness"—suggested "the only effective method of getting rid of an administration is consistently to roast its leader, where he is prime minister or president."

When Roosevelt beat Hoover by a wide margin, Joe Kennedy threw a huge victory party in New York, spread over two floors of the Waldorf Astoria. To his friends and family, Joe claimed credit for raising lots of campaign cash and convincing Hearst to endorse Roosevelt at the convention. These crucial factors were vital to FDR's win, he said, "but you don't find any mention of it in the history books." By then, Roosevelt's top "brain trust" aides had learned to keep their distance from the "fiery" Kennedy, who, the *Times* reported, "fights so hard in conferences for his proposals and his convictions that he sometimes arouses temporary enmity within the group."

On Election Night, Kay Halle joined James and Betsey Roosevelt at the family's Manhattan residence on Sixty-Fifth Street. Along with the new First Lady, Eleanor, they all traveled to the Biltmore Hotel, where Kay found FDR and campaign manager James Farley at "an oval table that contained about 48 telephones all going at once." FDR patted friends on the shoulders, accepting congratulations. "The drama of that room was unforgettable," Kay wrote in a letter to her mother, back in Cleveland. The celebration carried on until dawn. The following night, Joe Kennedy "gave a dinner at the Colony Restaurant—orchids champagne theater and night club," wrote Halle, who spent the evening with Kennedy's pals. "Mr. Herbert Bayard Swope was my partner—next table to us and talking to us all the time was Barney Baruch."

"Happy Days Are Here Again," the Roosevelt campaign song, played throughout the room, with Joe Kennedy determined to make the most of politics and his ties to the new president.

6

Across the Atlantic

What for most married men would seem an indelicate travel arrangement—cruising across the Atlantic with his wife and mistress—seemed nothing more than a cozy accommodation for Joe Kennedy aboard the steam-driven ocean liner, the SS *Europa*. Departing New York Harbor in late September 1933, the Kennedy entourage included his wife, Rose; his latest flame, Kay Halle; and his namesake eldest son, Joseph Jr. He also brought along a business associate with a dubious past named Henry Mason Day; and the lynchpin for his newest deal, James Roosevelt, the American president's oldest son.

As the huge ship shoved off, the young Roosevelt's mother, First Lady Eleanor; his grandmother Sarah Delano Roosevelt; and friends and other relatives waved good-bye from the dock. The president, who had dined with them earlier that evening, decided to remain at the family's Manhattan town house. Before leaving, Jimmy, as he preferred to be called, had told the press that "his trip was primarily for pleasure, but that he hoped to combine some business with it."

Ever the opportunist, Kennedy also planned to mix business and pleasure. His ultimate prize would be to gain the British rights to send Scotch whiskey, gin, and other imported liquors to a thirsty United

States, now that Prohibition appeared almost over. As part of his secret strategy, Joe had enlisted the president's twenty-five-year-old son
to help organize the private visit with Winston Churchill that underlined Kennedy's clout with the new administration. In their own ways,
Jimmy and Kay impressed upon Churchill the importance of Joe Kennedy, which led to a memorable visit at Churchill's Chartwell home.
In return, Jimmy Roosevelt landed the lucrative insurance contract on
the British liquor shipments, as Kennedy prepared to make a fortune
by legally selling booze in America. But no one seemed the wiser about
this deal. Despite the headlines surrounding this month-long journey
to Europe, the connections between the president's son, the Churchills,
and the Kennedys would remain unexamined for years.

Prohibition, the national social experiment in alcohol refusal that
began in 1920, finally collapsed after more than a decade with the 1932
election of Franklin D. Roosevelt. Prohibition's odd consortium of
"dry" supporters, from religious fundamentalists in the rural Bible Belt
to teetotaling Progressives in the cities, was slowly defeated, its lofty but
impractical goals gone horribly awry. In a classic boomerang of unintended consequences, this ban on alcohol had created an outpouring of
illegal bootlegging, rum running, moonshine stills, speakeasies, border
smuggling, and murderous organized crime gangs during the "Roaring
Twenties." Roosevelt, a recently converted "wet" Democrat, promised
a repeal of the Eighteenth Amendment by the end of 1933. That July,
experts predicted the impending change would "bring a flood of foreign liquors and wines into the United States." Waiting in the wings,
Joe Kennedy was as well positioned as anyone to cash in.

During Prohibition, Kennedy, who himself didn't drink, showed a
propensity for bending the alcohol laws his way. In 1929, for personal
use, he made sure to get a "Prohibition Service" permit to transport

liquor legally—roughly four cases (twelve gallons) of sherry—between "Father P. J. Kennedy" in Boston and his own house in New York. But as a businessman, he pushed things further, becoming part of a widening circle of alcohol distributors who provided whiskey and other liquor to customers for solely "medicinal purposes." Before Prohibition's finale, Americans would consume eight million gallons annually using this white lie, claiming they needed booze for health reasons. "Owing to the fact that in many centres medicinal liquor is being sold without even the formality of a physician issuing a prescription, consumption is expected to gain as the end of prohibition nears," the *New York Times* predicted shortly before the Kennedys climbed aboard the *Europa*. Through such medicinal permits, Kennedy was already an established supplier of alcohol by 1933. He had become well known to distillers and looked forward to the boom in business when Prohibition officially became a memory.

To nail down his advantage, just before leaving for England, Kennedy gained the exclusive New England rights to sell "various brands of alcohol beverages" handled by the National Distillers Products Corp., the firm headed by FDR campaign contributor Seton Porter. Prohibition had nearly killed Porter's business. It crawled out of bankruptcy court protection by selling wine for religious services, such as Catholic Masses, and through medicinal liquors. Now that the Roosevelt team ruled Washington, National Distillers expected to grow dramatically, eventually paying a "whiskey dividend" during the depths of the Depression. Shortly before his trip to London with Kennedy, Jimmy Roosevelt arranged for Porter to see his father at the White House. "Mr. Seton Porter has been very kind to me," Jimmy later explained to Missy LeHand, the president's private secretary, asking her to deal directly with any of Porter's concerns while he was abroad with Kennedy. "As you will remember, he [Porter] had a long talk with father last week."

Porter's letter to Kennedy, granting him exclusive sales for New England, detailed the prices of the more than two hundred thousand cases of whiskey, bourbon, and gin his company planned to handle. Porter signed off on the arrangement the week before Joe and Jimmy Roosevelt left for London. "We understand that you wish before sailing to get your skeleton organization in position," Porter wrote to Kennedy. "I only hope that the enclosed letter will be of assistance to you in formulating your plans."

According to this same letter, Henry Mason Day, Kennedy's shadowy associate who accompanied him aboard the *Europa,* was an intermediary helping with the liquor arrangements between Porter's National Distillers and Kennedy. In the past, the *New York Times* described Day as "a mystery man" who specialized in putting together lucrative international deals. A few years earlier, during the Teapot Dome scandal, Day was convicted of trying to cover up his Sinclair oil company's crimes by hiring detectives to spy on a jury reviewing them. He argued that a great miscarriage of justice had besmirched his name. "I am now and shall be able to look any man straight in the eye, as I have all my life," Day protested in 1929, just before leaving for jail. President Hoover declined his plea for clemency. As it turned out, Day and his similarly convicted partner, Harry F. Sinclair, a central player in the Teapot Dome investigation, didn't need an Oval Office dispensation. Instead, they made special arrangements behind bars to come and go as they pleased by providing gifts to their jailers.

Now, as a slightly older and presumably wiser senior partner in the brokerage firm Redmond and Company, Day wanted to seize on any "repeal stocks" that smelled of liquor, convinced that repeal of Prohibition would net the firm millions. Kennedy carefully masked his involvement with Day, though Joe's office could be found inside the Redmond firm. On documents, Joe concealed his own investments with Day's Redmond brokerage firm by using the name of Edward Moore—Joe's gofer and closest crony, for whom he named his youngest son. One joint get-rich-quick scheme handled by Day involved a "pool" investment in a shell company, Libbey-Owens Securities Corp., which sounded like the name of a then-well-known glassmaker. By manipulating the stock and promoting Wall Street rumors about a "booze boom" presumably requiring glass bottles, Day and others in the "pool" investment managed to raise its stock price exorbitantly, with Kennedy picking up sixty thousand dollars (about nine hundred thousand in today's currency).

Their scheme wasn't revealed until a 1934 Senate Banking and Currency Committee hearing about "alcohol pools" and investment fraud. During one February 1934 session, congressional investigators asked Day about Kennedy. What followed was a masterpiece of dissembling.

"Who is Joseph P. Kennedy?" asked Chief Counsel Ferdinand Pecora.

"Mr. Kennedy is a capitalist, or well-known private citizen," Day replied.

"Do you know what his business is?"

"I do not think he is in business," Day said.

"When you say he is a capitalist, does that cover your understanding of what his business is?" Pecora pressed.

"Well, I do not know," Day claimed. "My understanding of a capitalist is somebody who has considerable funds and does not have to work."

"I am not a capitalist," said Pecora.

"Neither am I, sir," said Day. "I have no objection to being."

Day's performance sounded more like Marx Brothers repartee than Karl Marx's *Das Kapital*. Until this testimony, Day had never mentioned Kennedy's involvement in a deal in which Joe earned a small fortune without investing a dime. (Four years later, in 1938, Day was forced out of Redmond and Company after the New York Stock Exchange censured the firm for financial irregularities, for which Day was blamed.)

The Senate hearing also revealed that, along with Day and Kennedy, the investor who'd "engineered" this 1933 Libbey-Owens "pool" was Elisha Walker, a wealthy New York speculator. With a robust mustache and slick hair parted down the middle of his scalp, Walker was described by *Time* magazine as "a bankless banker." Walker was an old pal of Kennedy's from his Hollywood days, when Joe asked him to run the Pathé studio. Among their circle of Wall Street speculators, it was Walker who first introduced Henry Mason Day to Kennedy. Jimmy Roosevelt became pals with Elisha Walker, too, arranging for him to get tickets to the president's 1933 inaugural. "Best of all was the delightful reception which your Father gave me," Walker wrote to Jimmy on May 13, 1933, after his private appointment with the president. "I had a most interesting talk with him and I appreciated immensely both his frankness and courtesy."

As it turned out, Walker and Kennedy were players in another noteworthy "pool" investment, the Brooklyn-Manhattan Transit Corp., a group organized by their mutual friend Bernard Baruch with his pal Herbert Bayard Swope. Together, Baruch, Kennedy, Walker, and Swope would control some 150,000 shares in the BMT, then a privately owned subway line in New York City, running trains mostly on elevated tracks through Brooklyn. Kennedy and Baruch expected the BMT to be bought out soon, in a government consolidation plan, for a handsome price. Jimmy Roosevelt let Walker know he wanted the insurance for the BMT firm, "which I feel we are qualified to handle."

Baruch, the mastermind of this particular subway deal, liked to combine politics and business. He had worked closely with Joe during the 1932 Roosevelt campaign and remained a close friend of Winston Churchill—whom the Kennedy entourage, including the president's son, would visit when the *Europa* landed in England. What role a smooth operator like Day would play on this trip, as Kennedy planned to gain the liquor rights from Great Britain, went largely unnoticed by the press and future historians. No doubt his awareness of Kennedy's involvement with National Distillers and BMT would prove significant. Presumably, Day wasn't just along for the boat ride.

. . .

Young Joseph Kennedy Jr., the aptly named mirror image of his father, accompanied his parents to England in 1933 to attend the London
School of Economics, another step in his education towards greatness.
Though he could be both gregarious and pugnacious with strangers,
Joe Jr. didn't rebel at the guiding hand of his father, whose opinions
he adopted as his own. "He was altogether different than Jack, more
dynamic, more sociable and easy going," their father recalled. While
in London, the eldest Kennedy son studied with Harold Laski, a highly
regarded economist and political science professor, and a prominent
Labour Party figure in government. Felix Frankfurter recommended
the arrangement to Joe, calling Laski the best teacher of his generation. Laski's visiting lectures at Harvard were widely admired. It didn't
matter to Joe that Laski, a socialist at heart, differed drastically from
Kennedy and his faithful son, who mouthed his father's conservative
capitalist views. "I never taught the boys to disapprove of someone just
because I didn't like him," Joe Sr. explained. "They heard enough from
me, and I decided that they should be exposed to someone of intelligence and vitality on the other side." The British don and his American
student managed to get along well. Laski was impressed by Joe Jr.'s
willingness to compete with more sophisticated British students. "It is
more interesting to talk to them than an American boy, because they
talk about important things and not on dances, etc. and it gives me a
chance to get their point of view," young Joe explained to his parents.
"I am just getting to the point where I can discuss matters intelligently
and not be like a dumb ham."

Laski, like other observers of the family, realized young Kennedy
dutifully carried the mantle of his father's outsize ambitions. "He had
his heart set on a political career," Laski remembered. "He has often
sat in my study and submitted with that smile that was pure magic
to relentless teasing about his determination to be nothing less than
President of the United States." Around this time, Eddie Moore, Joe's

trusted gofer, boasted to friends that "if we live long enough and he is spared, the first Irish Catholic in the White House will be one of this man's sons." Tommy Corcoran, another Irish American in FDR's circle, described Joe Kennedy Sr.'s "imperial instincts" as the leader of a clan. "Joe knew what he wanted—he wanted status and money for his children," explained Corcoran. "To Joe, his children were an extension of himself, and if you have this progenitor's sense, you play the game differently than if you want only for yourself."

Joe Kennedy, who spent his early adulthood trying to break free of Boston's provincialism, pushed his sons' education towards an amalgam of influences—worldly instead of parochial; secular rather than religious; a raw Irishness mixed with British tradition. "I think that the Irish in me has not been completely assimilated," he confided to a friend, "but all my ducks are swans." Family friend Kay Halle said the senior Kennedy steered his sons toward the best of this Anglo-American world. "He wanted his sons trained to serve their country in the British tradition," recalled Halle, whose own independence of mind and purse strings made her quite formidable. "This is what's so fascinating and strange, that the same British tradition among the advantaged classes in England should have imprinted itself upon an Irishman, and such an Irishman as Joe. This is a curious paradox."

By comparison, Jimmy Roosevelt was an oldest son devoid of any gravitas. He exuded missed opportunities and diminished promise, even though his father reigned at the top of American society. His younger brother Franklin Jr., touted as "the golden boy" of the family, had inherited his father's good looks and charm. Though still young by any measure, Jimmy appeared old, almost gaunt and prematurely bald, with wide, thick eyeglasses. Rather than an extension of his father's legacy, Jimmy often seemed a mere prop. At FDR's political rallies, Jimmy stood by his side, steadying his crippled father as he waved to the crowds. Jimmy, with his uncertain demeanor, always looked as if he were waiting to be noticed. During the 1932 presidential campaign, one of FDR's top aides, Ray Moley, who later became a sharp critic, noted how the candidate offhandedly teased his son. "And this is my little boy James," Roosevelt told the crowds. "I have more hair than he has." Usually "the crowd would roar," wrote Moley, who observed that after several of these performances Jimmy "grew rather depressed."

Joe Kennedy worked with Moley and Jimmy during the campaign, sharing laughs with the junior Roosevelt during train rides and in hotels. Joe seemed to sense this emotional gap between FDR and his eldest son: the overachieving parent and the dull but amiable progeny. He moved cagily to capitalize on it, acting as a big brother to Jimmy. Shortly before their European trip, Joe invited Jimmy and his wife, Betsey, to the Kennedy home in Hyannis Port, Massachusetts. He also bought him a horse as a gift. "Sell him or give him away if he is any expense," Joe offered. Jimmy considered Joe "a fabulous figure," a veritable Daddy Warbucks, with none of the wariness that FDR brain trusters showed toward Kennedy. Joe Kennedy had plenty of money and success, and Jimmy wanted both for himself.

Jimmy started his own insurance agency in Massachusetts, after disappointing his father by not finishing law school. As a favor, Joe Kennedy convinced some companies to switch their business to young Roosevelt. "I can't tell you how much I appreciate what you did for me," Jimmy wrote to Kennedy in May 1933, "and anyway words mean so little that I hope my actions will sometime make you realize how really grateful I will always be." Joe encouraged Jimmy to be his own man. He also asked him to advocate on his behalf with the president, aware of how personal gifts with Jimmy could provide influence. Kennedy expected a plum administration position for all his campaign efforts and fund-raising, not to mention a sizable donation from his own pocket. But by the summer of 1933, FDR gave no sign of bringing Kennedy into his government. In July, Jimmy urged his father to correct this injustice. "There is one person who, as I talked over with you the other night, feels that he has more or less been put aside now that his usefulness has come to an end," the president's son advised. "I am talking about Joe Kennedy."

Jimmy's note accurately distilled Kennedy's bitterness. No one needed to explain to FDR that Wall Street types such as Kennedy and Baruch had joined his election effort with the expectation of something in return. But Jimmy felt compelled to remind his father that Kennedy had been "a very useful man during the campaign, and when the bills had to be paid, he always came across. I believe today there is still $100,000 owed to him by the national committee."

Still, nothing happened. If Jimmy couldn't help at home, Kennedy decided, he'd enlist the president's son in his plan to make millions abroad. Having young Roosevelt in tow would surely be advantageous— akin to having an American Prince of Wales as an advocate—against the other American bidders seeking the British liquor import business.

Kay Halle's trip to England in the autumn of 1933 would be her second in as many years, offering another chance to visit with the Churchills. For all of her intimacy with the Roosevelts and Kennedys, spoken and unspoken, her relationship with Winston Churchill and his son, Randolph, would prove equally important to this excursion. Kay's first visit to Chartwell took place in the springtime of 1932. After her improbable romance with Randolph in America cooled, Halle decided to accept the Churchills' friendly invitation to visit London. She spent a few weeks in England and then returned later to America, serving as a volunteer on FDR's 1932 presidential campaign, where she met Joe Kennedy.

During her initial trip to England, Kay stayed at Chartwell for a

time, enchanted by the eccentric brilliance of Winston—"a noncon-
formist traditionalist," as she preferred to call him. Upon her arrival
with Randolph for tea, she found Winston "clad in overalls and muddy
boots," replacing the candles of a Waterford crystal chandelier. To reach
up, Winston stood on a satin-covered chair, upsetting Clementine to
no end about the mess. During Halle's weekend stay, former British
prime minister David Lloyd George came to Chartwell for dinner.
"They were talking about the origins of the First World War," Kay
recalled. "I sat listening, of course, but I simply did not have enough
background to know what they were talking about." At the head of the
table, Winston sat with "Renaissance splendour in an open-throated
silk shirt, a velvet smoking jacket and slippers with WSC threaded in
gold on the toes." Kay felt as if she had landed in the front row of a particularly scintillating parliamentary debate. "All during my visit it was
not only the projection and capacity of Mr. Churchill's intellect wres-
tling with the great issues that captivated me, but also the verbal felic-
ity and ingenuity with which he transposed his thoughts into so many
striking phrases and word pictures, blowing them into the air like so
many coloured bubbles," Halle remembered. "Unforgettable barbs and
humourous images punctuated the flow of his talk." She watched as
Randolph kept pace with the "highpowered and uninhibited" conversation presided over by his father at the family table, with all its verbal
pyrotechnics.

"Don't interrupt me when I'm interrupting!" Winston bellowed to
his son, to the roar of laughter among those seated around them. At
another point in this thrust and parry, when young Churchill seemed
to lunge at a weak argument, Winston barked comically, "Randolph,
lie down." At other times, Winston, savoring the moment, seemed to
devour his guests simply by listening with an intent stare affixed to his
bulldog face. At night, as Kay attempted to sleep in an upstairs guest
room, she could hear the muffled sounds of Winston and his associate
Brendan Bracken preparing for an important parliamentary speech the

following day. Past two in the morning, Halle listened to Winston in the adjacent room "tramping up and down, talking his speech into the long pier glass which served as a backboard for these practice runs."

During Kay's stay, Randolph tried to revive their close relationship, but she no longer had interest in him other than as a true friend. "Randolph called me yesterday—frantically wanting to see me, but I was engaged and it was just as well," Halle wrote to her father in April 1932. "I shall always be fond of him and think of him as I know he can be." Over the next few weeks, Kay took in the London sights with other friends, dining and going to the movies. She enjoyed the company of Churchill's nephew Johnnie, the artist son of Winston's only brother, Jack. With him, she visited Blenheim Palace, the ancestral Churchill home. After a few weeks of not seeing Randolph, Kay bumped into him while dancing with a new beau at Quaglino's, a posh nightspot for high society. Randolph, usually nursing a drink or two in these settings, sat down and joined their group of friends at a table. "When I got home he called me up and said he had something very important to tell me," Kay recounted in a letter to her mother. "Poor little R——— I do really adore him but he is different and really very naughty. He says he is furious that I have not tried to see him."

Kay made amends with Randolph, going out on the town with him, before she left in early June. At age twenty-seven, Halle heard that most of her female friends from home were married, and wondered if she would be "the only unplucked blossom in Cleveland," despite "serious (several) proposals" of marriage. "If only Randolph were more like Winston," she lamented to her mother. "He has such considerable gifts already but they can't hold out if he abuses his health. I fear he is cut on the unfortunate Lord Randolph pattern."

On this, her first trip to England, if she left disenchanted with young Churchill, Halle came away impressed with his father as a man of vision and action, even during these "wilderness years" of his political career. At Chartwell, surrounded by family, friends, and young research associates for his books, Winston showed "not a single sign of any inner anguish" that marked this era, she later recalled. She watched him perform with gusto in Parliament, even if other members didn't take heed. "Thank God for a man like Winston who sees and thinks in clear relationship and value and offers impartial solutions," Halle wrote to her parents. "When he talks and addresses himself to the various problems, his analysis and judgement seems [*sic*] so simple and right that one is amazed that it is not clear to everyone—as he sees it. He is a very great man. The greatest, I believe, of this age."

More than a year passed before Halle returned to Chartwell, in October 1933. Her once-narrow world was quickly becoming wider. Earlier that year, she stayed at the White House as a guest of her friends Betsey and Jimmy Roosevelt. Writing to her parents back home in Cleveland, she described waking up in a bedroom across from the one used by Mrs. Roosevelt and "looking out on to the broad spacious White House lawn—after a delicious breakfast brought in on a tray by a black butler." Her friendship with Betsey, a favorite of Franklin Roosevelt, allowed Halle to see the president in a close and candid setting. FDR even mixed the cocktails for them. "After a divine dinner, the Pres[ident] talked about his gr.gr.gr.grandmother [*sic*] being a Jewess—how he hated the Germans and Hitler," Halle recalled. "He talked more freely than he usually does said Jimmie."

For the European trip with Jimmy and Betsey Roosevelt and the Kennedys, Halle's friendship with the Churchills made her an invaluable companion. The social visit to Chartwell would be part of Kennedy's larger business effort to secure whiskey contracts. When they arrived in London, Kay called Randolph, and soon their group arrived for tea with his father and mother. "Winston was in perfect form, told me he wanted to have a long talk with me and said he had a very soft spot in his heart for Cleveland," Halle wrote to her family. "He was most cordial to Jimmy, took us all over the place, showed us his gardens, the new swimming pool he has built, his brick walls and was in top form. Betsey fell in love with him and Jimmy too."

Winston invited the president's son up to his study, where he autographed two copies of *Marlborough*, his new biography about the heroic Churchill ancestor. One copy was inscribed for Jimmy and the other for his father. In the past, Winston and Franklin Roosevelt had their differences. During the Great War, Franklin felt snubbed by Winston when he visited England, and Winston was aware that Roosevelt had declined to see him when he visited New York two years earlier. But on this 1933 visit, Winston let Jimmy know of his admiration for the president's efforts at national recovery with his New Deal programs. Churchill's inscription reflected that sentiment: "With earnest best wishes for the success of the greatest crusade of modern times."

Seated among his guests later that afternoon, Churchill impishly suggested a guessing game. He asked each to confess his fondest wish. "His guests fumbled and qualified their answers," Halle recalled. But Churchill, gazing at young Roosevelt, admitted quite candidly his ambition. "I wish to be Prime Minister and in close and daily communication by telephone with the President of the United States," he declared without hesitation. "There is nothing we could not do if we were together."

Churchill then motioned to his secretary to bring him a piece of paper. On it, he etched the British sterling pound insignia and then intertwined it with the American dollar symbol. He drew the union of the two with a great flourish.

"Pray, bear this to your father from me," Churchill beseeched the president's son. "Tell him this must be the currency of the future."

Jimmy looked perplexed. "What will you call this new currency, sir?" he asked.

"The sterling dollar," Churchill replied.

Roosevelt, who enjoyed a good laugh, teasingly asked, "What, sir, if my father should wish to call it the dollar sterling?"

"It's all the same—we are together," Churchill declared.

After that memorable afternoon, the Roosevelts would travel to Paris and then on to Rome. Rose Kennedy joined them on this relaxing trek, during which they would meet the Pope at the Vatican.

But Joe Kennedy had a much different agenda. Kennedy stayed behind in London to finish out the business deal for British liquor that he'd so carefully put together.

7

The Deal

"We are past the point where being a capitalist is the only way of becoming a politician, and we are dangerously near the point where being a politician is much the quickest way of becoming a capitalist."

—G. K. CHESTERTON

Winston Churchill tended to agree with Charles Dawes, the U.S. ambassador to the Court of St. James's, on most matters except one: alcohol. Until Dawes left in 1932, the U.S. embassy strictly enforced Prohibition, making sure the American outpost in London didn't serve liquor. "I admire him and dine with him every week," Churchill explained about the American ambassador. "But on leaving your Embassy, I always repair immediately to my Club, where I order each of the wines and brandys of which I was deprived at his table."

Churchill condemned Prohibition as sheer folly, an unnatural restriction on a most common human impulse. "All I can say is that I have taken more out of alcohol than alcohol has taken out of me," he joked, and was often seen in private with a glass in hand. He recognized drink as a social lubricant in times of peace, and as a salve and welcome diversion during war. "Whatever else they may say of me as a soldier," he told his World War I troops in his farewell, "at least nobody can say that I have ever failed to display a meet and proper appreciation of the virtues of alcohol." His troops heartily concurred.

Prohibition, tightly wrapped in religious orthodoxy and general extremism, never appealed to Churchill and caused one of his more notable defeats. To his utter mortification in 1922, he lost his seat in the House of Commons to Edwin Scrymgeour, a chaplain and son of the Scottish temperance movement. As the Prohibitionist Party's leader, Scrymgeour wanted to ban the manufacture and import of alcoholic refreshments, shut down all pubs, and allow liquor only for medicinal purposes—so long as the bottle was labeled "Poison." Though this loss proved a momentary blip in Winston's career, he never again underestimated the sober-minded zealotry of this God-invoking cause. As Chancellor of the Exchequer in the 1920s, he favored the collection of taxes from liquor sales to help float the government's budget rather than banning it. Until he left that post in 1929, he warned that any temperance movement in England would bring corruption and an "illicit traffic" in alcohol, just as it had in the United States.

During their trips through a so-called dry America, Churchill and his son had found the social experiment of Prohibition to be a duplicitous mess. "I must confess that on one occasion I was taken to a speakeasy," Churchill teased one American audience. "I went, of course, in my capacity as a Social Investigator." (Randolph's assessment was far blunter. "Prohibition is a complete farce," he declared in 1929.) Writing in *Collier's* magazine, Winston noted "the United States, far from being dry, is becoming an exporter of liquor on a large scale," and highlighted the growth of smuggled alcohol into Canada. He pointed to his experience in England as a better method to follow. "Why don't you tax alcoholic liquor and strike a three-fold blow at drunkenness, Prohibition and crime?" he asked at the New York Economic Club.

Churchill, by position and disposition, was a natural ally for Joe Kennedy's plan to profit from the liquor trade. By September 26, 1933, the day he and the president's son left for Britain, Kennedy had created a new firm called Somerset Importers (apparently named for Boston's WASPy Somerset Club, which kept Irishmen like him from joining) with an initial $118,000 investment. Somerset became his piggy bank for cashing in on Prohibition's demise. On this cross-Atlantic boat ride, Kennedy carried with him the letter from Seton Porter, of National Distillers Products Corp., appointing Somerset exclusive sales agent in New England for its liquor products.

When they arrived in London, Joe complained to Kay Halle that they needed to meet with "the very best people" during their stay. "Finally, perhaps through her intervention, they found themselves in the drawing room of the legendary Winston Churchill," wrote Joe's biographer David E. Koskoff. "Kennedy explained his purpose." Not much can be found in documents about these meetings. Instead, most historians have focused on Churchill's chat with Jimmy Roosevelt about the "sterling dollar," without considering Joe Kennedy's presence. But years later, in the early 1960s, Randolph Churchill insisted Joe Kennedy came to Chartwell with the rest of the Americans, including Kay Halle and Jimmy Roosevelt. Randolph later told *New York Times* columnist C. L. Sulzberger that he didn't know the purpose for this 1933 expedition underwritten by Kennedy, but quickly found out. Kennedy "assure[d] them Prohibition would shortly end and he wished to line up contracts to represent the best firms," Randolph said. Kennedy claimed he gave fifty thousand dollars to the Roosevelt campaign, Randolph recalled, and the presence of Jimmy Roosevelt on this trip seemed to underscore that point. In another conversation, Kennedy historian Arthur M. Schlesinger Jr. later recalled, "Randolph insisted that Joe Kennedy also was there" at the 1933 Chartwell meeting, though Schlesinger remained unconvinced. But *Times* columnist Sulzberger included Randolph's detailed account in his own 1970 memoir. "And he [Randolph] swears he can confirm its truth," Sulzberger attested.

Ultimately, there was one indisputable fact: Joe Kennedy pulled off an international coup that made him even richer. He landed the lucrative British importation rights to distribute Haig & Haig Scotch whiskey, Dewar's, Gordon's gin, and other imported drinks, all very desirable to customers in the no-longer-dry United States. ("Don't be vague, ask for Haig," proclaimed a favorite advertising slogan.) With young Roosevelt by his side, Kennedy beat out other potential rivals. "The British distillers were much impressed by Kennedy and the company he was keeping," observed Lord Longford, a chronicler of the Kennedys in England.

What Winston Churchill might have done to help Kennedy get the British liquor contracts isn't clear—perhaps a good word to the right person or just some friendly advice. As Prohibition historian Daniel Okrent noted, the same successful Kennedy-led group who met Churchill also conferred with Prime Minister Ramsay MacDonald and Neville Chamberlain, Winston's successor as Chancellor of the Exchequer. Clearly the Kennedy offer to become the sole American importer of British liquor contained a winning mix of politics and high finance. "If Joe Kennedy wanted to open political doors or commercial ones, he could have done worse than travel with the son of a president," explained Okrent.

Following the Churchill meeting, everything fell into place. Roosevelt's presence signaled the federal government's cooperation with whatever import regulations might be needed to enter America. Before leaving London, Jimmy Roosevelt joined Joe Kennedy for lunch with Sir James Calder, a major British distiller of top brands. Sir James gave his business to Kennedy and soon became a family friend, trekking that winter to Kennedy's newly purchased summer home in Palm Beach, Florida. From England, Jimmy cabled his father back at the White House: GRAND TRIP ALL WELL.

When Prohibition finally ended two months later, in December 1933, Joe Kennedy seized his chance. With the help of his pal Henry Mason Day (who had sold a distillery to National Distillers), he put

Somerset into full gear, blocking most potential competitors successfully and storing crates of "medicinal" liquor in warehouses. With this
new arrangement, Somerset saw its business in the United States soar,
selling 150,000 cases of Scotch whiskey in the first full year. "We have
done surprisingly well with contracts," Joe wrote his oldest son. By the
end of 1934, National Distillers Products Corp., including its New England franchise run by Kennedy, declared that its net profits had qua-
drupled in a year. When he sold the Somerset franchise a decade later,
Joe Kennedy earned $8.5 million (the equivalent of more than $100
million in today's currency).

Another set of finances surrounding this trip involved Churchill. In
September 1933, as the Kennedy group prepared to leave for London,
Winston began a series of stock investments in two seemingly obscure
American firms tied directly to Joe Kennedy: Brooklyn Manhattan
Transit and National Distillers Products Corp. These Churchill stock
investments were clustered around the Kennedy trip—executed both
shortly before the Chartwell visit and in the months afterward—and
were known only to a few, perhaps not even to Randolph. Where Winston got the money for such investments is not clear from available documents. On their face, however, these transactions seemed remarkably
risky for a man who had lost much of his fortune in bad investments,
who feared he might lose his beloved debt-ridden Chartwell Manor,
and who had previously relied on friends to bail him out financially.

Winston's involvement with the American liquor industry emerged
shortly after Kennedy began selling British whiskey, archival records
show. In March 1934, Churchill was able to invest $5,850 (approxi-
mately $101,000 in today's currency) in National Distillers Products
Corp.—the same American company that awarded its New England
franchise to Joe Kennedy. Later that year, Winston managed to buy
some more of the same stock for $4,375 (about $76,000 in today's currency). Soon after both purchases, Winston sold his National Distillers stock, earning a neat little profit, records show. The paperwork for

these transactions was handled by the Vickers da Costa brokerage firm, which included Churchill's brother, Jack, as a stockbroker and partner.

Winston's stake in BMT—the private New York City subway line associated with Kennedy, Baruch, and others in their speculative investment "pool"—was even greater and proved more complex. In the two weeks before Kennedy left for England, September 11–26, 1933, Winston repeatedly bought BMT in batches of 100 shares for a total purchase of $21,725 (approximately $380,000 in today's currency). Records show no other BMT exchanges for Churchill for another ten days, not until after the visit of the Kennedy entourage to Chartwell. The following day, however, Winston started cashing out. He quickly sold about two-thirds of this stock by October 11, 1933, making a substantial 10 percent profit within just a month of his investment.

The idea for Winston's BMT stock transaction apparently came from Kennedy's friend and business associate Bernard Baruch. "I bought seven hundred Brooklyn Manhattan T around 30, sold four hundred around 35, and am sitting on three hundred," Winston wrote to Baruch on October 15, 1933, shortly after entertaining his American visitors at Chartwell. "Many thanks for the fruitful suggestion." Baruch, Kennedy, and other "pool" speculators involved in BMT expected their 150,000 shares of private stock would boom if the subway company were merged into New York City's overall system. They managed to get Herbert Bayard Swope, the former newspaper editor who became Baruch's pal, onto the board of BMT along with another of their "pool" investors, Elisha Walker. Swope provided both Baruch and Joe Kennedy with inside information on the company's projected earnings and dividends. "In private life it was quite true that he [Swope] kept Baruch current on information that a later generation would call privileged," James Grant, a Baruch biographer, wrote about the BMT arrangement. They seemed confident of a big payday sometime soon.

Back and forth throughout 1934, Winston sold and bought BMT stock, at least some of which was purchased on margin with the hope that it would go up. The amount was much more than Winston previously said he'd ever invest on Wall Street. In the months surrounding the Chartwell visit, Churchill managed to purchase a total of more than $82,000 in BMT stock (about $1.4 million in today's currency) and sold a total of some $72,000 ($1.2 million today), according to available archival records. The BMT collection was among the biggest in his portfolio, which included a handful of other stocks in 1934. It also far exceeded the overall $12,000 that Churchill told his brother he was willing to wager in low-risk American overseas investments, particularly after losing a bundle in the 1929 Wall Street crash. "The more I study the stocks I know about," he advised Jack's brokerage firm prudently in 1931, "the more sure I am that the only way to recover the losses is to acquire some low priced solid securities without reference to any immediate dividends, and then put them away for two, three or four years."

Quite the contrary, Churchill's large stake in BMT stock posed a tremendous risk and broke every sensible rule of investing—unless someone had promised him it'd be a sure bet. Increasingly, this risky stake in one stock left Winston worrying that his anticipated bonanza might never happen. On November 18, 1933, he cabled Baruch: DO YOU STILL LIKE BWT [*sic*] KINDEST REGARDS WINSTON.

Baruch, like most speculators in discussing stocks, didn't leave much documentation. His telegram contained a one-word reply: YES.

Over the next year, Winston's anxious messages continued, as the situation surrounding BMT became only murkier. He wondered whether to cash out. ARE YOU STILL PLEASED WITH B.M.T. AROUND FORTY REGARD [*sic*] WINSTON, he cabled Baruch on October 27, 1934. That same day, he dropped a personal note to his brother, Jack, about his stock account. "I telegraphed Baruch about Brooklyn," he wrote, assuring Jack that he expected to make more money from his investments in the following year. But Baruch's telegram reply was decidedly mixed:

WHILE DISAPPOINTED DELAYED TRANSIT CONSOLIDATION FEEL BROOKLYN COM-
PARATIVELY BEST THING ON LIST ALTHOUGH AFFECTED BY POLITICO ECONOMIC
SITUATION. BERNIE.

Increasingly, the BMT investment by Kennedy and Baruch would
come under greater scrutiny. Their dream of a big payday soon evapo-
rated. Instead of a rapid merger that would dramatically increase the
stock's value, the BMT took years to be unified into a citywide system under municipal ownership. While Joe's initial half-million-dollar
stake swiftly doubled in value, it is not clear how much he finally
earned. Most biographers say Joe Kennedy lost money in the BMT investment, and presumably so did his partners.

How Churchill obtained money to invest in these two American
stocks so intricately linked to Joe Kennedy's quick-hit investment strategy remained part of the overall mystery shrouding this 1933 trip to
Great Britain and its lucrative alcohol deals. Winston's subsequent note
of thanks to Baruch about BMT suggests Kennedy's pal helped orches-
trate the buying of this particular stock. But Churchill's knowledge of
National Distillers Products Corp. seems unlikely to have been divined
from any other source than Kennedy and his circle of associates. Shortly
after this trip, records show, Churchill also managed in June 1934 to
buy shares in the distilling company of Sir James Calder—another of
Kennedy's business partners, who provided Haig & Haig whiskey—
which Winston soon disposed of at a slight loss.

For much of his career, Churchill—unencumbered by stock disclo-
sure rules and ethical "pay to play" restrictions that regulate much
of twenty-first-century government—wasn't inclined to refuse the
helping hand of a friend. Earlier, in 1929, Baruch provided money to
Churchill when the latter nearly lost his fortune in Wall Street's crash.
Following World War I, Sir Ernest Cassel, another rich financier, paid
for Churchill's home furnishings "as an act of spontaneous friendship" and provided him with "unlimited credit." A Churchill critic,

Lord Alfred Douglas, seized on Churchill's involvement with Cassel and lambasted Winston as "this ambitious and brilliant man, short of money and eager for power."

Churchill often relied upon private donors to help finance his personal lifestyle and political career. During his 1929 lecture tour in America, his travel expenses were paid by Baruch and Charles Schwab. In 1937, he relied on his friends' help when stock market losses and bad debts forced him to put Chartwell up for sale—one of the darkest days of his "wilderness years" era. "If we do not get a good price we can quite well carry on for a year or two more," he wrote to Clementine about their manor home. "But no good offer should be refused, having regard to the fact that our children are almost all flown, and my life is probably in its closing decade." At the urging of Churchill's top adviser, Brendan Bracken, his beloved Chartwell would be saved in the late 1930s by another friendly investor, Henry Strakosch, the South African mining magnate. Strakosch promised to pay Winston's debts, take over his troubled portfolio, and ensure that Chartwell remained his home "without distraction and anxiety," as Winston told Bracken. This generous bailout plan, considered more a gift than graft by Churchill and his benefactors, wasn't revealed until decades later. "The exact details of Strakosch's intervention remained secret for many years," wrote historian David Cannadine. "But it was widely known that Churchill did not seem able to manage his own finances."

For a time, Jimmy Roosevelt's role in Kennedy's British venture would remain hidden. Shortly after returning from Europe, Jimmy privately presented Kennedy's British distiller friends to U.S. alcohol control officials in Washington as a way of priming the pump for business. "It is almost as difficult for an Englishman to understand an American as it is for an American to understand an Englishman's customs, and

I am sure no fault can be found with either party for not thoroughly understanding one another at the first go-off," Kennedy explained to a Dewar's official about the new federal control board overseeing permits for liquor.

According to one biographer, Joe promised Jimmy Roosevelt a 25 percent stake in Somerset but reneged when they got back to the United States. "Kennedy put his arm around Jimmy and said, 'You know, I've been thinking about it, and with your father as president, if it ever got out that you were in the liquor business, it would be death,'" recalled a major Boston liquor distributor. "He [Jimmy] said, 'I don't think we should do this.'" Jimmy's brother Franklin Jr., no fan of Joe Kennedy, had a sense of the subterfuge surrounding the British trip. "Oh, I know he was a financial genius, but he was a rotten human being," said Franklin Jr. about Joe. "He once called in my brother to work out a deal with [a Scottish distiller], and Jimmy went and worked out the whole deal, then had trouble getting old man Kennedy to pay his expenses. And Kennedy made a pile out of that one."

Nevertheless, Jimmy Roosevelt made plenty of money through Kennedy's success in gaining the British import contracts. With Joe's help, the fledgling Roosevelt insurance firm in Massachusetts replaced another named W. T. Shackelford and Co., of Baltimore, with Jimmy providing the major insurance coverage for National Distillers Products Corp.—policies then estimated at more than $70 million. Rather than sell booze directly as Joe's business partner, Jimmy made his bundle by safeguarding the ships and their cargo of Scotch whiskey and other liquors delivered from Great Britain. Jimmy's tax disclosures showed that his income more than doubled—from $21,714 in 1933 to $49,167 in 1934 (about $850,000 in today's currency), a huge sum during the teeth of the Depression.

Emboldened by his coup in London with Kennedy, Jimmy Roosevelt came home bragging about nabbing the National Distillers account. He tried a similar strong-arm tactic with a Boston bank president, who learned that government checks would be pulled from his bank unless young Roosevelt handled its insurance coverage. "Your son James, engaged in the insurance business, is diverting accounts to himself from old established Insurance Brokers on the strength of not only the name of Roosevelt but implication that obtaining such business, favors will be granted by the administration," warned J. Henry Neale, a lawyer and banker who supported FDR. "This is said particularly to apply to National Distillers' account." After the White House received Neale's private letter about this "malicious rumor," the president demanded an answer from his son.

In an August 28, 1934, "Dear Pa" letter sent to President Roosevelt's private home in Hyde Park, New York, Jimmy apparently disclosed to his father his deal with the Kennedy-connected firm for the first time. "You wanted a statement of facts as to the National Distillers," he acknowledged. "It is true that I have this account, but I can't understand why I shouldn't have it."

Jimmy's two-page letter from Boston explained how he had approached Seton Porter of National Distillers, seeking his firm's insurance contracts, after he "got the idea prior to the repeal of Prohibition that when this was accomplished, the liquor industry would need to make some changes in the way of insurance." Jimmy didn't mention Joe Kennedy's name, but he probably didn't have to. He vowed to set things straight with Neale and firmly denied he was trading on the Roosevelt family name. He described Seton Porter, Joe Kennedy's partner in the liquor business, as his own good friend. "I think Mr. Porter would be willing to say that I have his insurance solely on the basis of merit, and I would only want it on that basis," Jimmy promised his father. "Also, I have never tried to do anything for them with the Administration and never will. Mr. Porter understands that completely, as I think he told you when he saw you" at the White House.

Jimmy only vaguely recognized the consternation Neale's warning letter had caused among the president's close aides, such as Louis

Howe. He seemed clueless about the political embarrassment the British liquor deal might cause his father if it were made public. "If you get any more letters like that, I wish you would tell Louis not to bother you with them, but refer them to me directly and I will give him any information that he desires," Jimmy wrote with a certain peevishness. "Incidentally, there is not a single piece of government business on my books . . . and if you ever hear anyone say what business I have because of any promised favors, I wish you would try to ascertain their names immediately and we will soon set them straight."

Neale received letters from both the president and his son denying the rumors. "I sent your letter to my boy James," FDR wrote. "There is, of course, not a word of truth in it." Neale was only too happy to accept their explanation, which seemed to put the matter to rest. But when reporters a few years later suggested that Jimmy had profited from insurance contracts steered his way, young Roosevelt again vehemently denied it, along with Kennedy. "Whoever started that is either purposely lying or just didn't want to investigate," Jimmy insisted. "I got into places I never would if I wasn't the son of the President. But son or no son, I got tossed out of a lot, too. Listen fellow, prospects don't wilt just because you're the son of the President."

Decades later, however, he casually admitted the truth during an oral history given in the twilight of his own career. "I did have the insurance account of the National Distillers, which I got basically through Mr. Joseph Kennedy who was as you may remember a good friend of my father," he told an interviewer in 1972. By then, no one seemed interested in the deal.

In enlisting the president's son as his ally, Joe Kennedy displayed more than financial acumen. In his calculated way, he understood the frailties of human nature, the weaknesses and soft spots in a family tree. He sensed the desire of those in a new generation to prove themselves and for an older generation still to view them as children. He ingratiated himself further with the president by befriending his family, making inroads of the sort that campaign cash could never achieve. With a rapier instinct, Joe could spot the fault lines in Franklin Roosevelt's personal life—in this case, the complex relationship between a great man and his son—and exploited them for his own purposes, all under the guise of friendship. Kennedy even described himself as "foster-father" to Jimmy, a young man only a few years older than his own son Joe Jr.

"You know I'm still cutting my teeth in a business way," Jimmy wrote gratefully to Kennedy in 1933, around the time of their British trip. The president's eldest son expressed his determination to follow through "with these big concerns" and show that he didn't have to rely "on the old man's reputation and have no guts of my own." In this deal, young Roosevelt agreed to Kennedy's wishes, naively and greedily, with the expectation of more benefits to come.

Ultimately, the secrecy surrounding Kennedy's 1933 trip obscured the origins of his relationship with Winston Churchill, which most historians say began later in the decade and was acrimonious from the start. However, documents show that the two men's shared friendship with Bernard Baruch, their contacts with Kay Halle and the Roosevelts, their political ambitions for profitable relations between their two countries, and their stake in two companies involved in Kennedy's business empire suggest a kindly alliance between them. Certainly in private, Joe gave the impression that he had a friend in Winston Churchill.

Only a few seemed to know of these initial friendly Churchill-Kennedy exchanges before everything changed so dramatically. Joe's granddaughter Amanda, in her 2001 collection of his letters, noted that Churchill "had been one of his earliest British political contacts, and had even suggested Kennedy's name for an award celebrating freedom and peace" in 1938. One of Joe's few trusted confidants, James A. Fayne, a Kennedy man in business and government, declared that Joe's "greatest friend in Europe" was Winston Churchill. "Before Mr. Kennedy was appointed Ambassador, his chief world contact was highly personal though it was Churchill," recalled Fayne in 1968, ". . . and then they became oceans apart."

8

The King of Wall Street

With his successful trip to London, Joseph P. Kennedy raised his expectations even higher—for his family, his church, his president, and particularly himself.

Much of his overweening ambition was focused on his sons. Kennedy urged his eldest, Joe Jr., studying at the London School of Economics, to travel throughout Europe as a way of preparing for his golden future. "You would be surprised how interested friends of ours are to see what you are going to learn out of this year abroad," he told his son. "I know you will be smart enough to keep your contacts with foreigners as much as possible. You have Americans to live with the rest of your life."

To burnish his image, Kennedy expanded his influence with the church hierarchy, partly to cultivate political favor among Catholic voters and partly to impress his devout wife, Rose. During their fall 1933 trip to Europe, Joe arranged a papal audience for Rose, while he stayed in London to finish up his business. At the Vatican, Rose was accompanied by Jimmy and Betsey Roosevelt, and escorted by Count Enrico Galeazzi, the Vatican administrator. Galeazzi enjoyed a close friendship with Francis J. Spellman, then an auxiliary bishop in Boston, who knew the Kennedys well.

"I shall remember the moments spent with His Holiness as the most precious ones of my life," Rose later wrote in thanks to Galeazzi. Arthur Houghton, one of Joe's cronies, known for his humor, also came along on the European trip and kept an eye on Rose and the Roosevelts in Rome. The president's son proved amiable yet tone-deaf about international protocol. Aware that Jimmy's awkward thank-you note had wished the ascetic pontiff "many years of happiness and pleasure," Houghton apologized to Galeazzi. "Well—it is the best I could get out of him," Houghton said of young Roosevelt. "I hope it will do."

Meanwhile, in England, Joe furthered his relationship with Kay Halle. After Rose and the Roosevelts left for Italy, Halle stayed on in London, ostensibly with Betsey's sister, for a short time. If she suspected an affair, Rose gave no indication that she was worried about Halle. Felix Frankfurter noticed the enviable attraction between the middle-aged Joe and this smart, personable young woman. "As for Miss Halle—I am sorry to have been somewhat mistaken about her," Frankfurter wrote to Joe, as if he'd been expecting some run-of-the-mill mistress. "I thought she had spirit as well as all else. And to think that she was cowed by you and didn't dare to come down here." When they returned to America, Joe stayed in touch with Kay. Soon she learned of the serious mystery illness, feared to be leukemia, that had forced the hospitalization of young Jack Kennedy in New Haven, Connecticut, near Choate. "Tonight Joe Kennedy called me from N.Y. where he came to [sic] his very ill son Jack," she told her family, without elaboration. From her previous hospital visit, Halle knew what it was like to watch Joe stare helplessly at his desperately ill and lonely boy.

Kennedy's greatest expectations, though, fixated on his own political career. For more than a year, he believed his tireless campaign efforts for Franklin Roosevelt, and his private dealings with Roosevelt's son

Jimmy, would land him a prominent position in Washington. Several in the president's inner circle opposed him. They worried that Kennedy's speculator background might undermine their efforts to clean up Wall Street—widely viewed as a corrupt Tower of Babel that had ushered in the Great Depression. FDR's top aide, Louis Howe, and others resented Kennedy's chumminess with the Roosevelts, suspicious of his motives. When he broke his leg riding a horse in April, Joe humorously noted to Louis Ruppel, a friendly reporter, "By strange co-incidence, the horse's name was 'Louis,' named after you I hope, not after the president's secretary. But then, after all, I have been thrown pretty consistently by Louises this year."

In reality, Kennedy was furious about his exclusion from Roosevelt's administration, where he expected to be treated as a big man, a figure of respect. He pushed Jimmy to remind his father of his desire for a top post, and threatened to demand repayment on his outstanding loans to FDR's 1932 campaign. But the White House's initial offers, diplomatic stations in Uruguay and the Irish Free State, seemed more like vague insults than rewards. "He thought it would be a very nice thing for me to go back as Minister to a country from which my grandfather had come as an immigrant," Kennedy recalled to his oldest son, Joe Jr., about the Irish offer. "I told him that I did not desire a position with the Government unless it really meant some prestige to my family."

Baruch complained to Kennedy that the anti–Wall Street fervor of some presidential advisers also hampered his influence with Roosevelt. Behind-the-scenes, however, Baruch and his savvy business associate Herbert Bayard Swope "lent a quiet, helping hand" in finding a government role for their pal. Eventually, after a Washington visit by Joe and Rose Kennedy orchestrated by Jimmy Roosevelt, the president came up with a high-visibility job. At a private meeting in June 1934, while sharing a beer with Baruch and Kennedy, Roosevelt decided to appoint Joe the nation's first chairman of the newly created Securities and Exchange Commission. Swope applauded the decision. "I don't believe any appointment you have made will yield a higher return in unswerving loyalty to you and more real service to the public than that of Joe Kennedy," Swope said in congratulations to Roosevelt. This new role, effectively as Wall Street's sheriff, offered Kennedy a chance to remake himself publicly, to turn his reputation as a devil-may-care speculator on its head. In a grand gesture, the president urged Rose to let her husband come to Washington. Joe feigned deliberation about the offer, but in fact, he jumped at it. When Ray Moley, a dubious Roosevelt aide, asked about any ghosts in his past, Kennedy exploded with a profanity and "defied anyone . . . to point to a single shady act in his whole life."

Many New Deal liberals objected to Kennedy's selection, which one called "setting a wolf to guard a flock of sheep." But Joe managed to win over the support of his doubters, including Ferdinand Pecora, the Senate's maverick Wall Street investigator, who agreed to join the commission. Convinced that he could rehabilitate his image, Kennedy swore his SEC chairmanship would be "a credit to the country, the president, himself, and his family—clear down to the ninth child."

Within a month, however, Kennedy's checkered Wall Street past began to haunt him. Reporters called attention to the Senate testimony of Henry Mason Day, who'd organized the deceptive pool in "alcohol stocks" that netted Kennedy a quick-hit profit in 1933. They wondered how Kennedy could regulate Wall Street abuses when he seemed so much a part of them. "He's independently wealthy and his associations with Henry Mason Day and Charles M. Schwab (the latter during the war) rank him in Grade A speculative society," wrote one columnist about Kennedy. Yet the press seemed to know only a little about Kennedy's hidden deals. They hadn't detected Day's involvement with Kennedy and the president's son to secure the liquor contracts for Somerset Importers. Nor did they seem unduly concerned when the SEC began a review of the stock transfers surrounding Brooklyn-Manhattan Transit—the obscure subway line whose investors happened to include Kennedy, Baruch, and an Englishman named Winston Churchill.

In September 1934, government officials blocked attempts by BMT to offer an eight-million-dollar bond issue on the New York Stock Exchange, claiming it violated the newly created federal securities regulations that the panel was charged with enforcing. In a press release, the SEC took pains to underline that Kennedy had recused himself from any proceedings examining BMT. The agency officials also noted that the value of Kennedy's BMT stock—all of which he held before taking on the SEC post—had no direct bearing on the bond issue. Federal investigators focused on whether BMT had improperly tried to avoid registering its bond issue and had taken advantage of rules requiring these bonds be sold only to New York State residents. The SEC probers learned that more than a million dollars' worth of bonds had found their way to investors outside of New York, in apparent violation of existing law. BMT argued that it had sold the bonds to New York bank distributing groups without violating any interstate commerce rules. But clearly, BMT had made a bold challenge to the rules Kennedy was now supposed to enforce.

Documents show that Kennedy's claim of noninvolvement in the BMT matter was less than sincere. A month before Kennedy's disavowal, Herbert Bayard Swope sent him a swath of press clippings about BMT and bragged how he'd managed to deflect the press's attention from anything that might prove embarrassing. "The way I handled it prevented any wild outburst, which readily could have happened under the circumstances," Swope wrote to Kennedy in an August 1934 note sent directly to his SEC office. Referring to their friend and partner Baruch by his initials, Swope's warned that "B.M.B. writes a long, rambling letter containing 'instructions' for you, which I shall tell you when I see you." By any rules, an SEC chairman (one supposedly recusing himself) didn't wait for "instructions" from a key principal in a company under investigation by the commission.

Kennedy, Baruch, and Swope were sitting on a potential powder keg. Although Churchill wasn't involved in the bond sale, an extended SEC investigation of BMT stock transfers outside New York State might have revealed Winston's substantial foreign investment in the subway firm. Investigators might also have found that the purchase of Winston's BMT stock occurred around the same time as Kennedy's successful liquor contracts were granted in Britain. Certainly these dealings, regardless of their legality, would have been politically embarrassing if exposed. Whatever the cause for concern, Swope tried to put Kennedy's mind at ease. He let him know that Baruch's explanation of the federal probe focused on the issuance of "municipal, county, state and national bonds, with which you have nothing to do." To Baruch, Swope complained that their trouble was being caused by other BMT investors who were "shooting not only at me, but also at you and Joe."

Fortunately for Kennedy and his pals, the BMT investigation soon faded away. In November 1934, Kennedy assured one U.S. senator that he had put all his stock holdings in a blind trusteeship prior to becoming SEC chairman, so that the agency could "discharge its very important and delicate work without the slightest embarrassment, even embarrassment generated by distortion of perfectly innocent facts." Other potentially embarrassing facts surrounding Kennedy's liquor business were also swept from view. Headed for a jury trial, a lawsuit by Boston brewer John A. McCarthy, who claimed Kennedy had promised to share his profits for help in setting up Somerset Importers, was dropped.

Still, rumors persisted that Kennedy had also cheated his buddies Jimmy Roosevelt and Swope, keeping them from getting their fair share of the Somerset liquor importing firm. "I did help him get the business going; I did help him get what he wanted from father," Jimmy

Roosevelt later explained. "But I did not expect to become part of the business. I have to make it clear that Joe and I never had any agreement to that effect." As for Swope, according to his biographer E. J. Kahn, Swope—who had advised Joe on his public comments as SEC chief just as he had helped arrange a New York speech for Churchill when he visited in early 1932—was offended when Kennedy offered to let him buy an interest in Somerset but refused any "free rides" for his previous services.

Remarkably, Joe Kennedy established a new regulatory framework for American business without letting the SEC become the bane of Wall Street, as many friends feared. "The feeling in local financial circles is that the reasonable attitude which the Securities and Exchange Commission has taken on most of the problems it has dealt with so far has been due to your common sense influence," lauded Edson B. Smith, a Kennedy friend, and editor of the *Boston Herald Traveler*.

Although Joe purchased a lavish countryside place in Maryland to stay during the week, he never moved his family to Washington. Instead, when weekends came, he traveled to Palm Beach, Florida; to Bronxville, New York; or to Hyannis Port, Massachusetts—wherever his wife and children happened to be at the moment. Jimmy Roosevelt said his father was pleased by Joe's SEC performance and valued his contrarian advice. "He was often critical of father's New Deal politics regarding big business, but he was, in a way, an old family friend, and when the chips were down he supported father," the president's son recalled.

By the time he resigned as SEC chairman in September 1935, Kennedy had finally gained the public respect he craved. Rather than be viewed with suspicion or contempt for his private deals, he was now praised by newspaper editorials after his first taste of public office. "I wanted power," Joe later explained. "I thought money would give me power and so I made money, only to discover that it was politics—not money—that really gave a man power."

The following month, Joe and Rose journeyed to England (for the second time in three years), where they visited Churchill at his Chartwell home. Their 1935 arrival was preceded by Baruch's note reminding Winston that Kennedy was an "important" American whom he might deal with in the future. Prior to leaving, Joe convinced Roosevelt to inform U.S. ambassador Robert Worth Bingham that Kennedy planned to "look into the question of foreign bonds listed in New York" and should be extended all courtesies. "He is anxious to meet one or two of the more important people in England, and I hope that you will be able to arrange it," Roosevelt directed. "Naturally he should see not only those in Government but also those in opposition."

After visiting Churchill and other officials in England, Kennedy would plan his next step in life. Though he promised that the SEC job would be his last in government, no one expected him to stay away for long. Nor did Joe's desire to remake his public image—he was now lauded as the vigilant protector of Wall Street ethics—mean he would abandon his shadier friends in private business. He made that intention clear before he left England for America.

"My trip is most interesting and quite exciting," he wrote cryptically to speculator Henry Mason Day at the Redmond brokerage firm on Wall Street where he himself once had a desk, "and I will tell you about it on my return."

Part II

FAMILY FORTUNES

"It is a wise father that knows his own child."
—WILLIAM SHAKESPEARE, *The Merchant of Venice*

"Don't hold your parents up to contempt. After all,
you are their son, and it is just possible that you may
take after them."
—EVELYN WAUGH

9

The Sons of Great Men

A crowd of smiling Englishmen, in derby hats and fedoras, gathered at a political rally in Wavertree, a suburb of Liverpool, and listened to the young candidate's aging father, Winston Churchill. "Two dogs are biting us but our dog is not biting back because it wears a socialist mussle," Winston growled, a canine reference to the two opposing parties, Labour and the Liberals. "The Conservative Party has been paralyzed."

This dog-eat-dog appraisal of Parliament in February 1935 caused the crowd to laugh. Winston, in bow tie and topcoat, accepted their applause. At age sixty-one, with a few thin hair strands covering his bald forehead, he was appreciated like an old vaudevillian whose best days were over. Standing beside him, with the biggest grin of all, was Randolph Churchill, his twenty-three-year-old son, a mere pup.

Quite to his father's surprise, Randolph had decided, impetuously and without much plan, to run in an uphill race against two parliamentary opponents. A similar constituency had first elected Winston to Parliament in 1900, at age twenty-six. To this admiring crowd, Randolph, an independent Conservative, vowed to capture the Wavertree seat "for keeps." With a flower in his lapel, his thick blond hair neatly combed over, Randolph presided over the rally as the scion of a new generation in the fabled Churchill dynasty. "A Chip Off the Old Block," declared the *New York Times*, repeating a nickname it had called him five years earlier. "He saw a chance to make trouble, irresistible to a man of his ancestry." Randolph's most notable asset was the Churchill family reputation, yet this appearance by Winston would be his one and only for his son's campaign. "My son has taken this step upon his own responsibility and without consulting me," Winston explained publicly.

In private, Winton remained upset about Randolph's "most rash and unconsidered plunge" into the Wavertree election. He felt his son's bid undermined the chances of another Conservative in the race, and realized a loss would damage Winston's own chances of getting back into the party's good graces. "With his personality and political flair he [Randolph] will undoubtedly make a stir," Winston wrote to Clementine. "But in all probability all that he will do is to take enough votes from the Conservative to let the Socialist in. All together I am vexed and worried about it . . . Randolph has no experience of electioneering and does not seem to want advice." Despite his father's amusing rhetoric on the stump, Randolph was determined to be the singular star of this campaign, a role for which he'd been preparing all his life. He felt his place in Parliament was inevitable. "If anybody had disputed my belief that I should enter the House of Commons and hold office by the time I was twenty-three, I should not have bothered to argue," he later explained. "For I regarded it as a certainty."

After his long lecture tour of America, Randolph had decided to become a political writer employed by Lord Rothermere, the press lord and political friend of his father, rather than return to Oxford as a student. Journalism seemed only a necessary prelude, a very public education, before Randolph ascended to his preordained role as a great man in politics.

On May 28, 1932, to mark Randolph's twenty-first birthday, the elder Churchill hosted a fabulous coming-of-age dinner at Claridge's (the same Art Deco hotel where Randolph had a party before departing for America), with the theme of "Fathers and Sons." Randolph shared the same birth date as William Pitt the Younger (the youngest leader in English history), and he didn't discourage a comparison that evening. With the exception of the elder and younger Pitt (as well as his own father and grandfather Churchill), Randolph conceded that few sons of famous men ever amounted to anything. "In most cases the son is a perfectly normal and intelligent youth, but, of course, everyone expects him to be at least as brilliant as his father, and if he falls short of the ideal there are not lacking those who will stigmatize him as a failure," Randolph later wrote in a 1932 newspaper essay. Of course, he didn't expect to fail. "I am not afraid to reveal . . . my two main ambitions," he admitted. "I wish to make an immense fortune and to be Prime Minister."

As guests at this birthday gala, several members of Parliament, high finance, and the media brought along their sons, including Winston's good friend Max Aitken, the renowned and often notorious Lord Beaverbrook of Fleet Street fame. The fathers and sons were invited to stand and give a speech. London's *Evening Standard,* which wrote extensively about this all-male affair, dubbed it " 'Great' Men and Their Sons." The paper's unnamed author (likely Beaverbrook himself) observed, "These 'great' men are convinced, needless to say, that their sons are also 'great.' The sons, or most of them, admire their parents' judgment in this respect." To be the guest of honor was heady stuff for Randolph, as it would be for any young man still untried and untested in the world. "It was a splendid occasion and far more than I deserved," Randolph later recalled. "The occasion was more suited to my pretensions than to my achievements or abilities."

At this dinner, drenched in cigar smoke and brandy, Randolph gave an impromptu speech "with great wealth of gesture and fluency of delivery," the *Sunday Times* reported, as if seeing a future national leader emerge before its eyes. "With all the energy and brains of the Churchills, lacking only as yet coherence of ideas, he has almost all the qualities that make for success." Winston's own rousing oratory invoked images of the torch, the flag, and the lamp being passed from one generation to the next. He paid tribute to his son's rapid-fire speaking abilities, which needed only a target or cause to be put to good use. As Lord Beaverbrook's newspaper recorded, Churchill described Randolph as "a fine machine gun, and it was to be hoped he would accumulate a big dump of ammunition and learn to hit the target."

The evening's over-the-top tone reflected Winston's own ambitions for his only son, which still overflowed with possibilities, justified or not. "Naturally I have high hopes for Randolph," Winston confided to a friend. "He has a gift and a power of presentation which I have not seen equaled in his age. Whether he will be noble and diligent has yet to be proved." Clementine worried that her husband's indulgence would ruin their son "because things came so naturally to him, he could not be bothered to work hard." Watching Randolph's skillful but unprepared improvisation that night, Lord Beaverbrook observed, "To him an old codger may say, 'Work, my boy, work! The way is wide open to you in politics if you do!' "

Winston did not view his son in such a pedestrian and ignoble way. In Randolph, he envisioned himself and all that was good about England. He presumed his son shared the same hardy self-reliance he had displayed after his own father, Lord Randolph, dropped dead, leaving him a young man with little money and repute. Adversity, not advantage, had been most character-forming for Winston. Although the once-massive fortunes of families such as the Churchills at Blenheim might dwindle, the glorious rule of Britain's gentry remained boundless. In Winston's heart, the sun never stopped shining on his country's empire. "The reason the historical English families have produced so many men of distinction is that, on the whole, they have borne great responsibilities rather than enjoyed great wealth," he contended. "Their younger sons, especially, have usually had to make their own way in the world, to stand on their own feet, to rely on their own merits and their own efforts. I am glad that I had to earn my living from the time that I was a young man. Had I been born heir to millions, I should certainly have had a less interesting life."

Even when family failed or disappointed him, Winston relied for support on a coterie of friends—all smart, quick-witted men of accomplishment. He had cultivated them over the years, none more so than Lord Beaverbrook. To a greater extent than Winston, W. M. "Max" Aitken was a self-made man, the son of a Presbyterian minister in Canada. He had assembled a fortune as a wily businessman, his fingers in everything from stocks to cement plants. When he came to England, Max began building a newspaper empire, including the London *Evening Standard* and *Daily Mail*. Soon he was knighted and dubbed "Lord Beaverbrook," the name derived from a place near his small Canadian hometown. Armed with his own barbed but fluid writing style, Beaverbrook considered himself a "master of his trade—a great newspaperman." Possessed of devilish eyes and a demonic grin, the bantam-size press potentate delighted and confounded his friends with humor and savvy insights. He also understood Winston better than most. "What a creature of strange mood [Churchill] is—always at the top of the wheel of confidence or at the bottom of an intense depression," he observed.

Beaverbrook joined Winston and F. E. Smith (Lord Birkenhead), who formed "the Other Club," a rogue alternative in 1911, after they were shut out of a fashionable London political dining society called The Club. Soon their club became a fashionable setting for "estimable and entertaining" men like them, including David Lloyd George, then Chancellor of the Exchequer and soon-to-be prime minister. Among Churchill's friends, Lord Beaverbrook was "the most compelling and consistently fascinating character in our life," recalled Sarah Churchill, Winston's daughter, even though there were periods when her father and Max "were barely on speaking terms. Yet throughout there ran a thread of intense personal regard. Max was a strange and difficult man to know. He inspired either deep affection or hatred. You certainly couldn't be indifferent to him."

The verbal exchanges between Churchill and Beaverbrook were always lively and bombastic, and often amusing, regardless of the political circumstances. In the 1920s, for example, the two laughed uproariously when a tense meeting of ministers concerned about calling a general election was interrupted by a talking parrot in the room. "You bloody fool! You bloody fool!" the bird cried, a remark that immediately froze the other politicians from going forward. For another three decades, both men continued to enjoy each other's company in the public arena. Beaverbrook, an astute observer of human nature, admired Winston's intellect and virtues as "exceptionally rare in politics—or, for that matter, almost anywhere."

Lord Birkenhead, an even more devoted friend to Churchill, initially despised him, at least by reputation, for leaving the Conservative Party. Not until he actually met Winston, in 1906, did they become fast friends. By nature, "F.E." was more pugnacious, outspoken, and daring than Winston. An accomplished attorney, Birkenhead saw his first speech in the House of Commons cause a sensation, enough so his oratorical skills became legendary. His placid, often bloodshot eyes looked out on the world with a droll gentlemanliness; his slicked-back hair pushed over his head, his narrow, drawn face halted by a pointed chin. Birkenhead and Churchill spent many afterhours in their club inside the Savoy hotel chewing over the issues of the day. "He had all the canine virtues in a remarkable degree—courage, fidelity, vigilance, love of chase," said Churchill of his dear friend. For his part, Birkenhead—a sportsman, stalwart debater, and all-around man's man—found Winston's love of luxury amusing. "Churchill's tastes are simple, he is easily contented with the best of everything," Birkenhead said, repeating his friend's credo. When Randolph Churchill was born, Birkenhead became his godfather; similarly, Winston served as godfather to Birkenhead's son, Freddie.

Winston's many nights cavorting with his friends left Clementine at home with a foul taste. In particular, she disliked the immense amount of time her husband expended with the "Terrible Bs": Beaverbrook, Birkenhead, and Brendan Bracken, Churchill's red-headed aide-de-camp, who encouraged the outlandish rumor that he was Winston's illegitimate son. "In all of them there was a touch of the buccaneer, and a streak of brashness and vulgarity, which jarred with Clementine and made her fear for the influence they might have with Winston," their youngest daughter Mary remembered. When young Randolph, spurred by his father's praise for Birkenhead, began to emulate his godfather's behavior, Clementine grew particularly alarmed. "She objected to the thoughtless encouragement he gave to his godchild, her already turbulent and outspoken son, Randolph," recalled Jock Colville, Churchill's personal secretary. "Whatever the justice of her complaints, the fact remained that her husband never had a truer, cleverer or more congenial friend." But in fact, Birkenhead, already known to most colleagues as a barely functioning alcoholic, left the door to drink wide open for Churchill's immature son—creating an emotional schism between father and son that only widened.

During his brief time at Oxford, Randolph visited Lord Birkenhead's nearby home with his own "smart bunch" of friends, where drinks flowed indiscriminately. Alcohol was mixed with genuine wit, fast repartee, and a funny, insulting brand of accusatory humor that became increasingly arrogant. Randolph's crowd at Oxford included Birkenhead's own son, Freddie, Seymour Berry (son of another press magnate, Lord Camrose), Tom Mitford (whose family would become friendly with both the Churchill and Kennedy families), and eventually, the gifted writer Evelyn Waugh. On weekends, about a dozen of Randolph's undergraduate friends gathered inside the Birkenheads' small paneled dining room like knights at their own round table. "It was F.E.'s habit to prompt us all to make after-dinner speeches upon which he would make caustic comments," Randolph recalled. "The atmosphere was gay and witty, and I seemed to be moving into an enchanted world: and expansion of that which I was now old enough to savour with full relish." With tumbler and shot glass in hand, Randolph could be like his father, surrounded by his own club of friends and their sterling, if sodden, wit and great ambitions.

Winston, comfortable with his own drinking habits, didn't share his wife's concerns about Randolph's chronic bouts of inebriation. Nor did he worry about the malevolent influence of Birkenhead, who soon died, at age fifty-eight, from cirrhosis of the liver. For Winston, the accoutrements of the pub, and his enjoyment of them, were part of his charming persona. Truth be known, he didn't inhale his Havana cigars very much, and he sipped his whiskey and brandy only between long intervals, leaving little damage to his body, as doctors were surprised to find years later in a post mortem. "He smoked matches and ate cigars," described a bemused Beaverbrook.

Political enemies learned to smear the Churchills together with the same brush. "I do not know which is the more offensive or mischievous, Winston or his son," said Conservative Sam Hoare in 1934, who opposed them bitterly over India. "Rumour, however, goes that they fight like cats with each other, and chiefly agree in the prodigious amount of champagne that each of them drinks each night." By 1935, even friends noticed the Churchill excesses. Lord Rothermere, Winston's patron and Randolph's newspaper employer, offered the senior Churchill a substantial sum of money if he pledged to give up whiskey and wine for the following year. Winston wouldn't hear of it. "I refused as I think life would not be worth living," he explained. Two years later, both Rothermere and Beaverbrook made a similar offer to Randolph. Each promised to pay him a thousand pounds if he stayed away from drink for a year. Randolph agreed to the wager, but asked for a one-day dispensation shortly afterward to celebrate the resignation of a political enemy. When he called his father, asking whether the dispensation was a good idea, Winston "chuckled with appreciation" and didn't object at all. His son's drinking never stopped.

In observing the Churchills, father and son, Evelyn Waugh was both intrigued and repulsed by the Churchill world of friends and political acquaintances. He and Randolph developed a love-hate friendship that lasted, off and on, for years. Among their Oxford friends, Evelyn shared Randolph's reverence for Tory politics and England's traditions—the aristocratic, romantic world later found in Waugh's *Brideshead Revisited*. In Waugh's novel *Scoop*, the newspaper publisher of the fictional *Daily Beast* resembled Churchill's friend Beaverbrook. But Randolph said Waugh "is not one of those who find the modern world attractive," even to the point of adopting "a formalism in his social life which borders on the ridiculous." In 1930, when Waugh turned to Roman Catholicism, he asked Father Martin D'Arcy, Britain's top Jesuit, who oversaw his conversion, whether Randolph might follow. "No!" D'Arcy shot back. "He'd be like a rogue elephant trumpeting in the sanctuary."

Although Winston initially looked favorably upon Waugh's writings and his friendship with Randolph, Evelyn never felt sanguine about the famous Churchill, whom he considered a fraudulent manipulator. Upon his first introduction to him, in the early 1930s, Waugh wrote to a friend that Winston seemed "six times better" than Randolph. A gifted artist and no stranger to sanctimoniousness, Waugh later concluded the senior Churchill was "not a man for whom I ever had esteem." In Waugh's book, Winston was "always in the wrong, always surrounded by crooks, a most unsuccessful father." Similar to Clementine's list, Waugh noted that Winston's "crook" associates all had *B*s in their surnames—and added Bernard Baruch as well. Whatever the petty differences between them, Waugh never stopped being sympathetic to Randolph and the primal difficulties a son might face in a world still influenced by his father.

During Winston's difficult years in the early 1930s, no one stood beside him more than his son. Randolph was "utterly loyal to him and made himself his lieutenant in all his political battles," Winston's grandson wrote decades later. Adopting many of the same views, Randolph dreamed of someday serving in Parliament with his father, fighting as comrades-in-arms for the same cause.

Randolph could be fearless. In 1933, shortly after Hitler became chancellor of Germany, the Oxford Union, the debating society that reflected the prevailing pacifist sentiment, approved a resolution that "refuses in any circumstances to fight for King and Country." Appalled, Randolph attempted to overturn this measure, but lost overwhelmingly after a vitriolic session. Winston was proud of his son's courage in taking such a principled yet unpopular stand. "Nothing is so piercing as the hostility of a thousand of your own contemporaries and he was by no means crushed by it," Winston told a friend.

India became another dividing line for the Churchills. For years, Winston's switch from the Conservative Party to the Liberals in 1904, and then back again to the Conservatives in 1924, caused much derision towards him. But in 1931, when Parliament allowed greater independence for India, Churchill found himself at odds with Conservative leader Stanley Baldwin, who made sure Winston didn't find a place in the Cabinet. Mohandas K. Gandhi's nonviolent struggle for India's freedom rankled every imperialist bone in Churchill's body. He worried about another key chunk of His Majesty's empire floating away. "It is alarming and also nauseating to see Mr. Gandhi, a seditious Middle Temple lawyer now posing as a fakir of a type well-known in the East, striding half naked up the steps of the Viceregal Palace, while he is still organizing and conducting a defiant campaign of civil disobedience, to parley on equal terms with the representative of the King-Emperor," Winston railed. In 1935, Baldwin's ascension to prime minister seemed to make Winston's chances of emerging from his wilderness ever more remote.

Despite this prevailing opposition, Randolph decided the time was right to launch his own political career, jumping into the three-way Wavertree by-election and putting opposition to India's independence at the top of his agenda. (Previously, he had called Gandhi the "little brown man in the loincloth"—in 1931, after meeting with him when his father wouldn't.) "Randolph was determined to blaze his own trail, both as a journalist and as a politician," recalled his sister Mary. "He was an aggressively loyal protagonist of his father's views, and was constantly drawing public attention to the scandalous exclusion of his father from office. Randolph's political skirmishes, however, were nearly always the cause of parental dismay or embarrassment—and sometimes both—and a constant source of noisy rows, for he would brook no moderating counsels, and forged ahead on his warpath regardless."

The 1935 Wavertree election proved a disaster for the Churchills, just as Winston had feared. Randolph's ill-prepared bid came in last, and many Conservatives were upset by Winston's apparent attempt as a "rebel Tory" to undermine the party's efforts. Then, in January 1936, Randolph decided to stand for a seat in another district, at Ross and Cromarty, convinced the first election had been an aberration. But the results were the same: another loss that seemed to doom his once-sterling and all-but-assured future in Parliament. "This was Randolph's first foray into the political arena where he had set his goal but which was forever to deny him any real success," recalled his sister Sarah. "Despite their disagreements, Randolph was to be everlastingly unhappy that he could not be as the younger Pitt to the elder, standing by his father in the House of Commons and fighting battles with him."

Winston, who once so adored Randolph and his potential, came away frustrated and more remote from his son. He had tried to be a better father than Lord Randolph had ever been to him and now felt hurt by his son's intransigence. Yet deep in his heart, he recognized how his own decision to linger on the public stage so late in life—waiting for years to see if his unrequited ambition to become prime minister could be realized—had stymied Randolph's career, perhaps more so than his son's own rash judgments.

Once, on a stroll around Chartwell, Winston as much as admitted this regret to his son. "My father died when I was exactly your age—this left the political arena clear for me," he told Randolph. "I do not know how I should have fared in politics had he lived on."

10

Menace on the Horizon

*"Adolf Hitler may be a 'clumsy lout,' as H. G. Wells says he
is, and it is certain that he is no Winston Churchill who can
pass from politics to authorship with the retention of any
quality of brilliance."*
—*New York Times* IN ITS OCTOBER 1933 REVIEW OF
HITLER'S MANIFESTO, *Mein Kampf*

As the world looked anxiously upon the rise of Germany's Nazi
leader, the Churchills and the Kennedys viewed this menace from
starkly different perspectives.

In nearby Britain, Winston Churchill attempted to warn his countrymen of the imminent threat—even though most preferred to think
that Hitler's war cries could somehow be mitigated, or would simply
blow away with time. In distant America, caught up in its isolationist
mood, Joe Kennedy paid little attention, except to wonder if the German leader should be embraced. The contrast between these English
and American mind-sets was particularly illustrated by their two eldest
sons, Randolph Churchill and Joseph Kennedy Jr.

In April 1934, eighteen-year-old Joe Jr. traveled through Germany,
just as his father suggested, to see for himself what Hitler meant for his
country. At the London School of Economics, Joe had heard his favorite professor, Harold Laski, and other academics criticize the growing
brutality of the Third Reich toward minorities, especially Jews. Laski

felt the Great Depression proved Karl Marx's critique of capitalism, resulting in an economic collapse that allowed political extremists such as the Nazis to come to power. However, Laski believed Hitler's reign wouldn't last long. Like many political leaders, Laski cautioned about military overreaction by Churchill, whom he called "one of the great anachronisms of our time . . . a gallant and romantic relic of 18th Century imperialism."

Mindful of Laski's teachings, Joe found his journey through Germany yielding conclusions much closer to his father's. "It was a horrible thing, but in every revolution you have to expect some bloodshed," he wrote to his dad. "Hitler is building a spirit in his men that could be envied in any country. They are not thinking of war, but of Germany through Hitler. They know he is doing his best for Germany, they have tremendous faith in him, and they will do whatever he wishes." In this Nazi world of Brownshirts, constant "Heil Hitler" salutes, and the Führer's photo in every shop, young Kennedy came to agree with some of the regime's most heinous theories. "He [Hitler] has passed the sterilization law which I think is a great thing," he wrote. "I don't know how the Church feels about it, but it will do away with many of the disgusting specimens of men which inhabit this earth." Jews were at the top of Hitler's unwanted list, Joe Jr.'s letter explained. "He saw the need of a common enemy. Someone of whom to make the goat," Kennedy wrote. "It was excellent physchology [*sic*], and it was too bad that it had to be done to the Jews. This dislike of the Jews, however, was well founded."

Hitler's institutionalized hatred was an extreme version of the anti-Semitism prevalent in American society, infecting the views of Joe Kennedy Sr. and several of his children, including Joe Jr., his daughter Kick, and his other eager-to-please son, Robert. The senior Kennedy's papers are littered with disparaging comments about Jews, even though, paradoxically, he counted Bernard Baruch, Felix Frankfurter, and other Jews among his friends. Some sentiments echoed his Boston Irish-Catholic background, where Jews were seen as a competing immigrant group or, by a narrow-minded clergy, as Christ killers. When he received this admittedly rambling note from his teenage son, Joe Kennedy applauded the young man's views on German politics. "I think they show a very keen sense of perception, and I think your conclusions are very sound," the senior Kennedy wrote. "Of course, it is still possible that Hitler went far beyond his necessary requirements in his attitude towards the Jews, the evidence of which may be very well covered up from the observer who goes in there at this time." Joe Sr. also wondered why Catholics wound up targeted by Hitler. "If he wanted to re-unite Germany, and picked the Jew as the focal point of his attack, and conditions in Germany are now so completely those of his own making, why then is it necessary to turn the front of his attack on the Catholics?"

Several months before young Kennedy, Randolph Churchill visited Hitler's Germany and arrived at far different conclusions. Instead of writing a docile private note to his father, Randolph provided a journalistic clarion call to the British public about the peril awaiting them.

While covering the German elections in July 1932, Randolph pulled off a coup for Lord Rothermere's newspaper, the *Sunday Graphic*, by meeting Hitler personally. Arranged by Ernst "Putzi" Hanfstaengl, Hitler's savvy Harvard-trained press aide, the son of Winston Churchill flew with the Führer inside his private ten-seater Ford-built plane. Randolph realized this special treatment was designed to impress him "so I could go home with some 'good' impressions and report to my father." Across the countryside, they hopscotched from one Nazi rally to the next. Randolph described these rallies as "a mixture between an American football game and a Boy Scouts' jamboree, animated with the spirit of a revivalist meeting."

When Hitler's plane landed in a field of clover, a dozen guards, all carrying concealed weapons under their black uniforms, drove him and his entourage to a nearby stadium with fifteen thousand people yelling, "Heil Hitler!" At another nighttime rally, in Berlin, no fewer than 120,000 people crammed into a stadium, many clutching flaming torches, shouting and chanting Hitler's name. Basking in the acclaim of this mesmerized crowd, Adolf Hitler stood in an open car rolling slowly in front of the stands and then gave a spellbinding speech that left the masses in a frenzy. Privately, Randolph asked a leading Nazi about Hitler's personality. "Well, he's really just like your father," the official replied. Randolph made sure not to share this comment with Winston. "It wouldn't have amused him," he explained.

In a gracious act he'd later regret, Randolph sent a congratulatory letter when Hitler won as chancellor. But at age twenty-one, well before most any Western journalist, young Churchill let the British public know about Hitler's ominous German threat.

"The success of the Nazi Party sooner or later means war," he warned in a July 31, 1932, newspaper article. "They burn for revenge. They are determined once more to have an army. I am sure that once they have achieved it they will not hesitate to use it." He predicted that "within three years at the most Europe will be confronted with a deadly situation."

A month later, in August 1932, Randolph returned to Germany, joining his parents in Munich. In researching his massive biography of Marlborough, Winston had decided to see firsthand the scene of his ancestor's greatest triumph, the place near the Danube River where the Battle of Blenheim was fought and won in 1704.

When Hitler's press aide, Hanfstaengl, found out about Winston Churchill's visit, he raised the prospect of a private meeting with the Führer. For nearly two years, Churchill had expressed worry about Hitler's brutalities and the threat posed by Germany, a view reflected in Randolph's recent reporting. "Why is your chief so violent towards the Jews? How can any man help how he is born?" Churchill asked the Nazi press aide. "Tell your boss from me that anti-Semitism may be a good starter, but it is a bad stayer." More out of duty than friendliness, Winston agreed to see Hitler, but the Führer demurred. "Hitler produced a thousand excuses," recalled Hanfstaengl. "With a figure whom he knew to be his equal in political abilities, the uncertain bourgeois re-emerged again, the man who would not go to a dancing-class for fear of making a fool of himself, the man who only acquired confidence in his manipulation of a yelling audience."

Hanfstaengl tried to convince his leader that meeting this British statesman-writer would be good international politics, but Hitler wouldn't abide such advice. He, too, knew Winston was in the wilderness of his career. After all, Churchill's visit to Munich wasn't as a diplomat or politician, but as a writer of history books about the distant past. "In any case, what part does Churchill play?" Hitler finally said. "He is in opposition and no one pays any attention to him." Hitler continued to fume about the proposed Churchill meeting during lunch with Joseph Goebbels, his minister of propaganda. "He criticizes Churchill very strongly," Goebbels recorded in his diary. "[Churchill] lives in the sixteenth century and does not understand at all the real needs of the English people."

As a British politician, Churchill continued his vigilance toward a Germany determined to rearm, warning in November 1933 of a "grim dictatorship" by Hitler. As a historian, though, Churchill wasn't entirely condemning in his writing about Adolf Hitler, as if believing, erroneously, that a few charitable words might defuse the Führer. Writing in his book *Great Contemporaries*, a 1937 collection of profiles of political figures, Churchill wondered aloud if Hitler would bring about another world war "or whether he will go down in history as the man who restored honour and peace of mind to the great Germanic nation." In his Hitler profile, Winston underlined the irony of how this onetime corporal and former Austrian house painter had revived Germany and "to a very large extent, reversed the results of the Great War." No matter what the outcome, Churchill, the historian, recognized Hitler as a figure of destiny. His lessons also seemed addressed to his many critics in Britain who didn't believe that building up their national defense should be a priority. "When Hitler began, Germany lay prostrate at the feet of the Allies," Churchill wrote about the looming menace. "He may yet see the day when what is left of Europe will be prostrate at the feet of Germany. Whatever else may be thought of these exploits, they are certainly among the most remarkable in the whole history of the world."

The power of words served as Churchill's greatest political weapon. In touring the Low Countries, where battles such as Blenheim once took place, he gained an invaluable sense of military strategy, the incalculable advantage of surprise attacks and daring secret operations. In his books, he pieced together the fascinating personalities and fateful decisions of war, seeing the broad tableau of historical events as a unified, understandable tale. "The story of the human race is war," observed Churchill, who, as a young man, once wrote, "A syndicate may compile an encyclopedia, only a man can write a book." Indeed, launching a four-volume biography like *Marlborough* was like going to war. With each new literary campaign, he said, "camps were set up; intelligence gathered; reports compiled." In literature as in life itself, Winston explained, "Everything is worked out by hard labour and frequent polishing."

Writing, for Churchill, aside from its remunerative considerations, became an exercise in self-revelation, with him recasting personal and national histories on his own terms with the stroke of a pen. His books aimed for "the graceful weaving of numerous original documents into the regular narrative," composed with a literary skill that few other politicians possessed or were inclined to try. He realized the value of his books in subtly setting a political agenda or enhancing the public's view of him personally. Describing his book *The River War*, he said, "I affected a combination of the style of [Thomas] Macaulay and [Edward] Gibbon, the staccato antitheses of the former and the rolling sentences and genitival endings of the latter, and I stuck in a bit of my own from time to time." A subtext within his biography of the Duke of Marlborough, who first supported the Catholic king before he switched to William of Orange, sounded vaguely like Winston's own switch in political parties. As historian Henry Steele Commager observed, Winston's "vindication of Marlborough from neglect and contumely was, in a sense, a vindication of himself." In *Marlborough*, Winston also summarized what could be his own epitaph: "Famous men are usually the product of an unhappy childhood."

Winston believed only great men with Olympian vision could see the true meaning of history as it unfolded. His massive books, humbly prefaced, were designed to make his own case. "A good knowledge of history is a quiver full of arrows in debate," he told his brother, Jack, about the time his first book appeared. None of Winston's works was more revealing than *Lord Randolph Churchill*, his 1906 two-volume biography of his father as a self-made man. The book starts at the magnificent Blenheim Palace, where Winston's own life began. "No glittering wheels of royal favour aided and accelerated his journey," Winston wrote, introducing the tale of his father as a misunderstood genius. "Whatever power he acquired was grudgingly conceded and hastily snatched away. Like Disraeli, he had to fight every mile in all his marches."

Aware that many of his contemporaries linked his own faults to his father, Winston produced "an imaginative portrayal of 'the best side' of his father which was also deliberately designed to serve Churchill's more immediate political needs," observed historian David Cannadine. A subsequent biographer pointed out that Winston never mentioned Lord Randolph's dependency on financier Nathaniel Rothschild, to whom he "turned for everything," as his closest adviser when Lord Randolph was Chancellor of the Exchequer. When he died, Lord Randolph owed sixty-six thousand pounds to Rothschild's family bank—an arrangement that sounded much like the helping hand Winston received from wealthy friends such as Bernard Baruch and Henry Strakosch. Winston felt that a "biographer of eminent persons" should not "slur over" such messy details. But as R. F. Foster concluded in his 1981 biography of Lord Randolph, Winston's written effort "conforms closely to what Churchill's emotions wanted to be true, as well as to what suited his politics; a great weight of minor alterations and major emphases combined to produce a portrait in the painting of which Churchill not only discovered his father but also refashioned him in his own image."

With Hitler's military on the march, a powerless Winston could only rely on his writings to curb its advance, to make his point in a public war of words. At times, he tried to enlist those who opposed him. In 1936, Harold Laski, once a skeptic of Winston's call for rearmament, sent him another author's new book about the persecution of Jews in Germany. Winston thanked him graciously, without seeking vindication. Though Churchill remained an outlier politically, his prescient warnings about Nazi Germany were now being embraced by former appeasement advocates such as Laski. Churchill promised to read the book, but implored Laski to "think a little meanwhile of how to preserve the strength of England, the hope of freedom."

11

London Calling

For news about Great Britain, Joe Kennedy often relied on the three *B*s in Winston Churchill's life: Bernard Baruch, Lord Beaverbrook, and Brendan Bracken. Baruch shared what he learned after his annual trips to Chartwell, Beaverbrook had stayed in regular contact with Kennedy ever since they negotiated British movie rights in the late 1920s, and Bracken, who didn't know Kennedy well, still found ways to court and flatter him.

After Franklin Roosevelt's 1936 reelection victory, for example, Bracken sent a note attached to a newspaper clipping written by Randolph Churchill. Young Churchill had covered the American campaign for London's *Daily Mail* and wrote a dispatch from New York mentioning Kennedy's possible future selection as secretary of the treasury or, "more likely," as head of the navy. Kennedy wrote back to Bracken to say he loved the "magnificent" Churchill piece free of "local prejudices" (even though Joe was apparently one of Randolph's sources). "It was easily the best analysis that had been made of the situation here." In his own radio talks and speeches, Joe quoted Randolph's analysis as a foreign correspondent.

Earlier in the 1936 campaign, Kennedy sent Bracken a copy of his book *I'm for Roosevelt,* one of several expensive efforts he made on behalf of the president. The pamphlet-like defense of Roosevelt's New Deal—much of it ghostwritten and edited by Kennedy's friend *New York Times* columnist Arthur Krock—was designed to rally support among ethnic Democrats influenced by the anti-Roosevelt radio priest Father Charles Coughlin.

For inside information about Washington, however, Joe Kennedy continued to rely on the president's oldest son, Jimmy. Wanting to return to government, Kennedy arranged for several FDR political fundraisers and personally financed a New England reelection campaign swing by the president's son. "After the 1936 campaign, he [Kennedy] made it clear he felt he deserved a reward—which he did—and he hinted broadly that the reward he had in mind was the post of secretary of the treasury—which was out of the question," Jimmy recalled. With Roosevelt's trusted friend Henry Morgenthau at Treasury, Kennedy instead became the head of the U.S. Maritime Commission. By late 1937, however, that job felt too limiting, and he pushed for a more high-profile position. The president sent his eldest son to placate him. After a lengthy talk one evening, Joe blurted out that he'd like to become ambassador to Great Britain, an idea that sounded preposterous.

Jimmy knew plenty about Kennedy's private dealings in England. Nevertheless, he didn't think Joe was serious. He laughed when Kennedy mentioned this new idea.

"Oh, c'mon, Joe, you don't want that," Jimmy protested.

"Oh, yes I do," Kennedy insisted. "I've been thinking about it and I'm intrigued by the thought of being the first Irishman to be ambassador from the United States to the Court of St. James's."

Jimmy promised to forward the request, though he predicted his father's reaction would be the same. "Sure enough, when I passed it on to father, he laughed so hard he almost toppled from his wheelchair," Jimmy recalled. After catching his breath, the president confirmed that Kennedy's request was out of the question.

Shortly afterward, though, Franklin called his son to say he'd changed his mind. The ambassadorship in London traditionally went to politicians, including five future presidents, or well-connected Anglophile supporters such as the departing incumbent, Robert Worth Bingham. But the president said he "was intrigued with the idea of twisting the lion's tail a little" by appointing an Irish Catholic. He instructed his son to invite Joe for a White House discussion about his possible appointment.

Upon arrival, Joe found the president in a jovial spirit—the kind of FDR bonhomie he'd displayed in Kennedy's company in the past, which kept Joe's inner animosity from surfacing. As always, Roosevelt was a masterful politician, able to balance and counter all sorts of conflicting interests—and still manage to get his way. He decided to tease Kennedy a bit, and Joe, desperate for the London post, couldn't resist taking the bait.

"Joe, would you mind stepping back a bit, by the fireplace perhaps, so I can get a good look at you?" Roosevelt dead-panned. A puzzled Kennedy, like a youngster awaiting a prize, followed along.

"Joe, would you mind taking your pants down?" the president further asked. The request stunned Jimmy, standing next to Kennedy. "I was as surprised as Joe was," Jimmy later recalled. "We couldn't believe our ears."

Kennedy asked the president if he'd heard correctly. The commander in chief said he had indeed. Kennedy unhooked his suspenders, dropped his suit pants, and stood there in his shorts, "looking silly and embarrassed," recalled Jimmy.

"Someone who saw you in a bathing suit once told me something I now know to be true," said Roosevelt, with a satisfied grin. "Joe, just look at your legs. You are just about the most bowlegged man I have ever seen. Don't you know that the ambassador to the Court of Saint James has to go through an induction ceremony in which he wears knee britches and silk stockings? Can you imagine how you'll look?

When photos of our new ambassador appear all over the world we'll be a laughingstock." He ended by telling Joe Kennedy he wasn't right for the job.

Mortified in his underwear, Kennedy asked Roosevelt if he'd send him to London if British officials agreed to waive their requirement of knee britches and instead allow him to wear a cutaway coat and striped pants.

"Well, Joe, you know how the British are about tradition," said the president. "There's no way you are going to get permission."

Within two weeks, however, Kennedy prevailed and obtained his waiver. "He'd called father's bluff, and father laughed and agreed to name him ambassador to England," Jimmy recalled.

Roosevelt's odd act of humiliation upset Kennedy. No other ambassadorial candidate would have faced such hazing. He believed the patrician president harbored bigotry toward Irish Catholics like him, which was brought out by Kennedy's upstart request to be sent to London. "I got the impression that deep down in his heart Roosevelt had a decidedly anti-Catholic feeling," Joe eventually wrote in his diary. "And what seems more significant is the fact that up to this time he has not appointed a prominent Catholic to any important post since a year ago last November." Kennedy concluded that "this [anti-Catholic] feeling [was] firmly imbeded [sic] in the Roosevelt family."

White House aides argued that Kennedy's appointment would prove disastrous, that he couldn't be trusted and was loyal only to himself. Some privately worried that his secret personal dealings with Jimmy Roosevelt would be exposed and could compromise the president's relationship with his eldest son. Thomas Corcoran, a close FDR aide, later said he knew that Kennedy had provided "help that Jimmy built up his insurance business that he had in Boston and amassed in a short time a fortune." For the president, getting rid of Kennedy, a constant prima donna, was worth the risk of sending him to Great Britain as America's representative.

"I have made arrangements to have Joe Kennedy watched hourly," the president told Henry Morgenthau, who doubted the move. "And the first time he opens his mouth and criticizes me, I'll fire him."

Kennedy's delight in being dispatched to Great Britain surpassed any lesser emotions. "I don't know what kind of a diplomat I shall be, probably rotten, but I promise to get done for you those things that you want done," he vowed to Roosevelt. "Rose and I are deeply grateful." Overjoyed by the appointment, Rose later said the Kennedys' time in London was "the most thrilling, exciting and interesting years of my life." While getting dressed for an evening at Windsor Castle soon after he arrived, Joe paused in momentary reflection and gleefully said to his wife, "Well, Rose, this is a helluva long way from East Boston, isn't it?"

Both Joe and Rose recognized the immeasurable long-term benefits for their family's future in politics. Perhaps someday Kennedy would become the sixth London ambassador to ascend to the American presidency, joining such old Boston names as Adams. More so, Roosevelt's selection of him (regardless of the practical joke attending it) was a giant step forward for Irish Catholics, the kind denied for decades in the United States. In his unpublished memoir, Kennedy acknowledged that the large public attention surrounding him "was heightened by the fact that my Irish-American background and my family of nine children were not in the normal tradition of our earlier envoys to the Court of St. James's." His selection was a barrier breaker, a milestone for his Irish-Catholic heritage. "You don't understand the Irish," explained Thomas Corcoran to another FDR aide, Harold Ickes, who wondered why Kennedy politically coveted this appointment abroad. "London has always been a closed door to them. As ambassador of the United States, Kennedy will have all the doors open to him."

Before leaving New York, Joe found out who had informed the president of his bowed legs. In a telegram sent to Kennedy, Bernard Baruch shared an inside joke between them in which the older man called himself "chairman," and the title "little chairman" went to the younger man. As Baruch wrote to Joe: I KNOW YOU CAN HIT A HOME RUN TOO BUT HOW ABOUT THOSE KNEE PANTS = CHAIRMAN.

At his father's request, Randolph Churchill acted like an old friend as the Kennedys took London by storm. He turned up everywhere with them.

When Joe arrived at Plymouth on a drizzly March 1, 1938, evening, Randolph joined a small contingent that rode with the new American ambassador on an overnight train to London. Randolph also appeared as an honored guest at an American Women's Club luncheon paying tribute to Rose Kennedy as the new ambassador's wife. He shared in the fun when the Kennedys hosted a large gala at the American embassy that lasted until three in the morning. And when Joe attended a Buckingham Palace ceremony, Randolph wrote about his impressions for his London newspaper. Young Churchill said Roosevelt "has charged Mr. Kennedy with the mission of advising him what part, if any, the United States can play in averting war without abandoning their traditional role of isolation." He praised Kennedy for offering "one of the most forceful and far-reaching declarations on Anglo-American relations in the recent history of the two countries," noting Anglo-American unity was a notion "he had borrowed from Winston Churchill." Enchanted with Kennedy's Hollywood background, Randolph wrote about the new ambassador's decision to bring "talkies" (via a movie projector) into his embassy. "Thus he will solve the problem of how to amuse his guests and at the same time satisfy his own unbounded appetite for film entertainment," touted Randolph's column, which featured a photo of "Miss Kathleen Kennedy," the ambassador's lively daughter. In a light reference to Kennedy's decision to avoid wearing the traditional knee britches, Randolph quipped that "the only trousers at last night's court were those worn by the American Ambassador and some of the less important waiters."

As much as he liked the Kennedys, however, Randolph realized the new ambassador's Irish-Catholic background might pose a problem. When Honey Fitz, the ambassador's seventy-five-year-old father-in-law, showed up in London for a short visit that spring, Randolph told Londoners that the former Boston mayor was known for "his excellent singing voice [and] was the first American politician to discover that the best way to poll the Irish vote was by twisting the tail of the British Lion."

The Kennedys' arrival in London caused a sensation, far more than anyone could have imagined except the publicity-minded Joe. Drawing on his experience as a Hollywood producer, he orchestrated press interviews, public appearances, gossip column "exclusives," photo sessions, and newsreels that sent images of his family's adventure overseas to theater audiences back home. If Churchill's political career was derived from the weight of history and book writing, Kennedy's seemed illuminated by the sound and images of film. The British public seemed fascinated with tales of the new wise-cracking American ambassador, his beautiful wife, and their nine kids living together at the official residence at 14 Princes Gate. "Kids Take Over the Embassy," proclaimed one London paper's headline. "King George Asks to See Kennedy's Nine Children," read another. The family was treated as innocents abroad—an amusing, rough-around-the-edges but totally American road show as they chatted with royalty and Cabinet ministers. In another rarity, soon after their arrival, Joe snared a hole in one while golfing at the new Stoke Poges course in Buckinghamshire. "Just fancy I had to come all the way over here to do my first hole-in-one," Kennedy said, laughing. As he later wrote, "I hoped it was a good omen."

The Kennedys appeared as a family of destiny, with lots of luck and familial love on their side. The sheer size of the brood fascinated the

British public, just as it would Americans years later. In feature articles, Rose invariably explained her system of keeping track of her nine children: writing each one's name neatly on index cards, listing who had been inoculated, had had their tonsils out, eyes examined, or needed to go to the dentist. Although she said having a big family was enjoyable, Rose, with a staff that included a family governess and a nurse, didn't offer any advice. "I am loath to answer that question until I see how my own family turns out," she said sagely, ever the mayor's daughter.

Joe wasn't as politic or discreet. When talking with reporters at the embassy, he plopped his feet on his desk and gave candid, off-the-cuff remarks. He chortled when the press referred to him as "Your Excellency." Unlike most ambassadors before, Kennedy gave the impression he would make American policy rather than follow dictates from Washington. "His favorite theme, on which he has been dwelling in many a talk with Britain's rulers, is the United States' refusal to consider any political tie-up abroad—and 'abroad,' he has made clear, naturally includes the fifth of the globe's surface called the British empire," observed a United Press reporter. "However inexperienced he may be in international politics, the belief that he enjoys the confidence of President Roosevelt to an unusual degree has endowed Kennedy with great influence in London."

Winston Churchill, who had felt his influence wane in recent years, had reason to believe his lunch with Joe Kennedy on March 10, 1938, might earn him a new ally. Previously they had shared friendships and mutual business interests, and Winston had hosted Joe and Rose at his Chartwell home. At this afternoon's meal, he invited Randolph along for the discussion. Despite their growing personal disagreements, the elder Churchill still respected his son's astute political judgments about others. This father-son collaboration was the kind Winston had always hoped for with his own father, Lord Randolph—the chance to act in tandem, sifting through state policy and the motives of other leaders. Meeting with men such as Ambassador Kennedy, up close in this type of private talk, would provide young Randolph with the same kind of opportunity, the same insights Joe wanted his own sons to acquire while in England. By the time of this luncheon, Randolph had dealt with Joe Kennedy more often than his father had—both recently in England and as a foreign correspondent covering politics in the United States.

Kennedy sought a meeting with Churchill undoubtedly because of their previous personal contact. Most important, he wanted to learn why Winston had a "pronounced and persistent opposition" to Neville Chamberlain, as Kennedy later wrote. Chamberlain, a rival within the Conservative Party, became prime minister in May 1937 when Stanley Baldwin retired. He, too, kept Winston out of the Cabinet, to Churchill's deep frustration. As with Baldwin, Chamberlain's approach to German aggression (allowing some concessions and seeking a possible alliance with Mussolini's Italy) relied on negotiations seeking peace rather than preparations for the likelihood of war. In his principled and often lonely opposition, Winston strongly believed Great Britain needed to bolster its defenses, which had deteriorated significantly since World War I. When Foreign Secretary Anthony Eden, an ally, resigned in a dispute about Chamberlain's overtures to Italy, Winston viewed him as a hero in their cause against appeasement. "One strong young figure standing up against long, dismal, drawling tides of drift and surrender," Churchill later described Eden.

Unaware of Kennedy's internal tensions with Roosevelt, Churchill tried to explain the reasons for his concerns to the new ambassador. "It was natural for Churchill to harp upon the basis of his differences with the Government," Kennedy recounted. "He regretted Eden's resignation for he and others believed that Mussolini had been headed for a fall and that Chamberlain's policy had rescued him." Winston argued that the prime minister's displays of weakness had allowed other, smaller nations to believe in Germany's growing supremacy. He said Chamberlain's refusal to confront German aggression immediately, and his waiting instead for England's arms buildup, was a big mistake. Churchill "made it clear to me that England's idea of delaying all action until they get stronger is a fallacy," Kennedy wrote. In the case of air power, he let Kennedy know that "their secret information is that Germany is gaining on Britain every month." Churchill argued that Chamberlain's acts of appeasement endangered the British Empire, and he rued "the fact that the Lion has had his tail wrung [and] has lost them prestige."

Their conversation underlined that the two luncheon partners were headed in different directions. Kennedy favored Chamberlain's position, rather than the bellicose course that Churchill felt necessary. In describing his first meeting with the prime minister, Kennedy described Chamberlain as "a strong character" with "a realistic, practical mind." Though Kennedy's notes from the luncheon do not specifically say this, one gets the impression that Winston realized that Joe favored Chamberlain's views rather than his own. Still, the Churchills and the Kennedys seemed determined to remain friendly, as they had been for years.

Clementine, the fiercest of her husband's defenders, made this clear a few weeks later, at a dinner hosted by Lord and Lady Astor. "My dinner companion was Mrs. Churchill and I had a very interesting discussion with her," Kennedy recalled. According to his diary, they mainly chatted about his objectives as the new American ambassador in London. As part of his job, Kennedy explained to Clementine, he needed to accurately inform Americans about the efforts of the British government. He particularly mentioned Chamberlain's negotiations with Ireland, an area of key concern to many Irish Americans back home. Clementine showed the same friendliness as when the Kennedys visited her home at Chartwell. She emphasized that Winston felt the same way. As Joe recounted, "She told me her husband liked me very much and would see me any time that I cared to see him."

12

Astor Place

In all of England, no one acted kinder toward the Kennedys than Lady Nancy Astor, the same powerful, wealthy woman whom Winston Churchill deplored. The legendary confrontations between Astor and Churchill, both sharp-tongued antagonists in Parliament, could be breathtakingly rude.

"If you were my husband, I'd poison your tea," she told Winston on one occasion.

"Madam, if you were my wife, I'd drink it!" he retorted.

Joe Kennedy, however, felt gratitude toward Astor. During their first year away from the United States, the ambassador's family was welcomed repeatedly at Cliveden, the lavish four-hundred-acre estate along the Thames River owned by Lord Waldorf Astor and his American-born wife. For years the Astors had hosted gala parties featuring the cream of European society, from George Bernard Shaw and Rudyard Kipling to Charlie Chaplin, T. E. Lawrence, and King Edward VIII. Nancy Astor befriended Rose Kennedy and her daughters as if their sponsor. She navigated them through various social circles, a test that they passed with flying colors. Lady Astor helped get Rose elected as honorary president of the American Women's Club of Great Britain, and she provided friendly advice to the Kennedy children, especially the second-oldest daughter, Kick. Rose later said her friend Nancy treated Kick as "a kindred soul, a younger version of herself."

In a world seemingly headed toward war, Astor viewed the Kennedys as a beacon of hope, and their children as filled with potential. "You have no right, at your age, to be gloomy," she'd tell young Jack Kennedy. "You young people will have a wonderful change [*sic*] to make a better world, but you have got to be very bold and very good to do it. You, Jack, particularly."

Joe Kennedy realized Lady Astor, one of Britain's most influential figures, had helped his clan gain acceptance in London in a stunning way. "My father impressed upon me that I would notice as I went through life that gratitude was mostly found in the dictionary," he explained in a December 1938 letter to Astor. "I would seem very unappreciative indeed if I didn't express to you my thanks for your many kindnesses to Rose, Kathleen and the children."

Lady Astor's life, with all its contradictions, fascinated the Kennedys. Born Nancy Witcher Langhorne in Virginia, the daughter of a former Confederate Army officer, she met her rich husband while traveling on a boat to England, seeking a new home after escaping her troubled first marriage to an alcoholic. When her new husband, Waldorf, was elevated to the peerage as Viscount Astor, Nancy took his abandoned seat in the House of Commons in 1919, becoming England's first female Member of Parliament. Her stinging humor and wide array of friendships throughout Great Britain made Lady Astor irresistible to the Kennedys, even if they had to ignore her occasional anti-Catholic remarks. "She is great fun any place, talks about everything, anything, intelligently and with gusto and to an inexhaustible sense of humor," Rose observed. Nancy assured Joe that her class-conscious bigotry didn't include his family. "I'm glad you are smart enough not to take my anti-Catholicism, which so many others make so much of, personally," she advised.

Politically, Lady Astor's home carried considerable significance for Joe Kennedy. On weekends, Cliveden often became a salon for politicians, aristocrats, and intellectuals opposed to England entering a war with Germany, with some openly admiring Hitler and his policies. These aristocrats with large fortunes were more concerned with the spread of Russia's communism than Hitler's brand of right-wing fascism. In private, Joe shared Nancy's penchant for anti-Semitic comments and avoiding conflict with Nazi Germany. At a May 1938 party among "the Cliveden set," as the press later dubbed them, Joe first met Charles Lindbergh, the famous American aviator, who had fallen under the influence of Adolf Hitler and his blitzkrieg to power. The ambitious new ambassador seemed galvanized by Lindbergh's all-American celebrity, and soon wound up heeding his advice on Germany's burgeoning military might. At Hitler's invitation, Lindbergh had recently toured Germany, inspecting their Luftwaffe airplanes. Lucky Lindy, as the world called Lindbergh after his daring 1927 transatlantic flight, concluded that America must, at all costs, avoid war against Hitler, whom he judged "a great man." Kennedy eventually forwarded an alarming report by the aviator to Secretary of State Cordell Hull in September 1938. That same night, Lindbergh listened to a radio speech by Hitler with a group gathered at Cliveden, where he and Nancy Astor agreed Britain must not confront Germany.

At the American embassy, Joe and Rose invited Colonel Lindbergh and his wife, Anne Morrow Lindbergh, to lunch alone. A few years earlier, the Lindberghs had suffered the 1932 kidnapping and murder of their toddler son. The discovery of his broken body resulted in one of the most highly publicized trials in history and the convicted killer's execution in the electric chair. Careful not to mention it, Rose nevertheless thought of the crime as she gazed at Lindbergh's still-youthful looks and Anne's girlish appearance with no makeup or lipstick. "She is small, gentle, terribly sweet in looks and manner with a wistful expression, all of which makes you seeth [sic] to know that anyone had hurt her so tragically," Rose wrote in her diary. After the initial pleasantries, their luncheon was consumed with ominous predictions about the German war machine. As documents later showed, Lindbergh's estimate of the number of German fighter planes had been exaggerated by the Nazi propagandists, but Joe accepted it without question. As Rose recalled, "The Colonel gave us a rude awakening by declaring from his observations that Germany could turn out dozens of planes to England's one."

Churchill fumed when he learned of Lindbergh's gathering with Kennedy at Cliveden. He realized how the American aviation hero and the new U.S. ambassador might push Prime Minister Chamberlain and the British government further down the road of appeasement. Giving ground to Hitler, he suggested, was similar to the person "who feeds the crocodile hoping that it will eat him last." For Winston, it was also another appalling example of Nancy Astor's malevolence in his life.

Once friendly, Lady Astor and Winston found their views sharply contrasting by the 1930s, even though they were in the same Conservative Party. Her pacifism had been shaped significantly by the Great War, when so many contemporaries came home maimed or not at all. "After two years in that first war, we did not look at the casualty lists any more—all our friends had gone," she lamented. In the public arena, she bristled at Winston's condescending remarks about women, and as a teetotaler, she favored an American-style Prohibition for Britain. "I have great regard and respect for the noble lady, but I do not think we are likely to learn much from the liquor legislation of the United States," Winston replied.

During the previous two decades in Parliament, the two could provide high entertainment for those watching their debates with a war-of-the-sexes dynamic. "Nancy, when you entered the House, I felt you had come upon me in my bath and I had nothing to protect me but my sponge," Churchill once declared, his chauvinism sugarcoated in humor. At a party they both attended, the owner of Chartwell, with all its animals, whimsically asked the crowd, "How many toes are there in a pig's foot?" Lightning-fast, Astor commanded, "Take off your shoes and count." Years later, as the comments became even more personal, Winston wondered aloud about what disguise he might wear for a masquerade ball. Astor sniffed, "Why don't you come sober?"

After a particularly acrimonious debate about India, Winston confronted Lady Astor in the House of Commons lobby. He vilified her in a way she felt he wouldn't have tried with her husband or his brother, both of whom owned influential British newspapers. "You hardly ever have a difference with me without calling me a Yankee (your mother was a Yankee—I am a Virginian) or asking me to get back to Virginia and leave British politics," she wrote to Winston. "As for my political life—dim tho it is—I would not change it for yours. But what I feel is, you would not dare use this kind of abuse [with a man]. I don't think it cricket that because I am a woman you should use it with me . . . so if our friendship is to continue, could you treat me as fairly as you would a man?"

Winston apologized for losing his temper. Like a chastened schoolboy, he explained, "I don't think you realise how keenly some of us who cannot take your detached views feel about our affairs, nor how wounded some of us are by the things you say."

Astor and Kennedy's involvement with Lindbergh alarmed Churchill, who remembered the scope of the hero aviator's celebrity. In 1927, after Lindbergh's plane touched down miraculously in Paris, Churchill declared that "he represents all that a man should say, all that a man should do, and all that a man should be." Through an intermediary in 1936, Churchill invited Lindbergh to Chartwell, but the latter never accepted. By 1938, Churchill realized that Hitler's charismatic brand of evil had infected not only naïve Americans like Lindbergh but also many Britons, including some in his own family.

During this time, Winston implored Sarah Churchill to visit Paris instead of Munich because, as she later recalled, he worried that his impressionable daughter "might be swept up in the enthusiasm of Fascism, which is what happened to my cousin, Unity Mitford." Unity was one of the well-known Mitfords (cousins on Clementine Churchill's side of the family), who frequently visited Chartwell in the 1920s. While growing up, Randolph felt "very much in love" with Diana Mitford, one of six remarkable sisters in the family. He also counted their brother, Tom Mitford, as his "greatest friend," one who became part of Randolph's crowd of friends at Oxford. The Mitfords tended toward the radical end of politics, either communism or right-wing fascist causes, and generally disapproved of Winston's brand of Tory politics. By the mid-1930s, the pro-Nazi sentiments of Unity Mitford, the fourth-oldest of the six sisters, particularly rankled Winston. After a trip to Germany, Unity became obsessed with Adolf Hitler, and the German leader used his bizarre relationship with this mixed-up young woman for his own twisted purposes. After the Nazis invaded Austria in March 1938, Unity told Winston how "everyone looked happy & full of hope for the future" in that conquered nation. This misguided relative, blind to the hateful frenzy of the Nazi movement, appalled Winston. "A large majority of the people of Austria loathes the idea of coming under Nazi rule," he corrected her. "It was because Herr Hitler feared the free expression of opinion that we are compelled to witness the present dastardly outrage."

The Kennedys became aware of Unity's dalliance with Hitler primarily through the friendship of Kick and her older brothers with the youngest Mitford sister, Deborah. (However, "Debo," as her friends called her, didn't share the extreme politics of her older sister.) During a tour of Germany in August 1939, Joe Kennedy Jr. bumped into Unity in Munich. "Unity Mitford is one of the most unusual women I have ever met," he wrote back to his father. "She is the most fervent Nazi imaginable and is probably in love with Hitler."

Eventually, despondent over her beloved Führer, Unity shot herself in the head, a botched suicide attempt that left her impaired for years until she died of infection. But in September 1938, when most British officials wanted to avoid conflict with Germany at almost any cost, Winston believed Unity Mitford was just a more virulent example of the growing number willing to appease Hitler. That same month, Churchill condemned Chamberlain for agreeing with Hitler to a peace pact at Munich, calling it a "disaster of the first magnitude." The agreement soon opened the door for the Nazis to run roughshod over Czechoslovakia, and left them hungering for more lands to conquer. "We have sustained a defeat without a war," Churchill thundered in Parliament, "the consequences of which will travel far with us along our road."

Even the royal court in Great Britain did not seem immune to this Nazi influence. In October 1937 the Duke of Windsor and his wife, the former American divorcée Wallis Simpson, traveled to Germany to pose for pictures with the Führer and flashed a "Heil Hitler" salute. As King Edward VIII, the duke had abdicated the throne only ten months earlier in order to marry Simpson. His visit to Germany was an incredible betrayal to Churchill. During the constitutional crisis surrounding a possible abdication, Churchill had loyally defended Edward when so much of Parliament wanted him to step down so his brother could replace him.

"You won't be satisfied until you've broken him, will you?" Winston shouted across the floor at Prime Minister Stanley Baldwin in an effort to save his king.

Lord Beaverbrook was one of the few to join his friend Winston as royal loyalists who struggled on until Edward finally lost heart in December 1936. As Beaverbrook succinctly told Winston, "Our cock won't fight." In the end, Churchill carefully helped the new Duke of Windsor prepare his national radio speech in which he famously renounced the throne "for the woman I love." With his quixotic defense of an unworthy king now ended, Churchill could be heard, in a barely audible tone, reciting lines from a famous ode by Andrew Marvell about the beheading of King Charles I. "As I saw Mr. Churchill walk off, there were tears in his eyes," the former king later recalled.

The abdication fight cost Churchill dearly among his fellow Conservatives—already upset enough to keep him out of the Cabinet. The Duke of Windsor had proved he wasn't worthy of Winston's loyalty. Against the advice of both Beaverbrook and Churchill, the duke journeyed to a Bavarian château, where Hitler greeted him like an old friend. After the two-hour meeting, Hitler suggested that relations between England and his country would have been better without the abdication. "If it had been possible for me to talk to King Edward VIII for just one hour, the abdication of His Majesty could have been avoided," Hitler insisted. The former king became an unwitting propaganda tool. During a German machine plant tour, workers even called out to the duke, "Heil Edward!" Observing the Nazi delight, a *New York Times* reporter observed that the duke had "lent himself, perhaps unconsciously but easily, to National Socialist propaganda." Covering the trip as a correspondent for Beaverbrook's *Evening Standard,* Randolph Churchill gained an exclusive interview with the duke that made headlines around the world.

When Joe Kennedy arrived in early 1938, controversy still swirled around the Duke of Windsor and his American-born wife. Asked his opinion, Joe typically dove in headfirst rather than seek diplomatic immunity. In his diary, he agreed with what former prime minister Stanley Baldwin had told him in confidence: "If a king wants to sleep with a whore, that's his private business, but the Empire is concerned that he doesn't make her their queen." In a less than charitable way, Kennedy also endorsed a provocative move by Rose, who snubbed the former Mrs. Simpson by declining a dinner invitation because of her presence.

"I know of no job that I could occupy that might force my wife to dine with a tart," Kennedy explained privately to the new queen.

Kennedy's aggressive role in the affairs of Great Britain surprised American foreign correspondents. "The British aren't accustomed to ambassadors expressing their frank opinions on international affairs in public," said CBS newsman Edward R. Murrow, a Churchill friend who detested Kennedy and his pro-appeasement stance. "American assistance and support, economic and moral, are welcomed in Britain, but advice as to how the war should be conducted or how the peace should be made is distinctly less welcome."

Back in Washington, FDR was annoyed at Kennedy's publicity hound approach and his involvement with those pleading the case for appeasement with Germany. Aides such as Harold Ickes were convinced that Kennedy "had been taken in hand by Lady Astor and the Cliveden set." To Morgenthau, another confidant, Roosevelt said, laughing, "Who would have thought that the English could take into camp a red-headed Irishman?"

Within a month after the Munich Pact, the dividing lines between Kennedy and Churchill became more distinct. Kennedy gave a speech supporting Chamberlain's pact and his promise that it would bring "peace for our time." Kennedy labeled his remarks as his own and not U.S. government policy, but they still got a lot of attention, as if Roosevelt approved, which he didn't. "There is simply no sense, common or otherwise, in letting these differences grow into unrelenting antagonism," Kennedy proclaimed about the threat of war with Germany. Churchill also spoke for himself, and not the government, about Great Britain's fate after Munich. For the moment, Kennedy's view was far more popular with the British people than Winston's.

"England has been offered a choice between war and shame," Churchill warned the House of Commons. "She has chosen shame, and will get war."

13

The Kennedy Women

At the appointed time, when the king and queen entered the white-and-gold ballroom of Buckingham Palace, a group of American debutantes awaiting presentation to the royal court began their curtsies. Elaborately, the young women bowed down before His and Her Majesty. King George VI, dressed as a field marshal, arrived arm in arm with Queen Elizabeth, glittering in diamonds, including the great Koh-i-Noor, the most magnificent of the Crown Jewels. Marching beside them were gentlemen-at-arms wearing scarlet uniforms with high helmets and white plumes.

Two young women in this royal assembly were Kennedys: Kathleen and Rosemary, the oldest daughters of the American ambassador. Rose Kennedy, wearing a satin gown with lace embroidered in silver and gold, accompanied them as sponsor for a handful of daughters of American officials.

"The girls all wore white, with three white ostrich feathers in their hair and no jewelry," recalled Deborah Mitford, then an eighteen-year-old debutante in that "coming-out" ceremony. Debo vividly recalled the Kennedy family's splash on the London social scene, especially her new friend Kathleen Kennedy, chosen as top debutante of the season.

"Vital, intelligent and outgoing, Kick was able to talk to anyone with ease and her shining niceness somehow ruled out any jealousy," Mitford remembered. "Suitors appeared instantly but I noticed from the start that none of the other girls was annoyed by her success and I never heard a catty remark made behind her back."

Kick's emerging circle of London friends included other debutantes from that season. Kick enraptured young men with her vivacious good looks and attractive personality, especially a refreshing American sense of humor that carried none of the solemn dreariness of British tradition. She could poke fun at herself as much as the stuffiness of her friends from aristocratic families such as the Mitfords.

"Oh, do go on—do speak English again, Kick," teased Veronica Fraser, a friend whose brother Hugh danced up a storm at the various balls and parties that season. At one weekend event, Kick was introduced to Winston Churchill but teasingly referred to his cousin, the Duke of Marlborough, as "Dukie Wookie."

At one of the coming-out galas, Jack Kennedy asked Debo to dance. "Rather boring but nice," Debo summed him up in her diary.

Debo's mother, a Churchill relative, sitting with the other chaperones, watched young Jack on the dance floor and saw something else in him. With the kind of premonition that only mothers may possess, she turned to a friend and reportedly predicted, "Mark my words. I would not be surprised if that young man becomes President of the United States."

England was familiar territory to Kick Kennedy, well before her father became ambassador. She landed in London with her parents and Jack in 1935, on her way to study at the Holy Child Convent outside Paris. It was in convent schools where Kick learned to curtsey. Ever daring and adventurous, she managed on one school vacation to travel secretly to Cambridge with a schoolmate so they could attend balls, dancing with handsome English students. In the Kennedy family, Rose generally oversaw the education and religious training of their five daughters (Rosemary, Kick, Eunice, Patricia, and Jean), while Joe watched over their sons' education and careers. Like many mothers of her day, Rose viewed "child rearing as a profession," molding the girls' character and behavior with constant lessons from the Bible, while Joe viewed his sons as heirs to his earthly domain.

During the summer of 1938, all nine Kennedy children lived together in the ambassador's residence in London, after years spent apart studying at various American schools. Princes Gate became a grand hotel for the Kennedys, where they posed for memorable family portraits on the back lawn. Even King George knew about the much-publicized American clan. When they met, he laughed and shared with Joe "the Music Hall joke about Kennedy being father of his country." To Page Huidekoper, then a young aide in the embassy who was friendly with Kick, the Kennedys were "hands-on parents" who cared immensely about their children's future. "They were incredibly close to the children," said Huidekoper in a 2011 interview, one of the few still alive from that era. "They demanded a lot of the children but they loved them unequivocally."

Others saw Joe's manipulative hand constantly at work. He presided over dinner conversation, often eclipsing or ignoring what Rose had to offer at the other end of the table. Invited for lunch at Princes Gate, Kick's friend Veronica Fraser noticed how the Kennedy boys reported everything to their father, from the status of their school grades to their "bowel movement," she recalled. "The girls got off more lightly but also reported in detail to their formidable parent." Even the 1938 debutante presentation before the king and queen bore Joe's imprint. Shortly after becoming ambassador, Kennedy stopped the longtime practice of allowing rich and well-connected American girls to come over to London for the ceremony, limiting the royal presentation only to the daughters of U.S. officials and Americans doing business in England. This decision brought more press attention to his wife and two daughters when they walked into Buckingham Palace.

The marriage of Joe and Rose Kennedy, united in raising their children together, remained a mystery for those who looked beneath the surface. In public and even in their handwritten notes, Joe treated his beloved "Rosa" with affection and respect, indulging her constant trips to Paris and elsewhere to see the latest haute couture collections. Rose's fidelity to her God and Church made her marital vows unbreakable, even though her husband often committed adultery. When visiting New York, Joe and Rose sometimes stayed at different hotels, purportedly because of his fondness for womanizing. Eventually, Joe's constantly philandering left Rose feeling diminished and sometimes powerless. For reasons all her own, she reacted in the same way her own mother did when she learned of Honey Fitz's career-crippling affection for a buxom showgirl named Elizabeth "Toodles" Ryan in 1913. Rose ignored her husband's affairs, even though they were far more flagrant; Joe even flirted with the queen. As he recorded in his diary, "I thanked her and said, 'I know one shouldn't say this to a queen, but may I say you look particularly beautiful tonight in that dress.' She blushed."

In England, Rose graciously followed her husband's social agenda without making much of a mark of her own. "She is an uninteresting little body, though pleasant and extraordinarily young looking to be the mother of nine," observed Sir Henry "Chips" Channon, a Conservative Member of Parliament. "She has an unpleasant voice, and says little of interest." Nevertheless, Rose made it her business to know the key figures in Great Britain's political debates. She felt warmly toward Winston, who'd hosted the visiting Kennedys at his Chartwell manor. After listening to him debate in Parliament, she would write in her diary, "Mr. Winston Churchill, who is said to be the most fascinating and brilliant orator, spoke attacking the Government policy. I found him fascinating, delightful and easy to follow."

In emulating their mother, Rose's daughters followed the strictures of a church that relegated women to a secondary role, much as American society did in general. "If Joe Kennedy's daughters had been sent to the very best Catholic schools, the better to retain the parochialism and tradition in order to pass it on to his grandchildren, his sons had been educated exactly for the opposite reason—to shed it," observed writer David Halberstam about this dichotomy. "There would be no Holy Cross, or Fordham, or Georgetown Law School in their lives. They were sent instead to the best Eastern Protestant schools, where the British upper-class values were still in vogue."

Eunice Kennedy, perhaps the smartest of the Kennedy children, seemed most inclined to follow her mother's lessons, especially in her devotion to the Catholic Church. She eventually graduated from Stanford University, but the goals and ambitions her parents held for Eunice were never the same as they were for her brothers. Joe Kennedy, keenly aware of bigotry against his own kind, didn't seem bothered by inequality facing his daughters. "If Eunice had balls, she would have been president," her father bragged, without a sense of irony.

Kick, with a keen native intelligence more than one derived from books, appeared to accept the male dominance of her 1930s world without question. Deftly, with a sardonic wit and an engaging smile, she maneuvered to exert her will on both her father and the other men in her life, including her two oldest brothers, Joe Jr. and Jack. She seemed unfazed by the sexual hunger of men, while keeping her own virginal sense of decorum, which she learned from her mother. "That's what all men do," she replied, when friends once mentioned men who cheat on their wives. "You know that women can never trust them."

Several friends of the young Kennedys were drawn from a small circle of Catholics in London and an even larger Tory group that over-lapped with the Churchills. Randolph Churchill was a regular fixture at several balls and parties they attended, including the Kennedys' splendid bash at the embassy. Further extended in this circle, Max Beaverbrook, the son of Joe's friend, fell in love and married Janie Kenyon Slaney, one of Kick's good friends. Many of Jack's buddies, such as Tony Rosslyn (actually Tony Loughborough, the Sixth Earl of Rosslyn), were enchanted by Kick when they weren't out with Jack chasing other women. Tony and Jack called themselves RossKennedy, as if a tag team in approaching the opposite sex. Tony, whose father committed suicide, also turned to Joe Sr. for paternal advice, and acted as one of the ambassador's biggest defenders among his growing number of British critics.

At Kick's urging, the Kennedys allowed her friend Sissy Thomas to live at the embassy after her father, Hugh Lloyd Thomas, was killed in a steeplechase accident. It was an act of kindness that would forever change the lives of Kick and, by extension, her brother Jack.

During the summer of 1938, Sissy's boyfriend, David Ormsby-Gore, the handsome and bright son of a Conservative politician, introduced Kick to his aristocratic best friend, William Cavendish, the Marquess of Hartington and future Duke of Devonshire. Kick and Billy immediately hit it off as a most unlikely couple. Tall and self-effacing, Billy stood nearly a head over this rambunctious American girl whose refreshing manner captivated him. To many, Billy seemed a more likely suitor for the king's daughter, Princess Elizabeth, than Joe Kennedy's Irish-Catholic spawn. The Cavendishes, proprietors of large estates in England and Ireland, ranked among "the twelve families that own England," with a family motto: *Cavendo Tutus* ("Safe by Caution").

Within weeks, caution was tossed to the wind. Kick and Billy began double-dating with Sissy and David Ormsby-Gore, who also was Billy's first cousin. They went out with Billy's brother, Andrew, and his love interest, Debo Mitford, whom he eventually married. "Kick had by now become part of the scene and was as much with Billy as I was with Andrew," Mitford recalled years later. Among their friends, Jack Kennedy enjoyed talking about politics with David Ormsby-Gore, whom he considered one of the most intelligent of his generation, more so than his friends back at Harvard. David's mix of everyday political concerns with an aristocratic air appealed to young Kennedy as the best of British tradition. "He was fascinated by English political society, with its casual combination of wit, knowledge, and unconcern," explained Kennedy biographer Arthur M. Schlesinger Jr. During this time, Schlesinger said, Jack read two books that further defined his future political style: David Cecil's *The Young Melbourne* and Winston Churchill's life of his father, Lord Randolph, in whom Kennedy found "as much historical sustenance" as in Lord Melbourne. Billy shared David's interest in Conservative Party politics, and both hoped to run for office someday. The two young men tended to agree with Churchill's critical assessment of the Munich Pact, and didn't share Ambassador Kennedy's unbridled enthusiasm for the agreement with Hitler put together by Prime Minster Chamberlain. Though momentarily relieved by Chamberlain's promise of peace, Billy and David were both familiar with Germany and doubted Nazi aggression could be contained without war. Although he still agreed mostly with his father, Jack Kennedy increasingly shared his friends' doubts. As the threat of war neared, he would later write to a friend back home in the States: "The big men of Berlin and London sit and confidently give their orders, and it is these kids—so far as I can see—who are the first casualties."

Travel through Europe became an essential part of the learning experience for the two oldest Kennedy sons, a grand source of education about the world outside America. They would also become the ambassador's unofficial eyes and ears, part of Joe's larger ambition to win the presidency someday. In April 1939, Joe Jr. went to Spain to observe the civil war between the fascist army of Generalissimo Francisco Franco and the flagging Republican resistance forces. He stayed for a while in the U.S. embassy in Madrid, just in time to see the Republican side collapse. The ambassador was so proud of Joe's insights that he read an account of what his son witnessed to a crowd at Lady Astor's Cliveden home. "His father thinks he [Joe Jr.] should write a book as the fact that a person who has written a book gives him a certain prestige," Rose wrote in her diary.

Still a student at Harvard, Jack went back and forth to London during holidays and vacations. He spent the summer of 1939 touring through Europe with David Ormsby-Gore and his Harvard roommate, Torby MacDonald, another Kick admirer. The ambassador implored Jack and his friends to "bend over backwards to stay out of trouble" in Germany, following their tour of Paris. By then, David's father, Lord Harlech, the former British colonial secretary, had split with Chamberlain over the former's weakness with Spain and Czechoslovakia, and favored Churchill's return to the Cabinet. When David showed up at the Kennedys' residence, Rose noticed that his heavy suitcases were weighed down with eighteen books. To her mortification, Jack didn't have any packed. Books soon became essential gear for all traveling Kennedys. While driving through Germany in a car bearing a British license plate, Jack and Torby, a star football player at Harvard, were attacked by rock-throwing Nazi Stormtroopers. "You know," Jack told his friend, "how can we avoid having a world war if this is the way people feel?"

Despite his dominating personality, the ambassador encouraged his sons to make up their own minds about international politics, letting them come to their own conclusions. Joe Jr. rarely strayed from his father's mind-set, a particularly dogged American brand of isolationism. Perhaps as part of his unspoken rivalry with his older brother, Jack seemed more determined to find his own way, displaying a greater influence from his British friends. Once, during a family debate, Rose became alarmed at how her two oldest sons were challenging their father. "I can take care of myself," Joe assured her. "The important thing is

that they fight together." As much as possible, Joe Sr. shared his diplomatic insights with his sons, preparing them for the days when they
might be in a similar position. "There is a very definite feeling here,
underground, that they would like to have Churchill as Prime Minister
pretty soon and Eden as Foreign Secretary, but Chamberlain's speech in
Parliament yesterday swept the boys right back in their corners again,"
Joe told them.

Through his private actions, Joe also taught his sons how to treat
women—not women of hearth and home like their mother and five
sisters, but the women with whom they could share an evening on the
town and an occasional bed. The ambassador was known among Kick's
girlfriends for being randy, with kisses on the lips to say hello and wandering hands. But his affairs often involved mature, attractive women
who were as bright and worldly as any he knew, including Gloria Swanson (who introduced Rose to haute couture in Paris) and Kay Halle, the
journalist friend of Randolph Churchill. Before he left for England in
1938, Joe responded to a friendly note from Halle that he hoped would
keep the embers of their earlier affair aglow. "While I read and hear
about you, I have almost forgotten that you ever knew one, Joe Kennedy," he wrote. "It looks as though I am leaving very soon for England
and that there will not be a chance for a reunion until I return or you
come to England. At any rate, keep thinking of us and I hope to see you
again."

The ambassador soon launched another secret affair with a brilliant
woman who shared a romantic history with Randolph Churchill. In
May 1938, Clare Boothe, now wed to Time Inc. publisher Henry Luce,
first focused on Kennedy at an official London embassy dinner party
hosted by Joe and Rose. Clare had married Luce in 1935, after a few
years as a divorcée in her twenties involved with such men as Bernard
Baruch and young Churchill. Following her departure as *Vanity Fair*
managing editor, Clare produced numerous articles and plays, includ-

ing a controversial hit called *The Women*, also made into a movie. With her upper-class accent and Southern Belle manner, she became known for her urbane wit and memorable aphorisms, such as "No good deed goes unpunished," which she had framed and hung on her wall. "As a bridge figure between the courtesan and the career girl, Clare has sometimes seemed a funny kind of feminist," her writer friend Wilfred Sheed observed. "She wanted to do all the things that men did, but if she didn't need a man under the bed, she needed one behind the throne."

Kennedy was one of Clare's occasional lovers during her marriage to Henry Luce, a right-leaning owner of one of America's most powerful media empires. Henry adored Clare, who shared most of his political views. He also listened to her editorial advice to create *Life*, the hugely successful pictorial magazine. But the Luce marriage, so fulsome in press clippings, was lacking at home, reported Clare's biographer Sylvia Jukes Morris, enough so that Henry was impotent with her. "I do not like to go to bed without you," Clare wrote her husband. "But somehow, lately, even when I'm with you, I seem to go to bed without you."

Whatever her reasons, Clare's sexual interest in Kennedy was set aflame at the embassy dinner party where Charles Lindbergh and his wife were also guests. During their trip abroad, Clare's husband met with British press officials, including Lord Beaverbrook and Brendan Bracken, while she drummed up support for a British production of her famous play. On their return trip to New York in June 1938, Joe joined them aboard the *Queen Mary*. "Clare made no secret of reveling in Joe's company," her biographer observed. "Harry enjoyed it less."

Kennedy's audacity, turning the Time-Life media potentate into a cuckold, didn't concern him much, even at the risk of seeming ungrateful. A month before this dinner party, *Life* featured a big photo essay about the Kennedys in London, calling them "the most politically ingratiating family since Theodore Roosevelt's." The magazine raised the prospect of Joe running for president—something that in 1938 undoubtedly irked another Roosevelt in the White House and his political aides.

Joe's long-distance affair with Clare had all the appeal of a winter's trip to Florida, with its brief flash of heat and enjoyment for a short, memorable time. When she returned to Europe in the summer of 1939, she let Kennedy know in advance. Traveling alone on this journey, Clare continued working on her new book, published a year later as *Europe in the Spring*, which mentioned Kennedy prominently. Her private notes to him were more revealing. SAVE ME LUNCH AND/OR DINNER CHAT ALONE LOVE CLARE, she cabled Kennedy in May 1939, before leaving New York. In another telegram, she gushed, YOU'RE ANGEL [*sic*] MAKE LIFE SO EXCITING FOR ME.

When not frolicking among the pillows, Joe and Clare could toss around their views on the world. Later in her book, Clare wrote that the British "felt it was a peculiar misfortune that (unlike other ambassadors who loved the countries they were in) England got an Irish-American isolationist like Mr. Kennedy." Clare took pains to explain Kennedy's position and underline that he, too, was critical of Germany. "We Americans can live quite comfortably in a world of English snobbery and British complacency, but we can't live—I should hate to live—in a world of Nazis and German brutality," Joe told her in endorsing the Brits. "Though they snub us or sneer at us, yet must we love them and aid them, because their heads may be a little thick, but they've got the right end of the stick. In the end, they stand for all the things we stand for, and if they go, we shall be the losers. Above all, they're the only crowd honest men can do business with."

On that same trip, Clare spent a weekend in the country with another familiar paramour, Randolph Churchill. The Churchills, father and son alike, shared Clare's loathing of the Nazis and those who would appease them. She first met Winston as an editor of *Vanity Fair*, when she arranged for the great man to sit for a photograph arranged with the help of Bernard Baruch. "She's the tops!" cooed Winston to his friend and financial adviser. At that time, Winston tried to convince Clare to marry an Englishman and that it should be his own son, Randolph.

Clare dallied with the golden-haired Churchill youth for a time. Randolph even chased her to Paris for a reunion at the Ritz. When he greeted her at the hotel, Clare appeared fully dressed wearing a trendy hat. "Now you can take them all off," she whispered. Her intermittent flings with Randolph, however, never seemed to satisfy. "Darling . . . you always seem to have a revulsion in the morning," Randolph lamented.

If Henry Luce knew about his wife's affairs with Joe and Randolph, it certainly didn't affect his magazine's flattering coverage of their two families. And as the Luces already knew, no good deed goes unpunished.

14

The Desire to Please

Before the Churchills, the family that would define much of her life, Pamela Digby knew the Kennedys. She first met Kick Kennedy in the spring of 1938, when they were debutantes together. At age eighteen, Digby arrived in London rather desperate to leave the English countryside and find the man of her dreams—preferably an interesting lad with a title and estate awaiting.

Although not terribly close at first, Pamela and Kick shared many friends and acquaintances, and attended the same parties and coming-out balls. One of the most unforgettable was the June gala at the American embassy hosted by Ambassador Kennedy and his wife, at which Pamela danced among three hundred guests. A swing band played "Thanks for the Memory" at night's end. "I knew her as anyone would know another girl friend," said Pamela about Kick, who turned out to be the grand hit of the debutante season.

Pamela wasn't nearly as fortunate, to her lasting chagrin. Freckle-faced and rather plump with puffy cheeks, she didn't attract the cool, sophisticated attention she hoped for, not the men of carefree gaiety who naturally gravitated toward Kick. Pamela blamed her evening dress for her lack of success. While Lord and Lady Digby deemed her garb quite sufficient for their daughter's entry into London society, Pamela considered it a poor second to the exquisite designer gowns worn by other debutantes. Her garment made her look frumpy and hardly scintillating.

The fault lay not in clothes or a lack of makeup, but in Pamela's pushy, calculating personality—a manipulativeness just below the surface that alienated other debutantes. With girls, Pamela's friendliness seemed forced and insincere; with boys, she couldn't be trusted with another debutante's beau. Not so charitably, Debo Mitford described Pamela as "rather fat, fast and the butt of many teases." The oldest Mitford sister, novelist and biographer Nancy, called Digby "a redheaded bouncing little thing regarded as a joke by her contemporaries." Even Kick Kennedy, the reigning American champ of this most British tradition, couldn't help take a poke at Pamela. To her brother Jack, Kick referred to Pamela as a "fat, stupid little butterball."

In her desire to please, Pamela, with light auburn hair and blue eyes, focused most of her attention on the young men in white formal wear who might ask her to dance, rather than on the judgment of other girls. As a sign of her suspect character, some debutantes whispered that Pamela had been found wearing silk knickers instead of the regulation navy blue cotton ones. During that summer's festivities, as Pamela tended to her weight and appearance, boys such as Hugh Fraser, a friend of Jack Kennedy's, took note of the Digby girl. "Although we talked endlessly about our figures (meaning bosoms and legs), we didn't notice anything particularly good about hers, and I was surprised when my brother Hugh told me, 'Pamela Digby has the most exciting body in Britain,'" recalled Fraser's sister Veronica. "I took another look, and decided that the plumpness was rapidly changing into something else. Pam lost no time in exploiting her assets." The stunning lack of social success for that debutante season motivated Pamela to improve herself with a vengeance. "My sister Pamela decided early on she was going to turn herself into a very glamorous person," recalled her younger sister, Sheila. "She had a lot of ambition."

The Digbys led a quiet, comfortable existence on a large estate with a dairy farm, where Pam learned to ride horses and yearned for a life in the city. Against her family's wishes, she read provocative accounts about Lady Jane Digby, a notorious nineteenth-century ancestor who gave up her privileged English marriage for a series of torrid affairs, eventually becoming the courtesan of a Middle Eastern sheik. "Our aunts couldn't bear it when we would discuss Jane Digby, but Pamela was always intrigued by her," recalled her sister. Pamela's proper father tore up all but a few pages remaining from the diary of their scandalized "very wicked" ancestor. Nevertheless, Pamela wore an old bracelet handed down from Lady Digby, inspired by her independent-minded example. Rather than going to university, Pamela was sent to a faraway (German) finishing school, like other upper-crust young ladies of her day. In Germany, Pamela was invited, through her friend Unity Mitford, to a tea featuring Adolf Hitler, she later claimed. "He was a cardboard figure," she remembered of the Führer. "It was a frightening experience."

After her debutante spring, Pamela traveled frequently, visiting Paris and Ireland, going back and forth to London to stay with friends, quickly learning the ways of the world. No longer a virginal ingénue, she engaged in discreet affairs with powerful older men while also dating men her own age. In October 1939, her life changed with a telephone call.

Inside the apartment of a friend, Lady Mary Dunn, she was asked to pick up the ringing receiver. The male voice on the other end identified himself as Randolph Churchill.

"Do you want to speak to Mary?" Pamela asked.

"No," Randolph announced. "I want to speak to you."

Soon it became clear Mary had conspired with Winston's son to get him a date with her auburn-haired friend, though they'd never met before. Randolph had hoped to spend the night with Lady Dunn, whose husband was away, but Dunn convinced him that Pamela would suffice.

"What do you look like?" Randolph claimed he asked Miss Digby.

"Red-headed and rather fat," Pamela replied, "but Mummy says that puppy fat disappears."

When she got off the telephone, Pamela asked Mary about this set-up. Mary vouched for Randolph as an old friend and assured Pam that she'd have a good time, if only for one evening.

"He's great fun, a bit too fat and drinks too much, but very amusing," Mary explained. "I told him I would try to persuade you to dine with him. Please do—you'll have a good time."

That night, Pamela and Randolph dined at Quaglino's, one of his favorite nightspots. The place was jammed with journalists and politicians, chatting away with him about the impending conflict against the Nazis. Pamela didn't say much, as Randolph virtually ignored her. Still, at age nineteen, she was enchanted with Churchill, seven years older and the personification of London sophistication in her eyes.

"I had certainly never met anyone like Randolph," she recalled. "What most appealed to me about him was his absolute certainty about everything—particularly about the war, which he believed was going to be extremely long and bloody, and that we should therefore enjoy life to the last bottle of champagne."

Within a matter of days, Pamela Digby and Randolph Churchill decided to marry.

Clementine Churchill disapproved of her son's rash, if not reckless, choice to wed a woman he barely knew, just as she looked with disfavor at all family misbehavior that might upset her husband. "She was always worried that any of the children might do something that would reflect badly on Winston," Pamela recalled. Throughout the 1930s, as the Churchill children grew into adulthood, Randolph wasn't the only one who gave them trouble.

Sarah, their third child, inherited Winston's sense of showmanship and her mother's good looks. Most considered Sarah her father's favorite, though Winston nicknamed her the Mule, for her strong-willed obstinateness. "Sarah is an oyster, she will not tell us her secrets," Winston said. As soon as she could do so legally, Sarah entered the theater business, starting in one of its lowest rungs—the chorus line of C. B. Cochran's "Young Ladies" troupe of lovelies, featured in a 1935 revue called *Follow the Sun.* Cochran, no fool, made sure his young performer secured her famous father's permission, which Winston granted reluctantly with Cochran's promise to "keep an eye" on her. Sarah had studied music at a well-respected school of dance, but her main attributes for this job seemed her flowing light red hair, pretty face, and winsome figure. (In his polite evaluation, Cochran let Winston know Sarah's voice was "very tiny.") Cochran's show offered London audiences "girls who danced fairly naked—as naked as you could get in those days," recalled Pamela. "That was really not what her parents had in mind for their daughter." But Sarah, wanting to make her own mark, "was never to feel alone or strange in the chorus line," she later wrote. In one musical number, she and the other chorus girls turned around, bent over, and showed their "befrilled bottoms" to the audience. Teasingly, the girls asked in a song, "How low can a chorus girl go, before she is called a so-and-so?" Sarah was aware of her father's discomfort at her career choice, but had no intention of acceding to him. "How much I love you, and how much I will try to make this career that I have chosen—with some pain to the people I love, and not a little to myself—worthy of your name—one day," she inscribed in a note to Winston.

Clementine also didn't like that her oldest daughter, Diana, who studied at the Royal Academy of Dramatic Art, had her heart set on the theater just like Sarah. Cochran's opinion of Sarah's voice was a far more generous finding than Clementine's assessment of her two daughters' abilities. "It's very strange that both she [Sarah] and Diana should have this passionate wish to go on the stage without the slightest talent or even aptitude," she confided to her secretary. Diana's showbiz dream faded after her December 1932 wedding to John Bailey, the son of a very wealthy South African diamond tycoon. Diana later said she married "to escape from all the endless talk around the Chartwell dinner table." In 1935, after three unhappy years, Diana divorced Bailey, a spouse she'd barely known before taking her vows. For her, this marital failure was compounded by another unvarnished realization: that her mother had been correct as well about her lack of theatrical talent. Eventually, she gave up that dream, too. These two profound disappointments in Diana's life wound up permanently souring her relationship with her mother—perhaps the price Clementine had to pay for being right. During the 1935 by-election, Diana met and soon married Duncan Sandys, a handsome young Conservative Party politician whom the Churchills found more agreeable than Bailey. "I like my new son-in-law," Winston wrote. "He & Diana are very much in love. That is all a great relief."

By 1936, Sarah threw the family into an even greater tumult when she decided to marry the comedian Victor Oliver, one of the stars of her revue. Vic, previously married and nearly two decades her senior, became Sarah's Svengali, exerting a powerful influence. Hoping to gain her parents' blessing, Sarah initiated a visit to Chartwell with Vic, which proved a sorry misjudgment. Winston and Clementine asked Sarah for more time to ponder her decision. They employed every tool to forestall Sarah from marrying her beloved showman, including some prudent words from C. B. Cochran himself. Winston pointed out that Oliver, born Jewish in Austria, had never become an American citizen, despite more than a dozen years living there, and could be deported back to his homeland, now under Nazi control. Holding a British passport in his hand, Winston stood before his daughter to issue a firm warning. "If he does not take American citizenship, in three years' time you will be married to the enemy—and I will not be able to protect you once you have lost this," Winston bellowed, as if addressing another Member of Parliament.

Shortly after, Vic Oliver went to America on tour, and Sarah hastily followed him, with barely any notice to her family. On her ship ride over, Sarah bumped into another passenger, Lady Astor, her father's old parliamentary adversary. "Sarah, what are you doing here?" Astor asked.

"I am going to America," Sarah said.

Astor quickly deduced, "You're running away!"

"No," Sarah corrected, "I am running *to*."

When Sarah arrived in New York, Lady Astor advised Churchill's daughter how best to handle the awaiting press corps at the dock. News of Sarah "eloping," with no more than four pounds in her pocket, had already swept across the ocean as an international gossip story of forbidden romance. Graciously, Lady Astor allowed herself to be identified as Sarah's "chaperone," though the circumstances were clear: her famous father didn't approve of this trip. Sarah stayed at a Waldorf Astoria hotel suite as guest of her father's friend Bernard Baruch, alerted by Winston to this family crisis through a transatlantic telephone call.

In the meantime, Winston dispatched Randolph—already leaving on another boat to New York to cover the 1936 presidential election—to act as the family's voice of reason in preventing Sarah's marriage. It was both a sign of confidence in Randolph and moreover a measure of Winston's desperation. Clementine cautioned Winston not to act as heavy-handedly with Sarah as he had when Randolph wanted to marry his American friend Kay Halle. During this new crucible, she reminded Winston of "the effect of the letter you wrote to Randolph 5 years ago. He was very near marrying Miss Halle when I was with him in New York."

After his ship arrived the following day, Randolph quickly caught up with his sister but feigned ignorance to fellow journalists about her love affair. "I didn't know anything about this until now," he claimed.

Randolph thought he'd pulled off a diplomatic coup by convincing his sister to wait until Vic's divorce was ratified before going ahead. "We have gained two months in which there is a chance that one of them might change their mind," Randolph reported home to his father. Randolph remained silent as the New York press hounded him for more comment, calling him "the man who wants to trip Cupid."

Vic, the thirty-eight-year-old vaudevillian, knew when to take a bow after a successful performance. "If the family is willing, I would be very honored to become connected with the name of Churchill," he said, after first denying any interest in marriage.

On Christmas Eve 1936, Sarah and Vic took their vows in the chapel of the Municipal Building in New York, then left on a cruise liner back to England. Sarah smiled when asked if the Archbishop of Canterbury or another cleric might repeat their marriage vows in a church upon their return. "That's a good joke," she replied.

Winston Churchill had always vowed to be a good father, unlike his own. But by the time his four surviving children were adults in the 1930s, his shortcomings and failures were evident, with painful consequences for all. As his parliamentary career progressed, his duties of parenthood at Chartwell had been mostly delegated to his wife and her help, especially those unpleasant tasks needed in a family to keep order and any sense of discipline. "Winston was more relaxed and indulgent, greatly enjoying his children in the brief moments he could spend with them," explained their youngest daughter, Mary. "But the burden of bringing up and disciplining their brood was always left to Clementine."

Unlike most parents able to see each of their children grow to maturity (including the Kennedys, then living together at the London embassy), the Churchills endured the worst tragedy, the death of a child, early in their marriage. In August 1921, when both Winston and Clementine were away in Scotland on summer holiday, their nearly three-year-old daughter, Marigold, left in the care of their French governess, contracted a fatal throat infection. The little girl, affectionately called Duckadilly by Winston, died shortly after her parents reached her bedside. The agony of watching their daughter slip away before their eyes was unbearable. "She said 'So tired' and closed her eyes," Winston remembered of his daughter's last words. "And I thought that Clemmie would die in the violence of her grief. She screamed like a creature under torture."

Clementine could not bring herself to mention her daughter's name again. Marigold's painful absence, however, didn't curb Winston's constant travel, his days and nights away from his family. Three weeks after the little girl's death, he went off to a speaking engagement in Scotland, treated royally at Dunrobin Castle by his friend the Duke of Sutherland. "I wish you could have come as there is constant lawn tennis and many pleasant things to do," he wrote his wife at home. "Alas I keep on feeling the hurt of the Duckadilly." Soon after, Winston remained in France when Clemmie collapsed from nervous exhaustion. Doctors ordered her to bed for a week, while the other Churchill children suffered influenza with high fevers. From France, Winston applauded Clemmie's "Napoleonic" response to this family crisis. Letters between them suggest Clementine agreed that Winston, already grieving the recent death of his mother, Jennie, when their daughter succumbed, must have some distance to gain his equilibrium, to ward off the "black dog" of depression that stalked him at other trying times.

Nevertheless, Clementine keenly felt the burden of running their household without much help from her husband. His priority, as always, remained his public life. Frequently, Winston enlisted Clementine in his political causes, which she obliged as if their prime duty together. Gradually, her response was to pull away from her remaining children, who were tended by household help or essentially not at all. "As children, we soon became aware that our parents' main interest and time were consumed by immensely important tasks, besides which our own demands and concerns were trivial," recalled Churchill's daughter Mary. "We never expected either of our parents to attend our school plays, prize-givings or sports' days. We knew they were both more urgently occupied, and any feelings of self-pity were overborne by a sense of gratification that their presence was so much required elsewhere. When our mother did manage to grace any of these (to children) important occasions, we were ecstatically grateful. Her elegance and beauty were a source of great pride to us, as her high standards in all things were a cause of anxiety, lest we should fall short of her expectations."

In the eyes of some Churchill aides, Clementine's demands could be overbearing. "Mrs. C. considers it one of her missions in life to put people in their place and prides herself on being outspoken," Winston's personal secretary, Jock Colville, later complained in his diary. Mary's assessment of her mother, probably the most gentle of that of her four siblings, implicitly factored in her father's lack of emotional support at home. Clementine "had no real understanding of the childish mind or outlook, and applied her own perfectionist standards not only to manners and morals, but to picnics or garden clothes," Mary wrote. Winston rarely spoke up, even as his children seemed to need him as a father more than an occasional pal, visiting parliamentary minister, or literary philosopher. "Modern young people will do what they like," he rationalized. "The only time parents really control their children is before they are born. After that their nature unfolds remorselessly, petal by petal."

Throughout the 1930s, the public man calling for order and the rule of law to an endangered world was, in private, remarkably mute to the violent reproaches of his son, Randolph, or the disorder in his two eldest daughters' lives. "Winston never backed Clementine up," said cousin Diana Mitford about the frustrating Churchill household. "It would have been better if he had bashed Randolph, but he always let him rip."

Even mild-mannered Mary longed for her father to exert his authority and not let his wife face the storms of family life alone. "This lively boy manifestly needed a father's hand; but the main task of controlling him fell almost entirely upon Clementine, and so right from the early days Randolph and she were at loggerheads," she lamented.

For all his misbehavior, Randolph still sought ways to please his father, to gain his approval as a son, if a prodigal one. By 1938 he offered valued advice to Winston (such as encouraging his father to speak in a more casual and contemporary style), which his father didn't heed. In turn, Randolph received little counsel from his father. Winston's aides viewed Randolph as a tool of his father's agenda, with little regard for the impact of this on his own once-propitious career. Two of Winston's top advisers, Brendan Bracken and Lord Beaverbrook, encouraged Randolph to publicly attack the "Municheers," the appeasers who lauded Chamberlain's fateful pact with Germany, even if young Churchill endured "an occasional blast" of criticism himself. Often with abandon, Randolph would fight his father's battles as very much his own. At an elegant dinner party, when a Chamberlain supporter suggested they all forget about the Nazis and worry about getting richer, Randolph bolted out the door, outraged. "You're all a lot of quislings," he spewed. "You'd all be happy if you could make a deal with Hitler!"

By comparison, Winston's relationship with Randolph was far more complex and ambivalent than Ambassador Kennedy's unabashed admiration for his eldest son, Joe Jr. Though only a few years apart, Randolph showed far more gifts than young Kennedy—bursting with knowledge of the world, a swashbuckler in the public arena, a successful writer and speaker on both continents. Randolph's early political defeats could still be viewed as part of a talented prodigy's gradual coming of age. On his own, he showed grit and individual nerve, more than the stolid steadiness of Joe Jr. waiting for his daddy's approval to run someday. Unlike the Kennedy boys, Randolph already knew the unbearable weight of public expectations as the son of a publicly recognized great man.

Whether as a writer or a politician, he found his achievements measured in the shadow of those of his father. Even Randolph's first book was not his own. He edited a collection of Winston's speeches, published in 1938 under the title *Arms and the Covenant*. (The American version offered a catchier name, *While England Slept*, which particularly caught the attention of Jack Kennedy.)

For all his rising visibility as a possible presidential candidate, Ambassador Kennedy never treated his sons, neither Joe nor the less accomplished Jack, as consultants or comrades-in-arms. Their dreams and ambitions weren't tempered by their father's immediate political goals. In advising his own father, Randolph found himself in a far more competitive atmosphere. He jockeyed for Winston's ear and private counsel with top associates such as Brendan Bracken and Anthony Eden, and now with Diana's new husband, Duncan Sandys, touting his own considerable political ambitions. For the Kennedy sons, the generational lines were cleaner, less blurred—even if the ambassador seemed, at that moment, to have a better chance than Winston of leading his nation someday. Joe Kennedy didn't yet turn to his sons for actionable advice, the policy and political decisions on which a whole career can turn. He didn't invite his sons to lunch with other foreign dignitaries to get their candid assessment, as Churchill had done when the new American ambassador first arrived. Kennedy let his boys into the tent of state as an educational device, as a summer training ground for a future time when they would be ready for public life. The difference between the families could be found also in their humor. The Churchills, with their pointed quips in public, revealed a certain tension between father and son. More fondly, Kennedy's two oldest sons, still both at Harvard in early 1938, could directly challenge their father, without any of Randolph's rancor. They could poke fun at his blusterous claims, albeit in private. In their colloquial American style, they expressed doubts when they read of their father's golfing exploits in England. DUBIOUS ABOUT THE HOLE IN ONE, cabled Joe Jr. and Jack from the States.

When Randolph tried to be funny or ironic, he ran the risk of being misunderstood, based on his record of rash and inappropriate statements. Increasingly, Winston grew tired and resentful of the *monstre sacré* he'd created in his own household. At a Chartwell dinner in February 1938, Randolph attempted to joke with war secretary Leslie Hore-Belisha about a gift Winston had given to him, implying it was a cheap attempt to ingratiate himself with the secretary. The implication infuriated his father, enough so that he remained silent for the rest of the dinner. Randolph had crossed an indelible line with Winston. The remark was "singularly unkind, offensive & untrue; & I am sure no son should have made it to his father," he later chided.

Despite Randolph's attempt to apologize, Winston suggested instead that they not see one another for a while. More letters crossed between them, only to dig up past grievances. Randolph reminded his father of how, with a remark meant to be humorous, he had once publicly belittled his only son. "When I was thirteen and fourteen years old you paid me the compliment of treating me as if I were a grown-up," Randolph wrote. "Now that I am nearly twenty-seven you treat me as a wayward and untrustworthy child." In reply, Winston said he considered the comment to Hore-Belisha neither "jocular" nor "ironic," terms Randolph had used to explain his admittedly "stupid" and "absurdly untrue" remark. "It was grossly rude, & as such wounded me deeply," Winston wrote back. "I do not see why at my age I sh[oul]d be subjected to such taunts from a son I have tried to do my best for."

Shortly after this calamitous dinner, Randolph went to Parliament, attempting to seek forgiveness in person. He spotted Bracken standing beside Winston. True or not, he resented how this professional rival for his father's attention seemed to gloat at his misfortune. Randolph never got near enough to his father, who acted cold. Winston left without a word between them.

Randolph's visit had been prompted by a conversation with Clementine Mitford, a first cousin of the Mitford sisters, to whom Randolph had confided what had happened with his father. She reproached him for his thoughtless comment. As they talked near a window, she suddenly realized Randolph was crying, staring out through the pane. "That was what was terrible" about the moment, Clementine Mitford later said, watching this grown man weep about his father and his own misdeeds. Another cousin, Anita Leslie, who detailed the incident in her biography of Randolph, underlined the lasting consequences of his remark. "What had really happened was that Winston had grown afraid of his son's political ventures and of what he regarded as Randolph's indiscretions as a journalist," she judged. The father and son soon spoke again, part of the regular transmission of family and political business as needed. But the wound between them never fully healed, remaining there to be reopened again and again. The most painful lesson from this episode was the one most glaringly apparent for Winston: he needed to disavow, or at least disengage himself from, his son's future in order to obtain what he wanted most in life.

After so much family unrest, Randolph's wedding plans with Pamela Digby in 1939 appeared a hopeful sign of maturity, that a wife's influence might shape and lend direction to his life. Unfortunately, Pamela didn't seem to have much judgment herself. "One of the reasons I fell for him originally was [that] he was a very overpowering person," she recalled, an "extremely attractive" trait that endeared Randolph to her. "He always knew—he *seemed* to know—what was going to happen. He was a very bright guy and he could twist anything around to his advantage."

With the world on a path toward war, Pamela figured she could depend on this bold young man with the celebrated surname, Churchill. Still ruggedly handsome in a boozy way, Randolph had recently signed up for the Fourth Queen's Own Hussars, his father's fabled military unit, expecting he'd be on the front lines of battle sometime soon. In an oddly romantic fashion, he convinced Pamela to marry him so that he might carry on the Churchill legacy regardless if he got shot in battle afterward. As she recalled, Randolph said "he would probably be killed & desired to leave a son for posterity." It was a convincing offer that seemed to guarantee widowhood. She said yes, for no dearth of bad reasons, and then wavered for a time about the wisdom of her decision. "I was getting so upset by seeing all my friends going off, as they dramatically thought, to be killed, and I thought how marvelous it was to be going out with somebody about whom I didn't give a damn," she later recalled.

Charmed, befuddled, and a bit bored with her own life, Pamela agreed to become Randolph's wife as quickly as possible. The initial howls of protest from friends and her parents, Lord and Lady Digby, didn't deter her or give her second thoughts. Instead these awful tales and stern warnings about Randolph's randy exploits "rather egged me on," she admitted.

At Chartwell, Clementine expressed her objections to Randolph's plans, despite the hasty origins of her own marriage to Winston. Pamela wasn't the only young woman to whom Randolph had proposed the half-baked idea of getting married. His wartime intimations of mortality, fueled by a pint or two, spurred these offers of marital bliss. His would-be fiancées all sensibly declined his offer except Pamela.

Only Winston seemed to think their wedding was a glorious idea. He pooh-poohed those who suggested the young couple wasn't adequately prepared. "What you need is a double bed, champagne and cigars," he retorted merrily, inventing a memorable phrase even for an occasion such as this. But he did have one reservation, which he posed to Pamela in private the first time they met at Chartwell. She remembered seeing Winston come out of his studio, a short distance from the main house, and walk up the grassy hill toward Randolph and his intended bride.

"Your family, the Digby family, were Catholic but I imagine you are not still a Catholic?" he said, looking at her very severely. "Are you Catholic?"

"No, I'm not," Pamela replied.

The agnostic in Winston, unaffiliated with any church or particular deity, surely didn't mind. But the historian in Winston seemed vaguely to remember that the Digbys were Romanists. As a royal monarchist looking for a rightful heir, this possible variance from the Church of England was something he needed to know. He didn't want to see religion become an issue. Jack Churchill, Winston's stockbroker brother, had married a Catholic, and their children were being reared in the Church of Rome. Winston's inquiry about her religion seemed to carry a slight distasteful implication: that he was part of "the majority of that type of English person who is anti-Catholic," she later explained.

Pamela assured Winston that he needn't worry. She had been baptized at infancy in the Church of England. While their papist affiliation was true centuries before, the Digbys had been Protestants in good standing for years among the peerage, and faithful Conservative Party members, too.

"Yes, you had your heads chopped off in the Gunpowder Plot," Winston now recalled.

"That is right—Sir Everard Digby," Pamela replied. (Actually, Sir Everard, converted to Catholicism by a Jesuit, was hung, drawn, and quartered at the Tower of London for his involvement in the 1605 attempt to blow up the House of Lords and kill King James I.)

Winston appeared relieved. "That being out of the way—that I was not a Catholic—he became very much on our side," Pamela recalled. "But the rest—Clemmie and my family—were very practical and didn't think it was a good idea."

Love in haste prevailed. The Churchills presented Randolph's proposal as grandly as possible. "Since the age of 19, Randolph Churchill has had a varied and sometimes spectacular career in politics and newspaper work," the *New York Times* reported about the nuptials. On the way to the altar, it was learned the Digby home at Minterne, Dorset, had once belonged to Gen. Charles Churchill, a brother of the great Duke of Marlborough. Wedding chroniclers noted that the two families shared this fateful association with Winston's hero, the subject of his massive biography, as if they were joined by fate rather than mere coincidence.

On October 4, newsmen and a large crowd assembled outside St. John's Church, craning their necks for the real star of the show, Winston Churchill, who showed up in a black felt hat rather than his naval cap. Many friends and relatives cheered on the newlyweds, including the toast-making lord Freddie Birkenhead and Vic Oliver, the comedian son-in-law. Randolph appeared gallant in his Hussars uniform, while the voluptuous Pamela, no longer frumpy, wore a blue dress and a convincing smile. As they left the church, the couple marched under the raised swords of Randolph's fellow Fourth Hussars, a splendid exit for a man presumably off to war.

The day's majesty and exchange of eternal vows didn't sweep away all doubts, however. After their wedding, Randolph confessed to Pamela that he had nearly married another woman because of the confusion surrounding their three-week courtship. When Pamela seemed to waver in her acceptance, Randolph had decided to keep searching for a bride to sire his heir. On September 19, he finally found another woman agreeable to marriage and "would have done so but for the refusal of the Archbishop of Canterbury to grant a special license for that day." Looking for an advocate to convince the Anglican head of the Church of England, Randolph enlisted the most unlikely of arm twisters: Joseph P. Kennedy, the Irish Catholic from Boston. Although Randolph was increasingly critical of Kennedy's appeasement position, documents show that young Churchill did privately approach the American ambassador for this extraordinary favor—most likely to Joe's Machiavellian delight. As with Jimmy Roosevelt, Joe had tried to cultivate a friendship with Randolph, as a subtle way of influencing sons and compromising their fathers. "In middle age he began to take on younger proteges," his granddaughter Amanda Smith later described in her own fashion. "Often these were the children of extraordinary famous and very busy parents." Contrary to most historical accounts, Pamela said, Randolph "rather liked" Joe Kennedy originally. Randolph attended many social events with the Kennedys and undoubtedly knew of Joe's friendship with Baruch and Beaverbrook, both wealthy fixers close to his own father. More so, Randolph's job as a political writer made the headline-grabbing ambassador fascinating, even if Randolph was gradually repulsed by his views. "In fact, at one moment, Randolph saw quite a lot of Kennedy," Pamela later explained. "I guess he didn't really *like* him, but he was a good source. He was working for a newspaper."

To his wife, Rose Kennedy, the ambassador explained that twenty-eight-year-old Randolph had sought advice about marrying an actress and that he'd been turned down—only to wed Pamela Digby instead a week later. "Nuts! I call it," Joe concluded in a September 26, 1939, letter home, sparing his Catholic wife any details about the Archbishop of Canterbury. The decision to seek Joe's help underscores Randolph's personal desperation as well as his ill-informed judgment. Joe didn't consider himself particularly friendly with the archbishop. Rather, Joe was a friend of the new king, George VI, who had confided that the archbishop and Winston Churchill had cruelly drawn attention to "the defect in his speech" during the abdication crisis, according to Joe's diary. Over brandy one night, the king told Joe he felt vindicated after finishing a successful speech at Guildhall in front of them. "I made that speech straight at Churchill," the king told him. (This version differs substantially from the relationship portrayed in the 2010 movie *The King's Speech*, in which Churchill encourages the stuttering king.) Thus, with no particular patron on his behalf, Joe could not likely have convinced the archbishop to change his mind about a special allowance for Randolph. Years later, Pamela said, she eventually learned about Randolph's frantic request to Kennedy. "My husband has asked him, the American Ambassador, to use his utmost endeavours with the Archbishop of Canterbury to obtain such a special license," she recounted in annulment records.

Before her own vows, Pamela also harbored doubts about this marriage. She had hedged her bets on success with Randolph in a way that appalled more than one friend and family intimate. Her father's good friend Lord Margesson, the Conservative Party's chief whip, a man known for getting his way in Parliament, "took me for a long walk in the country & did his utmost to dissuade me," she recalled. Another girlfriend, who'd known Randolph her whole life, tried to persuade Pam beforehand to reconsider. "He has tried to marry every girl in London for the last two years," she implored.

No longer a debutante, Pamela gave the most practical of replies. Her answer would set the stage for the Churchills' family life for the next several years. "Well, if he [Randolph] is not killed & we do not get on well together," she declared, "I shall obtain a divorce."

15

Breach of Faith

The prospect of war in 1939—a "gathering storm," as Winston later called it—loomed over the Kennedys, the Churchills, and everyone else who lived in Great Britain. Looking back on the previous year, Rose Kennedy savored the peaceful memories of her family's triumphant introduction to London, filled with castle dinners, royal encounters, and joyous celebrations. In a January 1939 note, she personally thanked President Roosevelt for "all the interesting and stimulating experiences . . . made possible through the honor which you had conferred upon Joe."

The ambassador, conversely, showed his appreciation in an odd way. Since his arrival in Great Britain, his crude double-dealing and reckless efforts to create his very own foreign policy convinced the president and his administration that the choice of Kennedy had been an awful mistake. Getting rid of Joe Kennedy, though, would be more complicated and protracted than anyone ever imagined.

On his first visit home to America in June 1938, expecting to be hailed as a hero, Joe immediately encountered trouble. As he debarked from the *Queen Mary,* he denied speculation he might run as a political successor to Roosevelt in 1940—when the president would finish his second and presumably last term. To reporters waiting at New York Harbor, Joe refuted the very rumors he'd created behind the scenes. "If I had my eye on another job, it would be a complete breach of faith with President Roosevelt," he insisted.

During his nine-day return, Kennedy faced one bitter disappointment after another. At Harvard, he hoped to receive an honorary degree at the same commencement ceremony where Joe Jr. would be graduating cum laude. Instead, his private lobbying for this honorary degree backfired, leaving him with "considerable personal embarrassment." Once again, he felt snubbed by the Brahmins at Harvard, just as he had as an undergraduate hoping to earn his way into their exclusive clubs. "It was a terrible blow to him," Rose recalled. "Suddenly he felt as if he were once again standing in front of the Porcellian Club, knowing he'd never be admitted." Joe claimed to reporters that he'd turned down the honor. "Can you imagine Joe Kennedy declining an honorary degree from Harvard?" FDR said incredulously to his secretary of the interior, Harold Ickes. Mortified, Joe couldn't bring himself to attend his oldest son's graduation. He claimed that he needed to see to a medical crisis involving his other son, John F. Kennedy, ill at their Cape Cod home.

Meanwhile, Kennedy learned that the president's press secretary, Stephen Early, had planted a disparaging article about him in the *Chicago Tribune*, emphasizing "the chilling shadow of 1940" between the president and his ambitious ambassador. The article quoted an unnamed Roosevelt aide who criticized the London publicity surrounding Joe's family as part of his political sales plan. "He'd put them in an orphanage one by one to get himself into the White House," said this New Dealer to the right-wing *Tribune*. Before leaving for England, Joe went again to Washington to find out where he stood with Roosevelt. "It was a true Irish anger that swept me," Kennedy wrote in his diary. He bitterly confronted Early and demanded to see the president. In his paternal fashion, Roosevelt "assuaged my feelings and I left again for

London," Kennedy recalled, "but deep within me I knew that something had happened."

Whatever their differences, Joe admired Roosevelt for his steely will and sunny optimism, which seemed quintessentially American. Miles away in London, he once described FDR's "gallantry" to the wife of Edward F. L. Wood, best known as Lord Halifax, Britain's foreign secretary. "The man is almost paralyzed yet he ignores it and this forces others to overlook it," Joe explained. "He dominates a room. I have seen him, when he is determined to win an argument, rise to his full height and, bearing his weight solely upon his arms braced against the desk, make the point to bring him victory. This always brings a lump to my throat, although I consider myself pretty hard-boiled."

Despite nagging reservations about his ambassador, Roosevelt sent Joe back to England. During their private chats together, Joe had disparaged British defenses against the Nazis and argued the need for America to stay clear of any European conflict. He even suggested FDR not criticize the Fascists in Italy. Yet for reasons not readily apparent, Roosevelt didn't heed the advice of his more liberal aides to rid himself of Kennedy. Politically, the president realized he might need Joe's support if he indeed sought a third term in 1940. Kennedy, touted as the most prominent Catholic layman in the country, might even suit his need for a vice-presidential candidate to consolidate the Democratic Party. But the far more compelling reason to keep him was personal.

For years, the president accommodated Kennedy because of his close friendship with Roosevelt's oldest son, James. By 1937, Jimmy's importance to the president had become even more apparent. Jimmy resigned from his insurance company in Boston (though keeping part ownership) and joined the Roosevelt administration, appointed as "secretary to the president," with a great deal of oversight of federal agencies and political decisions. For all of Jimmy's character flaws and lack of judgment, his father loved him very much. The president relied on his son's presence to bolster his spirits in a family where he and his wife, Eleanor, were often apart. Dutifully at New York Harbor, Jimmy had boarded the approaching ship to warn Joe Kennedy of the swarm of reporters waiting to ask about his 1940 presidential ambitions, providing enough time so that Joe's replies were tailored to mend fences with Roosevelt's father. Before returning to Great Britain, Joe faced questions about his past business dealings with Jimmy, including the 1933 British liquor contracts. *The Saturday Evening Post,* a widely read magazine, published an exposé alleging that Jimmy had helped Kennedy land his ambassadorship because of past favors that made the president's son rich. It detailed how Jimmy's firm profited by underwriting the insurance on the ships carrying the Haig & Haig bottles across the Atlantic, allowing Kennedy to become "the premier Scotch whisky salesman in America." Jimmy protested that he had had no part in the liquor deal or in Joe's appointment to London. "Being the President's son, they'd have been calling me a crook no matter what business I'd enter," he complained. On the departing *Normandie* liner, accompanied by his two sons Joe and Jack, Kennedy grabbed a copy of the article and flashed his gleaming smile to the press. "Kennedy needs help from no one," he said brashly. Once again, the ambassador denied what he knew to be true. He called the story a "complete unadulterated lie," and slipped out of a tight situation with an exiting quip: "I admit I am the ambassador but I deny that I am the premier Scotch whiskey salesman in this country," Kennedy said, then added with a pause, "I do like, however, to be the best in everything I do."

Taking advantage of the relationship between fathers and sons, Kennedy's corrosive influence over Jimmy became a wild card for Franklin Roosevelt, a potentially explosive arrangement not easily dismantled or defused. Joe's actions underlined the demonstrably poor judgment of the president's son. Aides to FDR worried Jimmy might hurt his father's presidency because of his greediness.

Franklin Roosevelt seemed well aware of the character flaws in his son that invited corruption and favor seekers. When Jimmy tried to influence William O. Douglas, then chairman of the SEC, on behalf of a client being investigated by the agency, an alarmed Douglas visited the White House and threatened to resign. After Douglas explained what had happened with Jimmy, he recalled that the president "cradled his head on his arm and cried like a child for several minutes" and then told Douglas to ignore his son. When Jimmy pushed his father to declare a national Life Insurance Day, in another example, press spokesman Stephen Early gently reprimanded his boss's son. "Washington gossips, among whom are several newspapermen, letter writers and readers in general have been connecting your name, referring to your relationships and to your business, in a way that makes some of your friends money," wrote Early, without mentioning Kennedy by name. "Untruthful and exaggerated reports are easy to circulate and once circulated are difficult to correct. Some people are always ready to believe the worst about any one, facts and evidence to the contrary notwithstanding. I would not be a true friend of yours if I did not tell you these things. I want you to know that I do it for this reason only."

But Jimmy preferred his own friends, not his father's protectors. He admired self-confident, outspoken men like Joe Kennedy who treated him like a peer rather than an appendage. Helping to arrange for Kennedy to go to London was a gift through which Jimmy could show his appreciation, and prove he was a political player just like his dad. Joe flattered him and treated him like part of the Kennedy clan. "Well here is your old pal, spending the weekend with the King and Queen and Mr. and Mrs. Neville Chamberlain," Joe enthused from London early in his stay. "I wish you had been there at the dinner last night." Despite ample warnings from others, Jimmy kept helping Joe and the friends he vouched for—such as Joseph Schenck, a shadowy former business associate in Hollywood. In July 1939 the president became a "good deal upset" about his son's visit to the treasury secretary in an attempt to intervene in a criminal investigation of Schenck that eventually wound up in a conviction.

Within President Roosevelt's family and inner circle, Jimmy wasn't the only one feeling beholden to Joe Kennedy. He helped FDR's son-in-law John Boettiger land a top editorial job at a Hearst newspaper in Seattle, where the president's daughter, Anna, also worked in the Women's Features section. Boettiger sent Joe notes about Haig & Haig whiskey ads appearing in the rival paper. Privately, in notes between them, Boettiger called Joe "the great war-buster" and expressed relief about Chamberlain's agreement at Munich. "Now that the immediate threat is over, some people are wondering whether Hitler was bluffing," Boettiger wrote, hardly expressing the official Roosevelt administration view. Always looking for favor, Kennedy spoke to the president's son-in-law in the same chummy way he did with Jimmy, complaining about press rumors of a troubled relationship with FDR. "I am *persona non grata* to the entire Roosevelt family," Kennedy wrote. "Well, of course I know a lot of this is hooey, but it is damned annoying three thousand miles away."

With two of the closest women in Franklin's life, Joe also ingratiated himself. The president's wife, Eleanor, wrote Kennedy to thank him for "all you have done for my children. You have been so kind and interested and such a real friend and I have come to believe in your judgment and integrity. I hope that you might be willing to count me as a friend also." Despite this endorsement, Kennedy probably sensed the emotional distance between the First Lady and her husband. ("I realize more and more that FDR is a great man," Eleanor wrote to a friend in 1936, admitting Franklin "is nice to me but as a person I'm a stranger and I don't want to be anything else.") Kennedy established his own close ties with Missy LeHand, FDR's personal secretary and another intimate who helped run the White House. During the Depression,

Missy's brother was out of work, and Joe found him a job at Somerset Importers, earning her gratitude forever. "My brother is just a different human being—happy beyond words and working like the devil, and, confidentially, boring us all to death talking about Gordons, Haig and Haig etc.," Missy wrote to Joe. "This letter almost sounds maudlin, but just tear it up and remember that I appreciate it." Missy kept in contact with Joe, another set of eyes and ears for him in Washington.

The press scrutiny surrounding Jimmy Roosevelt's dealings with Kennedy didn't prevent the American ambassador in London from overseeing his liquor business back home. One British writer called Joe "our Ambassador to the Court of Haig & Haig." In September 1938, Joe sent a critical note to Ted O'Leary, his top official at Somerset Importers, calling the company's performance "disgraceful," and insisting that "I don't intend to see this lost to the family." Earlier, O'Leary had written to the boss inquiring about rumors that Kennedy planned to sell Somerset because "the fact that you were in the liquor business would be embarrassing and that you were contemplating the disposal of your interests." Kennedy's private interest in making money from Somerset remained undaunted, causing conflict with his official role. His embassy aide Harvey Klemmer raised some eyebrows among the British by arranging for shipping space for about two hundred thousand cases of whiskey destined for the United States. "It got so bad that a friend in the Ministry of Shipping came to see me and said, 'You'd better go easy because one of his competitors is threatening to raise a question in Parliament about the improper activities of the American embassy,'" recalled Klemmer. "So we pulled our horns in a little after that."

Eventually critics claimed Kennedy cared more about preserving his own fortune than about the fate of Europe. Russian ambassador Ivan Maisky complained of "Capitalist Kennedy seeking personal concessions on imports of Haig and Haig whiskey and Gordon's gin, for which he holds exclusive distribution rights in the United States, in exchange for his help in obtaining American supplies, a crude form of blackmail." Even the FBI, despite Joe's friendship with chieftain J. Edgar Hoover, created a file on his liquor business activities, with a note containing a confidential source's tip that Kennedy "made a very profitable deal through the influence of XXXX," a name still blacked out today in the agency records.

As Joe Kennedy boarded the *Normandie* with his two sons in June 1938, hounded by reporters about his liquor dealings with the president's son, another passenger, Bernard Baruch, stepped onto the ship without much notice. By the time of this trip back to England, the once-close relationship between Baruch and Kennedy had changed. More subterfuge existed between them than Kennedy apparently realized. Joe knew Baruch enjoyed an annual vacation trip to Europe, usually seeing Winston Churchill during his travels. But on this visit, Roosevelt charged Baruch with a secret mission that seemed to undermine Kennedy. In essence, the president asked Baruch to verify his ambassador's questionable estimates of German military strength and whether Britain had enough firepower to withstand a Nazi attack. Kennedy told the president that Britain's defenses were inadequate and strongly advised the United States not to engage Germany in a European fight. But Roosevelt didn't trust Joe's judgment, which relied too heavily on Chamberlain's policy of appeasement. In going around Kennedy, Baruch came to a very different conclusion about America's future, siding with Churchill. "Bernard Baruch is planning to sail to England with a group of colleagues who are in complete disagreement with the policies of Prime Minister Chamberlain," the *New York Post*, then a liberal newspaper, reported as the ship departed. "Their backing will be offered to Winston Churchill."

After meeting at Chartwell, Baruch came away convinced that

America must prepare for conflict against Hitler. "War is coming very soon," Churchill told him. "We will be in it and you will be in it." Ruefully, Churchill didn't expect to be at center stage in protecting his country. "You will be running the show over there," Winston explained to his old American friend, "but I will be on the sidelines over here." Baruch agreed with Churchill on the need for immediate rearmament, just as the two worked together on munitions during World War I. Baruch already knew he differed sharply with Kennedy on this matter. A few months earlier, Joe told him, "As much as I dislike saying it, Germany is really entitled to what she is asking for" in seeking reunification with lands lost during World War I, and that the root of the current crisis was economic rather than military. For Baruch as a Jew, the Nazi crisis became personal when he realized he couldn't secure the evacuation of his relatives from Germany. The Nazis had already linked Baruch to Churchill. In a report home, the German ambassador said Churchill's "friendship with the American Jewish millionaire Baruch leads him to expend all his remaining force and authority in directing England's actions against Germany." Convinced fighting would soon start, Baruch offered to let Churchill's pregnant daughter, Diana, and other family live in the United States for safety reasons. Winston wouldn't think of it. Instead he urged Baruch to push Roosevelt to end his neutrality. "Many thanks, but Diana is air-raid warden in London," Churchill wrote his friend. "Now is the time for your man to speak."

As Joe realized what happened behind his back, he began criticizing Baruch to Roosevelt. He blamed Baruch as a key source for newspaper columns portraying Kennedy as Chamberlain's lackey and as a constant critic of the president with his London friends. At a February 1939 White House meeting, Roosevelt recounted to Joe how Baruch complained to him that the ambassador's staff had ignored Baruch's request to stop by before leaving London. FDR loved to play one against the other and seemed amused at Kennedy's reply.

"I said there wasn't a word of truth in the whole story," Joe recounted in his diary. "He was just too damn jealous. The President said he knew that and he had got a great laugh out of the whole story."

After spending a few winter weeks in the warmth of his Palm Beach home, Kennedy was prepared to quit as ambassador. The speculator in him usually knew when to get out of a situation, and it was clear the good times in England were over for him. He told Roosevelt he didn't want to stay in London if he didn't have the president's confidence. Roosevelt assured him of his support. "He knew the way I felt about him and I wasn't the kind to be any good unless I was on good terms," Kennedy wrote in his diary. "He said that he knew all that and not to worry—people just liked to make trouble."

A few months later, Kennedy's complaints against Baruch spread to Herbert Bayard Swope, his former friend and New York business associate. Like Baruch, Swope staunchly supported Churchill's stance against the Nazi threat and objected to Kennedy's advocacy of appeasement with Roosevelt. Swope, snubbed on the Somerset deal, later claimed he was offended that Joe had kept running the liquor firm while ambassador. "He did not believe that it was ethical that a man whose fortune was largely based upon trade with a country (importing large quantities of whisky) should represent his own country there," wrote Swope's biographer, Alfred Allan Lewis. Joe strongly denied rumors from America that he was still speculating on stock as an ambassador, and blamed Baruch and friends for stirring up trouble. When Roosevelt telephoned London, he started with an odd reference.

"Hello, Joe," the president said, "I have a few things to discuss and it won't make any difference even if the Germans listen in." They chatted quickly about some matters. Then Joe decided to settle a score with his onetime friend, Baruch, and threw in Churchill's name as well.

"Baruch is trying to get an appointment of some kind that has to do with Britain's purchases in USA and is being helped by Churchill," Kennedy said. "I want to know if you know about it and whether it is anything you are interested in."

Roosevelt clearly wasn't. The president alluded to needing Baruch's help with the upcoming Senate vote on the 1939 Neutrality Bill, which would eliminate a previous congressional arms embargo to nations at war such as England. Kennedy acceded but soon followed up with a cable that emphasized how much he disagreed with men such as Churchill and Baruch. "Of course, the real fact is that England is fighting for her possessions and place in the sun, just as she has in the past," Kennedy wrote to the president. "I personally am convinced that, win, lose or draw, England never will be the England that she was and no one can help her to be . . . There are signs of decay, if not decadence, here, both in men and institutions." In his cynical, flinty-eyed way, Kennedy said he didn't view the impending European conflict "as a holy war. Democracy as we now conceive it in the United States will not exist in France and England after the war, regardless which side wins or loses."

To his father-in-law, Honey Fitz, Kennedy's assessment was more candidly from the heart, placing the oncoming conflict in the only way he truly understood—as a threat to his family and his dreams. He feared losing his sons in a conflagration that he felt wasn't America's business. In a devil's bargain, Joe admitted, "I hate to think how much money I would give up rather than sacrifice Joe and Jack in a war."

Rather than keep his mouth shut, as he swore to friends and Roosevelt he would do, Kennedy continued a stream of comments in London that both hurt his reputation and revealed his personal bigotries. Since an October 1938 Trafalgar Day dinner for Britain's Navy League, Joe had supported Chamberlain's Munich peace agreement as the best way to avoid conflict. "The democratic and dictator countries differ ideologically, to be sure, but that should not preclude the possibility of good relations between them," he declared. "After all, we have to live together in the same world, whether we like it or not." His freelance remarks—expressing "a pet theory of my own," as he called it—contradicted FDR's efforts to quarantine dictators such as Hitler and caused a firestorm of criticism in America. Privately to German foreign officials, Kennedy stressed his "understanding and sympathy," further undermining the president's position. "As in former conversations, Kennedy mentioned that very strong anti-Semitic tendencies existed in the United States, and that a large proportion of the population had an understanding of the German attitude toward the Jews," Herbert von Dirksen, the German ambassador in London, reported back to Nazi leaders in Berlin. He added that "from his [Kennedy's] whole personality I believe he would get on well with the Fuhrer." Kennedy's personal anti-Semitic comments didn't prevent him from publicly trying to find havens for German-Jewish refugees in places such as South America. But when criticized about appeasement, Joe reverted to anti-Semitic slurs, as did his sons. Having returned to Harvard that fall, Jack wrote to his father to express his support for the Trafalgar Day speech as a reflection of support for Chamberlain's policy. "While it seemed to be unpopular with the Jews, etc., was considered to be very good by everyone who wasn't bitterly anti-fascist," wrote young Kennedy, blaming the intense media criticism on "internationalists" and Jewish publishers and journalists.

Perhaps his biggest critic, though, was Winston Churchill, undoubtedly disappointed at how the once-amiable relationship with the Kennedys had been soured by the ambassador's defeatism—a virtual death wish for the future of Great Britain and everything Winston held dear. Through the intervention of mutual friends such as Baruch and Kay Halle, Winston had made a special effort to cultivate a friendly alliance with the American ambassador. Kennedy had visited his Chartwell manor as an honored guest, and members of their family traveled in the same circle of friends and acquaintances. Churchill's son, enlisted as a social envoy to the ambassador's family, remembered the sense of bitterness at how things had turned out. "Word was passed around (before his arrival) to be nice, consequently the establishment went to work," Randolph later explained. "He was invited to house parties, dinners, golf, and shooting by dukes and earls. However, war came, and it soon became apparent that Kennedy thought England was dilapidated and done for; he indicated a private personal preference for the Germans. This became quietly known and the government told the establishment it was no longer necessary to be nice. Suddenly Kennedy found himself isolated and alone."

Kennedy's acid betrayal, however, spurred a dramatic political turning point for Winston. At a June 1939 dinner honoring Churchill, American newspaper columnist Walter Lippmann asked him about Kennedy's prediction that England would "be licked" in a war with Germany. Hoisting a drink in one hand and a cigar in another, Churchill defiantly explained how Great Britain would prevail, even if France fell to Hitler and England itself were invaded. His words carried an unforgettable fury.

"Yet supposing—as I do not for one moment support—that Mr. Kennedy were correct in his tragic utterance, then I for one would willingly lay down my life in combat rather than, in fear of defeat, surrender to the menaces of these most sinister men," Churchill warned. "It will then be for you, for the Americans, to preserve and to maintain the great heritage of the English-speaking peoples. It will be for you to think imperially, which means to think always of something higher and more vast than one's own national interests."

Churchill's splendid, memorable rhetoric expressed the growing feeling among his countrymen that Hitler's threat could no longer be ignored. In the months to come, Churchill would remain cordial to the ambassador and, at times, still displayed touches of personal warmth toward members of the Kennedy family. But the ambassador had unwittingly lit a fuse rallying public support for Churchill, slowly ending his "wilderness years" of political disrepute. The British people, who had applauded Chamberlain's Munich Pact less than a year earlier, now began to realize that Churchill's deadly assessment of the Nazis was correct. The Third Reich on the march had seized Czechoslovakia, and Poland seemed next for invasion. If Hitler were not stopped, all would be lost in their beloved England.

In the depths of his defeatism, Kennedy had provided the contrast in bas-relief to Winston's soaring defiance, to his courageous refusal to let his nation succumb to evil. In this paradoxical sense, Joe Kennedy had performed his greatest favor to Churchill: provoking a furious response that awakened the world to just what was at stake.

16

The Cross and Double-Cross

*"The 'cousinhood' of intelligence gathering and espionage
forms one of the most absorbing subtexts of the 'special
relationship.' It embodies the shared blood and toil of
wartime camaraderie, the mutual exchange of secrets
(sequestered from all non-Anglo-American eyes), the
bonding that results from confronting common enemies,
stretching from the Great War to the Cold War."*

—CHRISTOPHER HITCHENS

Ever since the Boer War, when he performed a bit of reconnaissance
work posing as a civilian riding a bicycle, Winston Churchill believed
resolutely in the power of spies and secret intelligence to decide great
battles and to move the seismic tides of history. "Our intelligence service has won and deserved world-wide fame," he observed after the
Great War in *The World Crisis.* "More than perhaps any Power, we
were successful in the war in penetrating the intentions of the enemy."

As much as any politician of his generation, Churchill relied on
British intelligence reports, from tracking the Dervish in the Sudan
to exposing terror plots by the Irish Republican Army. He loved the
"Great Game," as he called it, the contest of ciphers, cryptology, and
schemes on the grandest scale. During his years out of power, Churchill
collected secret service information about German aircraft strength
and Hitler's intentions. He sifted through dozens of carefully prepared
reports by code breakers (gleaned from intercepted cables and radio

messages) and made sense of them all. He used this information in the House of Commons to criticize existing policy and argue for bolstering military defense. He called his British code breakers "the geese who laid the golden eggs and never cackled." Churchill reveled in these spy stories. "In the higher ranges of Secret Service work, the actual facts in many cases were in every respect equal to the most fantastic inventions of romance or melodrama," he recounted. "Tangle within tangle, plot and counterplot, ruse and treachery, cross and double-cross, true agent, the bomb, the dagger and the firing party were interwoven in many a texture so intricate as to be incredible and yet true."

By 1939, however, the world's busiest and most complex spy center wasn't found in London, but rather in Vatican City, the 110-acre, postage-stamp-size home to the Roman Catholic Church, buzzing with rumors of impending war. Hugh Wilson, the departing U.S. ambassador in Berlin, called the Vatican "the best information service in Europe." Vernon Kell, the chief of MI5, the British military intelligence agency, believed the Church in Rome had the most developed network, dating back centuries and motivated as much by religious belief as by bribes and other tools of spycraft. Kell refused to hire Catholics as British agents lest his own spy agency be infiltrated.

The Vatican had listening posts in virtually every nation, with its mix of concordats and papal nuncios keeping the Church's intelligence arm well informed. Hitler and the Nazis tried to place their own spies within the Church's midst. For years, the American government seemed ignorant of the Vatican's preeminence in espionage. But as war approached, Joe Kennedy pushed the Roosevelt administration to catch up. "Experiences in London had taught me the value of being in touch with Rome with its vast sources of intelligence reaching almost every corner of the world," Kennedy recalled. "The information that the Vatican had with reference to conditions in Germany, in Austria and in Italy had peculiar value to us."

The Vatican connection proved an important political asset for the

Kennedys in years to come. Joe used his discreet, largely unknown ties to Rome to buttress his position as one of America's leading lay Catholics in public life, helped by his personal friendship with top clergy and his generous charitable donations as a wealthy man. His dream of seeing a Kennedy someday elected as the first Catholic president relied in part on the Church's implicit support and on millions of ethnic Americans who identified with this barrier-breaking goal. In the late 1930s, however, Kennedy's main effort with the Vatican focused on gaining secret intelligence for the U.S. government. To underline his unique contributions, the London ambassador once again entrusted his cause with the president's son Jimmy. In April 1938, Kennedy sent young Roosevelt "a strictly confidential memorandum which I have received personally from Cardinal Pacelli," then the Vatican's secretary of state (and future Pope Pius XII), and asked him to pass it along to the president. A State Department document later said Pacelli's memo outlined "the relations of the Vatican with various countries." How Joe Kennedy obtained the memo isn't clear, though Jimmy portrayed it as a small coup, a reminder of Joe's unique contacts.

Cardinal Eugenio Pacelli, a thin-faced, austere man with thick eyeglasses, had been the Church's chief diplomat since 1930, creating written treaties with several nations that allowed Catholics to practice their religion and run schools, hospitals, and church organizations without state interference. His 1933 concordat with Hitler's Germany raised some concerns about Pacelli's view toward the Nazis. Years earlier in Pacelli's career, Sir Samuel Hoare, then the British ambassador in Rome and a frequent source of intelligence to MI5, considered Pacelli "a convinced pro-German." Winston Churchill, a political adversary of Hoare's, had known Pacelli on a friendly basis since they first met in London in 1908 and likely held a more nuanced view of the Vatican diplomat. Both Churchill and Pacelli shared a similar dread about the Bolsheviks in Russia. They feared communism would lead to the spread of godless dictatorships as threatening as the Nazis. In his memo to Kennedy, Pacelli said the Church felt "at times powerless and isolated in its daily struggle against all sorts of political excesses from the Bolsheviks to the new pagans arising from the 'Aryan' generations."

Historically, many criticized Pacelli for a slowness or silence in confronting the Nazis, especially over their persecution of Jews both before and during World War II. But Pacelli's 1938 memo makes clear his opposition to the Nazis and the embattled position Catholics faced with Hitler, despite the protections agreed upon with the concordat. "No matter what pretexts are set forth by the German government, the real fact is that since the early time after the Concordat was signed a more or less open attitude against all clauses accepted in the Concordat was adopted by the German government," Pacelli wrote in the translated version from Italian sent to the White House. "The Holy See has used all possible ways to protect the freedom of the Church and of the Catholics, keeping itself ever ready to do the best in order to avoid any more bitter conflict, and being always prompted by the desire of avoiding to make the situation more and more difficult."

In his own note to Jimmy, Joe Kennedy pointed to portions of Pacelli's memo that underlined the Vatican's role as a beehive of intelligence and the strategic need for America to be more present in Rome. The future pope's note to Kennedy read, "It will be very fine if you will convey to your Friend at home these personal private views of mine," and he urged President Roosevelt to appoint a U.S. diplomat to the Vatican. Pacelli underlined that "in this very crucial moment of the European political life that the American Government is without a direct source of information from and a straight and intimate connection with the Vatican circles." As the world inched toward war, this memo bolstered Kennedy's argument for a better U.S. presence in Rome.

For nearly a century, the American government had refused to send a diplomat to the Vatican, an opposition largely fueled by the nineteenth-century Know-Nothing movement and lingering anti-Catholic bigotry. Kennedy tried to convince Roosevelt to send an American envoy to the papal state, both as a practical improvement to U.S. intelligence abroad and good politics at home among many Catholic Democrats. In the long run, Kennedy shared Pacelli's fear that the Communists might prove more dangerous than Hitler or Italy's Mussolini. While the Axis persecuted Church members, the Communists dismantled the Church entirely in Russia. "He thought the Communists would be the winners in Europe if there was war," recalled Kennedy's former London aide Page Huidekoper. "But Joe was never pro-Nazi—I'm sure of that."

As both Jimmy Roosevelt and his father probably realized, the Vatican go-between for Kennedy was Count Enrico Galeazzi, the top aide to Pacelli, who would become a powerful behind-the-scenes figure in Rome. An elegant man with a finely trimmed mustache and an astute sense of diplomacy, Galeazzi served as Pacelli's closest aide. The press often identified him as the Vatican's "architect," though more accurately he served as the Vatican's administrator. The future pope depended greatly on Galeazzi, whose half-brother became Pacelli's physician. Jimmy Roosevelt had a better understanding of Galeazzi's role than most Americans. He first met the count in 1933, on the same European trip where he also met Winston Churchill. (Shortly after his Chartwell visit, Jimmy traveled to Rome with his wife, Betsey, Rose Kennedy, and others in their entourage, while Joe remained in London to tie up loose ends with his British liquor deal.)

Kennedy's biggest secret triumph with Galeazzi occurred in 1936. In the waning days of FDR's reelection campaign, Kennedy, Galeazzi, and then–auxiliary bishop Francis J. Spellman of Boston arranged for Cardinal Pacelli's trip to America. After being politically berated on the radio by Father Charles Coughlin, the infamous demagogue priest, Roosevelt wanted to shore up his support among Catholic Democrats with this historic visit by the Vatican's top diplomat. No papal figure had ever visited the United States, because of public opposition to any alliance with Rome. In his splendid robes, Pacelli visited FDR's home along the Hudson River in Hyde Park, New York. Kennedy and

Spellman joined the president and the future pope, and the controversial idea of a U.S. envoy was discussed. For Kennedy, the trip became a personal triumph, especially when Cardinal Pacelli stopped for tea at Joe and Rose's home in Bronxville. The red cushion placed underneath the future pope that day would take on a special status in the Kennedy home for years afterward.

The 1936 visit sparked a lifelong friendship between Kennedy and Galeazzi, and catapulted Spellman eventually into becoming cardinal of the New York archdiocese, the top job in the American-Catholic hierarchy. Kick Kennedy made sure to see her father's Vatican friend when she visited Rome in 1936, and Jack did so in 1937. Galeazzi drove Kennedy's second-oldest son out to Castel Gandolfo, the papal summer residence, for a dinner with Cardinal Pacelli—a future president meeting a soon-to-be pontiff. "Started out in Galeazzi's car and went to the Pope's summer Palace," Jack wrote in his diary. "Had a private audience with Cardinal Pacelli first who asked after Mother and Dad. He is really a great man although his English is rather poor."

During his Roman holiday, Jack Kennedy visited St. Peter's Basilica—the "terribly impressive" spiritual home of the Church, with its Michelangelo-inspired domes, paintings, and marble sculpture— and was part of a papal audience before going to dinner at Galeazzi's home, where they discussed politics. "He gave me quite a talk about the virtue of fascism," Jack recounted in his diary, "and it really seemed to have its points—especially the corporative system which seems quite an interesting step forward."

Despite his growing differences with President Roosevelt, Joe Kennedy pushed to represent America at the March 1939 coronation ceremonies for Pacelli as the incoming pope Pius XII. "When the new Pope is elected and the ceremonies take place, I am going to try and find some reasons to be sent to Rome," he alerted Galeazzi, after the death of Pope Pius XI that February. In that same note, Kennedy hoped Pacelli would be selected as the new pontiff and he mentioned he'd talked with both President Roosevelt and Prime Minister Neville Chamberlain, who felt the same. After some lobbying by Jimmy, the president agreed to send Kennedy as a political favor. He knew how much the special ceremony would mean to Joe, Rose, and their Catholic family. Nearly all the Kennedys attended, including John F. Kennedy, with seven-year-old Edward M. Kennedy receiving his First Holy Communion from the new pope. Rose appeared so moved by her private chat with the pontiff that Joe thought she might faint. "I had a great time in Rome and I deeply appreciate the President's having sent me," Joe wrote to Jimmy, after returning to London. "It was really a wonderful experience and you will be interested to know that it probably has driven me back to the Church. It's too bad you didn't go; it might have driven you back too."

During his time in Rome, Kennedy gained a sense of the intrigue and outright spying that surrounded the Vatican. In a private tour of the Sistine Chapel, the beautiful art-filled place where the cardinals had met in private to choose Pacelli as the new pope, Galeazzi let Kennedy know "in great confidence" of some of the apparent spying that took place with the papal vote. According to Kennedy's diary, the Vatican administrator explained how he had made "a thorough search" for any hidden Dictaphone recording devices in the room where the conclave took place, and actually found "a very small" microphone connected to the overhead wires. Only Galeazzi and Pacelli knew of this concealed listening device, he wrote. Kennedy also learned Boston's cardinal William O'Connell—who had married Joe and Rose many years before—was the only American who hadn't voted for Pacelli on the first ballot. At their hotel, Kennedy received a visit from the cardinal's nephew Joe O'Connell, a Kennedy family friend who stood as godfather for their firstborn son, Joe Jr. The cardinal's nephew let him know that "Number One," as the cardinal was called in Boston, didn't like the idea of a U.S. envoy to Rome. ("The Hierarchy, I think, are afraid they will lose some influence," Joe noted in his diary.) The cardinal's nephew provided another piece of advice for the ambassador, which Joe wrote down: "Don't trust any one in Rome. No one was your friend."

Nevertheless, Kennedy trusted Galeazzi, perhaps the most secretive man at the Vatican, enough to continue sending him private letters and personal donations to pay for expenses as he saw fit. "Please remember that I am yours to command and that if there is anything you think I can do to be of any service, you have only to go to the [American] Embassy and either deliver to them a letter, which will come to me by pouch, or ask them to send me a wire," Kennedy told his Vatican friend. After "a couple of talks" with the new pope, Kennedy assured Sumner Welles, the U.S. undersecretary of state, that the Vatican was decidedly against the German regime. Joe said Pius XII displayed "a subconscious prejudice that has arisen from his belief that the tendency of Nazism and Fascism is pro-pagan and, as pro-pagan, they strike at the roots of religion."

Galeazzi continued to be an important source of intelligence for Kennedy. A year later, this Vatican friend would alert Kennedy to the surprising news that the Pope "had just been approached by the German Government with a request to receive [Foreign Minister Joachim von] Ribbentrop who wanted to talk about peace." The bold German move was designed to outfox American efforts to convince the Vatican to end its official position of neutrality and instead publicly condemn Nazi aggression. On his own, Kennedy dispatched his crony, Edward Moore, to Rome to meet secretively with Galeazzi and learn the contents of Ribbentrop's conversations with the Pope and also with Mussolini. "Moore proved to be a good spy," Rose Kennedy later recalled. Eventually Joe flew to Paris to debrief Moore, and later tried to explain the Vatican's quandary to American officials. "What can the Pope do?" Kennedy said. "He can not turn down any suggestion of peace and yet is suspicious because they [the Nazis] are always mealy mouthed just before they do something dirty." Indeed, Hitler was already making plans for his invasions.

. . .

Foreign intelligence played a significant role also in the Irish question, another matter of political and cultural consequence where Kennedy and Churchill differed greatly. One of their sharpest contrasts revolved around the Irish leader Éamon de Valera.

For decades, de Valera and Churchill had nurtured a bloody dislike for each other, ever since Eire's 1920s war for independence. Among the Irish, Churchill remained notorious for overseeing the Black and Tans' reprisals in combating the IRA's violence. No doubt with de Valera in mind, Churchill declared, "The Irish have a genius for conspiracy but not for government."

For his part, Kennedy took an instinctive liking to Ireland's combative Taoiseach, who was eager to cultivate the American ambassador as an ally. During the Pope's coronation, Joe and Rose Kennedy sat next to de Valera, a tall, defiant man born in New York but who had spent much of his life fighting British control of Eire. "Rose, De Valera and I talked all the time, principal subject England should permit Northern Ireland come in with the Southern," Joe scribbled in his diary, after conversing with de Valera in Rome. "He thought there would be many Irish against him in the USA."

From the beginning, President Roosevelt expressed hope that Kennedy, as an Irish American, might help broker a lasting peace between the Catholics living in an independent Ireland in the south run by de Valera, and Northern Ireland, controlled by a Protestant majority loyal to the British Crown. When he appointed Kennedy as the new U.S. ambassador to the Court of St. James's in early 1938, FDR indicated to British prime minister Neville Chamberlain "how happy I should be if a reconciliation could be brought about." Soon after Kennedy's arrival, Chamberlain agreed to a new treaty with de Valera's Irish Free State, a move that made Churchill furious. The deal allowed Ireland to regain control of three naval ports at Cobh (formerly Queenstown), Berehaven in West Cork, and Lough Swilly in Donegal. These were the same three ports that Churchill had helped keep in British control, as part of the 1922 Irish treaty that created the Free State. During the Great War, Churchill, then First Lord of the Admiralty, had felt they were vital to England's defense against German U-boats. In the event of a new conflict, he didn't want Great Britain's western flank exposed to foreign invasion by sea. Already appalled by Ireland's determined neutrality against the German threat, Churchill believed Chamberlain's give-away would recklessly endanger British warships and particularly submarines in the event of war. What was perceived as Kennedy's American meddling only added fuel to Churchill's fire. "I say that the ports may be denied to us in the hour of need and we may be hampered in the gravest manner in protecting the British population," warned Churchill, then still a political outsider in Parliament. "Who would wish to put his head in such a noose?"

Kennedy praised Chamberlain's action and soon accepted de Valera's invitation to visit Ireland in June 1938—"the land of my forefathers," as he called it—where he received an honorary degree from National University in Dublin. He also took a sentimental journey with his eldest son to County Wexford, to visit the homestead where his grandfather Patrick Kennedy lived before coming to Boston. "I must say I enjoyed my trip to Dublin probably more than anything I have done since I have been here," Joe later wrote. "They were all very kind to me and made me feel at home."

During a state dinner held at a Dublin castle, de Valera shared with the new American ambassador "his deep resentment against Churchill because of the bitter attack" leveled against the port treaty, a feeling expressed by other Irish leaders. Remembering his own slights felt in Boston, Kennedy identified with the Irish cause. When later asked why he didn't get along with certain Englishmen, Kennedy replied he "could not forgive those who had been responsible for sending the infamous Black and Tans into rebellious Ireland." A British Foreign

Office memo later underlined Kennedy's perceived loyalties, a remarkable view of the American ambassador in London given an imperiled England's need to secure more U.S. support. "To pacify the East Coast Irish Mr. Kennedy was given his present appointment," it read. "From Mr. Kennedy's point of view, he owes his position to the fact that he represents a Catholic, Irish, anti-English group. He must therefore continue to exhibit this attitude."

Giving any credence to de Valera undoubtedly annoyed Churchill. Winston privately called de Valera "that murderer and perjurer," likely responsible for the assassination of fellow Irish leader Michael Collins. He suspected de Valera might aid Hitler against England if given the chance. When the IRA launched a major bombing attack against England in 1939, Churchill's suspicions only heightened. Why would de Valera allow Germany to keep an embassy office open in Ireland if not to spy and cause fatal mischief?

Churchill pushed hard for British intelligence to infiltrate and monitor Irish communications for any signs of collusion with the Nazis. In particular, the security service, MI5, kept its investigative eye on Dr. Eduard Hempel, the German minister in Dublin, who secretly traded thousands of telegraph and shortwave radio signals with Berlin until his hidden transmitter was discovered. "It would seem that money should be spent to secure a body of trustworthy Irish agents to keep most vigilant watch," Winston advised. Wary of subversion from within, Churchill warned about "plenty of traitors" among Irish Catholics living in Glasgow, Scotland, near where British battleships were docked. He rehired an old bodyguard to protect him from assassination. But most of all, his old grudges and fears about Ireland arose once again, enhanced by his historical knowledge of how France and Spain once used the Emerald Isle as a launchpad for attacks against England. Churchill discounted assurances from British security officials who vouched for G2, the Irish intelligence agency, as helpful and willing to share information. He felt de Valera's claim to neutrality was merely a pretense to treachery, an invitation for Germany to attack by U-boat or from the air. "What does intelligence say about possible succouring of U-boats by Irish Malcontents in West of Ireland inlets?" he demanded.

The fear of secret plots, even assassination, as possible targets of intrigue, consumed the Kennedys' thoughts in London. Privately, they worried a single headline-grabbing act of violence—attributed to the Germans, fairly or not—could tip America from a studied neutral stance and send it headlong into war. Shortly after their trip to Rome, Rose wrote in her diary about Kick's conversation with her British friends who were upset about the impending conflict "and thought she was so lucky to be American." They "playfully" suggested that the United States might join the Allied cause and save Great Britain "if the American Ambassador or some of his family were shot."

When Kick relayed this tale, perhaps lightheartedly, Rose didn't seem amused. "Therefore, perhaps some Englishman may take it upon himself that one or two of us be accidentally (?) killed in a supposedly German air raid," she wrote in an April 7, 1939, entry. The paranoia of the times even infiltrated the way the ambassador viewed Churchill. Filled with diabolical concerns, Kennedy told his diary just what he thought Churchill was capable of in the name of the Crown.

"He kept smiling when he talked of 'neutrality' and 'keeping the war away from U.S.A,'" Joe wrote of his exchanges with Winston. "I can't help feeling he's not on the level. He is just an actor and a politician. He always impressed me that he'd blow up the American Embassy and say it was the Germans if it would get the U.S. in. Maybe I do him an injustice but I just don't trust him."

17

The Last Dance

Romance filled the warm summer night's air at Blenheim Palace, a place always special, almost magical, throughout Winston Churchill's life. Decades earlier, at this historic home where he'd been born, Winston proposed to Clementine, and the newlyweds spent part of their honeymoon there. At Blenheim, Winston declared, the two most important events in his life happened: "to be born, and to marry, and I never regretted either."

On this night in July 1939, the Churchills gathered once again, for the coming-out party of young Sarah Spencer-Churchill, the debutante daughter of Winston's cousin the Tenth Duke of Marlborough, whose family hosted a lavish celebration. Blenheim's grounds were aglow with floodlights, like moonbeams shimmering off the lake, porticos, and terrace. In the gardens, Japanese lanterns floated like fireflies in the trees.

Most of the nine hundred guests arrived in livery and private cars, attended by footmen in powdered wigs. As they entered the palace, a troupe of strolling players dressed in Tyrolean costumes serenaded them. As if on angels' wings, couples in the ballroom danced a lively foxtrot to London's favorite swing band. Lilies and pink and white hydrangeas replaced the books in the library, which had been converted into a dance floor, with brilliant chandeliers above. Eventually the crowd joined in unison, waltzing to "The Blue Danube." One of the guests, Henry "Chips" Channon, later described the "rivers of champagne" that flowed, as though they might never sip again from such a cup. "I have seen much, traveled far and am accustomed to splendor, but there has never been anything like tonight," he wrote in his diary. "Shall we ever see the like again?"

Winston and Clementine first joined the family dinner inside Blenheim's stately banquet hall, with its elaborate furnishings, paintings, and a domed ceiling. Later in the evening, Winston, the growing object of political speculation amid rumors of war, could be seen on the terrace. He shared a drink with Anthony Eden, his Conservative comrade-in-arms in Parliament. On the dance floor, Mollie Acland remembered her partner spotting Churchill chatting and smoking in the distance. "Oh look at that poor old has-been," the young man said in disgust. "My father says he's still a potential trouble-maker, but he won't get any more public life now!"

Randolph Churchill, brimming with alcohol, argued about the looming prospect of war and was discreetly escorted away. "Randolph, you've been drinking," exclaimed the estranged wife of a lord in rebuffing his advances.

"Who hasn't?" he said. "Anyhow the food is ghastly and the whole performance at a time like this is a disgrace."

The young Kennedys, however, imbibed the British traditions as if their own. The accoutrements of England's castles and class structure appealed to these nouveau riche Americans. Mingling in the crowd were twenty-two-year-old Jack Kennedy and his sister Eunice, delighted to have her turn this season as a debutante. Eunice had become friends with Sarah Spencer-Churchill and stayed the whole weekend at the palace. One of her beaux was Hugh Fraser, a British friend of Jack's. A few days after this party, Eunice would be presented to the king and queen along with all the other debutantes. In her diary, she remembered how her name, Miss Kennedy, was called out in a strong rich voice. Eunice expressed happiness "in the realization that I had achieved the aim of every young girl—that of being presented at the Court of St. James's—the world's greatest empire—'The Empire upon which the sun never sets.'" Like her brother, Eunice was well read and knew of the English history surrounding Blenheim Palace and John Churchill, the first Duke of Marlborough. "There is something very English about the way it retires from the rest of the world behind a grey stone wall and a gateway which alone gives indication of its character," Eunice wrote about the Churchill ancestral home. "It is no ordinary country house; it is a national monument raised to commemorate the victory from which it takes its name." With its 320 rooms and 2,700 acres of parks and gardens, Blenheim seemed "nearly as big as Versailles," wrote Jack to his friend Lem Billings, saying he "never had a better time."

The ambassador and his wife also attended the party and, from Rose's diary entry, appear to have seen Winston inside Blenheim and perhaps said hello. "The British to me live in the past so much," Rose noted after the Blenheim gala. "They pride themselves on living in houses centuries old, they talk about their ancestors who have been so famous in the past and they know their history so well." Like so many others that night, the Kennedys sensed that nothing would ever be the same after this magnificent party, already retreating swiftly into memory. "Some felt that it might be their last chance before another world cataclysm to show to their friends the lovely treasures of the past, to give to the young people a fling and a chance to enjoy luxuries which might never be allowed them again—and how right they were," wrote Rose.

Her son shared the same sentiment of that night. "You had the feeling of an era ending," Jack explained, "and everyone had a very good time at the end."

.   .   .

In the dark, lonely waters of the Atlantic, a German torpedo pierced the side of the SS *Athenia*, ripping a gaping hole into the giant steamship. The explosion hurled crewmen's bodies into the air and illuminated the night sky of September 3, 1939—the same day England entered into war against Germany.

The unarmed British liner, carrying fourteen hundred passengers, sank two hundred miles off the Irish coast. Mistakenly, the commandant of a German U-boat had perceived the *Athenia* to be a warship and fired, killing more than a hundred on board, including twenty-eight Americans. "The boat lurched to the port side and everyone went hurtling across the floor," recalled a young surviving American passenger, Barbara Rodman. "The fumes were so thick we thought we'd be asphyxiated. Everyone was crying 'Oh my God!' There were many dead lying around."

Hours before, Prime Minister Neville Chamberlain had declared Great Britain would join France at war against Germany, following Hitler's refusal to remove his Nazi troops from Poland. The September 1 invasion of Poland had finally convinced Chamberlain that his policy of negotiation with the Führer, what Churchill and other critics called "appeasement," had failed miserably. Chamberlain admitted "the long struggle to win the peace" was over. Sitting in the public gallery of the House of Commons, Ambassador Kennedy and his family (Rose and their adult children Jack, Joe Jr., and Kick) watched this momentous debate. "Everything that I have worked for, everything that I hoped for, everything that I have believed in during my public life has crashed in ruins," Chamberlain declared.

The prime minister assembled a new War Cabinet, with Winston Churchill in his old role as First Lord of the Admiralty, the same position he held during World War I. Finally, after years in political exile, Winston had returned to the arena, called by his countrymen to the center of a struggle between forces of evil and his beloved British Empire. In his mind, this life-or-death equation was simple, stark, and urgent. After Chamberlain spoke, the House listened next to Churchill, who expressed what the majority now felt certain. "We are fighting to save the whole world from the pestilence of Nazi tyranny and in defence of all that is most sacred to man," he proclaimed. Still saddened by Chamberlain's words, Joe Kennedy sat up in the gallery and "felt no wish to cheer."

Excited by that rarest of opportunities in life, a second chance, Winston rushed to his old Admiralty office, which appeared the same as when he'd left after the Dardanelles disaster. Royal Navy officials cheered his arrival with a signal to all hands at sea: "Winston is back." Like an energetic youngster, he pushed open a hidden panel. It revealed a situation map, untouched since the Great War, with tiny ship markings frozen in time. "It was a strange experience, like suddenly resuming a previous incarnation," Churchill described.

The sinking of the huge *Athenia* might have resembled the *Titanic* tragedy, but Churchill realized it was closer politically to the May 1915 *Lusitania* attack, also by a German U-boat, prompting America's entry into the Great War. At a War Cabinet meeting, after learning of the *Athenia*'s fate, Churchill predicted the tragedy might wake up Americans to the dangers posed by Hitler. "The occurrence should have a helpful effect as regards public opinion in the United States," he said. Although *Athenia* survivors had witnessed only a submarine's periscope cresting above the waves, they could only assume it was the Nazis who'd attacked. In denying any German responsibility, Joseph Goebbels, Hitler's propaganda chief, implied the *Athenia* sinking was instigated by British saboteurs and pointed directly at Churchill. "Your impudent lies, Herr Churchill," Goebbels accused on the radio. "Your infernal lies!"

After Chamberlain's declaration of war, air-raid sirens went off in London—a false alarm but a cry that reflected the public's anxiety. With Europe moving toward battle, Ambassador Kennedy recommended Americans return home. Privately, he took measures to send

Rose and their children back to the United States and out of harm's way. To assist the *Athenia* survivors who were brought back to Scotland, Kennedy sent his second-oldest son to Glasgow as his personal representative, along with his trusted aide, Eddie Moore. For Jack Kennedy, it became his first experience with government during a crisis. "He was the son of the Ambassador and he came to talk with us," Barbara Rodman Wilson recalled seventy-five years later, at the age of ninety-seven. "It was so good to see an American, no matter who it was!"

Inside the Beresford Hotel lounge, young Kennedy met with about a hundred surviving *Athenia* passengers. Many had suffered bruises and burns from their ordeal. Jack offered assurances that two large vessels would soon bring them back safely to America. Already the crowd had learned President Roosevelt wouldn't allow U.S. naval convoys to escort them—essentially leaving them vulnerable to another attack by German U-boats festering in the North Atlantic seas.

"You can't trust the Germany Navy!" they shouted at Jack. "You can't trust the German government!"

The crowd wasn't placated by the ambassador's skinny son, who looked like a teenager. Some survivors had waited hours in the open seas to be rescued. They watched helplessly as lifeboats were swamped and drowned bodies floated on the surface. Jack learned many third-class tourist passengers had been trapped belowdecks and died. To this huddled group of survivors, young Kennedy tried to explain the president's decision, noting that the United States was still a neutral nation, and that his suggested solution was best.

"It is much better to be on an American boat now than on a British boat, even if it was accompanied by the whole fleet," Jack argued.

Indignantly, a woman bellowed, "I don't believe it." And the rest of the crowd voiced their disapproval, refusing to leave without an accompanying U.S. convoy. Jack visited survivors at hotels and hospitals in Glasgow, displaying what one London newspaper called "a wisdom and sympathy of a man twice his age." Though he remained unflaggingly courteous, Jack soon left for London, to brief his father on what he had seen and heard.

Back at Princes Gate, Ambassador Kennedy faced resistance from those in his family, especially Kick, who didn't want to leave when it seemed England needed them most. Kick, a blend of worldliness and innocence, expressed the sense of loss and yearning among a generation afflicted by this war. "It is an eerie experience walking through a darkened London," she described about the initial days of the government-ordered blackout. "Gone are the gaily-lit hotels and nightclubs; now in their place are sombre buildings surrounded by sandbags. You wander through Kensington Garden in search of beauty and solitude and find only trenches and groups of ghostly figures working sound machines and searchlights to locate the enemy. Gone from the parks are the soap-box orators and the nightly strollers. But yet the moon shines through and one can see new beauties in the silent, deserted city of London. It is a new London, a London that looks like Barcelona before the bombs fell."

The senior Kennedy insisted his family leave immediately, though in separate departures, so it wouldn't look to the British press that they were fleeing. "Oh, we must get back to school, but we shan't go until all other American citizens have gone," Jack assured reporters. Both he and Joe Jr., starting his first year at Harvard Law, were back in Cambridge, Massachusetts, by the end of September.

Rose missed London but was pleased that the romance between Kick and Billy Hartington, whose Protestant family looked askance at Catholics, might fade with the family's return to the United States. By the time the SS *Washington* returned to New York, Kick seemed to accept that her time in England was over. "It can't be eighteen months since we were on this boat going in the other direction," she wrote her father. "Thanks a lot Daddy for giving me one of the greatest experiences anyone could have had. I know it will have a great effect on everything I do from herein [*sic*]."

The ambassador also ordered young embassy staffers such as Page Huidekoper to go home, keeping a promise to Huidekoper's father that he'd look out for her safety. Years later, Huidekoper recalled how much the Kennedys and Churchills, once so friendly, now seemed at fateful loggerheads. "Joe was determined that the U.S. not get involved in the war, and that was the one thing that Winston wanted—to get the U.S. into the war," Huidekoper said in 2011. "It changed because of their innate differences. Joe Kennedy was an isolationist when he came to England and became more outspoken about isolationism as it got closer to the war."

With the declaration of war, everything seemed different for Joe Kennedy, even with his two good friends in England, Lady Astor and Lord Beaverbrook, who once favored Chamberlain's policy of appeasement. During an October 1939 weekend after his family departed, the ambassador visited Cliveden, the magnificent country estate of the Astors, and chatted with Nancy Astor and a group of her British acquaintances about the war. "Of course they all wanted to know when America was coming in and of course I told them they weren't coming," he wrote to Rose back home. "So perhaps, dear, you went home at the height of your husband's popularity." During their talk, Astor exhibited a real change of heart about her longtime political detractor Winston Churchill, and told Kennedy that Winston might replace Chamberlain soon as prime minister. "If he does, then I certainly think England's march down hill will be speeded up," Kennedy wrote his wife. "Churchill has energy and brains but *no* judgment." Lady Astor maintained her friendly relations with the Kennedy women, especially Kick and Rose, but increasingly disliked the ambassador's defeatism. In Parliament, she admitted she'd been wrong about Churchill's dire warnings about the Nazis and urged Chamberlain to put him in the

Cabinet. "The Astors surprisingly enough, take a strong pro-Churchill line," observed Henry "Chips" Channon. "Lady Astor, frightened by anonymous letters and gossip about the so-called 'Cliveden Set,' has thrown over her principles and is urging Chamberlain against his better judgment to take the plunge."

Kennedy's affinity with Max Aitken, Lord Beaverbrook, the press lord and friend of Winston's, formed perhaps the ambassador's closest alliance in England. The American business tycoon liked Beaverbrook's cunning and sharp instincts in all facets of life—enough so that Randolph Churchill's friend writer Evelyn Waugh (who fashioned his novel *Scoop* on the bold and crafty press magnate), once quipped that he "had to believe in the Devil if only to account for the existence of Lord Beaverbrook." If pushed, Kennedy agreed that Max could be "a treacherous little bastard."

For much of Kennedy's time at the embassy, he and Beaverbrook agreed with Chamberlain's appeasement policies, hoping their respective nations could somehow avoid war with the Axis powers. Churchill believed them both dangerously wrong. "There would be a great deal to be said for [Beaverbrook's] policy of a pacific isolationism if we could arrange to have the United Kingdom towed out fifteen hundred miles into the Atlantic," Winston chided. During their decades-long friendship (reaching back to the Other Club), Winston and Max had often differed on politics. After one of their frequent friendly arguments, Beaverbrook said of Churchill, "He is strictly honest and truthful to other people, down to the smallest detail of his life—yet he frequently deceives himself."

As British public opinion turned acrid about Kennedy's defeatism, Beaverbrook seemed determined to stay in his good graces, just like another Churchill loyalist, Brendan Bracken. At an October 1939 gathering with reporters at Beaverbrook's place, Bracken praised Kennedy: "He's a great friend of England's. Greatest ambassador we ever had." While Bracken's statement probably was just tactical, Beaverbrook's fidelity to Kennedy seemed sincere. Even when England declared war against Germany, Beaverbrook ordered his newspapers not to turn on his American friend. Instructions from Lord Beaverbrook's editors insisted that "Mr. Kennedy is not to be criticized in the columns of our papers, but that he is to receive favourable comment."

Like birds of a feather, Beaverbrook realized Joe wanted mostly to protect his investments—in his family and his own future. Between them, Kennedy offered a kind of shelter for the rich British lord, who was afraid of losing everything as well. When the Russians entered Poland in September 1939, Beaverbrook sounded "frightfully disturbed" in calling Kennedy at his weekend country home with the news. Max said he'd move his fortune to America in Joe's care if necessary, according to Kennedy's diary. "All my papers, my money, and everything else I own is yours to do as you wish with," Beaverbrook told him, "There are only three men in England who know what the real situation is: first you—second, [British secretary of state for war, Leslie] Hore-Belisha—and third—(you may be surprised)—Winston Churchill."

For an imperiled British nation, Kennedy thought Beaverbrook would make a better leader, and so did the press lord himself. Joe's cables praised Beaverbrook to the president—just as Beaverbrook said he did on Kennedy's behalf when he visited the White House. "If he [Beaverbrook] had his way, he would like to turn over the British Empire to you to straighten out," Joe enthused to Roosevelt. During a trip to Washington around this time, Beaverbrook stopped in to see the president, and they chatted about Kennedy, Churchill, and the war. "Beaverbrook told me that in his conversations with you, you were most complimentary in discussing me and I am deeply grateful to you for this," Kennedy wrote to FDR. "One's influence on this Country is primarily dependent on how they think one stands with the President."

Kennedy still hoped Prime Minister Chamberlain might stay in place, but in a note to his sons Jack and Joe Jr., back at Harvard, admitted that this might not be possible. Chamberlain, a cautious man by nature, didn't know how to handle Churchill. In July 1939, Chamberlain had assured Kennedy that he "had no intention of putting Churchill in Cabinet." Former prime minister Stanley Baldwin agreed, citing Churchill's erratic and headstrong behavior years earlier as a prominent Member of Parliament. "If he was a lot of trouble outside the Government," Baldwin complained about Churchill, "he was 20 times more trouble inside." By September, however, Chamberlain reversed himself, allowing for Churchill's return as First Lord of the Admiralty. Chamberlain remained wary of Winston and admitted as much to the American ambassador. "I could see he [Chamberlain] bitterly distrusts Churchill and is well aware he is after his job," Kennedy recalled in his diary. "He thinks he is better in the Cabinet than out. Easier to handle. He didn't think there was one man in his Cabinet who would vote for him for Prime Minister. I said I thought that was true . . . He hates it all but is 'tough' and is not going to let Churchill get away with it."

While both Churchill and Kennedy still shared smiles when in public together, they worked privately at undermining each other. In his secret memos sent to the White House, Kennedy did his best to cast doubt on Winston's character. Forgetting his role as a British liquor distributor, the ambassador complained, without any hint of irony, that Winston always seemed to be nursing a whiskey in his glass. "He has developed into a fine two-handed drinker and his judgment never proved good," he informed President Roosevelt. Kennedy warned of Churchill's friendship with those favoring intervention in Europe, without mentioning Baruch or others by name. "Remember, Churchill has in America a couple of very close friends who definitely are not on our team," Kennedy advised.

Instead of heeding his warning, Kennedy was thunderstruck to learn, President Roosevelt reached out directly to Churchill himself, providing an open invitation to go behind his ambassador's back. A few weeks after it was written, Churchill received FDR's September 11 missive congratulating him on returning to his old post. "It is because you and I occupied similar positions in the World War that I want you to know how glad I am that you are back again in the Admiralty," Roosevelt wrote to Churchill, in classic rapprochement. "What I want you and the Prime Minister to know is that I shall at all times welcome it if you keep me in touch personally with anything you want us to know about."

Ever practical, Roosevelt now seemingly forgot his critical view of Churchill's attitude toward him during World War I. That same month in 1939, Felix Frankfurter, a New Deal insider appointed to the U.S. Supreme Court, returned from a trip to London and told the president that his meeting with Churchill "was one of the most exhilarating experiences I had in England—it made me feel more secure about the future." Roosevelt listened intently to Frankfurter's advice the same way Joe Kennedy once had when Frankfurter suggested Harold Laski teach his sons at the London School of Economics. Ending his private note to Churchill, FDR alluded to the Marlborough biography that Winston had inscribed as a gift when his son Jimmy Roosevelt visited Chartwell in 1933. As the president told Churchill, he was "glad you did the Marlboro [*sic*] volumes before this thing started—and I much enjoyed reading them."

Kennedy became the delivery boy for the president's letters and for Churchill's replies, which Winston signed impishly with his own anonymous code name, "naval person." Joe learned of their provocative content only when Churchill decided to share it with him, more as a personal courtesy than by political necessity. Both knew Kennedy was being circumvented. "I resented this by-passing of me and my position as the Ambassador," Kennedy later wrote. "I lost none of that resentment when Churchill two days later asked me over to the Admiralty and there read me the letter from the President recalling their association from the last war and inviting Churchill to communicate directly with him at any time that he might feel the urge to do so."

In October 1939, Roosevelt again kept Kennedy in the dark with secret intelligence about another possible crisis, similar to the *Athenia* disaster. Warned that a time bomb might be on board the *Iroquois*—a U.S. steamship that had left Ireland with a boatload of returning Americans—FDR personally telephoned Churchill about the matter. The Germans first alerted the U.S. naval attaché in Berlin, based on information its spies picked up in Ireland, and suggested "the purpose of this plot was to bring the United States into the war," Kennedy recalled. U.S. officials sent a convoy to escort the *Iroquois*, already halfway in the Atlantic, home to America. No bomb was ever found. But again Kennedy learned he'd been kept in the dark on this matter only after talking with Churchill rather than his president. "It was an embarrassing moment for me," Kennedy wrote. "Churchill naturally assumed that the President had kept me aware of the situation, whereas I actually was in complete ignorance of every fact."

For the next two months, Kennedy kept in constant contact with Churchill. They talked about the German U-boats that threatened to sink more ships, and other matters concerning the war. On his own, Roosevelt kept sending Churchill a steady stream of private messages— the start of more than two thousand correspondences between them during the war. The only way Kennedy knew about their exchange was when Churchill asked him to send his reply by coded transmission or in the diplomatic pouch bound for America. In a spirit of cooperation, Churchill offered to share with Roosevelt the secret technology of British radar devices used on their destroyers "whenever you feel they would be of use to the United States Navy and are sure the secret will go no further."

Before Kennedy left for the Christmas holidays in America, the ambassador stopped again at Churchill's admiralty building, attached to Whitehall, the administrative center of power. Kennedy walked into the First Lord's office, with its paintings of famous British battles and Winston's favorite blue octagon table in front of his desk. Churchill, in a confident mood but looking "somewhat pasty," immediately offered him a whiskey and soda. "I declined somewhat to his disappointment as I felt he wanted one," Joe recorded in his diplomatic diary. Nevertheless, Churchill's mastery of military matters, far beyond Kennedy's expertise, was evident throughout their long conversation. Realizing how Kennedy had been usurped, Churchill smartly enlisted the bruised ambassador in one mission. Before their talk ended, he explained how the British planned to mine the Norwegian territorial waters as the only way of stopping ore from Swedish mines from reaching Germany's war machine.

"What do you think the President's reaction to such a proposal would be?" Churchill asked.

Feeling out of the loop, Kennedy seemed happy to have his opinion considered. "I don't know," he replied, "but I can ask him."

Winston and Joe agreed upon their own secret code, based on the good times their two families had shared in the past in places such as Blenheim. When Kennedy got back to Washington, if Roosevelt agreed with the Norwegian plan, Joe would send a message to Churchill stating, "Eunice would like to go to the party." If the president felt the mining plan would cause too much controversy in the United States, Kennedy would cable, "Eunice would not like to go to the party."

On December 8, 1939, when Kennedy finally visited Roosevelt at the White House, he complained bitterly about feeling left out of the president's contacts with British leaders, especially Churchill. During this meeting, Roosevelt confided to Joe that he didn't trust Churchill, either. "I'm giving him attention now because of his possibilities of being P.M. and wanting to keep my hand in," the president explained. As always, Roosevelt knew how to play to Kennedy's strong opinions about keeping America out of the British fight. "I'm willing to help them all I can but don't want them to play me for a sucker," Roosevelt assured him. To aides, Roosevelt later explained how he placated Kennedy by flattering him and keeping him busy, realizing his rambunctious ambassador needed some "plates to keep spinning on sticks." Like a kid with a decoder ring, Kennedy cabled Churchill with their prearranged secret code about Eunice's partygoing, relaying Roosevelt's okay for the Norwegian mining.

After nearly two years away from home, Kennedy didn't want to go back to London. He wanted to stay with his growing family, relax at his Palm Beach house in the Florida sunshine, and contemplate whether he should run for president as an isolationist Democrat. Immediately upon arriving in the United States, he told the press that he favored a third term for FDR. "I cannot go against the guy," he admitted privately. "He's done more for me than my own kind. If he wants it I'll be with him." Yet Joe stood ready if Roosevelt decided not to run, and encouraged press speculation about a Kennedy candidacy. While he was still in London, Roosevelt told him over the telephone, "After 1940 I am going to look at the performance instead of acting in the play." Nonetheless, Joe sensed the president wanted to stay in office (even though no predecessor had gone beyond what George Washington considered the appropriate limit of two terms) and that he wanted Kennedy to return to London.

Once Great Britain's favorite American, with his smiling family and roguish charm, Kennedy had become irritating to the British public and its leaders. Before he left for New York, he'd even managed to anger the king and queen with his doubts about England's chances in the war and his defense of Charles Lindbergh's defeatist comments—enough so that Joe felt compelled to apologize in writing to his royal highness the king. Both Churchill and Chamberlain counseled moderation in their infuriated king's reply. While he was home in America, Kennedy also upset the British with a deeply pessimistic speech. "Don't let anything that comes out of any country in the world make you believe you can make a situation one whit better by getting into the war," Kennedy told a crowd of fellow Irish Catholics in Boston. "There is no place in this fight for us. It's going to be bad enough as it is."

But for all the trouble Kennedy had caused in Britain, Roosevelt decided to stick with him. It seemed better to keep Kennedy in London, thousands of miles away, than to see him cause more mischief at home, especially if Roosevelt intended to run for an unprecedented third term. Joe explored every possible excuse to get out of his commitment, including a doctor's note saying he suffered from stomach ailments requiring hospitalization and rest. Though England and France had declared war against Germany, outright fighting had yet to start. This stretch of quiet months in late 1939 and early 1940 would be later called "the Phony War." To another friendly diplomat, Joe complained about "his discontent over returning to London, his belief that everything he could do there could just as well be done by a $50-a-month clerk, that he wanted to quit but didn't see how he gracefully could before the elections."

For three months, Kennedy stayed in America, dawdling and delaying over his future, while his embassy post remained conspicuously empty during a time when England was technically at war. In February, Joe returned to London, unhappy about his fate and trapped by his sense of duty. As much as he had once coveted the appointment to the Court of St. James's, Kennedy now wanted out in the worst way.

18

While America Slept

In public debate, the heirs of Winston Churchill and Joseph Kennedy carried on their family legacy while trying to establish voices of their own.

With the outbreak of war, Randolph Churchill felt proven right. Presciently, he had warned about the evils of Hitler long before the Nazis marched into Poland. In 1933, he challenged the Oxford Union's refusal under any circumstances to "fight for King and Country" and endured boos and hisses; security guards escorted him out of the debate hall. While his private excesses attracted scorn, his sharp acumen about the world eventually earned him grudging respect. By 1939, he had returned to Oxford for a very different resolution—pushed by its president, Hugh Fraser, a friend of Jack Kennedy's—one that welcomed the government's conscription of young men to fight the Nazis. The Oxford Union now agreed that peace could be obtained only through military strength and a willingness to go to war. Randolph turned this triumphant, redemptive moment into a bit of merriment, reminding those gathered who'd been correct all along.

"Onward Conscript Soldiers, marching as to war, you would not be conscripts, had you gone before," young Churchill bellowed to the sizable audience, which roared its approval. They would soon follow his father into battle.

A dutiful son, Joe Kennedy Jr. didn't venture very far from the political views of his namesake. He realized his father's appointment to London was part of a larger generational dream for the Kennedys—becoming the first Catholic president of the United States someday. "He claims that he would give it up in a minute if it wasn't for the benefits that Jack and I are getting out of it," Joe Jr. said about his father. "He doesn't like the idea of taking orders and working for hours trying to keep things out of his speeches which an Ambassador shouldn't say." Privately, Joe Jr. echoed the ambassador's anti-Semitism and believed Jews in America were the major advocates with Roosevelt for war. Though handsome and energetic, Joe Jr. didn't embrace London's sophisticated social world, which viewed him as a crude and more common-stock American. With his abrasive manner, "Joe was received less enthusiastically" than his siblings, observed Kick's biographer Lynne McTaggart. "His humor often [seemed] uncomfortably sharp-edged. He lacked the finesse that had enabled Jack and Kick to adapt so readily to British ways . . . Some aristocratic young women were shocked by what occasionally surfaced as sexual aggressiveness and a violent temper."

When he returned to America, Joe Jr. became a delegate to the 1940 Democratic Party National Convention but didn't support the president. Instead of FDR, the ambassador's oldest son boldly endorsed James Farley, the estranged political kingmaker who had masterminded the winning New Deal coalition of urban ethnics, labor, racial minorities, and rural poor. Young Kennedy came out for Farley once he knew his father wouldn't run for president. At the convention, Harry Hopkins and other top White House aides skillfully orchestrated a draft movement for Roosevelt's third term. Pressure was placed on Joe Jr. to change his mind—including a telephone call to London asking his father to intervene.

"No," replied Joe Sr., "I wouldn't think of telling him what to do."

With little variance, Joe Jr. echoed his father's isolationist views. At Harvard Law, he joined the Harvard Committee Against Military Intervention in Europe and was quoted in the press as one of its leaders. He opposed any talk of U.S. entry into the war, perhaps more so than his father. Even later, when he began training as a navy pilot, Joe Jr. said his isolationist views hadn't changed, though he conceded he "ought to be doing something." In December 1940 an internal FBI memo claimed the ambassador's "appeasement sentiments were shared by his two sons." The Bureau's chief, J. Edgar Hoover, sent to the White House foreign intelligence received from British officials that quoted Ambassador Kennedy's scathing criticism of Roosevelt in London. The FBI report about Kennedy's appeasement, however, was correct about only one son.

After traveling through Europe, Jack Kennedy returned to Harvard for his senior year, still reflecting on all he'd seen and heard abroad. Writing to his father in London, Jack let him know his honor's thesis would examine British foreign policy since 1931 and "discuss class influence in England." For young Kennedy, his provocative choice, particularly given his father's sensitive position, would pose an exhilarating personal challenge and crystallize his thinking about Winston Churchill.

While in England, young Kennedy had witnessed Churchill's urgent call in Parliament for rearmament against the Nazi threat. He was intrigued by Churchill's capacity to convince with the power and cadence of his words. "I wouldn't say my father got me interested in it," Jack later said of his Harvard project. "They were things that I saw for myself." Jack read Churchill's best-known books and turned to the Hansard, the official Parliament transcripts, to study some of his lesser-known speeches. There was also a linkage between sons. Jack read Randolph Churchill's preface in *Arms and the Covenant,* the 1938 collection of Winston's rhetoric that Randolph had edited, and used the Churchill book as a touchstone for his own work. Kennedy reexamined the role of Churchill's political contemporaries who held power during those years, especially prime ministers Stanley Baldwin and Neville Chamberlain. Most memorable to young Kennedy was Churchill's 1936 speech concerning the "Locust Years," what Winston called the period of British indifference while Germany built up its war machine.

During early 1940, Jack worked on his project in a mad dash. He employed five stenographers and handed in the final draft within hours of his deadline. It was sloppy enough that his graders commented on its typographical errors. But the thesis, entitled "Appeasement at Munich," contained enough intellectual vigor and critical analysis to earn him a cum laude distinction at graduation in June. Jack conceded it "represents more work than I've ever done in my life."

In his paper, Kennedy examined the pacifism throughout British foreign policy after World War I and the rise of German militarism. He blamed the appeasement policies of British leaders as a reflection of public sentiments and the way political systems operate. He argued that the nature of a liberal democracy is fundamentally different from a dictatorship—and that an unchecked figure such as Hitler could easily fan the winds of war by controlling the press and bending other freedoms to his will. Jack credited Churchill's foresight in recognizing the Nazi threat and calling upon his nation to prepare for possible attack. "In light of the present-day war, we are able to wonder at the blindness of Britain's leaders and the country as a whole that would fail to see the correctness of Churchill's arguments," he wrote. Yet the Harvard undergrad also suggested "to blame one man, such as Baldwin, for the unpreparedness of British armaments is illogical and unfair, given the conditions of Democratic government." He defended Chamberlain's Munich Pact with Hitler, which he said provided enough time for Britain's military to catch up to the Germans. His thesis paper offered a dry, detached analysis, not an impassioned treatise or an indictment of political leadership. As Arthur M. Schlesinger Jr. later noted, Kennedy's thesis "was a singularly dispassionate statement to be flung into America's most passionate foreign policy debate of the century—so dispassionate, indeed, that it was impossible to conclude from the text whether the author was an interventionist or isolationist."

In reaction, Jack's father and older brother, both wholehearted isolationists, took exception to some of his findings though, in the interest of family loyalty, they endorsed his overall effort. "I read it before he had finished it up and it seemed to represent a lot of work but did not prove anything," Joe Jr. told his father. "However, he said he shaped it up the last few days and he seemed to have some good ideas so it ought to be very good." In his own lengthy critique from London, the ambassador praised Jack's hard work and generally agreed with "the fundamentals" of his thesis. Even though he opposed American involvement in the war, the ambassador suggested Baldwin should be taken to task for ignoring Churchill's call for restoring Britain's military might. "I think that you better go over the material to make sure that, in pinning it on the electorate, you don't give the appearance of trying to do a complete whitewash of the leaders," he said. "For some reason, Britain slept. That means pretty much all Britain, leaders and people alike."

Ever the promoter, Joe Kennedy decided his son's thesis should become a book. He recruited his friend *New York Times* columnist Arthur Krock to spruce up his son's prose and find a publisher; Krock knew the ambassador would buy plenty of copies. Krock suggested a new title *Why England Slept*, a sly reference to Churchill's book *Arms and the Covenant*, which had been published in the United States with the name *While England Slept*. This newly minted volume from Kennedy's progeny would be touted as "an answer to Winston Churchill's *While England Slept*." Jack requested his father check with Churchill before they used the cheeky title. Initially, the Kennedys asked Harold Laski, the British politician and professor, to write a preface, but eventually

Henry Luce, the *Time* magazine publisher and husband of Clare Boothe Luce, did it. "If John Kennedy is characteristic of the younger generation—and I believe he is—many of us would be happy to have the destinies of this Republic handed over to his generation at once," wrote Luce, who built a fortune spotting future trends.

When Joe received advance copies from the publisher, he sent one book each to Churchill and Laski. But Laski chastised Joe for foisting Jack's undergraduate thesis as a hyped-up literary success. "For while it is the book of a lad with brains, it is very immature, it has no real structure, and it dwells almost wholly on the surface of things," the professor complained. "I don't honestly think any publisher would have looked at that book of Jack's if he had not been your son, and if you had not been Ambassador. And those are not right grounds for publication. I care a lot about your boys. I don't want them to be spoilt such as rich men's sons are so easily spoilt. Thinking is a hard business, and you have to pay the price of admission to it. Do believe that these hard sayings from me represent more real friendship than the easy praise of 'yes men' like Arthur Krock."

Joe, as proud as if he'd written the book himself, didn't want to hear any criticisms. His son's book became part of the ambassador's diplomatic oeuvre. In a copy sent to Brendan Bracken, Winston's top associate, Kennedy underlined the points with which Churchill might surely agree. "It occurs to me that there is a lesson for America in the dilemma in which this country found itself as a result of inadequate armaments at the time of Munich," Joe observed. Along with the book, Kennedy also asked Bracken if Winston could autograph posters for all his kids. Bracken said he'd be delighted to arrange it with Churchill, adding "but in view of the number of your children, he may easily develop writer's cramp!"

Unlike Churchill, Joe Kennedy's aspirations for his sons began to exceed his own political ambitions. After officially informing Churchill that President Roosevelt intended to provide at least fifty desperately needed destroyers to the embattled British, the ambassador mixed in some personal business before he left, mentioning his son's *Why England Slept.* "I told him [Churchill] that young Jack had finished his book and it was receiving almost universal approval in the United States and that it had paid very great tribute to the Prime Minister," the senior Kennedy wrote, "and he evinced a great interest in it and I said I would send it around to him this afternoon." Churchill's personal secretary later thanked the ambassador for his son's book and said Winston had read it with "great interest."

The ambassador, so puffed with pride at his son's achievement, didn't seem to notice Jack had agreed with Churchill about the Nazi threat more than with him. "A defeat of the Allies may simply be one more step toward the ultimate achievement—Germany over the world," JFK wrote in his book, a view not shared by either his father or his older brother.

Churchill apparently did read young Kennedy's new book. At a staff lunch a month later, he talked about it, then turned to a young aide who'd once worked for Neville Chamberlain. "You slept too, didn't you!" Churchill said to the aide, with a jovial jibe.

At age twenty-three, Jack Kennedy saw *Why England Slept* establish his writing credentials and subtly distance him from his father's strident isolationist politics. In the equally important realm of family politics, Jack moved to the head of the line, no longer seen as frivolous or secondary in the eyes of his parents. As his father told him, "You would be surprised how a book that really makes the grade with high-class people stands you in good stead for years to come."

19

We Shall Fight

With his Scotch highball noticeably in hand, Winston Churchill boasted how many Englishmen supported his combative stance against Hitler. "Take the workman, for instance," he said, his commanding voice in full annunciation, holding court at a small stag dinner hosted by Prime Minister Chamberlain at Downing Street. "His back is up. He will stand for no pulling of punches against Germany. He's tough."

Ten guests filled the smoke-filled stateroom, but Churchill's comments seemed aimed at only one, Joe Kennedy.

Throughout early 1940, Churchill met frequently with the American ambassador, careful not to exacerbate their sharp differences. Winston remained convinced that "the twilight war," as he called it, would eventually break out into full-fledged combat requiring America's intervention. At this dinner among friends and rivals, Churchill felt Kennedy could be handled deftly through flattery, jokes, and a determination to show Britain's willingness to fight against the Nazis at all costs.

Kennedy, the perpetual discounter, wasn't buying it. "Well, if you can show me one Englishman that's tougher than you are, Winston, I'll eat my hat!" he laughed.

During this evening, Kennedy showed his own skill at banter among men of power, what another guest later described as his ability "under the cloak of horseplay" to "get across many unpalatable home truths regarding Anglo-American relations. It was superbly done."

Any back-and-forth with Winston was always entertaining, and the ambassador, who favored humorous comments at his own family table, showed a comfort with this exchange. Kennedy made sure Churchill and the prime minister understood the American desire not to stumble into the conflict by having one of its steamships attacked in the crossfire between combatants. With his own wink of an eye, Kennedy recalled how he told Secretary of State Cordell Hull that the United States should not enter the war even if his ship were sunk on the way back to London.

"I thought this would give me some protection against Churchill's placing a bomb on the ship!" Joe cracked.

The whole room laughed, as did Winston, who savored a witty remark as much as any.

"Not I," replied Churchill, with apparently a smile still on his face. "I am certain that the United States will come in later anyway."

At this March 1940 dinner, Churchill showed particular concern with another American guest, Undersecretary of State Sumner Welles. Roosevelt's decision to send Welles on a "fact-finding" mission to London had unnerved Churchill, accustomed to successfully going around Kennedy to deal directly with the president. He realized that Welles, a longtime friend of Roosevelt, could conceivably prompt a peace negotiation with the Axis powers that Britain would feel compelled to accept, regardless of the long-term consequences. Churchill felt adamantly that Hitler could be no longer accommodated or appeased. He sensed Roosevelt agreed with him. But like so many who dealt with FDR on both sides of the Atlantic, he wasn't certain if the president would ever commit American troops to war in Europe.

Inside his Admiralty office a few days later, Winston expressed to Kennedy his misgivings about Welles's trip and any thought of a presidential peace plan. Roosevelt shouldn't bother with such an effort, he suggested. "It would just embarrass us, and we won't accept it," Churchill explained. "In fact, I would fight Chamberlain if he proposed to accept it."

As their chat progressed, Churchill asked Kennedy if the president might seek a third term.

"Probably he would, if it were necessary to keep things right in the United States," Joe replied.

By this time in early 1940, Kennedy had endorsed FDR's reelection bid and publicly disavowed any interest of his own. Churchill knew of the ambassador's presidential ambitions, but his question suggested he didn't know of Kennedy's White House conversation with a tired-looking Roosevelt during the yuletide holidays. "I just won't go for a third term unless we are in war," Roosevelt told Kennedy. Before he left for England in February, however, Joe met again with Roosevelt, who appeared more certain to seek a third term.

Keenly aware of Roosevelt's importance to Britain, Churchill appeared happy with the ambassador's reply. "Of course, we want him to run, but we must take care that the United States does not know that," said Winston, mindful of not inflaming the already volatile American isolationist sentiments. "If we stirred up some action here in July, which seems more than likely, Roosevelt might then be more inclined to run."

During his London stay, Welles visited Churchill's Admiralty office along with Kennedy. They found Winston sitting in a big chair in front of a fireplace, reading the afternoon paper, with a cigar and drink by his side. Winston soon pulled out charts on ship sinkings and argued how well his navy could withstand U-boat attacks. He called the Nazis a "monster born of hatred and of fear" and expressed confidence that "we will, of course, win the war and that is the only hope for civilization."

After hearing Churchill's attempts to convince Welles of their noble cause, Kennedy showed his unease. "For Christ's sakes, stop trying to make this a holy war, because no one will believe you," Joe groaned at Churchill. "You're fighting for your life as an Empire, and that's good enough."

Privately, the ambassador attempted to convince Welles that if some peace accord with Germany weren't reached, the British faced disaster. But Welles walked away from Churchill's presentation very impressed, writing to Roosevelt about Winston's "cascade of oratory, brilliant and always effective, interlarded with considerable wit."

Although Welles came to London at Roosevelt's behest to check out his ambassador's gloomy assessments, Kennedy didn't act resentful. He personally liked Welles, and they had worked well together before. In the past year, Welles helped convince FDR to send Kennedy and his family to the Vatican for the Pope's 1939 coronation, and Welles pushed successfully to have Roosevelt appoint Myron Taylor as his personal envoy to the Holy See. Kennedy hoped Welles's extensive travels around London, Paris, Rome, and Berlin might result in some compromise toward peace. Before Welles's plane left the airport for America, precariously taking off on a snowy morning, Kennedy wished him Godspeed with his mission, believing that "thousands, perhaps, millions of lives hung on that chance."

By May 1940 the "Phony War" erupted into a very real one. German advances in Denmark, Norway, and elsewhere undermined support for Prime Minister Chamberlain's government, enough that Conservative Party members talked openly of finding his replacement. Before his appointment to the War Cabinet, Churchill had been quite critical of Chamberlain, particularly his Munich Agreement. "Churchill was vociferous in his belief that Germany had been bluffing and continued to do so," Kennedy recorded in March 1939, after sharing a lunch with Winston. As First Lord of the Admiralty, Churchill proposed several fighting measures, which Chamberlain ignored or dismissed, to Winston's great frustration. The fall of Norway was only the latest humiliation. "If Chamberlain had shown more strength at Munich," Churchill asserted, "Germany would have been crushed."

Yet when others called for a new prime minister, Winston displayed a certain loyalty to Chamberlain. He would not allow himself to be part of this intraparty mutiny. Harold Macmillan, then a young Conservative MP, recalls Churchill telling him that "he had signed on for the voyage and would stick to the ship." Despite their differences, Churchill retained a fondness for Chamberlain dating back to his father, Joseph Chamberlain, a prominent Parliament member. The elder Chamberlain had been friends with his own father, Lord Randolph Churchill, a generation earlier. As a young man stunned by his father's rapid demise, Winston had turned to Joseph Chamberlain for advice and support. "I must have had a great many more real talks with him than I ever had with my own father," he wrote, and later lionized Joseph Chamberlain among the profiles in his book *Great Contemporaries.* When young Winston first ran for office, fresh from his famous Boer War escape, Joseph Chamberlain appeared at rallies to endorse him. Winston never shared the same rapport with Neville, who told friends such as Kennedy that Churchill was out for his job. However, at this most vulnerable moment for the prime minister—when a chant went up in Parliament calling for seventy-year-old Chamberlain to "Go! Go! Go! GO!"—Winston would not stick the knife in.

Watching from the gallery on May 8, 1940, the American ambassador hoped for Chamberlain's survival, though he realized from Churchill's behavior that change was imminent. "I could not help but feel at the time that for all his protested loyalty to the Government, he saw in the distance the mantle being lowered on his shoulders and that he took pains, despite an occasional loss of temper, not to encourage too much enmity from any quarter," Kennedy wrote in his diary about Churchill. When Joe spoke privately with Lord Beaverbrook, Max showed him a handwritten letter from Chamberlain thanking the press lord for his editorial support. "It's the letter of an old man and a rattled one," concluded Beaverbrook, who let Kennedy know he'd be pushing for Winston to become the new prime minister. Brendan Bracken, another Churchill confidant, told Joe that Winston would never work for Lord Halifax, then considered the only alternative choice for prime minister.

The following day, Chamberlain's fate was sealed when Germany invaded Holland and Belgium, extending its grip throughout Europe. Chamberlain resigned on May 10, and the king called upon Churchill to form a new government. Observing this drama from a diplomatic distance, Ambassador Kennedy visited Churchill to extend America's best wishes. In a light, congratulatory moment, Joe told Winston that he "felt partly responsible for his new job." Before Churchill could fathom a reply, Joe recalled the secret code used between them in relaying Roosevelt's approval for the mining of Norwegian territorial waters a few months earlier. "Eunice went to the party," Joe said, laughing; "Hence Norway, hence Prime Minister."

At age sixty-five, Winston Churchill rode to Buckingham Palace with his wife, Clementine, in a moment of great personal triumph and solemnity. All the decades of sacrifice and dedication—especially in recent years, when he felt his pleas to save the British Empire had gone unheeded—had culminated in this moment. "I felt as if I were walking with destiny," he remembered, "and that all my past life had been but a preparation for this hour and for this trial."

The Churchill family understood how much this honor meant to Winston. Away on military training, Randolph had called his father immediately when he heard news of the German offensive and inquired about his father's chances of becoming prime minister. "Oh, I don't know about that," Winston told his son. "Nothing matters now except beating the enemy." But when the formal announcement of Churchill's selection was made, his extended family rejoiced, including Randolph's wife, Pamela, who was living with her in-laws. "I am so delighted over our new Prime Minister," she wrote to Winston. "And I feel that now England will be put into full motion, & that Hitlerism will be crushed forever." On his way home from Buckingham Palace, Winston's bodyguard congratulated him on the "enormous task" he'd taken on. "God alone knows how great it is," Churchill replied, with tears welling in his eyes. "All I hope is that it is not too late. I am very much afraid it is, but we can only do our best." Only a man of intense humanity like Churchill could raise the spirits of Great Britain, staring into the abyss of loss and annihilation, and deliver them from a modern evil as threatening as the world had ever known. Better than most, Randolph understood his father's sacrifices to get to this point, especially his political estrangement because of principle. He believed his father uniquely suited to lead the nation away from devastation. "At last you have the power and the authority out of which the caucus have cheated you and England for nine years," Randolph wrote to him. "I cannot tell you how proud and happy I am. I only hope that it is not too late."

After decades of watching his exploits, Churchill's countrymen would now rely on his "pluck, his courageous energy and magnificent English," observed fellow Conservative MP Sir Henry "Chips" Channon, who noted that "his humour too, although often in doubtful taste, is immense." Churchill never lost his upbeat disposition in the face of defeat. "This war will be won by carnivores," he declared with a snarl. In his rousing, heartrending speeches as prime minister,

Winston rallied his nation by offering his "blood, toil, tears and sweat" toward victory. Though not a religious man, he suggested that a divine power had made his miracle selection possible. "Go and pray for me," he asked aides as they went to church. "Ora pro nobis. (Pray for us)." When Clemmie walked out of a church where the minister had given a pacifist sermon, Winston acted outraged, declaring, "You ought to have cried 'Shame'—desecrating the House of God with lies! Tell the Minister of Information with a view to having the man pilloried." Even when called upon by the king to lead, he managed a moment of wit. "I suppose you don't know why I have sent for you?" the monarch asked. Churchill didn't miss a beat: "Sir, I simply could not imagine," he replied, before attending to the business at hand.

In this time of crisis, Winston turned once again to his ablest, shrewdest, most talented friend, Lord Beaverbrook. Their personal loyalty dated from three decades earlier and had survived endless dinner arguments and verbal battles. Now he placed Beaverbrook in charge of fighter plane production, the most essential task needed to ensure Great Britain's survival. Churchill fully appreciated Max's "power to inspire and drive, his ability to get at the heart of a problem at speed, his refusal to despair or admit defeat," wrote one of Beaverbrook's biographers.

Beaverbrook had helped his friend Winston overcome dark moments before. In 1915, when Churchill was pushed out of the Admiralty following the Dardanelles fiasco, Beaverbrook's support sustained him. "I was glad to be able sometimes to lean on him," said Churchill. He looked to Max to come up with innovative answers to the crushing Nazi attack. "I need his vital and vibrant energy," admitted Winston, who worked sixteen-hour days himself. Though Chamberlain had dismissed Beaverbrook's selection as Winston's "pet suggestion," once he gained power Churchill immediately installed his friend in this key position. Beaverbrook quickly increased the number of planes produced by the government in the same way he'd built a fortune by relentlessly manufacturing Fleet Street newspapers. Within weeks, Jock Colville told his diary, "Lord Beaverbrook is producing the goods in an astonishing way."

Joe Kennedy noticed the distinct change in Beaverbrook, no longer a voice for appeasement. "He didn't talk like his old self," Kennedy bemoaned in his diary. "He talked as a Minister of the Churchill Government should, I suppose, and seemed to be doing his best to sell me on the idea that things were still all right." After they spoke of Beaverbrook's efforts to strengthen British air defenses, Max finished with a moment of candor. No one could get to the bottom line like he could: "After all, if we can't think we are going to win," he concluded, almost philosophically, "there is no point in going on."

In the days ahead, Kennedy continued to heed Beaverbrook's advice and insights, despite their disagreements on the war. Joe understood why Winston relied so much on their mutual friend, even if the king recommended that Beaverbrook not be appointed to such an important post.

"He is really a very peculiar man," George VI confided to the American ambassador.

"Yes," Joe conceded, "but a great hustler."

On May 14, Kennedy learned of Beaverbrook's formal appointment. After returning from the theater that evening, Joe stopped to talk with his friend and showed Max a cable he'd just received from the U.S. ambassador in Rome. The message indicated Mussolini's Italy would no longer remain neutral as hoped, and instead was likely to join the Axis forces, particularly given Hitler's successful drives through Europe. Hours later, Beaverbrook called Kennedy and asked him to come to Admiralty House for a late-night meeting with the new prime minister. When Joe arrived, he saw there were no shimmering lights from the windows of Admiralty House, which was completely blacked out. A large platoon of soldiers stood guard, but quickly let him up to Churchill's old office. Winston "greeted me warmly," Kennedy recalled.

He found Churchill relaxing in one of his favorite comfortable chairs, again with cigar and Scotch highball in hand. He was seated next to Beaverbrook; his new secretary of state for war, Anthony Eden; and other top aides. "I couldn't help but think as I sat there talking to Churchill how ill-conditioned he looked," Kennedy wrote in his diary. "The affairs of Great Britain might be in the hands of the most dynamic individual in Great Britain but certainly not in the hands of the best judgment . . . I would say that a very definite shadow of defeat was hanging over them all last night."

Churchill proceeded to survey the bleak picture, while insistent England would not be beaten. If Italy joined Hitler's side in the fight, Churchill said, "it certainly will decrease our chances." He admitted that the British couldn't afford to lose any troops defending the French, who were soon to be overrun by the advancing Germans. Instead, Britain needed every bit of military muscle to fight a Nazi invasion of its own shores, especially with much of Europe's western coast available for U-boat bases.

"We need the troops in England anyway, for within a month we too are likely to be vigorously attacked," Churchill told Kennedy. "The whole situation is far from happy—almost desperate." He asked for Joe's help in convincing Roosevelt to send up to forty old destroyers "and all the airplanes you can spare."

Kennedy's response remained dubious; he was defensive about America's own security needs. If England didn't think it could survive a German onslaught, how could Winston expect Roosevelt to expend his own limited military resources? "It isn't fair to ask us to hold the bag for a war that the Allies expect to lose," Kennedy argued, a contrarian view undoubtedly alone in the room. "If we are to fight, under these circumstances it seems to me we would do better fighting in our backyard." He pointed out that most American warships were in the Pacific, and there weren't enough U.S airplanes to protect America's vast coastline from attack. "Even if we wanted to help, what could we do in a war that is likely to be over in a few months?"

Rather than take offense at this blunt assessment, Churchill continued to discuss his request to the president, calling Joe by his first name in a friendly tone. He warned that a lack of support from America might mean Franco's Spain would follow Italy in joining the enemy coalition. Then Churchill paused for a moment, both for effect and to gather his parting message about the future of the British Empire.

"Regardless of what Germany does to France, England will never give up so long as I am in power, even though England is burned to the ground," he asserted roundly. "The Government will move if it has to and take the fleet to Canada and fight on."

Over the next two days, Churchill and Kennedy talked repeatedly, with Roosevelt's reply indicating that he needed congressional approval to send even aged warships to aid Great Britain. Churchill expressed gratitude with the president's response, especially in light of Roosevelt's recent announcement to build up America's own air defenses. Churchill urged Joe not to be too depressed about the dire situation. "We have all got to put on a good front," he cautioned.

Late one night, Roosevelt called Kennedy on the telephone. The ambassador repeated his gloomy assessment contained in a private cable he'd sent to Washington. In his secret and personal diplomatic dispatch sent from the U.S. embassy, Kennedy had ended with what appears an allusion to Beaverbrook. IT IS THE VIEW OF MY FRIEND THAT NOTHING CAN SAVE THEM FROM ABSOLUTE DEFEAT UNLESS BY SOME TOUCH OF GENIUS AND GOD'S BLESSING THE PRESIDENT CAN DO IT, he wrote. Then Joe retreated to his country estate in Windsor for the weekend—a place away from the expected bombing in London—and hoped for some relaxation, knowing his wife and children were safe in America.

For Churchill, however, the outset of war meant a relentless effort to save his beloved homeland and family, virtually everything in life dear to him. His hope of gaining America's help in this struggle never faded, no matter how remote the odds, regardless of how many doomsayers he might encounter. Even his son, Randolph, wondered how he might achieve this goal, as they discussed it one morning in a family bathroom.

Looking in the mirror, Winston lathered his face and carefully shaved himself with his Valet razor. Then he turned with great intensity.

"I think I can see my way through," he told his son, as if he'd had an epiphany. "I shall drag the United States in."

20

A Spy in Their Midst

Keeping an eye on Joe Kennedy, spying on the American ambassador, posed a number of hazards for the British. Any action involving Kennedy, personally or professionally, presented the danger of unintended consequences, possibly affecting America's willingness to help Great Britain in her time of crisis. These undercover concerns came to a boiling point soon after Winston Churchill became prime minister in May 1940.

For several weeks, Churchill had known of a British secret service investigation of a serious security leak at Kennedy's U.S. embassy. Top-secret messages between Washington and London were winding up in the hands of the Nazis. His Majesty's agents kept Kennedy in the dark as they monitored the ambassador's whereabouts—along with suspected British "fifth column" advocates favoring a pact with Hitler instead of war.

British intelligence discovered many aspects of the ambassador's private life in London while his wife and family were back home. Churchill's advisers learned of the ambassador's secret extramarital affair with American writer Clare Boothe Luce—who, when in town, also happened to be seeing the prime minister's married son, Randolph.

Winston's top aide, Brendan Bracken, quite skilled with deception, addressed his concerns in a very private letter to the PM's son.

Bracken prayed Randolph would not consider this "a pompous lecture," and jocularly mentioned that "I believe you are even more indiscreet than I was at your age!" As the letter progressed, the true offense didn't seem to be infidelity, for Bracken made no reference to Randolph cheating on his bride, Pamela. In his dressing down, he also didn't comment on the hypocrisy of Kennedy as the self-promoting family man. Instead, he scolded Randolph for the great crime of conversing with his paramour about Kennedy and the prime minister in a way that could impact matters of state. "After you last saw your friend Mrs. Luce, she went to the American ambassador and told him that you had declared that your father 'hated Kennedy,'" Bracken related. "Kennedy is a very sensitive man, and believing what Clare said to be true, he has turned very sour. This is a most unfortunate development. Whatever you may think about Kennedy, he has influence with the Government of the United States, and believing as he does that your father is hostile to him, he is not likely to go out of his way to be over helpful in presenting any suggestions made by your father to the Government of the United States. I have not, of course, had a word with your father about this matter. My job is to minimize his difficulties. But I do beg of you to be a good boy, and above all, to be discreet."

Kennedy likely considered himself already discreet. On the trip back to Europe in March 1940, Joe mentioned casually, in a letter to Rose, that he had bumped into Clare aboard his ocean liner. His diary added "her gay conversation was a contrast to the greyness of sea and sky." With their spouses back home in America, Joe and Clare, two restless souls attracted to each other, resumed their affair. Joe later flew to Paris to spend a weekend with Clare in April 1940, at the Ritz. "JPK in bedroom all morning," she wrote cryptically in her diary. After talking together about the state of the world, Joe and Clare usually wound up in bed. "He couldn't keep his mouth shut or his pants on, a combination of weaknesses that no doubt added to his pleasure but detracted from his work," columnist James Reston later said of Kennedy's carousing in London.

Though accounts vary, several historians say Clare was enjoying dinner with Kennedy in May 1940, relaxing at his rented weekend English countryside estate in Windsor, when Joe received an urgent telephone call about a spy scandal inside his embassy.

Kennedy's top diplomatic assistant, Herschel Johnson, said Scotland Yard had just stopped by his office with terrible news. Because the lines might be tapped, "Johnson's language was guarded," Kennedy recalled, "but I gathered enough from what he said to learn that one of our clerks was suspected of having given out confidential information to sources allied to the Nazis." Given the lateness of the hour and the sensitivity of matters at hand, the ambassador asked Johnson to meet him the next morning at his Windsor country estate. It was then that Kennedy first heard the suspected spy's name: Tyler Kent.

Benedict Arnold didn't have a better pedigree than Tyler Kent. Claiming former U.S. president John Tyler as a distant cousin, Kent was a product of two of America's finest private schools, St. Alban's and Princeton University, and appeared to have a bright future ahead in government diplomacy. No one on Kennedy's staff thought him capable of espionage. If anything, Kent seemed simpatico with the ambassador's isolationist views. "He was always very well dressed—his suits were expensive and probably handmade—but there was certainly no reason to suspect him," remembered Page Huidekoper, one of the ambassador's aides, who saw Kent regularly going in and out of the top-secret file room. "I don't think anyone had a clue that he was sending messages to the Nazis."

At age twenty-eight, Kent had come to London in October 1939 and worked as a code clerk, a post that gave him extensive access to secret documents. Years earlier, his father had served as the U.S. consul in Manchuria, and those State Department connections helped Tyler land his first job in Moscow. With curly dark hair slickly parted on the side, he appeared a sophisticate, and was capable of speaking several languages. By nature, though, he remained strangely naïve. Inside the bowels of the Grosvenor Square embassy building, Kent carefully read and deciphered highly confidential messages between Washington and London, most notably the friendly exchanges between President Roosevelt and Winston Churchill. The more documents he read, the more Tyler Kent became outraged. At the time, three-quarters of the U.S. electorate opposed intervention and supported neutrality. Kent felt the Germans were a necessary bulwark against an even larger threat, Communist Russia. These confidential papers revealed how much the president favored Churchill as a replacement for Chamberlain, and the former's meddling in the internal politics of a foreign nation. If America knew of these secret dealings, Kent convinced himself, the political uproar would prevent Roosevelt from gaining a third term. Despite Roosevelt's well-publicized promises not to send American soldiers to fight in Europe, the papers examined by Kent also showed how much the president was preparing for war against Germany. "It was a complete lie of course—he [Roosevelt] was elaborately preparing to come in," recalled Malcolm Muggeridge, a British journalist who attended Kent's trial as an official observer. "But had it been possible to publish those details, and to show the complete contrast between what he [Roosevelt] was saying and what he was doing, I think it might have been the end of him."

Kent began squirreling away copies of the secret memos and messages (more than fifteen hundred documents in all) and kept them inside his London flat. He waited for the right moment to expose this duplicity between the American president and Churchill-led British officials. He envisioned giving these purloined papers to an isolationist congressman or a hungry newspaperman, and once the truth about this chicanery appeared, he, Tyler Kent believed, would be hailed as a national hero.

Inside the embassy, Kent wasn't the only one making duplicates of these top-secret papers. "Ambassador Kennedy was having copies of, shall we say, important political documents made for his own private collection," recalled Kent in a BBC interview forty years later, "and it was quite easy to slip in an extra carbon." Privately, both Kent and the ambassador, who knew each other barely if at all, were appalled by the prospect of an American war. Both disliked Jews and Communists, and increasingly distrusted Roosevelt to keep U.S. forces away from Britain's conflict. Kennedy later suggested that his copies of the documents were meant only for a future memoir, and there is no clear evidence that he intended to use them against Roosevelt. But at the time, British intelligence didn't take any chances. When Scotland Yard detectives spotted Tyler Kent meeting with a suspected German agent in October 1939, they launched a full investigation of his contacts and never told Kennedy. Instead, British agents kept Kennedy under surveillance for months, suspecting that Kent might be working at his boss's behest. "We had reached the point of bugging potential traitors and enemies," Randolph Churchill later recalled. "Joe Kennedy, the American ambassador, came under electronic surveillance." Even after British intelligence officials concluded they had enough evidence to arrest Kent, they deliberately waited to see if Kennedy could be ensnared.

The obsessive head of this MI5 investigation, Maxwell Knight, was a master of intrigue. A womanizer and an avid naturalist who kept parrots in his kitchen and garden snakes in his bathtub, Knight invented code names and held secret meetings in seedy hotels to avoid detection. One of his agents, Ian Fleming, later wrote the James Bond novels and based the character M on Knight, who signed his memos with that same sobriquet. By early February 1940, Churchill assumed a spy leak when his confidential cable to Roosevelt promising to stop searching

American ships was quickly learned by other nations. Churchill kept his distance from this highly volatile investigation, but there's no doubt he learned of the espionage taking place under Kennedy's nose. He kept quiet, though, acting none the wiser in the ambassador's presence. "Churchill was exceptional among British statesmen of his time for his familiarity with intelligence and his consuming interest in it," wrote British spy historian F. H. Hinsley. Kennedy wasn't forthcoming with Churchill, either, as the diplomatic dispatches clearly showed. While he was sympathetic to the British fight when conversing in London, his private dispatches sent home to Washington were devastatingly pessimistic. They predicted German victory and cautioned Roosevelt not to try to save England.

Kent's circle of like-minded friends included members of the Right Club, the secret society founded by Archibald Maule Ramsay, an archconservative Member of Parliament opposed to Churchill. Most Right Club members were anti-Semitic and favored diplomatic ties with Nazi Germany rather than war. They gathered often at the Russian Tea Room, a small café in South Kensington. At this place, Kent became friendly with Anna Wolkoff, the owner's beautiful daughter, who wound up introducing Kent to Ramsay. Inside the Russian Tea Room, Tyler shared his story about the secret transmissions between Roosevelt and Churchill, acting as if he were an unappreciated American patriot. Ramsay and Wolkoff, though, had other, more nefarious purposes in mind. One night in April, all three went to Kent's apartment to scrutinize the documents taken from the U.S. embassy. Wolkoff returned to make photographic copies of key documents, which she later gave to an Italian source, who relayed them into German hands. By then, British intelligence was already aware of their deceit. Knight and his team prepared to pounce and arrest them all. Winston knew of this espionage several weeks before he became prime minister in May, but the approval to end this plot came within days of his taking office.

As MI5 determined, the dragnet of spies in their midst included Sir

Oswald Mosley, an odious British fascist politician married to Diana Mitford, one of the Mitford sisters and a second cousin of Clementine Churchill. Mosley projected himself as a Hitler-like figure for England. With the Nazis as models, Mosley and his British Blackshirt followers attempted a similar assault on British democracy, without much success. Nevertheless, Diana's involvement with Mosley caused the Churchills a great deal of discomfort because of their previous close relationship with her. During the 1920s, when the Mitford family and the Churchills shared holidays together at Chartwell, Randolph felt romantic toward Diana; both had brilliant blue eyes characteristic of Clementine's family. In 1932, Mosley was on good enough terms with the Churchills to be invited to Randolph's "fathers and sons" dinner at Claridge's celebrating his twenty-first birthday. But by 1936, Diana had secretly married Mosley at the Berlin home of Nazi propaganda chief Joseph Goebbels, with Adolf Hitler as a guest. The Germans seemed enraptured with her blonde, Aryan looks. At the same time, Diana's sister Unity had all but committed herself to the Führer in an even more public way.

Despite his horror at this spectacle, Winston Churchill had asked Diana for her opinion of Hitler when he gathered material about the Führer profiled in his 1937 book, *Great Contemporaries*. Diana explained the German leader didn't like dealing with democratic leaders. "One day you are speaking to one man, the next day to his successor," Hitler complained to her. By 1940, in Churchill's estimate, Mosley's political extremism had become a security risk. British intelligence showed Mosley was part of the Right Club crowd that included Ramsay. Though there didn't appear to be any evidence linking them to the Tyler Kent case, both Mosley and his wife, Diana, were arrested. They spent three years detained without trial in a British facility. Swept up in the fear of a Nazi takeover, Winston told the War Cabinet that he worried a puppet government run "under Mosley or some such person" could turn Britain into "a slave state." Urged on by war secretary

Anthony Eden and others in British intelligence, Churchill used the Kent case to round up dozens of "fifth column" suspects, out of fear of another internal spying plot. "If any doubt existed the persons in question should be detained without delay," Churchill declared, invoking Regulation 18B of the Emergency Powers Act. He vowed to find other fifth columnists and root out "the malignancy in our midst."

For Kennedy, the Tyler Kent case caused even more embarrassment. When embassy aide Herschel Johnson arrived at Kennedy's country estate, he explained to Joe the sordid details of the British investigation as previously outlined by Knight and Guy Liddell, his MI5 counterespionage supervisor. In order to arrest Kent along with Anna Wolkoff, the British government needed Kennedy to waive Kent's diplomatic immunity. Incensed by Kent's actions, the ambassador quickly approved.

Late in the morning of May 20, Knight and a handful of Scotland Yard detectives descended upon Tyler Kent's apartment. Kennedy sent along Franklin Gowen, his embassy's second secretary. "In case Kent says his rooms cannot be searched because of his diplomatic immunity, tell him to take the matter up with me," Kennedy instructed. When they arrived and knocked on the door, a voice twice yelled, "Don't come in." The authorities rushed through the entrance. They found Kent getting out of bed with his mistress, Irene Danischewsky, a Russian-born redhead married to a British merchant. "Both were scantily attired," Kennedy mentioned in his unpublished memoir.

Scattered throughout the apartment were confidential papers. Files were labeled "Germany," "Russia," "Jews," and "Churchill." Detectives discovered photographic plates of two highly confidential memos involving the president, including a telegram from Roosevelt in May about fighter planes, anti-aircraft equipment, and steel purchases requested by Churchill. A padlocked, heavy-leather-bound binder contained the names of the Right Club members. Gowen, the ambassador's man at the scene, thought Kent's calm mistress might be a secret agent for British intelligence. "From the way she behaved and looked at the police officers she made me think that perhaps she had been 'planted' on Kent by Scotland Yard," he reported. But Danischewsky cooperated with detectives, concerned her husband might find out about her dalliances with Kent for "admittedly immoral purposes."

Knight and the Scotland Yard inspectors then whisked Kent from his apartment to the American embassy, where an interrogation took place in Kennedy's presence. The ambassador sounded almost as incredulous as his clerk.

"This is quite a serious situation that you have got your country involved in," Kennedy told him. "From the kind of family you come from—people who have fought for the United States—one would not expect you to let us all down."

Kent remained defiant. "In what way?" he asked.

"You don't think you have?" Kennedy demanded. "What did you think you were doing with our codes and telegrams?" He knew Kent had recently applied for an embassy transfer to Berlin.

"It was only for my own information," Kent insisted.

Kennedy likely realized this lowly clerk's betrayal had exposed his own high-stakes double-dealing. When Churchill virtually begged for old American destroyers to protect his country, Joe promised to help push Roosevelt within the restraints of the neutrality law. Instead, as documents stolen by Kent revealed, Kennedy had predicted Britain's downfall to the president: "If we had to protect our own lives," he advised, "we would do better fighting in our own backyard."

Kent wasn't the only aide poorly serving the ambassador. Three months earlier, British authorities tipped off Herschel Johnson that a spy, code-named "The Doctor," was operating inside the U.S. embassy. All Washington-bound messages, they warned, were being intercepted and obtained by the Germans. At that time, Kennedy was still in Florida and apparently learned nothing about the warning. Rather than tell his boss, Johnson, a career diplomat who disliked the brash ambassador, went over his head. He informed Assistant Secretary of State James Clement Dunn in Washington that "practically everything from Ambassador Kennedy's dispatches to President Roosevelt, including reports of his interviews with British statesmen and officials," were winding up in Nazi hands. During the height of the Kent investigation, another Churchill ally in British intelligence, William Stephenson (famously called Intrepid), informed FBI director J. Edgar Hoover of the espionage plot during an April visit to the United States. But in his own memoir, Kennedy claimed he had no idea of "this extraordinary story" until Johnson alerted him that late May weekend in Windsor.

For nearly seven months, while agents followed Kent's movements around London, the American ambassador was kept in the dark. "I was naturally distressed by the incident and by the failure (that I had no hesitancy in commenting on) of the Scotland Yard Officials to bring their suspicions about Kent to our attention months before," Kennedy said in his memoirs. "Their failure had led us to the dissemination of much confidential information as well as spreading broadside data in the form of true readings that would make insecure our most secret codes."

Kennedy's petty objections must have sounded absurd to Knight, the rest of British intelligence, and Churchill himself, all of whom knew better. American officials were shocked at the security breach inside Kennedy's embassy, the heart of their foreign intelligence in Europe. "Nothing like this has ever happened in American history," declared Assistant Secretary of State Breckinridge Long, worried how the broken codes had exposed U.S. thinking to the Germans. "It is a terrible blow—almost a major catastrophe."

Over the next six weeks, while Roosevelt and Secretary of State Cordell Hull struggled to repair the damage, Kennedy blamed Kent solely, acting like a victim rather than an inept administrator. "The

Germans did not need any secret service in Europe; they didn't have to guess about anything," Kennedy later explained. "They could just read the facts about Great Britain and America and most European countries by reading the secret London–Washington diplomatic dispatches and cable traffic since the London Embassy was the clearing point for nearly all European matters on the continent." Roosevelt ordered "a diplomatic blackout" at embassies around the world until a new set of secret codes for transmitting secret information could be put in place. Aware of his vulnerability, Kennedy entrusted his own duplicates of these key documents to his loyal aide Edward Moore, who secretly returned with them to the United States. Kennedy pleaded with Churchill's aides to protect him from scandal with reporters. "They have discovered that one of the American Ambassador's Confidential Clerks is a spy and has been furnishing Miss Wolkoff (Russian agent) with photostatic copies of all Kennedy's most confidential correspondence, including the Prime Minister's personal messages to President Roosevelt," wrote Harold Nicolson, chief censor at Churchill's Ministry of Information, in his diary. "Kennedy begs us to keep this out of the press but the American journalists have already got the scent of something of the sort."

Kent, as an American abroad, soon went to trial in England and was given a seven-year prison sentence in November 1940. The general public wasn't allowed into the private proceedings, which were surrounded by a secrecy strictly enforced by Churchill's government. "If America had been at war I would have recommended that he be sent back to America and shot as a traitor," Kennedy later claimed. "But in the circumstances prevailing we had to leave it to British justice."

The ambassador wasn't in any position to argue. The whole haphazard, unprofessional nature of Kennedy's stewardship seemed stunningly on display with this criminal case. Without drawing much public scrutiny to the volatile contents of Kent's stolen documents, Churchill had managed to neutralize the troublesome American ambassador and his remaining influence in Washington. Because key testimony and papers remained secret for decades, historians have struggled to gauge just how much Churchill affected the Kent investigation. In his book about Churchill and British intelligence, David Stafford suggests Knight's actions were influenced by his good friend Desmond Morton, Winston's top military intelligence aide, concluding that "Churchill may well have known what was going on and ordered the trap closed at a moment that suited him." Kennedy considered the young clerk "a traitor as well as thief," but the ambassador "was effectively silenced" because of the Tyler Kent matter, observed Kent biographers Ray Bearse and Anthony Read. "Although he may have agreed with Kent's stated motives for stealing the documents—and indeed he was also collecting copies of signals for his own purposes—as ambassador he was outraged at actions that he regarded as disloyal to himself," they concluded. "The chief of mission is ultimately responsible for overseeing security precautions, so Kennedy found Kent's treachery a deep personal embarrassment."

Roosevelt no longer trusted his ambassador's judgment or competence. In August 1940 the president sent over another special envoy, William "Wild Bill" Donovan, to assess the British situation. Donovan came away impressed by Churchill's war effort, while trying to avoid the discredited American ambassador. "Frankly and honestly I do not enjoy being a dummy," Kennedy complained to FDR, threatening again to resign. But Roosevelt backed Donovan and, mindful of the Tyler Kent fiasco, asked him to put together an American intelligence service, eventually called the Office of Strategic Services (OSS), patterned on the British model. From now on, the president's secret messages back and forth to Churchill would be sent through naval channels, rather than normal diplomatic ones through Kennedy's embassy. As FDR's top aide, Harry Hopkins, explained, "Ever since the Tyler Kent case, the Boss doesn't trust State." The same could be said of Joe Kennedy.

21

Grace under Fire

The distant moaning sound of a wounded Nazi plane falling from the sky grew louder until it became an overpowering din, destined to end with a deadly explosion. The plummeting aircraft appeared headed straight for the Windsor country home of Ambassador Joseph Kennedy.

Not far away, British anti-aircraft fire had sliced through the German Messerschmitt's propeller, causing the fighter plane to tumble virtually out of control. It soared over oak trees and skimmed over the top of Kennedy's roof, looking for a place to land. On the ground, Joe and a journalist pal from *Collier's* magazine watched as the Luftwaffe pilot, visible through his plane's windshield, frantically tried not to crash.

"We could see the fuzz on the pilot's face and almost count his buttons," Kennedy attested. "I thought for a time that it was going to land on my home." Instead, at the last minute, he said, the Nazi piloted the plane into a nearby park and was presumably arrested.

The bloody war Joe Kennedy never wanted had a constant way of finding him. By September 1940, the Battle of Britain—Churchill's succinct name for the German terrorist attacks designed to break England's will—arrived in full force, steadily taking its toll. During the months-long aerial combat, thousands of British civilians lost their lives. Many worried Hitler's ground forces would soon invade England, just as Kennedy privately predicted. Roosevelt mostly ignored his ambassador's advice, but asked Kennedy to stay in London during this fateful crisis, at least until the American presidential elections were over in November.

At the Windsor country home where he spent weekends (and where critics said he hid like a coward from bombs falling on London), Kennedy remained trapped in a fate determined by the politics of war. "It is by far the most unsatisfactory method of doing business that I have ever seen, and if it weren't for the possibility of invasion I would resign today," he fumed.

Overhead, Nazi planes unleashed bombs in relentless waves, devastating enough so no one felt safe. One evening, Kennedy climbed atop the seven-story American embassy building and stared past midnight at the illuminated clouds. Towering flames from explosions on the ground accompanied a chaotic spray of British anti-aircraft fire and flailing searchlights seeking the enemy up in the sky. Kennedy felt certain the world, as his family had known it, was coming to an end. "The last three nights in London have been simply hell," he wrote to Rose. "Last night I put on my steel helmet and went up to the roof of the Chancery and stayed up there until two o'clock in the morning watching the Germans come over, in relays every ten minutes, and drop bombs, setting terrific fires."

Earlier that day, as Kennedy walked along a London street, a bomb fell nearby. "We heard it coming and dove into the bushes," he recalled in his letter home. "It struck with a dull thud." Another explosive smashed the barracks near the American embassy—the same place where his family once hosted lively parties with the future Duke of Devonshire and other British royalty before the war. Looking out from the roof, Kennedy remained transfixed by the defiant image of

London's largest cathedral, still standing amid the smoky destruction. As he described to Rose, "You could see the dome of St. Paul's silhouetted against a blazing inferno."

Kennedy felt very much alone in London. He'd become a pariah among many once-friendly acquaintances and party-givers who now hated him, not necessarily because his judgments had been in error but because they feared he might have been right. "I trust that Joe Kennedy, the jaunty American ambassador, is wrong, for he prophesies the end of everything, and goes about saying that England is committing suicide," wrote Sir Henry "Chips" Channon in his diary. "My reason tells me he is wrong, that everything is on our side, but my intuition warns me that he may have something."

Aware of the random dangers facing Kennedy, the father of nine children, Roosevelt called his ambassador for his fifty-second birthday. They spoke only in vague generalities. "Taking into account that everybody might be listening, he made rather a perfunctory inquiry as to how we were all getting along," Joe wrote in his diary. He resented how Roosevelt had lied to him so freely—claiming the State Department wanted him to remain in London, when the real reason was FDR's desire to keep the vituperative Kennedy from muddling up his ongoing reelection campaign. To his wife, Kennedy conceded he felt abused by the man he had helped put in the White House. "I haven't the slightest doubt," he said of Roosevelt's top advisers, "that they would turn around tomorrow and throw me in the ash can."

What Kennedy couldn't figure out, however, was Churchill's geniality toward him, a warmth of spirit and personal courtesy that even Joe knew wasn't deserved. Immediately after the Tyler Kent debacle, Winston kept his distance, avoiding meetings requested by Kennedy. From his intelligence sources, Churchill learned of Kennedy's cables, especially those aspersions concerning Winston's drinking and overall judgment, mixed with hopelessness about England's chance for survival. Many in Churchill's circle, including Randolph, could no longer abide the dissembling American ambassador and considered him a traitor. "I thought my daffodils were yellow until I met Joe Kennedy," was one apocryphal joke attributed to Churchill's camp at the time. But after conferring with Beaverbrook, Winston decided to change his tack toward the irascible ambassador. Joe complained bitterly to Max that he'd not seen Churchill for more than three weeks. Beaverbrook admitted that "Randolph had poisoned his father against me," Kennedy recounted. "I told Beaverbrook to hell with Churchill. I didn't give a damn." (This conversation apparently prompted Bracken's rebuke to Randolph to keep his mouth shut about Kennedy when entertaining Clare Boothe Luce.)

From then on, Winston adopted a different approach. Rather than keep the ambassador in political isolation, Churchill decided to include him in war meetings and personal conversations. With almost indefatigable optimism and surprising candor, Winston kept trying to convince Kennedy to support his cause, as if these attempts were still friendly gestures rather than smart tactics. When Kennedy asked pointblank about England's chance of surviving Hitler's threatened invasion, Churchill answered in a pragmatic way that Kennedy could appreciate: "In the secrecy of this room, I don't know," he confided to Kennedy. "I can't see anything beyond the defense of this island. I think, however, that if he [Hitler] licks us, he will take you on next."

Churchill knew Kennedy resided in the president's doghouse, effectively banished from the administration's war planning, even though he served in the thick of battle in London. Churchill "knows quite well that I have no standing at the moment" with the Roosevelt crowd, Kennedy acknowledged in his diary. Over the past several months, Churchill's allies, such as Baruch, had successfully persuaded the president to ignore his London ambassador's defeatist predictions. Kennedy suggested Britain might agree to a negotiated peace settlement with Hitler, something that Churchill took pains to correct with Roosevelt. "Our intention is, whatever happens, to fight on to the end in this Island," he insisted. Deliberately, Winston included Kennedy in the exchange of diplomatic correspondence between himself and the American president. Joe couldn't figure out the underlying motivation for Winston's courtesy. "It is of course apparent that we are being kept completely in ignorance of what Roosevelt is doing," Kennedy wrote in his diary. "I am interested to find out, and I will if possible, just why it is Churchill sees any reason at all for keeping me advised; because if he didn't send me these cables occasionally I would have no conception whatsoever of what is going on . . . Why he bothers to count me in is a mystery."

In close proximity, Kennedy often witnessed Churchill's grace under pressure. On the Saturday night in June when they learned Italy's Mussolini had joined Hitler in the fight against England, a blow that might have bowed another leader, Churchill managed to share some humor with the American ambassador, inviting him into the Cabinet room.

"Well, you certainly picked a nice time to be Prime Minister," Kennedy said, in his smart-alecky American way.

Rather than being offended, Winston replied candidly, with his own sense of wit: "They wouldn't have given me the Prime Ministership if there had been any meat left on the bone," he conceded.

Kennedy, the Wall Street pro but amateur diplomat, seemed oblivious to Churchill's more subtle manipulations of power. Only vaguely did Joe appear to grasp Churchill's masterful understanding of Europe's military conflicts, the historian's sweeping vision of events as they unfolded, and the anticipation of how he might effectively turn potential massacre into a national victory. Mostly, what Joe couldn't understand about Churchill was his magnanimity, his personal appreciation for someone who had lost out in the public debate and now found himself alone and discarded. No one in London seemed more in the wilderness now than Joe Kennedy, the unreconstructed advocate of appeasement. In his remaining time in England, Kennedy would witness one of history's most remarkable chess masters at his peak, faced with a daunting enemy at his doorstep and his empire on the brink of extinction. Yet between Kennedy and his sons, only Jack seemed to recognize Churchill's greatness.

The Battle of Britain culminated a bloody summer for Churchill's government, starting with the miracle at Dunkirk, France. In late May and early June 1940, more than three hundred thousand British and French troops, unable to stop the advancing Nazi army and fighter planes in France, evacuated successfully from Dunkirk's beaches, crossing the English Channel to safety. Worried the British Expeditionary Force sent to help the French might all be captured, Churchill dispatched navy ships to Dunkirk and assembled a flotilla of fishing boats, pleasure craft, and virtually every floatable transport imaginable to save his fighting forces from death and imprisonment. It was an ignominious retreat, but a painfully necessary one. Churchill turned a potential disaster into a triumphant rescue, enlivening his nation's spirit for the rest of the war. Doubters, though, compared Dunkirk to Churchill's disastrous World War I decisions in the Dardanelles, which forced his resignation from the Admiralty. This time would be different, however. In churches and on the radio, the nation prayed for the troops' deliverance. Beaverbrook, who buoyed Winston in the worst of times, argued pragmatically for the evacuation and to stop further Royal Air Force combat flights over France. "Let's get along home," Max urged, so the British could regroup their forces and fight another day.

By July 1940 the aerial attacks of the German Luftwaffe extended into England. After the French government fell, putting most of western Europe in Axis control, Nazi warplanes began a relentless bombardment of London and other cities. Churchill rejected any plans to send the royal family or government to Canada in case of German invasion. "I believe we shall make them rue the day they try to invade our island," he vowed. Winston advised his Cabinet to be ready to lose their possessions, and perhaps their lives, if necessary, to save their beloved nation. He rejected foreign secretary Lord Halifax's suggestion of a negotiated peace settlement with Hitler, an idea favored by Ambassador Kennedy. In a splendidly defiant June 4 speech, Churchill declared, "... We shall fight on the beaches, we shall fight on the landing-grounds, we shall fight in the fields and in the streets, we shall fight in the hills. We shall never surrender." As the crowds cheered this rallying cry, Winston provided a wry addition, delivered sotto voce to reporters such as Edward R. Murrow: "... And if they do come, we shall hit them on the head with beer bottles, for that is all we shall have to fight them with!"

Winston's wit and cool resiliency, even when confronted with the cruel tasks of war, made him beloved by his soldiers and generals, his staff and colleagues, and his desperate nation yearning for leadership. As Jock Colville, his personal secretary, wrote in his diary at the time, "It is refreshing to work with somebody who refuses to be depressed even by the most formidable danger that has ever threatened this country." Churchill's never-say-die attitude, Winston claimed, reflected the greatness of the British Empire rather than of him. "It was the nation and the race dwelling all around the globe that had the lion's heart," he later wrote. "I had the luck to be called upon to give the roar."

Unlike other statesmen so dour and gray, Churchill, captured vividly in press photographs, projected his roused feelings about the war. In one memorable picture, the prime minister, ever the showman, wearing his pinstripe suit and bowler hat, cradled a Thompson submachine gun in his arms with a menacing grin. The Nazi propagandists said Churchill looked like a Chicago gangster with his tommy gun, but the image indelibly expressed the new British mood to fight rather than negotiate. When Churchill heard about King George VI practicing his shooting in the royal garden, intending to kill a German himself in case of an invasion, Winston upped the ante. "If he felt that way about it, he [Churchill] would get him a Tommy gun so he could kill a lot of

Germans," as Brendan Bracken recalled the story for Kennedy, well aware of the power of images. The next time Kennedy talked with the king, who had nearly been killed by one bombing attack, the monarch confirmed he was the proud owner of a submachine gun provided by Churchill.

These heroic images and rallying cries by Churchill provided ballast for the English people, emboldening them to carry on rather than capitulate. They overcame the sinking feelings of doom inflicted by the stark realities of war. Many feared Hitler's planned invasion—called Operation Sea Lion—would be unleashed any day. By September, when Hitler launched the London Blitz, German fighter planes began attacking urban neighborhoods as well as military targets. Schools, houses, and churches were shattered, burned, and turned into rubble. Thousands slept in the Underground at night. Flames and smoke consumed the skies, as the streets of London became a hellish cosmorama. More than four hundred citizens of London were killed during the first night of intense bombing, part of the nearly thirty thousand lives lost over the next several months.

In stirring speeches and radio broadcasts, Churchill's rhetoric displayed all the ingenuity he brought to other facets of his leadership. His words included everything from biblical themes of sacrifice and redemption to literary and historical references known to most schoolchildren. His tribute to the brave RAF pilots defending the British Isles against Nazi fighter planes ("Never in the field of human conflict was so much owed by so many to so few") resonated with Shakespeare's famous St. Crispin's Day speech in *Henry V* ("We few, we happy few, we band of brothers"). Perhaps most memorable was his June 18 speech, after the fall of France, in which he eloquently but bluntly underlined the high stakes:

> Upon this battle depends the survival of Christian civilisation.
> Upon it depends our own British life, and the long continuity

of our institutions and our Empire. The whole fury and might of the enemy must very soon be turned on us. Hitler knows that he will have to break us in this island or lose the war. If we can stand up to him, all Europe may be free and the life of the world may move forward into broad, sunlit uplands. But if we fail, then the whole world, including the United States, including all that we have known and cared for, will sink into the abyss of a new Dark Age made more sinister, and perhaps more protracted, by the lights of perverted science. Let us therefore brace ourselves to our duties, and so bear ourselves that, if the British Empire and its Commonwealth last for a thousand years, men will still say, "This was their finest hour."

Despite their sharp differences, Joe Kennedy couldn't help but admire Churchill's performance. He obtained a copy of this speech, and another, both autographed personally by the Prime Minister, and sent them home to his family, enclosed with his letter describing London's bombing. "I had them all signed for the children," he advised Rose, "as I think they will be important historical documents." He knew his son Jack, an admirer of Churchill, would be especially pleased.

Between the families, there were other courtesies and kindnesses, such as when Clementine thanked the ambassador for sending her and Winston a copy of America's *Vogue* magazine featuring a photo of their youngest daughter, Mary. During Winston's laborious wait to get the United States to send old destroyers to buttress Britain's defenses, Joe enclosed a small personal gift to tide over the prime minister: a Virginia ham, which arrived on the American luxury liner SS *Washington*. "While I know there are things you would rather have from the States than hams, still a 'ham what am' is better than something what ain't, and I hope you will like it," wrote Kennedy, with his own version of the wordplay Churchill enjoyed. Eventually, Winston felt comfortable enough in Kennedy's presence to tease him about his constant refusals to share in a drink of Scotch and a good smoke. "My God, you make me feel as if I should go around in sack cloth and ashes," Churchill joked.

Between Joe and Winston, there were enough genial exchanges that, if not for the current life-or-death crisis, might have cemented a lasting friendship. As is, they shared a very close mutual friend in Lord Beaverbrook, who continued throughout the Battle of Britain to include Joe in private conversations about the war. In September, Churchill and Beaverbrook met for dinner with Kennedy, accompanied by three U.S. military advisers sent to London by Roosevelt without consulting his ambassador. The two nations finalized details of the destroyer deal, while Kennedy once again vented his frustration about being circumvented by Roosevelt. "I made it clear in the presence of all that I had never been asked about the condition of these destroyers and I didn't know much about them anyway, but the deal seemed to me to be an 'as is' deal," Kennedy later recorded.

The arrangement was very advantageous to the United States, which acquired long-term leases to run military bases on British territory in the Caribbean and Newfoundland in return for fifty mothballed American destroyers left over from World War I. Faced with the advancing Nazi danger, England had no real choice but to accept. During their meeting, Churchill asked if the destroyers needed to be overhauled and if they possessed such basic modern equipment as submarine detectors. Roosevelt's advisers were of little help.

Beaverbrook turned to Joe. "Will they be able to come across the ocean on their own power?" Max asked.

"Perhaps," said Kennedy, his air still petulant.

Near the end of the evening, Winston and Joe talked about the deadly bombing in London and surrounding cities. "Churchill asked me how many people I thought had been killed by air raids in this country," Kennedy recalled. Winston expressed confidence that the RAF would maintain air superiority over Germany, shooting down more planes than Hitler could afford to lose, especially if he intended to launch a Russian front. Thanks to Beaverbrook's extraordinary job increasing production, Britain had twenty times the reserve planes it had had when Churchill became prime minister four months earlier. Even if Hitler's troops intended to invade England soon, Max's Spitfires would ensure their failure. "It was very apparent, watching Churchill and Beaverbrook, that Beaverbrook has very great influence with Churchill and is more than likely to have great weight in any ultimate decisions," Kennedy observed. Before they were through, Joe broke out a box of cigars and gave them as a gift to Winston. He joked that this "would even up the destroyer-bases deal."

The meal was reminiscent of their October 1939 luncheon together, when Kennedy first learned of Roosevelt's plan to go around him and deal with Churchill directly. At that earlier lunch, Joe had raised the question of German bombing of English cities (exactly as it happened a year later), and Winston explained the need for America to enter the war as soon as possible to keep the Nazi threat away from U.S. shores. Presciently, Churchill also explained the strategic need for a two-front war that would include the Soviet Union as an ally rather than an enemy. "The danger to the world was Germany and not Russia," Winston told Kennedy privately, "and it was therefore the Nazi regime that must be finished off."

Now, as prime minister overseeing the battle for Britain's very existence, and with the evil intentions of the Nazis made clear, Churchill insisted on carrying through to victory. Nothing less would do. He felt confident Roosevelt, as soon as his reelection was secured in November 1940, would join the fight against Hitler. "You know that I was the only one who wasn't discouraged at the outlook when I took this job and now most people are coming around to my way of thinking," Churchill reminded Kennedy. "We are going to beat this man."

As the world watched Britain rally its forces, however, Joe Kennedy remained unconvinced. He considered England a lost cause and was ready to go home.

22

Crash Landing

A sense of urgency filled Clare Boothe Luce's private correspondence with Joe Kennedy throughout the summer and fall of 1940. The imminent threat of Hitler overwhelming all of Europe, and perhaps America, drove her discreet relationship with the isolationist U.S. ambassador to another level.

"I'd rather see you, my sweet, stay right in dangerous old London than to come home and identify yourself with the Third Term campaign," she wrote.

As much as she supported Churchill, Clare strongly opposed a third term for President Roosevelt and hoped to enlist Kennedy in the campaign to stop it. Dripping with a playwright's sarcastic humor, her letter from New York sounded as if she might as well have said "Third Reich" instead of "Third Term." In an earlier draft of the letter, Clare clearly worked on this mocking phrase, "the Third Term campaign," until she got it just right, enough to draw a laugh out of Kennedy an ocean away. What Joe might do next, however, seemed anyone's guess.

At age thirty-seven, Clare Boothe Luce was at the height of her powers, one of the best-known women in America. She was finishing up her book about Europe's battlefronts, called *Europe in the Spring,* based on her reporting for *Life,* the glossy periodical owned by her wealthy publisher husband, Henry Luce. She detailed the fight against the Nazis across the Continent as a wake-up call for America. Her book later climbed to the top of the best-seller lists and proved her most widely praised. Previously, she penned another hit Broadway play, *Margin of Effort,* a prophetic spy satire about the murder of a Nazi agent inside a German consulate in an American city. Her play underlined the evils brewing in Hitler's regime and how fascism could infect the United States.

Both "Harry" and Clare Luce were appalled by what they witnessed of Nazi Germany when they visited Berlin in 1938, and their internationalist views differed from Kennedy's isolationism. Both ardent Republicans, the Luces detested Roosevelt personally and were determined to stop a third term. Some of their dislike stemmed from FDR's condescension when the couple had visited him at Hyde Park. The president—perhaps recalling when she was Bernie Baruch's girlfriend in 1932 rather than the wife of a media potentate—"treated Clare cavalierly as just a young, pretty (silly) thing," described author David Halberstam. Using all their influence, the Luces hoped to convince Joe Kennedy to support their favorite 1940 candidate for president, Republican Wendell Willkie. A Democratic defection by Kennedy could bring thousands of ethnic Catholic voters from the cities along with him. Henry Luce considered Willkie to be a great man. His Time-Life magazines treated Willkie with the same abundant coverage accorded Winston Churchill and later John F. Kennedy. Harry's magazines also flattered Joe Kennedy, though Clare's attention was even more direct.

"I think of you constantly and pray with Churchill that it will come out all right in the end," Clare wrote to him shortly after war in England began and she had returned to the United States. She called his son Jack's book "a masterpiece," and later enclosed a copy of her newly completed book about Europe faced with war, which included Joe's comments. Like the famous men she favored, Clare knew how to compartmentalize sex and politics. With beguiling style, she could also combine them to her advantage. "Did anyone ever tell you, Mr. Ambassador, that you have a very fine smile?" she teased. "I hope you are having plenty of occasions to use it, but from what I read in the papers, Mr. Hitler is still doing his best to wipe it off." Yet when bombing began in London, she sent a most sobering message: "We are tormented with worry about you. God keep you safe."

When Clare's book arrived on October 1, the ambassador sent her a letter of thanks. "Of course, I immediately turned to the part that spoke about me," he admitted. As part of their pithy showbiz-influenced banter, Joe feigned annoyance at his portrayal, only to quickly forgive Clare's literary transgressions. "I am sure you couldn't or wouldn't write anything about me that would be half as bad as the things you know about me," he jested. Against the backdrop of war, they sounded like characters from the nation's popular movie *Gone with the Wind*, with Joe as a gruff Rhett Butler to Clare's coquettish Scarlett O'Hara. "So maybe I should be mad," he concluded about her book, "but I really don't give a damn."

Clare tried to persuade Joe away from his rigid stance against joining Great Britain in war. Throughout Europe, she'd seen too much of Hitler's destruction to believe in Kennedy's hope for a negotiated peace. "Oh all right! I'm an internationalist—and you are an isolationist—so we can never, perhaps on this, agree," she wrote in one note. "You will see darling Joe that there can be no progress, no peace, no security until we make up our minds, as Germany has made up its, where the hell for the next thousand years we think we are going," she concluded.

By October 1940, Joe decided to leave for America as soon as possible. He realized Churchill had successfully pushed back German air attacks. The much-feared invasion of England's shores would not take place. "I've just got the teeniest, weeniest suspicions that nobody would like to have me home at this time, but with the invasion prospect eliminated they are going to have me, whether they like it or not," he wrote to Clare. "Frankly, everything has happened to me so far except really being hit, and I don't think I need have any hesitancy now about going home after experiencing 136 air raids."

Clare also wanted to see Kennedy stay in London, at least until November's presidential election was over. She shared the same view of Kennedy as the White House insiders, though for very different reasons. When she heard her discreet lover might be coming home to endorse Roosevelt publicly with a radio speech, she tried frantically to persuade Kennedy otherwise. While not particularly faithful in marriage, Clare shared a strong political bond with her husband, Henry Luce, both avowedly committed to FDR's Republican rival, Willkie. After all her pillow talk with Joe—hearing his rage about Roosevelt, his ungrateful patter, and his self-absorbed slights, which appalled so many Londoners but which Clare devoured as gossipy catnip—she believed some twisted deal with the president's camp was compelling Kennedy to be two-faced. She urged him not to go on the radio and rally Catholics for a third FDR term.

"I know too well your private opinions not also to know that half of what you say (if you say it) you really won't believe in your heart," she implored. "Please remember that the rift that the election of FDR will drive through the national heart is the same rift your speech in support of a third term is going to drive through mine tomorrow . . . Holy God, the thing I can't bear is everybody telling me . . . 'See, what we told you about Kennedy is true!'"

At this crucial point in history, both Roosevelt and Churchill worried what Kennedy might say upon his return to America. Top advisers such as Harry Hopkins and Brendan Bracken did all they could behind the scenes to influence the ambassador's decisions and make sure he had as little effect as possible. It seemed the only person who wanted Kennedy home, without reservation, was his wife. Though their children were mostly grown or away at school, Joe's absence had been difficult for Rose and the whole family, especially with their knowing London's dangers. After so many memorable times living together at the embassy, the Kennedys had been apart for much of the past year. "We read in the paper this morning that a plane crashed very near you," wrote fourteen-year-old Bobby to his father. "It said that over here now you are called 'The worst bombed Ambassador' . . . We have missed you an awful lot."

With considerable savvy, Rose advised her husband about the murmurings back in the States. "Between you & me, it is the same old story," she wrote. "They think the Pres. [*sic*] does not want you home before the election due to your explosive—defeatist point of view, as you might so easily throw a bomb which would explode sufficiently to upset his chances." She leavened this blunt assessment with her own brand of humor, the kind they always enjoyed regardless of the distance apart. "I wanted to go to the W[hite] H[ouse] as a wife, say I am worried about your health, think you have done enough—guarantee to chloroform you until after the election, & say you should be brought home."

Warned about Kennedy's plans, Roosevelt invited him on October 17 to return home for consultation. The president extended the offer in an ever-so-friendly way, before his embittered ambassador could insist on an ultimatum. "I know what an increasingly severe strain you have been under during the past weeks," the president began, "and I think it is altogether owing to you that you get a chance to get away and get some relief." His note clearly instructed Kennedy not to speak to the press, not say anything when he arrived in New York, and to remain quiet "until you and I have had a chance to agree upon what should be said," after a White House meeting.

Kennedy left England on the first day of Tyler Kent's secret trial for spying. Officials on both sides of the Atlantic were aware of the case's potential explosiveness, particularly if the Churchill-Roosevelt correspondence became known. The Allies had done a good job of keeping the lowly embassy clerk under wraps, out of the glare of publicity. Yet the ambassador—who had his own copy of the secret exchanges— remained a wild card, leaving an uncertainty how he might react if provoked. Churchill stroked Joe's ego, assuring him of his personal support. He invited the departing ambassador to 10 Downing Street, where the two posed together with stilted smiles for photographers. Winston said he assumed Joe would help the president with his reelection campaign. In Kennedy's bidding farewell to the prime minister, there existed a feeling that his departure for America might become permanent and the two would never see each other again.

"I don't want a new man over here," Churchill told Kennedy during their private meeting, "and you can be of great help as this thing progresses." Winston claimed he would send a letter to FDR asking to retain the same London ambassador during the war. Kennedy let him know of his unhappiness. "I reminded him that I was having a row with Roosevelt because of the manner in which the White House ignored the Embassy and did business with the Prime Minister direct," he later wrote.

In reality, Churchill wasn't sorry to see Kennedy go. For the past several months, Churchill's team had steadily undermined Kennedy with the White House. During the Tyler Kent investigation, British intelligence monitored the American ambassador's activities and became well acquainted with his private views, especially about Roosevelt. At one point, Brendan Bracken, Winston's most discreet confidant, gathered intercepted cables and telephone calls containing Kennedy's most critical comments and forwarded them to White House aide Harry Hopkins, who then informed the president. It was proof positive of the rumors Roosevelt had heard about Kennedy's disloyalty and dangerousness.

With surprising naïveté, Kennedy seemed unaware of these betrayals. He didn't know Bracken—the friendly Irishman who cheerfully obtained Churchill's autograph for the Kennedy kids back home—was his most devastating critic. Similarly, Joe counted Harry Hopkins as a friend, and didn't know of his part in this passage of documents. Two years earlier, Kennedy had let Hopkins convalesce at his Florida residence after doctors removed two-thirds of Harry's cancerous stomach. But in this perilous time of emerging world war, neither Bracken nor Hopkins was willing to see the Churchill-Roosevelt alliance endangered.

The most surprising betrayal, however, involved Joe Kennedy's closest friend in Great Britain, Lord Beaverbrook. When Joe mentioned privately about possibly endorsing the GOP's Willkie, Beaverbrook sagely advised sticking with Roosevelt. Although he'd once agreed with Kennedy about appeasement, Beaverbrook became Churchill's chief defender of the skies, ramping up plane production to ward off German attacks. Beaverbrook now agreed with Churchill that to prevail in the war, Great Britain desperately needed a third Roosevelt term. "These plans depend on keeping the right man in the White House," Beaverbrook warned. "Kennedy claims he can put 25 million Catholic votes behind Wendell Willkie to throw Roosevelt out." Without tipping his hand, Beaverbrook wouldn't let his American diplomat friend sink England's chances.

As his "adieu" conversation ended with Churchill, Kennedy wished England well but underlined that his chief concern was with America's future. He asked the prime minister if he still "did not want the United States in the war," as Joe remembered Winston saying on a previous occasion. Churchill answered "sharply," Kennedy recalled. Once again, Joe had misunderstood everything.

"Of course, as soon as they want to come in, I do want them in," Churchill insisted.

There could be no longer any doubt in Kennedy's mind that the prime minister was pushing for the same special alliance between the United States and the United Kingdom that Winston had extolled the first time they met at Chartwell.

A few nights later, with the air-raid sirens blaring in London, Kennedy left for New York City.

At LaGuardia Airport, reporters, photographers, and other onlookers watched as the Pan American Clipper plane carrying Ambassador Kennedy landed in Flushing Bay on Sunday, October 27—a week before the presidential election. With four large swirling propellers, the giant craft taxied along the water to the pier. Everyone anticipated a momentous announcement when Kennedy got off the plane. Wearing a dark overcoat and homburg hat, Joe carried his bulging leather briefcase filled with papers. He looked a bit thinner, but just as ebullient as when he first left for London.

At the dock, two particular women waited separately and anxiously, uncertain of what he might say. Newspaper stories predicted Kennedy's last-minute defection for Wendell Willkie. In the crowd, the presence of Clare Boothe Luce seemed to confirm this rumor. WHEN YOU LAND TELL THE PRESS AND THE PEOPLE THE TRUTH AS YOU HAVE ALWAYS TOLD IT TO ME, she'd cabled to him. Randolph Churchill would later say Clare and her husband, Henry Luce, had secured radio time so Kennedy could address the nation, endorsing Willkie as the best way of avoiding America's entry into the war.

As he emerged from the plane, Kennedy tried to shoo away the press people without comment. He also kept his distance from Clare, who wanted to talk with him urgently. Kennedy's mind still wasn't made up about his much-publicized meeting with the president, expected to take place as soon as he arrived.

"I can't tell you now, but I'll have a lot to say when I finish," Kennedy finally said to reporters, hustling into the airport's marine terminal.

There, inside a private room, Joe spoke with the other woman waiting for him, Rose Kennedy, and some of his closest advisers, huddled to discuss the biggest political decision of his life. At various stops along the long trip home, first in Lisbon and later in Bermuda, Kennedy had received cables from the president directing him to see Roosevelt immediately upon his return. At LaGuardia, another Roosevelt letter, handed to him by Max Truitt, a maritime commissioner and old Kennedy pal, contained the same message.

Rose counseled patience and coolness to her hotheaded spouse. Kennedy bristled with anger at his treatment by the Roosevelt crowd, swearing that he'd vote for Willkie. The daughter of Honey Fitz, the leader of Boston's Irish-Catholic Democrats for so many years, wasn't ready to endorse her husband's idea of ratting, as Churchill might have called it, in favor of the Republican candidate for president. In doing so, Joe would effectively be resigning from the Democratic Party, along with dashing all the political hopes and dreams of their family. As the mother of three sons eligible for the military, Rose felt as strongly as her husband about American intervention in the European conflict. "One may wonder what I thought about all this—I hated it," she'd recall. "War always seemed to me the ultimate insanity. There was nothing I could do but put on a cheerful face. To hope and to pray." Perhaps she hadn't seen copies of the cables her husband had in his possession, the hard proof showing Roosevelt's secret intent of aiding Churchill. Rather than oppose her party's president, however, Rose preferred to believe in the sincerity of Roosevelt's oft-stated promise of not getting involved in the war.

Joe knew Roosevelt's invitation to stay for the night at the White House, extended to Rose as well, would make it hard, if not impossible, to quit and go against him.

"The president sent you, a Catholic, as ambassador to London, which probably no other president would have done," reminded Rose, who flew with him immediately to Washington. "You would write yourself down as an ingrate in the view of many people if you resigned now."

When the Kennedys arrived at the White House, Roosevelt greeted

Joe effusively. The president focused on Kennedy's greatest and most vulnerable asset: his family. Franklin asked Rose about her father, Honey Fitz, and immediately inquired about Kennedy's sons. "For a man as busy as you are, your relationship with your boys is a rare achievement," the president said. Both knew Joe traded on the fault lines of Roosevelt's own relationship with his family, especially Jimmy. Solemnly, the president promised to help Kennedy's sons if they ever ran for elective office, a consideration that remained paramount in Joe's mind.

Over a dinner of scrambled eggs and sausages, in deference to Joe's delicate stomach, Roosevelt listened to his guests. "Joe did most of the talking," Rose recalled in her personal notes. "The president looked rather pale, rather ashen, and I always noticed the nervous habit he had of nervously snapping his eyes." Sen. James F. Byrnes, a friend of Joe's and another carefully scripted actor in this high-stakes presidential drama, interrupted with "a great idea" that had supposedly occurred to him spontaneously. After listening to Kennedy's tales of wartime London, Byrne suggested Joe go on the radio and endorse the president. Joe ignored Byrne's hint, having expected to talk confidentially with Roosevelt. Frustrated that this would never happen, he finally burst out, "Since it is not possible for me to see the president alone, I guess I'll just have to say what I am going to say in front of everybody."

Kennedy then launched a tirade about his alleged mistreatment by the State Department. He complained how visiting emissaries such as Sumner Welles and William Donovan had undermined his job as ambassador, and finally how Churchill had gone around him while dealing directly with Washington. "We then discussed the status of the war and I told him frankly that I thought Churchill had but one real idea and that was to get the United States into the war," Kennedy recalled in his memoir. Although he attacked the State Department bureaucrats, Joe never criticized the president personally. Roosevelt, in his best "soft-soap" manner, simply agreed with Joe, thus defanging the latter's venomous attacks. The president promised to clean out his government after the election, and acted most sympathetically to his ambassador and adoring wife. Eventually, Joe gave in. He agreed to the radio speech, under one condition: he would pay for it and say whatever he wanted.

Clare and Henry Luce kept lobbying Kennedy to pull a last-minute surprise against the president, to no avail. "Clare tried to get hold of him and he wouldn't answer the phone," Henry Luce later recalled. "We were appalled when he came out for FDR as the man to keep us out of war." Just before the speech, Charles Lindbergh visited Joe at the Waldorf, where the ambassador still seemed to be waffling, and told him the "war would stop if it were not for Churchill and the hope in England that America will come in." But Roosevelt, always the great persuader, assured Kennedy that he had no intention of sending American boys into the European conflict. He repeated that promise to the American people right up until Election Day.

"I have said this before, but I shall say it again and again," Roosevelt vowed to a cheering crowd in Boston on November 4, "your boys are not going to be sent into any foreign wars."

Looking on, Kennedy didn't believe a word of it. There was little he could do, however, especially if he didn't want to ruin his family's political name. When he finally spoke publicly, in an October 29 speech heard over 114 stations of the CBS radio network, Kennedy underlined the need to send armaments to England as a way of keeping the war away from America. He cited his son Jack's book as a lesson for all to follow. He still portrayed himself as a friend of Prime Minister Churchill and his policies.

"Those of us who know the stuff of which Churchill and the British leaders are made, those of us who know the courage and the calibre of the officers and men of the Royal Navy, can feel completely assured that surrendering the fleet to Hitler is a thought so fantastic that it is beyond the basis of belief," said Kennedy. In conclusion, he emphasized his family, his most prized possession. "My wife and I have given nine hostages to fortune," he said. "Our children and your children are more important than anything else in the world."

On Election Day, Roosevelt overwhelmingly beat back Willkie's challenge. As a reward for his strong public endorsement, the press expected Kennedy to find another prominent position in FDR's third-term administration. At the White House on the day after the election, Joe visited with Roosevelt, who appeared tired but happy.

"Well, you've got it," Kennedy told the president, who indeed carried the weight of the world on his shoulders. "I certainly don't begrudge you the next four years."

Roosevelt asked him to stay on as ambassador until he could find a suitable replacement, Kennedy said in his diary. When Joe suggested one possibility for London, socialite and former ambassador Anthony Biddle, the president wondered aloud about the prime minister's reaction. "How about Churchill?" he asked Kennedy. They both knew Roosevelt dealt directly with Churchill, but this nominal deference to diplomacy was part of the ruse between them.

"If there is a Chinese nigger, Churchill would talk to him now if you sent him," Joe said, a crude comment that made Roosevelt laugh reflexively.

"Mr. President, Churchill is keeping this fight going only because he has no alternative as Churchill the fighter, whether there is any hope in the future or not," Kennedy continued, "but his real idea is that he'll get the U.S. in and then U.S. will share the problems."

For a time, the two men discussed the war in Europe and America's plans before turning to a personal conversation about their sons. The president complained the press had shabbily treated his second-oldest son, Elliott Roosevelt, during the campaign. Questions of favoritism arose about how Elliott, already possessing a high-paying job with Hearst's chain of radio stations, had gained a commission as an army captain buying supplies that allowed him to avoid the draft affecting millions of other young men. The president then asked about Jack. Ambassador Kennedy said that the draft board had rejected his son because of his health. He didn't tell FDR about Jack's chronic illness—a secret the Kennedys kept closely guarded. The president offered his own reasons for Jack's poor condition. "He [Roosevelt] said he had a theory that the stomach trouble of these kids was due to drinking," Kennedy recalled in his diary notes. "I said that mine didn't drink."

Kennedy always suspected Roosevelt held a bias against Irish Catholics like Joe, and his comment probably assumed that grandsons of a Boston barkeep were perennially sloshed. Indeed, shortly after, Roosevelt privately called Kennedy a "temperamental Irish boy" who was "terrifically spoiled at an early age by huge financial success: thoroughly patriotic, thoroughly selfish, and thoroughly obsessed with the idea that he must leave each of his nine children with a million dollars apiece when he dies (he has told me that often)."

At this meeting, however, Roosevelt quickly ended his own moment of Irish cultural stereotyping. "Well that explodes that theory," he replied rather blithely.

On Saturday morning, November 9, Kennedy agreed to a bull session with a group of reporters. As he always did, the ambassador believed himself off the record and able to speak freely. "The best informed men that I have met in twenty-five years of a varied career are not statesmen, diplomats, or college professors, but American newspaper men," he told his son Jack, about that time. Despite what he said publicly in his radio speech, Joe reverted back to his old cutting ways in private with these reporters. He launched potshots at the British Cabinet and, most damningly, he claimed "democracy is finished in England" and probably in America as well.

The next day, the *Boston Globe* ran a story with his stunning comments, creating a furor that essentially killed his political future. Joe tried to coerce a retraction from the paper, threatening to pull liquor ads for his Somerset Importers firm. The *Globe* editors didn't budge. Kennedy's comments as "an appeaser" angered many in America, especially Roosevelt's closest political aides, who let the press know the ambassador had been fired rather than resigned. But the harshest reaction came from Great Britain, where, in the fight of their lives, Kennedy had cavalierly doomed them to defeat. "While he was here, his suave, monotonous smile, his nine over-photographed children and his hail-fellow-well-met manner concealed a hard-boiled business man's eagerness to do a profitable business deal with the dictators and deceive many English people," London columnist A. J. Cummings fumed.

Worst of all, from the Kennedy perspective, Joe's disloyalty and rash comments toward Roosevelt had undercut his sons' political futures. Rose was stunned at how her husband ignored her pleas to curb his intemperate comments. The Kennedy sons winced at rumors of cowardice mentioned behind their backs. Aware that his family's once-sterling reputation had been tarnished, Joe Jr. decided to enlist in the navy's Air Corps, rather than finish at Harvard Law School. "I think in that Jack is not doing anything, and with your stand on the war, that people will wonder what the devil I am doing back at school with everyone else working for national defense," Joe Jr. admitted to his father. "As far as the family is concerned, it seems that Jack is perfectly capable to do everything, if by chance anything happened to me."

Jack tried to remedy the situation by offering a proposed article for his father to publish under his own name. Rather than his dissembling pre–Election Day speech on FDR's behalf, in it the ambassador would offer a more critical, truthful view. Jack hoped that speaking plainly to the American people would be his father's lasting legacy. With an eye toward the future, he also had a sense of how his father's sullied reputation might impact his own ambitions. Despite his prescient book about England, Jack was surprised to find himself personally attacked in the press "for being an appeaser and a defeatist," he wrote to his father. "It must be remembered continually that you wish to shake off the word 'appeaser.' It seems to me that if this label is tied to you it may nullify your immediate effectiveness, even though in the long run you may be proved correct."

Jack's article, never made public, invoked a familiar name. "It may be unpleasant for America to hear my views but let me note that Winston Churchill was considered distinctly unpleasant to have around during the years 1935 to 1939," his father would say in this rendition. "It was felt he was a gloom monger. In the days of the Blitzkrieg the optimist does not always do his country the best service. It is only by facing the reality that we can hope to meet it."

History might still prove his father right, Jack Kennedy suggested, just as it had with Winston Churchill.

Part III

WARTIME

"And how can man die better
Than facing fearful odds,
For the ashes of his fathers,
And the temples of his gods?"
—THOMAS MACAULAY

"Arm yourselves, and be ye men of valour, and be in
readiness for the conflict; for it is better for us to perish in
battle than to look upon the outrage of our nation
and our altar."
—WINSTON CHURCHILL, *with a reference to the King James*
Bible during a BBC broadcast, May 1940

23

The House of Churchill Bears a Son

In the House of Commons, that ancient temple of British democracy, Randolph Churchill stood regally to claim his place. The prime minister's son looked resplendent in his blue Hussars uniform with gold trim, the scion of a family that had given its all to the Crown and empire. The reedy tenor voice, operose language, and combative approach toward his fellow Members of Parliament all seemed quite familiar. His words reminded them of his father, just as Winston once stood in this chamber and invoked the name of Lord Randolph in his first address. Yet this was a new Churchill, come of age in the twentieth century, ready for a modern war.

"I hope the House will pardon me for striking this personal note, but I today have the personal privilege and satisfaction of having my father here," Randolph began to appreciative laughter. "Therefore, I would like to ask an extra measure of indulgence, on account of the added embarrassment occasioned by paternal propinquity."

Gracious at the outset, Randolph's first parliamentary speech, on November 26, 1940, was pure Churchillian. He soon described the dangers faced bravely by those in uniform, defending England every day in battle. Then, with his own filial retribution, he reminded those in the chamber who had once argued that Hitler could be appeased that his father had been right and they terribly wrong. "We were giving in to evil, and today we are resisting it," he said defiantly. When Randolph finished, the chamber cheered.

After three unsuccessful tries, Randolph finally had gained a House seat through an uncontested by-election in Preston, filled after a Conservative Party member died. At age twenty-nine, a bit older than he intended to enter Parliament, young Churchill said he "hoped that at Preston he had found a political home for all time." Randolph's selection was more a tribute to his father's wartime leadership than due to any attribute of his own. Nonetheless, both Churchills, who had waited years for this moment, were pleased. "The sample he has given us today of his powers shows that he is going to act up to the traditions of the greatest of all his forebearers," declared Major-General Sir Alfred Knox, the speaker who followed Randolph.

On the front bench, Winston sat with his back turned as Randolph addressed the House, so as not as to embarrass him. When his son finished his speech, the prime minister, a sentimentalist at heart, was visibly moved. The Churchills appeared born to lead now and for decades to come.

During much of 1940, Randolph prepared himself for battle. The expectation that he, like much of his generation, faced butchery even more grinding and devastating than that of the Great War, had compelled his impulsive move to marry Pamela (to secure an heir to the Churchill lineage) and to join the Queen's Fourth Hussars (to die a glorious death). Pamela quickly learned her husband's view of destiny. While in bed together during their honeymoon, he read aloud from Edward Gibbon's *The History of the Decline and Fall of the Roman Empire,* intent that his new bride absorb its lessons.

"Fancy trying to read me *Decline and Fall*!" Pamela recalled decades later with amusement. "Even worse, he would stop and say: 'Are you listening?' When I said 'Yes I am,' he would demand: 'Well what was that last sentence?' Can you imagine! Hilaire Belloc was fine, but Gibbon was too much!"

Sent to Hussar training in Yorkshire, Randolph dragged along Pamela, wedded to his wish to become a father and an officer. At the base, about 180 miles north of London, the younger soldiers teased Randolph for being out of shape. Senior officers resented his pontifications about military strategy, learned at the foot of his father. Winston's influence was never far away. During Randolph's training, Lord Beaverbrook, his father's ally, continued his salary at the *Evening Standard* newspaper, while Winston's right-hand man, Brendan Bracken, helped find the semi-detached house where Randolph and Pam spent a snowy and unhappy winter.

At first no one seemed to question Randolph's bravery—only his good sense and, as it turned out, his timing. Traditionally, the Hussars were expert in the art of swordplay, as Winston on horseback once witnessed with awe in India. However, eighteen months before Randolph arrived, the Fourth Hussars were converted from a cavalry into a mechanized unit. "This meant that our horses had been taken away from us but no tanks had been supplied in their place," Randolph recalled years later. "So we did not have very much to do." Indeed, it became clear the Hussars wouldn't see combat anytime soon, not with the prime minister's son in their ranks. "All the sergeants' wives were saying: 'Of course we are all safe as long as Mr. Churchill's son is in the regiment—none of our husbands will be sent abroad,'" recalled Pamela. "One thing that Randolph never lacked was courage. He was desperate to go abroad, yet every regiment except the Fourth Hussars seemed to be sent."

Randolph vented his frustrations to his wife, and to his father during London visits, complaining about the generals and the lack of equipment. The prime minister's son was "one of the most objectionable people I had ever met: Noisy, self-assertive, whining and frankly unpleasant," observed Jock Colville, personal secretary to Churchill. "At dinner he was anything but kind to Winston, who adores him." Of course, Randolph's military life was very much defined by his father, who intimated he couldn't carry on the burdens of the war if his only son were killed. For all his intelligence and ability to make what Colville called "shrewd and penetrating comments," Randolph seemed oblivious to the unspoken directive of these same generals to keep the prime minister's son away from combat. Instead, he readily accepted his father's claim of noninvolvement. When Randolph pushed for assignment to the battlefront, Winston deflected him, advising patience and compliance. "I am sure y[ou]r best & indeed *only* course is to obey with good grace, & do whatever duty is assigned to you," his father instructed. "In this way you will win the confidence of those in whose power you lie ... I am always on the look out for any compliment or pleasure I can give you, as you know; but so far as the service is concerned you must make y[ou]r own way. I am always thinking about y[ou]r interests & y[ou]r fortunes."

As if following her own assigned duty, Pamela soon became pregnant. When informed of the news in January 1940, Randolph's parents were delighted. They invited Pam to move into Admiralty House with them. "Of course, Old Winston was very much hoping that I was going to have a boy," she recalled. "It meant a great deal to him." When a Marlborough cousin attempted to name their own new baby "Winston Spencer Churchill," Pam became distraught. She convinced the prime minister to prevail and secure that special name for his first grandson. Both Clementine and Winston grew fond of their vivacious daughter-in-law, knowing full well that life with their randy son wasn't easy. In particular, Clemmie listened with sympathy as Pamela worried about the gambling, pub, and restaurant bills run up by Randolph, known for undeterred drinking and indiscreet womanizing.

When Winston became prime minister, Pamela followed her in-laws to 10 Downing Street (ostensibly to be closer to her doctor), where she stayed in a downstairs bomb shelter during the Battle of Britain's worst moments. Clemmie slept in a full bed inside this shelter, while her expectant daughter-in-law shared a double-decker with Winston. "I had to get my sleep between 9 and midnight or 1 in the morning, because once he got into the upper bed, the snoring was terrible," Pamela recalled. "I had young Winston kicking inside me and old Winston snoring above me."

In the Churchill house, Pamela learned about politics from the master. From a short distance, she observed conversations between wartime leaders. She began to understand the personal qualities that made Winston inspiring to his nation. At a family dinner, Churchill talked of a possible invasion by the Nazis and that they might have to kill a German soldier bursting through their door. Pamela, full-bellied in her final month of pregnancy, realized her father-in-law "was in dead earnest and I was terrified."

"But Papa, what can I do?" she asked anxiously, explaining that she didn't know how to fire a gun. In a way somehow reassuring, Winston growled humorously, "You can always get a carving knife from the kitchen and take one with you, can't you?"

Pamela came to appreciate Winston as another young woman once did with the same first name—Pamela Plowden, an old flame he met before Clementine, who observed, "The first time you meet Winston you see all his faults, and the rest of your life you spend in discovering his virtues."

Randolph's parents hoped his election to Parliament, his military service, his marriage, and imminent fatherhood might set him on the right course in life, a path toward greatness. On the day of his installation, Pamela and Clementine rejoiced in the visitors' gallery as

Randolph joined his father on the floor of the House of Commons. Pamela's doctors ordered that a canister of "laughing gas" accompany her in case she suddenly went into labor. When Randolph left again for military training, Pamela yearned as a good wife for his return. "Darling I miss you so terribly & just feel I can't wait until next weekend," she wrote. "Let's have one day all to ourselves. I am so selfish about you—angel—but you're just all I want." She even tried to defend Randolph when he deflated his family's grandest hopes with his indefensible behavior.

During a forty-eight-hour leave to visit home, he escaped a family dinner for a "quick drink" of brandy with an American journalist friend. He wound up carousing all night at the Savoy, boasting of his political ascension and predicting that he'd be a better orator than his father. After sunrise, he arrived home drunk. Pam had to undress her husband and put him to bed. Meanwhile, a security official had found several secret maps and military papers in his unlocked Jaguar outside 10 Downing, which they returned to the mortified prime minister. Randolph apologized profusely. "His father was furious," Pamela recalled. "He promised his father he would never drink again."

But on the night before Pamela gave birth, Randolph was out again enjoying himself, with another woman. By five o'clock the next morning, when his blue-eyed infant son arrived, Randolph remained missing. "They couldn't find him the night the baby was born and he confessed to me later on that he was in the arms of Richard Tauber's wife, Diana," recalled Pamela, referring to the English actress married to the famous Austrian tenor. Nevertheless, the joyous start of a new Churchill generation—another male heir to the Marlborough legacy, a grandson named for the prime minister, Winston Spencer Churchill— took precedence over Randolph's transgressions. Pamela, slowly coming out of the haze of anesthesia, asked deliriously, over and over, about the baby's gender.

"I've told you five times—it's a boy," a young navy nurse assured her.

"It can't change now," Pamela exclaimed gratefully. "It can't change now."

Pamela felt she had done her duty to God, country, and the prime minister. "I'd at least been able to produce a boy for him," she remembered. "And of course, Winston was utterly delighted. He used to come and watch the baby, feed him, and was just thrilled to death with him."

The next two months were perhaps the most joyous time for the Churchill family, despite the many deaths and other tragedies of war surrounding them. Pam recovered enough to attend Randolph's first lauded speech at Parliament. At the baby's christening on December 1, the day after Winston's sixty-sixth birthday, Lord Beaverbrook and Brendan Bracken stood as godfathers. Pamela's parents and brother beamed. Journalist Virginia Cowles, who was godmother, heard a teary-eyed Winston say softly, "Poor infant, to be born into such a world as this."

At Christmas 1940, the new baby was the center of attention as Winston and Clementine hosted a festive holiday dinner at Chequers, the prime minister's country retreat. All their children and their spouses gathered, including Diana and Duncan Sandys, Sarah and Vic Oliver, Randolph and Pamela, as well as eighteen-year-old Mary. Whatever past troubles they had among themselves seemed to fade into a moment of glorious harmony. "I've never seen the family look so happy—so united," Mary wrote in her diary. "I wonder if we will all be together next Christmas?"

The moment proved memorable because the Churchill family would never gather again like this during the war.

24

New Alliances

Brendan Bracken's eyes stared intently through thick, oval-shaped glasses, as if he could barely abide the world's horrors. His mop of curly red hair seemed electrified. A grim smile stressed the intensity of his personality. Always by Churchill's side, like a faithful son, Bracken translated the prime minister's intuitive, epigrammatic words into action. While Winston envisioned the big-picture puzzle, Bracken always manipulated the little pieces into place. When, for example, Churchill, ruminating about a difficult personnel matter, uttered, "You should never harness a thoroughbred to a dung-cart," Bracken, the fixer, knew exactly what horse he meant.

What to do about America, however, was a far greater dilemma.

After the Joe Kennedy debacle, Bracken worried Great Britain couldn't afford another messy arrangement with its reluctant ally. Although Britain had fended off the Luftwaffe's attacks, at least for the moment, the future of the empire depended on whether that isolationist giant, the United States, could be persuaded to enter the war. Kennedy was gone, in a fury of self-immolation, yet the newly reelected Roosevelt remained coolly uncommitted. In private, he promised Churchill that the American government would do everything, short of declaring war, to keep the British defenses afloat. But to appraise the European situation once again, like Baruch and Welles and Donovan before, the president dispatched another envoy: presidential aide Harry Hopkins, a sober-minded, chain-smoking New Dealer. One writer described Hopkins as looking like "an ill-fed horse at the end of a long day." His arrival in mid-January 1941 couldn't be good news, Bracken feared.

Churchill ordered every possible courtesy extended to Hopkins in the hope of winning him over. "Brendan said that Hopkins, the confidant of Roosevelt, was the most important American visitor to this country we had ever had," recalled Jock Colville. "He had come to tell the President what we needed and to form an opinion of the country's morale. He could influence the President more than any living man."

In the basement of 10 Downing, Hopkins first met the prime minister for lunch, a four-hour affair complete with port and brandy. Though hardly opulent, the bottom floor was considered safe from bombing and a bit cozy, especially compared to surrounding buildings with their windows blown out. "His man Friday—Brendan Bracken met me at the door—showed me about the old and delightful house that has been home of Prime Ministers of the Empire for two hundred years," Hopkins later described to FDR. The initial exchange began awkwardly, particularly when Kennedy's name arose. "I told him there was a feeling in some quarters that he, Churchill, did not like America, Americans or Roosevelt," Hopkins recalled. "This set him off on a bitter tho' fairly constrained attack on Ambassador Kennedy, whom he believes is responsible for this impression."

In the company of Americans, Churchill usually weighed his words carefully. Certainly he didn't know if Hopkins and the former ambassador might be friends. But Winston couldn't restrain his pent-up anger at Kennedy, years of frustration that boiled over. Hopkins later gave his own explanation of Kennedy to the prime minister. While figures such as Charles Lindbergh "wanted a German victory" and a negotiated peace, Kennedy was a garden-variety American isolationist who, he said, believed "Help Britain, but make damn sure you don't get into any danger of war."

As the two men chatted over the next several days, Hopkins became increasingly impressed with Churchill and the need to support Britain's fight against Hitler. Churchill took Hopkins on a tour around England, displaying his embattled nation's ports, military outposts, and attempts to defend itself. "I have never had such an enjoyable time," wrote Hopkins. ". . . God, what a force that man has." Bracken brought Hopkins, the son of an Iowa bowling alley operator, to the legendary Blenheim Palace, the scene of Winston's noble birth and a reminder of Great Britain's resolve in previous wars. At their first luncheon together, Churchill heeded Bracken's reconnaissance on Hopkins, said to be a most liberal New Dealer. Winston blathered on about the social programs he intended to create after the war for the working poor living in cottages. Warned that Churchill could be long-winded, Hopkins showed little patience. After a certain point, he cut him off. "I don't give a damn about the cottages," he said. "I have come here to find out how the hell we can lick Hitler." Rather than offend him, Hopkins's plainspokenness delighted Churchill. Perhaps this was the kind of relaxed man with whom Winston could play poker, just like Beaverbrook. "Hopkins," Churchill replied, rising from his chair, "you and I had better talk." They did privately, until the wee hours of the next morning.

During one weekend visit to the prime minister's country home, Pamela Churchill observed Hopkins in action as he arrived with Bracken. "This little shriveled creature with a dead cigarette out of the corner of his mouth, huddled in an overcoat, in the great hall at Chequers, saying, 'If ever this damn war is over, I will see to it that the American government gets central heating in Chequers,'" she recalled with a laugh. Hopkins forged a special alliance with Churchill, serving as a vital intermediary between his president and the prime minister—or, as Harry put it, "a catalytic agent between two PRIMA DONNAS." Their long series of talks eventually helped create the Atlantic Charter, a statement of shared Anglo-American principles signed in August 1941 by Roosevelt and Churchill aboard a ship in Newfoundland, the first time the two met face-to-face during the war. "Harry had an extraordinary faculty of explaining president to prime minister and I think prime minister to president, so that when they met, Churchill thought he knew Roosevelt," Pamela recalled. Almost as important, she added, Harry "served in a position preventing Churchill from doing things which he knew would annoy Roosevelt, and told Roosevelt not to do the things which he knew would annoy Churchill."

Winston desperately wanted the United States on his side, though Roosevelt avoided any commitment to war, even after their carefully planned first meeting. For Churchill, the special relationship between the two nations was deeply personal. "He was fascinated by America and Americans, feeling that he was half American," Pamela recalled years later. As a sign of his goodwill in America, Winston pointed to an issue of *Life* magazine that appeared during Hopkins's January visit, with a stunning photograph of Pamela and his namesake grandson on its cover. No longer plump and pregnant, she posed with a cool sensuality for photographer Cecil Beaton, who later described her "Raeburn-esque red curls and freckles, looking radiant and triumphant." Inside, a lengthy article lionized Churchill and his "great bulldog jaw and penetrating stare which today inspire the most stubborn and successful resistance that freemen have yet made to Nazism." After a month of observation, Hopkins came to a similar conclusion, repudiating Joe Kennedy's invective.

"I cannot believe," he wrote back to Roosevelt, "that Churchill dislikes you or America—it just doesn't make sense."

After the Churchill family's peaceful Christmas, Randolph returned to war, on terms more to his liking. Hoping for heroic feats of his own, rather than the reflected glory of his father, the second lieutenant learned of a newly created commando unit being put together by charismatic colonel Robert Laycock and looking to add officers. When Randolph's reassignment came through, however, his Hussars superiors didn't wish him a fond adieu. Tired of his loutish behavior, they instead flogged him with recriminations and a good riddance. "Randolph, who had thought he was well-regarded, burst into tears," wrote his cousin Anita Leslie. "That was one of his endearing traits—his honest childlike desire to be loved and his amazement when he discovered that he wasn't."

Without the prime minister's son in their ranks, the Fourth Queen's Own Hussars were soon ordered into battle, in Crete, and suffered heavy casualties. "All the wives said it was because Randolph Churchill had been taken away so now they knew that their husbands would all be sent to their deaths," recalled Pamela. Meanwhile, the British Commandos, after a short time training in Scotland, were dispatched to Egypt. The original idea for the commandos derived from Winston, who wanted a well-trained force in the Middle East to carry out menacing raids against Nazi encampments along the eastern Mediterranean, keeping the enemy off balance. With dark skullcaps and their faces blackened, they would surprise-attack on moonless nights. "How wonderful it would be if the Germans could be made to wonder where they are going to be struck next, instead of forcing us to try and wall in the Island and roof it over," said the prime minister, then busy defending England from air attack. Apparently, Winston had no inclination his son would soon be one of the unit's volunteers.

Another commando recruited by Laycock was novelist Evelyn Waugh, a pal of Randolph's at Oxford, who embraced the experience as fodder for his next novel. (Indeed, Waugh fashioned a fictional character on Laycock, just as he supposedly did with Beaverbrook and Bracken in other works.) By late 1940, Waugh had gained fame for his novel

Vile Bodies, though his best work was soon to come. The combative friendship between Randolph and Waugh had drifted since Oxford, though they resumed it with gusto as wartime companions. "We seem to have gone different ways and it was not until 1940 when the war had begun in earnest that we got to know each other very well and made the friendship which had many ups and downs and many coolnesses followed by reconciliations," Randolph later remembered.

Waugh harbored a private disdain for the prime minister, especially for his tortured relationship with his son. But these misgivings didn't prevent the novelist from using Churchill's influence in applying to the Royal Marines in 1939, before volunteering for the commandos. In November 1941, Waugh penned a glowing firsthand account in *Life* magazine about the Churchill-inspired commando unit. "A good commando fighter, known jokingly as a 'Churchill Marine,' should have the imagination of a mystery writer, the cunning of a burglar, the endurance of an Olympic athlete and the patriotism of a hero," wrote Waugh. With some literary license, he suggested the presence of Randolph and other commandos with famous surnames "showed how the sons of the last war's leaders saw in the commandos the chance of reliving their father's achievements." When Waugh got in trouble for the unauthorized *Life* profile, he claimed it'd been arranged by Churchill's chief aide Brendan Bracken, by then formally installed as minister of information. Waugh recognized his personal link with Churchill's son was good for business.

By February 1941, the overcrowded commando ship carrying Randolph and Waugh set out around the coast of Africa, including a short sojourn in South Africa. The entire trip took a month. "We have been at sea a week now & face the long voyage with patience," Waugh wrote to his wife, complaining that Randolph "brought luggage enough for a film star's honeymoon." Although many dedicated soldiers graced the commandos, most were dilettantes "drawn from various famous regiments and included the cream of the British aristocracy," recalled

Kenneth T. Downs, an American journalist who befriended Randolph. "They were a rake-hell lot who performed incredible feats in action. When idle, they were given to high-stakes gambling, drinking and other activities which made them the despair of the military establishment in the Middle East, whom the Commandos dubbed 'The Gabardine Swine.'"

With his wicked wit, Waugh found plenty to write about in this military madhouse. He dedicated his comic novel about the Phony War, called *Put Out More Flags,* to his friend Randolph. Waugh later claimed his whole unit of well-educated, well-heeled cut-ups defied military authority and confounded any Freudian-tinged attempt to understand or control them. "The company's commander's course is so up to date that we are all psycho-analysed," he teased. "I enjoyed myself prodigiously with my analyst. He complained later to the CO that I seemed under the impression that I was psycho-analysing him."

Randolph fancied himself both a brave warrior by day and a merry comrade after hours. Without regard for his wife and baby at home, Randolph acted with abandon, convinced he had no future as a man on his way to the front. "He did not care if he was killed now that he had a son," wrote his cousin Anita Leslie. On the trip to the Middle East, his comrades upped the ante for Randolph. During a poker game, he lost a small fortune—three thousand pounds, the equivalent of several years' wages. Half that money he owed to Peter Fitzwilliam (then known as Peter Milton, until 1943, when he became the Eighth Earl Fitzwilliam), a dashing, roguish friend from White's, a club in London, where they all cavorted before the war. Even though Peter was one of the richest men in England, Randolph's honor wouldn't allow him to welch on this debt.

Desperately, Randolph sent a letter seeking help from his twenty-one-year-old bride, asking her to figure out a solution. "You must promise me not to tell my mother and father about this," he pleaded ashamedly. Pamela was stunned by this "bombshell" turning her life upside down.

She'd already moved into a small house in Hitchin with Randolph's sister Diana (whose husband, Duncan Sandys, was also away at war), to catch up on their debts. Along with baby Winston, she thought she might be pregnant again, and hoped for a daughter they'd call "little Jenny." In the past, Winston had helped pay some of his son's outstanding bills. But this time Pamela knew she couldn't go to her in-laws, to whom Randolph had sworn he'd never drink or gamble again. "I thought, 'What the hell do I do?'" she recalled. "I can't go to Clemmie and Winston. What will I do? I went to Max."

Unbeknownst to her husband or any Churchill, Pamela called Lord Beaverbrook at his ministry office and began sobbing over the telephone. Max was little Winston's godfather, and she felt Beaverbrook, by reputation, could get anybody out of a jam. If he could revive Britain's lagging air force, perhaps he could do the same for her marital finances covered in red ink. Max listened and then told her to come for a visit. As she drove her Jaguar to Beaverbrook's offices, she remembered Randolph's warning about his father's manipulative friend: "You must not get under the Beaverbrook spell because nothing amuses Beaverbrook more than to have complete control of people's lives, smash them or put them together as he sees fit. And one thing I ask you is not to come under his spell."

Inside Beaverbrook's office, Pamela attempted a bargain, what she later called "my first sort of adult lesson." She asked if Randolph's reporter's salary, being paid by Beaverbrook while her husband was away in the military, could be obtained in advance to relinquish his gambling obligations. Max wouldn't have it. Instead he offered a gift.

"If you want me to give you a check for 3,000 pounds, I will do it— for you," said Beaverbrook, with almost Mephistophelian glee.

Pamela later said she "smelled danger" in the proposition. Realizing her vulnerability, she said no to the outright payment, fearing that she'd become more beholden to him than she intended. "Max had to have control of the people around him, whether it was Brendan Bracken or even Winston Churchill," she later said. "He had to be in the driver's seat."

Their negotiations resulted in Pamela getting a job at the Ministry of Supply, necessitating a move to a nearby place and little Winston's staying most of the time with a nanny at Cherkley Court, the press magnate's estate. Pam sold off her diamond earrings, bracelets, and all their wedding presents. "Poor Pamela will have to go to work," Evelyn Waugh relayed to his wife. "Poor Randolph has had a letter from Pam about his losses at cards. She is very vexed with him."

Randolph's recklessness ended whatever hope Pamela had for their marriage. "That was the first realization in my life that I was totally on my own and that the future of my son was dependent on me, that I couldn't rely ever again on Randolph," she recalled. "I knew it was over, but that I had to try and deal with it the best I can."

Despite her anger with Randolph, Pamela continued as a convivial guest at many government occasions with her in-laws, including a luncheon in late March 1941 held at Beaverbrook's Cherkley with another special guest, W. Averell Harriman.

Harriman's arrival was the direct consequence of presidential aide Harry Hopkins's visit. For months, Churchill, Beaverbrook, and Bracken had worked feverishly to enlist Hopkins's support for their war effort. "Winston often speaks about you," Bracken cabled Hopkins after the latter's six-week trip ended. "And so indeed do all the friends you made over here." Upon Hopkins's return to Washington, he persuaded President Roosevelt to send Harriman to London as a special expeditor working directly with Beaverbrook in fighter plane production. "Nothing will be kept from you," Churchill promised Harriman, eager to please as he was with Hopkins. Along with his political instructions, Hopkins gave Harriman a piece of advice before he left. He suggested Harriman get introduced to Pamela Churchill, the prime minister's daughter-in-law, as soon as he landed. "She knows everything in London," counseled the presidential adviser, "and she is very good looking."

Beaverbrook knew that Harriman, a personal friend of Roosevelt, would be an important key to Britain's success. Averell's wife stayed behind in New York, so he had plenty of time for meetings with Beaverbrook. "He [Max] made a great fuss over me, always trying to induce me in a very clever way to recommend the things which he thought were important," Harriman recalled years later. "He was very anxious to bring the United States into the production."

At the luncheon inside Beaverbrook's Cherkley estate, another guest also became intrigued with Harriman. Sitting across the dining room table, the prime minister's daughter-in-law gazed at the suave middle-aged American diplomat with his taut and tanned skin, slicked raven black hair, and urbane manner. As she later recalled, young Mrs. Churchill thought Harriman was "the best-looking man I had ever seen."

By then, Pamela had moved to a sixth-floor room at the Dorchester, a luxurious London hotel, one of the few not in wartime shambles. She managed to afford it by renting her old place and getting a job with Beaverbrook's intervention. She wanted to create a new life for herself, without requiring anyone's approval. "It was pretty tricky because I couldn't really tell Clemmie and Winston why suddenly, from living happily in Hitchin with my baby, I suddenly up and separated myself from my baby and wanted a job in London," she recalled. At the Dorchester several days later, she attended a lively party for Adele Astaire, elder sister and former dance partner to Hollywood's Fred Astaire. (Adele left showbiz to marry Charles Cavendish, part of the Duke of Devonshire's family and cousin to Billy Hartington.) At this party, Pamela chatted with Harriman, who was eager to learn about Churchill and his advisers.

"Tell me about these people," Harriman asked her. "Tell me about Max Beaverbrook."

It was an extraordinary position for a twenty-two-year-old woman to be put in, offering her opinions to a virtually unknown foreigner considered vital to her country's defense. But Pamela did so freely, in a tantalizing mix of sexual and international politics. The two conversed for a time, until Harriman suggested they get away from the crowd. "Why don't you come back to my apartment and we can talk easier and you can tell me more about these people," he said.

The party's lively, festive mood had countered the gloom of nightly air raids until a harrowing bomb blast on nearby Park Lane blew out the hotel windows. Pamela decided to stay the night with Harriman, inside his apartment at the Dorchester, rather than return to her own on the sixth floor. Their affair began that night. In the morning, they got up and walked as a couple in the surrounding neighborhood, surveying the damage from the bombing. Churchill's personal secretary, Jock Colville, spotted Randolph's wife and the American diplomat strolling along the Horse Guards Parade. Colville kept his mouth shut about his suspicions, though he made a special note in his diary.

After their walk, Harriman followed Pamela to Cherkley, where they would spend a weekend together with Beaverbrook. "That kind of suited everybody because Beaverbrook was perfectly happy to get to know Averell at the very early stages," Pamela remembered. Beaverbrook, the social conniver, sensed "immediately" the sexual tension between Harriman and the prime minister's daughter-in-law, she recalled. "No fool, but, you know, that was fine by him."

Beaverbrook seemed to understand nothing could be gained by confronting the two lovers, both married to others. With the press baron, Randolph's employer and godfather of their son, there was no hiding the truth of her affair, not as she was able to do with Winston, Clementine, and even her own husband. As she'd learned from experience, Max knew everything.

25

"The Masters of Our Fate"

"Men are not prisoners of fate,
but only prisoners of their own minds."
—FRANKLIN D. ROOSEVELT

In Washington for Christmas 1941, Winston Churchill felt a bit lonely and not very well. This yuletide far away from home would be very different from the last, spent contentedly with his whole family in London. Yet looking out at the tree-lighting ceremony on the White House Lawn, he knew he'd been given the best gift of all.

With the Japanese attack on Pearl Harbor on December 7, America declared war against the Axis powers, a decision Churchill had been waiting for since 1939. Finally, Great Britain would be joined in a grand alliance with the United States and all its might. To plan the war, both Churchill and Lord Beaverbrook rushed across the ocean for a series of strategy meetings with President Roosevelt and his military advisers. "This is a strange Christmas Eve," Churchill said in a White House speech broadcast internationally. "Almost the whole world is locked in deadly struggle, and, with the most terrible weapons which science can devise, the nations advance upon each other."

Churchill had been dining at Chequers with Averell Harriman, the president's expeditor, when news of Pearl Harbor arrived. The prime minister immediately called the White House to voice his support. "We are all in the same boat now," Roosevelt told him. Winston's study of American history, especially the Civil War, had taught him that the United States was traditionally slow to go to war, but once engaged in conflict, "fought to the last desperate inch." "I went to bed," he wrote that night of Pearl Harbor, "and slept the sleep of the saved and thankful."

During the Christmas meetings at the White House, Churchill helped convince Roosevelt to focus first on beating Hitler in Europe, rather than immediately launching a second front against the Japanese in the Pacific. Proclaiming that the war would be won by machines, Beaverbrook argued successfully with the president for a sharp increase in production goals. Both Roosevelt and Churchill enjoyed their wide-ranging strategy sessions and witty conversation over drinks. "They looked like two little boys playing soldier," observed Eleanor Roosevelt, knowing that the administration's focus would now turn from a domestic New Deal to an international war creating a new world. "They seemed to be having a wonderful time—too wonderful, in fact. It made me a little sad somehow."

During his three-week White House stay, Churchill amply displayed his sense of humor. One day, the wheelchair-bound president was abruptly rolled into the prime minister's room, expecting another meeting. Instead he found Churchill just emerged from his bath, naked as a baby without a towel. As Roosevelt's chair began to be turned around, Winston made the best of the moment. "Pray enter—the Prime Minister of Great Britain has nothing to hide from the President of the United States," he beckoned with amusement. The British visit helped forge a respectful friendship between the prime minister and president, which lasted throughout the war. Winston flattered, cajoled, urged, and inspired his American counterpart as much as he knew how. Years later, Churchill admitted, "No lover ever studied every whim of his mistress as I did those of President Roosevelt."

On the day after Christmas, Churchill addressed a joint session of Congress—the first time for a British prime minister—with a speech as rousing as any by his onetime American hero Bourke Cockran. "I cannot help reflecting that if my father had been American and my mother British, instead of the other way around, I might have got here on my own," he said. "In that case this would not have been the first time you would have heard my voice." The Congress cheered him on. He reminded them that Germany could have been stopped earlier, perhaps without bloodshed, if an Anglo-American alliance had been forged. With a vow they'd win the war together, Churchill ended his fiery message. "Now we are the masters of our fate," he implored. As he turned to leave, his right hand rose in the air, with two fingers forming a confident *V* for victory. The speech drew hosannas from editorialists on both side of the Atlantic and praise from a familiar voice in Cairo. "I thought your Washington speech the best you have ever done," Randolph wrote to his father from his army office in Egypt, "particularly the delivery, which was wonderfully confident and clear."

That night, Winston felt a sharp pain in his chest, radiating down his left arm. In his White House bedroom, he opened a window for some air and soon became short of breath. His physician, Charles Wilson (later named Lord Moran), was called. He listened to Winston's chest with a stethoscope and realized that the sixty-seven-year-old prime minister had suffered a heart attack. Yet the doctor decided to say nothing. On his own, Moran decided it was better to run the risk of further endangering Churchill's health rather than ordering a "disastrous" treatment of six weeks' rest. "That would mean publishing to the world—and the American newspapers would see to this—that the PM was an invalid with a crippled heart and a doubtful future," Moran later wrote in his memoir. "And this at a moment when America had just come into the war, and there is no one but Winston to take her by the hand ... Right or wrong, it seemed plain that I must sit tight on what had happened, whatever the consequences."

When Moran removed the stethoscope from his ears, Churchill immediately quizzed him. "Is my heart all right?" he asked.

"You have been overdoing things," Moran replied, advising him to slow down.

Churchill refused to be thrown off his pace. He discounted any chance the pain emanated from his heart. In early January, he traveled to Florida for a few days' rest before returning again for a last round of negotiations with Roosevelt in Washington. On January 14, 1942, Churchill flew with Lord Beaverbrook in a Boeing flying boat from Virginia to Bermuda, and then again in the same large plane on their way home to England.

During the flight, Max and Winston moved up to the control deck. They looked out at the starlit sky and the tops of clouds. Both men told the pilot how they envied his job. They had ignored the king's warning that the empire's top leaders not travel together in the same aircraft. Beaverbrook didn't lose sight of the gamble. After all the other passengers, including the prime minister, fell asleep on the long flight home, Max told the pilot, "If we lose Churchill, we lose the war."

Right after Pearl Harbor, Joe Kennedy cabled Roosevelt, hoping to become an American version of Lord Beaverbrook by boosting arms production for the war. Although he'd opposed entry into the European conflict, Kennedy always remained a strong proponent of military buildup for defense. In recent months, one New York newspaper had even suggested he would be selected to "head up the National Defense Advisory Commission, just as Barney Baruch did in the last war." In a surge of patriotism after the Japanese attack, Joe volunteered his services to the president, ignoring their differences. "In this great crisis, all Americans are with you," he wrote to Roosevelt. "Name the battle post. I'm yours to command."

While in America with Churchill, Beaverbrook contacted Kennedy, more for social reasons than political. No matter how much the British wanted to appear cooperative, little chance existed they would encourage Kennedy's return to the American government. Churchill knew from his intelligence network about Kennedy's scathing criticisms inside the United States. In recent years, British officials had attempted discreetly to influence American politics, hoping isolationist objections to the war could be overcome. British agents gained access to secret U.S. diplomatic documents, and only after Pearl Harbor did Churchill warn FDR that "our enemies" could probably do the same. "From the moment we became allies, I gave instructions that this work should cease," he informed Roosevelt in February 1942, after returning home. That same month, Churchill relayed to the Foreign Office a private letter sent by J. J. Astor quoting Kennedy saying, "I hate all those goddamed Englishmen from Churchill on down."

Since leaving London, Kennedy had been carefully monitored by British intelligence, with updates on his activities collected by its New York office at Rockefeller Center. "More evidence of regrettable activities on the part of Mr. Kennedy, which should be added to our dossier on the subject," said one January 1941 memo summarizing the former ambassador's recent trip to Hollywood. While in California, Kennedy stayed with his son Jack for two nights, as a guest of William Randolph Hearst, at the same Santa Monica house where Churchill and his son visited in 1929. Joe addressed a group of Hollywood producers, many of them Jewish, whom he knew from his showbiz days. According to a confidential memo sent by the British consul in Los Angeles, Kennedy upset fourteen film producers and executives by claiming "there was very strong anti-Jewish activity in England and that they had better not make any more pro-British pictures or even anti-Nazis pictures." Of all things, a Three Stooges comedy short, *You Nazty Spy!,* in which comedian Moe Howard plays Hitler, reportedly provoked Kennedy's speech.

Though Kennedy "seems to have given little evidence" for his Hollywood warning, he "caused what was tantamount to a panic amongst his almost entirely Jewish audience," said British consul Eric

Cleugh in his memo sent to British intelligence agents in New York and the British embassy in Washington. The memo outlined possible malevolent reasons for Kennedy's outburst, including "current gossip that Mr. Kennedy wishes to re-enter the motion picture industry and his campaign of terrorism may be prompted by a hope that it will cause some of the Jews to get out of the business, so leaving a gap for Mr. Kennedy." The British dossier on Kennedy says he tried unsuccessfully to stop a handful of films from appearing, including *London Can Take It!*, a documentary produced by Bracken's Ministry of Information, and the Hollywood dramas *I Married a Nazi* (released as *The Man I Married*) and *The Mortal Storm*.

In a war of propaganda, Britain could not afford for a former U.S. ambassador to endanger its survival. Just as they investigated him in London during the Tyler Kent episode, British intelligence expanded Kennedy's dossier with other 1941 memos describing him as "embittered and in a vicious frame of mind" and claiming "he has no sense of the importance of what he says . . . he has no loyalties except to his own pocket." Cryptically, Cleugh advised that if Kennedy's impact lingered in Hollywood, "it would probably be advisable for some countermeasures to be taken by an unofficial visitor here." The document doesn't say who that "unofficial visitor" might be, or what this British agent might do regarding Kennedy's actions inside his own country.

At the same time, actor Douglas Fairbanks Jr. privately sent what he called a "tattle tale" note to President Roosevelt. Alarmed by Kennedy's Hollywood remarks, he warned that the former ambassador claimed "the Lindbergh appeasement groups are not so far off the mark when they suggest that the country can reconcile itself to whomever [*sic*] wins the war and adjust our trade and lives accordingly. He did maintain, however, that we should continue aiding Britain, but not at the expense of getting ourselves into trouble." In a reply to the actor, Roosevelt conceded that "what you say fits in with the general picture" about Kennedy.

Though no longer in government, Kennedy remained a volatile political figure, determined to hold Roosevelt to his promise of keeping America out of the war. "We should never take such a grave step just because we hate Hitler and love Churchill," Kennedy said in a May 1941 commencement speech in Atlanta. "The people who must suffer and give up their lives are entitled to know all the facts before their judgment can be won over to the interventionist cause." Kennedy still looked to the increasingly shrill aviator Lindbergh for his own set of facts about the German war machine, as well as a political ally in preventing American participation. The ambassador's hand was seen in the one-hundred-dollar contribution given by his son Jack to the America First Committee, a large antiwar group that featured Lindbergh as its most prominent spokesman. "What you are doing is vital," Jack wrote in April 1941, attaching the money.

During congressional debate over the Lend-Lease bill, Joe Kennedy initially joined with Lindbergh in opposing it. Joe generally favored aid to the British, but he felt Lend-Lease, with its huge amount of wartime aid and materiel, would effectively end America's neutrality. When he testified on the bill before the House Committee on Foreign Affairs, however, he appeared fuzzy and conflicted, perhaps influenced by the chummy conversation he had just had with Roosevelt. Once again, the president had managed to placate his truculent former ambassador and moneyman. "His whole attitude was very friendly," Joe wrote about Roosevelt in his diary. "I said numerous times that I couldn't understand why so many people were so anxious about our not being friends."

At their White House meeting, the president solicited Kennedy's opinions about nearly everything, including those in Churchill's inner circle such as minister of labour Ernest Bevin and Lord Beaverbrook.

"Would you trust either one of them?" Roosevelt asked.

"Well, not too much but I would have much more confidence in Beaverbrook than in what any one else told me," Kennedy replied, "but I would always be gun-shy of both of them."

Roosevelt had long ago discounted what Kennedy said in favor of the opinions of men such as Hopkins and Harriman. Yet for all their political rancor, there remained a personal attachment between FDR and Kennedy as they talked about the president's son Jimmy. Kennedy had taken an overnight train from New York and met the president that morning in his bedroom, where he found FDR in gray pajamas sitting in his wheelchair. As the president shaved in the bathroom, Joe sat on the toilet seat. "We talked about Jimmy and the fact that he would have to be careful about losing too much money in the moving picture business," Kennedy wrote in his diary. "He said that he would talk with him and then with me later."

In recent months, Jimmy Roosevelt had moved out to Hollywood and divorced his wife, Betsey, which deeply chagrined the president, who admired his daughter-in-law. The controversy surrounding Jimmy's insurance company (set up in Boston with Joe's help) had caused constant problems for the administration, prompting Jimmy to resign as a presidential aide. In Hollywood, he became a vice president for producer Samuel Goldwyn and United Artists, though he continued to rely on Joe for advice. "Why don't you take over my United Artists contract??!!" Jimmy beseeched Kennedy.

Joe gently declined, saying getting involved in Hollywood again "offers worse trials and tribulations than bombings in London." But he offered to help the president's son with his business matters, especially now that Jimmy was headed toward active duty in the military. "Remember that I am always interested to hear how you are doing, boy, socially and financially," Kennedy assured him. "A lot of people don't realize that there are a great many problems and not pleasant ones that go with being the President's son." Not sure what the future would bring, Jimmy thanked Kennedy for "your straightforward and frank assistance," and then waxed nostalgic about their friendship, "remembering always the fun I've had with you and the many things we have done together and which you have made possible for me."

Roosevelt's son-in-law, John Boettiger (whom Kennedy had be-friended and helped land an executive job at the Hearst newspaper in Seattle), seemed sympathetic to Joe's isolationist views. In bitterly com-plaining about White House aides surrounding the president, Kennedy showed his naïveté: "I am still one of those guys who believes that when President Roosevelt says he isn't going to get us into war, he means he isn't going to get us into war and that is a whole hell of a lot more than many of his so-called friends believe." At first, Boettiger seemed recep-tive, treating Joe like a family friend. "Somehow or other, I feel sure we are all thinking along the same lines, and that Roosevelts, the Kenne-dys and Boettigers will be struggling shoulder to shoulder first to keep America out of war, but always to keep America free!" Boettiger wrote on January 31, 1941.

Following the Lend-Lease debate, however, Roosevelt seemed dis-gusted with Kennedy's antics and disloyalty. To his son-in-law, the president's devastatingly candid appraisal painted Kennedy as virtu-ally a Nazi sympathizer. "It is, I think, a little pathetic that he worries about being, with his family, social outcasts," Roosevelt explained to Boettiger in March. "As a matter of fact, he ought to realize of course that he has only himself to blame for the country's opinion as to his testimony before the Committees . . . To him, the future of a small capi-talistic class is safer under a Hitler than under a Churchill. This is sub-conscious on his part and he does not admit it. Personally, I am very fond of Joe and he is wrong in referring to being hurt by my 'hatchet men.' I have none of course, though there are lots of people who speak out of both sides of the fence!"

After Pearl Harbor, Kennedy's offer to volunteer for a vital gov-ernment position went nowhere. He never heard back from Roos-evelt. When Massachusetts congressman John McCormack asked the president if he'd like Kennedy to serve, Roosevelt feigned ignorance of Joe's cable and acted interested in his offer. Feeling spurned, Kennedy thanked McCormack for his intervention and decided to forget the whole thing.

Nevertheless, Kennedy kept a constant running dialogue about the war with his friend Beaverbrook, just as they had done in London. During his visit to America with Churchill, Beaverbrook traveled to New York and met with Kennedy on January 17, 1942, at the Waldorf Astoria. Beaverbrook confided about the extraordinary damage to the U.S. fleet inflicted at Pearl Harbor and expressed worry about America's "very serious" vulnerability to future attack. Max expected bombings on the West Coast and "token bombings" along the Atlantic shoreline. "He said we had practically no defense and no anti-aircraft guns," Kennedy recalled. "He is disappointed at our production and amazed at our complacency."

Joe asked if Max might stay longer, after the prime minister returned to England, presumably to help America jump-start its aircraft production, but Beaverbrook replied that "Churchill did not want him to leave his side." At the White House, whenever Joe's name arose, Max said Roosevelt "always told him of the great affection he held for me," Kennedy recalled. The president "practically admitted" that Joe had been "an important factor" in his 1940 reelection. Then, "with that baby stare of his," Beaverbrook asked how well Joe got along with FDR's top aide, Harry Hopkins. Joe tried to act nonchalant, with a nondescript reply. Watching Beaverbrook's reaction, he wondered if Max had figured out who his main detractor in the White House was. "I am convinced that he knew it's Hopkins who is keeping my services from being employed, and he just wanted to know my reaction," Kennedy later deduced.

Beaverbrook promised to bring up the job offer again with Roosevelt's staff when he returned to Washington, but Joe instructed him to forget it. Pride, once more, got the best of him. "They are very well aware of what I can do and that I am ready and willing to do it—and that's all that's needed," Kennedy insisted. Max warned that America and Britain could lose the war, and Kennedy agreed. "I still have very little confidence in the business ability of Churchill and Roosevelt to decide these terrific matters," Joe admitted in his diary. "When you consider the Japanese situation, our attitude toward them, and that Roosevelt knows they have been preparing for 20 years, our unpreparedness is nothing short of insanity."

Unlike his father and older brother, Jack Kennedy privately supported Lend-Lease. In a series of letters, he urged the former ambassador to do the same. Jack had realized the lessons he outlined in *Why England Slept* could now be applied at home. While in California, young Kennedy had attended a series of roundtable discussions about world affairs and become convinced, like Churchill, that an Anglo-American alliance was needed to stop Hitler. "There is a real feeling here," Jack observed at the conference, "that outright and total support for Great Britain is not only preferable but essential for long-term survival and stability here in the States. There is near unanimity that we have no choice now but to make ourselves, and our friends, strong."

Two months before Pearl Harbor, Jack signed up as a navy ensign, ignoring his earlier rejection by the military for medical reasons. With nearly all his generation signing up for the imminent war, including his elder brother, Joe Jr., Jack said, "I do not intend to be the only one among them wearing coward's tweeds." The Kennedy sons were keenly aware of the former ambassador's reputation for cowardice because of his opposition to American intervention. That same month, Jack learned of his father's horrendous decision to arrange a lobotomy for his mildly retarded sister, Rosemary, hoping to improve her condition but rendering it profoundly worse. The tragedy "confirmed that vital part of me, that has always been, at heart, a fatalist," Jack wrote to a friend, speaking of the character trait that made him "confront unavoidable facts, grim realities, and awful possibilities about the times in which we find ourselves abandoned. It has also made me realize something more simple. Father does not always know best."

Jack Kennedy wound up at the Office of Naval Intelligence in Washington. He served under a captain who was once posted in the London embassy and who admired Jack for his handling of the 1939 *Athenia* incident. This desk job was originally arranged by his father for Joe Jr. Instead, young Joe had insisted on a far more dangerous task flying navy planes. For Jack, the office assignment seemed a perfect way to get into the war, given his poor medical condition and the captain's help in getting a doctor's cursory exam to allow his enlistment. After he arrived in Washington, Jack socialized often with his sister Kick. She'd recently joined the *Washington Times Herald* as a researcher/secretary. To her chagrin, Kick had learned that her old London beau Billy Hartington was about to get engaged to another woman back in England. There seemed nothing she could do about this romantic rival. "I haven't heard from him for simply ages and that no doubt is the reason," she lamented to her father.

In Washington, both Kick and Jack soon found new loves in their lives. Among Kick's colleagues at the newspaper, Jack met reporter Inga Arvad, a blonde-haired Danish graduate of Columbia University's Journalism School, who was four years older and immediately charmed him. Inga's beauty would attract many men, including Bernard Baruch, whom she called "the old goat" behind his back. "He [Baruch] can help me a lot," Inga wrote to her mother, according to her FBI file, "but it won't do any good for him to be so much in love." At the *Times Herald*, Inga became fast friends with Kick, whose virginal all-American-girl quality contrasted with the sultry style in Inga that had enticed her brother. Before long, Jack Kennedy, at age twenty-four, wanted to marry her. What he didn't know about "Inka Binga," as he friskily called her, was that the FBI suspected her of being a German spy. Columbia class-mates told federal investigators of Arvad's "pro-Nazi" views and blatant anti-Semitic comments. A photo even turned up of Inga inside Hit-ler's private box at the 1936 Olympics, which she later claimed to be covering as a journalist. The FBI file reported that the Führer called her "a perfect Nordic beauty." Inga's estranged second husband, angry about Jack, was apparently the source for columnist Walter Winchell's provocative item in January 1942 about the romance. "Pa Kennedy no like," Winchell commented, in what proved an understatement. Try-ing to salvage his own political career and cultivate his sons' futures, Joe Kennedy erupted and rushed down to Washington. When he con-fronted his son and daughter, Kick tried to defend Jack's wish to marry her friend for love. "Damn it Jack," the patriarch exploded. "She's *al-ready* married."

Initially Jack defied his father, and the affair quickly got him bounced out of Washington by the navy and transferred to a post in South Carolina. When Inga visited Jack at a local hotel, FBI agents with devices picked up their lovemaking while listening through the walls. In this struggle for Jack's soul, Inga knew who would win. "I am not going to try and make you change—it would be without result anyway—because big Joe has a stronger hand than I," she concluded.

Privately as in public, Joe Kennedy knew how to masterfully cover up and mitigate damaging evidence, motivated by what he insisted was love for his family. There was no doubting Joe was the emotional cen-ter of his family's existence, the galvanizing force that provided the money and energy to fuel their dreams. He could spin a new version of reality out of whole cloth if necessary, just as he did in justifying the lobotomy on his daughter Rosemary. All his life, he'd been dissembling with a salesman's grin—with business partners, with government of-ficials including Roosevelt and Churchill, with Rose, and now with his adult children, whose romantic partners he could check out, wary that his progeny might be exploited or taken for a bundle. In writing to his oldest son, Joe ignored the FBI's investigation of Jack's affair with a possible Nazi spy, instead foisting a very different reason: Jack's wanting to go to sea. "He has become disgusted with the desk jobs and all the Jews," his father claimed, "and as an awful lot of the fellows that he knows are in active service, and particularly with you in the fleet service, he feels that at least he ought to be trying to do something."

Determined to put his own spin on history, Joe began putting together a memoir of his diplomatic career in Great Britain, hiring two ghostwriters at different points. The versions left among his papers recount Kennedy's numerous meetings with Churchill, and portray him not as a cowardly appeaser in London but as a diligent and farsighted patriot only looking out for his country's best interests. In January 1942, word of Kennedy's memoir leaked to syndicated columnist Drew Pearson. "If Joe is frank—and he usually is—the book ought to be a bestseller," Pearson predicted. When Roosevelt heard of the impending book, he asked for an advance look at the manuscript. He immediately found plenty of offensive material, toward not only the British but also FDR's inner circle of advisers such as Harry Hopkins. The president invited Joe for a White House visit, and the two men argued for an hour about the book's publication. Given the wartime circumstances, Kennedy agreed to hold off, acceding to the commander in chief's concern that Joe's diplomatic memoir "would play into the hands of Axis propagandists," as Pearson later reported.

With his sons now in the military, Kennedy again offered to serve Roosevelt in any capacity, the same open-ended volunteering he'd sent in a cable immediately following Pearl Harbor. "I don't want to appear in the role of a man looking for a job for the sake of getting an appointment, but Joe and Jack are in the service and I feel that my experience in these critical times might be worth something in some position," Joe wrote on March 4, 1942. "I just want to say that if you want me, I am yours to command at any time," he repeated. As Roosevelt likely knew, Joe wanted to be put in a grand expeditor's role, an American version similar to the broad task performed by Lord Beaverbrook. Certainly, Joe's experience with Beaverbrook—along with his personal knowledge of how Baruch excelled in a similar role in World War I—made him better situated for such a high-profile post than as a diplomat. Roosevelt, who'd ignored him the first time, responded promptly. Three days later, the president asked Joe to help oversee "stepping up the great increase in our shipbuilding—especially in getting some of the new production under way. I know, for example, that you do not want to be merely a member of one of the many Commissions—that you do want actual, practical and effective responsibility in turning out ships. [Admirals] Land and Vickery are keen to have you do this. Will you?" But the task required running shipyards rather than acting as an important decision maker on military production, like Beaverbrook.

After telling the president he'd take on any job, Kennedy refused Roosevelt's request. "Without a definite assignment and authority, I'd just be a hindrance to the program," he explained.

Whatever chance Joe had of shedding his "appeaser" label—of gaining political rehabilitation with Roosevelt's crowd or of presenting his own version of the facts in a book—now seemed lost. He had been rendered mute, boxed into a corner, by his own missteps and by a clever president unwilling to put him in a sensitive role again. Joe would spend the rest of the war in political exile, unable to affect great events or grand alliance policy as his sons went off to war. Friends in the press would float rumors of a comeback, but nothing happened. Much of what Joe learned about Roosevelt and Churchill's special relationship came from letters with his friend Beaverbrook. "I am withstanding all efforts to get me to make speeches or to write articles, because I don't want to do anything that won't help us all win the war and get out of this mess," Joe confessed to Beaverbrook on New Year's Eve 1942, "and they expect criticism from me, so I am suffering in silence."

26

Replacements

John Gilbert Winant came to London as the perfect replacement. Arriving in February 1942 on a transatlantic flight, the new U.S. ambassador to the Court of St. James's offered a welcome contrast to his predecessor, Joe Kennedy, and a bit of relief for the Roosevelt administration.

The press heralded Winant as "the New Hampshire Lincoln," a shy and homespun former governor with bushy eyebrows, deep-set eyes, and a granite-like chin worthy of Mount Rushmore. "He is almost the antithesis of what a diplomat should be," Associated Press correspondent Jack Stinnett observed. "He's a slow talker, and in debate has the habit of gazing down his shirt front for seconds before he makes a statement."

In contrast to the brash, self-promoting Babbittry of Kennedy, Winant didn't carry out his own personal foreign policy. He didn't publicly embrace aviation heroes turned appeasers, or hobnob with German sympathizers among the Cliveden set. He didn't oversee shipments of Scotch whiskey to his own firm back in the States. Most important, the fifty-two-year-old millionaire was grateful to the president, rather than contemptuous; more New England Protestant than big-city Irish

Catholic; and a Republican more favorable to the ideals of the New Deal than capitalist Kennedy would ever be. "Send us John Winant as ambassador and, even more, secure the permanent end of Joe Kennedy's political career," urged Harold Laski, no longer tolerant of Kennedy's glib bombast. FDR's friends made sure Laski wasn't disappointed.

With the Churchills, Winant made an equally favorable impression. In his first few months, the ambassador spent almost every weekend at Chequers, the prime minister's country home during the war, listening to Winston's pleas for America's help. Eager to please, Churchill's top assistant, Brendan Bracken, aided Winant in finding a place to stay in London. "House agents have an exaggerated notion of the wealth of Americans," Bracken advised. "If you think the house suitable to you, we will take over the job of negotiating terms." Winant grew to admire Churchill's vantage on world events even as he defined them: "You have taught me that the great historians have a true sense of lasting values," he later told the prime minister. Winant was at Chequers when Churchill learned of Pearl Harbor.

However, the Churchill most impressed with Winant was the Prime Minister's beautiful redheaded daughter, Sarah. She also viewed Winant as a welcome replacement. The American ambassador's entry into the Churchill inner circle, and the heart of Sarah's affections, coincided with the disintegration of her marriage to entertainer Vic Oliver. "Winant had fallen rather ethereally in love with Sarah Churchill, then in her late twenties, which helped attract him to the Churchill family, to the British cause in general and to Chequers in particular," recalled Churchill biographer Roy Jenkins, then employed as a young researcher for Winant. "He was a helpful ambassador, but his look of calm asceticism concealed inner seething."

Winston Churchill's amorphous, uncorralled love for his children was particularly reflected in Sarah, who, as an actress, dancer, and dramatic spirit, often defied convention and her parents' wishes. With the war, though, she joined her father's ranks. She signed up for the

Women's Auxiliary Air Force and later accompanied her father and Winant on an important trip to Cairo for a strategy conference with Roosevelt, as the early stages of war played out in North Africa. These military assignments helped keep Sarah away from Oliver. When she told her father of her divorce plans, Winston seemed amused rather than downhearted. "You cheeky bitch! I wouldn't let you leave me!" he bellowed. Winston never liked Oliver. When he later heard that Mussolini had arranged for the firing squad killing of Italian foreign minister Count Galeazzo Ciano, married to Mussolini's daughter, Churchill muttered acidly, "Well, at least he had the pleasure of murdering his son-in-law." Perhaps because Sarah was his unspoken favorite, Winston could confide to her some of his deepest fears, the kind he couldn't say aloud as undaunted leader of his people. "War is a game played with a smiling face, but do you think there is laughter in my heart?" he asked his daughter while in Cairo. "We travel in style and round us there is great luxury and seeming security, but I never forget the man at the front, the bitter struggles, and the fact that men are dying in the air, on the land, and at sea."

Like the man himself, Winant's wartime relationship with the prime minister's daughter was quiet and circumspect. Gil and Sarah were both still married to others, though Winant's wife remained mostly in America. The affair certainly complicated matters for the U.S. ambassador. The prime minister made no effort to interfere with a "love affair which my father suspected but about which we did not speak," Sarah recalled. It was a remarkably precarious position for Churchill to have his daughter in love with Winant and for his daughter-in-law, Pamela, to be engaged in an affair with Harriman, the other American emissary sent to Britain. Yet Winston, ever the navigator, got along famously with both men. Winant even enjoyed the amusing code name that Churchill used with the president. "A certain naval person has spent a great deal of time in trying to familiarize Averill [*sic*] and myself with the naval situation," Winant enthused to Roosevelt soon after he arrived in London.

By his first year, Winant was beloved by the English people, and famous for his compassionate visits with bombing victims living among the city's ruins. Rather than spending weekends in the countryside as Kennedy had, he stayed in a simple flat rather than his stately official residence, and lived on British rations. However, he soon found himself eclipsed by Harriman, who broadened his portfolio after Pearl Harbor beyond Great Britain to include critical negotiations with the Soviet Union, all demanding Churchill's constant attention. Far more energetic than Winant, Averell couldn't help stepping on the ambassador's toes, claiming ever more responsibilities. While Harriman served as a vital link between his friend Roosevelt and Churchill, Ambassador Winant became "almost an appendage of the Prime Minister," recalled Jock Colville. "Averell not only took the glamour out of Winant's job," observed American journalist Harrison Salisbury, "he substantially undercut his relationship with Churchill." Ambassador Winant found himself in a very familiar frustrating place. Cut out of the flow of information, and replaced in the decision-making by a special fixer sent by Washington, he lost influence with Roosevelt. "I have been by-passed continuously," Winant complained.

It was the same sorry lament of Joe Kennedy, the man he had replaced.

Pamela Churchill never admired Winant, certainly not the idealized version of the American ambassador portrayed in the British press by those relieved to be rid of Kennedy. She thought Winant's humble, halting manner rather dull and pathetic. Privately, she remained partial to the old Kennedy crowd and to the new American in town,

Averell Harriman, whose demeanor she found most enticing. If the bond between Winant and Sarah was imperceptible to most, the passion between Pamela and Harriman could be more readily detected. Randolph's cousin Clarissa Churchill confessed to a longtime friend that "Randolph's wife had no intention of sticking to him; and that Mr. [Winston] Churchill would be very sad if their marriage broke up."

Since 1939, the most stable part of Pamela's marriage had been her relationship with her in-laws. With young Mary finishing school, Diana Sandys with a husband and family of her own, and Sarah and Randolph active with the military, the Churchills often relied on Pamela and their grandson young Winston for weekend company. "I was kind of the only one at home and they kind of treated me as the daughter at home in those days," Pamela recalled. "Clemmie was marvelous—she took me right into the heart of the family." Though perfectly cordial to her, Pamela never understood why Clementine was so "very pessimistic" toward her only son. "She decided early on to make Winston her entire life. One of the problems, because she so lived for Winston and protecting him, [was] that even her children became a challenge to that," Pamela later reflected. "I think her problem with Randolph was it was the only thing that came between her and Winston—his love for his son. This was very hard for her to take, especially when Randolph was making life difficult for Winston." Singular in her affections, Clementine appeared distant with the rest of her family, including her new grandson. "She didn't ever have any really cozy relationship with her children and grandchildren—I don't know why she didn't," Pamela recalled. At dinners with her adult children, Clementine took great pains to serve a proper cup of tea "and was just very correct but they were total strangers."

Neither Diana nor Mary particularly liked Pamela, though she did befriend Sarah. They talked about Randolph, and Pamela shared some of her difficulties with him as a husband. Pamela could see how much the prime minister lit up in his daughter Sarah's presence, despite his emotional limitations as a parent. "I think in his own family he was devoted to his children and there were problems all the way through," Pamela recalled. "But he loved Sarah deeply. Sarah in those days was a marvelous person—she was not only beautiful but she was poetic, she was enchanting." However, neither married Churchill woman, Pamela nor Sarah, confided to the other about her secret extramarital love. In wartime Britain, romances like theirs might be discerned in public but never discussed.

Pamela soon found a convenient way to hide her affair with Harriman and see him after hours, beyond those diplomatic weekends spent with the prime minister at Chequers or with Lord Beaverbrook at Cherkley. She befriended Harriman's daughter Kathleen, who had moved to London to be near her father. The two young women in their early twenties, though from different nations and backgrounds, went everywhere together. In Kathleen's eyes, Pamela was "a wonderful girl, my age, but one of the wisest young girls I have ever met—knows everything about everything, political and otherwise," Harriman's daughter wrote to her older sister back home on Long Island.

An expert horsewoman and skier who had recently graduated from Bennington College, Kathleen Harriman enjoyed her father's pride as she became accustomed to the consequences of his complicated personal life. Kathleen's mother, Kitty, had been Averell's first wife, whom he divorced in 1928. A governess would raise Kathleen and her sister. Averell then courted Marie Whitney, a witty and glamorous married woman whom he met while playing polo. The breakup of the Whitney marriage sparked some New York tabloid headlines that included Harriman in the mix. Yet his interest in beautiful women continued after he married Marie. When President Roosevelt decided in March 1941 to send Harriman to London, Marie remained in New York, attending to her art gallery, her health, and her own matters. After a brief time, Harriman invited Kathleen to visit him in London, and with the intervention of Harry Hopkins, she received State Department approval to do so, as a traveling journalist for the Hearst news service. Kathleen decided to stay and assist her father, deeply engaged in his important work for the president. Although she admired Marie, Kathleen remained devoted to her father, whom she called "Ave," more like a friend than a parent.

Introducing his daughter to Pamela Churchill, Averell asked that she show Kathleen around London, especially when he was away on diplomatic business. Tactfully, Kathleen didn't say anything when she learned of her father's affair with the prime minister's daughter-in-law, who was half his age. Living in an upstairs apartment at the same hotel as "Ave," Pamela assumed Kathleen had figured out their subterfuge. A few months transpired until she finally broached the subject with Kathleen. "Of course, I'm not a fool!" Kathleen replied. As she later recalled: "Within a couple of weeks of being in England, I realized what was going on and I had to decide whether I would go home. I figured that it was important to stay and protect him."

When Harriman and his daughter moved to a bigger suite in the Dorchester, Pamela joined them, taking a bedroom of her own, subsidized by Averell. Among their London social circle, Pamela and Kathleen were known as roommates, with Averell portrayed as the munificent daddy figure. "Who do I go around with? People I've met through Pam, mostly older men," Kathleen explained to her sister Mary. "You can't imagine how interesting life over here is." No longer was Pamela the plump debutante or, at least for the moment, the pregnant Churchill Madonna affixed to a drunken husband. Though two years older, Kathleen was fascinated by Pamela's way of handling men, a power she projected with what Evelyn Waugh described as "kitten eyes full of innocent fun." With remarkable self-awareness, fostered by Cecil Beaton photos of her plastered to the walls of her room, Pamela became a combination of deference and manipulation, sensuality and jocularity, a sparkling concoction alluring to many men. "Pam is also a bitch," Kathleen wrote. "I like her and think we'll get on OK."

During that summer, Harriman paid for a country cottage Kathleen had secured outside London. Just as she learned to accept Beaverbrook's largesse, Pamela relied on financial help from her newest benefactor, the fourth-wealthiest man in America, heir to the railroad and banking fortune of robber baron E. H. Harriman. ("There's a very rich American coming to London for Roosevelt," Beaverbrook advised her before Ave's arrival.) Pamela and Kathleen stayed together when Harriman went on a long inspection tour of the war effort in the Middle East. "We were already ensconced in this cottage by the time Averell came back," Pamela recalled of her free, fun-loving time with Kathleen Harriman. "So that was kind of a good alibi. She was wonderful."

Six months before Pearl Harbor, Harriman became increasingly aware of Great Britain's tenuous grip on its empire and Churchill's nagging fear of losing to the Nazis if America didn't enter the war. During a trip to Cairo, Harriman carried a letter from Churchill directing British commanders to cooperate completely, assuring them that the American special envoy "enjoys my complete confidence" and that "no one can do more for you."

Up until then, British fighting around the Mediterranean Sea had been a mess, from defeats of the Royal Navy in Crete to German general Erwin Rommel's menacing sweep through North Africa. As a matter of strategy, Churchill placed much of Britain's military might in the Middle East in order to protect shipping and the flow of oil, keeping it away from the Nazi war machine. Winston had personally escorted Harriman around bombed-out London when he first arrived, to show him how the English were standing up to attacks. By July 1941, Churchill urged the presidential adviser to visit Cairo and see for himself why more American assistance was so desperately needed. As a sign of the trip's importance, the prime minister asked his son, Randolph, then an underused officer stationed in Cairo, to personally show Harriman around. Over the next few weeks, Harriman toured across hundreds of miles in the Middle East, listening to young Churchill's opinions about destroyed British tanks and other weaknesses in the desert. Averell seemed to formulate his own judgments. "Randolph thought him shrewd and wonderful," recalled his cousin Anita Leslie, then an ambulance driver serving in Cairo. "He did not yet know that his wife Pamela thought the same."

The Churchills were heartened by positive reports they received about Randolph's military work in Cairo, though their son complained of his father's meddling inquiries to the generals about him. "It really has been v[ery] embarrassing," he explained in a letter to Pamela. "He ought to know that in war 'no news is good news.'" However, Winston took heed of Randolph's note complaining about the poor job being done by the local commander, and replaced the man. And while his drinking and philandering persisted, Randolph did a fine job on duty promoting British interests. "Randolph's post as officially described sounds thrilling & terribly responsible—His duties seem multifarious & will require discrimination, judgment & tact," Clementine wrote to Winston. "But I think Randolph has these qualities—I must write & congratulate him." The prime minister impressed upon his son the need to win over his "good friend" the visiting American, in the best interest of their nation. As Harriman left for Cairo, Churchill wrote a personal letter to his son, which first mentioned Pamela and little Winston and then talked about matters of war. "The United States are giving us more help every day, and longing for an opportunity to take the plunge," he wrote. "Whether they will do so or not remains an inscrutable mystery of American politics. The longer they wait, the longer and more costly the job will be which they will have to do." Winston directed his son not show the letter to strangers and, after digesting its contents, to burn his copy.

Randolph soon agreed with his father about Harriman. After a few days together in Cairo, Randolph strongly endorsed him as a crucial on-the-ground strategist. "I have been tremendously impressed by Harriman, and can well understand the regard which you have for him," Randolph wrote back to his father. "In 10 very full and active days he has definitely become my favourite American . . . I have become very intimate with him and he had admitted me to all the business he has transacted. I am sure you would do well to back his opinions on the situation out here to the limit." In Randolph's assessment, Harriman's political advice about Roosevelt was correct and should be followed. He let his father "know what a tremendous admiration he has for you," Randolph added. "He clearly regards himself more as your servant than R's [Roosevelt's]."

Harriman cheered Randolph with news that his father looked "well and vigorous," and that Pamela and his daughter Kathleen got along famously. Randolph had no idea of the intense affair between his wife and the American envoy, even if his letter home to Pamela seemed to hint at it. "I found him absolutely charming, & it was lovely to be able to hear so much of you & all my friends," he wrote of Harriman's visit. "He spoke delightfully about you and I fear that I have a serious rival."

After several weeks, Harriman returned home to Washington to meet with Roosevelt. He briefed U.S. military commanders, who questioned Churchill's bold gambit in the Middle East. But Harriman proved the prime minister's newest and perhaps most potent ally in attempting to sway American leaders in 1941, until Pearl Harbor decided their fates. Like Harry Hopkins, Harriman could be counted upon to smooth out the initially uneasy relationship between Churchill and Roosevelt. At the Atlantic Charter conference, before meeting Roosevelt as president for the first time, Winston turned anxiously to Harriman and asked, "I wonder if he will like me?" Using Pamela as his back channel, Harriman delivered the answer. She relayed the message to the prime minister that "the President is intrigued and likes him enormously."

. . .

As Churchill knew, nothing in intelligence work compared to human sources. His daughter-in-law, though not conscripted, performed superbly in relaying the private thoughts of the visiting Americans, especially Harriman. During his first two months in England, Ave spent seven weekends with the Churchills, mostly with Pamela. One of her biographers, Sally Bedell Smith, quotes "a man who knew Pamela intimately after the war" as saying that Churchill, the son of Jennie, not only condoned this sexual affair but recognized its political value. "I know Churchill put Harriman in her way so they would go to bed, so she could find things out and tell him. I am convinced of that as anything," this unnamed man said to Smith, whose other biographies include that of William Paley, another of Pamela's later intimates. "It was done in the seventeenth and eighteenth centuries by kings. Why not Winston Churchill? He was ruthless. She was living openly in the flat with Harriman. Of course Winston knew, even though his own son was away at war. Pam was useful to him."

Whatever Churchill sensed about this *amour sucré* remains one of historical conjecture, but enough to pique the curiosity three decades later of Kennedy friend Arthur M. Schlesinger Jr., who asked Pamela if the prime minister ever confronted her. "He only mentioned it once," she told him.

"You know they are saying a lot of things about Averell in relation to you," Winston said, as Pamela recalled years later.

At that moment, Pamela felt that "her blood froze." The Churchills had treated her as their daughter, opening her eyes to a world she had never imagined. She adored the prime minister, even if her marriage to his son was impossible. According to Schlesinger, "She thought that old Winston was the one person she could not lie to about it." Perhaps Winston, even if he knew the truth intuitively, wasn't ready to face the consequences of knowing with certainty, of having to lie deliberately to his son.

"Well, a lot of people have nothing else to do in wartime but indulge in gossip," she replied to her father-in-law.

As the explosive question hung in the air for that moment, Churchill apparently decided to dismiss rather than detonate it. "I quite agree," he concurred. As Pamela recalled, "Then he said something about the triviality of gossip in the midst of the mighty concerns of war."

Whatever personal honor may have been at stake perhaps seemed minuscule to the demands of his nation facing a mortal enemy. "That was the end of the conversation," Pamela recalled of this short but tense chat with the prime minister. "It was the one moment when I thought he was going to talk about it . . . And he never mentioned it again."

If Winston provided the tacit atmospherics for Pamela's affair with Harriman, Beaverbrook urged them on purposefully. Both Winston's longtime ally and friendly protagonist, Max was the true puppet master, perceiving a Machiavellian advantage. He used these two lovers as conduits for information, as a means to gain more power for himself. "In retrospect, Pam feels that Beaverbrook engineered the whole thing in order to get something on Averell and thereby influence American policy," Schlesinger recorded in his journal. She said that Harry Hopkins, who initially encouraged Harriman to meet her, eventually became "disturbed, fearing stories to the effect that the President's envoy was breaking up the Prime Minister's son's marriage." Part of Hopkins's concern may have been that sensitive information Pamela derived from pillow talk with Harriman was later shared with Beaverbrook as well as the prime minister. "I described Max to him. I described Winston to him," admitted Pamela four decades later. "I've always maintained that Max was the only person who had any real influence with Winston during the war. They were so totally different [in] what they admired in each other, it was sort of fascinating."

Harriman spent as much of his time with Beaverbrook as anyone in England. The American millionaire envoy and the British press magnate worked feverishly together on building up arms supplies under the Lend-Lease program. In September 1941 they traveled together to Russia to negotiate more aid for the Soviet resistance against the Nazis. Like her father, Kathleen Harriman was mesmerized by Lord Beaverbrook, writing home that "even his best friends are scared of him, because he's got a fearful temper and no one seems to know when it will break." While watching tough-guy actor Edward G. Robinson in a film, Winston chuckled and said the actor was "just like Max."

Ever the poker player, Beaverbrook valued Harriman as a special chit, which he could play with Churchill as well as Roosevelt, as if he were running his own foreign policy. When they were all together, Harriman noticed Winston's special regard for his old friend Max, no matter how troublesome or demanding the latter was. "The PM considers that Beaverbrook can do a lot of things which he cannot, such as building up his successful newspapers, financial acquisitiveness, gambling, etc. and he does not understand what is back of them," Harriman wrote. "Beaverbrook realises this and never gives himself away. Winning from the PM at poker is an essential part of their relationship." As part of his ceaseless networking, Max kept in touch with many Americans, sending FDR historical manuscripts as a holiday gift ("1943 will be the best year we have had for a long time," the president wrote back in thanks) and candid comments about the prime minister and his son. "It is the general view that Bevan will do Churchill no harm," Beaverbrook wrote to FDR, referring to Aneurin Bevan, a Labour Party critic of Churchill's handling of the war. "And certainly at the moment though he [Bevan] is trying to achieve the parliamentary style of Winston when he wished to demolish an opponent, he is attaining only the platform style of Randolph." In personal letters with Joe Kennedy back in the States, Beaverbrook and Joe compared notes on Churchill. Kennedy, too, saw Max as a man of action. "Favored as I was with a ringside seat at that Armageddon, I can testify as an eyewitness that Lord Beaverbrook, as much as any one individual, can be credited with having forged victory out of the molten lava of defeat that seemed irresistibly to be submerging proud Britain," Kennedy later wrote. "For the war was won in the air, by the RAF in September 1940; and Lord Beaverbrook, as Minister of Aircraft Production, gave to 'the few,' who contributed 'so much,' the planes with which they won the Battle of Britain for 'so many.' "

When Churchill, so grateful for what Beaverbrook had achieved, dubbed him "Lord Spitfire" for his plane production, Max responded with a sense of history that undoubtedly the prime minister appreciated. "You will be talked of even more widely after you are dead than during your lifetime," Beaverbrook wrote prophetically. "But I am talked of while I live, and save for my association with you, I will be forgotten thereafter."

Despite these humble words, Beaverbrook prepared himself should Churchill stumble as prime minister and the Parliament turn to him as a replacement. By early 1942, Churchill faced sharp criticism for the fall, immediately after Pearl Harbor, of British-held Singapore to the Japanese, resulting in the loss of hundreds of men and two battleships. Still others within the government, including Beaverbrook, grumbled for more aid and cooperation with the Soviets, which Churchill, almost as wary of the Communists as the Nazis, opposed. Ironically, some critics panned Churchill for bringing the mercurial Beaverbrook into his coalition government. With her own political antennae, Clementine Churchill warned her husband about Beaverbrook's mischief-making, his constant threats to quit unless he got his way, and his lust for power.

Clementine "never liked or trusted Max," Pamela recalled. "She, I think, probably quite rightly, as Winston's wife, knew that Max would use Winston to the maximum but throw him to the wolves if he felt inclined." In February 1942, Clementine urged Winston to remove Beaverbrook from his government. Better to replace him, she argued, before Beaverbrook gained more political leverage. "It is true that if you do he may (& will) work against you—at first covertly & then openly— But is not hostility without, better than intrigue & treachery & and rattledom [*sic*] within?" she contended in a letter. "My Darling—Try ridding yourself of this microbe which some people fear is in your blood—Exorcise this bottle Imp & see if the air is not clearer and purer."

After one letter too many threatening resignation, Churchill accepted Beaverbrook's request on February 26, 1942, which blamed his asthma as the cause. Many thought the old fox would rest on the sidelines, waiting for his moment to pounce as an acceptable substitute for Churchill. Privately, Beaverbrook confided his interest in the top job, both to those in Parliament and to Harriman. "Beaverbrook tried to take advantage many times of Churchill," recalled Harriman, "and I never thought he was as loyal to Churchill as Churchill was to him."

For now, Max was gone from the government, though, in Winston's mind, never replaced.

27

The Churchill Club

*"The winds and waves are always on the side of
the ablest navigators."*
—EDWARD GIBBON, *The History of the
Decline and Fall of the Roman Empire*

By 1943, Winston Churchill believed the war, which had killed so many and threatened England's very existence, would soon be won and Hitler's Nazis vanquished. Victories at El Alamein, in the Egyptian desert, and German surrender at Stalingrad, sent the Axis forces into a slow retreat, the kind of turning point that a student of history like Churchill recognized so well.

"I always avoid prophesying beforehand, because it is much better policy to prophesy after the event has already taken place," Winston jovially told the press in February 1943, when asked about the future outcome. Informed with a scholarly view of world history, Churchill knew twists of fate, personality quirks, and unforeseen circumstances could humble any strategist. How else to explain Hitler's megalomaniacal decision to invade the huge Soviet Union rather than an already weakened England, creating a bloody Eastern Front that drained Germany's resources? Or the Führer's bumblings in North Africa in the battle for oil, for which, Winston mockingly told the U.S. Congress in May 1943, "we have to thank the military intuition of Corporal Hitler."

Upon becoming prime minister, Churchill interrupted writing the large multi-volume *A History of the English-Speaking Peoples*—his paean to Great Britain's shared heritage with America and other former colonies—so his belief in this special alliance could be put into action during the war. History provided perspective when faced with many frustrations, not only with Roosevelt but also with U.S. generals and his own. "Never forget that when History looks back, your vision & your piercing energy, coupled with your patience & magnanimity, will all be part of your greatness," Clementine reminded him after some discouraging setbacks. "So don't allow yourself to be made angry—I often think of your saying, that the only worse things than Allies is *not* having Allies!' "

Many he once considered friendly, including Lord Beaverbrook, constantly questioned his judgment and tactics. On his own in May 1943, Beaverbrook traveled to the United States, as a former minister without portfolio, to assess Roosevelt's chances for reelection in 1944. During his stay, Max contacted Joe Kennedy in Cape Cod and asked him to meet in Washington, where they dined alone in Beaverbrook's suite. For nearly two hours, Max chastised his friend for not supporting Roosevelt enough, suggesting he either join the administration or run for public office himself. Joe sensed Max had visited the president, though he denied it when Kennedy asked directly. "He is a candidate for the fourth term," Beaverbrook said in his "straight-forward but very debonair" way, according to Kennedy's diary. Beaverbrook added that Roosevelt "of course, wants you in [the administration] and would be very happy to get you in and would pay a big price if you went in." By then, Kennedy had been out of government service for two years. He remained convinced Roosevelt didn't want him back, even if they met occasionally at the White House for a seemingly friendly conversation. As a man of considerable wealth himself, Beaverbrook suggested Joe must be bored with private life. He insisted the White House would offer Joe "a big carrot" for the taking.

"I can honestly say that I have no further desire for public office," Kennedy replied. As he later wrote in his diary, "I let him talk and said I never heard more bunk because I could get all the thrills and excitement watching the careers of my children. I do not have to have it centered on me any more. I have had mine."

On the chance he might be sincere, Beaverbrook didn't press the issue with Kennedy. This generational baton-passing wasn't something Beaverbrook wanted for himself, not with the war in full gear. Beaverbrook's own son, a decorated fighter pilot, aspired to politics and was later elected to Parliament after the war. But Max, still a bundle of energy and willpower, keenly wanted to remain in the limelight, even though he was a decade older than Kennedy. While out of office, Beaverbrook—far more than his American friend—wanted desperately to get back in, on his own terms.

"We would like to see Roosevelt re-elected," Beaverbrook said, in the imperial *we*. "We know he is our friend and we naturally feel that we would be much better off with him than anybody else." Then, after a pause, Max added, "Of course, I like Roosevelt very much."

"That's a damn lie," Kennedy burst out, "you never liked him and if you like him now you like him because he is giving you everything you want."

Max and Joe, as friends, valued such candid talk. After discussing Roosevelt, their dinner conversation turned to Churchill, the other touchstone in their lives. For several weeks, Churchill felt snubbed by Roosevelt, concerned that the Americans might not cooperate in the same European war strategy as he envisioned. Once he heard of the president's private invitation to Max to visit him, the prime minister decided to travel on the *Queen Mary* to the United States with Beaverbrook and others for an official visit. "In Washington, Churchill certainly seems to have feared that Roosevelt and Beaverbrook would combine against him over his Mediterranean strategy," observed Beaverbrook's biographers Anne Chisholm and Michael Davie. Like Soviet leader Joseph Stalin, Beaverbrook believed the Allies should immediately create a second front in western Europe, rather than wait to secure the Middle East. So Churchill declared the need for another strategy session with Roosevelt, always capable of his own intrigue, while keeping an eye on his estranged colleague, Beaverbrook. Harriman joined them on the *Queen Mary*, also wary of Beaverbrook's influence with Roosevelt. "I had two fights with him [Churchill] while on the ship going over," Beaverbrook recounted to Kennedy, "when he didn't speak with me for a day and one in Washington when he didn't speak to me until the following morning when he opened up the conversation by remarking that we haven't changed much, we still argue and fight, but it only shows that we are vital people and we must continue in our regular way."

Despite Joe's fondness for Max, there didn't seem much loyalty in this special Anglo-American alliance. "I reminded Beaverbrook that I had a long conversation with Roosevelt before I resigned about Churchill and Beaverbrook and at that time neither stood particularly high in his regard, but at that time I knew that he didn't stand very well with them, so it was all even," Kennedy recorded. In his own notes, Beaverbrook said Kennedy predicted that the likely Republican 1944 candidate, New York governor Thomas Dewey, would defeat Roosevelt. "Kennedy makes attacks on the President for yielding to Churchill's strategy [regarding the Middle East]," Max recalled about his American friend. "This is bad business for the Americans, and damaging to the President."

Soon after this 1943 trip, Churchill convinced Beaverbrook to rejoin his government as Lord Privy Seal, a nebulous job formalizing his preferred role as a minister without a defined role. Better to have Lord Beaverbrook in Churchill's closest circle than run the risks of him outside of it. "Max is back in the Government again," Pamela Churchill wrote to Harry Hopkins, "so I guess the fireworks will soon start."

. . .

Kick Kennedy's desire to return to England became a reality in mid-1943, as the German bombing ebbed and her father's opposition subsided. The ambassador's much-criticized decision to send his family home when the bombs started falling in London had left a foul taste in the mouths of his children, particularly Kathleen. Unlike her father, she favored American intervention to save Britain. By early 1940, she had enlisted her brother Jack in her cause. "Kick is very keen to go over—and I wouldn't think the anti-American feeling would hurt her like it might us—due to her being a girl—especially as it would show that we hadn't merely left England when it got unpleasant," Jack wrote to their father, without success.

In recent years, while Kick enjoyed her time at the *Washington Times Herald,* she longed to resume her love affair with Billy Hartington in London. "I know when she was working in Washington, she was very anxious to get back to England to see him [Billy]," recalled Page Huidekoper seventy years later. "They were clearly crazy about each other before that."

News from England of Billy's rumored fiancée left Kick crestfallen— until a few months later, when she learned he'd broken the engagement. She resolved to go back to London as soon as possible. When she spotted a recruitment ad for the American Red Cross, which was planning to establish after-hours recreation clubs for U.S. servicemen overseas, she quickly signed up. Page endorsed her enlistment forms, vouching that, in applying, Kick wasn't merely looking to join a boyfriend. But both knew she hoped for an assignment where she could reunite with Billy. Her father pulled enough strings with the army so Kick was assigned to the Hans Crescent Club, for officers only, known for its Saturday jukebox dances in the heart of London. A society newspaper column reported on the departure of the former ambassador's daughter for England: "She is heart-whole and fancy-free, however, and determined to make her own mark in the world *sans* her famous father's influence."

In Great Britain, Kick's old friends rejoiced at her return. Billy Hartington took her on a date as soon as he could get leave from the Guards Armoured Division, where he was stationed about an hour away from London. Lady Astor welcomed her with open arms, though Kick remained apprehensive about the overall reception. "Everyone is very surprised and I do mean surprised to see me," she confided to Jack. "There's much more anti-Kennedy feeling than I imagined and I am determined to get my stories straight as I think I'll get it on all sides." Gratefully, no one in England "mentioned a thing about Pop," except a cranky old Labour politician, Kick later reported. At the club, one man vaguely familiar with the Kennedys "thought all the Red Cross girls (30 strong) were my sisters," Kick laughed. The man told the club member that he'd heard Kick had a lot of sisters, "but I didn't think she had that many!"

Ever the social butterfly, Kick went out on the town with William Douglas-Home, who'd become a well-known playwright. ("He's very good company but that's about as far as it goes," she wrote in a letter home.) Douglas-Home was more impressed with her, later writing a long-running play with a not-too-fictional character based on Kick. Another admirer from her first stay in England, Tony Rosslyn, sipped champagne one night with her as they toasted the United States and the idea of a unified victory. "She is surrounded by her old friends and others from both sides of the Atlantic and I have lent her a push bike to get about on," Tony wrote to Kick's father, praising her charms. "Kick is my ideal of what a girl should be for a wife but I wouldn't let her know it."

The Kennedy patriarch, always sentimental about his daughter, replied that Kick is "the steadiest battler that there is for England. She seems to be very happy, and while we miss her like the devil, whatever she wants is always all right by me." Attempting to influence his children through their peers, Joe asked Rosslyn to relay some advice to his daughter. "I wish you would say to her sometime as I've said to Jack—that he doesn't have to win this war all by himself any more than she has to entertain the entire American Army or be the focal point for British-American relations, just do a little, that's enough." His note also alluded to the surprise appearance of Hollywood star Bob Hope at Kick's Red Cross club, arranged through Joe's entertainer friend Morton Downey. Her father made sure photos of Kick, dressed in her Red Cross uniform, appeared in newspapers on both sides of the Atlantic.

Traversing London on weekends, Kathleen Kennedy increasingly shared the same social circles with Pamela Churchill, whom she no longer mocked as a "fat, stupid little butterball" from their debutante years, but as a lively young woman whom she considered a friend. This second-generation friendship between the Kennedy and Churchill families contained its own ironies. To their mutual amazement, Kick informed her brother Jack that Pamela, at age twenty-three, had transformed into "London's glamour girl." In this description there wasn't any of the cattiness that Kick might have employed years earlier as a teenager. After all, she and Pamela were both performing the same task at different clubs. At the suggestion of Brendan Bracken, Pamela helped to create the Churchill Club in London—a place where British women and American soldiers could meet, dance, and get to know one another, perhaps forming lifelong special relationships. "We find that the majority of American soldiers want more than anything else to meet their opposite British member," she explained to Harry Hopkins. As its secretary, Pamela arranged for lectures about English history and culture, described by the club in Churchillian lingo as "the cherished heritage of the English-speaking peoples."

Working in this world of men away from home, Pamela, with her luxuriant auburn hair and bosomy figure, was Rita Hayworth seductive to Kick's Katharine Hepburn earnest. "I must say," Evelyn Waugh described to his wife, "Pam Churchill is a very tasty morsel." Although

Kick and Pamela landed in their positions at least partly because of their ties to powerful men, both possessed an industriousness and ambition they admired in each other. Years later, Pamela insisted Kick's club was populated by "the chic ones who had the good food, the American Red Cross. They were the glamorous ones." But with Pamela as a celebrated greeter, the Churchill Club attracted many top generals and politicians, including U.S. Supreme Commander Dwight D. Eisenhower and the prime minister himself. "When we opened, Eisenhower was at the club and, in fact we were rather shorthanded, and he came in and helped me in the kitchen," Pam recalled. "He was wonderful."

Another visitor to the Churchill Club, American songwriter Irving Berlin, was invited by Clementine to 10 Downing Street to see the prime minister, who mistook his name for that of the philosopher Isaiah Berlin. Winston enjoyed reading Isaiah's political analysis in a weekly column but had never met him; Irving was a complete mystery to him.

"Mr. Berlin, what is the most important piece of work you have done for us lately?" asked Winston.

"I don't know, it should be 'White Christmas,' I guess," said the Tin Pan Alley author of one of America's most popular melodies, especially among U.S. servicemen abroad.

After several comical misfires, Churchill finally asked Irving Berlin when he thought the war in Europe would end.

"Sir, I shall never forget this moment," said Berlin, a thin and tiny man, in his squeaky New Yorkese. "When I go back to my own country I shall tell my children and my children's children that the Prime Minister of Great Britain asked me when the European War was going to end."

Frustrated and bewildered, Winston got up from their lunch table. "That man Berlin," he later exclaimed, "he's better on paper."

. . .

During this time in London, Pamela's life was far more complicated than Kick Kennedy's. As the mother of the prime minister's grandson, she remained married to Randolph, even after her drunken husband arrived home on leave with a spotted face and overweight figure. Her affair with Averell Harriman suddenly ended when Ave announced he'd accepted Roosevelt's offer to serve as ambassador to the Soviet Union. The White House hoped Harriman would take advantage of his long-nurtured ties with Russian leaders during the war. Harriman asked his daughter Kathleen, by then writing for *Newsweek*, to follow him to Moscow immediately, which left Pamela alone and dejected. He continued to help pay Pam's rent but asked his daughter, less than gallantly, to relay a good-bye message to her. "Help Pam straighten herself out—poor child," Harriman instructed. "She is in a tough spot. Tell her I am sure she will do the right thing if she follows her own instinct. Give her my best love and to you. P.S. Destroy this letter or keep it locked up."

For days afterward, Pamela sulked around the Churchill Club. She later tried writing cheery letters to Ave, with the intent of making him jealous. "Incidentally the Harriman Mission practically lives at the Club," she wrote, mentioning their friends still there. "All the American generals have been so helpful. In fact there isn't one that I'm not on the most intimate terms with!" No matter how romantic their forbidden torrid affair might have seemed, Pam eventually realized the value of moving on to the next man in her life. "The fact that I was in love with Averell had nothing to do with the fact that I never thought I would spend the rest of my life with him, nor did I think he was there to protect me," she later reflected. "There was no real sense of faithfulness involved either, really. I was totally free because, obviously, I mean, he had no, could have no demands on me. Both of us knew that one day I had to go out and find somebody else."

At her club, Kick mingled with the British men, just as Pam socialized with the Americans at the Churchill Club. Joe Kennedy's daughter went to dinner with Lord Beaverbrook after turning down his invitation to spend a weekend at Cherkley because she couldn't leave the club on Saturdays. "This admirer is the combined age of all your other admirers," Beaverbrook kidded. Kick was very aware that London had endured a state of war for four years, while the conflict for the United States seemed new. "It certainly is going to be a tough job to get the British out to your part of the world to do any fighting," she wrote to Jack, already dispatched by the navy to a PT boat in the Pacific. "I can't imagine some of these boys who have been out in the Middle East for four years or more going on to fight in the Pacific. You're probably wondering why they don't send some of the boys like Lord Hartington and Rosslyn don't go [*sic*] but apparently there is a great thing over here about keeping the experienced men in battle."

Kick's love for Billy Hartington carried on unabated, though she remained pessimistic about their families of different faiths agreeing to see them married. "Of course I know he (Billy) would never give in about the religion and he knows I never would," she explained to Jack about her dilemma. "I can't really understand why I like Englishmen so much as they treat one in quite an off-handed manner and aren't really as nice to their women as Americans, but I suppose it's just that sort of treatment that women really like. That's your technique isn't it!"

28

"His Heart's Desire"

"Courage is the ladder on which all other virtues mount."
—CLARE BOOTHE LUCE

Weeks before leaving for the Pacific, Ensign John F. Kennedy, accompanied by a buddy from the Charleston naval intelligence office, paid an impromptu visit to a family friend, Clare Boothe Luce, at her nearby South Carolina plantation. Though it was not very late in the evening, one of America's most celebrated beauties had covered her face in cold cream and was wearing a plaid night robe when a servant announced young Kennedy at the door.

"He looked very handsome and he's such a bright clever boy," Clare later wrote to her daughter, Ann.

How much Jack may have known of his father's relationship with Clare—or her affairs with Randolph Churchill or Bernard Baruch before that—seemed secondary to her status as the wife of publisher Henry Luce and, even more so, as part of the Kennedy family's rarified world of money and fame. Ostensibly, Jack had stopped by on a whim, just to say how much another friend admired her daughter, Ann, calling her "swell" and "pretty." Ann was already studying at Stanford University in California, where Jack himself attempted some graduate work before the war began. Clare suggested her daughter would look up Jack's sister Eunice, beginning her own studies at Stanford. "Do what you can to see that her [Eunice's] first weeks are not too lonesome," Clare later asked her daughter in a February 1942 letter.

During the previous summer, Jack had dated Ann Brokaw, Clare's only child from her first marriage, more as family friends than anything serious. Like most of Ann's prospective boyfriends, Jack seemed taken by Clare's presence. "When the future President appeared to collect his date, he showed more interest in mother than in daughter," recounted Clare's biographer Sylvia Jukes Morris. "Her daughter was not actually a debutante, but she came out at the time that John Kennedy was making the rounds, escorting young ladies about New York and, in fact, took out her daughter on several occasions. Ann always got the feeling that her beaus were really more interested in her mother, who just had so much more charm and was better looking, too."

When he was not battling illness or injury, Jack's affection for women seemed boundless. In fact, he'd been quietly banished to the naval intelligence field office in Charleston following the FBI's discovery of his intense relationship with Inga Arvad, the suspected Nazi spy. Along with his handsome appearance, Jack's humorous, carefree demeanor carried the day with most women, even those in his family. Kick usually confided in him more than her older brother Joe Jr. Jack could even tease his mother, Rose (a stickler about proper English usage and her son's health habits), for her exacting ways. Jokingly, he said that millions could be made by publishing Rose's round-robin letters summarizing all the comings and goings of their far-flung family. "Its [*sic*] enough to make a man get down on his knees and thank God for the Dorchester High Latin School which gave you that very sound grammatical basis which shines through every slightly mixed metaphor and each somewhat split infinitive," he wrote. "My health is excellent—I look like hell, but my stomach is a thing of beauty—as are you, Ma,—and you, unlike my stomach—will be a joy forever."

Clare Boothe Luce was charmed by Jack, more by his intellect and political potential than anything else. After the two families spent a

December 1940 evening in New York, Jack sent a "Dear Mrs. Luce" note thanking her for "the great time I had last evening ... I certainly enjoyed meeting you and Ann. Those 6ft 4—220-pounders from Stanford will give her no trouble at all." After their 1942 encounter, Clare sent Jack two books by turn-of-the-century writer Homer Lea, an American who overcame his physical disabilities to become an author-adventurer in the young Winston Churchill mold. Lea's *The Day of the Saxon* predicted the breakup of the British Empire, while his *The Valor of Ignorance* foresaw a war between America and Japan. (Churchill read *Saxon* in 1912 and decades later called it "a great and prophetic book. It said that we should be fighting again on the fields of Flanders. I did not believe it then, but we have fought there twice since.")

Clare spent a little time at her southern home before heading to South America and then the Middle East on assignment for *Time*. On the way, she stopped in Florida to visit Joe Kennedy. According to one of Rose Kennedy's round-robin letters, Joe "spent several hours with her [Clare] and enjoyed it immensely," arranging for Ann and Eunice to spend Easter together at Stanford. Clare gently chided Joe, though, for being too pessimistic about the war with his second son, Jack, whom she called "a darlyn." After Pearl Harbor, the Luces had publicly urged a full-out assault by the United States, lest the Nazis and Japanese prevail in the war. In their conversation in South Carolina, Jack had let Clare know of his disappointment with his father's opposition to the war. Joe Sr. blamed the Roosevelt administration for cutting him out and, in a moment of pique, had actually offered to Beaverbrook to work for the British instead. Jack wanted to distance himself from his father's appeasement but found it difficult. He hoped to leave Charleston soon to fight in the Pacific, like so many other young men of his generation. "He has everything a boy needs to be a great success in the world, and one of the things which gives me comfort is the thought that no set of circumstances can lick a boy like Jack," Clare wrote in her note to Joe Sr. "He is vaguely unhappy with your pessimism. It alarms him ('so unlike Dad') and dispirits him, and I do think that you . . . and I have no right to add the burden of doubt to the other burdens that he, and a million like him, must carry from here out."

Joe Kennedy knew Clare was right. He sent a copy of her note to Jack, though he didn't like one word of it. Not only did Kennedy have grave misgivings about a war for his sons and country, but also he now felt muzzled. "Heavens knows, I don't want any pessimism of mine to have any effect on you, but I don't know *how* to tell you *what* I think unless I tell you *what* I think," he wrote his son in an attachment. Jack carefully read Clare's entire note, which expanded on the military threat America faced and the price his generation might face. "After all, Jack and all the other boys are the ultimate recipients of all the errors which we—and the men of our times have made," Clare had written to his father. "If Mr. FDR's foreign policy is to be implemented, it will be with the very bodies of these kids. And it's so tragically true that it's not theirs to reason why, they've just got orders to take."

Later in 1942, when Clare Boothe Luce decided to run for Congress in Connecticut as a Republican, Joe Kennedy reported to his friend Lord Beaverbrook that she "has much better than an even chance to win." Privately, Joe seemed intimidated by Clare's relentless energy and ambition, as if speaking to a mirror image. He admitted he didn't see himself taking a "big job" anytime soon in Washington, and seemed intent on disparaging her ambitions as a woman in the limelight. "I don't think women . . . are ever going to like you too much," he advised Clare, mainly, he said, because of her beauty and literate intelligence, and because "you never put yourself out for women as much as you do for men."

After she won her congressional seat, Clare became an outspoken critic of FDR's policies, far more than Joe dared in public. "One of the most astute people they have is our friend, Clare Luce," Joe said in a note to Beaverbrook about the Republican Party. "She certainly thinks ahead of anyone I've seen that they've produced to date." Inga Arvad, who read Clare's note containing her political appraisal of young Jack, appreciated Clare's instincts. "You will get there; as Clare says, 'He has everything to make a success.' Right she is, and I like her for discovering it so quickly," Inga wrote to Jack. "You have more than even your ancestors and yet you haven't lost the tough hide of the Irish potatoes. Put a match to the smoldering ambition and you will go like wild fire."

Clare's influence on Jack prompted him to support a much greater military effort by America, rather than an endurance of early defeats that could lead to a stalemate. Jack warned that "Churchill might be thrown out of office on the recoil" of more military setbacks against Germany and Japan, pushing the British Parliament to seek a no-confidence vote (as it did shortly afterward, without success). As Jack observed, "Beaverbrook might be the logical successor to Churchill, a strong man, a man who has the confidence of the people, and yet a man with an appeasement background, a former leading isolationist, and a man who might see a greater chance for Britain in a peace—however difficult—than in a war sure to extend for years and one whose chances for success would appear slight."

But the only real choice, as Jack knew, was to fight. He sought again to join the battle by getting reassigned from Charleston. His views now echoed Churchill's words, rather than his earlier isolationist stance so reflective of his father. "We are embarked on a war that will bring either certain defeat or such blood, such sweat, and such tears as no one in America from the White House to the man in the street has ever imagined," Ensign Kennedy wrote, employing the British prime minister's memorable phrasing. By the fall, Jack had completed his training at the Motor Torpedo Boat Squadron Training Center, in Rhode Island, and was promoted to lieutenant, junior grade. Visiting his family in Hyannis Port during that time, Jack discovered in the mail a gift from Clare Boothe Luce, a lucky coin that he promised to clip to his military dog tags.

"I couldn't have been more pleased," he wrote to her. "Good luck is a commodity in rather large demand these days and I feel you have given me a particularly potent bit of it to wear. Now, however, for me St. Christophers [a Catholic medal traditionally worn in prayer for safe travel] are out—I'll string along with my St. Clare."

By March 1943, Jack was on his way to serve on a PT boat in the Solomon Islands. That same month, Rose wrote a friendly letter to Clare, saying her husband and Kick kept her informed of Clare's new life in Congress. "Jack has been sent to the Pacific," Rose added, "his heart's desire."

Since 1893, the Solomon Islands, an archipelago of nearly a thousand small swampy islands, had been a protectorate of the United Kingdom, though, by the time Jack Kennedy arrived, the British had mostly stopped protecting it. Only the British resident commissioner and a few others remained, hidden in the tropical jungle brush by local natives. They provided a coast-watching service, a crude local form of British intelligence that alerted American commanders to enemy ships nearby.

It would be up to U.S. forces to begin pushing back the Japanese assault in the Pacific, just as Britain had fought mostly alone against Germany and Italy in the early years of the war. Winston Churchill had convinced Roosevelt to prevail first in Europe—including the sweep through the Middle East known as Operation Torch—before America's full attention returned to the Pacific. "Although we had little knowledge of American Pacific plans, we realised that an intense crisis had arisen in the Solomons," Churchill recalled. "It was obvious that no [British] carriers could reach the scene for many weeks. I earnestly desired to help in this heroic struggle, but with the main naval responsibility for landing the Anglo-American Army in North-West Africa upon us we could make no immediate proposal." Not until December 1942 did Churchill—now calling himself the "former naval person" in private notes to FDR—dare risk sending a handful of British ships to the Pacific. By the summer of 1943 they had joined an embattled fleet of American battleships, carriers, and small wooden craft known as PT (for "patrol torpedo") boats, one of which would be commanded by twenty-six-year-old John F. Kennedy.

Back in the United States, Kennedy's family worried greatly about his safety, especially with news of intense combat against the Japanese, seemingly determined to fight island by island. Rose enlisted nuns to pray for her son's cause. Jack, with his own sense of grace under pressure, tried to make light of the very real prospect he'd soon be killed. "Kathleen reports that even a fortune-teller says that I'm coming back in one piece," he wrote home. "I hope that it won't be taken as a sign of lack of confidence in you all or the Church if I continue to duck."

On August 2, Kennedy's *PT-109*, with a crew of thirteen aboard, cruised quietly into the thick blackness of night. Without warning, a Japanese destroyer cut through their boat, slicing it in half with everyone hurled into the water. Two crewmates died within moments. "This is how it feels to be killed," Jack thought to himself, as he later recalled. While some later blamed the crash on his inexperience or neglect, Kennedy's actions immediately afterward were unquestionably heroic. Despite hurting his back, the ensign swam around the flaming debris. He helped pull his surviving crew members up onto the boat's wreckage, still floating in the water. Knowing his band of survivors couldn't stay, and risk capture by the Japanese, he convinced his crew to swim toward a small island three miles away. He gave the most injured sailor, who didn't know how to swim, a large life preserver and towed him to safety. When the Japanese neared, the group moved again to another island.

Back at the PT base on Rendova Island, most believed Kennedy and his crew had been killed. The commander held a memorial service and didn't send any boats looking for their bodies. "Jack Kennedy, Ambassador's son, was on the same boat and lost his life," one officer at the base wrote home. Eventually after three days of fear and brutal conditions,

Kennedy and his crew discovered some local natives willing to carry a coconut back to the PT base. Jack carved a message on its greenish shell: "Nauro Isl . . . commander . . . native knows pos'it . . . He can pilot . . . 11 alive . . . need small boat . . . Kennedy."

The coconut wound up in the hands of Reginald Evans, an Australian coast-watcher, the last remnants of the British Empire's presence on the islands. Evans arranged for a group of natives to travel back to the island by canoe, carrying enough food to feed the Americans. Jack was handed a letter by the native group's leader, Benjamin Kevu, who spoke the King's English perfectly, with instructions on how to return to safety.

"You've got to hand it to the British," Jack told one his crewmates, amazed at their good fortune.

Then Kennedy left his men and returned with the natives in their canoe, which had enough room for only one passenger. They covered this battered young American with palm fronds, to avoid detection as Japanese fighter planes flew overhead. Soon Kennedy met Evans at his secret hideaway, and two PT boats, alerted by the coast-watcher, left Rendova and picked up Jack. He showed them where to find his stranded crew.

When his surviving crew arrived at Rendova, Kennedy took the old gold coin from around his neck, the gift from Clare Boothe Luce, and gave it to the native scouts who'd carried the coconut with his message. He later thanked the congresswoman again for the "good-luck piece," as he called it, which "did service above and beyond its routine duties during a rather busy period."

For four days, Joe Kennedy knew his son was missing in action, but he chose not to tell Rose or anyone else in their family. He'd always feared one of his sons might be killed in this war—the conflict he never wanted, always dreaded, which had ruined his public reputation. Then, on a car ride home, while listening to the radio, Joe heard a news alert of Jack's rescue. Overcome with emotion, he drove off the road and into a field. When he arrived back at the house, Rose fell into his arms and rejoiced. "He is really at home—the boy for whom you prayed so hard—at the mention of whose name your eyes would become dimmed—the youngster who you would think dead some nights & you wake up with sorrow clutching at your heart," Rose later wrote in her diary. "What a sense of gratitude to God to have spared him."

After witnessing death all around him in such brutal form, Jack found his carefree attitude chipped away. In seeing friends killed, he became more bitterly ironic about the pretense of war, and more philosophic about fate and mortality. He had come to the Pacific partly to show that he wasn't a coward, wasn't an appeaser, as they said about his family behind his back. His own instincts proved right—and quite ironic when his round-robin letter to his family, written obviously before the *PT-109* disaster, was received at home on August 10, containing this assurance: "I myself am completely—and thoroughly convinced that nothing is going to happen to me." His letter mentioned one of the two men lost on his boat, Andrew Kirksey—a married man with three children—who nearly got killed during a bombing shortly before the *PT-109* accident. "He never really got over it, he always seemed to have the feeling that something was going to happen to him," Jack recalled. "When a fellow gets the feeling that he's in for it—the only thing to do is let him get off the boat—because strangely enough they always seem to be the ones that do get it. I don't know if it's coincidence or what."

Jack was upset to find how quickly his Navy superiors had given up in their initial search for the *PT-109*'s crew. He worried his family may have heard of his presumed death. "This is a short note to tell you that I am alive—and *not* kicking—in spite of any reports that you may happen to hear," he wrote home immediately after being rescued from the *PT-109* debacle. "It was believed otherwise for a few days—so reports or rumors may have gotten back to you. Fortunately they misjudged the duration of a Kennedy."

After the *PT-109* incident, Jack Kennedy disdained politicians who embraced the rhetoric of war. "People get so used to talking about billions of dollars and millions of soldiers that thousands dead sounds like drops in the bucket," he wrote to his parents. "But if those thousands want to live as much as the ten I saw—they should measure their words with great care."

Back in the States, however, his father prepared to wrap Jack in public relations glory. Joe Kennedy took advantage of his son's crash in the Pacific to burnish his reputation as a war hero, with an eye toward the family's political future. "Kennedy's Son Is Hero in Pacific as Destroyer Splits His PT Boat," declared a front-page story in the *New York Times*. The *Boston Globe* called Kennedy's rescue of his crew "one of the great stories of heroism in this war." A few months later, writer John Hersey, a friend of Jack's, turned the *PT-109* tragedy into a daring and compelling narrative for *The New Yorker*. Joe Kennedy arranged for a condensed version to be later reprinted in *Reader's Digest*. Father Kennedy also pushed for a medal for his son, and lobbied his friend in Congress, Clare Boothe Luce, for it. "I wrote within a few days of speaking to you on the phone about Jack," Clare assured him. "I am sure there will be some results. So just be patient." Soon afterward, Jack received his navy medal, with Admiral William Halsey citing that Kennedy's "courage, endurance and excellent leadership contributed to the saving of several lives." Though grateful for the acclaim, Jack wasn't fooled by the publicity arranged by his father. He knew better, and deeply grieved the loss of the two men on his watch. Years later, when asked how he became a war hero, Jack offered a wry but realistic assessment. "It was involuntary," he said. "They sank my boat."

News of Jack's exploits reached around the world. In London, Lord Beaverbrook, who had once shared Joe's misgivings about the war, cheered the latest news in a letter to his friend. "What a splendid story it is of your son John's gallantry in the Pacific," Max wrote him. "I read it the other day when a copy of 'Time' reached me. And how proud a father you must be, and how thankful that his great bravery was not in vain. I am so glad for you." Joe even heard praise from Kay Halle, who'd kept in contact with him just as she had with the Churchills. Kay spent much of the war in the Office of Strategic Services, working for American spymaster William "Wild Bill" Donovan, who kiddingly called her "Mata Halle," a reference to the notorious double agent of World War I. By the time her note arrived, Jack had returned to the States, where the back pain from his injury on the *PT-109* required surgery at the Chelsea Naval Hospital near Boston. "I was terribly moved by John Hersey's story and I really can't read it over without filling up a little myself," Joe told Halle, suggesting they get together in Washington the next time he came to town. "Jack has just had an operation, the result of the smash-up out there, but he seems to be getting along very well."

Clare Boothe Luce also wished Jack a speedy recovery. The congresswoman sent him a copy of *Primer of the Coming World*, by Leonid Schwarzschild, similar to Jack's earlier book, *Why England Slept*, in its call for a strong national defense. "You will wish that you had written it," Clare wrote to young Kennedy; "it is your type of mind." Winston Churchill had touted the book as a "must read" for the British Cabinet. "Never again must we succumb to the myth that power and armaments and compulsion are of themselves sinful," warned Schwarzschild about the postwar world still emerging. "All order, all civilization, all law and dignity, rest on the existence of weapons and power."

Clare told Jack that she hadn't yet read "the wonderful articles in the

New Yorker," because of preparation for an upcoming speech attacking Roosevelt before the Republican Convention. As the convention's only key female speaker, Clare issued a blistering critique of FDR's foreign policy, calling for a new president "who loves his country more than he loves power." She blamed the deaths of many American men on Roosevelt's "decade of confusion and conflict that ended in war." In her letter to Jack, Clare credited some of the speech themes to young Kennedy's experiences. "You were in my mind while I wrote it," she told him. With Father Joe, Clare collected on a one-hundred-dollar bet that his son would get the navy medal, just as he'd hoped and planned. She suggested to Joe that it was better that his war hero son was back home convalescing from back surgery than facing enemy fire in the Pacific. "What a wonderful boy Jack is, but isn't it lovely to have him tucked away safely in a plaster Paris Cast for a few months, anyway?" she asked.

The Kennedys were aware of their good fortune, especially compared to the tragedy that would befall Clare Boothe Luce. Driving in a car from Stanford in January 1944, Ann Brokaw, Clare's only child, was killed before her twentieth birthday in an accident that flung her body into a tree. All the Kennedys were stunned by the news, especially Eunice, who had become friends with Ann, and Jack, who expressed shock about the death of the girl he had once casually dated. "I thought that I had become hardened to losing people I liked—but when I heard the news today—I couldn't have been sadder," he wrote to Clare. "She was a wonderful girl—so completely unspoiled and thoughtful—and so very fond of you—I can't believe it."

Back in London, Kick read the news about Ann Brokaw's death and, for a moment, contemplated life's fateful twists. In a letter home, she recalled how Clare had helped her efforts with the Red Cross and how the congresswoman had given good luck coins to soldiers like Jack going off to war. So far, Kick considered herself one of the lucky ones, with two brothers and her beloved Billy Hartington in combat without getting killed. "It just shows how ironic life can be when one thinks she gave good luck pieces to three soldiers exposed to all sorts of dangers," Kick told her family, "and her own daughter is killed in an automobile accident."

29

Stratagems of Hell

"The Father knows the Son; therefore secure

Ventures his filial virtue, though untried,

Against whate'er may tempt, whate'ver seduce,

Allure, or terrify, or undermine.

Be frustrate, all ye stratagems of Hell,

And devilish machinations come to naught."

—*Paradise Regained*, BOOK I, JOHN MILTON

A few days before Christmas 1943, after many feared he would die, Winston Churchill roused himself out of bed to play a late-night game of bezique with his son, just as they always had done in the past. The card game was one of the first signs of normalcy returning to Winston's life after a near-fatal bout of pneumonia.

There was something about this pleasantly diverting French game of chance—with its stratagems of kings and queens on cards manipulated across a tableau—that both found pleasing, as a tonic for whatever ailed them. At 11:30 p.m., after nearly two hours of play, a nurse caught Winston's attention, peeking her head into his room.

"Have the doctors gone to bed?" the prime minister asked, almost bumptiously. When the nurse affirmed that they had, Winston replied, "Good . . . I hope they sleep well."

His illness had nearly consumed the prime minister, following his stressful strategy meeting in Teheran with President Roosevelt and Soviet leader Joseph Stalin. During exhaustive negotiations, the "Big Three" agreed upon Operation Overlord, the massive Allied invasion of France that would take place the following spring and become known as D-day. On December 11, Churchill flew to Tunisia to discuss these plans with General Dwight D. Eisenhower, the supreme Allied commander. On the way, he became desperately sick.

"I am afraid I shall have to stay with you longer than I had planned," the sixty-nine-year-old prime minister confided to Eisenhower, when riding with him in a car from the airport. "I am completely at the end of my tether."

Churchill soon collapsed, and stayed for several days inside Eisenhower's North African headquarters, a large white villa near Carthage that Ike's aides called "the White House." Winston's doctor, Lord Moran, detected pneumonia in his lung after an X-ray was taken. Moran called in every available specialist to save the prime minister's life. Winston also suffered another heart attack, his second since Christmas 1941 inside the real White House. Alerted by Lord Moran, Clementine rushed to her husband's side, as did Randolph. Daughter Sarah, traveling with her father as an aide, feared the worst as she watched him sleep. "Once he opened his eyes, and must have caught my troubled look before I had time to mask it," she recalled. "He looked at me without speaking for a moment; then said, 'Don't worry, it doesn't matter if I die now, the plans of victory have been laid, and it is only a matter of time,' and fell into a deep sleep once more."

The game of bezique with Randolph reminded father and son how much they could enjoy each other's company, and bolster each other in the most trying of times. Despite their thunderous arguments in private, Randolph always defended his father in public with the fiercest devotion. Such staunch duty to his father's honor was the same Winston had once shown to Lord Randolph, the kind of Churchill fidelity assumed to flow in their bloodline, from one generation to the next. Loyalty was the family's most prized possession.

Despite his shortcomings, Randolph's sharp mind, keen instincts, and understanding of Winston's vision proved helpful to the prime minister at various points in the war. Winston entrusted his son with some of his most closely guarded views. "I think they [Germany] are now convinced they cannot win," Winston confided in April 1943, appreciating the Allied progress since the Nazi takeover of France in June 1940. "It would be folly to indulge in comfortable hopes of an early ending," Winston warned, but "what a change this is from the days when Hitler danced his jig of joy at Compiegne."

In recent years, the two Churchills could be formidable as a tandem, though never with the impact they'd envisioned. For instance, during one parliamentary session, Randolph sprang to his feet in the middle of a confidence vote debate aimed at the prime minister. While on a short leave from the Middle East, he denounced fellow Conservatives who blamed his father for early setbacks in the war stemming from insufficient weaponry. "This is the Parliament of Munich," rebuked Randolph, dressed in his military uniform; "it is the Parliament that failed to rearm the country in time." But in that debate, the angriest defense belonged to Winston. At one point in the parliamentary session, a Churchill critic, Sir Archibald Southby, took note of Randolph in uniform and wondered aloud why the prime minister's son was not with the troops rather than the MPs. "Before the honorable and gallant Member leaves that point," Southby interrupted, "he speaks with such authority as a soldier—will he tell me on what occasion he has been, as a soldier, in a battle where he has been shot at by the enemy at 1,500 yards?"

Furious at the insinuation, Winston confronted Southby to his face once they were outside, in a corridor. As Southby attempted to explain, the prime minister rattled his fist in his face and shouted, "Do not speak to me. You called my son a coward. You are my enemy. Do not speak to me!"

The fear of being called a coward rankled the Churchills, just as it did the Kennedys, whose sons felt compelled to prove themselves in war because of their father's much-reviled appeasement. Randolph joined the commandos hoping to see action but eventually wound up in a desk job dealing with wartime press correspondence. "It was maddening for him that everyone was so nervous of using Winston's son in battle, and that he was not considered suitable as a soldier," wrote Randolph's cousin Anita Leslie. "Nothing could have been worse for him than to be sent around the desert in charge of a bunch of newspaper men."

The past two years for Randolph had been full of frustration. When he volunteered in April 1942 to join a secret parachute unit of the Special Air Service, Randolph learned just how protective the cocoon had been around him. The unit was the brainchild of David Stirling, a commando friend of his and a habitué of White's. As in the film *The Dirty Dozen*, later made by Hollywood, Stirling planned for small bands of a dozen marauders to jump well into enemy territory near airfields and carry out risky plots that eventually destroyed ninety planes and other vital military equipment. In theory, Winston Churchill loved the idea of unconventional warfare behind enemy lines—ever since his own hair-raising experience in the Boer War, when he was captured and escaped in South Africa. But when Randolph dared to prove his own bravery in war, convincing Stirling to let him join his crack unit of parachuting commandos, Clementine quickly disapproved and complained to Winston. Rather than applaud her son's courage, she dismissed Randolph's move as irresponsible and focused on the worry it would cause her husband.

"I grieve that he has done this because I know it will cause you harrowing anxiety, indeed, even agony of mind," Clementine argued to Winston. "I feel this impulse of Randolph's . . . is sincere but sensational. He could have quietly and sensibly rejoined his Regiment & considering he has a very young wife with a baby to say nothing of a Father who is bearing not only the burden of his own country but for the moment of an un-prepared America it would in my view have been his dignified & reasonable duty."

Parachute training indeed was dangerous. During the early test runs in the Egyptian desert, Stirling watched in horror while two men in his unit fell to their deaths when their parachutes failed. Friends asked Randolph, out of shape and without much training, if he feared jumping from a plane. "Not at all," he said. "I have no imagination, so action doesn't bother me in advance."

When Randolph finally went up for his first launch, Stirling, ever the adventurer, told him to follow him by leaping out the cabin door. Randolph tried not to show the slightest fear or trepidation. In advance, he bribed the dispatcher on the plane with a five-pound note and strict instructions. "Just in case I hesitate, give me a good push," he commanded.

At the assigned moment, the thirty-one-year-old Churchill lunged into the blue sky. From below, Stirling looked up and watched as Churchill's parachute popped open. He began floating toward the ground, with a big rapturous look on his face as he neared Stirling.

"Thank God the bloody thing opened!" Randolph bellowed, as if speaking to his parents' concerns. Undoubtedly, Clementine's prior words of warning embodied the deepest concerns of the prime minister, though his father didn't try overtly to stop Randolph. "Of course I do not wish to hamper you in any way, but I am told that parachuting becomes much more dangerous with heavy people," advised Winston, hardly a champion of his son's cause to prove himself.

Whether Stirling knew of these parental concerns, he teased Ran-

dolph as he descended at a more rapid clip than the rest of the para-
chutists.

"Why are you going so much faster than the others?" asked Stirling,
while in midair. "Are you just too heavy?"

As they approached the ground, Stirling couldn't help his bemusement in seeing the young Churchill slam into the desert sand, landing
awkwardly in the wrong position. For several moments, Randolph lay
on the ground dazed, and with the wind knocked out of him. He struggled to get back on his feet and recovered on his own. Stirling agreed to
let him come along on a raid a month later.

Benghazi would be different. Rather than blowing up airfields, this
British raid into Libya was meant to attack two enemy ships in the harbor. Instead of parachuting into hostile territory, Stirling and the other
superior officers decided that a land route was best—and drove more
than four hundred miles in a converted Ford utility car made to look
like a German staff car.

Their covert operation went well until about fifty miles outside
Benghazi. A corporal preparing some explosives suffered a hand injury
when a detonator exploded, leaving him unable to join the squad of six
who would enter Benghazi. With the injured corporal, an opening occurred, and Randolph, part of the support team meant to stay outside
the city, pushed himself into the squad of six. All the squad's members
were highly trained, none more so than Fitzroy Maclean, a brilliant
desert commando and a Conservative MP from Lancaster. "The crack
of the detonator had hardly died away when Randolph appeared, ju-
bilant," Maclean recalled. "Already he was oiling his tommy-gun and
polishing his pistol in preparation for the night's work."

Randolph climbed into the backseat of the Ford, which Stirling drove for another forty miles until they reached a smooth tarmac road that led to the heart of the city. Once on that road, however, the car's unbalanced wheels and slightly bent axle made a frightful noise, loud enough to announce their arrival. They stopped and tinkered with the wheels, only to make things worse. "We could hardly have made more noise if we had been in a fire engine with its bell clanging," Fitzroy recalled later in a book. When they approached a roadblock guarded by an Italian sentry, Randolph remained frozen with the others, gripping grenades and guns, as Fitzroy first tried a linguistic bluff.

"Staff officers," he cried in his best Italian, ". . . in a hurry."

The sentry paused menacingly, then let them go with a warning to fix their headlights. He didn't seem to notice their British uniforms.

Their adventure was only beginning, prompting "the most exciting half hour of my life," Randolph later explained to his father. After being chased at eighty miles an hour by another car into the city, Stirling ditched their disguised Ford along a narrow side road in the much-destroyed Arab quarter. Stirling turned off the lights, and they sat in the dark and silence, only to hear an air-raid siren go off.

The British Commandos planned to explode enemy ships in the harbor, knowing that an Allied aerial bombing was scheduled for a specific time. As they crept through shadows, however, they noticed one of the ships aflame. A large crowd had assembled around the burning hulk, which illuminated the entire harbor. It eliminated any chance of a surprise attack to finish their task. Stirling decided not to make their presence known. They returned prudently to Alexandria in the squeaky Ford.

Disaster struck, ironically, when they returned safely behind Allied lines. On their way between Alexandria and Cairo during the night of May 27, Stirling tried maneuvering the car past a long convoy of trucks, only to have it struck by the last lorry, which suddenly darted into their lane. As he swerved to avoid it, the truck hit their back wheel, causing the car with Prime Minister Churchill's son in it to flip over a couple of times. All occupants were thrown from the car. A *Daily Telegraph* war correspondent, who had hitched a ride, got pinned under the vehicle and soon died of head fractures. Randolph told his parents that he had suffered only severe bruises in the crash. In fact, he had seriously crushed vertebrae, requiring several weeks in a Cairo hospital. Doctors put his battered back in a plaster cast until he could heal, just as Jack Kennedy endured in the Pacific. A friend who visited while Randolph convalesced, photographer Cecil Beaton, was impressed by his upbeat prognosis. "The situation's splendid," Churchill insisted as they chatted about the war. After so many initial setbacks for Great Britain, Randolph expressed confidence that they would prevail against the Germans. "Randolph's stout heart makes me feel ashamed of my anxieties," Beaton wrote in his diary. "Just to hear such exuberance is encouraging."

Randolph had proven his mettle as a war hero. In the desert of North Africa, on a daring raid, he was willing to stare down the enemy with unflinching bravery—both in the hardened eyes of comrades such as Stirling and Maclean and perhaps in his father's grateful estimation as well. "It is very disappointing that we failed to achieve anything," Randolph admitted to his father in a secret note. "On the other hand, it has filled us with confidence for future operations of a similar kind."

After leaving the hospital in July 1942, Randolph returned home from the Middle East, taking a long way through America. At a New York press conference at the Waldorf Astoria, he predicted the Allies would win the European war, "if we're lucky," sometime in 1943. "And if we're unlucky," he added, "we'll win by the end of 1944." Wearing a back splint and nervously rubbing out his cigarettes, Randolph assured Americans that victory "is in the bag."

When he arrived in England, Randolph managed swiftly to stir the pot politically, upsetting his fellow Conservatives by suggesting their party had become too subservient to the upper class. Perhaps most remarkably, he gave a speech calling for the British Empire to subsidize the procreation of babies as a way of maintaining its dominion. "I do not think it is generally realized that if the present tendency continued there would be only 4 million people in the British Isles in little more than a hundred years," he warned, "and Britain cannot remain a great power on the basis of that population." His plan would provide a paid allowance by the government for every third child born to a couple and all subsequent toddlers. Randolph scolded British parents for being part of "one of the most class-conscious and snob-ridden nations in the world," afraid to bear more children if they couldn't afford to send them to the finest schools. It was their duty, he urged, to go forth and multiply for the empire's sake.

In Randolph's own home, though, there seemed little prospect of more than one child. While away at war, the prime minister's son seemed oblivious to his wife, Pamela, and their young son, to the consternation of his parents. Winston tried to rally Randolph's interest by describing a tranquil home front waiting for his return, in contrast to a life of jumping out of planes on commando raids. Pamela "is a great treasure and blessing to us all," the elder Churchill wrote in May, mentioning that baby Winston "was in the pink when I saw him last. He has not so far grown old enough to commit the various forms of indiscretion which he would be expected to inherit from his forebearers." But Randolph remained too engrossed in proving himself the conquering hero to pay attention to the rather hellish condition of his marriage.

When he came home, his presence became unbearable for Pamela, accustomed to living very much on her own. She couldn't handle his drinking, with his all-night binges. Her own father was a teetotaler, while her mother sipped an occasional glass of sherry at dinner. "I had absolutely no knowledge of anybody who drank too much and Randolph did and this caused problems," she recalled—problems that sparked loud public arguments between the couple. In one of their last intimate times together, Randolph spent a weekend with Pam in a Scottish castle, reading aloud at night from Winston's biography of his father, Lord Randolph Churchill. He discovered a copy in the bedroom and seemed more captivated by his father's literary voice than his wife's literal presence—the same self-absorbed indulgence he had performed during their honeymoon. "She hates him so much she can't be in a room with him," observed Evelyn Waugh after a visit with them. "She could not look at him and simply said over her shoulder in acid tones, 'Ought you not to be resting?' whenever he became particularly jolly. She was looking very pretty and full of mischief."

Both sides of the family tried to salvage their marriage. Pamela's father, Lord Digby, came to London and counseled his daughter ("I suppose urging her to bear her burden bravely," Waugh surmised). By then, however, the couple was firmly going their separate ways. Pamela's relationship with Harriman had cooled when he left for Russia as ambassador, and especially after Marie, Harriman's wife in America, found out and threatened to divorce him. By the time Randolph returned home from the war, Pamela had spent much of the year having an affair with American Jock Whitney (then married to Jimmy Roosevelt's ex-wife, Betsey), and later with CBS newsman and devoted Churchill fan Edward R. Murrow. Pam became the diva of the Churchill Club. At night, she slept with some of the richest and most famous American visitors, including Murrow, whose gripping radio broadcasts nationwide illuminated Britain's fight for survival. "There was an aura about her because of Churchill," recalled a Murrow friend to biographer Ann M. Sperber. "Of course, he loved Janet [his wife] very, very much. But he wanted Pam. Really thought he wanted her." When Whitney departed London, but before her affair with Murrow, Pamela slept with Maj. Gen. Fred Anderson, the top American bombing commander, and relayed every strategic tidbit she learned from him to her father-in-law, Winston Churchill. "Pam liked to go around with men, and she liked sex and she was attractive," an American journalist later told the *Los Angeles Times.* "The American men gave her the nicknames 'Porcupine' and 'Spam,' but her lovers were 'reasonably discreet.'"

For Randolph's part, his infidelity ran the gamut from prostitutes he hired in brothels while off duty in the Middle East, to passionate but futile offers to marry his beloved Laura Charteris, the beautiful divorced wife of Lord Dudley. To the elusive Laura, Randolph composed some of his most honest letters, pouring out his feelings and fears from the Middle East. Laura's instincts, perhaps for self-preservation, kept her from committing to anything more. Her friendship with Randolph became a constant in his life, though she remained resolved to wed another man. Randolph possessed "that very strong Churchill quality of determination," she later explained, "so whatever I said or did made not the slightest difference to his attitude and determination to marry me."

Clementine seemed intent on keeping Pamela in the family, regardless of her daughter-in-law's indiscretions. She turned to her as a confidante and consistently sided with her daughter-in-law in all matters. "Randolph is treating our darling Pamela badly," Clementine complained to Winston. Most important, she wanted Randolph to settle down—to stay at home with his young wife and toddler son—so his behavior wouldn't upset his father, her first and only concern. "I rather think Randolph is trying for a 'rapprochement' [*sic*] with Pamela," Clemmie wrote in May 1943, when her son was still in the Middle East. "He sent little Winston an 'airgraph' letter & said at the end 'take care of your Mother'—How I wish that could happen. Perhaps it will."

Although Pamela initially believed that her mother-in-law's support was based on the merits, she gradually realized Clementine wanted a psychological wedge between her son and Winston. "Through the years I realized that her relationship with Randolph was a problem," Pamela recalled. "And I think she found in me an ally, which I didn't realize until many years after my marriage." Burdened with four years of war and his own flagging health, Winston treated Pamela like one of his own daughters, as a pleasant companion when Clementine couldn't be with him. On the July 1943 night when the Allies launched their invasion of Sicily, the prime minister asked Pamela to play a game of bezique with him, to keep his mind away from worry. At one point, she remembered, Winston looked up from the game as if thunderstruck. "So many brave young men going to their death tonight—it is a grave responsibility," he lamented.

Winston and Clementine realized the burdens Pamela faced with their son. Using "that wonderful understatement," they seemed to forgive Pam for seeking solace in a more mature, married man such as Harriman, at least in her account. "They were very, very understanding about that," she later explained. "Very supportive of me. Though it was never, never, ever discussed, they knew perfectly well, I think, that I was in love with Averell. It was fine, and nobody really blamed me either, because they understood how difficult Randolph was."

Nearly everyone seemed to know of his wife's infidelities except Randolph. Certainly in Washington, President Roosevelt and his aides were well aware of Harriman's dalliance with the prime minister's daughter-in-law. "Harry Hopkins always told me that the President knew all about it, and laughed about it," recalled Pamela years later. "It was wartime and there wasn't any press gossip in those days, but the people from Roosevelt down, knew about it. It didn't seem to bother them. Harry used to talk to me about it quite openly." The subject also came up with William Walton, a Time-Life war correspondent and close friend of the Kennedys, who relayed to Pamela his conversation with President Roosevelt during a White House visit. Impishly, Walton told FDR that "the most beautiful woman in London had his [Roosevelt's] picture in her drawing room," next to a photo of Winston Churchill. "He [President Roosevelt] was pleased to hear it was you and said he hoped to meet you someday because he'd heard so much about you," Walton wrote to her. "Then with a great roar of laughter he said, 'But that R___, what a handful he is! What a handful!' I think for the PM to have such a problem child rather delighted him [FDR] since he had so many of his own."

Randolph Churchill wasn't amused. He seemed most hurt, however, by the perceived disloyalty of his parents rather than the infidelity of his wife. He'd spent much of his young adult life trying to emerge from the shadow of a great man, while still being loyal to his father. In his eyes, Winston and Clementine "had condoned adultery beneath their own roof," Randolph told Jock Colville. Randolph had suspected Pamela's affair as early as 1942, just before he upset his parents and wife by volunteering for dangerous parachute training. He felt himself played for a fool by having treated Averell Harriman so well during his earlier Middle Eastern trip, when Randolph innocently called him his "favourite American." By October 1943, when Randolph returned home again from North Africa—expecting to be hailed as a commando raid hero, as he had been treated recently in America—he instead was mortified to learn this well-known secret and felt deeply betrayed by his family. "It was extremely painful to him to overhear American soldiers whisper on his approach, 'Here comes Mr. Pam,'" explained his cousin Anita Leslie. "He felt the knife thrust—it was not as 'Mr. Pam' that he had regarded himself in Benghazi, and he could not help resenting his parents' fondness for their pretty daughter-in-law." Stewing over this complicated betrayal, Randolph "felt he had been forced into the wrong role—that of disregarded husband instead of wartime hero."

Undoubtedly for Randolph, the biggest question centered on his father. How could Winston, with his finely tuned understanding of human nature and his penchant for learning secrets, not have known of the Harriman affair and the inherent risks of public exposure involving Pamela and the U.S. envoy? Had his father's desire to bring the United States into the war and save Great Britain come at the expense of his own honor? Why had he not stopped Harriman with the same force with which Randolph attacked anyone who dared sully his father's name? "Not only did these events destroy my parents' marriage, but they had a devastating impact on Randolph's relationship with his father," reflected Winston S. Churchill, the prime minister's grandson, decades later. "Randolph found it impossible ever to forgive his parents for, as he saw it, condoning what had happened and, worse still, seeming to take Pamela's side by telling Randolph to be kinder to his young wife, of whom they were both so deeply fond."

The bitterness in Randolph spilled out in family conversations at 10 Downing Street, where he rather piously accused Winston of disloyalty and not protecting his flank from disrepute. Winston became so incensed by his son's accusations that Clementine, fearful of her husband having another heart attack, banned Randolph from speaking about such things to his father. His sisters were sympathetic about Randolph's crumbling marriage but horrified by the emotional burdens he placed on their father at a time when the whole world looked to him for leadership. Youngest daughter Mary reproached Randolph for his behavior, but in her diary she gave a more evenhanded assessment: "I think the greatest misfortune in R's life is that he is Papa's son—Papa has spoilt and indulged him & is very responsible."

The only answer for Randolph was a return to war. The existential emptiness that seemed to plague him could be filled only by action and deeds. As soon as his injuries eased, Randolph traveled back to the Middle East, and eventually joined his father at the Teheran Conference. Randolph prepared for his new military assignment, another high-risk adventure, this time in Yugoslavia, authorized during the Teheran meeting. But he was quickly called back to his father's side when Winston developed pneumonia in December 1943.

For all of their acrid father-son confrontations, Winston's spirits were buoyed by Randolph's presence. Randolph shared stories with him that he had heard in his travels, and they played endless games of bezique. Somehow, hundreds of miles away from the tensions of home, their comradeship resumed, just as it had when they journeyed together in America a decade earlier. The good humor between them even emerged during discussions about the Allied invasion plan, Operation Overlord, designed to get rid of the Nazi rulers if they didn't surrender.

"I have made it clear that, as regards the present Government, all resignations will be gratefully received!" Churchill joked about the Germans to one of his wartime ministers, Harold Macmillan, as his son stood nearby.

"Does that mean that anyone can join who wants to?" Randolph teased.

Winston grinned at his son. "No," he replied, "but you can join the queue."

Randolph's personal life would remain a sea of troubles, however, and he never gained the respect he yearned for. His estrangement from wife Pamela caused many stresses within their family. While Pamela might be an agreeable daughter-in-law, "the trouble, which you always seem to overlook, is that she declines to be in any way a satisfactory wife," Randolph explained to his father. "You will only make all of us unhappy if you create illusions about her in your mind." Randolph expressed remorse that his marriage breakup had led to "bitter words between you and me—I can never forgive her for that," he explained. "How can she endeavour to have all the fun of being your daughter-in-law while fulfilling none of her obligations as my wife passes my comprehension, and that you should aid her in this, to say the least undignified procedure, makes me most unhappy."

Money played a controlling factor between father and son. Winston continued to assist financially both Randolph and, to Randolph's annoyance, his estranged wife. In agreeing to a seven-year arrangement to provide Randolph with more funds, Winston indicated that any future generosity would depend on his behavior. "If I should survive so long, we shall have to consider the matter afresh from the point of view of your conduct and my resources," Winston informed his son. "As you were so angry when I made a similar arrangement for Pamela because you were not told beforehand, I shall be glad to have a telegram from you approving of this particular transaction."

Despite their disagreements, however, Winston possessed compassion for his son—barely recovered from wartime injuries to his knees and spine. "No reference was made by either of us to family matters," Winston wrote to Clementine after seeing his injured son in Italy near the end of the war. "He is a lonely figure by no means recovered as far as walking is concerned."

As the divorce papers were filed, Winston expressed regrets and blamed the war for destroying his son's marriage. In his view, Pamela was a "splendid" mother in bringing up his grandson Winston, and he appealed for family unity "to shield him [the boy] from the defects of a broken home." Even though Randolph asked him not to take sides, Winston left much of the fault at his son's doorstep. "I grieve so much for what had happened which put an end to so many hopes for Randolph and Pamela," he lamented to Pamela's mother. "The war strode in however through the lives of millions. We must make the best of what is left among the ruins."

30

Tests of Faith

*"I know that one goes into a war for reasons of honour &
soon finds oneself called on to do very
dishonourable things."*

—EVELYN WAUGH

War tested Winston Churchill's lifelong affinity for the United
States as never before. By early 1944, with the impending D-day invasion across the English Channel, Churchill faced many competing
national interests, Allied military demands, and prodigious egos to balance, including his own. "If we are together, nothing is impossible—if
we are divided, all will fail," he had implored a few months earlier in
a speech at Harvard, after mapping out strategy with President Roosevelt in Washington.

In Churchill's grand vision, Italy held the key for victory. Before
a massive assault along the western French coastline, he believed the
Axis powers must be weakened from the south—at the "soft underbelly of the crocodile"—with Italy providing a pathway to recapturing
"Fortress Europa" from Hitler. Many disagreed with his plan. But even
when his strategy prevailed, Winston had to be constantly mindful of
American politics.

One delicate example was the Allied air raids planned over Rome.
Back in the States, Catholic churchmen expressed fears about the
Vatican's safety to FDR, who needed Catholic support in running for

a fourth term that fall. Roosevelt sent several messages to Churchill echoing these concerns. "We must be careful not to bomb the Pope; he has a lot of influential friends!" Winston joked at one point to his British generals.

Indeed, Pope Pius XII sent his top aide, Count Enrico Galeazzi, Joe Kennedy's close friend in Rome, to Washington to meet with Roosevelt and Churchill. New York's then-archbishop Francis J. Spellman, already America's most prominent Catholic cleric, joined Galeazzi to express concern that holy and historic places not be damaged. Always the discreet insider, Galeazzi denied to the press what was obvious: that he'd been sent on a diplomatic mission. During the same September 1943 U.S. visit in which Churchill spoke at Harvard of Anglo-American unity, the British prime minister met privately with Roosevelt, Spellman, and Galeazzi to reach an accord without upsetting Allied plans to seize Rome. To placate the president, Winston wound up reversing himself.

In prosecuting the war, Churchill and his foreign policy lieutenant Anthony Eden believed the Italian capital shouldn't be spared from its bombing campaign, a view shared by Allied supreme commander Gen. Dwight D. Eisenhower. "I cannot see any reason why, if Milan, Turin and Genoa are to be bombed, Rome should be specially exempted," Winston complained to Eden. Roosevelt initially told Churchill that he didn't want to interfere with Eisenhower's bombing strategy, though the president eventually said further air raids shouldn't continue while they were negotiating with the Vatican. Although he disagreed, Winston appreciated Roosevelt's political needs.

"I am sending the following message to the Pope and feel that this should come from me instead of from both of us because of the large percentage of Catholics here, and because the Pope and I have a rather personal relationship, especially during the last few months," FDR explained to Churchill. "I know you will understand this and I hope the message will have a good effect." To the Pope, Roosevelt promised

Allied bombers wouldn't go within a twenty-mile radius of Vatican City, but warned that the Nazis might not do the same and to blame them for any damage.

As always, Churchill kept the long view. He didn't wish to create domestic difficulty for Roosevelt or any more personal strain than necessary. Winston suspected Franklin's health was worse than his own.

"In my long talks with the President I naturally discussed American politics," Winston explained to Clementine. "Although after 12 arduous years he [Roosevelt] would gladly be quit of it, it would be painful to leave the war unfinished and break the theme of his action. To me this would be a disaster of the first magnitude. There is no-one to replace him, and all my hopes for the Anglo-American future would be withered for the lifetime of the present generation—probably for the present century."

By dawn on June 6, 1944, hundreds of boats, tanks, armored trucks, barrage balloons, and amphibious landing craft dotted the Normandy coastline, part of a massive flotilla the likes of which the world had never seen. Up on the beaches, thousands of Allied soldiers—Canadian, French, British, and American—rushed into the teeth of the Nazi defense. Above this blood-drenched scene, fighter planes flew sorties in unison, dropping paratroopers behind enemy lines. Among the pilots in the sky to the north was Joe Kennedy Jr., who flew on patrol in a grid, protecting ships from German submarines. Out his window, Kennedy could see the invading ships on the distant horizon.

After many months of preparation for Operation Overlord, Churchill insisted on being there to witness the invasion. D-day embodied his dream of an Anglo-American partnership, the joining of two great democracies, against Nazi tyranny. Finally, this decisive blow was his answer to Hitler, like thunder from an avenging god, the liberation for his

The Kennedys in London. The family's glorious experience in prewar Great Britain had a lasting impact, especially in forming the worldview of a future president. Gathered together in the back of their London residence are (left to right) Eunice, John, Rosemary, Jean, Joe Sr., Edward, Rose, Joe Jr., Patricia, Robert, and Kathleen. *JFK Library*

The Churchills in America. After World War II, Winston enjoyed worldwide acclaim for stopping the Nazi threat. He was joined by wife, Clementine, son, Randolph, and daughter, Sarah, on a 1946 trip to America in which he warned about a future cold war with the Soviet Union. *National Archives*

Winston's family life. Winston and Clementine Churchill produced five children—
including daughters Diana (seen here), Sarah, Marigold (who died at age two in 1921),
and Mary. Their only son, Randolph, was touted in the press as a golden heir to the
Churchill political dynasty. *Corbis*

Churchill political legacy. A father-son tandem in Parliament was envisioned for
Winston and Randolph Churchill, though never to the extent that his son hoped. To
the crowd's delight, Winston made a rare public appearance in support of Randolph's
unsuccessful political campaign in 1935. *Getty*

Marriage of Randolph and Pamela. Desiring a Churchill heir before going off to war, Randolph married Pamela Digby in October 1939, after a brief courtship. Their troubled marriage would lead to divorce and haunt Randolph for years, while Pamela became good friends with the Kennedys. *Associated Press*

Chartwell guests. At his Chartwell home in the 1930s, Winston Churchill welcomed the Kennedys and other visitors such as movie star Charlie Chaplin. Pictured left to right are two of Randolph Churchill's friends, Tom Mitford and Freddie Birkenhead, Winston, Clementine Churchill, Diana Churchill, Randolph, and Chaplin. *Associated Press*

Masters of the deal. Wall Street tycoon Bernard Baruch (left) became longtime friends and business associates with both Joseph P. Kennedy (right) and Winston Churchill, often acting behind the scenes to wield his own influence.

Princeton University Library

The Court of St. James. As payback for his political help, Joe Kennedy convinced President Roosevelt to appoint him as U.S. ambassador to Great Britain in 1938, a great coup for an Irish Catholic from Boston. "I got the impression that deep down in his heart Roosevelt had a decidedly anti-Catholic feeling," Joe wrote in his diary.

Library of Congress

Dreams of dynasty. When his own presidential ambitions fell apart, U.S. ambassador Joseph P. Kennedy poured his drive and huge fortune into seeing one of his sons elected as the first Irish Catholic in the White House. Seen here arriving in England in 1938 with sons Joseph P. Jr. and John F. Kennedy. *JFK Library*

Royal splendor. Posing for the press in their formal gowns, Rose Kennedy accompanied her daughters Kathleen and Rosemary for their royal presentation in May 1938 at the Court of St. James, London. Constant coverage of the Kennedys helped build their celebrity, both in America and the UK. *JFK Library*

Vatican power. Ambassador Kennedy and his family represented the United States at the 1939 coronation of Pope Pius XII. Joe's secret dealings with Vatican administrator Count Enrico Galeazzi was aimed at enlisting the church's support someday for his family's White House ambitions. *JFK Library*

Bittersweet farewell. U.S. ambassador Joseph P. Kennedy visited 10 Downing Street before returning to America in October 1940. Once friendly with this Irish American, Winston Churchill grew to despise his isolationist appeasement views. *Associated Press*

Unsteady alliance. To help save his embattled nation, Winston convinced U.S. president Franklin D. Roosevelt to overcome the doubts of Ambassador Joseph P. Kennedy. Years later, Churchill admitted, "No lover ever studied every whim of his mistress as I did those of President Roosevelt," seen here with his son Elliott and Churchill in 1941. *FDR Library*

Star-crossed romance. Despite a family clash over religion, Kathleen Kennedy married William "Billy" Cavendish, the Marquess of Hartington, in May 1944. A few months later, Billy was killed in battle. The only other Kennedy to attend the wedding, Joe Jr., would later die in a wartime plane explosion. *JFK Library*

The millionaire's daughter. Kay Halle, the daughter of a Cleveland department store owner, was an intimate of both Randolph Churchill and Joe Kennedy Sr. in the 1930s and remained friendly with both dynasties for four decades. In 1963, she convinced President Kennedy to award honorary U.S. citizenship to his longtime hero Winston Churchill.
Library of Congress

Brilliant Lord Beaverbrook. Wily and unpredictable, publishing tycoon Max Aitken, aka Lord Beaverbrook, was Winston's lifelong friend who helped him win the Battle of Britain. Beaverbrook also became a close confidant to Joe Kennedy Sr., sharing some of his deepest secrets. *Library of Congress*

JFK at war.

Ignoring his poor health and his father's opposition to the war, Jack Kennedy signed up for the military soon after Pearl Harbor, following his brother Joe Jr.'s example. Here Lt. (jg) John F. Kennedy poses as a newly commissioned naval officer in 1942. *JFK Library*

In the Pacific, Jack Kennedy (right) commanded his crew aboard the *PT-109*, a vessel later destroyed in a fatal 1943 collision with a Japanese cruiser. "This is how it feels to be killed," Jack thought to himself. Later the much-publicized *PT-109* ordeal turned Kennedy into a celebrated war hero. *JFK Library*

When Jack's *PT-109* was reported missing, his father feared him dead. "This is a short note to tell you that I am alive—and not kicking—in spite of any reports that you may happen to hear," Jack wrote home after being rescued. "Fortunately they misjudged the duration of a Kennedy." *JFK Library*

During the Cold War, JFK campaigned for the presidency in 1960 by calling for more military defense. But after a nearly catastrophic nuclear showdown with the Soviets, Kennedy favored peaceful coexistence. "Winston Churchill said it is better to jaw-jaw than war-war," Kennedy insisted. *JFK Library*

Winston at war.

Young Churchill, seen here in uniform of the 4th Queen's Own Hussars in 1895, witnessed many battles that later affected his views as a politician. "In war, you can only be killed once, but in politics many times," he quipped.

11819—Winston Spencer Churchill, the Famous War Correspondent, Bloemfontein, South Africa.

Winston became world famous from his books and writings about war. After surviving capture during the Boer War in 1899, he wrote his mother, "I believe I am to be preserved for future things." *Library of Congress*

With his knowledge of war, Churchill marveled at the German military in 1906 while observing maneuvers alongside Kaiser Wilhelm II. Churchill later oversaw Great Britain's fight against Germany in two world wars. *Library of Congress*

Churchill's leadership and bold vision guided Great Britain through its long-running conflict against Hitler's Nazi Germany. He convinced the Allies to first take control of North Africa before attempting a huge D-Day invasion at Normandy in 1944.

Politics in their blood. During his 1946 race, congressional candidate John F. Kennedy shared a light moment with his father, former U.S. ambassador Joseph P. Kennedy and his grandfather, John F. "Honey Fitz" Fitzgerald, Boston's former mayor. *Library of Congress*

The family enterprise. At their Hyannis Port home in 1948, the Kennedys managed to rally as a family despite the wartime death of son Joe Jr. and recent plane crash that killed daughter Kathleen. Seen from left to right: JFK, Jean, Rose, Joe Sr., Patricia, Robert, Eunice, and Edward (kneeling). *JFK Library*

Three brothers in politics. At the height of their power together in August 1963, President John F. Kennedy posed at the White House with his two brothers, U.S. attorney general Robert F. Kennedy (left) and U.S. senator Edward M. Kennedy of Massachusetts (middle). *JFK Library*

Churchills honored by Kennedys. President John F. Kennedy awarded honorary U.S. citizenship to Winston Churchill at an April 1963 White House ceremony attended by (clockwise around JFK) the ambassador of Great Britain Sir David Ormsby-Gore, his wife, Sylvia ("Sissy"), grandson Winston Churchill, First Lady Jacqueline Kennedy, and son Randolph Churchill. Winston was too infirm to attend but watched on television from his home in England. *JFK Library*

JFK's many sides. Historian Arthur M. Schlesinger Jr. became a top Kennedy aide and also a friend to Randolph Churchill, with keen personal insights into both dynasties. "Kennedy never tired of quoting Winston Churchill: 'We arm to parley,'" Schlesinger wrote. Privately JFK told him the family's success "was due to my father." *JFK Library*

Grand manipulator. Shipping magnate Aristotle Onassis befriended members of both the Churchill and the Kennedy families, often with private intentions of his own. Onassis seen here with Winston Churchill in 1959, cruising the Mediterranean aboard his giant yacht, named for his daughter, Christina. *Associated Press*

Sons of great men. Former first lady Jacqueline Kennedy, seen here in New York in 1966, understood both Randolph Churchill and her son, John F. Kennedy Jr., were defined by the lasting impact of their fathers' legacies. *Condé Nast Archive/Corbis*

Kennedy on history. As a Pulitzer Prize–winning historian, President Kennedy learned many lessons about world crises from reading Winston Churchill. "The people of the United States and of the world will never forget your valiant leadership in their darkest hours in the fight against tyranny," he told Churchill. *JFK Library*

Churchill on history. As a future Nobel laureate in literature, Winston's study of American history, especially the Civil War, taught him that the U.S. was traditionally slow to war but "fought to the last desperate inch" once engaged in conflict. Upon learning of Pearl Harbor, Churchill wrote, "I went to bed and slept the sleep of the saved and thankful."

Library of Congress

embattled nation that he'd worked so tirelessly to achieve. "In my view it is the Germans who will suffer very heavy casualties when our band of brothers gets among them," he assured Roosevelt with Shakespearean imagery. No one seemed able to dissuade him from visiting the battlefront. Only after King George VI insisted that he stay in London did Winston reconsider.

In his underground war rooms near 10 Downing Street, filled with maps and telephones, Churchill kept track of each minute development during the invasion. Enthusiastically, he reported to the House of Commons that initial Allied casualties seemed lighter than expected, though the total deaths would eventually reach ten thousand. Winston, so aware of history's lessons, never underestimated what would be the grim reality of this massive attack of men and machines. When Clementine bid him good night inside the Map Room, Winston seemed stricken at the magnitude of human loss. "Do you realise that by the time you wake up in the morning twenty thousand men may have been killed?" he asked her.

The hard-fought success of D-day along the western coast of France created a "second front" against Hitler. The Führer was now squeezed in a fateful stranglehold, with the Soviet Union to the east, allowing the Allies to move decisively toward Berlin. Stalin had lived up to the bargain forged at the Teheran Conference, creating a series of deceptions to keep the Germans off guard before the Normandy attack. For nearly two years, Churchill had kept Stalin's demand for a western invasion at bay, until the Allies had gained control of Italy and there had been sufficient time to construct enough planes and ships to succeed with a massive assault from the sea. To his closest aides, Winston remembered the disastrous World War I losses at Gallipoli, the failure of his invasion planning at the Dardanelles, and remained determined not to repeat these.

Looking ahead to a postwar world, Churchill remained deeply troubled by Stalin's expansion plans, though Roosevelt seemed unwilling to confront the Communist leader. The slow buildup to D-day allowed the Soviet Union to grab control throughout Eastern Europe, including Poland and Czechoslovakia. "The Americans could not understand that it was of little avail to win the war strategically if we lost it politically," lamented Bernard Montgomery, Churchill's field marshal. But the British didn't seem to comprehend how much FDR still needed the Soviet Union's help to finish out the war in Japan, especially if it required a long ground war rather than the sudden finality of a still-undetermined atomic bomb. What Winston touted as the Anglo-American "special relationship" became strained. The war had chipped away at whatever closeness Churchill had forged with Roosevelt, perhaps the inevitable consequence of their different personalities and national needs. "He [Churchill] began the connection with the highest hopes for mutual trust and friendship," observed historian Richard M. Ketchum, "only to be disappointed at the end that he had never quite penetrated Franklin Roosevelt's shell."

Ironically, one American who agreed with Churchill's concern about the Soviet leader was Joe Kennedy, who, in his own way, also felt Roosevelt's faded loyalty. In a Boston speech two weeks before D-day, the former ambassador warned that "forces have been unleashed which may require years to control" and that America's postwar future "lies not in the State Department nor in the Foreign Office, but in the mind of a single statesman in Europe today—Mr. Stalin."

While the Allies moved toward ending this war, Winston anticipated the next. In surveying the map of Europe, Churchill knew the fight for freedom was taking place well beyond Normandy's beaches. With Greece, he overcame FDR's reluctance and pressed hard to keep the Communists from taking power in this strategically important cradle of democracy. A generation of Greeks would remain grateful to Churchill for making sure they didn't fall into the Soviet bloc of nations in the postwar world. And when the Communist guerrillas threatened to take control of Yugoslavia, Churchill underlined his concern by sending his only son, Randolph. This mission would be another chance for young Churchill to demonstrate his bravery.

Bursting into White's one spring morning in 1944, Randolph appeared on a frenzied manhunt, crying out the name of his prey.

"Where's Evelyn Waugh?" he demanded in this stately gentlemen's establishment, the unofficial London headquarters of Tories like him. "I've got to get hold of him! Where the devil is he?"

He stumbled into an old Oxford friend, who said Waugh was training in Scotland with his own regiment, and wondered why the prime minister's son seemed so rushed.

"Because my father has agreed to me taking charge of a mission to Croatia under Fitzroy Maclean," Randolph explained, with utter honesty if not discretion. "I can't go to Croatia unless I have someone to talk to."

When Randolph outlined the high-risk assignment to Waugh, the famous author "was delighted" to accept, and his superiors in Scotland weren't sorry to see him go. "His courage, coupled with his intellect, might have won him a distinguished military career," Randolph later said of his notoriously moody friend. "But he was usually more interested in driving his immediate superiors mad than in bringing about the defeat of the enemy."

Randolph's Yugoslav adventure had begun a few months earlier. Coming out of the Teheran Conference in late 1943, Winston agreed to send a commando unit led by Maclean into Yugoslavia, partly to stir sabotage and help the resistance against the German puppet government. The prime minister admired Maclean's charismatic, often inventive leadership in North Africa and had heard about his personal heroism from Randolph after their Benghazi escapade. Maclean would be Churchill's "warrior-ambassador," charged with figuring out for the

Allies how best to deal with the polyglot Yugoslavia—with its Croats, Serbs, Bosnians, Macedonians, Slovenians, and all their cultural in-fighting when not resisting German invaders. Initially, Churchill backed the royalists, whose prince had fled to London. But listening to Maclean, Winston realized he needed to know more about Josip Tito, the then-obscure leader of the daring Communist partisans, who had killed Germans in greater numbers.

In putting together a team, Maclean welcomed Randolph's request to join his mission. The prime minister's son had just finished serving as his father's temporary aide in Teheran, and Maclean's approval brought a certain validation, allowing Randolph into a rarified club determined by sheer cunning and fortitude. Randolph wasn't cut out for a desk job, "but for my present purposes he seemed just the man," Maclean later wrote. "On operations I knew him to be thoroughly dependable, possessing both endurance and determination. He was also gifted with an acute intelligence and a very considerable background of general politics, neither of which would come amiss in Jugoslavia. I felt, too—rightly, as it turned out—that he would get on well with the Jugoslavs, for his enthusiastic and at times explosive approach to life was not unlike their own." Carrying a letter from his father to Tito, Randolph and a few others flew with Maclean on their first mission, from Italy to Yugoslavia, in January 1944.

High above the mountains, their American-built Dakota transport plane managed to avoid any enemy planes or anti-aircraft fire. As they neared their designated parachute location in west Bosnia, signal fire and billowing smoke showed the way. The plane lowered closer to the ground, enough so Maclean could distinctly see people's faces below when the cabin doors opened. He worried the plane might be too low. Nevertheless, he jumped out first when the dispatcher's green light flashed. Randolph followed in descent. He nearly hit a telegraph pole before landing in a tumble of muddied snow. Tito's soldiers greeted them, impressed by the bravery of Churchill's son. During the remaining winter months, Randolph remained stationed in the woods, inside a house where he read Tolstoy's *War and Peace* to pass the time. In March, a German surprise attack on the Partisans forced Tito to flee his headquarters. He relocated temporarily with Randolph and the others in Italy. When Tito returned to Yugoslavia in May, Randolph stayed behind in newly liberated Rome and was granted an audience in early June with Pope Pius XII.

Inside the Vatican, the pontiff expressed concern about the growing strength of the Communists in Yugoslavia and their church repression. Randolph explained why his father's government now favored the Partisans as the most effective force against the occupying Nazis. Perhaps overly impressed by Tito and his patriotic soldiers, Randolph discounted any lasting Soviet influence. "I explained to him that the whole trend to-day is away from Communism and that private property and religious institutions are guaranteed and respected by the movement of national liberation," he wrote to Winston after the papal visit. He said that the internal strife in Yugoslavia stemmed from religious differences, not politics, and that Tito was the best hope "to bring all these discordant elements together." Both Churchills believed that Catholics, particularly those in Croatia, where Randolph promoted Britain propaganda, would keep communism from spreading. At the end of his talk with Pius XII, Randolph, rather awkwardly, decided to mention his favorite Catholic in England—his friend novelist Evelyn Waugh. What did the Holy Father think of Waugh and his writings? he asked. The mystified pontiff said he'd never heard of him. Randolph appeared nonplussed.

"I thought Captain Waugh's reputation might be known to Your Holiness because he's a Catholic too," Randolph blurted out, a near-comic exchange later repeated for the amusement of his detractors and drinking mates.

After spending a few snowy, dull months in the Yugoslav hinterlands, Randolph asked Maclean if he could invite some more interesting friends to join their unit. "The trouble, you know, is that so few of your officers are my social and intellectual equals," he explained to Maclean. "Couldn't I bring a few amusing chaps back with me to Yugoslavia?" As long as they were fighting men at heart, Maclean said he wouldn't mind.

With that sly permission, Randolph was soon searching for Waugh in White's, the club where the novelist had vouched for him as a member. Playing on his Churchill connections, Waugh already had been granted a three-month leave to finish his literary masterpiece, *Brideshead Revisited*. The prime minister's son also arranged for another old friend, Freddie Birkenhead (son of Winston's deceased friend Lord Birkenhead, best known as F. E. Smith), to leave his unit. In June 1944, the same month when thousands lost their lives on the D-day beaches of Normandy, the indulgence accorded Randolph's demands angered some in the ranks, but there seemed little choice. Soon, his time with Waugh in Yugoslavia proved dangerous enough. Flying into Croatia in mid-July 1944, their Dakota plane crashed, killing ten passengers, including Randolph's local aide-de-camp. Sitting in the plane's rear with Waugh, Randolph forced open parts of the burning fuselage, enough so he and others could escape the flames. For his heroism in saving lives, he later received an MBE, Most Excellent Order of the British Empire, with its gold Grand Cross. Waugh, who suffered a concussion, remembered wandering in a cornfield by the light of the burning plane. He was carried away on a stretcher, hearing screams and "confused talk about who had escaped and who hadn't." When President Roosevelt learned of the crash, he immediately sent a personal note to the prime minister, one father to another, aware of their common vulnerability to having a son killed in war. "I am very happy that Randolph has come through all right," Roosevelt wrote. Churchill's short reply underlined that his son was among the fortunate few. "Thank you so much," Winston responded. "Ten died and nine survived."

In Croatia, novelist Waugh and young Churchill "were very close, almost inseparable, and the reasons were clear," recalled John Blatnik, an American OSS officer who worked with them. "Randolph enjoyed using the English language as an admirably refined mechanism for precise expression of thought." By that time, Freddie Birkenhead had joined them, sharing a room in the British local headquarters with Randolph, where they imbibed endless drinks. As weeks passed, Waugh tired of listening to their stories, "the retelling of memorable sayings of their respective fathers," interlarded with Birkenhead's earthiness and Randolph's obnoxious banter. Evelyn bet the prime minister's son he couldn't read the Bible in a fortnight and pass a quiz on its contents. Randolph accepted the task with all the fervor of a convert. Sitting rapturously in a chair, he found delights and abominations from Genesis to the Apocalypse. At the end of one tale about divine intervention, he burst out laughing, "Christ, God is *a shit!*"

Annoyed by such impudence, Waugh attacked the godhead figure in Randolph's own life. When asked by Randolph if his father's much-praised *Life of Marlborough* was worthy, Evelyn called it nothing more than drivel. "As history, it is beneath contempt, the special pleading of a defense lawyer," Waugh described sourly. "As literature it is worthless. It is written in a sham Augustan prose which could only have been achieved by a man who thought always in terms of public speech."

As always, Randolph assaulted anyone who dared impugn his father's reputation. He, of course, could say anything he liked to make Winston's blood boil, but no one, not even a writer he venerated like Waugh, could utter a disparaging word.

"Have you ever noticed it is people who are most religious who become the most mean and cruel?" Randolph asked accusingly at Evelyn.

"But my dear Randolph, you have no idea what I would be like if I weren't a Catholic," he replied.

Catholicism, particularly the High Mass ritualism he embraced in 1930, was only a part of Waugh's mystifying composition. His off-again, on-again, love-hate relationship with Randolph, bonded by élite eccentricities and anything but common experiences, took advantage of Churchill's name yet returned little true loyalty. "He [Randolph] is not a good companion for a long period," judged the forty-year-old Waugh, "but the conclusion is always the same—that no one else would have chosen me, nor would anyone else have accepted him." Waugh's writerly gift for delving into character flaws found a lodestar in the Churchills. Although he dedicated his earlier novel expressly to Randolph, Waugh discreetly plumbed the Churchill world to come up with fictional characters, such as Rex Mottram in *Brideshead Revisited*. (Waugh's galley proofs for *Brideshead* landed by parachute in Yugoslavia during a mail drop in November 1944, while the author was decamped with Randolph and Freddie.) Though some likened Mottram to Max Beaverbrook or Brendan Bracken in this drama set in 1930s England, the character also bore striking similarities to Winston himself. In Waugh's portrayal, Mottram is a Conservative Party politician "on the fringe of Government, prominent but vaguely suspect," who "said the sort of thing which 'made a story' in Fleet Street, and that did him no good with his party chiefs; only war could put Rex's fortunes right and carry him into power." In Waugh's sly references, Mottram's friends even included "Max" and "F.E."

With the real characters in Randolph's life, Waugh could be far less discreet. Despite the failure of his first marriage, when he learned of his wife's adultery, the bisexual Waugh delighted in gossiping about Pamela's infidelities and Randolph's marital difficulties with her. Waugh "had a way of making you tell all and he would discover all these intrigues between the wives and the various husbands and he would 'stir the pot' for trouble," Pam recalled. Waugh married again in 1937, to Laura Herbert—a younger woman whom he met indirectly through Father D'Arcy, his Jesuit baptizer—and they had a succession of children, though Evelyn, chauvinistically and by preference, preferred the company of men. "So fiercely had he fought for his 'masculinity' after his broken marriage that he had tried to thrust away all that was homosexual in him," wrote Waugh biographer Martin Stannard. "It would not die. 'Pansies,' along with kippers and mothers-in-law, had to remain the subject for jokes even though Waugh frequently felt closer to the male homosexual community in spirit than to abrasively masculine figures like 'Randy' Churchill. There was often a deep divide between Waugh's private and public life, between an almost religious tenderness and aggression."

Randolph, consumed by his own family complexities, probably knew little about the intimacies of Waugh's marriage or sexual inclinations, and cared even less. With his own fragile ego, he sought to be liked by friends such as Waugh and Birkenhead, not to critique or condemn them. After years of witnessing his friend's behavior, Waugh knew Randolph to be fearless, whether in a pub or in a parachute. He admired that the prime minister's son had sought ways to join the war rather than evade it. That willingness to confront danger was tested before they left Yugoslavia, with the war winding down, when the three friends from Oxford awoke one morning to an enemy air raid.

"Get up, you fool—the Germans are overhead and they are trying to get me!" Randolph yelled, quickly putting on his pants as he roused Birkenhead. "They have this house pinpointed."

Randolph's instincts were likely correct about the farmhouse that served as their headquarters. Its sole luxury, as the only house with an indoor toilet, was a sure sign the prime minister's son was staying there. Randolph had become the symbol of British support for the Yugoslav resistance. Even a fearless warrior such as Maclean worried about

Randolph's vulnerability if the Germans learned of his whereabouts and wanted revenge on the son of the man engineering their impending demise. "Do take care not to be captured," Winston warned when he last saw his son. "The Gestapo would only try to blackmail me by sending me your fingers one by one—a situation I would have to bear with fortitude."

As the German planes roared overhead, spraying the ground with gunfire, Randolph alerted everyone in the area to take cover. He half-expected Nazi paratroops to descend from the sky. From a protected spot in a slit trench, Randolph looked out on a field behind the farmhouse. He was horrified to see Evelyn Waugh, in a white sheepskin coat, standing alone defiantly before the planes. Waugh later claimed his honor required it, if sanity did not.

"You bloody little swine, take off that coat!" Randolph screamed, from a nearby trench. Waugh remained unmoved. "*Take off that fucking coat! It's an order! It's a military order!*"

In a strange and slow reaction, Waugh finally sauntered over to the trench and then paused. He looked with disgust at Randolph lying on the ground. "I'll tell you what I think of your repulsive manners when the bombardment is over," he hissed in, joining the rest.

Like red cloth to a bull, Waugh's white duffle coat served as a highly visible incendiary target for the German fighter planes. They saturated the farmhouse with bullet holes and then dropped bombs on the nearby village, killing several Croatian civilians. As the planes flew away, Randolph and Evelyn fell into a cold silence that lasted for days.

Finally, Randolph apologized if his manner had been a bit gruff. As mission commander, he explained, every life in their headquarters was his responsibility. Glaring with dark, condemning eyes, Evelyn remained unmoved.

"My dear Randolph, it wasn't your manners I was complaining of: it was your cowardice," Waugh declared.

Freddie chortled at this "devastating rejoinder," which made its merciless way back to White's for the constant retelling and amusement of their friends. From firsthand observation, Waugh certainly knew of Randolph's unflinching valor and that any suggestion to the contrary was a blood libel. "Churchill had many faults," concluded Stannard, Waugh's biographer. "Cowardice was not one of them." Still Waugh persisted with the joke at Randolph's expense, with a lack of loyalty too often displayed by those closest to the young Churchill.

For much of the war, Winston claimed that if Randolph were killed, he, the prime minister, "would not be able to carry on" his work, which prompted Winston's generals to usher his son discreetly out of risky duties that most men could not have escaped. Randolph's brushes with danger, by volunteering for assignments such as Benghazi and Yugoslavia, were of his own volition. But the stinging whispers of cowardice, like that of adultery involving his wife, haunted his sense of manhood.

By 1944, Prime Minister Churchill seemed more prosaic when his generals again suggested shielding his son from danger. Perhaps now with a grandson, he realized, the family's legacy was secure for another generation. "If it is thought he is doing no good where he is and an opportunity comes of bringing him out, do so," Winston instructed Gen. Henry Maitland Wilson, a close confidant overseeing the Mediterranean operation. "But do not bring him back out of any consideration for me or because a price has been put on his head. Let Service considerations alone prevail. This is what I know he would wish."

When he got wind of possible special treatment, Randolph let his father know it wasn't necessary. "It is kind of your Generals to be so worried about my welfare," he advised.

Unlike thousands of other Englishmen, Churchill's son had survived after five years of war. Try as he might, he failed to become a dead hero. Instead, he'd return to civilian life with the cruelest of indignities attached to his name: cuckold and coward.

31

Love among the Ruins

" 'Have you news of my boy Jack?'
Not this tide.
'When d'you think that he'll come back?'
Not with this wind blowing, and this tide."
—RUDYARD KIPLING, "MY BOY JACK," 1916

Unlike Rudyard Kipling in the Great War—and so many other heartbroken fathers in this second, larger conflict—Winston Churchill narrowly escaped having a son die in combat. By early 1944, Joseph P. Kennedy felt that he, too, had been spared such a wretched fate. Kennedy's eldest son, Joe Jr., was due home soon after flying more than his fair share of sorties over embattled France. His second-oldest, Jack, was already in Boston, recovering from his injuries aboard the *PT-109* in the Pacific. Perhaps considering himself lucky, Joe empathized with fathers facing the greatest misfortune.

"I have just heard today of the loss of your boy," Kennedy wrote to a friend, Harry Hogan, in February 1944. "As one father to another, who, although he has not had the total loss, has had his boys missing in action, I can feel in a small way how you must be suffering."

Kennedy knew other fathers cursed by this most harrowing loss. Before the month ended, the son of Harry Hopkins—the broker of war plans between the president and Winston Churchill—died in battle.

Stephen Hopkins, an eighteen-year-old Marine, lost his life on an obscure, tiny Pacific island called Namur, felled by a Japanese sniper's bullet. For the Kennedys, the death of Lord Halifax's son Peter Wood, killed in action in Egypt, landed the biggest emotional impact. Peter and his brother Richard had been part of the young Kennedys' social circle in London in the late 1930s, while the aristocratic Lord Halifax and his wife remained friendly with Joe and Rose. As Kick told her parents, "Richard really is the soul of honesty and I think one of the best and most understanding friends I have in all this world."

Lord Halifax, like Kennedy, had disagreed previously with Churchill about the necessity of war. When Chamberlain stepped down, many favored Halifax for prime minister but he deferred to Winston. Halifax was serving as the British ambassador in Washington when news came of Peter's death in November 1942, killed in a war his father had tried to prevent. Both Joe and Rose Kennedy admired how Halifax, in such emotional pain away from home, remained in his post undauntedly for his nation. As Rose observed, "Like so many other British fathers whom we knew, he continued bravely, uncomplainingly, working probably harder than ever in order to keep his mind so occupied that he would not dwell on the sorrowful, heart-breaking picture of seeing so many of the bright, gay, well-educated young men, who the year before had so confidently talked and planned their futures in the professions or in politics, to see them all killed in the skies or in the trenches."

Despite these wartime tragedies, the lasting effects of love, more than death, preoccupied the thoughts of the Kennedys in early 1944. From a continent away, Rose and Joe Kennedy watched, almost helplessly, as Kick's romance with Billy Hartington blossomed in London, the place where the two had first met in 1938, at a garden party attended by Princess Elizabeth. After being forced apart by war, with Kick spending nearly three years in America, the young couple vowed never to separate again, to overcome the ruinous odds against their love. During the war, Billy and his military unit had survived the 1940

Dunkirk evacuation. Now they faced the impending invasion across the English Channel, which would kill thousands of troops. Whatever their future odds, Kick dreamed of a wedding day with her Billy, the future Duke of Devonshire, and never to let him go. "I suppose I really always expected to marry Billy," she admitted to her mother. "Some day— some how."

Her closest brother, Jack, wasn't impressed with Billy. He considered his title and nobility part of a fading order. "I would advise strongly against any voyages to England to marry an Englishman," he wrote to his sister in March 1942. "For I have come to the reluctant conclusion that it has come time to write the obituary of the British Empire. Like all good things, it had to come to an end sometime, and it was good while it lasted. You may not agree with this, but I imagine that the day before Rome fell, not many people would have believed it could *ever* fall." Jack privately felt Churchill had understood that the empire was nearing an end, and he blamed him "for getting this country into war," knowing the only salvation from Nazi annihilation was America's military might. Winston Churchill remained a touchstone in the Kennedys' lives. In a lighthearted letter to his family, Jack compared his mother jokingly to the British prime minister, referring to one of his famous lines: "Never in history have so many owed so much to such a one—or is that quite correct?" he teased her. "If you would look in that little book of yours under Churchill Winston—I imagine you can check it." Kick let Jack know of her determined interest in Billy Hartington, regardless of his dissent. "Billy Hartington wants to know if you still think the British are decadent," she wrote her brother. "Do you?" Typical of her usual banter with Jack, she made light of her chance of marrying Billy. "I doubt it—but it would be rather nice as I believe it would give me some title or other," she cracked, before she returned to England to work for the American Red Cross.

In January 1944, Kick attended a dinner at London's Connaught

Hotel, hosted by the Devonshires, and spent the night enchanted by Billy and other young men in their full-dress uniforms. It was an exciting time for Billy, who remained in the military but, at his family's insistence, had resigned his commission as a British Army captain in order to vie for a seat in Parliament. A Conservative Party member running as the wartime coalition candidate, Hartington carried the endorsement of Winston Churchill in the by-election. On her days off, Kick helped Billy at campaign stops by handing out leaflets that read: "A vote for Hartington is a vote for Churchill." That night at the Connaught dinner, Kick spotted the prime minister's youngest daughter among the crowd. "Mary Churchill wore a light blue crepe dress with an aquamarine necklace," Kick reported home. "She has lovely blue eyes but is rather chubby. However, she laughs a lot and seems quite merry."

Kick also conversed with one of Randolph's writer friends. "The best part of the evening was when I was talking to Evelyn Waugh, who has written a lot of very funny books," she told her parents. Though witty herself, she had a hard time keeping up with a sophisticated intellect like Waugh, admitting, "all in all the conversation made me realize just how much I had to learn." Waugh came away with far less admiration toward the former ambassador's daughter. By then, rumors abounded of an interfaith marriage between Kick and Billy, a struggle between their Catholic and Anglican religions, sparking the novelist's moralistic wrath. "Kik [*sic*] Kennedy's apostasy is a sad thing," wrote Waugh, who blamed "her heathen friends" for persuading her away from the Catholic faith. "It is second front nerves [that] has driven her to this grave sin and I am sorry for the girl."

Looking for a way to marry Billy and remain in the Church, Kick consulted Father Martin D'Arcy, S.J., the London Jesuit who inspired Waugh's conversion a decade earlier, but he offered few solutions. After failing to get a dispensation from a bishop recommended by D'Arcy,

Kick wrote her parents, "I suppose it will [be] practically impossible." At age twenty-four, she was certain of the man she loved and wanted to marry, yet neither family seemed ready to compromise on religion.

During Billy's campaign for Parliament, Kick's presence seemed a mixed blessing. In talking about the Anglo-American couple, one British newspaper later noted Kick's Irish "Home Rule" background, the historical opposition of Billy's ancestors, and mused "Parnell's ghost must be smiling sardonically." Indeed, the two families held starkly different views of Ireland's struggle for independence and religious conflict with Great Britain. The 1882 assassination of Lord Frederick Cavendish—Billy's paternal granduncle, then the British chief secretary for Ireland in Dublin—by knife-wielding Irish extremists in Phoenix Park became a bitter legacy for his family, and one of Winston Churchill's first shocking memories as a child. Billy's crusty old father, Edward William Spencer Cavendish, the Tenth Duke of Devonshire, was the proud resident of Chatsworth, a lavish estate elegant enough to rival Blenheim. In January 1943, the duke joined Churchill's government as undersecretary for colonies. As a Freemason with a long memory reaching back to Phoenix Park, the duke had little use for Irish Catholics, even those as warm and engaging as Kick Kennedy. Over lunch, Sir Henry "Chips" Channon listened with unease as his friend "Eddie" Devonshire insisted his eldest son not abandon their family traditions. "He will not budge," wrote Channon about the duke; "the Kennedy alliance is not to his liking; he has an anti-catholic mania, and has forbidden the match."

Faced with the duke's bigotry, Kick tried to fob off his obstinacy with humor and her own steeled will. She also tried to placate her family in the United States, especially her deeply religious mother, Rose. "Of course the Dukie is very worried about having *A Roman Catholic* in the family," Kick wrote her parents in April 1944. "In fact, he's a fanatic on the subject. In their eyes the most awful thing that could happen to our son would be for it [*sic*] to become a Roman. With me in the family that danger becomes immediate even though I would promise that the child could be brought up as an Anglican."

Deferring to his father's wishes, Billy refused to marry in the Catholic Church. He wouldn't repeat the recent example of his cousin David Ormsby-Gore, who wed his Catholic wife, Sissy, a friend of Kick's, without any difficulty. Ironically, if Billy had won a seat in the House of Commons, he would have given up his peerage, making it easier for him to marry outside the Church of England. But Billy lost his election in February 1944, to the Independent Socialist challenger, a firm repudiation of his family's historic control of that district. "Churchill wrote him [Billy] a letter which didn't help," Kick wrote to her parents, explaining the defeat. "I don't know what the people want," the duke complained to his son. "I do," Billy shot back; "they just don't want the Cavendishes." Billy looked forward to perhaps running for Parliament again, after the war. "I am going out now to fight for you at the front," he promised his supporters in defeat. "After all, unless we win the war[,] there can be no home front."

Before he returned to battle, Billy hoped to marry Kick, if some agreement could be reached. "I have loved Kick for a long time, but I did try so hard to face the fact that the religious difficulties seemed insurmountable," he explained in an almost apologetic letter to Rose Kennedy. "But after Christmas I realized that I couldn't bear to let her go without ever asking her if we couldn't find a way out and I knew that time before I should have to go and fight was getting short." One of the Kennedys' best friends in London, Lady Nancy Astor (another American who fell in love with England), counseled Kick like a daughter and suggested she follow her heart. "Of course, she still hopes I'll marry Billy and keeps telling me I'll only be happy in England," Kick wrote home.

Back in America, the Kennedys confronted their daughter's religious dilemma as best they knew how, given the wartime travel restrictions. If she married Billy under terms he wished, they feared Kick would no longer be a Catholic in good standing. She'd be unable to take Communion and, perhaps mostly alarmingly, would have repudiated the Kennedys' political base. As Kick's biographer Lynne McTaggart concluded, "Because of the family's ambitions and its Irish American constituency, Billy was probably the worst possible marriage partner for her."

Rose sought a spiritual solution from an all-knowing God, while Joe relied on his earthly connections for a last-minute fix. His influential friends Count Enrico Galeazzi, administrator for the Pope in Rome, and Archbishop Francis J. Spellman in New York searched for some catechistic allowance for Kick to marry and still stay in the Church's good graces. While Joe's machinations proved limited, Rose aimed her powerful appeals at her daughter's conscience. "Galleazzi's [*sic*] pal said of course the authorities were always the same and frankly I do not seem to think Dad can do anything," fifty-three-year-old Rose wrote in a "Dear Kathleen" letter. "He feels terribly sympathetic and so do I and I only wish we could offer some suggestions. When both people have been handed something all their lives, how ironic it is that they cannot have what they want most. I wonder if the next generation will feel that it is worth sacrificing a life's happiness for all the old family tradition."

The Kennedys turned to Lord Halifax, the British ambassador in Washington, to confer with Kathleen when he returned to London for a visit. If any compromise could be reached with the Devonshires, they felt Halifax would find it. Halifax's father once pushed for a union of the Anglican and Roman Catholic Churches. When serving in London, Joe Kennedy often relied on Halifax, then foreign secretary, as a friend to explain Churchill's erratic behavior or soothe his own bruised feelings. Kennedy considered the diplomat as "almost a saint" in demeanor. Yet in this circumstance, Halifax remained evenhanded, recognizing Billy's obligations to his titled family and religion. Halifax introduced Kick to an Anglican monk, who discussed her marriage plans but ultimately convinced her to marry at a government registry, rather than in church. Others consulted by the Kennedys, including Spellman, who talked to Joe Jr., advised much the same. "His attitude seemed to be that if they loved each other a lot, then marry outside the Church," Joe Jr. informed his father. "He didn't seem to be disturbed about it creating a bad example."

Within ten minutes on a Saturday morning in May 1944, Kick Kennedy married Billy Hartington inside the austere Chelsea Registry Office, far from the majestic churches she once envisioned for a wedding. No vows were exchanged, and no one from the Kennedy family attended except her oldest brother, Joe Jr., who gave her away.

Billy wore his Coldstream Guards army uniform, and Kick appeared enchantingly in a light pink crepe dress, assembled with the help of wartime clothing coupons donated by friends. Kathleen Cavendish, the new Marchioness of Hartington, no longer seemed that girlish Red Cross volunteer on a bicycle darting past the bombed-out buildings of London, but rather an attractive young woman content with her difficult choices in life. Reporters and photographers, alert to the controversial wedding, hounded the newlyweds. They smiled dutifully for the cameras outside the redbrick registry building, before shuttling to a reception of champagne and cake. In the press photographs, the Duke of Devonshire stands stoically beside the beaming couple. Reporters noted their wedding "was the first time since 1694 that an heir to the dukedom of Devonshire had been married outside the family chapel."

Lady Nancy Astor and Marie Bruce, another friend of Rose Kennedy, attended the wedding as the bride's only guests. DEAREST ROSE, YOU WOULD REJOICE IN THEIR YOUNG HAPPINESS, they cabled. ONLY GRIEF YOUR SORROW. In America, an emotionally distraught Rose Kennedy checked herself into a hospital, partly to avoid the badgering questions about her daughter's marriage outside the Church. "I was very worried about a newspaper report here that you were very ill," Kick wrote to her mother three days later, while on her honeymoon. "They made out that it was because of my marriage. Goodness mother—I owe so much to you and Daddy that nothing in the world could have made me go against your will . . . Please don't take any responsibility for an action, which you think bad (and I do not). You did everything in your power to stop it. You did your duty as a Roman Catholic mother. You have not failed."

Initially, Joe Kennedy mirrored his wife's opposition to a wedding outside the Church. His rejection slowly melted, though, as he realized the depth of his daughter's love for Billy. As he explained to Jack's friend Tony Rosslyn, "When Kathleen feels that strongly about anything, I go along with her." To Sir James Calder, his associate in the British liquor business, Joe conceded, "Rose and I finally came around to your point of view—that they will get married and settle things afterward." With Lord Beaverbrook, Joe was at his most candid: "I see now that I've lost one of my daughters to England," he admitted. "She was the apple of my eye and I feel the loss because I won't have her near me all the time, but I'm sure she's going to be wonderfully happy and I can assure you that England is getting a great girl." The war had claimed his daughter's affections, but Kennedy's main concern remained his oldest son's safety as a combat pilot. In this same letter to Beaverbrook, he mentioned that Joe Jr. planned to stay in England for now. "Young Joe is still over there—has just volunteered for an extra month's duty before he's sent home, which will give him forty missions," he told Beaverbrook. "Although he's had a large number of casualties in his squadron, I'm still hoping and praying we'll see him around the first of July."

During Kick's wedding, Joe Jr. performed at his finest. With a few hints of gray in his hair, the twenty-eight-year-old displayed a subtle maturity in this family crisis that suggested the kind of man he might become, far different from his earlier brashness and arrogance as a rich man's son. On his sister's behalf, he handled the financial arrangements of the marriage agreement with the Devonshires' lawyer. He also made

sure Kick didn't sign any paper agreeing to bring up children as Angli-
cans, even though the duke pressed for it, and successfully discouraged
the idea of a blessing on the couple from the Archbishop of Canterbury.
Despite his own previous concerns about Billy, Joe Jr. unflinchingly defended his sister's decision to marry. ("I am much more favorably impressed with him than I was the last time I was over here," he wrote
to his parents. "I think he really has something on the ball, and he
couldn't be nicer. I think he is ideal for Kick.")

Joe Jr. seemed genuinely shocked by the Kennedys' lack of support
for Kick, including the diffidence of brother Jack. THE POWER OF SILENCE
IS GREAT, he scolded his family in a one-line telegram sent a day after
the wedding. In a sense, young Joe had the most to lose by standing up
for his sister, joking as the press photos were taken that he was "finished
in Boston." Given his budding political career in Massachusetts, where
he'd already been a delegate to the 1940 Democratic Convention, he
realized that Kick's marriage to British nobility wouldn't sit well with
many Irish Catholics back home. They condemned it as some tribal
betrayal or abandonment of the Church. But Joe Jr., always the protective older brother, wouldn't have it. "As far as Kick's soul is concerned, I
wish I had half her chance of seeing the pearly gates," he wrote to his
parents. "As far as what people will say, the hell with them. I think we
can all take it."

Joe Kennedy Jr.'s noble actions belied a reality he didn't want his
parents to know. Staying in England meant one last desperate chance to
be a hero, and more time to continue his affair with a married woman,
Patricia Wilson—a secret shared with no family member other than
Kick.

Months earlier, Joe had attended a dinner with Kick at the Savoy
in London, arranged by William Randolph Hearst Jr., the son of the

famous publishing tycoon. A guest at his table included Pat Wilson, a dark-haired beauty with an infectious laugh. Joe found himself terribly attracted to this previously divorced mother of three children whose second husband had been gone for a long time as a British Army major in Libya. With abandon, Joe and Pat began an intense extramarital affair, just as other young English wives did while their husbands were away. Somehow, in the chaotic uncertainty of war, such relationships seemed more like companionship than cheating. Occasionally on weekends, Kick and Billy spent time with Joe at the farmhouse where Pat lived with her children, not far from Joe's military station. In her letters home, Kick professed ignorance about whom her older brother might be dating. Wary of what his parents might think, Joe portrayed Pat as merely a member of their circle of friends. He revealed nothing more.

His parents' judgment affected Joe Jr. in an even more troubling way, in a gnawing sense that perhaps he'd overshadowed his brother Jack in their lifelong rivalry. Growing up, Joe Jr. had always dominated his younger, skinnier brother, sometimes punishingly so, prompting Jack to affect the carefree attitude that others found so winning. When the war began, Jack still appeared envious of his athletic older brother, and vied with him for their parents' approval. "Jack bought me a miniature Torpedo Boat done in silver in the form of a tie clip," recalled their father. "He is really terrifically jealous of the fact that I wear Joe's gold wings all the time and is bound that I have one of his insignias, and so I am to turn this tie clip into a pin some way or other." When he later became a war hero, Jack fashioned tie clips into the form of his *PT-109* boat and gave them away as mementos. "In their long brotherly, friendly rivalry, I expect this was the first time Jack had won such an 'advantage' by such a clear margin," observed their mother. "And I daresay it cheered Jack and must have rankled Joe Jr."

Before leaving for England after a short stay home, Joe Jr. attended a large party in Boston and seemed visibly upset when the crowd toasted his brother's heroic *PT-109* exploits. "By God, *I'll* show them," he swore.

Later in London, Joe Jr. (his very name an appellation that invited father-son comparisons) confided this driving motivation to Angela Laycock, the wife of a British Commando leader, who was aware of the towering ambitions in the Kennedy clan. "She had the feeling Joe was in awe of Jack's intelligence and believed that his own was no match for it, particularly since his younger brother's recent triumphs," observed Kick's biographer, after interviewing Laycock. "He was sure it was his brother Jack who would ultimately be President."

Instead of leaving in July, Joe Kennedy Jr. volunteered for a dangerous secret mission called Operation Aphrodite, bound to win him the navy's highest honor if successful. Operation Aphrodite stemmed from Churchill's concern with development of a new Nazi weapon: a long-range multi-barrel gun dug into a bunker near Mimoyecques, along France's Pas de Calais, theoretically capable of hurling devastating rocket bombs at London every few minutes. Earlier in the war, German bombing from planes had destroyed buildings and killed thousands of civilians, until British air pilots stopped their advance. The new long-range attacks threatened London again. Unbeknownst to Churchill, the dreaded new Nazi rockets didn't work. Every time they were tested, the projectiles "toppled" to the ground, miles from their target. "We did not know this until afterward, and as a precaution our bombers repeatedly smashed the concrete structure at Mimoyecques," Churchill recalled later in his history of the war. At the time, however, he felt that defensive raids were necessary. He enjoyed inspecting the airfields where Allied bomber pilots such as Kennedy took off across the English Channel. "I hate to see brave men killed and the smoking planes fall out of the sky, but I am old and have to be near the fun," the ancient warrior admitted to a cousin.

On August 12, 1944, Joseph Patrick Kennedy Jr. became one of those pilots who fell from the sky. His risky mission called for guiding a plane loaded with explosives toward Mimoyecques. As they got near, Kennedy and copilot were expected to bail out. Two planes behind them would use sophisticated radio technology to steer their craft into the target. Instead, twenty minutes into their flight, Kennedy's plane exploded into little pieces of shrapnel. His body was never found. FDR's son Elliott Roosevelt, flying a photoreconnaissance plane behind them, witnessed the giant conflagration, which nearly threw his own plane off course. ("Elliott has returned to this country and he had told me of your boy's great bravery," Eleanor later wrote Rose Kennedy.) What the Kennedy patriarch feared most about the war—the lasting threat he perceived to his sons and all his dreams of glory—was lost in those British skies, just when he thought he might escape such tragedy.

Two priests arrived at the Kennedy summerhouse in Hyannis Port to break the news to the former ambassador. Nearly all the family spent that Sunday afternoon there, including Jack, home for the weekend from a nearby naval hospital, where he was recuperating from an unsuccessful back operation for his wartime injuries. Joe was napping in an upstairs bedroom when Rose rushed in. When he came downstairs, Kennedy learned from the priests that his oldest son was dead. "Children, your brother Joe has been lost," said the man who'd never wanted this war, whose worst nightmare had come true. His eyes brimming with tears, he briefly told Jack, Bobby, Eunice, Pat, Jean, and little Teddy, "I want you all to be particularly good to your mother." Perhaps remembering his friend Lord Halifax's countenance after one son died in war and another son lost both legs, Joe instructed his family, "We must carry on like everyone else . . . and take care of the living, because there is a lot of work to be done." The other children, as their father urged, followed through on their plans for sailing. Jack, however, spent the rest of the day walking the beach by himself, lost in memories.

For the next several weeks, Rose took solace in early morning Masses and prayers for her beloved son. "He was so keen about politics too. Joe was hoping he would be governor of Massachusetts," Rose told family friend Clare Boothe Luce. "I have prayed that one day he would be happy and glorious in heaven and I now feel that God has fulfilled my wish in His own Holy way."

The Kennedy patriarch struggled to make sense of his son's incomprehensible death by replying to sympathy cards and notes. He felt in simpatico with a political rival, Massachusetts's Republican governor, Leverett Saltonstall, whose own son, Peter, had been killed that same month on patrol in the jungles of northern Guam. "Eventually, we may think of Peter and Joe as great heroes who fought and died for their country, but today they are our two boys who are gone," Joe wrote, after receiving the governor's condolence note. "My respect for the Deity that rules our destinies beyond our understanding makes us truly accept His course as wiser than any we can contrive for ourselves and our loved ones. (There must be something more to all this world than what we see; otherwise, it would not make any kind of sense.)"

From the White House, Franklin Roosevelt sent sympathy to his former ambassador for "your great sorrow and wish it were in my power to say a word that would lighten your burden of grief. I do want you to know that I am thinking of you." Though Kennedy privately blamed FDR for dragging America into war, he answered his president as graciously as he knew how. "I had always imagined, as you state, that words were powerless in the face of personal tragedy but now, in the valley of the shadow, we find sustaining comfort in expressions of sympathy," Kennedy acknowledged. That same day, to Roosevelt's aide Grace Tully, Joe expressed more candidly what his son's death meant. "Of course, it has been a terrible blow to us both, particularly as he was the oldest boy, and I had spent a great deal of time making what I thought were plans for his future," he wrote. To Tully, Joe also expressed concern about the future of Jack, already suffering through operations at the naval hospital for his own war wounds. "He is in quite bad shape and weighs as much as his twelve-year-old brother."

Kathleen returned home on an army transport plane after learning of her brother's death. At Boston's airport, she was met by Jack, who tearfully embraced her. She felt stunned by Jack's scarecrow-like appearance; he was terribly thin, with his face drawn and a jaundiced cast to his skin. Kick spent the next few weeks at Hyannis Port, attempting to comfort her parents and siblings with cheery words and constant activity that hid her own grief. But she realized nothing would ever be quite the same in the Kennedy family. During a painful moment on Labor Day, while Jack entertained some of his boisterous navy pals, the Kennedy patriarch suddenly leaned out an opened window and yelled, "Jack, don't you and your friends have any respect for your dead brother?" With his oldest brother gone, Jack particularly felt all the expectations of his father's ambitions. "I am now shadowboxing in a match," Jack admitted to his friend Lem Billings, "where the shadow is always going to win."

For a few moments on September 16, Kick forgot about the war, with all its material deprivations and human sacrifices, to go shopping at Bonwit Teller, the elegant New York department store, where she planned to meet her sister for lunch. When Eunice arrived on the second floor, however, Kick quickly sensed something was wrong. Overwhelmed, Eunice would only reply, "Why don't you go talk to Daddy."

They rushed to the former ambassador's suite at the Waldorf, where Joe gave Kick the telegram from England informing her of her husband's death. On a Belgian battlefield, a German sniper had shot Billy through the heart, instantly killing him. "Come on you fellows, buck up," Major Hartington urged his fellow soldiers moments before he lost his life. Kick and Billy had barely had a honeymoon together before he returned to the war. His death stunned family and friends on both sides of the Atlantic. "Very sad news in the paper tonight that Billy Hartington has been killed in action in France," Pamela Churchill wrote on her Churchill Club stationery to Averell Harriman. "He only married Kick Kennedy in May, after having wanted to do so for five years— her brother Joe Kennedy was also killed about four weeks ago. She at the moment is back in the States." Lord Beaverbrook immediately contacted Joe to offer condolences and help to Kathleen. "It is indeed a cruel blow to follow so soon after the loss of your own boy," Max wrote his friend.

While Kick's parents and Kennedy siblings rallied to her side, the Duchess of Devonshire offered perhaps the most meaningful words. "I want you never, never to forget what complete happiness you gave him," Billy's mother told Kick the day after the fateful telegram arrived. "He wrote that to me when he went to the front. I want you to know this for I know what great conscientious struggles you went through before you married Billy, but I know that it will be a source of infinite consolation to you now that you decided as you did . . . My heart breaks when I think of how much you have gone through in your young life." Jack Kennedy, in a revealing four-page sympathy letter to the Duchess of Devonshire, emphasized what Billy had meant to his beloved sister. "I have always been so fond of Kick that I couldn't help but feel some of her great sorrow," he wrote on September 21, 1944. "Her great happiness when she came home which even shone through her sadness over Joe's death was so manifest and so infectious that it did much to ease the grief of our mother and father."

From the White House, President Roosevelt sent a condolence letter to Joe Kennedy ("Please tell Kathleen I am thinking of her in her crushing sorrow") and later invited his former ambassador the following month for a private White House visit. Inside the Oval Office, Kennedy was startled by the president's tired, sickly appearance and slipping memory, his magnificent voice now faded. The two old New Dealers talked about the war, about Churchill, and about the president's reelection bid for a fourth term. "In speaking about Kathleen's husband, he spoke of him as Billy Harkshire or some name like that," Kennedy recalled in his diary. "He asked Churchill what kind of boy he was, and Churchill told him he was one of the most promising lads in England."

Rather than rue the past, Kennedy now pushed his second son's advancement forward. To the president, he complained that Jack had lost out on a better medal for his *PT-109* heroics "because I was *persona non grata* to the powers that be in Washington." Roosevelt immediately turned the conversation to one of his own sons. "Well, those things happen," he explained. "In fact Elliott was recommended for the Congressional Medal of Honor. The board turned it down because they felt it would look as if he had been given it because he was the President's son."

With Roosevelt, Kennedy didn't dwell on his anger for prosecuting a war that had claimed so many lives. Kennedy's visit would be the last with the president who had transformed his life, who had given him so many political opportunities, and who ultimately took away his oldest son. Only with Churchill's friend Lord Beaverbrook, whose own son was serving as a British fighter pilot, did Kennedy reveal his true feelings. "For a fellow who didn't want this war to touch your country or mine, I have had rather a bad dose—Joe dead, Billy Hartington dead, my son Jack in the Naval Hospital," Kennedy concluded. "To have boys like ours killed for a futile effort would be the greatest reflection on all of us."

32

Victory and Defeat

From all of England, more than one hundred thousand people, many of whom heard the announcement of victory in Europe on the radio, swelled around the gates of Buckingham Palace on May 8, 1945. Cheering, crying, dancing, and waving, they waited for hours until the king and queen walked out onto the flag-draped balcony. The sustained roar of a nation filled with gratitude, relief, and sheer joy greeted the royal family. Few, if any, moments in the long history of the British Empire were more glorious than this. After nearly six years of war, many thousands killed, and parts of London and other major cities bombed into rubble, their island nation had survived.

With due deference, the royal couple turned and motioned to the man most responsible for this victory, Prime Minister Winston Churchill, to stand between them at the balcony's edge. As the king and queen saluted the multitude below, Winston just stared at the crowd and beamed paternally. Earlier in the day, he rode in an open-air car and raised his two fingers in a V symbol as his countrymen rejoiced around him. To another throng in front of Whitehall, Churchill declared, "This is your victory" to which the thankful assemblage shouted back, "No, it's *yours*!"

At this most triumphant time at Buckingham Palace, when all about him knew how much he'd saved them from destruction, Winston stood quietly, as if in reflection. He seemed humbled by this mass affirmation—not only for all he had done in war, but for all he had been in life. "All my thoughts are with you on this supreme day my darling," wrote Clementine, traveling in Russia on a goodwill tour and well aware of what this victory meant to her husband. "It could not have happened without you."

As Churchill and the royals celebrated V-E Day on the floodlit balcony, the American widow Kick Kennedy watched from a distance, among the British crowd behind the palace gates.

"I must say that it was a most moving sight," recalled Kick, a widow now called The Marchioness of Hartington. She came along to Buckingham Palace with her friends David and Sissy Ormsby-Gore and Jack's friend Hugh Fraser. She noticed the playwright Noël Coward close behind in the crowd. They gazed at enormous bonfires, fireworks, and dancing in the street. "We want the king!" the crowd demanded, until the royal couple finally appeared. "We roared ourselves hoarse," Coward recounted. "I suppose this is the greatest day in our history."

By the next day, the joyous reception to war's end underlined for Kick what she had lost and her sobering future ahead. That evening, she dined with Billy's mother, the Duchess of Devonshire, who "feels as we all do that one must really now settle down to facing life without the best ones, who will never come back," Kick told her parents. "That is what is difficult."

After Billy's death, Kick had returned to England. It was a way of carrying on her own life, while her father in America continued to bitterly blame Roosevelt and Churchill for the death of his son Joe Jr. In April 1945, when America mourned FDR's death from a stroke in Warm Springs, Georgia, the Kennedy patriarch watched contemptuously as Churchill praised the president, whom Winston later described as "a very great man who was also a warm-hearted friend." Joe, privy to so many past discussions between these two leaders, felt he knew better. "I don't think it made any very great impression in America to read that Churchill, when speaking of him in Parliament with tears in his eyes, talked of what a great friend Roosevelt had been to England and mentioned some of the nice things he had done," he bristled to his daughter, now permanently in London. Kick couldn't bear the bitterness and remorse from the past year—including her mother's lingering moral condemnation of her marriage to Billy. Still, Kick remained true to her family. She recounted for her father, as only she could, how she had defeated Elliott Roosevelt, the president's strapping two-hundred-pound son, in a friendly game of gin rummy. "He wanted to beat me just once," Kick recalled. "I told him nothing gave a Kennedy more pleasure than beating a Ro———up. He was very nice and I must admit that I liked him."

A month after V-E Day, Jack Kennedy arrived in England as a roving correspondent for the Hearst newspapers. He let his father know he was "quite thrilled with the job" arranged for him. As a returning war veteran, Kennedy provided a seasoned perspective to his reporting and analysis, much as young newspaper correspondent Winston Churchill did in covering the Boer War and other faraway conflicts early in his career. The recent deaths of Joe Jr., Billy, and so many other bright, promising fellows during the war hung over Jack's visit and invited comparison with World War I. In his European diary, Jack cited one of his favorite books, *The World Crisis*—the same gripping history book Kay Halle had spotted him reading as a sickly teenager recuperating in the Boston hospital bed. In it, Churchill underlines "the terrific slaughter of the field officers of the British Army—two or three times higher than the Germans," Kennedy observed. "This tremendous slaughter had its effect on British policy in the 30's when Chamberlain and Baldwin could not bring themselves to subject the young men of Britain to the same horrible slaughter again."

In London, twenty-eight-year-old Jack visited with Kick and their friends from the old days, especially Hugh Fraser, who was now standing for election. "Everyone here thinks he [Jack] is only about 18," his sister reported back to their parents. "I think he's getting a little bored with being thought so young." Jack appeared fascinated by Fraser's campaign for Parliament, "picking up a pointer or two for his own struggle to win a seat in the House of Representatives," recalled Hugh's sister, Veronica, a friend of Kick's who would later marry Fitzroy Maclean. On the social circuit, the beautiful Veronica took note of Jack's cavalier style. "He was charming and debonair and quick-witted as ever and danced beautifully with all the right ladies at the fund-raising Tory ball, and flirted with all the wrong ones whenever our backs were turned," she later recalled. "If anyone had said, 'Fifteen years from now Jack will be the President of the United States,' I would have thought them barmy." Another British friend, Alastair Forbes, later compared young Kennedy, a millionaire's son with an intellectual streak, to another figure born in a palace. "He had a detachment which reminded me very much of Winston Churchill in the sense that his life had been protected by money," Forbes said. "Money was the great insulator."

With Kick's help, Jack struggled to put together a privately published book in 1945 called *As We Remember Joe*, a collection of essays dedicated to his older brother's memory. At times, the whole endeavor seemed part of his father's intent for Jack to live up to the expectations of a ghost rather than to reality. While several family and friends readily contributed, including grandfather Honey Fitz, others found it difficult. Harold Laski, Joe Jr.'s famous former teacher at the London School of Economics in the early 1930s, was suggested as a possible contributor, but Kick had to inform her brother Jack that "Joe didn't see anything of Harold Laski when he was over here" during the war. More problematic was Pat Wilson's contribution, which Kick dutifully sent along to Jack, clearly wondering whether to include a remembrance by their brother's adulterous lover. "Mrs. Wilson's piece on Brother Joe . . . I don't think it really good enough, do you?" Kick asked Jack. "Either she didn't have the time to do a proper piece or she just couldn't. I don't think she thought it very good either." Shortly after Joe's plane explosion, Pat Wilson's British Army husband died fighting in Libya. Pat didn't object when her words failed to appear in the book. "She quite understands about your leaving out her little piece," Kick explained to Jack. "I think she is going to marry someone next summer. She admits that it isn't like Joe and nothing ever will be. Of course, the Voice of Experience, Kick, says she shouldn't marry anyone on that basis but you never can tell what will happen."

For inspiration, Kick suggested Jack pattern this memorial book on another favorite, John Buchan's *Pilgrim's Way*, with its brave, chivalrous presentation of combat heroes such as Raymond Asquith, the prime minister's son, who died in World War I. Jack had already memorized what Churchill's *Great Contemporaries* recalled of Asquith's death: "He went to his fate, cool, poised, resolute, matter-of-fact, debonair." In his sympathy note to the Duchess of Devonshire, Jack had compared the loss of her son Billy to this fallen British hero. In reading the "letter about the cool and gallant way Billy died, I couldn't help but think of what John Buchan had written about Raymond Asquith—'Our roll of honour is long, but it holds no nobler figure. He will stand to those of us who are left as an incarnation of the spirit of the land he loved . . . He loved his youth, and his youth has become eternal. Debonair and brilliant and brave, he is now part of that immortal England which know not age or weariness or defeat.' I think those words could be so well applied to Billy." In putting together the memorial book about Joe Jr., Jack drew upon stirring quotes from both Buchan and Churchill books, but his own words seemed frank. "A slight detachment from things around him—a wall of reserve which few people ever succeeded in penetrating," Jack wrote in describing his older brother, with whom he had a lifelong rivalry. "I suppose I knew Joe as well as anyone and yet I sometimes wonder if I ever really knew him. He was very human and most certainly had his faults: a hot temper, intolerance for the slower pace of lesser men, and a way of looking—with a somewhat sardonic half smile—which could cut and prod more sharply than words. But these defects—if defects they were—were becoming smoothed with the passage of time."

Jack's own perspective evolved during his European trip, though not far from his father's idiosyncratic worldview. Like his father, he supported financial help to Great Britain to emerge from the postwar destruction. Yet in one February 1945 article entitled "Let's Try an Experiment in Peace," Kennedy proposed that the Big Three (Churchill, Stalin, and Roosevelt) work together to avoid the need for a big postwar defense spending buildup (a notion somewhat at odds with his *Why England Slept* lessons). Jack's tolerance for another war was tempered by having witnessed so many deaths himself. "When I think of how much this war has cost us, of the deaths of Cy and Peter and Orv and Gil and Demi and Joe and Billy and all those thousands and millions who have died with them—when I think of all those gallant acts that I have seen or anyone else has seen who has been to war—it would be a very easy thing to feel disappointed and somewhat betrayed," he admitted. Despite his admiration for Winston Churchill's bluster and linguistic dexterity, Jack still shared his father's belief that Chamberlain was a more important figure. "Of the two, I think that the latter did the most," Jack wrote in his diary. "He is given scant credit for it, particularly by the English people themselves, but perhaps history will be more generous."

While in England, Jack decided to hear for himself Harold Laski, the much-vaunted teacher whom his father and older brother had once so admired. Most probably, Jack knew of Laski's refusal to write a preface for *Why England Slept*, but remained unaware of Laski's loathing of his father's time in London. ("Send us John Winant as ambassador and, even more, secure the permanent end of Joe Kennedy's political career," Laski had urged FDR's friends, convinced Kennedy was nothing more than a dangerously right-wing smorgasbord of Hollywood glamour and White House ambition.)

At a political rally, Jack watched as Laski, now a leader of the Labour Party, "spoke with great venom and bitterness" before a crowd. Like his father and Churchill, Jack worried "whether a dictatorship of the Left could ever get control in England, a country with such a great democratic tradition." After interviewing Laski, young Kennedy came away unimpressed. "I think that unquestionably, from my talk with Laski, that he and others like him smart not so much from the economic inequality but from the social," he wrote in his diary. "In speaking of Boston, he said, 'Boston is a state of mind—and as a Jew, he could understand what it is to be an Irishman in Boston.' That last remark reveals the fundamental, activating force of Mr. Laski's life—a powerful spirit doomed to an inferior position because of his race—a position that all his economic and intellectual superiority cannot raise him out of."

Joe Kennedy later echoed this contempt for Laski, the man once sought as a teacher for his sons. In a December 1945 speech before the Chicago Economic Club, the former ambassador criticized Laski for suggesting that American capitalism would be replaced by socialism. "How can Laski have the gall to assert that capitalism is dead when the British empire has been twice saved in thirty years by the capitalist United States," Joe chided. "I know Laski and he is an arrogant apostle of anarchy who has spent his time shuttling between Moscow, London and New Haven peddling his particular brand of socialism."

On the same European trip, Jack mirrored his father's sympathies about Ireland and its mercurial leader Éamon de Valera. Young Kennedy interviewed de Valera, who'd been scorned by Churchill for his studied neutrality during the war, particularly his courtesy call of sympathy to the German legation in Dublin upon the death of Adolf Hitler. Furious, Winston charged that de Valera preferred to "frolic" with the Germans and had recklessly endangered Allied naval ships by denying them access to Irish ports. Criticism from Churchill only added to "Dev's" appeal in Ireland. "Mr. Churchill's threats do not affect us," de Valera replied. "We deny the right of any English authority to prescribe what an Irishman shall and shall not do." Aware of Ireland's importance back in Boston, Jack Kennedy treaded lightly with the aging Irish leader. Unlike Churchill, he never condemned his actions, even the outrageous condolences for the Führer. "Churchill's speech at the end of the war, in which he attacked De Valera, was extraordinarily indiscreet—made things much more difficult for [U.S. ambassador to Ireland David] Gray and pulled De Valera out of a hole," Kennedy observed.

Jack's diary contains other comments reflecting his father's views, especially those penned while the younger Kennedy was traveling to Germany with Secretary of the Navy James Forrestal, a family friend. Despite the stunning evidence of Nazi brutality and death camps, Jack still hadn't lost his awe for the German war machinery. He judged comparable German PT-like boats as superior to his own in the Pacific. And after visiting Hitler's Eagle's Nest hideaway in the mountains, he wrote the most inexplicable note in his diary. "You can easily understand how that within a few years Hitler will emerge from the hatred that surrounds him now as one of the most significant figures who ever lived," Kennedy concluded. "He had boundless ambition for his country which rendered him a menace to the peace of the world, but he had a mystery about him in the way that he lived and in the manner of his death that will live and grow after him. He had in him the stuff of which legends are made."

This baffling comment, published fifty years after first written, left many historians puzzled. Even his longtime admirer journalist Hugh

Sidey called his observation "bizarre" and said it "gives no hint that Kennedy sees that the legend is one of a monster." Perhaps young Kennedy was influenced by Churchill's *Great Contemporaries*, which he turned to in putting together *As We Remember Joe*. In that 1937 book, published two years before war began, Churchill pointed to Hitler's "frightful methods," including his reprehensible actions toward Jews, but left open the possibility that the Führer could still redeem himself as a "great" figure in history. By 1945, however, Jack Kennedy should have known better.

The political prescience of John F. Kennedy emerged in covering Winston Churchill's 1945 election campaign. Weeks after V-E Day, the wartime coalition government headed by Churchill was dissolved, at the Labour Party's insistence, so a new election could be held in July. Few Americans doubted Churchill's Conservative Party would prevail. "After leading Britain through six of the most crowded and perilous years in her long history, this indomitable man is marching through an old-fashioned political campaign as though it were no more than a stroll in the woods of his beloved country place, Chartwell, in Kent," observed U.S. columnist Marquis Childs, who sensed a victory for Churchill, the odds-on favorite.

However, Jack realized the Tories were in trouble, more than they realized, after watching Hugh Fraser's campaign and several Labour Party rallies in Britain. "Churchill is fighting a tide that is surging through Europe, washing away monarchies and conservative governments," Kennedy explained in one of his columns. "While everyone knows Churchill's strengths, they are not sure that he can buck the recent strong surge to the left," he said in another. Though Labour Party candidates uniformly praised Churchill for winning the war, they emphasized better domestic social programs to help voters recover after so much destruction in their lives. "The Conservative Party, fat and happy with years of victory, let their political ace, Mr. Churchill, carry the ball," Kennedy later explained. "Instead of a vigorous campaign on the virtues of private enterprise, they offered a watered down version of blood, sweat, and tears for the years of peace. Blood, sweat and tears was fitted to the desperate days of 1940 but not to 1945 to a people whose chronic fatigue and exhaustion had brought them to a sharp-tempered dissatisfaction with life in England."

The roster of Conservative Party candidates up for reelection featured Randolph Churchill. After sending a telegram to his father for his "splendid" V-E speech, he had flown home immediately from Croatia and begun his campaign. With characteristic enthusiasm, Randolph shook many hands, fielded all questions, and performed impromptu speeches with admirable ability. He even tried to hire an elephant to march down streets harnessed with a loudspeaker, until the Conservative leaders in his district rejected the idea as undignified. An old commando leader, Robert Laycock, campaigned with him, though the biggest rally featured his father. Arriving in an open car, with Randolph seated on the hood, the prime minister offered a twenty-minute speech urging why his son should be returned to Parliament.

The Churchills, triumphant from war, seemed poised to reap its rewards from a grateful citizenry. Both Randolph and the other Conservative Party candidate running for the two available seats from Preston "thought themselves undefeatable—for they had returned from the war carrying youth and valour emblazoned on their shields and the name of Churchill had become famous throughout the world," wrote Randolph's cousin Anita Leslie. In Parliament, the long-ago dream of two Churchills active in politics, serving in the House of Commons, would become a reality once again. Winston always hoped to stand with his own father in the House of Commons. Now with Randolph by his side, that dream seemed destined to continue for years, much to their mutual delight. One splendid moment occurred in June, during a boisterous debate with Labour Party MPs, as Winston bobbed and weaved with a grim smile through a cascade of verbal darts. When his Conservative colleagues argued back, Winston grew more impatient and finally capitulated to an interrupter demanding to be heard.

"Let him make his point of order," Churchill commanded, swinging around from the Labourites to defer to the noisy Conservative member behind him. As he turned, the prime minister realized this objector was his son, Randolph. The surprise on both faces amused everyone. "Father and son were taken aback for a second, and then simultaneously burst into loud laughter, which was shared by the whole House," observed one reporter.

A few minutes later, a Labour member gave faint praise to Winston before bitterly complaining that whatever good feeling existed in the chamber had been spoiled by the prime minister's recent attack on socialism.

"Hear, hear," Randolph chimed in, loudly and blithely seconding his father's attack. His audacious timing was perfect, drawing another round of laughter.

Yet Randolph's lack of judgment and poor influence on his father also seemed on display. A week earlier, he did little to discourage his father from giving one of the most controversial speeches of his career. In a June 4 wireless speech, Winston charged that if the Labour Party came to power they would use "some form of Gestapo" tactics to enact their policies. "The Gestapo speech was one of the worst-judged acts of Churchill's political career," historian John Keegan later declared. Both father and son worried some form of socialism might spread to Britain, especially after witnessing Communist expansion in Eastern Europe at the end of the war. On the advice of his old friends Lord Beaverbrook and Brendan Bracken, Winston attacked Harold Laski, the professorial Labour Party chairman and former Kennedy friend, and suggested he would be the director of such a "socialist Gestapo." Winston's remarks were remarkably facile, hardly the magnanimity he had preached in victory. Nor were they worthy of the respect his opponents had shown toward him. Indeed, as the Holocaust atrocities had become known, Laski suggested a public statue be erected to honor Winston for his fight against the Nazis. "As I look at the Europe Hitler has devastated, I know very intimately that, as an Englishman of Jewish origin, I owe you the gift of life itself," Laski wrote to him in September 1944.

The "Gestapo" speech was an appalling slap in the face to both Laski and Labour Party leader Clement Attlee, who stood resolutely in support of Churchill's fight against the Nazis. It also backfired among a weary British public, reinforcing Winston's reputation as a warmonger pining for his next fight. Many blamed Lord Beaverbrook for instigating Churchill's speech, especially when the headline "Gestapo in Britain if Socialists Win" appeared in his *Daily Express* newspaper. "After ripping the Gestapo out of the still bleeding heart of Germany, will you stand for a Gestapo under another name at home?" asked the newspaper, drenched in Beaverbrook's hyperbole. Attlee publicly made the connection: "The voice we heard last night was that of Mr. Churchill but the mind was that of Lord Beaverbrook." From other accounts, Beaverbrook wasn't directly involved in the "Gestapo" speech, with Beaverbrook biographer A. J. P. Taylor contending that Randolph had "approved" of the "Gestapo" speech before his father delivered it. Youngest daughter Mary Churchill later claimed her mother tried to excise the odious "Gestapo" comment from Winston's speech "but he would not heed her."

The day after the July 1945 election results were made known—one of the most disastrous in Conservative Party history and certainly for the Churchill family—Randolph took solace in the friendship of Evelyn Waugh, who, typically, had not bothered to vote.

During the war, the two friends from Oxford had quarreled through the Middle East and haggled their way through occupied Eastern Europe. Yet once home in London, they returned to good spirits again, especially when at White's, their favorite nightspot. Coming by Waugh's place at 7:30 the morning after the results were known, Randolph kept up a buoyant mood, trying to hide his hurt from another shocking rejection. However, when they later arrived at Randolph's makeshift home, the same where Pamela had once lived, the painful emptiness in his friend's life seemed clear to Waugh. "Randolph's house . . . has only the furniture which Pam chose not to take," Waugh noted. "My heart sank."

Despite his confident campaigning, Randolph lost by a wide margin in Preston, crushing his fondest hope to remain in Parliament with his father. And while Winston faced little opposition in his own district, many Conservatives were swept away in a Labour Party landslide, including Churchill's son, his son-in-law Duncan Sandys, and his top aide Brendan Bracken. That evening, Winston ate a quiet dinner together with Randolph and the rest of their family. Dressed in the blue siren suit that he wore so often during the war, he then retired to the Map Room, lit up a cigar, and awaited his fate. Though he had some premonition of defeat, Winston never appeared worried. The final tally, however, left the prime minister stunned and out of power.

The world couldn't believe the news. "Winston Churchill sat tonight in the study of the prime minister's official residence at No. 10 Downing Street and surveyed the crashing ruin in which a political career of 46 history-crowded years had ended," declared the *Boston Globe*. Writing to Jack Kennedy back in America, Veronica Fraser, the sister of his friend Hugh Fraser (one of the few Conservatives in their circle to survive the Labour Party rout), gave credit to young Kennedy's political savvy. "Your guess was better than ours after all!" she wrote to Jack. "I wonder how many seats the poor old conservatives would have held without Winston? It's a great chance for Hugh and it will be much more fun for him, firing broadsides from the opposition backbenches—but that's a rather selfish view."

After acting with such dispatch, the British public seemed surprised that Winston Churchill, a steadfast fixture in their lives and arguably the savior of their embattled nation, might suddenly disappear. In London, the *Times* insisted "no one will dream of interpreting the crushing defeat inflicted on his party as bringing in any way into question his place in history, in national pride or in the affection and gratitude of the people." Yet Winston, now age seventy, couldn't help wondering why his leadership had been rejected. Graciously, he said the right of a democracy to decide its fate by election, rather than through the barrel of a dictator's gun, was precisely the point of the war. To confidants such as Anthony Eden, however, he conceded, days after the loss, that "it hurt more, like a wound which becomes more painful after the first shock." His family particularly felt his anguish. "It was not so much the loss of power that he minded but the sudden loss of a job to do," his daughter Sarah observed. "Six years geared to the utmost mental as well as physical exertion, and suddenly nothing." Upon her father's spirits, Mary saw "with near desperation a black doom descend."

As always, Clementine, who wanted her husband to retire, attempted to put the best face possible on a bad situation. "Winston, this may be a blessing in disguise," she suggested gently.

Wit provided the necessary balm. "At the moment," he replied, "it seems quite effectively disguised."

Part IV

MAKING PEACE

~

"Kennedy never tired of quoting Winston Churchill:
'We arm to parley.'"
—ARTHUR M. SCHLESINGER JR.

"What is the cause of historical events? Power. What is
power? Power is the sum total of wills transferred to one
person. On what condition are the wills of the masses
transferred to one person? On condition that the person
expresses the will of the whole people."
—LEO TOLSTOY, *War and Peace*

33

Feeling the Heat

Pink flamingos fluttered around the infield lake at Hialeah Park, one of the world's most magnificent racetracks, as vacationing millionaires and railbirds flocked together in Florida's winter sun. Royal palm trees, high above the crowds, fanned the lush tropical breezes that swept across the grassy esplanade. In this sport of kings, visitors passed through gates leading to the ornate Renaissance-style clubhouse and to the grandstands where twenty thousand watched the thoroughbred horses galloping by. No longer at war, America embraced idyllic places like Hialeah, where the blood, toil, tears, and sweat of the past could be easily forgotten.

At the start of the season in January 1946, one of Hialeah's owners, Joseph P. Kennedy, relaxed in his favorite box, tending to his usual interests. He and his wife, Rose, shuttled to the track with friends aboard a special train from Palm Beach, where the family maintained its huge white mansion along a stretch of oceanfront known as Millionaires' Row. Kennedy's stake in Hialeah, when made known three years earlier, drew as much curiosity as his earlier investments in liquor. "I don't understand why anybody should be interested," he discounted to the press. "It's just as if I had purchased shares of stock in a company."

In his Hialeah box that day, Kennedy chatted with Rose and his two daughters Eunice and Patricia, all smartly dressed in brightly colored clothes with white trim. Someone asked if he wanted to say hello to a distinguished guest who'd just arrived, Winston Churchill.

Kennedy paused uneasily. "Fine, a little later in the afternoon," he replied.

Several hard years had passed since "the ambassador," as he still preferred to be known, shook hands with the British leader. When they parted in London in 1940, Kennedy's diplomatic career was in tatters while Churchill's power was on the ascendancy, each man's situation rooted in his views on the war. In the ensuing years, history had proved Winston, with his grand vision of Anglo-American unity saving the world from tyranny, right; yet Kennedy's fear of what war would mean for his family had been true as well. Though the war had ended, neither man had yet to recover from its consequences.

Churchill welcomed his long American trip, spending several weeks in a place where the population greeted him with unmitigated glory and adulation. As with past visits, the United States was a land where Churchill found deep personal meaning. Still stunned by his electoral loss in Britain, he remained agitated. "Papa has not yet settled down to painting, and is a little sad and restless, poor darling," Clementine wrote home to her daughter Mary. "I hope he is going to begin writing something." While on this trip, Churchill received an honorary degree in February at the University of Miami and laid a wreath at President Roosevelt's grave in Hyde Park, New York. Most significantly, in March, while in Missouri with President Truman, he would present his "Iron Curtain" speech warning about the Soviet threat.

During his time in Florida, though, Winston acted much like a tourist. His traveling entourage included former daughter-in-law Pamela Churchill, who stayed with her friend Kick at the Kennedys' winter mansion. The social ties between their two families made it difficult for Joe Kennedy to avoid greeting Winston when he strutted smilingly into Hialeah, cigar in hand, wearing a light gray business suit and fedora and carrying a walking stick.

Eventually Joe joined the former prime minister in a grandstand box, where he'd been sitting quietly and contently scanning racehorses through binoculars and picking the winner in the fifth race. Looking up, Winston appeared happy to see Kennedy again. He immediately recalled their old days together in London.

"I remember that one of the last times we met we were having dinner during an air raid," Churchill said, with the usual swagger in his voice. "It didn't bother us much, though, did it?"

Kennedy must not have been impressed by such bravado between old men because he said nothing in reply, according to his notes of the encounter.

Winston then expressed sadness at what the ambassador's family endured. "You had a terrible time during the war; your losses were very great," said Churchill. "I felt so sad for you and hope you received my messages."

Kennedy said he had received the prime minister's condolence note, and thanked him for his sympathy. Their conversation quickly turned from the personal to the political. "The world seems to be in a frightful condition," Winston offered, expecting a similar assessment from Joe, as if they were chatting about the weather.

But Kennedy would have none of it. The memories of Joe Jr. being blown up in his plane, of his family's sobs and yearning for their lost eldest son, were too strong for him to keep his comments at bay.

"Yes—after all, what did we accomplish by this war?" Kennedy demanded.

Churchill answered sharply, almost in rebuke. "Well, at least we have our lives," said the British wartime leader.

"Not all of us," Kennedy admonished.

Perhaps the pain on Kennedy's face was too much to bear for either man. Churchill "dropped the subject at once," Kennedy recalled, and returned to world affairs and relations between their two countries. They talked about the political future of Anthony Eden, who most thought would be Churchill's successor within the Conservative Party, and about the need for a U.S. loan to help Great Britain recover after the war. Aware of England's sacrifices, Joe told Winston he thought the money should come as a gift rather than a loan.

The two men spoke not as friends but as wartime intimates, with Churchill confiding that "to all intents and purposes, his political career was finished," Kennedy recalled.

Joe found it necessary to interrupt, suggesting Winston might have been fortunate to have been defeated.

"He smiled and said he wasn't sure but that was right," Kennedy recalled. "He said he intended to now enjoy himself as best he could until he died. Of course, it was apparent that he really didn't mean that, but that was what he said."

After the war, Kick Kennedy and Pamela Churchill's friendship grew closer. They were no longer vaguely familiar debutantes with little in common but rather an American widow and British divorcée, both in their mid-twenties, whose experiences and social circles in war-torn London had bonded them together.

With her family in America, Kick still maintained the good-girl veneer that her mother insisted upon. On her own in London, she'd become more independent-minded, especially after Billy's death. Though she didn't approve of every adulterous move by Pamela, Kick appreciated the other woman's spirited, devil-may-care approach to life. For all the friendship and favors Pamela Churchill provided in London, Kick

Kennedy felt compelled in 1946 to invite her for an extended winter-time vacation in Florida. Kick "was my close friend and that's how I came into the Kennedy family," Pamela recalled decades later. "The first time I ever came to America, I stayed with the Kennedys down in Palm Beach."

As an honorary Kennedy, Pamela found herself enthralled by the family's dinner table conversation about politics. She went shopping with Rose Kennedy and appeared in the local newspaper columnist's list of "Best Sundressed Women in Palm Beach," even though she appeared "quite pale when near the other deeply tanned beauties." With Kick and her parents, Pamela also enjoyed the Sunday races at Hialeah. After enduring so many wartime hardships and material restrictions in England, Pamela was amazed by the extravagant wealth and undisturbed beauty of America.

When the former prime minister arrived in Florida, Kick joined the Churchills as part of their entourage. She rode with them in a special car, escorted by twenty policemen on motorcycles, to the Orange Bowl stadium, where they watched Winston receive his honorary degree from the University of Miami. Afterward, Kick joined the Churchills at the Surf Club. Under a cabana at this private resort, Winston took out his oils and composed a painting of the endless blue-green Atlantic and darkened clouds on the horizon giving way to daylight. On this warm afternoon, the Churchills brought along their bathing suits and decided to go for a swim. "Winston presented a very comical sight, bobbing around in the surf," Kick wrote in her diary. "He adores the water though I must say I wouldn't enjoy swimming in such a public spot every day."

As they entertained themselves at the Surf Club, Kick laughed along with the prime minister, flashing her wry smile and throwing back her thick and curly auburn hair. Unlike during her war years riding a bicycle in a Red Cross uniform around crumbled London, Kick, with her distinctive beauty in the Florida sun, now appeared more womanly than girlish, whether wearing pearls with a summer dress or all wet in her polka-dot swimsuit.

Eventually, Winston inquired about Kick's father, whom he hadn't seen since their tense encounter a few weeks earlier at Hialeah Park.

"He sends you best regards," Kick answered.

Winston's face soured. "He makes an exception in my case," he said with a harrumph.

The ambassador wasn't pleased when his daughter, with some bemusement, repeated Winston's comment to him. "Daddy took umbrage at this remark," she noted in her diary.

Along with the inviting sun, Pamela Churchill sought refuge in Florida with the Kennedys for another reason besides getting a tan. As Kick knew, her friend had flown to America partly on the expectation of getting married to her wartime lover, CBS broadcaster Edward R. Murrow. While in London together, Pamela fell deeply in love with the suave, older American journalist, who promised to divorce his wife when he returned home to New York. Murrow, who admired Winston Churchill, detested Joe Kennedy as an appeaser. He chastised Pamela for vacationing at his Florida home, which he likened to "staying with [Nazi Gestapo leader Hermann] Goering."

In Palm Beach, however, Pamela heard from Murrow that he'd decided to remain with his wife and his newly born son, Charles Casey Murrow. CASEY WINS, he telegraphed to Pam, who was shattered by the news. Her divorce from Randolph, filed in December 1945, had left her free to marry Murrow after their long affair. Even Winston and Clementine seemed to wish for Pamela's happiness away from their son. "Never forget not only are we devoted to you but you are the mother of my grandson," Churchill told her.

While in Palm Beach, Pamela obtained a better sense of Joe Kennedy and his commanding grip on the lives of his children, now well into adulthood. Much of the talk touched on Jack's impending congressional race in Massachusetts and how the family would rally behind him. Kick idolized her father and laughed off any suggestions about his questionable behavior. When a British tabloid portrayed the former U.S. ambassador as a playboy in Palm Beach, Kick couldn't help sharing it with the rest of the family in one of their round-robin letters. "I think it shows there's a lot of life left in that old man of ours if he can start being a playboy at his ripe old age!" she teased. Whether Old Joe was attracted to Churchill's former daughter-in-law later became a source of conjecture. Writer Truman Capote, a social friend with Pamela in the 1960s, suggested one of his novel's characters was based on Pamela's stay at Palm Beach, when the senior Kennedy allegedly slipped into her room in the middle of the night and pressed her into having sex with him. "The sheer ballsy gall of it—right there in his own house with the whole family sleeping all around us," says the character Lady Ina Coolbirth in Capote's book, repeating the story, never proven, he claimed Pamela recounted over lunch. For whatever reason, Pamela abruptly decided to leave Palm Beach. She stayed with another American friend, Betsey Whitney (the former wife of Jimmy Roosevelt who had married Jock Whitney), and then returned to New York, where Murrow attempted to renew their affair, without success. Determined to return to Britain, Pamela contacted Lord Beaverbrook, seeking his advice as she had done since her marriage to Randolph. The press lord offered Pamela a job writing society articles for one of his London newspapers, and she traveled back on the *Queen Mary.*

Like some real-life novella, Pamela Churchill's arrival in England coincided with another twist in her love life: the return of Averell Harriman. In April 1946, President Truman appointed Harriman U.S. ambassador to the Court of St. James's, the same post once held by Joe Kennedy. Harriman replaced Gil Winant, whose bouts with depression had ended whatever effectiveness he once had in the job. Ave returned to London without his wife, Marie, or his daughter, Kathleen, and soon resumed his indiscreet affair with Pamela. The rumors started circulating again (with Randolph complaining to friends that he should have named Harriman as a co-respondent in his divorce proceedings), though Harriman's tenure didn't last long. While having lunch with Winston Churchill in September, the White House called looking for him. The former prime minister guessed correctly that Truman wanted Harriman to fill the open job of U.S. commerce secretary, a Cabinet position in the postwar years far more advantageous than London. When Ave asked if he should accept the president's offer, Winston didn't hesitate. "Absolutely," he replied. "The center of power is in Washington."

The politically ambitious Harriman quickly accepted and jumped to Washington. Pamela remained in London while Marie Harriman continued living in New York. Ave's wandering eye soon found another object for his affection, in the nation's capital. He spent nights with Kay Halle, the heiress friend of both the Churchills and the Kennedys, with many Democratic Party connections of her own in town. Friends soon heard rumors that Harriman wanted to leave his wife for Halle. "On weeknights, the commerce secretary's limousine was frequently parked at Halle's house in Georgetown," wrote Harriman biographer Rudy Abramson. "The proximity—and Halle's high visibility and earnest intentions—made the matter more irritating to Marie than the wartime affair with Pamela had been." But Halle never harbored a serious intention of marrying Harriman, her friend Timothy Dickinson told another biographer. "She knew if she married Averell she would be bullied beyond belief," Dickinson explained.

Passion with the men in Pamela's life was often mixed with sexual hypocrisy and double standards. Certainly Murrow's withering criticism of her friendship with the Kennedys carried an odd stamp of moral disapproval. And at a chance meeting, Harriman "rather sanctimoniously blurted out that she was ruining her life" by flitting from one powerful man to another, implying that she was patterning her life on that of Lady Jane Digby, her ancestor often described as a courtesan. That stigma was unfair, insisted Pamela's brother Edward. "While she was actually in a relationship, Pam was never unfaithful to her lovers," Lord Digby said years later; "in most cases it was the man who strayed while Pam was entirely focused on that man."

For Pamela, no friend seemed better able to understand these contradictions than Kick Kennedy, who returned to London soon after her Florida vacation. In their short existence, both young women had witnessed tragedy beyond their control, yet continued to define daily life on their own terms. "Mother and I were talking it over last night and decided nobody in the world twenty-five years of age has had the kind of life you've had or as interesting," Joe wrote his daughter, suggesting her diary could become a best-selling book. Rather than spend her life in postwar America, though, Kick felt most comfortable in England, in the *Brideshead Revisited* world portrayed by her friend Evelyn Waugh. "I know it is unfair that so few should have so much etc. but there's a certain grandeur, tradition, strength that is very much part of the England that would disappear without them," she explained about the old homes and castles, especially the Devonshires' Chatsworth estate. "I know my little brothers will think 'Kick has gone more British' than ever, my persecuted Irish ancestors would turn over in their graves to hear talk of England in this way but I don't care. I think a landed aristocracy can be an instrument of good just as much of evil and when it is the former then —'preserve it.' (You'd better not let Grandpa Fitz see the above.)"

In this world, the Churchills were the defenders of a way of life that now existed mostly in words and memories—a paradox that the Kennedys (especially Kick), as Catholics bound by a sense of tradition, understood better than most. She teased and joked about many of the ironies, yet wished to remain a part of postwar England. In a letter home, she mentioned one of Randolph's commando pals, Robin

Campbell, who talked to her about his two years in a German prison camp, and spoke of the influence of religion on her friends. "Apparently Robin was so impressed by the Catholic Chaplain in the prison that he is thinking seriously of becoming one, much to the amazement and shock of his various relatives," Kick wrote her parents. "Have heard the same thing about Randolph Churchill. Can you imagine him as a pillar of the Church?"

When Kick chatted with Lord Hugh Cecil, who had been best man at Winston Churchill's 1908 wedding, she mentioned her own tragic marriage to the future Duke of Devonshire. In the eyes of her Catholic Church, Kick explained, "Billy and I had been living in sin."

Lord Cecil, a strong Anglican capable of outdebating Winston in their early days, merely rolled his eyes. "But so many of one's friends are nowadays," he sighed.

Shortly after returning north from his Florida winter home in 1946, Joe Kennedy decided to get out of the business of alcohol. His British friend Lord Beaverbrook was among the first to find out. Kennedy provided the same reason he'd later foist on the American public.

DEAR MAX YOUNG JACK WAS NOMINATED FOR CONGRESS TUESDAY, he cabled in June. I AM SELLING OUT SOME OF MY BUSINESS, INCLUDING THE LIQUOR . . .

As usual with Joe, there was much more to it than this simple explanation. Somerset Importers had been a cash-rich galleon of Scotch whiskey, gin, and other top imported blends. On his initial one-hundred-thousand-dollar investment, Kennedy "realized immense profits," said biographer Richard J. Whalen, enough to include Somerset in the trust fund that he established for Rose and their children. After the war, Somerset continued to draw attention because of Jimmy Roosevelt's involvement with the British liquor deal. Jimmy steadfastly denied everything. In September 1945, he let Kennedy's crony Arthur Hough-

ton know that U.S. Senate investigators, working for Republicans looking for scandal, had paid him a visit. Houghton, one of Joe's closest pals,
had traveled with the Kennedys and Jimmy Roosevelt when they visited London in 1933. To these prying Senate investigators, Jimmy said
he'd never gotten any money from Somerset officials and "that anything that has transpired between them was on purely a friendly and
social basis and in no way connected with business," records show. (The
Justice Department's antitrust division later asked the FBI in 1953 to
investigate these same rumors involving Kennedy and Roosevelt's son,
without any luck.)

Kennedy's involvement in the liquor business was bound to hurt his
son's budding political career. In a July 1946 note to Sir James Calder,
chairman of Distillers Company, Joe detailed a few financial reasons
for selling Somerset but alluded to more pressing concerns. "There are
lots of odds and ends, which I don't care to write—some to do with England and some to do with my own organization—but when I see you I
will tell you about it," he explained to Calder. By then, Jack Kennedy's
political opponents were already pointing to his father's liquor interests
and questioning if they affected the former ambassador's support for a
British aid package after the war. "They made the real issue my support of the British Loan and said that the only reason for it was that I
had a franchise from Haig & Haig," he wrote to Calder. "It occurs to me
that from here in it is going to be necessary for me to take a great many
positions for England as against Russia, and it is silly to have wrong
interpretations put on my actions."

Democrats who disliked Joe Kennedy, such as President Harry Truman, also used his liquor interests to sully his reputation. During the
1944 campaign, then-vice-presidential-candidate Truman threatened
to throw Kennedy out the window of Boston's Ritz-Carlton hotel for
disparaging President Roosevelt. "Harry, what the hell are you campaigning for that crippled son of a bitch who killed my son Joe?" Kennedy demanded. The raw wound of his son's death haunted Kennedy,

but Truman wouldn't forgive such party disloyalty. A few years later, sharing a bourbon with Truman, California politician Oliver J. Carter remembers how Truman refused any whiskey. "He never drank Scotch because every time he paid for a drink of Scotch he was putting some money into Joe Kennedy's pocket and he wouldn't have any part of that," recalled Carter. "He thought Jack was a fine guy, but he didn't think that Joe was worth two bits. All he just said was that old Joe Kennedy had blamed Franklin for young Joe's being in the service that brought on his death. And this he thought was an unfair accusation."

Money from his father's fortune fueled Jack Kennedy's successful 1946 campaign for Congress, creating the prototype for a "Kennedy political machine" that would propel Jack throughout his career. Kennedy money financed newspaper ads, radio spots, billboards, and circulars touting the name of this political unknown—including copies of John Hersey's article turning JFK into a *PT-109* hero. It paid for Jack's strongest possible opponent, the less-than-honorable James Michael Curley (a former mayor known as the "Purple Shamrock"), to go away and seek another office, and it compensated the staff salaries and campaign experts who groomed the ambassador's uncertain son into a victorious candidate. "It takes three things to win," advised Joe Kane, an old Boston political operative recruited as the campaign's tactical mastermind. "The first is money and the second is money and third is money."

Joe Kennedy learned this lesson in soliciting huge contributions from men such as William Randolph Hearst during FDR's 1932 campaign. While ideals and rhetoric might move some in politics, cash was its universal language, the coin of the realm Joe Kennedy knew best. Yet he made a point of telling the press he would make no campaign speeches on his son's behalf. "He's doing this on his own," Joe insisted.

With his father's largesse, John Fitzgerald Kennedy, a twenty-nine-year-old navy veteran, regained the U.S. House seat his namesake grandfather, John F. "Honey Fitz" Fitzgerald, held at the turn of the century before returning to Boston to become mayor. Though Jack still listened respectfully to his well-known eighty-three-year-old grandfather, a master of the old Irish-Catholic political clubhouse system built on patronage, he stayed beholden to his wealthy father, who had once bitterly fled Boston to make his fortune on Wall Street and in Hollywood. After a shaky start, Jack showed a natural affinity for campaigning, prompting Kane to suggest that Joe Kennedy invest heavily. "Your Jack is worth a king's ransom," assessed Kane. "He has poise, a fine Celtic Map. A most engaging smile."

As in the case of Winston Churchill and his father, Jack Kennedy's political career seemed a reaction to Joe Kennedy's own failures in the public arena, his own stunted ambitions. Jack confided to friends that he felt "my father's eyes on the back of my neck," though he remained quietly determined to forge his own path. As Kenneth O'Donnell and Dave Powers, two close aides who became part of the Boston "Irish Mafia" around Kennedy, later observed, "After getting a close look as a reporter at the postwar political leaders in action, he decided that he might be able to find more satisfaction and to perform more useful service as a politician than as a political writer or teacher of government and history, the two careers that he had been considering up to that time."

Along with money, Kennedy's campaign depended on religion. His campaign sought to rally the Irish, Italian, and other ethnic Catholics in the working-class neighborhoods of his congressional district, partly by currying favor with clergy who knew of Joe Kennedy's close ties to the Church hierarchy. Along with generous donations to church charities trumpeted in the newspapers, Joe cultivated Boston's archbishop, Richard Cushing, suggesting subtly in letters that he could help him get elevated to cardinal by putting in a good word with his friend Count Enrico Galeazzi, the top aide to Pope Pius XII. Cushing was well aware of the leapfrog career move by Francis J. Spellman in becoming New York's cardinal. Through his longtime friendship with Galeazzi and Kennedy, Spellman emerged as, in effect, "the American pope." For Joe Kennedy, these favors paid off, particularly when Cushing and other Boston priests introduced his little-known son at Communion breakfasts and other functions as a friend of the Church as well as a suitable congressman.

Ironically, the Kennedy experience in Churchill's England posed the biggest political drawback among local Hibernians and Boston electorate sympathetic to de Valera's Ireland. A primary opponent's camp even claimed that Jack's sister Kick, the widow of the would-be Duke of Devonshire, had married a descendant of Oliver Cromwell, the scourge of Ireland during its centuries-long oppression by England. Eventually, Jack convinced his opponent to drop the hurtful rumor and back off. But in a humorous note, he asked his family members to be more mindful of their British connections. He pointed to a recent newspaper photo of his mother with Lady Astor, coverage of Kick as "Lady Hartington," and Father Joe's public support of a postwar loan to Britain. "Let's not forget," Jack urged gently, "that I'm running for Congress not Parliament."

Kick returned to London while the rest of the Kennedy clan worked fervently in Boston for Jack's election. In quasi-British style, Rose and her other daughters hosted tea parties for women voters as a way to draw supporters. All the extended family was delighted when Jack won the Democratic primary, the only race that mattered. In victory, Grandpa Honey Fitz jumped on a table and sang "Sweet Adeline." Joe and Rose rejoiced in Jack's impressive achievement, a joy perhaps easing the sting from their oldest son's death. "I did not know he had it in him," said Joe about his second son, who he once worried might fritter away his life. Aware of how death and fate played a deciding hand, Jack felt the weight of family expectations mixed with his own. "I'm just filling Joe's shoes," he confided. "If he were alive, I'd never be in this."

From the other side of the Atlantic, Kick reminded her brother, the newly elected freshman congressman, not to let his head swell. "The folks here think you are madly pro-British so don't be destroying that illusion until I get my house fixed," she joked. "The painters might just not like your attitude!" In postwar London, Kick enjoyed being called Lady Hartington, as an Irish-Catholic American who became Anglicized by marriage and by choice. As her prominence in the city's social scene grew, she traded gossip with friends such as Pamela Churchill about what they'd heard in the States. She even went to lunch with former prime minister Churchill and Lord Beaverbrook, knowing this courtesy would get back to her father. "It's rather nice not having to be a Kennedy," she told a friend. "Lord knows there are enough of them as it is."

34

The Coldest War

Old Glory and the Union Jack draped the streets of Jefferson City, Missouri—the perfect symbolism for a visit by President Harry Truman and the man who Truman said had saved Western civilization.

In an open-air limousine convertible, Winston Churchill sat beside Roosevelt's successor while thousands of Missourians waved and greeted them at the train station. The two grinning politicians were surrounded by dour security agents (standing guard on the running boards) as the limo drove through the state capital on March 6, 1946. After a long train ride from Washington, the seventy-one-year-old former British prime minister was careful not to exert himself too much. When asked that year about his secret of success, the old warhorse advised, "Conservation of energy—never stand up when you can sit down, and never sit down when you can lie down."

Only months after being turned out of high office, Churchill journeyed to a college gym in nearby Fulton to give one of the most significant speeches of his career. With the American president's blessing, his clarion call for Anglo-American resistance to the Soviet Union's "Iron Curtain" (his metaphor for the spread of communism dividing up Europe) would launch the decades-long Cold War. But this address in

Fulton, entitled "The Sinews of Peace," also provided another turning point in Churchill's long life. Instead of retirement, he chose vigorous, almost defiant engagement. Rather than fade away with his glorious victories of the past, he decided to embrace, almost prophetically, the future of the postwar world with its atomic dangers. He would reinvent himself once again as a world statesman, his voice both familiar and brand new.

Not everything about this trip was high stakes, however. On the ride to Missouri, Truman and Churchill demonstrated their personal diplomacy with a card game.

"Mr. President, I think that when we are playing poker I will call you Harry," Churchill announced.

"All right, *Winston*," Truman replied.

For more than an hour, they played with a handful of aides and reporters aboard the *Ferdinand Magellan,* the specially made presidential train car with a thick concrete floor to protect against explosions. Churchill's pile of chips dwindled as he lost each hand, downing sips of drink along the way. When the former prime minister, wearing one of his siren suits, excused himself for a momentary bathroom break, Truman quickly issued an executive order.

"Listen, this man's oratory saved the western world," Truman commanded the group, which included a young reporter named David Brinkley. "We are forever indebted to him. We're not going to take his money."

"But, Boss, *this guy's a pigeon*," cried one of the players, Harry Vaughan, the president's military aide.

The president wouldn't allow anything to trump this special relationship. As if a matter of national security, the card sharks were defanged. Winston's fortunes suddenly turned for the better, Brinkley recalled years later, after "Truman ordered us to let him win."

Before the evening aboard the presidential train ended, Winston displayed his considerable understanding of American history and wondered aloud about fate. "If I were to be born again," he mused, he wished to become a citizen in "one country where a man knows he has an unbounded future."

Truman's entourage asked what nation that might be.

"The USA," Churchill declared solemnly, ". . . even though I deplore some of your customs."

Puzzled, the Americans wondered what Yankee habit so appalled him.

"You stop drinking with your meals," Winston replied.

At the packed Westminster College gymnasium in Fulton, Churchill rewarded Truman's confidence with a stellar performance. Winston wanted to wake up America, content with victory in World War II and ready to return to its isolationist slumber. He warned that if the West didn't act swiftly and with determination, another conflict, with the totalitarian Communist regime looming in Moscow, awaited them.

"An iron curtain has descended across the Continent," Churchill lectured, wearing the honorary cap and robes of an Oxford don before a nationally broadcast audience. "This is certainly not the Liberated Europe we fought to build up. Nor is it one which contains the essentials of permanent peace." Truman, who appeared next to Churchill onstage, had reviewed and approved the speech beforehand. Plainspoken Harry indicated its important message needed to be heard.

Churchill argued that Stalin's unchecked expansion in Central and Eastern Europe posed the same risk for world conflict as Hitler's aggressive Germany once did in the 1930s, when Winston was a lonely voice in the political wilderness. "Last time, I saw it all coming and cried aloud to my fellow-countrymen and to the world, but no one paid any attention," Churchill recalled, almost melodramatically. "There never was a war in all history easier to prevent by timely actions than the one which has just desolated such great areas of the globe. It could have been prevented in my belief without the firing of a single shot . . ." Now, one by one, Churchill called off the names of European capitals lost to the "Soviet sphere." He worried that this growing Communist bloc of nations would expand in the world unless a "fraternal association" (the United States, Great Britain, and the rest of the "English-speaking world") stopped its Cold War appeasement. He urged a negotiated settlement with the Soviets, to prevent tensions from bursting into an active war neither side wanted. "From what I have seen of our Russian friends and Allies during the war, I am convinced that there is nothing they admire so much as strength, and there is nothing for which they have less respect than weakness, especially military weakness," he said, as if reciting lessons from history as he experienced it. "If these all-important years are allowed to slip away," he concluded, "then indeed catastrophe may overwhelm us all."

Truman stood and applauded, appearing pleased. Unlike his tempestuous relationship with Roosevelt, Churchill appreciated Truman's frank, direct manner and the bold way he'd brought World War II to an end. He supported Truman's use of atom bombs on Hiroshima and Nagasaki (killing some two hundred thousand civilians) in order to avoid an estimated quarter of a million Allied casualties that would have taken place by an invasion of Japan. The decision to drop the bomb had been "unanimous, automatic, unquestioned," and made with barely a moment's thought, Churchill later recalled. Earlier in the war, the British agreed to work cooperatively with the Americans on the bomb's development, but said they wouldn't use it unless both sides agreed.

"Let me know whether it is a flop or a plop," Churchill wrote to Truman in July 1945 about the first atomic test in the New Mexico desert.

"It's a plop—Truman," the message came back. That same year, when Stalin's expansion plans became clear, Churchill first used the term *Iron Curtain,* in a private message to Truman.

Public reaction to Churchill's Fulton speech, however, swiftly turned negative. Newspaper editorials condemned his speech as rogue bluster, and columnist Walter Lippmann called Truman's invitation an "almost catastrophic blunder." The new president soon learned his nation wasn't ready for another war against its recent ally Stalin and his Russian army. Going after the Soviets in peacetime was far different from finishing off Japan in war. Truman "pulled back into his shell, even declared that he had not known in advance what Churchill was going to say," *Time* magazine reported. Backpedaling away from Churchill's comments, Truman eventually offered to send the battleship *Missouri* to pick up Stalin so he could come to America and refute the charges.

Winston didn't waver, however, for his true feelings against the Soviets were even stronger than his Fulton rhetoric. Since the 1917 Russian Revolution, he felt Lenin's Bolsheviks were extremists, intent on a dictatorship that did not recognize God, property rights, or human freedom. "The strangling of Bolshevism at its birth would have been an untold blessing to the human race," Churchill declared. He'd made similar comments throughout his career. "Bolshevism is not a policy; it is a disease," he railed. "It is not a creed; it is a pestilence." In comparing Stalin's Soviet Empire to the defeated Axis powers, Churchill wondered if the Anglo-American alliance had simply replaced one great evil with another.

Although his own empire's resources were depleted, Churchill wanted the United States to control the Soviets in Europe through the use of nuclear weapons. No longer a backwater colony of the Crown, America was now "at the highest point of majesty and power ever attained by any community since the fall of the Roman Empire," Churchill judged with a historian's eye. Possessing the most deadly device ever seen, the United States would "dominate the world for the next five years," he predicted, providing an opportunity for America to act swiftly to set a course for future peace. The Soviets still appeared far away from developing their own atomic weapons, and would respect American dominance if exerted. Dropping the bomb—or at least "a showdown" with the implied threat of doing so—must be a vital tool in curbing Soviet communism, Churchill argued. He expressed these views on his own, certainly without approval of Labour Party leaders running the British government. Letting the isolationists, pacifists, and appeasers prevail would only ensure another world war, he contended. "The argument is now put forward that we must never use the atomic bomb until, or unless, it has been used against us first," Churchill said. "In other words, you must never fire until you have been shot dead. That seems to me a silly thing to say and a still more imprudent position to adopt."

Privately, Churchill suggested that America strike first, before it was too late. According to FBI records, he urged Sen. Styles Bridges, a conservative Republican from New Hampshire active in foreign affairs, to back a preemptory and devastating attack on Moscow. "He [Churchill] pointed out that if an atomic bomb could be dropped on the Kremlin wiping it out, it would be a very easy problem to handle the balance of Russia, which would be without direction," Bridges told the FBI. During a "private conference with Churchill" while visiting Europe in the summer of 1947, Bridges claimed the former prime minister had "stated that the only salvation for the civilization of the world would be if the President of the United States would declare Russia to be imperiling world peace and attack Russia." If this wasn't done, according to the FBI report, Churchill predicted "Russia will attack the United States in the next two or three years when she gets the atomic bomb and civilization will be wiped out or set back many years."

A full-fledged nuclear attack on the Kremlin didn't seem to faze Bridges, who'd been a sharp policy critic of Roosevelt and Truman. Bridges mentioned this conversation with Churchill only while talking to a G-man about "other matters," according to the agent who compiled the report. It noted that Bridges "concurs in Churchill's views and that he sincerely hopes that our next President will do just that before Russia attacks the United States." Others close to Churchill heard similar bellicose sentiments. His personal physician, Lord Moran, recalled that Winston advocated a nuclear knockout blow against the Soviets during a conversation in 1946. "We ought not to wait until Russia is ready," Churchill said. "America knows that fifty-two percent of Russia's motor industry is in Moscow and could be wiped out by a single bomb. It might mean wiping out three million people, but they [the Soviets] would think nothing of that." Winston paused and smiled as he thought of this grotesquerie. "They think more of erasing an historical building like the Kremlin," he added.

A few years later, before Churchill gave a Boston speech, Averell Harriman warned U.S. State Department officials that his old friend might make "politically embarrassing statements," urging aggressive use of the atomic bomb as a negotiating stance against the Soviets. Undoubtedly remembering Truman's retreat at Fulton, Harriman suggested that the administration get an advance look at Churchill's address. Inside a crowded Boston Garden, Churchill didn't call for an attack on the Kremlin but condemned the Soviet Politburo as "something quite as wicked but in some ways more formidable than Hitler." He reprised his "Iron Curtain" warnings and portrayed the atom bomb as Western democracy's most potent weapon. "I must not conceal from you the truth as I see it," he said in a speech offered on television as well as on radio. "It is certain that Europe would have been communized, like Czechoslovakia and London under bombardment sometime ago, but for the deterrent of the atomic bomb in the hands of the United States."

Since his days watching the sword-wielding Dervish warriors slaughtered on the hills, Churchill had understood the supremacy of machinery in war, over the courage and glory of individual soldiers. Some were surprised by his callousness about such butchery. "War has always fascinated him; he knows in surprising detail about the campaigns of the past captains; he has visited nearly all the battlefields and he can pick out, in a particular battle, the decisive move that turned the day," Lord Moran wrote in his diary. "But he has never given a thought to what was happening in the soldier's mind, he has not tried to share his fears. If a soldier does not do his duty, the P.M. says that he ought to be shot. It is as simple as that."

At Boston's Ritz-Carlton before that night's speech, Winston chatted about the atomic bomb with his longtime American friend Bernard Baruch—who later introduced him to the crowd as "the greatest living Englishman"—and with family friend Kay Halle. By his side were his wife, Clementine, and son, Randolph, seated at a circular table holding teas, buttered scones, sandwiches, and Scotch whiskey. Winston mentioned that in the New Mexico desert site, where the first Trinity bomb had been ignited, a monument was being built in memory of those who died at Hiroshima.

"Do the Americans have a bad conscience because the atom bomb was dropped?" he asked.

Kay Halle remembered Winston's "unblinking X-ray eyes" as he stared at her, looking for an answer. Kay was now an accomplished woman in her midforties and far different from the fun-loving blonde-haired department store heiress from Cleveland whom Randolph wanted to marry nearly two decades earlier. Since then, she had worked as a broadcaster, a newspaper feature writer, and for the Office of Strategic Services, the wartime predecessor to the CIA. Though Kay revered the former prime minister, she was confident enough to give an answer he might not want.

"Very many," Halle replied, about the number of Americans who felt guilty about this nuclear holocaust.

Winston dismissed such claptrap, arguing that the A-bomb posed "the only deterrent to the Soviets." He showed little patience with those who asked if he worried what God might say about the atom bomb. "I shall defend myself with resolution and vigour," he argued, as if the Gates of Heaven might resemble the well of the House. "I shall say to the Almighty, why when nations were warring in this way did

You release dangerous knowledge to mankind? The fault is Yours—not mine!" Yet in private, Churchill seemed disturbed by the moral consequences of this new warfare and wondered if its true meaning might be beyond his grasp. "Do you think that the atomic bomb means that the architect of the universe has got tired of writing his non-stop scenario?" he wrote George Bernard Shaw. "The release of the bomb seems to be his next turning point."

Publicly, Randolph supported his father's Fulton speech about the Soviet "Iron Curtain" and his firm resolve against communism in Eastern Europe. But in their private conversation in Boston, Randolph, always able to find his father's weak spot, suggested that British "saturation bombing" of Germany during the war "was an almost equal horror" to Hiroshima, Halle recalled. Aerial bombs from Allied planes obliterated cities such as Dresden, Hamburg, and Cologne, reducing them to rubble and flames. To his family and friends at this Boston hotel, Winston recalled his moral reservations about these raids in which "tens of thousands of lives were extinguished in one night . . . old men, old women, little children, yes, yes, children about to be born." Kay watched her hero speak with true humanity, "with tears brimming in his extraordinary eyes."

From his own experience, however, Randolph knew the Russians didn't fear that the Americans would strike first with the atom bomb. During a November 1945 visit to Moscow, he heard Soviet officials complain that the United States didn't share its nuclear technology, but they didn't seem overly alarmed by the "imperialistic purposes" of Uncle Sam. "I asked them chaffingly whether in fact anyone in the Kremlin has lost a single minute's sleep worrying about whether the Americans were about to drop an atomic bomb on Red Square," Randolph recalled. "They were all too honest to pretend they had."

Little did they know his father would drop the bomb if he could.

· · ·

Painting provided Winston Churchill with the chance to reimagine a chaotic world as he would have it. Gardens, gentle seas, and sunny skies filled his landscapes, in bold blues and living shades of green, usually with no humans in sight. While immersed in oils during the winter of 1947, Winston tried his hand at portraiture, repainting an old image of Lord Randolph Churchill. Sitting in his studio at Chartwell, he suddenly experienced an apparition of his father. According to Winston's apocryphal account, which he called "The Dream," the ghostly figure wanted to know which nation was the leading power in the world.

"The United States," Winston replied.

"I don't mind that—you are half American yourself," this spirit said.

The ghostly figure asked his son what he had done with his life. "Fathers always expect their sons to have their virtues without their faults," the apparition told him. The image faded before Winston could mention he'd been prime minister of Great Britain, the great goal each had set for himself. Churchill's account of his father's ghost appeared in the *London Daily Telegraph* but was quickly forgotten. Years later, Pamela Churchill pointed to Winston's dream as evidence of the emotional burdens of legacy. "It did disturb him obviously deeply when the British public rejected him in the 1945 election," she theorized. "And it brought to Winston's mind a kind of failure ... His father never had confidence in him, and somehow the two things Freudianly became connected." Winston wasn't the only Churchill who felt the weight of paternal expectations and a desire to redefine himself. After the war, Randolph still believed his destiny was to become prime minister someday, and that the name Churchill alone would carry the day, regardless of the mounting evidence against his chances. "Dear Randolph, utterly unspoiled by failure!" satirized writer Noël Coward.

Despite his braggadocio and overt confidence, Randolph looked tired and older than his thirty-four years. His smooth blond hair had begun to thin and gray, and his overweight body was still recovering from his wartime injuries. Unlike with his father, the election in 1945 had left him without a seat in the House of Commons and suddenly looking for a job.

In the past, Randolph had relied on journalism, particularly for newspapers owned by Lord Beaverbrook, just as his father had used writing to earn some cash and promote his views in between political posts. But Randolph, caught in the maelstrom of divorce and a shortage of funds, returned to another, easier way to make money. Near the end of 1946, he traveled to America to give lectures, hoping to repeat his successful speaking tour from the early 1930s. Americans still tended to view Randolph as the heir apparent, the next Churchill to assume power, unlike many in Britain with less regard for him. "It was perhaps just as well that America existed for Randolph," remarked his cousin Anita Leslie. "It was such a large country to jaunt around in giving lectures—and Randolph remained excellent on the platform if not in private life." On the lecture trail, Randolph kept himself amused at night by excessive drinking and boorish gestures to women. "Britishly drunk all the time, soliciting respectable women at luncheon parties, etc.," Evelyn Waugh complained to his agent after meeting his friend in Hollywood. Randolph's penchant for rapid mood changes—a sudden, almost violent intensity in his speech, followed by a period of mildness seeking forgiveness—suggested problems beyond alcohol abuse.

Only Kay Halle, who'd known him since his golden-haired Apollo-like youth, seemed to recognize a deeper cause in Randolph's psyche. To Kay, Randolph confided that "he could *feel* whenever an illogical tantrum was going to overwhelm him," Anita Leslie later described in her biography of him. Leslie didn't seem to consider this "illogical tantrum" a symptom of mental illness, but mentions Randolph's description to Halle of "a physical sensation that arose from the earth" and left him feeling out of control. "If I can stop it before it reaches my knees I will be all right," Randolph explained to Halle, his loyal friend, "but once it gets above them a black fog envelops me and I just don't care what I say." Randolph Churchill's behavior displayed signs of bipolar disorder (then called manic depression) as defined in today's medical literature: very elevated emotional highs with racing thoughts and talkative outbursts followed by remorseful "black fogs" and feelings of worthlessness; irritable moods and little temper control; impulsive decisions and spending sprees; binge drinking and overweight eating; compulsively seeking sex with many different partners; and a false overestimation of self-importance. In retrospect, Lady Juliet Townsend, Randolph's goddaughter, said many of these symptoms were evident in his demeanor though never diagnosed professionally. "He certainly was a person who was very up and down," she recalled in 2012, "and got more down than up as time went on." His contemporaries, including Waugh, dismissed these problems as part of Randolph's eccentricity or buffoonery, without regard for a deeper cause. "Randolph's friendships were not very close friendships because he was so wild—people didn't like to get too close to him," recalled Adrian Berry, grandson of newspaper baron Lord Camrose. "My uncle Freddie [Birkenhead] regarded Randolph in slightly comic terms, not a person whom he'd confide in."

Neither Clementine nor Winston was much for psychological analysis, and none of their correspondence about Randolph's behavior suggests it. Perhaps the nagging sense of a family link (that his son's erratic nature too closely resembled that of his late father) was too uncomfortable for Winston to consider. Even Halle seemed ill-equipped to deal adequately with Randolph's raw admission. "Kay tried to train him to check this crazy creeping temper at the ankle stage," Leslie described. "But it was no good." Kay's well-intentioned but amateur methods—as if his "crazy creeping temper" could be put on a leash—were no match for the "illogical tantrums" that continued to haunt his existence.

Across America, Randolph's bad-boy antics were followed by gossip rather than political columnists. In December 1946 he was arrested for reckless driving after addressing a women's club in Connecticut. Rather than hire a lawyer, he unwisely conducted his own defense. He argued that his eighty-mile-an-hour speed along the Merritt Parkway wasn't necessarily "reckless" because the highway was "one of the safest in the world." The judge failed to see his logic and fined him fifty dollars. Back in England, the verdict was even harsher. Both his parents, Winston and Clementine, could no longer hide their disappointment in him and his adolescent behavior. Randolph's acts of genuine heroism during the war, his insightful advice as Winston's eyes and ears in other nations, and the deaths of friends and colleagues in battle had somehow failed to mature him or season his judgment. In his wake, all he seemed to leave behind were unpaid bills and a broken marriage, with a six-year-old son who barely knew him. Unlike Winston at this same age, who spoke of life's brevity after his father's death, Randolph acted as if the party would never end.

Upon his son's return to England, Winston let it be known he didn't care to see him, an emotional wound Randolph could not bear. In February 1947, Randolph composed a heartfelt letter admitting his faults and acknowledging his father's disappointment in him. "As you know the only career in which I am seriously interested is politics," he said. "While fully realizing that I have made my full share of mistakes I believe also that circumstances have not so far been propitious. But I am still young & fortune may yet come my way." Randolph conceded he should have become a lawyer, just as Winston suggested, but needed to work as a journalist to pay his debts. What he could not afford emotionally, though, was the estrangement of his father. "Please don't expect too much of me now," Randolph beseeched. "Believe instead, I beg you, that I have no other ambition than to be ultimately judged an honorable & faithful son. No day passes but that you are constantly in my thoughts & I am grateful that you think so often of me. Give me your confidence & I shall not fail you."

At home, Randolph felt eclipsed, no longer the sun king in waiting. Within the extended Churchill family, Christopher Soames, the newly married husband of Winston's youngest daughter, Mary, acted as a trusted unofficial aide to Winston, just as Diana's husband, Duncan Sandys, had done during the war. Both sons-in-law seemed only too happy to serve as surrogate replacements to Winston's own son.

Over time, Diana's marriage to Sandys showed increasing signs of trouble, weighed down by her husband's infidelity, his political ambitions, and her sullen reaction. Among Winston Churchill's adult children, however, Sarah most closely rivaled Randolph.

During the war, Sarah's relationship with the U.S. ambassador John Gilbert Winant—which overlapped her divorce from comedian Vic Oliver—always seemed a matter of political convenience, never displaying the passion of Pamela Churchill's affairs. Both Sarah and Gil were still married, at least technically, and were far more discreet. While traveling at her father's side during the war, Sarah penned "Dear Gil" letters that were friendly but contained few hints of intimacy. By 1945, whatever passion they shared had passed. Their occasional meetings, as part of the affairs of state, remained merely cordial. "I have had occasion to think of you often," she responded to Winant in one letter. "You have been greatly missed—but I have unerring faith that things happen for the best."

The following year, President Truman replaced Winant as ambassador with Harriman. The avuncular, Lincolnesque Republican Winant seemed lost in this new postwar world, left only to write his memoirs. "The former's book is due for publication quite soon," Kick Kennedy wrote home after a dinner party that included Winant and Anthony Eden. Kick knew her father had never liked his replacement. "I find him more bogus each time I see him," Kick added. In his book, Winant didn't mention Joe Kennedy but recalled Churchill's steely explanation to him "that power has to be used irrespective of anyone's feelings. If we win, nobody will care. If we lose, there will be nobody to care."

A few weeks later, on the publication date of his book, Winant committed suicide, firing a bullet into his head. "What a waste—what a waste," said Edward R. Murrow, one of those who'd pushed for Winant to replace the appeaser Kennedy. Clementine Churchill, always fond of Winant, had to convince her reluctant husband to attend his London memorial. As the war progressed, Churchill had ignored Winant and his figurehead status, just as his daughter had disengaged herself from their affair.

Shortly afterward, Sarah began another ill-fated relationship, with society photographer Anthony Beauchamp, which drew her father's ire when she introduced them at a Monte Carlo hotel. Winston's contempt for Beauchamp wounded her deeply. Her response reflected the emotional pain inside the Churchill family. "Am I not a human being?" she implored. "Can you not call me into your room, tell me you do not like him, and for the love that you say you have for me, extend him just the common courtesy that you do to the maitre d'Hotel or chef d'orchestre, & trust me to see that the visit is terminated quickly ... I assure you I shall never again, subject you to any of my friends, nor indeed them, to your contempt. I do not understand how you can say you love me—when you are so very, very unkind."

Defying her father's wishes, Sarah married Beauchamp in 1949 and moved with him to America. She would land minor roles on Broadway and in Hollywood movies, dancing with Fred Astaire in *Royal Wedding*, but always identified by the press as Winston Churchill's daughter.

The Churchills were no longer one big happy family, not as they seemed at Chartwell during Christmas 1940, when everything was at risk, including the British Empire itself. With bombs falling on London, the need to stick together was then so clear and urgent. But now, with the end of war, his humiliating ouster as prime minister, and his unresolved financial woes, Winston found himself at bay. Once again, he endured a dizzying fall from power. It was similar to his sudden removal from office after the 1915 Dardanelles disaster, when, he recalled, "The change from the intense executive activities of each day's work . . . left me gasping . . . Like a sea beast fished up from the depths, or a diver too suddenly hoisted, my veins threatened to burst from the fall in pressure."

To return to power, Winston needed to stay in the limelight through his writings and speeches, mostly warning about the Cold War. And to underwrite these activities, he would need a source of funding as befit a great man. Rather than depend on his own wits, he usually relied on others (especially Brendan Bracken and Lord Beaverbrook) to find a solution for him. This time, however, his son, once again reconciled with his father, came up with an answer in America.

The Churchill family had been always cast in a favorable light by *Life* magazine, including its wartime cover featuring Pamela holding Randolph's infant son, Winston. The Time-Life media conglomerate based in New York was a natural place for Randolph, the freelance writer, to raise money for his father. Owner Henry Luce had admired Churchill's heroic leadership during the war, and his celebrated wife, Clare Boothe Luce, enjoyed a personal relationship with Randolph that by war's end was still fond if no longer intimate. In October 1945, after the family's disastrous results at the polls, Clare teased Randolph about newspaper coverage summarizing his love life, military service, and political ambitions. "How unfair to accuse you of preferring Hussies to Hussars when everyone knows Hurrahs are your real preference (being a politician!)" she joked. Clare admired the Churchills, perhaps more than her husband. "I have thought of you and your gallant father very often since the elections," she wrote. "In or out of office, he stands incomparably the world's greatest man—maybe its only great one now. The price of being right is always persecution. In politics or religion, Barabbas will always be 'the free democratic choice of the people.'"

Randolph called the London bureau of Luce's media empire and proposed that *Life* magazine run a photo gallery and text about Winston's paintings. The editors frowned on the idea, but Luce jumped immediately, paying $20,000 with the hope of eventually snaring Winston's wartime memoirs. The gamble paid off. By the spring of 1947, Churchill agreed to a whopping $1.15 million (nearly $12 million in today's dollars) for the unprecedented serialization in *Life* and the *New York Times* of his long-awaited history of World War II. For his own political reasons, Luce urged Winston to criticize Roosevelt's "two-faced" weakness during the war, particularly with Stalin during the 1945 Yalta Conference. The Big Three divided up much of the postwar world at that meeting, held two months before Franklin's death. Winston bitterly disagreed with the creation of the Soviet Communist Bloc from that fateful meeting. But while Churchill gladly accepted Luce's advance, he didn't heed his advice. By then, Winston was already planning his return to the top, by arguing his Labour Party usurpers were too weak, too inadequate to deal with the Soviet tiger.

From his bed at Chartwell, Winston Churchill dictated his manuscript, based largely on his own recollections and official papers he had taken with him upon leaving office as prime minister. At age seventy-four, he looked to his future by coming to terms with the past. "Let us stop our melancholy recriminations and apply ourselves to the business at hand," he chided during a 1947 House of Commons debate dragged down by criticism of Yalta. "Let us leave hindsight to history—that history which I am now, myself, in the process of writing!"

Delighted by the prestige of obtaining Churchill as one of *Life*'s star writers, Luce did everything to keep him happy. He paid for vacations and hosted gala events in his honor, reminding the public of his greatness. "It can be worth the space plus the money if, in some sense, Churchill becomes 'our author,' " Luce explained to an associate before paying the ransom-like sum.

Typical of this royal treatment was the March 25, 1949, dinner hosted by Luce at the Ritz-Carlton in Manhattan, toasting the former prime minister. Winston arrived by special train from Washington, where he'd given Truman a red leather-bound edition of his Marlborough biography. While in New York, Winston stayed as always at the home of his American friend Bernard Baruch, who accompanied him to this Luce dinner. Outside Baruch's apartment, protesters held signs and chanted, "Churchill wants war, we want peace." By then, America's anticommunist scare was in full bloom. When reporters asked if he felt vindicated regarding his prophetic warnings of a Cold War with the Soviets, he nodded. "I read the Fulton speech over again the other day to see what I had said," he explained. "I'm bound to say I don't feel inclined to go back on any of it."

Flashing his familiar V sign, Churchill left for the Ritz. Inside the hotel, a restless black-tie crowd waited to hear him speak, including an admiring young congressman already in his second term: the Honorable John F. Kennedy from Massachusetts.

35

Circles of Friends

In postwar London, several of Randolph Churchill's Oxford friends and commando veterans visited the white Georgian house on Smith Square owned by Kick Kennedy, the widowed Lady Hartington, a lively parlor for politics, the literary arts, and forgetting the heartbreaking past.

In Kick's new home, located near St. John's Church, where her friend Pamela Churchill had married Randolph years earlier, the two young women shared many laughs and gossipy stories about the Churchills and the Kennedys. "Kick's house is really very cute, very nicely furnished," described her sister Eunice during an October 1946 visit. "We hold a salon every night from 6 to 8 here at home; otherwise you can't tell where we might be." One constant visitor, Seymour Berry, the best man at Randolph's wedding, dated Kick frequently enough that some friends thought they might get married. In this same circle of friends was Freddie Birkenhead (son of Winston's best friend, the late F. E. Smith), who had served in Croatia with Randolph and Evelyn Waugh. By far, Waugh was the best known of Randolph's friends to attend Kick's dinner parties, and the most opinionated. While he found Kick attractive, Waugh thought the sentimental oil painting she kept on her wall of her dead husband, Billy (commissioned from an old photo of him in uniform) was "most God awful."

As a Catholic convert, Waugh considered the Hartington wedding as unholy, a selfish act of apostasy. At one party, he sat next to Kick and gave her a lecture on Catholic marriage law. She seemed amused enough by this celebrated novelist not to take offense. Evelyn, who'd regained the roly-poly weight he lost during the war, mistook her attention for infatuation and noted, "The widow Hartington is in love with me, I think." With Frank Waldrop, her old Washington newspaper editor, she later laughed about Waugh's moralizing until she suddenly stopped. "You know, Frank, I had only five weeks with my husband," she lamented, "and now he is gone."

Inside her London group of acquaintances, William Henry Lawrence Peter Wentworth-Fitzwilliam, the Eighth Earl of Fitzwilliam (simply "Peter Fitzwilliam" to friends) emerged as the most intriguing and fateful for Kick. Her attraction to this swashbuckling, wealthy, and married war hero—far different in character from Billy Hartington— would lead to a secret love affair that once again caused conflict within the Kennedy family. Kick first met Fitzwilliam, the son of one of England's richest families, at a June 1946 victory ball honoring the commandos. During the war, Randolph, Waugh, and Fitzwilliam, all drinking buddies from White's, served together in the Middle East. Indeed, on the boat ride to Cairo, it was Fitzwilliam to whom Randolph lost a huge sum in a poker game—a financial crisis that ruptured Randolph's marriage with Pamela and only added to Fitzwilliam's notoriety as a gambler. In a begrudging tone, Waugh referred to Fitzwilliam as "king dandy and scum."

At the commandos ball, Kick turned plenty of heads with her pale pink gown, an effervescent smile, and a sense of humor that could captivate a room. That night at the Dorchester Hotel, Fitzwilliam's wife, Olive, an heiress to the Guinness brewery fortune, served as president of the ball fund. Among the honored commando veterans, Fitzwilliam was singled out for a brave special mission during the war. Basking in the limelight, Peter nevertheless spent enough time with Kick to spark a romance, brazenly in front of his wife. By that point in their marriage, Olive had learned to look the other way when her husband flirted with other women. At such gatherings, she'd down drink after drink, enough so that she eventually became an alcoholic.

After the commandos ball, Fitzwilliam became a favored visitor at Kick's home in Smith Square. Friends worried for her reputation with such a charming adulterer, and that she might wind up hurt. "You don't know him—*you don't know him*," Kick insisted. Both lovers tried hard to keep their affair private, escaping London to the Fitzwilliam family's estates throughout England and Ireland. A dashing man with thick dark hair, Peter showed enough business acumen with his outside investments to rival Joe Kennedy. His family, whose wealth was the stuff of legend, had the largest residence in England, a three-thousand-acre estate. This huge Georgian mansion, called Wentworth Woodhouse, contained 365 rooms (one for every day of the year), enough so that, in the eighteenth century, Peter's ancestors gave guests paper wafers to leave in the hallways to retrace their way to its dining hall. Despite his many financial investments, Peter's greatest interest centered on thoroughbred horse racing. He owned one of the best stud farms in England, and invited Kick to join him in racing excursions to France. Pamela Churchill came along with Kick as a sidekick and camouflage. "Kick was the perfect friend for Pamela, non-judgmental and fun-loving," wrote biographer Sally Bedell Smith. "As the daughter of Lord Digby, Pamela knew her way around racecourses and fit in comfortably with turf society." In her letters home, Kick gave her parents glimpses of this glamorous world, mentioning a week-long trip to Paris with Pamela and Virginia Sykes, a former girlfriend of her late brother, Joe. In her correspondence, Kick could be catty and gossipy, the way all Kennedys enjoyed dishing in private. Aware of his mother's disapproval of American Wallis Simpson and her affair forcing King Edward VIII's abdication, Kick wrote of seeing the Duchess of Windsor and her husband on the social circuit and painted the woman he loved in pathetic tones. "Really, no one here takes any notice of them & the extraordinary thing is that I actually feel that she is jealous of what I, as an American, have got out of England and which has always been denied to her," she told her parents. Kick played to the Kennedy family's competitive streak in her Anglo-American exchanges. "After Pam's dinner party, we went to her sister's debutante party," she wrote. "It gave me quite a turn to see all the ugly girls. Americans of that age certainly have them all beat."

While visiting Ireland in November 1946, Kick's more serious-minded younger sister Eunice stayed with her at Lismore Castle, the Irish estate owned by Billy's family. They went to the races with a soft Irish rain falling, much different from the climate at the always sunny Florida track their father owned. "It was certainly the furthest possible cry from Hialeah," Kick wrote to her parents. "But the characters around an Irish racecourse certainly make the whole day worthwhile." The letter home mentioned Fitzwilliam, but did so misleadingly, avoiding any parental upset. Though Eunice accompanied her, Kick dared not explain to her sister the true nature of her relationship with the Eighth Earl of Fitzwilliam.

At Lismore Castle, Pamela Churchill joined Kick's other high-powered friends from London when her brother Jack visited in September 1947. While on a European fact-finding mission with other House members, Congressman Kennedy tacked on his own extended holiday in Ireland joining his sister. "I hope Jack will let me know when he is planning to arrive at Lismore and if anyone is coming from America," Kick wrote home several weeks beforehand. "I don't want everyone to arrive at once."

Lismore, built centuries earlier, felt like a step back into history, a time when the British Empire dominated Irish Catholics in their own land. With some amusement, Kick reminded her family that she was now living in the place where Billy's great-great-uncle was "brought in here, dying, when shot by Irish patriots in 1882." With its ancient stone walls and turrets along the River Blackwater, the castle offered plenty of beauty and spacious rooms for Kick's various guests. The list of invitees included Winston Churchill's cousin Sir Shane Leslie, and most notably Anthony Eden, Churchill's top foreign adviser, who had suffered the same family tragedy during the war as the Kennedys. In July 1945, Anthony lost his beloved fighter pilot son, Simon, in Burma. Yet Eden's judgment of Churchill was far different from that of the embittered former ambassador Kennedy. "It is you who have led, uplifted and inspired us through the worst days," Eden wrote Winston on V-E Day. "Without you this day could not have been."

Despite their differences, Kick knew her father liked and respected Eden and would enjoy knowing of her invitation to meet Britain's future prime minister. "Anthony Eden arrives today so by the end of the week he and Jack will have fixed up the state of the world," she wrote home whimsically. Eden, a handsome man known for his distinctive clothing style, had already made an impression on Jack years earlier: Jack wrote to a friend that he'd been "sporting around in my morning coat, my 'Anthony Eden' black Homburg and white gardenia." Talking politics at Lismore was part of the guests' relaxation. "Anthony Eden, who was very easy to entertain, arrived loaded down with official looking Conservative documents but when he had been here only a few days got into the Irish spirit," Kick reported. "Jack liked him enormously."

Though nearly twice her age, Eden courted Lady Hartington with a fair degree of romantic interest. At a dinner party the year before, society hostess Lady Cunard had kept leaning toward them and asking loudly, "Anthony, don't you think Kick is pretty?" followed in another breath by "Kick, don't you think Anthony is wonderful?" Three months before his Lismore trip, Eden had escorted Kick to the Ascot Racecourse outside London, where he received a polite reception from the crowd. "They'll cheer but the blighters won't vote for us," he whispered to Kick. The couple dined at Eden's house, where Kick learned more about his troubled marriage. Eden's wife, Beatrice, hated his political career, and she moved permanently to the United States after their son was killed in the war. "She [Mrs. Eden] is in America and refuses to return so he lives in a rather squalid little house with very few comforts," Kick described. "He is a nice man and fascinating to talk to for me." If Eden knew about Peter Fitzwilliam, it didn't stop him from showing an interest in Kick even after the Lismore visit. "I long to see you," Eden wrote in a lengthy missive to her. "I love your letters, especially when you write as you talk, for then I can imagine that you are here. How I wish that you were, and I do believe that you would enjoy it too."

Strolling Lismore together, Kick let Jack know of her romance with Peter Fitzwilliam. She spoke glowingly of Peter, as if he were standing right before them, with an intensity Jack had never really known in his own love life. Jack listened fraternally, and didn't prod or condemn. For now, Kick's older brother was the only Kennedy family member she'd tell. Jack could be trusted to keep her secret.

While in Ireland, Congressman Kennedy remained intent on discovering his family's roots. During his earlier 1945 trip, which included meeting Éamon de Valera, Kennedy had packed several books about Irish-American history. But on this trip, Jack planned an unannounced personal visit to the old Kennedy homestead in nearby County Wexford. While Kick's other guests played golf, Jack convinced Pamela Churchill to accompany him for the four-hour journey in his sister's American-made station wagon. Pamela shared the same sharp social antennae as Kick, but she wasn't attracted to her successful brother. "In England we dated very much older men and Jack seemed, well, boyish," Pamela recalled, though the congressman was three years her senior. "Skinny and scrawny, actually. Kathleen's kid brother. Not eligible, so to speak."

The road to Wexford was a long one. A century earlier in 1848, in the teeth of the Irish famine that claimed a million lives, Jack's great-grandfather Patrick Kennedy left his family's homestead (a drab whitewashed stone house with a thatched roof and only thirty acres on a tenant farm in a small area known as Dunganstown) to begin a new lease on life in a poor immigrant section of East Boston. What happened to the succeeding generations of Kennedys would be nothing less than miraculous. They became emblematic of the rise of Irish Catholics, as America's first large wave of immigrants who redefined their adopted nation. Rather than the British class lines of peerage or inherited wealth, Jack's two grandfathers relied on their two faiths, Catholicism and the Democratic Party, to gain power in New England. Certainly Honey Fitz and P. J. Kennedy learned that hand shaking at parish Communion breakfasts, patronage deals through the political clubhouse, and the constant courting of ward bosses and Church hierarchy would pay off at the ballot box. Despite his millions from Wall Street and Hollywood, Joe Kennedy's greatest triumph was his appointment to the Court of St. James's, overcoming the strictures of his Irish-Catholic immigrant background. Nothing defined the differences between American and British society more starkly than this social ascendancy through Yankee ambition rather than noble blood and class distinctions. The Kennedys' climb to the top proved "the hardest and longest move of all—inching up the rungs of the class ladder until the Kennedys stood near the top and could look as equals on the dukes and earls whose ancestors had ruled their native land," JFK's earliest biographer, James MacGregor Burns, explained. Joe Kennedy made sure his sons understood these lessons, prompting Jack's curiosity to learn more about his family origins.

At the Kennedy farm in County Wexford, accompanied by Pamela,

Jack discovered not much had changed since his great-grandfather left. "I'm John Kennedy from Massachusetts," he said after his knock on the door was answered. "I believe we are related." His distant cousin Mary Kennedy Ryan seemed dubious at first but eventually invited the two strangers in for tea.

The Kennedys who remained in Ireland had spent much of the past century trying to regain the land rights to their tenant farms from the British and supporting Ireland's independence movement led by such politicians as de Valera. Mary Ryan herself had been a member of the old IRA's women's auxiliary during the 1920s conflict against the British, carrying guns and money, either in carts or under her dress, to a secret hiding spot near their farm. "Jack kept pressing on about his ancestors going to America and so on, trying to make the link," recalled Pamela. As a treat, Jack took the Irish Kennedy cousins for a short ride in Kick's shining new station wagon, accompanied by the former Mrs. Randolph Churchill. "They never could figure out who I was," recalled Pamela. " 'Wife?' they'd ask. I'd say no. And they'd say, 'Ah, soon to be, no doubt!' "

After nearly two hours "surrounded by chickens and pigs," Jack recalled, he "left in a flow of nostalgia and sentiment." The trip reaffirmed the Irish stories he'd heard from his parents and grandparents. Neither Pamela nor Kick, however, seemed impressed. As their car pulled away from the Kennedy farm, Pamela turned to Jack with a remark meant as witty. "That was just like *Tobacco Road*!" she tittered, referring to the popular novel about rural life in Georgia. Jack wasn't amused. "The English lady," he later recounted, ". . . had not understood at all the magic of the afternoon." To Dave Powers and Ken O'Donnell, his Irish-Catholic political aides from Boston, he was much blunter: "I felt like kicking her out of the car." At Lismore, Lady Hartington was even haughtier. After listening to her brother's wondrous account of the Kennedy homestead, Kick mustered only a bemused question. "Well, did they have a bathroom?"

Throughout his Irish trip, Jack suffered an unexplained, debilitating illness with little relief. Eventually he flew back to London, staying at the Claridge's hotel in Mayfair, where he collapsed. He sought help from Pamela, who had also returned to the city. "I need a doctor," Jack told her desperately over the telephone. Pamela convinced her doctor, Sir Daniel Davies, also used by Lord Beaverbrook, to go see him immediately.

Kennedy's wartime back injury and malaria usually provided a plausible public explanation for his often sickly appearance and yellowish skin tone. Pam's doctor first diagnosed Jack's symptoms as those of Addison's disease, a chronic disorder of the adrenal glands with symptoms of weight loss, dizziness, nausea, diarrhea, and muscle fatigue. Sir Daniel kept him at the hospital, where Jack received lifesaving cortisone injections. "That American friend of yours, he hasn't got a year to live," the doctor informed Pamela.

Ravaged by his strange illness, Kennedy remained in a London hospital for weeks and was given the last rites of his church. In mid-October 1947, he traveled home with his mother across the Atlantic, confined to the sick ward of the *Queen Elizabeth*. He was then flown by charter plane from New York to Boston, and carried on a stretcher, drawn and pale, into the New England Baptist Hospital until he could recover. Misled by Joe Kennedy's publicity men, the press claimed the congressman suffered from "a malarial attack." No one suspected otherwise.

Friendship with the Kennedys required keeping secrets. As Kick's confidante, Pamela Churchill became privy to Jack Kennedy's biggest secret: the potentially fatal medical condition that could keep him from his family's vaunted political goals. Yet there was no doubt she could be trusted, just as she was with so many intimacies about the Churchills. "I knew the Kennedys very well," Pamela explained a half century later. "Kick was my closest friend in those days." Pamela understood the power of such information. As the friendly siren of the Churchill

Club during the war, she listened carefully to the conversations of American military brass, politicians, and prominent U.S. journalists— and then reported the most significant details to her father-in-law, the prime minister. "Basically, I'm a backroom girl," Pam explained. "I've always said this and I've always believed it."

In February 1948, Kick wanted Pamela Churchill to come with her again to Florida, just as she had when Winston visited in 1946. Visiting Palm Beach in winter gave Kick the chance to catch up with her family, to let them know more of her new life on the other side of the Atlantic. But this year the complicated love lives of these two young women didn't allow for such an idyllic trip together in the sun. Kick had hoped Pamela's presence might make it easier for her to tell her parents about her intention to marry Peter Fitzwilliam. Kick convinced Elizabeth Cavendish, her late husband Billy's sister, to come with her to Palm Beach, as a false sign the Devonshires approved of Kick's new love. In fact, Elizabeth harbored strong doubts and offered support only because Kick seemed "terrified" of confronting her mother. Among Kick's London circle of friends, few believed Fitzwilliam would bring her anything but heartache. At dinner the night before she left for America, Kick burst out crying when David and Sissy Ormsby-Gore condemned Peter's dishonorable character. Like the Jesuits she consulted, Kick heard the Ormsby-Gores predict excommunication from the Catholic Church if she married Peter.

A sexual passion unlike any she'd ever known before apparently compelled Lady Hartington to risk everything dear. "Her friends began to suspect that she had begun sleeping with him," wrote her biographer Lynne McTaggart. "She didn't seem to care anymore whether the affair was kept a secret or her reputation remained unsoiled." Her old newspaper friend John White noticed a change in Kick's demeanor;

she was no longer the virginal Kennedy princess. Instead of duty, desire now motivated her actions; instead of obedient faith, a blinding happiness. "I was overjoyed to see that she had finally been awakened," White observed. "Rarely in life do you see someone so bubbling over with love, everything that love should be, every bit of it. Poor old Billy Hartington. But again he probably would have been blown away if she had felt that way about him." As word of her affair spread within her Smith Square salon, even Evelyn Waugh weighed in with advice. He'd later claim to Clarissa Churchill, Winston's niece, that Kick sought his opinion about what to do about "*le scandale* Fitzwilliam." Waugh suggested to Kick that having sex with a married man was relatively venial compared with the cardinal sin of leaving the Church. "If you want to commit adultery or fornication & can't resist, do it," Waugh cautioned, "but realize what you are doing, and don't give the final insult of apostasy."

During her nearly two-month-long stay in Florida, Kick never mentioned Peter's name. Not until the last day of her trip, when the Kennedys were all together for a joyous occasion, did the twenty-eight-year-old Lady Hartington inform her parents like a wayward child. At the Greenbrier hotel in White Sulphur Springs, West Virginia—where Joe and Rose spent their 1914 honeymoon—the family gathered among some three hundred celebrities, wealthy tycoons, and society types to attend an April 17, 1948, gala hosted by the hotel's owner. Hollywood star Bing Crosby sang "White Christmas" and other well-known tunes, while Kick convinced the band to play her favorite "How Are Things in Glocca Morra," from *Finian's Rainbow,* a new show on Broadway. Recovering from his illness, Jack flew in from Washington to join the fun.

Near night's end, Kick stunned her mother by announcing her love for Fitzwilliam and their plans to marry when she returned to England. Kick's adamant resolve was met by an even sharper, firmer rebuke from Rose. To this deeply religious matriarch, it seemed unconscionable that her daughter would break up an existing Fitzwilliam family to wed a divorced man. All Kick's conciliatory letters from England—the effort to reconcile herself with her religion and her mother after marrying Billy Hartington, seeking her approval by attending religious retreats—now sounded hollow. As Rose realized, she'd been betrayed by both her daughter's adulterous behavior and the apparent complicit knowledge of her son Jack and her own husband. No longer would Rose Kennedy look the other way. If Kathleen married this man, she emphatically told her daughter, she would no longer have anything to do with her, she'd be dead in her mother's eyes. And if her husband went along with this unholy arrangement, Rose indicated there would be dire consequences for their own union. In a rare instance, Joe Kennedy kept silent. He knew Rose's threat endangered their "family enterprise"—the magnificent Kennedy clan they had invested their whole lives in—and would shatter his relationship with his daughter Kathleen, who, Rose once told Lady Astor, was her husband's "favorite of all the children." Joe weighed his options as Kick left the next day for London.

In a sense, Joe Kennedy faced a similar predicament as Winston Churchill did with his favorite child, actress Sarah Churchill. She married two rakish husbands of whom the prime minister fundamentally disapproved. But whereas Winston did not seem able to keep his hurtful comments at bay, Joe proved far more adept and diplomatic with his children, even in the most inciting moments. He didn't explode or risk the permanent expulsion of his daughter. "The measure of a man's success in life is not the money he's made—it's the kind of family he has raised," he insisted to a reporter in 1943, when his own political wilderness seemed to have no end. "In that, I've been mighty lucky." At least for the moment, Joe honored his wife's principled stand and did nothing to contradict her. Rather than fight, he soon left for Europe as part of a government commission study of the Marshall Plan. Kick contacted her father and pressed for a May 15 meeting in Paris. She felt strongly that if her father met Peter Fitzwilliam, he might recognize qualities similar to those in himself and give his tacit approval of, if not his blessing for, their marriage. To persuade her father, she planned to ask her British friend Janie Kenyon-Slaney and her husband, Max Aitken (Lord Beaverbrook's aviator hero son), to join them in Paris. Max knew Peter; perhaps Beaverbrook's son could ease the senior Kennedy's objections. It was her father's love, more than that of anyone in her family, that Kick didn't want to lose.

Impulsively, a few days before this fateful meeting, the couple decided to fly from London to southern France, to spend a Whitsun holiday in Cannes drinking up the sun along the Riviera. Halfway into the journey, their chartered plane stopped in Paris because of stormy weather ahead. Peter impatiently called some horse owner friends, who agreed to share an impromptu leisurely lunch at a Paris café. When he and Kick returned to the airport, the plane's pilot warned them that dangerous clouds remained in the skies, near the mountains leading to Cannes. Unaccustomed to not having his way, Fitzwilliam convinced the pilot to run the risk anyway, and he and Kick climbed back into the plane. Kick urged Pamela Churchill, who had come to the airport with them, to join them for the short trip. For reasons of her own, Pam declined. Instead, she "put them on the plane together," as Pam recalled, and watched as they flew away.

Several hours later, Joe Kennedy received a call from the press at his Paris hotel suite letting him know that his daughter was dead. The small ten-person plane had lost control and crashed, killing everyone aboard. Kick's battered body was carried by oxcart from the mountainside scene. The wartime widow's search for happiness, the hope that her father might like Peter and support her decision to marry, was now over, covered up in misleading accounts of why they were together in the first place.

Alerted about the missing plane, Congressman Kennedy waited

on a sofa in Washington, listening to Kick's favorite song from *Fin-ian's Rainbow*, until the telephone rang again and he and his sister Eu-nice received the final word. Jack cried and eventually left the room to mourn alone. He later flew to Boston to gather with his mother, Rose, and siblings at the family's Hyannis Port home. In his sorrow, Joe ac-cepted a gracious offer by the Duke and Duchess of Devonshire al-lowing Kick to be buried near their Chatsworth castle, the scene of so many happier times before the war, rather than have her remains brought back to the States. Billy's parents knew of Kick's secret affair with Fitzwilliam and shared the Kennedys' desire to keep it out of the obituaries. The ambassador had come to Paris with one of his favorite fixers, Boston's former police commissioner Joseph F. Timilty—exactly the kind of gruff, bushy-eyebrowed accomplice Joe needed to tell a man he couldn't marry his daughter. He'd even visited his Vatican friend Count Galeazzi, for an ecclesiastical solution to Kick's dilemma. Shat-tered by her death, Joe scribbled a note on his way to claim her body: "No one who ever met her didn't feel that life was much better . . . We must not feel sorry for her but for ourselves." At Kick's funeral, the for-mer ambassador was the only Kennedy in attendance. Rose's adamant condemnation of Kick's behavior chilled the idea that the whole family might attend. At first Jack tried to go, but passport problems made him stay home. More than two hundred mourners paid their respects. Joe Kennedy, dressed in a rumpled suit, barely spoke. Many still viewed him as the appeaser who'd abandoned England at its most desperate hour. "He stood alone, unloved and despised," recalled Alastair Forbes, one of Kick's friends.

Despite their past antagonisms, Winston Churchill sent his written condolences on a wreath placed at Kick's grave. Winston's note seemed to acknowledge the loss of Kennedy's oldest son in the war, the battle-field death of his son-in-law, and now the loss of his charming daugh-ter the prime minister remembered so well. "Pray accept my sincere sympathy on your renewed grievous loss. Winston Churchill," read the cable. The former ambassador thanked Churchill, acknowledging the way their families' paths had crossed. "Rose and I are exceedingly grateful for your kind thoughts," Joe wrote to Winston. "We know how greatly you admired Kathleen and that you will appreciate how we cherish the memory of her beautiful character." Her funeral reflected how much of Kick's life—flawed but always vividly intense—had been spent in England rather than America. Unlike her father, she'd been accepted by the British aristocracy as one of their own. Looking at her grave were several men who had loved her at separate times and in different ways: Seymour Berry, Tony Rosslyn, William Douglas-Home, Anthony Eden, and even Evelyn Waugh. Surrounding her coffin were other friends, such as Lady Nancy Astor and Brendan Bracken, and couples who had been part of her married life with Billy, including David and Sissy Ormsby-Gore, who had warned Kick about her involvement with Fitzwilliam.

Randolph Churchill represented his family as well as himself. Everyone knew of his divorce from Pamela, arguably Kick's best friend at the time of her death, but Randolph had decided to come anyway. During the funeral services, he and Pamela spoke once again, not with rancor or any bitterness but with a tenderness they had not shared in years. Both seemed shaken by death's sudden claim on Kick, the lively hostess of her Smith Square salon full of their friends, someone they'd known for most of their adult lives. The Kennedys had been a touchstone, part of their understanding of what it meant to be American. As his father's representative, Randolph first met Kick upon the Kennedys' 1938 arrival in London, before any other Englishman or Pamela had heard her name as a debutante. Now, a decade later, Lady Hartington, known as Kick, the embodiment of this special Anglo-American relationship, was gone. The twisted wreckage had left both Pamela and Randolph searching for answers.

To her divorced husband, Pamela admitted her life had been tougher than she expected after leaving the Churchill family's protective bubble. Floundering in his own way, Randolph recognized how much both his parents still adored Pamela with their young son, Winston, and that perhaps his own rudderless life might be given new direction if they got back together as a family. Following Kick's burial, Randolph proposed a reconciliation with Pamela. He arranged for a weekend getaway at the castle-like home of a friend, with champagne at the ready. Like a newlywed, Randolph hoped for a second honeymoon with Pamela, and used all his oratorical skills to plead his case. They talked about their mutual employer, newspaper baron Lord Beaverbrook, and how Winston's wealthy ally had come to control so much of their lives, just as Randolph once feared. The war had ruined so many marriages, but Randolph argued that theirs could be salvaged, if only she believed in him.

As they drove a sedan into the countryside, however, Randolph got lost, and Pamela slowly came to her senses. She realized he was no longer the charismatic Adonis figure of his youth, but a lonely, bloated thirty-seven-year-old man with receding gray hair and an uncertain future, who seemed not to have learned any lessons from the past. For all his kindnesses, Randolph could easily revert to being a self-centered lout, looking for a maid rather than a wife. No matter how vulnerable she might feel, Pamela concluded that she was better off without him.

Memories of Kick remained buried with her at Chatsworth. With no more familial ties in London, Joe and Rose Kennedy focused their attention almost exclusively on Jack's career in America and the admirable lives of their other children—such as Robert, for whom England was a more distant memory. "He [Bobby] is just starting off and has the difficulty of trying to follow two brilliant brothers, Joe and Jack," the senior Kennedy wrote to Beaverbrook in 1948, thanking him for an encouraging note sent to his third son. "That in itself is quite a handicap, and he is making a good battle of it."

Jack's memories of Kick and Joe Jr. in England taught him to embrace the immediacy of life, rather than any doctor's prediction of imminent death. No one had believed in Jack more than his favorite sister, Kick. He had trouble sleeping at night, dreaming about her. "If something happens to you or somebody in your family who is miserable anyway, whose health is bad, or who has a chronic disease or something, that's one thing," Jack explained years later to James MacGregor Burns. "But, for someone who is living at their peak, then to get cut off—that's the shock."

Jack returned to London that summer but found it too wrenching to visit Kick's grave at Chatsworth, which bore the epitaph "Joy She Gave, Joy She Has Found" etched on her tombstone. It fell to Jack to help settle Kick's estate. He sorted through various entanglements of his sister's life even more complicated than his own. After meeting with Kick's housekeeper, learning more details of his sister's love affair with Fitzwilliam, he instructed, "We will not mention her again." In years to come, the loss of Kathleen remained too painful for Joe and Rose Kennedy to discuss among themselves or with others, including their children. Rose turned again to her Church for solace and, ironically, relied on her newfound friendship with the Devonshires, the Protestants she once dreaded as in-laws, to settle the remaining loose ends of Kick's life. "We have received most of the things in America, except two pictures given to her by Pamela Churchill," Rose told a lawyer disposing of Kick's belongings in London. "I believe the Duchess of Devonshire is holding them for me." Without the deep faith his wife sustained, Joe never felt more despondent. The grand dreams built around his most stellar children no longer existed. "The sudden death of young Joe and Kathleen within a period of three years has left a mark on me that I find very difficult to erase," Joe explained to Beaverbrook. "What a horrible mess the world is in. I am afraid I see very little hope on the horizon."

At Christmas that year, when Pamela Churchill contacted him, Joe Kennedy was still morose. Yet he tried acting cheery for his daughter's friend, giving out his overfamiliar brand of fatherly advice. "I am afraid that Palm Beach is never going to be the same without Kick," he confided. "Of course, I hear about you every now and then, but usually that some rich fellow is passionately in love with you. I don't blame them, but it is about time you gave some of these Americans a chance. Unless you hurry, there won't be any rich ones left."

36

Warrior Historians

The old boy, dutiful as ever on his seventy-fourth birthday, walked quietly into the House of Commons to take his usual place. Until that moment in November 1948, the parliamentary session had been lulled into slumber by a Labour Party member's dull questioning of the minister for "town and country planning." As Winston Churchill shuffled toward his seat, every Englishman in the chamber suddenly broke into cheers, giving him a standing ovation.

No one offered any proclamations or speeches, nor did they have to. Churchill's newly published wartime memoir, *The Second World War, Volume 1: The Gathering Storm*, reminded them of what Winston had done for their nation. The applause seemed a graceful note of thanks for this man of history, still living in their midst but seemingly in retreat. On this sentimental day, his colleagues didn't realize how much these printed words about the past would reenergize Churchill and point him toward the future. *The Gathering Storm*—printed in England and the United States, with excerpts in *Life* magazine, the *New York Times*, and the *London Daily Telegraph*—turned his rendition of the world's most monstrous conflict into a personal triumph. As always, Churchill presented history as a morality tale: a battle of eternal verities, of courage and rectitude rewarded, of embattled democracies valiantly facing evil despots, and of individual vision and daring as the truest test of greatness.

Following his sharp rebuke at the 1945 polls, Churchill once more transformed defeat through his mastery of language. While composing at his Chartwell desk or dictating from bed, he could build "an impalpable crystal sphere around one of interests and ideas," he described. "In a sense, one felt like a goldfish in a bowl; but in this case, the goldfish made his own bowl." Winston's prolific literary production—more than two million words over his lifetime—aided his return to 10 Downing Street, just as his 1930s writings had led him to become prime minister the first time around. Writing books remained for Winston an instrument both of power and of indelible self-expression. "Words are the only things that last forever," he explained.

Over the next five years, *The Second World War* appeared in four successive volumes, like sizeable waves upon the public's consciousness. With his team of researchers and typists, Churchill also published *A History of the English-Speaking Peoples*, the book he'd begun in the late 1930s but set aside when he became prime minister. In his own style of romantic formalism, Churchill walked readers through a vast time period, from Caesar's invasions of Britain before the birth of Christ to the beginnings of the Great War. Stressing his Anglo-American roots, he wrote extensively about the U.S. Civil War and Lincoln's admirable qualities as a leader. With an empathy borne of his own experience, Churchill described the beleaguered American president at war: "It is sometimes necessary at the summit of authority to bear with the intrigues of disloyal colleagues, to remain calm when others panic, and to withstand popular outcries. All this Lincoln did." Writing allowed Churchill, during the miserable approach of Hitler's war machine, to consider the heroic Joan of Arc, the legendary War of the Roses, and other redemptive moments from the past. History provided ballast for Winston in assessing his own world of constant upheavals. "On the whole I think I would rather have lived through our lot of troubles than any of the others," he admitted to Lord Beaverbrook, "though I must place on record my regret that the human race ever learned to fly."

Critics later complained that Churchill emphasized the impact of the British Empire chauvinistically, at the expense of the rest of the world. In his Anglicized portrayal of America, observed author Peter Clarke, Churchill "unthinkingly talked up the extent to which a common ancestry was actually the experience of a large proportion of American citizens," ignoring the millions of immigrants from ethnic groups, including those such as the Kennedys from Ireland. Labour opponent Clement Attlee quipped that Winston should have called this impressionistic work "Things in History Which Interested Me." But as biographer Paul Johnson later explained, Churchill revealed "a historian's mind, eager to grapple with facts, actualities, to answer the who, how, where, when questions, rather than a philosopher's, mesmerized by abstractions with their whys and wherefores."

By far, *The Gathering Storm* and his other World War II volumes had the most historical impact, largely because of Churchill's personal possession of many key government records from the conflict, copies of which he secured while in high office. These documents acted as fact-laden bricks for the edifice he constructed. In coming years, other popular histories, such as William L. Shirer's *The Rise and Fall of the Third Reich*, would generously cite Churchill's account. As the appraiser of the war he helped engineer, Winston alone decided who would wear the white hats and the black ones in his good-versus-evil drama, even among the Allies. *The Gathering Storm* would bolster Churchill's contention that this deadly conflict was "an unnecessary war," caused by the blunders of his prime minister predecessors, Stanley Baldwin and particularly Neville Chamberlain. In seeking peace at Munich, Chamberlain had committed a "long series of miscalculations, and misjudgments of men and facts," Churchill declared, opening the door to Hitler's rapid rearmament and aggressive march through Europe. Though the book was sold as the definitive account of the war, not everyone agreed with its conclusions.

Former ambassador Joseph P. Kennedy, still resentful of his "appeaser" label, criticized Churchill's book publicly at a time when most were hailing it as a masterpiece. "The significance that will be attached to Winston Churchill's memoirs leads me to observe that they should be handled with great care," Joe warned in a lengthy September 1948 letter to the *New York Times*. "They are replete with serious inaccuracies on the basis of which judgments are made that are unfair to individuals and events." Kennedy's harsh and prickly rebuke appeared only four months after his daughter Kathleen's death, when the former ambassador had thanked Churchill for his kind sympathy note. Now a long-held animus emerged in public. Kennedy defended his deceased friend Chamberlain against Churchill's hypocritical attacks and called "somewhat more perverse" Churchill's distortion of a speech by Home Secretary Samuel Hoare. "Numerous" other Churchill judgments "suffer from the same cavalier treatment of recorded facts," Kennedy charged.

Perhaps most revealingly, Kennedy indicated Churchill had access to many confidential documents still out of bounds, under secrecy laws, to other historians, which had granted the former prime minister an unchallenged role as the arbiter of this prewar era. Winston could not be trusted with the truth, not without steering it to his own advantage with overhyped prose, Kennedy suggested. "Churchill's misquotations of documents that are public make it difficult for one to rely on his quotations from documents that are not generally available," Kennedy concluded. "Other facts not yet made public may further bring into question Mr. Churchill's position as a raconteur of history. They will not, of course, derogate from the vividness of his style."

A month later, on his father's behalf, Randolph Churchill replied with his own blast at Kennedy's "serious and offensive allegations." The same young man who had recently stood at the gravesite of Kathleen, who had once asked Ambassador Kennedy for marriage advice, now charged in the *Times* that Kennedy's letter was written in "so jumbled and incoherent a fashion that it is difficult to judge what it is all about." He rebuked Kennedy's criticisms with a lengthy letter of his own that quoted from his father's book. But Randolph, the editor of an earlier volume of his father's wartime speeches, did concede two errors of fact—including the misreporting of the date for a speech Chamberlain made on March 14, 1939, in the House of Commons; his father's cited date, March 12, was a day Parliament would have been closed for Sunday religious observance. In the *Times,* Randolph never called the ambassador an appeaser, as he did in private, but implied that the world would be worse off if Kennedy's wrongheaded proscriptions had been heeded. "Future historians may perhaps decide that it was lucky for the world that Mr. Churchill did not often make mistakes less easily corrected," Randolph ended.

Privately Kennedy sought to rally the support of Chamberlain's widow in this debate, without success. He sent her a copy of his *New York Times* rebuttal and attached a letter complaining about "the misinformation that surrounds Munich and its aftermath." He noted Lord Halifax recently voiced similar concerns about Churchill's portrayal of the prewar era and felt that "those of us who participated in it had a responsibility to do something about it" by objecting to Churchill's account. His *Times* letter was too brief to counter all Winston's errors, he claimed; "that must be left to a later day."

Ground fire between the Churchill and Kennedy camps emerged again in 1952, when Randolph complained that *Time* magazine had referred to Czechoslovakia as Britain's ally prior to the war. "Though some of us thought at the time of Munich that it was in Britain's interest to fight in defence of Czechoslovakia's freedom, our country had no more moral or legal obligation to do so than had the United States," Randolph wrote to *Time* in June 1952. "The 'holier than thou' attitude adopted by some Americans towards the English in regard to Munich is wholly unwarranted, the more so since—a fact seldom adverted to in the United States—President Roosevelt was among those who sent a telegram to Signor Mussolini congratulating him on the calling of the Munich Conference."

As if to pick a fight, Congressman John F. Kennedy, serving as a surrogate for his father in a similar way, replied that Randolph was in error. "President Roosevelt never sent congratulations to Mussolini for arranging the Munich Conference, as alleged by Randolph Churchill," wrote JFK to *Time* the following month. "The President's telegram to Mussolini on Sept. 27 was a final appeal asking Mussolini to intervene with Hitler." To back up his point in this internecine debate, Jack quoted from Winston's book *The Gathering Storm* and said that "the illustrious father of Mr. [Randolph] Churchill has admitted that Great Britain was deeply involved."

The lingering wartime acrimony between the two families was never more on display than in this exchange.

For years, Joe Kennedy planned his own historical account, a memoir of his tenure as U.S. ambassador leading up to the war, but the book never materialized. Since leaving London, the former ambassador had continued his gadfly-like array of intense, often contradictory political views, increasingly out of step with those of his sons and the rest of the Democratic Party. In 1945 he chastised Harold Laski for suggesting that capitalism was dead in America and should be replaced with socialism. But then, in 1947, while in Palm Beach with Bernard Baruch and their friend *New York Times* columnist Arthur Krock, Kennedy floated a unique idea in opposition to President Truman's active policy of containment against communism. "Kennedy had his own proposal," *Time* magazine reported. "Let Communism spread, meanwhile keep the U.S. fat. After the little nations had a bellyful of Stalin's totalitarianism they would renounce it and rush joyfully to the U.S." Though Kennedy may have been right about the long-term prospects for the Soviet Bloc, such isolationist "let 'em go to hell" ideas at the height of the Cold War underlined to many why Joe shouldn't be president.

In coming up with his own lessons drawn from World War II, Joe Kennedy believed in a strong fortress-like defense for America, with few, if any, foreign entanglements. "To prevent World War III, we should keep our military forces strong, work with Great Britain, support Nationalist China, encourage a Western European bloc—and tell the Russians exactly where we stand," he wrote in the March 18, 1946, issue of *Life* magazine, soon after Churchill's "Iron Curtain" speech. Approvingly, Kennedy even quoted Churchill's description of the Soviet Union as a "riddle wrapped in a mystery inside an enigma." But by December 1950, he renounced "suicidal" U.S. foreign aid that seemed useless in preventing another worldwide conflagration or building allies. "Where are we now? What have we in return for this [postwar] effort? Friends? We have far fewer friends than we had in 1945," Kennedy complained at a University of Virginia Law School forum. "In Europe they are still asking for our dollars but what kind of friendship have we bought there?"

In Kennedy's view, virtually nothing seemed worth expending American lives and treasure. He urged a quick withdrawal from the Korean War. Berlin, divided among the Allies, wasn't worth going to war over with the Russians, he said. "It may be that Europe for a decade or a generation will turn Communistic," he conceded. "But in doing so, it may break of itself as a unified force . . . This policy will, of course, be criticized as appeasement. No word is more mistakenly used . . . I can recall only too well the precious time bought by Chamberlain at Munich. I applauded that purchase then; I would applaud it today."

To secure a place in history, or least provide his own version of events, Kennedy began preparing a memoir of his London years with the help of syndicated newspaper columnist Paul Mallon. Like Churchill, Kennedy kept personal copies of many important documents but also maintained a diary, kept correspondence, and wrote lengthy recollections to serve as the foundation for a future book. His press aide at the embassy, Harold Hinton, a former *New York Times* reporter, huddled together fragments of this early work, intended to be a fond, proud testament to his appointment as the first Irish Catholic to the Court of St. James's. But after his stormy departure from the Roosevelt administration, Kennedy wanted vindication and his own form of revenge. The early prewar drafts, his granddaughter Amanda Smith later described, began "as a breezy chronicle of the new ambassador's first forays into international politics and society," but soon turned bitter. The final editions of this work, Smith said, "would emerge after the war in large part as a careful accounting of what he had come to see as the Roosevelt administration's increasing circumvention, intentional public humiliation and general ill usage of its ambassador in London as Europe staggered toward war." Most pointedly, Kennedy wanted Mallon to show readers that Roosevelt and Churchill had lied to get the United States into war.

Over the telephone with the former ambassador, Mallon agreed to ghostwrite the book for an upfront five-thousand-dollar payment. As he sorted through Kennedy's papers, however, Mallon found that the task of making an acceptable memoir was becoming increasingly impossible. In his version, Kennedy insisted that FDR had supported the 1939 Munich Agreement more than the public realized. He believed Churchill had "deceived" the French and was less than honest about Dunkirk. But most problematic was Kennedy's account of the 1940 Tyler Kent spying affair inside his own embassy, which his notes indicated "had never been related fully."

The Tyler Kent case reemerged as a point of contention after the war, between the Democratic Truman administration and isolationist Republicans in the Senate. Following a five-year stay in a British jail, the former embassy code clerk had been deported back to America, where he alleged that he'd been imprisoned to keep the secret 1940 Roosevelt-Churchill correspondence from being revealed to the public.

State Department officials didn't provide details of the case until September 1944, after Hitler's defeat, when they said Kent likely would have been found guilty of treason had the United States been at war when he was arrested. The cloak-and-dagger narrative of Kent (copying documents late at night in Kennedy's embassy) "read like an espionage thriller," the *New York Times* reported.

Arriving home in December 1945, Kent stood next to his mother and declared that he had had a "moral right" to make copies of the FDR-Churchill correspondence, which he'd intended to supply to isolationist-minded senators. "He might have kept us out of the war at a saving of God knows how many lives and prevented the horrors of the cold war with Stalin and his successors," conservative columnist Westbrook Pegler later wrote of Kent. Though Kennedy had shared the aim of keeping America out of the war, he had no intention of supporting his clerk's betrayal. He called Kent's claims "all pure unadulterated bunk" and rejected his demand for an apology for his having waived Kent's diplomatic immunity, thus allowing the British prosecution. "As far as withdrawing anything I have ever said about him, the answer to that is 'nuts,' " Kennedy said defiantly.

Yet, as his private papers show, Kennedy remained concerned about the Kent case, especially its long-term impact on his family's reputation. Even Churchill was drawn into the debate. When Winston visited Florida in January 1946, Senate GOP members of a Pearl Harbor investigating committee asked the former prime minister to testify about Tyler Kent's claims and "if some parallel British-American actions had in fact been agreed on" prior to the war. Winston deflected the offer as a nuisance not worthy of comment. Joe Kennedy tried to steer a midline course as both a defender and revisionist of what happened in those waning days of his ambassadorship. In drafts of his memoir, he denied Kent's assertion that there was ever a note sent by Churchill to FDR saying, "Were I to become Prime Minister of Britain, we could control the world." Yet any Kennedy memoir, prepared by the best ghostwriter money could buy, still faced a hard time trying to cast the Kent fiasco in any favorable light.

Eventually, Joe reached out to his friend Beaverbrook for help in getting a transcript copy of the secret spy trial against Kent in England. In a November 1950 letter to Max, Joe admitted the press "has always made something terribly diabolical about the Tyler Kent case and the only reason it did not create a smear against me was because I was able to smash back at Kent rather strongly. Of course, it may be impossible to get any of this material, but the story will never be correctly put forth unless I have it in my possession. Whether I use it or not is a different matter. Of course I would like to use it, but I would be satisfied to have it and use it for my protection when I really go after Kent. Can you help me?"

A year later, Kennedy again pressed Beaverbrook, the best fixer he knew in London, for results, after he assigned a reporter to do his sleuthing. "Have you been able to dig anything up for me?" Joe inquired in November 1951. "I hate to bother you but this is one of the cases that some day I am going to have difficulty with and I would like to be as well protected as I can be." Beaverbrook didn't have any luck in obtaining this secret trial transcript and told Kennedy that "the Tyler Kent business will have to stand over for the present."

Kennedy's intention of following in Churchill's footsteps with a memoir steeped in World War II drama fell by the wayside, however. No matter how great his desire to aggrieve the wrongs to his reputation or the humilities he felt had been inflicted by Roosevelt, he knew that a published book would dredge up embarrassing facts that could only hurt him. Unlike Winston, Joe didn't have possession of needed documents to cast a compelling version of events, to spin his own version of history with himself in a central, heroic role. Instead, he deferred to his son's rising political ambitions and to the unflattering reality about his past.

For at least two months in early 1948, Paul Mallon reviewed rough drafts and asked Kennedy's secretary to provide more documents, if possible, to bolster his contentions, just as Churchill's memoir relied on his former public papers. "Out of the events with which we are dealing came the war and the unsatisfactory peace," Mallon explained. "The question which we must answer in the book is Why? You must begin to read your documents and your opinions toward answering this overall question."

After several weeks of work, however, Mallon received bad news from the ex-ambassador's office. Kennedy called his ghostwriter and told him he'd decided to suspend the project after the start of the first draft. The ambassador told Mallon he could hang on to the five-thousand-dollar payment. But the ghostwriter refused.

"I cannot accept payment, as I told him on the telephone, for work which did not meet his satisfaction," said Mallon, in returning the check and documents to a Kennedy aide. "I guaranteed that it would . . . His graciousness in offering it nevertheless cannot relieve me, in good conscience, from my obligation."

From time to time, Joe thought of reviving the project, but ultimately Kennedy's memoir never appeared, and his unpublished manuscript remained secreted away with the rest of his personal papers.

Randolph Churchill hoped to gain permission to write his father's life story, the official biography of one of the grandest English lives ever, but first he needed to establish himself as a reliable person in his father's eyes and not just simply as a facile writer.

For more than a decade, Randolph had pondered the idea (and the sizeable literary riches it might bring him), though the reaction of his father and potential book publishers seemed uncertain. In 1932 a group of publishers dangled an advance of four hundred pounds for what Randolph described as a "light biography" of his father, whose political career then seemed virtually over. But others advised Randolph not to squander his chance. "I think it's a great opportunity either for brilliant success or ghastly failure," warned one friendly publisher. "The money does not count in proportion to the fame or infamy that will attach to you. Do it. Don't take a *penny* (double underlined) till you deliver the manuscript and *before delivering it submit it to at least two people*." By the late 1940s, Winston was still wary about handing over his life and valuable papers. Randolph's attempt to gain his father's permission and cooperation to accomplish what Winston had a generation earlier— that is, write a magisterial biography of his father that would help cast his own public image—remained painfully amiss. In effect, Randolph would have to audition for the role as his father's biographer.

Following his messy breakup with Pamela, Randolph's life wandered aimlessly, often lacking contact with his own son, Winston. Constantly away, Pamela wasn't much of a parent, either; she left bringing up their son to a nanny. Pamela moved between love affairs with wealthy Aly Khan and handsome Italian millionaire industrialist Gianni Agnelli, enjoying a lifestyle that Randolph Churchill could never have afforded with his journalist's income. When little Winston came to visit in the South of France, his mother's lovers bought him his own motorboat to putter about in. "I can't afford to give my son motor boats, but you have friends who can," Randolph said jealously to her. As Pamela recalled later, "Kids become battlegrounds."

Ironically, in a failed attempt to marry Agnelli, Pamela became interested in Catholicism and decided to convert, even though she'd never walk down the aisle with Gianni. Biographer Christopher Ogden said Pamela's spiritual "knowledge about the religion came primarily from three Catholic friends": Clarissa Churchill, the daughter of Winston's brother Jack, who had married a Catholic; Hugh Fraser, the Tory MP who was a friend of Jack Kennedy; and Kick Kennedy, who had clung to her Catholic heritage throughout her tempestuous love affairs. Pamela also was impressed with Clare Boothe Luce's conversion, encouraged by Monsignor Fulton Sheen in New York. Although both women were whispered about for their affairs of the flesh, Ogden wrote, "Pamela discovered, as Clare Boothe had, that her new Catholicism offered a tremendous solace and a sense of strength." When Pam later decided to marry Hollywood producer Leland Hayward (already with a wife and children), she enlisted Joe Kennedy's help with New York archbishop Francis Spellman to get her future husband an annulment. Kennedy was impressed with Clare's spiritual devotion. When Clare sent a heartfelt note after Kick's death, Joe wrote back, "Your cable was a help on a dark day."

Marriage offered the promise of a steadying influence for Randolph in 1948 as he wed June Osborne, a beautiful but high-strung woman eleven years his junior. Clementine and Winston embraced their son's remarriage plans, without the brazen doubts expressed by Randolph's pals at White's. "I do not know the young lady but she must be possessed of magnificent courage," Evelyn Waugh suggested, in his humorous, backhanded way. He had read the wedding announcement in the newspaper and asked Randolph to "give me the opportunity of doing homage to the heroine." Waugh teased Randolph about his reputation. A few months earlier, he pointed out, the White's crowd had speculated that "you are entangled with a woman and once more about to become a father." Waugh said he immediately rose to his defense: "I have loyally maintained that you are doing time in Sing Sing or El Cantara for some minor homicide & that you have chosen to suffer under a pseudonym rather than bring further disgrace on your name."

After Waugh met June for lunch two weeks later, he sent her a friendly-sounding note in his ever-complicated way, offering advice about Randolph and his father:

> I have known him for a long time; perhaps before you were
> born, certainly before you could read & write, and have always
> felt that he had a unique natural capacity for happiness which,

one way and another, has never yet been fully developed. I am sure you will be able to do this for him. He is essentially a domestic and homeloving character who has never had a home. My observation has taught me that the best possible guide for choosing a husband is to go for the child of a happy marriage. That has been a huge source of strength to Randolph's father & I am sure it will be so to him.

Waugh, of course, knew nothing about June, who soon exhibited her own emotional problems. At a party shortly before their wedding, Randolph slipped a few Benzedrine tablets to her so she could overcome the effects of the flu. Instead, with a few drinks, she began to hallucinate wildly. She screamed that she wanted to commit suicide, and ran to the banks of a nearby river, where Randolph caught up and tried to stop her. June hit him repeatedly with her fists. Eventually, as Waugh recalled, she settled down, weeping on Randolph's shoulder as he kissed and comforted her. When the police arrived, June jumped into a car and ordered the driver to whisk her away. Before the night was through, Randolph and Waugh went out on their own, for more drinks at White's.

One year after the couple's wedding—attended by all the Churchills, including little Winston—their only child, Arabella, was born, in December 1949. At the christening, Randolph's old friend Seymour Berry stood as godfather. Beneath their joy, however, more difficulty brewed among the parents. "Randolph, June and little W came for the night—All passed off well, but there is evident tension," Winston relayed to Clementine, away on a tour in Italy. "She [June] never looked prettier, but is on the verge of tears. R[andolph] I thought seemed 'masterful.' However I think they mean to have another try."

Along with Randolph's choice of wives, Winston sometimes wondered about his son's friends, notably Evelyn Waugh. For all his native intelligence and lancing wit, Waugh could be both cruel and jealous of

Randolph. Evelyn could sting like a school bully poking fun at someone less nimble. With marksman-like accuracy, he knew how to hit
Randolph's emotional spots, especially vulnerabilities about his father.
Yet when convenient, Waugh readily cashed in on the Churchill name.
Using Randolph as a willing agent, Waugh had met Clare Boothe Luce,
who eventually arranged for the novelist to write an extended essay
about American Catholics for *Life* magazine. With the lucrative assignment in hand, Waugh dashed off a note to Randolph: "Thanks to your
kind offices I am off to USA as soon as the Luce family can get me a
cabin."

The elder Churchill may have known or suspected how bitterly
Waugh felt about his political actions, especially in Yugoslavia, where
the once-friendly Tito became a Soviet Communist puppet persecuting
the Catholic Church. But he questioned the loyalty of his son's friend.
After Waugh helped Randolph get into the posh Beefsteak Club, the
novelist sent the younger Churchill a cheeky note of congratulations; it
claimed to know why his friend Randolph had been granted member-
ship. "The Duke of Devonshire sent a message that your chief characteristic was pious deference to older men; I said you would not use the
club very often," Waugh quipped.

Although Winston once shared this same sort of humor with his
own contemporaries, razor tongues such as Max Beaverbrook and Lord
Birkenhead, he didn't share Randolph's delight with Waugh's letter. His
father was "quite taken aback," Randolph recalled.

"I thought this man was your friend," Winston inquired of his son.

"So he is," Randolph answered, defensive once again. "I've lots of
other very funny sorts of friends."

In recalling this conversation years later, Randolph explained that
his father "had a naive view about friendship; it was all or nothing."

So it was in deciding on a future official biographer. Gaining Winston's total, unreserved approval to tell his life story would have to wait.

37

Great Contemporaries

Kay Halle's spacious redbrick house at 3001 Dent Place in Georgetown was a perfect haven for the powerful and well connected from both sides of the Atlantic. In 1952 the Democratic era of Roosevelt and his successor, Truman, was ending, with the election of former general Dwight D. Eisenhower, a Republican, as president. But the good times at Halle's place remained distinctly bipartisan.

Visiting British friends often joined Halle in Washington, along with influential Americans who had worked with her during the war in the Office of Strategic Services. CBS newsman Ed Murrow, diplomat Averell Harriman, writer Clare Boothe Luce, historian Arthur M. Schlesinger Jr., and dozens of other notables turned her comfortable place into a salon. "It was," she liked to say, "the greatest collection of brains ever gathered under one roof."

The wealthy department store heiress had retained her sharp, angular beauty and the vibrant charm that attracted so many men. Former lovers such as Randolph Churchill, her would-be fiancé, were now friends who never lost touch. "Roy Jenkins, a very brilliant and charming right wing Labour M.P. is arriving in Washington," alerted Randolph, suggesting Kay invite Jenkins over to her home. "You might ask a few friends to meet him, the Alsops [syndicated columnist Joseph Alsop and his brother, Stewart], [historian Arthur M.] Schlesinger, and of course Scotty [*New York Times* Washington columnist James 'Scotty' Reston]."

On the Washington social circuit in the 1950s, the Kennedys were among other old intimates whom Halle saw regularly. Joe's sons increasingly made their presence known in town. No longer was Jack Kennedy a scrawny, sickly boy reading Churchill's *The World Crisis* in his hospital bed, but rather a successful U.S. senator from Massachusetts with his eye on the presidency. "I was very impressed with the way he had developed and his independence of thought," she recalled.

During a cocktail party at journalist Drew Pearson's house, Joe Kennedy waved over Halle to a corner, where he was already huddled in a vigorous debate with his second-oldest son.

"Kay, I wish you would tell Jack that he's going to vote the wrong way," the senior Kennedy insisted, displaying the same frank cockiness she admired when they first met during the 1932 Roosevelt campaign. "I think Jack is making a terrible mistake."

Halle long ago forgot the contents of the legislative bill, but she remembered how well Jack floor-managed his mercurial father.

"Now look here Dad, you have your political views and I have mine," Jack countered, with his brother Robert silently by his side. "I'm going to vote exactly the way I feel I must vote on this. I've great respect for you, but when it comes to voting, I'm voting my way."

Between Jack and his father, there was none of the tensions, recriminations, or angry words that so often marred the Churchill exchanges, as Halle witnessed firsthand. Winston Churchill and his only son still did not share a singular goal as the Kennedys did. Rather, the Churchills remained a union of competing interests so long as the senior septuagenarian was still a top player in the political arena. "I always believed in staying in the pub until closing time," Winston quipped about his future.

Jack Kennedy's campaigns took center stage because his father realized there was no hope for a political comeback of his own. The younger Kennedy's stunning 1952 upset victory against Republican incumbent U.S. senator Henry Cabot Lodge Jr. proved a great turning point—a vast sea change, as one of the last Protestant Brahmins to hold statewide power finally gave way to their longtime Irish-Catholic rivals from the Democratic Party. This Senate race reprised another battle between these two family dynasties: Jack's grandfather, Boston mayor John F. "Honey Fitz" Fitzgerald, lost a 1916 Senate bid against Lodge's namesake grandfather. In the art of politics, Jack showed a golden touch, just as Joe had in making money. When the Kennedys differed, as they displayed that night while Halle watched, Joe seemed more bemused than infuriated by his sons. "Well, Kay, that's why I settled a million dollars on each one of them," Joe boasted, referring to the trust funds he'd set up for his children, "so they could spit in my eye if they wished."

While Joe Kennedy could revert to the crass stereotype of an Irish hack, his son impressed with his quick wit and coolheaded, sophisticated presence. Halle compared Jack's "reserved" style to that of an English squire. Jack had grown into a handsome, complicated man with many sides to his winning personality. From his father, Halle knew of Jack's constant illnesses, his life-threatening operations, and she realized how much Jack could mask his pain. She witnessed his steely determination at a Washington party when he leaned against a chair and it suddenly moved. He collapsed to the floor, landing on his spine. "He turned white as a sheet," Halle recalled. "He rose, righted himself and went right on talking to me. I knew that he must have been in desperate pain, but he just went straight on with the conversation. I thought that was the most remarkable demonstration of his iron courage and power to dominate the physical with his will." He brought that remarkable will to politics in his own unique way, she said. In a predominantly white Anglo-Saxon Protestant nation, Jack Kennedy seemed a more assimilated brand of Irish Catholic, a few generations and millions of dollars away from the immigrant ship. "I always had a curious feeling about him that he had a sense of his own destiny in a curious way, that, perhaps, he was not going to have as long a time as he might wish to do all he wanted to do," Halle recalled. "There was some curious sense in him that every moment seemed keenly important and was not to be wasted."

Three blocks from Kay Halle's house, Jack Kennedy rented an apartment in Georgetown, living the life of an eligible bachelor whom many women found appealing. "He was the golden boy . . . every girl in Massachusetts wanted to date him, and I wasn't any exception," recalled Margaret Coit, winner of the 1951 Pulitzer Prize for her biography of John C. Calhoun. As a potential girlfriend, Coit would see another side of Jack's personality, different from that which his father's friend Kay Halle observed.

In the spring of 1953, Coit came to Washington to research a new book about Bernard Baruch, and feigned a reason to interview the thirty-five-year-old Massachusetts senator. "I thought up what possible excuse I would have to meet him because he was not a friend of Baruch's although his father had been," recalled Coit, who'd read Jack's *Why England Slept.* Previously she'd tried asking Jack's father about Baruch, but the former ambassador was appalled by her sleuthing. "He frightened me to death, kind of barking at me, roaring at me," Coit recalled. Her biography never mentioned Baruch's financial involvements with Joe Kennedy—including their Brooklyn Manhattan Transit Corporation stock investment together. She spoke with the younger Kennedy in the senator's outer office, where they discussed his recollections of England before the war. "I took down my notes, but all the while he was looking me over," she recalled. When they finished, Kennedy invited her to a party a few days later at his Georgetown town house, where he barely paid any attention to her, lost in conversation with another senator. At night's end, Jack put his arm around Coit and said aloud to his sisters at the party, "Isn't she the prettiest thing you ever did see?" Margaret, though only two years younger, blushed with embarrassment. His sisters sighed, perhaps for Coit's benefit, and wished Jack "would meet some nice girl."

Coit didn't hear from Kennedy for a few more days, not until he asked her again to his office. He quizzed her about Baruch and offered "something very penetrating about Clare Boothe Luce's private life and a little malicious." Then Jack sat next to Coit on an office love seat, put his head back, and nearly passed out. "It was as if all the energy had drained out of him," she recalled. "I thought he was going to faint, and I was so scared I didn't know what to do." As he recovered, they agreed Jack was too tired to go out on a date that night and instead would drive her home. Kennedy stood up gingerly and reached for his crutches, leaning against the wall. Together they walked through the empty corridors of the Senate Office Building and got into Jack's open convertible with its faded blue paint and fair share of dents. They drove wildly through the Washington streets until they reached the rooming house where Coit was staying. She invited him in, thinking he might want to rest for a moment. Inside, Jack collapsed on the living room sofa, and then tried to drag Coit down beside him. "Don't be so grabby," she said, moving away. "This is only our first date. We have plenty of time."

Kennedy lifted his head and, for a moment, stared at her with his penetrating gray eyes.

"But I can't wait, you see, I'm going to grab everything I want," Kennedy insisted. "You see, I haven't any time."

Coit didn't understand this driven, very complicated young politician and the aggressive way he apparently treated women. "We had been talking about books and ideas and my concepts of the books on Baruch, and then he had seen me as one kind of person," she recalled.

"He had seen me as a mind; and now he saw me just as something female. He couldn't fit the two together, and it was as if he were two parts. He was like a fourteen year old high school football player on the make; and he was like an elder statesman of sixty in his intellectual process—the two together and it was the cold machine-like quality that scared me so."

Eventually, the young couple jumped back into Kennedy's convertible for another spin. This time, while driving along, Jack's mind returned to the world of books.

"My brother Bobby told me you had won the Pulitzer Prize," he said, with the wind rushing by, blowing through their hair. "You never told me that. You are very modest. I would rather win a Pulitzer Prize than be president of the United States."

They drove around some more until Jack's mind turned to another subject.

"Tell me something else," he said, with steering wheel in hand. "How did Bernard Baruch make his money?"

Still feeling feisty, Coit remembered Joe Kennedy's silence and tried to enlist his son in her literary cause. "Pretty much the way your own father made his, I would imagine," she replied drolly. "Why don't you ask him?"

Jack staked his own claim. "I want to make millions," he vowed. "I am going to outdo my father." When they drove past the White House, Jack appeared quite serious as he looked through the gates. "I am going to go there," he stated with determination.

Kennedy seemed surprised that Baruch had convinced Coit to write her next biography about him. "What I am interested in is me," he kidded. "Why don't you write a book about me?"

"You are not important enough yet," Coit replied.

Jack smiled, undaunted. "Well, you could put me in a book—*Men I Have Known*," he teased.

After a while, Jack dropped her off again at the rooming house and assured her, "I'll call you." Coit felt relieved. She had dated aggressive men but no one as erratic as Jack Kennedy. "It was the coldness that frightened me and the fact that he was out of a much more sophisticated background than anything that I knew," she recalled. "I just wanted out of there." She did take Kennedy's advice, however, and read Churchill's magnificent biography of Marlborough, Winston's glorious ancestor.

The day following her date with Jack, as part of her research for the Baruch book, Coit talked with Arthur Krock, the *New York Times* columnist who often flacked as Joe Kennedy's ghostwriter and political adviser and as a secret literary agent for his son. Krock had won a 1951 Pulitzer for his commentary, the same year as Coit did for her book. She mentioned to Krock that she'd met the young senator.

"John Kennedy—what a tragedy that boy is," Krock announced, mostly solemnly.

Surprised by his reaction, Coit asked the *Times* man to explain himself.

"Don't you know he is going to die?" he asked, incredulous at her ignorance.

Coit didn't believe him. "What are you talking about?" she demanded.

Krock remained quite resolute. "His father told me that he had only four years to live," he replied.

Suddenly, Jack's rash and seemingly inexplicable statements about impending doom and eternity made sense to her. "That explained a lot to me, particularly those things—'I am going to grab everything I want. You see, I haven't any time,'" she reflected decades later.

The grand style Churchill presented in his Marlborough biography inspired Jack Kennedy's sense of himself, of his view of great men seeking their destiny, of history made up of "heroism, romance and drama," as his daughter, Caroline, later described. Kennedy's congressional aide Mark Dalton remembered his enthusiasm for the Marlborough book, asking aloud, "Did you ever read anything like that in all your life?" Churchill's personal example also seemed to influence Kennedy, particularly his decision to marry only after he had established his public life in government. "I don't mean that he decided he'd marry when Churchill did, but I know he had decided that he wasn't going to get married terribly early," recalled his navy pal Chuck Spalding.

Not long after his encounter with Coit, Jack became engaged to Jacqueline Bouvier, a beautiful "Inquiring Photographer" for the *Washington Times-Herald* whom he had met several months earlier at a dinner party set up by friends. Bouvier shared his love of books, and her Catholic heritage made her an acceptable choice to both Jack's parents and his Boston Irish constituency. Their fashionable wedding and reception—at the Newport, Rhode Island, home of Jacqueline's mother and stepfather, Janet and Hugh Auchincloss—was touted in the media by the Kennedy publicity machine. The couple eventually moved to a rented house on Dent Place, in Georgetown, not far from Bobby and his wife, Ethel. With her wit and charm, Jackie seemed to fill the hole in Jack's heart left by his sister's death—"a substitute for Kick," said friends such as Chuck Spalding's wife, Betty, who had once roomed with Jackie in Washington. Columnist Joseph Alsop, a frequent guest in Kennedy social circles, said he "always felt that that time in England and Kick, to whom he was closer than any of the rest of his family, all this had more influence on him than most people thought." But Jackie later claimed her husband's affinity for Churchill and the British came more from his choice of reading material than from his actual time spent in London. One of the first books Jack gave his new bride was *Pilgrim's Way*, by John Buchan. "The part for which he cared most was a portrait of the brilliant Raymond Asquith—eldest son of the British Prime Minister—who was killed in action in World War I," Jackie later recalled. "The poignancy of men dying young always moved my husband—possibly because of his brother Joe dying in World War II."

Kennedy wasn't the only one who felt this way about this princely figure. Churchill prominently mentioned Asquith's death and his aplomb in life as part of a portrait of his father, British prime minister Herbert Henry Asquith, contained in his *Great Contemporaries* book. "Everything seemed easy to Raymond," described Winston, who met young Asquith near the French battlefront in December 1915, a few months before this "presumably invulnerable" young man was shot dead in war. "The brilliant epigram, the pungent satire, the sharp and not always painless rejoinder, a certain courtly but rather informal manner, distinguished in youth the son, as they had his father before him." Jack absorbed the lessons of Asquith's brief but brilliant life by reading both books, by Buchan and Churchill. (During the Great War, Buchan was friendly with Churchill while working at the Ministry of Information, but considered him "mischievous.") The style and format of Churchill's *Great Contemporaries* (which featured well-known figures from Hitler to FDR, Leon Trotsky to Lawrence of Arabia) would soon influence one of JFK's literary efforts, written during the mid-1950s, when he, too, confronted the prospect of an early death.

After his first year of marriage, Jack's deteriorating back required major surgery in New York, a 1954 operation dangerous enough that he was once again given last rites by a priest. "I can't go on like this," he told his new wife. Jackie Kennedy slowly grasped how much her husband's infirmities defined his existence. "I always thought of him as this enormously glamorous figure whom I married when he was thirty-six," she recalled. "I thought he'd had millions of gay trips to Europe, girls, dances, everything. And of course, he had done that, but I suppose what he meant was that he had been in pain so much."

During the long recuperative period, Jack tried to get his mind off his troubles by trying painting, just as Winston enjoyed at Chartwell, and by reading aloud from Churchill's *A History of the English-Speaking Peoples,* with what Jackie later called Winston's "wonderful sort of seraglio prose." Eventually, lying in his bed surrounded by books and research, Jack launched a Churchill-like book project published in 1956 as *Profiles in Courage,* which quickly led to literary fame. His language and tone bore a distinct resemblance to that in Churchill's *Great Contemporaries.* "Courage is rightly esteemed the first of human qualities because it is the quality which guarantees all others," Winston wrote in 1937. Two decades later, Kennedy began with "This is a book about the most admirable of human virtues—courage."

Profiles in Courage became a best-seller, extolling the fortitude shown in the U.S. Senate by such figures as John Quincy Adams, Sam Houston, and George Norris, the independent-minded Republican from Nebraska who supported Al Smith for president in 1928. Although Kennedy hatched the idea, his aide Ted Sorensen pulled together the research for the book, edited his longhand drafts, and provided a Churchillian polish. The book won the Pulitzer for biography in 1957, after Joe Kennedy pushed his friend Arthur Krock to lobby the board on his son's behalf. When newsman Drew Pearson suggested Sorensen had ghostwritten the book, Joe Kennedy erupted, threatening to sue. Jack objected, too—"I cannot let this stand," he told Clark Clifford, his father's lawyer. Jacqueline didn't speak to Sorensen for two years after rumors floated that he'd composed the whole thing. "I really saw Jack writing that book," she insisted, still upset long after the controversy faded. But true to form, Jack remained cool and showed none of the vehemence of his father and his wife. Somehow, he always evaded trouble, no matter what political difficulties or compromising personal problems befell him. "Remember I've always said he's a child of fate, and if he fell in a puddle of mud in a white suit he'd come up ready for a Newport ball," Joe explained to Jackie, advice from the old enabler to the new.

As his father once advised, writing a book kept his son in very good stead. *Profiles in Courage* would help set the stage for his presidential bid in 1960, a reminder that his Harvard-trained intellect made him something more than another Irish Paddy off the street. Even Margaret Coit was impressed, congratulating the senator on his prize.

"Thanks for thinking of me—but don't count on a repeat performance!" Kennedy wrote to his fellow Pulitzer winner on official Senate stationery. Scribbled next to his signature, Jack added a personal aside: "When are we going to meet again?"

38

Winners and Losers

"I would my father look'd but with my eyes."
—WILLIAM SHAKESPEARE, *A Midsummer Night's Dream*

At the Old Vic Theatre in 1953, moments before his performance in Shakespeare's *Hamlet* would begin, actor Richard Burton received unsettling news. Winston Churchill was in the audience.

"Do be good tonight, dear boy," the theater director admonished, "because the old man is in front."

Suddenly in terror, the young Welsh actor looked through a spy hole and spotted the prime minister. After six years as the opposition leader in Parliament, Churchill had returned to 10 Downing Street. He'd also just won the Nobel Prize in Literature for his lifetime devotion to memorable writing and rhetoric. For those like Burton, who came of age during the war, Churchill was a paterfamilias, an embodiment of the British Empire.

A bit buzzed from drink, Burton quickly doused his head in cold water, a necessary tonic "to bring myself to my senses." Every bristle of his hair seemed to stand up on its own until he flattened it with grease. Then he stepped out onto the stage to recite the Bard's words, keenly aware of his childhood hero in the front row.

As the play progressed, Burton could hear a murmuring in the darkness, a voice from the audience reciting every line of Hamlet just as he was saying it, word for word. "It was Churchill speaking the lines with me," he recalled, "and I could not shake him off." Burton sped up, slowed down—to no avail. When he tried cuts in the Bard's play to get Churchill to stop, he could hear a growl at the diversion. "He knew the play intimately," recalled Burton, who a decade later would perform *Camelot* in front of John F. Kennedy and his wife, Jacqueline. Eventually Burton learned that Churchill, the writer-statesman, knew several Shakespeare productions by heart.

At intermission, Burton spotted Churchill's empty seat and thought he'd left for the night. Backstage, however, the prime minister was waiting in his dressing room. The actor hoped Churchill might praise his performance, but instead the latter had been motivated by nature's demands.

"My Lord Hamlet, may I use your lavatory?" the Nobel winner beseeched. And without any shilly shally, he did.

Winston Churchill's return to power once again entailed a family drama, one of almost Shakespearean dimensions, played out with his son, Randolph, and the weight of his own ambitions.

Defying political expectations, Winston refused to be put out to pasture after his 1945 defeat. Nothing in his life indicated he would fade away. When reporters suggested a prized gray thoroughbred he owned, Colonist II, be retired to stud, the old warhorse in him seemed appalled by any such notion. "To stud?" he mocked. "And have it said that the Prime Minister of Great Britain is living on the immoral earnings of a horse?" Instead Churchill waited for the Labour Party to slip and for his Conservative Party to regain an advantage. In October 1951, at age seventy-six, Winston returned as prime minister, the fruits of a carefully engineered victory in which Labour gathered far more votes, but the Tories managed to gain more seats in the House of Commons.

Churchill had learned his lesson: in postwar England, he determined to be more accommodating than combative. "There are always a lot of bloody rows in politics—that's what politics is for," he explained. "A lot of fires blaze up, and it's my job to put them out. You get habituated to the heat." His return to power brought sweet vindication for a terribly bitter loss in 1945, without any illusions about voter whims. "I always remember," he explained, "if instead of making a political speech I was being hanged, the crowd would be twice as big."

While his father returned triumphantly as prime minister, Randolph's attempts to join him in Parliament failed. The longtime dream of two Churchills in the House of Commons, father and son, lingered. Despite Winston's campaigning for him, Randolph lost a 1950 by-election in Devonport, in southwest England, and then again, most decisively, in October 1951. In both contests, he faced Michael Foot, a former newspaper colleague turned Labour candidate. Foot portrayed him to the locals as a carpetbagger from Liverpool, while Randolph spoke as if a prince. Before one large crowd, gathered to see Winston as much as the candidate, Randolph joked in introducing his father: "He bustled in like something not merely from another world but another century, talking as if the place belonged to him, as the Churchills have often done, from the great Marlborough and his Duchess onwards." On a makeshift stage, nine-year-old Winston Spencer-Churchill, the son of Randolph and Pamela, sat next to his father. Young Winston beamed with a handsome smile and a full head of blond hair, just like Randolph once appeared in his youth. Now in his fortieth year, Randolph had thin hair, his jowls were plump, and his belly rounded. He no longer appeared a maverick full of potential but rather a middle-aged disappointment who had never lived up to his promise. His appeal remained rooted in his family name rather than his own deeds. In his introduction, his voice carried by loudspeakers to the crowd, he described his father as "all that is linked with the fortune, glory and romance of England and her Empire." After his first Devonport visit, Winston appeared again during the 1951 campaign, the same that had brought the Conservative Party back to power, but without success for his son.

The defeat in Devonport became Randolph's sixth and final attempt for public office. Despite his ancestral heritage and training, he didn't seem cut out for retail politics. He had spent most of the past twenty years as a freewheeling journalist seeking scoops and punchy phrases for Beaverbrook's newspapers rather than as a backbencher weighing his words and movements. "Along with his honesty ('Lies are so dull,' he would say) and his streaks of kindness, it was his reckless courage which shone most brightly," recalled Foot admiringly. Typical of his candor, Randolph infuriated the Oxford Union by vigorously opposing the debating society's motion that regretted "United States domination of the democratic world." In this debate, Randolph combated the familiar charge of Churchills as warmongers—just as he had in the 1930s, when he condemned Oxford Union members for a measure against fighting "for King and country" despite the Nazi threat. "The members of this house have since expunged that disgrace with their blood on a hundred battlefields," Randolph scolded and then provocatively urged them to "accept the fact that America is a greater nation."

Despite his brave façade, Randolph couldn't hide the emotional toll of his crushing loss. No longer would friends such as Evelyn Waugh make light of Randolph's travails. "Your failure and the generally wretched outcome of the election makes it more plain than ever that the present system wont & cant work in present conditions," Waugh wrote him. "This is not the moment for a dissertation on politics, but for a friend to tell you how much he grieves at your most undeserved misfortune."

The Churchill name that had once emboldened Randolph now seemed only to imprison him. No longer was he compared to Pitt the Younger, destined to march to the prime ministership. His father's appearing at campaigns on his behalf, applauded by the crowds, had a way of making Randolph seem weak and feckless. "Winston worshipped his son and was trying to, at every possible means, give his son any help or advantage that he could," said Pamela, who for years observed the dynamic between Churchill fathers and sons. "So much so that, in the end, it acted against poor Randolph because Randolph in turn worshipped his father. One thing he wanted to do was make his father proud of him."

However, Randolph enjoyed none of the organized family effort typical of John Kennedy's congressional campaigns, nor the marshaling of donations and political favors by his father, certainly not as Joe Kennedy did for his son. Except for the singular appearance by Winston in this race, Randolph found himself very much on his own.

Failure became the accursed word between them. Winston's disappointment in his son, at least as Randolph perceived it, was exacerbated by his electoral losses. The success of Winston's sons-in-law Christopher Soames, married to Mary, and Duncan Sandys, married to Diana, both elected to Parliament as Conservatives, only compounded Randolph's shortcomings. In an achingly candid letter in October 1952, Randolph begged his father for another chance, decrying Winston's view of him. "I realize too that you regard me as a failure & that you cannot disguise this view entirely successfully from other people," he wrote. "My view for what it's worth, is that I am not a failure in any terms."

Randolph sensed Winston no longer trusted his judgment and merely tolerated his son's presence. Randolph begrudged the paternal fondness and loyalty his father displayed toward older contemporaries such as Brendan Bracken and Anthony Eden—somewhat close to Randolph in age but not temperament. "I believe that a single episode with Anthony Eden in the Mediterranean (about which you were much too busy to understand the psychological background) has convinced you that I am wholly unfit to be in your company when persons of consequence are present," he argued in that lengthy letter, a *cri de coeur* to Winston. "But the fact that I am never invited when you have any official guests shows the world as well as myself how low a view you take of me."

In his painful self-appraisal, Randolph described himself as his father's creature, weaned on the jargon of political jousting and bon mots, once so encouraged by Winston. "I know that I often say provocative—& needlessly provocative—things," he explained. "But where, except at your table & at your feet did I learn to think that levity & frivolity & an unexpected heterodoxy were the proper terms . . ." Did Winston not remember how they'd enjoyed those dinners for great men's sons, the lectures in America, the debates at Oxford Union, and the ripostes in the press against Hitler and those bloody appeasers? Did he not remember Randolph's fierce, undying loyalty when Winston was in the 1930s political wilderness and his son's future seemed so bright? "Those days of our friendship & instinctive understanding are now nothing but precious memories—more irrevocably etched in my mind than any other experience," Randolph bemoaned. Yet now, when he opened his mouth about politics, Randolph claimed, his father's response was often abject rejection. "In place of the tolerant comprehension I knew, my portion is snubs & insults, flouts & jeers, cries of 'shut-up' which you never address to anyone else & which no-one else would ever address to me."

In withering detail, Randolph charted how their once-close relationship had changed dramatically since Winston realized his dream in 1940 to become prime minister. Randolph's rage seethed between each raw allegation in the letter: "It has been a growing sense of grief to me that ever since you first became Prime Minister you have repeatedly made it clear to me—& to others—that you no longer have that same desire for my company in private or in public which between 1923 & 1940 was the chief delight & pivot of my existence," he wrote. "Can't you understand the maladjustment, the frustration, yes even (recently) the jealousy that urges the bile of resentment when one's love is scorned as worthless & the person one loves scarcely troubles to hide from friend or foe the indifference or hostility which he feels?"

Randolph beseeched his father, upon whom he still so depended, to see things from his perspective and not merely his own. "I ask something now: that you should try to understand me as I am (and not as you imagine I am or think I ought to be)," he ended.

Winston tried to reconcile with his son by sending a generous gift for Christmas. He congratulated Randolph on his first book (not a compilation of his father's writings, as he'd done before), its publication timed to coincide with the 1953 coronation of Queen Elizabeth. But the return to 10 Downing demanded the full attention of Winston, who exuded the gratitude of a man given a second lease on political life. No longer would he beckon as a prophetic voice warning of doom. Instead Churchill's new administration sought a peaceful economic recovery for his war-torn nation, just as President Dwight Eisenhower favored in the United States during the early 1950s.

Humanity living under a nuclear cloud troubled Winston increasingly and prompted a change in his views. Although he still railed against socialism, Churchill no longer believed the Allies should try a preemptive nuclear first strike against the Soviet bear. As a staunch supporter of Anglo-American cooperation, he backed Eisenhower's proposal to consider the "limited use" of atomic weapons if North Korea advanced beyond its existing boundaries. But after America's 1954 test blast of the "Bravo" hydrogen bomb in the Pacific, Churchill seemed sobered by the bomb's ability for annihilation well beyond the impact of conventional weapons. He considered the new H-bomb "as far removed from the atom bomb as the atom bomb was from the bow and arrow" and that a nuclear conflict "meant effectively the end of the human race." Churchill worried about Cold War hawks in America who pushed for a nuclear confrontation with the Soviets. "I always feared that mass pressure in the United States might force them to use their H bombs while the Russians still had not got any," Winston confided, before the Soviets detonated their own in 1955. Churchill sought détente with the Soviet leaders who succeeded Stalin but showed a profound ambivalence with power and its ability to prevent catastrophe. His doctor, Lord Moran, remembered Winston holding a copy of *Hamlet* that he'd been reading since his visit to the Old Vic, and speaking with a world-weariness resembling the Dane's. "Bloody world," he exclaimed. "No human being would have come into it if he had known what it was like."

The glory days of the British Empire were over—with the empire now encumbered by huge debts and austerity—though Churchill remained its greatest advocate. During the war, he had convinced Roosevelt to underwrite the United Kingdom's defense with a seemingly endless supply of battleships, aircraft, and soldiers. Under Eisenhower, though, America was reluctant to commit to alliances around the world, bearing the costs and burdens of imperialism. "Winston is trying to relive the days of World War II," Eisenhower observed. "In those days he had the enjoyable feeling that he and our president [Roosevelt] were sitting on some rather Olympian platform with respect to the rest of the world and directing world affairs from that point of vantage."

Despite his affinity for Americans, Winston showed little enthusiasm for the revolutionary spirit of independence among those living in former colonies of the British Empire such as India, South Africa, Kenya, or even neighboring Ireland. A patronizing tone of British superiority could be found in his humor. "We English have always needed a place like this to come for the sunshine," he told an American consul in Morocco during World War II. "Why don't you give us Morocco, and we shall give you India. We shall even give you Gandhi, and he's awfully cheap to keep, now that he's on a hunger strike." Earlier in his career, Churchill favored using poison gas against "uncivilized tribes" such as the Kurds in Iraq and setting up concentration camps in South Africa, mirroring the intensity his Black and Tans armed forces had brought against rebelling Irish Catholics in the 1920s. Even with the United States, Winston seemed puzzled by the former British colony's willingness to absorb so many non-Caucasians and didn't seem to understand its civil rights "problem" in the 1950s with African Americans. "After all, you can't take twenty million of them into your belly like that," he told *New York Times* columnist C. L. Sulzberger. "Nonsense to say the black is the same as the white."

None of this ugliness arose, however, when Churchill received the 1953 Nobel Prize for Literature (rather than Peace). His antiquated views about colonialism and race, stuck in the Victorian era, when the sun never set on the British Empire, were overshadowed by more recent public memories of his defiant yet eloquent expressions of human freedom in the face of Nazi tyranny. The award cited his "brilliant oratory in defending exalted human values" as well as his literary works. "This award says words well chosen, uttered at the right time, bravely spoken, are the most powerful things in the world," the *New York Times* commented. "They can drive men to madness, as Hitler's words did. They may inspire them to acts of utter heroism and self-sacrifice, as Churchill's did." Winston dispatched Clementine to pick up the prize, along with a charming message of acceptance. "I do hope you are right," he informed the Nobel Committee about the merits of its decision. "I feel we are both running a considerable risk and that I do not deserve it. But I shall have no misgivings if you have none."

Increasingly, Clementine urged her husband to retire, causing some contentious scenes between them. Winston would have none of it, intent on holding the reins of power as long as he could. "Winston himself could be maddening, and on occasions behaved like a spoilt child," observed their daughter Mary, "but now there were times when Clementine harried him too much, and could be unreasonable and unkind." By April 1955, Winston's health had faded and his boundless energy seemed gone. He resigned as prime minister after nearly four years. Whether the Churchill legacy would endure remained an open question. Randolph vaguely hoped of running again for public office but felt his father's image loomed too large in the mind of the British for him to advance on his own. Rather mournfully, Randolph explained to a friend, "I could do nothing while he is alive." Waiting in the wings, Anthony Eden, the loyal and hardworking foreign secretary in Churchill's government, intended to become Winston's anointed successor. Randolph realized his father would probably resist Eden's ascension as well.

In his last great speech before the House of Commons, Prime Minister Churchill warned the world about nuclear proliferation and the lethal threat posed by the hydrogen bomb. Unlike his past call to arms, he recommended a negotiated sober-eyed disarmament with the Soviets, best achieved through Anglo-American unity. "Which way shall we turn to save our lives and the future of the world? It does not matter so much to old people; they are going soon anyway; but I find it poignant to look at youth in all its activity and ardour and, most of all, to watch little children playing their merry games, and wonder what would lie before them if God wearied of mankind." Keenly aware of his own mortality, Churchill left his best, most rigorous prescription for the future. "The day may dawn when fair play, love for one's fellow-men, respect for justice and freedom, will enable tormented generations to march forth serene and triumphant from the hideous epoch in which we have to dwell. Meanwhile, never flinch, never weary, never despair."

On behalf of a grateful nation, Queen Elizabeth offered to make Winston a duke, but he begged off, preferring to stay in the House of Commons until he died. "Besides, he said, what good would a Dukedom be to Randolph; and it might ruin his and little Winston's political careers," recalled his private secretary, Jock Colville. Randolph appreciated his father's thoughtful gift of turning down the peerage. A few months after Winston left 10 Downing Street, Randolph expressed his gratitude in a letter, both philosophical and admiring. "Power must pass and vanish," he wrote. "Glory, which is achieved through a just exercise of power—which itself is accumulated by genius, toil, courage and self-sacrifice—alone remains. Your glory is enshrined forever on the unperishable plinth of your achievement; and can never be destroyed or tarnished. It will flow with the centuries. So please try to be as happy as you have a right and (if it is not presumptuous for a son to say it) a duty to be. And, by being happy, make those who love you happy too."

The vacuum left in power's wake, however, made Winston restless and "sometimes lonely." To intimates, the Nobel laureate for literature admitted he "no longer had the zest to write." Instead, he painted landscapes at the villas of Lord Beaverbrook and his literary agent, Emery Reves, both located along the Mediterranean Sea. Mostly, Winston looked for restful ways to fill his days. "I have now retired from literature," he informed Bernard Baruch, his American friend and patron, "and am endeavouring to find ways of spending pleasantly the remaining years of my life."

39

Black Knights on a Chessboard

To Churchill's son, Aristotle Socrates Onassis always looked "like the black knight on a chessboard." The Greek shipping tycoon of enormous wealth, "with his dark skin, curved nose and blinkered eyes," held a certain fascination for Randolph Churchill.

From the time they first met around 1954, Randolph was never certain who was manipulating the other in a match of wits. "Like the knight at chess, he is given to sudden unexpected shifts of mood and emphasis—two steps forward and one step sideways," he wrote of Onassis. "His most characteristic stance is with shoulders slightly hunched, arms spread out, and swaying a little on the balls of his feet like a bantamweight watching which way his opponent is going to move."

Though only five years older, Onassis seemed far more accomplished—a self-made man who had reaped a fortune and determined his fate—in a way the prime minister's son had never achieved. Onassis grew up in Greek-controlled Turkey after World War I, where his family had been tortured and his parents lost their property; he eventually became a successful businessman. Using guile and skill, Onassis built an armada of tankers and freighters to service his oil-rich Saudi Arabian clients and a world hungry for petroleum. The rootless shipping magnate likened himself to Odysseus, the mariner of Greek mythology. With silver hair and a jackal's smile, Onassis charmed men and seduced women. On his giant personal yacht, the bar stools were covered with whale foreskin, allowing him crudely to tell female guests such as Greta Garbo that they were "sitting on the biggest penis in the world." From his base in Monte Carlo, selected for its tax-free status rather than any national fidelity, he spent lavishly on anything he desired. "They say I have no class," he explained. "Fortunately people with class are usually willing to overlook this flaw because I am very rich."

A few years earlier, Onassis had come to Randolph's attention through his former wife, Pamela. As a way of helping her financially, Lord Beaverbrook had sent Pamela to the South of France to interview Onassis and his Greek shipping rival, Stavros Niarchos, on a plum assignment for the "Londoner's Diary" column in his *Evening Standard* newspaper—the same popular feature for which Randolph worked as a columnist. Though she couldn't write much, Pamela's beauty and natural curiosity could squeeze the secrets out of rich and powerful men, as the Fleet Street newspaper baron knew from their World War II experience. During Pamela's stay on the Riviera, Onassis later claimed, they had an affair, though Pamela insisted to her biographer that Onassis was "too earthy, vulgar and ugly for her tastes." At New York City's Plaza hotel in spring 1953, Pamela hosted a cocktail party where Onassis first met one of her guests, Robert Kennedy, who seemed to instinctively dislike him. Adding to his buccaneer image, federal officials arrested Onassis in February 1954 while he sipped a luncheon martini at a posh Manhattan restaurant. Investigators claimed he had illegally purchased American surplus ships without being a U.S. citizen, as required by law, and they impounded some of his tankers.

As his own association with Onassis developed, Randolph Churchill journeyed to the South of France. Along the beachfront, he spotted another Beaverbrook confidant, Joe Kennedy. As he often did, the Kennedy patriarch spent part of August at a rented villa in Monaco, not far from Beaverbrook's place. If Randolph's greeting was sincere, Kennedy wasn't impressed. "My cup is filled to overflowing!" Joe wrote to his son Bobby, sarcasm dripping from his August 1954 note. "Randolph Churchill came up to me in Monte Carlo and asked me how I was, and told me that he was going to stay with Beaverbrook a couple of days. He did, and Beaverbrook said he was the most insufferable bore he has ever listened to and only tolerates him on account of his father. He is fat and just as repulsive as ever. Winston is expected here but they don't know when."

Onassis made a pretense of friendship with Churchill's son. As a working journalist, Randolph understood the news value of being close to one of the world's most colorful businessmen. In this Mediterranean playground for the rich, Onassis acted like a king. The glamorous parties on his 322-foot super yacht the *Christina* (named for his daughter)— with its heated pool, mirrored walls, and elaborate furnishings—often featured royalty, entertainment stars, and international figures. "I don't think there is a man or woman on earth who would not be seduced by the sheer narcissism of this boat," said actor Richard Burton when he visited. Randolph knew Onassis intended to use him for his own purposes, just like others who had befriended the prime minister's son because of his family name. In return, Randolph accepted this master manipulator's generosity without illusions, well aware of the mysteries surrounding him. "He's a Turk—he pretends he's a Greek because that was the side to be on," Randolph bluntly told another writer about Onassis. During this difficult time for his tanker business, Onassis carefully soaked in all the political insights and accumulated gossip Randolph Churchill had to offer. He settled the American government's lawsuit for illegally purchasing surplus vessels, agreeing to pay seven million dollars so he could continue his business on the high seas. But for Onassis, the most important transaction of all was the chance to meet Winston Churchill himself.

At La Pausa, Winston Churchill found himself immersed in beauty and creature comforts. The luxurious home of his literary agent, Emery Reves, filled with paintings by Monet, Rodin, Cezanne, and van Gogh, was carefully presided over by his attractive young wife, Wendy Russell, a former *Vogue* model. Already a wealthy man before he represented Churchill, Reves and his wife treated Churchill as a visiting potentate accustomed to only the best. They catered to his every whim. Winston seemed enchanted by Wendy's beauty and attentiveness. His weakness for such unabashed treatment had always worried Clementine, who feared its consequences on her husband's judgment and reputation. In January 1956, Clementine remained home sick in London as Winston wrote to her about his latest excursion. "Randolph has arrived and is staying with the Onassis [*sic*] on the monster yacht," Churchill explained. Randolph soon convinced his father to meet the Greek tycoon one evening at La Pausa. Randolph touted his new friend's gregariousness as "a born orator with a poetic sense" and his lifelong admiration for Winston. When he arrived at the Reveses' villa, Onassis fumbled and fawned in front of the old man, acting nervous and seemingly in awe. "He made a good impression upon me," Winston relayed home. "He is a v[er]y able and masterful man & told me a lot about whales. He kissed my hand!"

Initially, Onassis upset Churchill by talking about Cyprus, where some presiding British troops had been killed. Before leaving, though, he deftly extended Churchill an invitation to join him on the yacht *Christina*. Reves was dubious about Onassis's offer that they inspect his yacht, but Wendy convinced them to accept. "That is a man of mark," Churchill concluded. "I would like to see him again." As they boarded the yacht, Randolph appeared delighted with this new alliance. Ari wore his dark shades but smiled as press photographers captured, from a distance, the former prime minister coming aboard. "Randolph seemed to miss the hint of hoodlum, the rough customer, behind those black lenses," his sister Sarah recalled.

Winston enjoyed the yacht's splendor immensely, calling the craft "the most beautiful structure I have seen afloat." Onassis offered to lend the vessel to Churchill so he could soon travel to Ceylon. Winston urged his wife to join them for "a little Easter cruise." Like others who were surprised to see newspaper photos of Winston with this notorious ship owner, Clementine diplomatically expressed interest but added, "Somehow I don't want to be beholden to this rich and powerful man, & for the news to be blazoned." Nevertheless, both Churchill father and son enjoyed the Onassis opulence too much to refuse the offer. For a time, Ari even proposed building a villa for Winston in Monte Carlo, on land owned by one of his companies near the casino.

In London, another loyal Churchill friend, the newly chosen British prime minister, Anthony Eden, considered Onassis "a rather unsavory character," but his concerns were overshadowed by the prospect of war in the Middle East, over the Suez Canal. This crisis along the Nile would be Eden's great test as Churchill's successor and whether the British could maintain an empire in the late twentieth century.

Winston always liked Eden, a Conservative ally twenty-five years younger, who had served him faithfully as foreign secretary and deputy prime minister. "I regard you as my son," Churchill told him during World War II, an affinity that Randolph deeply resented. Randolph might be given various assignments by his father, but never earned the confidence Eden enjoyed. Matters became only worse when the handsome diplomat divorced his first wife and, in a 1952 civil ceremony, wed Clarissa Churchill, the daughter of Winston's brother, Jack. Randolph and his friends disapproved vehemently. Evelyn Waugh, aware that Clarissa was Catholic like the rest of Jack Churchill's family, took her to lunch and warned her about marrying Eden outside the Church. Apocryphally, Waugh told Clarissa of another young woman, Kathleen Kennedy, who had disregarded his similar advice and wound up being killed in a fateful accident. "Clarissa's apostasy has upset me more than anything that had happened since Kick's death," Waugh moaned. "I can't write about it or think of anything else."

Before Winston retired in 1955, he harbored second thoughts about Eden. Churchill deliberately avoided stepping aside for his loyal deputy, who'd waited years for his turn. "Winston will probably bury Eden," Randolph crowed to friends, "and then he will deliver himself of a magnificent oration in which he will talk of the sad and premature death of this promising young man." Churchill's delay in succession became obvious to insiders such as Beaverbrook, who confided as much to Joe Kennedy in August 1954, as they relaxed together in Monte Carlo: Beaverbrook "told me that Anthony [Eden] is annoyed as the devil that Churchill doesn't get through, and the other day Churchill, talking to Beaverbrook, said there is a chap named Eccles working for Churchill and he said to Max he would give him a better appointment in a year or two, and then looked at Max and chuckled and said, 'Don't tell Anthony,' which indicates he knows Anthony is expected to be prime minister but Churchill gives him no satisfaction," Kennedy wrote his son Bobby in August 1954.

On his last night spent at Downing Street, Winston paused silently for a few moments and confided solemnly in Jock Colville, his longtime private secretary. "I don't think Anthony can do it," he said vehemently. After nearly sixty years in the limelight, Winston seemed unable to leave the public stage, the way that most men fear death.

A year later, Prime Minister Eden faced his most vexing challenge when Egyptian president Gamal Abdel Nasser decided to nationalize the Suez Canal, a vital passageway more than a hundred miles long carved out of the desert. Since the nineteenth century, it had allowed ships and tankers to carry goods between the Mediterranean and the Red Seas, enabling Europeans to avoid the much-longer journey around Africa to trade with Asia. Nasser's provocative move followed a decision by the British and Americans not to fund construction of the Aswan Dam—a rebuke for Nasser's growing support from the Communists in the Soviet Union and China. When Nasser took over the Suez Canal in July 1956, British Tories urged Eden to intervene militarily in their former colony. They warned this Cold War crisis could result in the kind of appeasement Chamberlain had agreed upon at Munich in 1938. However, U.S. president Dwight Eisenhower refused to go along, upsetting the Anglo-American unity shared by the Allies since World War II. In London, Eden called upon his old mentor Churchill for advice. "Eden says he wants to see me, as he has much to tell," Winston wrote from Chartwell to Clemmie, who was away. "Personally, I think that France and England ought to act together with vigour, and if necessary with arms, while America watches Russia vigilantly." During a briefing, Winston learned of Eden's military plans with the French, joined by the Israelis, to wrest control of the canal away from the Egyptians. "Anthony told me everything," Winston informed his wife on August 3, 1956. "As I am well informed, I cannot in an unprotected letter tell any secrets."

Secrecy and state security, however, didn't prevent Randolph Churchill from telling what he knew to his friend Aristotle Onassis. Soon after Nasser nationalized the canal, Randolph alerted Onassis about the strong possibility of British military action. The business timing couldn't have been better for Onassis. For several months, U.S. oil companies had been unofficially boycotting Onassis, upset with his arrangement with the Saudis, and thus pushing his firm toward bankruptcy. But with Randolph's inside information, Onassis was poised to make a fortune when the Suez Crisis erupted in October 1956. With forty ships sunk in the canal, commercial traffic came to a standstill. Oil firms suddenly relied heavily on Onassis's large fleet of tankers to avert an economic catastrophe. For months, Ari raked in exorbitant fees until the canal reopened in March 1957.

For Anthony Eden, the Suez Crisis ended in political fiasco. At the behest of the American government and the rest of the world, United Nations officials convinced the British and French to withdraw from the canal. They oversaw a cleanup and returned the waterway to the Egyptians. By keeping British military plans a secret from Eisenhower, who was busy running for reelection, Eden seriously strained the "special relationship" between America and Great Britain that Churchill had spent his life nurturing. Mostly, the incident underlined the end of an era for the British Empire when Her Majesty's forces could impose their will on a misbehaving former colony such as Egypt, as though nation-states were children. Eisenhower threatened financial pressure if England didn't go along with the return of the canal. Winston, as "an Anthony man," publicly supported the new prime minister, knowing his doubts about Eden had been confirmed. Unlike in the past, though, Churchill was no longer well enough to come back to 10 Downing and save the day. "I am not the man I was," he acknowledged. "I could not be Prime Minister now."

By January 1957, Eden's political standing had deteriorated enough to hurt his health and force his resignation as prime minister. Randolph broke the news of Eden's departure with an article in Beaverbrook's *Evening Standard*. His loathing for his father's successor metastasized into an ill-considered book called *The Rise and Fall of Sir Anthony Eden*. Critics condemned the bileful screed as inaccurate and unfair. "Readers of this book will not learn much about Sir Anthony Eden, but they should get a full appreciation of Mr. Randolph Churchill," chided former PM Clement Attlee in a review. The book mortified Winston and Clementine, raising questions again whether Randolph could be entrusted as his father's official biographer.

Meanwhile, all the courting of Winston Churchill and his son paid off handsomely for Onassis. The great man continued to cruise the Mediterranean on Onassis's yacht while Randolph remained a confidant. "Randolph's a drunk but he's the best informed drunk in London," Onassis told one of his associates as his Suez gamble unfolded. He later sent Randolph the cover of a German magazine featuring Onassis as the true victor of the Suez conflict. Over the image, Ari had inscribed, "To my favourite spy!"

40

Friends in High Places

*"The television has come to take its place in the world; as a
rather old-fashioned person I have not been one of its
principal champions."*

—WINSTON CHURCHILL, 1952

The flickering television images, beamed to millions of Americans
from the 1956 Democratic Convention, portrayed John F. Kennedy in
the most dreaded way possible for a politician: in defeat.

For the first time in a career full of successes, Kennedy had lost,
to Tennessee senator Estes Kefauver, in a last-minute bid to become
Adlai Stevenson's vice-presidential running mate. The young senator
from Massachusetts had ignored his father's advice, risked his future
chances for the White House, and now soberly faced the consequences.
"What has happened today bears out the good judgment of Governor
Stevenson in deciding that this issue should be taken to the floor of the
convention," Kennedy said at the podium before bowing out. "I hope
this Convention will make Estes Kefauver's nomination unanimous,
thank you."

Television, still in its infancy, captured the convention drama inside
Chicago's International Amphitheatre. One after another, delegates
holding signs and placards for Kefauver jumped on his bandwagon
until Kennedy graciously but grimly conceded. In black-and-white
images, Jack could be seen clapping dutifully, thin-faced and looking

younger than his thirty-nine years, as the cheering crowd embraced another candidate.

Joe Kennedy, who strongly cautioned his son from entering the 1956 vice-presidential fray, once considered Stevenson, the bald erudite Illinois governor, the new political darling of the television age. In 1952, when Stevenson first faced Dwight Eisenhower for president, Joe called him "a great friend of mine and the family," telling Lord Beaverbrook that Stevenson was "the hottest thing we have in America on television. He delivers speeches that you want to read because of his great sense of humor and his great capacity for phrase making. He runs Churchill an even race."

Churchill held a more reserved opinion of Stevenson, regarding him as a philosopher rather than a king. "In America, when they elect a President they want more than a skillful politician," Winston said in 1955. "They are seeking a personality: something that will make the President a good substitute for a monarch. Adlai Stevenson will have to build himself up gradually if he is to do any good." Once, Stevenson asked Winston how he had obtained his famous oratory skills. Churchill credited a long-forgotten American, Bourke Cockran, "who inspired me when I was 19 & taught me how to use every note of the human voice like an organ . . . He was my model. I learned from him how to hold thousands in thrall."

In 1956, Randolph Churchill attended both the Republican and Democratic Conventions, as not a visiting diplomat but rather a scribe for Beaverbrook's newspaper. He came away impressed with the incumbent vice president, Richard Nixon. "Quite grown up," Randolph observed about Ike's junior exec, a sort of American Tory four years older than Kennedy. "I'm the only man in the world who supports a Stevenson-Nixon ticket."

At the Democratic event, Randolph watched as New York governor Averell Harriman—the same man who'd undermined his ill-fated marriage to Pamela a decade earlier—had his name put into contention for

U.S. president. Truman and the New York delegates backed Harriman, who paid for an expensive "spontaneous" demonstration on the convention floor, complete with "scores of beautiful models, a twenty-piece band, [and] hundreds of placards of the Governor's smiling face four times bigger than life," observed Russell Baker of the *New York Times*. The only thing Harriman lacked was votes.

Randolph's appearance on behalf of Lord Beaverbrook was somewhat surprising in itself. In 1952, Churchill's son had publicly condemned the press lord as a "false friend" of his father's, and as an enemy of Great Britain's monarchial institutions. Beaverbrook seemed not to believe his ears when a reporter reached him at his winter home in Nassau, the Bahamas, for a response to this. Max asked for Randolph's remarks to be read twice, then paused for a moment. "Much obliged," Beaverbrook said. "I have no comment to make at all." In America, Joe Kennedy read about the kerfuffle and made light of it. "We never were very far apart on world affairs," he joked to Beaverbrook, "and I am satisfied we are closer together now, even as far down as Randolph Churchill." Nevertheless, Max respected Randolph's journalistic abilities and the way his surname would open doors to the powerful. "I have always pursued politics as an art rather than a science," Max wrote to Joe shortly before the Democratic conclave began.

During the convention, Stevenson allowed the party to pick his running mate. Already tapped to give the nominating speech for Stevenson, Jack Kennedy, with his brother Bobby as campaign manager, believed this decision might provide his chance for higher office. When the two brothers came to that joint conclusion, Jack asked Bobby to inform their father over the telephone, rather than face his wrath himself. "Call Dad and tell him I'm going for it," Jack said.

When reached at his rented summer villa in Cap d'Antibes, Joe blew up. He ranted that their move would bring disaster, that Stevenson's second presidential bid was doomed and that Jack's future would go down with it. Most alarmingly, he insisted, the defeat would be blamed on Jack's Catholicism. Joe Kennedy and Jack's own advisers knew full well how potent anti-Catholicism was in America, a land where Irish Catholics such as Al Smith had learned they were still viewed in some states as papist aliens. How could his sons risk everything so willy-nilly, Joe argued, with a poor strategic choice destined to undermine all that their family had worked so hard to achieve in seeking the White House?

"Whew, is he mad!" Bobby said after getting off the phone. Jack later admitted he suffered "a momentary paralysis" in defying his father's advice.

As the delegates' votes were counted, Jack's chance faded. Though Lyndon Johnson's Texas delegates and those from New York supported Kennedy's bid, some expected support didn't come through. The inexperience of Kennedy's youthful team—including Theodore Sorensen, Kenny O'Donnell, and Jack's thirty-one-year-old brother, Bobby—became apparent. Their head counting, an essential in politics, had been mistaken. Before the vote counting on television was finished, Jack rose from a chair in his suite and called it quits. "That's it, let's go," he declared, marching off to the amphitheater to accept his fate.

Following the convention, Jack went to France to visit his father, just as he had promised, and then spent time with his playboyish pal, Florida senator George Smathers, on a Riviera yacht tour. His pregnant wife, Jackie—spotted at the convention by television cameras rooting for her husband—begged him not to leave. She had a history of troubled pregnancies. While her husband was gone, Jackie began hemorrhaging and was rushed to a Newport hospital. Doctors performed a caesarean section, but the Kennedys' baby girl was stillborn. For another three days, Jack couldn't be found on the Mediterranean. When finally reached by telephone, he rushed home, but a breach of trust with Jackie had done its damage. "The death of the baby placed a real strain on Jack and Jackie's marriage," his lifelong friend Lem Billings later recalled.

Politics that year also didn't proceed as planned. As a sign of the Kennedys' goodwill with fellow Democrats, Bobby traveled with the Stevenson campaign during the fall but was quickly disenchanted with Adlai's effete manner. Bobby "learned what not to do," recalled another aide, Newton Minow, and later applied those lessons in the 1960 campaign. Quietly, Bobby wound up voting for Eisenhower, rather than his party's standard-bearer. Fortunately for Jack, the fallout from his vice-presidential defeat didn't last long. Many watching the televised convention found the young senator appealing, gracious in defeat, and worthy of another try the next time. Television would be key. While Adlai asked his media adviser at the convention to fix the broken TV set in his hotel room, Jack absorbed the visual mastery of this new political medium. He learned Americans wanted some majesty with their presidential politics, as Churchill knew so well. "Honey, vigor, compassion, intelligence—the presence or lack of these and other qualities make up what is called the candidate's 'image,'" Kennedy explained in a November 1959 issue of *TV Guide* magazine. "My own conviction is that these images or impressions are likely to be uncannily correct."

Eventually Joe Kennedy simmered down and began planning again for Jack's future. Despite his two sons' faulty decisions at the 1956 convention, he didn't chastise them or dwell on the rightness of his advice. Whenever his sons were down and their errors obvious, Joe seemed to tack in a different direction than expected and deliberately boost their spirits. The old movie producer in him realized the potential of his telegenic son to win over an audience. "He came out of the convention so much better than anyone could have hoped," Joe told one of his showbiz pals, Morton Downey. "As far as I'm concerned you know how I feel—if you're going to get licked, get licked trying for the best, not the second best. His time is surely coming!"

. . .

In politics as in finance, Bernard Baruch liked to be an insider from the beginning. His work for Woodrow Wilson in World War I had introduced him to that rising British star Winston Churchill, just as his association with Joe Kennedy had led to his involvement with Franklin Roosevelt's first presidential campaign. "Maybe B.M.B. has the common failing of liking to be on the winner [sic] when the choice is otherwise not so clear," joked Arthur Krock, the Times columnist paid by both Baruch and Joe Kennedy as their private publicity man. As a journalist, Krock quoted Baruch's folksy wisdom as a park bench philosopher, but never exposed his behind-the-scenes deals. Only insiders knew of Baruch's connections between the Kennedy and Churchill worlds. And now that Kennedy's son seemed headed for the White House in 1960, Baruch wanted influence again. In his late eighties, Baruch still liked to know that his voice and money could be heard in Washington.

Baruch had sent Jack Kennedy a congratulatory letter after his 1952 Senate upset over Henry Cabot Lodge Jr. More important in terms of loyalty, the old philanthropist came to see the young senator at the hospital in 1954, when Jack's back problems were at their worst and his political career in doubt. Jacqueline Kennedy learned that Baruch had left a note at the hospital's front desk when he apparently couldn't get in after hours. "Just knowing that someone like you was thinking about him was so much better medicine than any doctor could give—because he has been feeling so sick all these weeks," explained Jackie, who hoped to meet her father-in-law's rich and famous friend. "I know Jack is miserable—because he would have adored to have seen you—but I am sure I am much more—because I would rather meet you than anyone in the world," she gushed, the dashes in her letter seeming like the breathy purring pauses in her speech, "and now I feel that you are a ship that has passed in the night—and unless Jack gets operated on all over again next year—my dream will never come true." Despite their past differences, Joe Kennedy tried to keep his connection with Baruch as well. When Baruch bowed out of Joe Kennedy's offer to speak at Notre Dame University—"I would say, my dear friend, that you had better count me out," wrote Bernie at age eighty-five; "the spirit is willing, but I am afraid the flesh will be weak"—Kennedy instead endowed a chair in Lord Beaverbrook's name at the Catholic school. "When courage was given out, your father was sitting right in the front pew," Baruch wrote to a very deferential Bobby Kennedy in 1956. "He and I have been friends for a long time and have had many a good laugh together."

Similarly, as Churchill's best friend in America, Baruch stayed in contact with Winston's friends and family. Like his father, Randolph Churchill asked for stock advice from Baruch. When Randolph revealed that his ex-wife Pam Churchill had undergone a hysterectomy in New York, Bernie sent her a note "to let you know of my deep interest in your recovery and my continuing affection." On his annual fall trips to London, Baruch met with Beaverbrook, always visiting him along with Winston. "Politics is a fascinating thing," Baruch wrote to Max in 1956, "but to a man who has principles or who cannot get away from his reasoning powers—that two and two make four—the holding of office is not very attractive except like the one you held in war."

Baruch also shared candid comments with Brendan Bracken, Winston's trusted aide. Bracken had declined to join Churchill's second government for health reasons, telling Baruch that Winston must make a fresh start with new people. "By nature he is, as you know, the kindest of men[,] but a Prime Minister, in putting a government together, must of necessity drop people who have been former colleagues," Bracken explained in 1951. "This is an inevitable duty but it has been very painful to Winston." Bracken's health continued to deteriorate, until he died at age fifty-eight. Despite their differences, Randolph wrote a touching tribute in Beaverbrook's newspaper to the redheaded aide whom Winston had once treated like a son. "You were always on the good side: you loved truth and honour: you hated cruelty and injustice," Randolph recalled. "Fare thee well, my gifted, true and many-sided friend."

Brendan's death fell heaviest on Winston and Max, the surviving part of the dynamic trio whose actions early in the war had helped save Great Britain. Soon after Bracken's passing, Churchill felt moved to thank Max for his own enduring friendship. "I am very glad that you like my companionship. It has now become very feeble, though nonetheless warm," he wrote, underlining "that the ties we formed so many years ago and strengthened in the days of war have lasted out our lifetime."

From both sides of the Atlantic, Baruch and Beaverbrook worried about Winston's newfound friendship with Aristotle Onassis and its effect on his reputation. Throughout the late 1950s, newspapers carried photos of the former prime minister lounging on Onassis's yacht and at his Monte Carlo casino. When Baruch expressed wariness, knowing the precarious state of Winston's finances in the past, Churchill dismissed the press coverage and said they'd "put in fairy tales about Onassis. He is a friendly kind of man, but I did not depend on his invitation to go there." Privately, Beaverbrook considered Onassis a cad as well as a buccaneer. "Oh, he's an amusing dog," Beaverbrook concluded. "An amusing dog. He takes care to get hold of all the important people who come into his bailiwick. Takes the ladies out on his yacht."

Onassis courted Churchill with lavish attentiveness, almost as his servant. He drove him in his sports car, escorted him up his yacht's gangplank, served him caviar and Dom Perignon champagne, sang him Greek songs, and covered him in blankets when Winston felt a chill. He played cards with him and learned bezique. Ari even chased after Toby, Winston's prized white canary, when the bird flew away. At the Monte Carlo casino, Ari made sure Winston never lost his money. After Churchill placed a bet at the roulette table, Onassis doubled it discreetly. "We must remember that it was he, the man of our century, who saved the world in 1940," Onassis insisted to the yacht's other guests. "Where would we all be today and in what state if it were not for this man!" Even when Winston returned to England, Onassis would tell his other guests, "As the great man once told me . . ."

Aboard the *Christina,* Winston toured the Mediterranean, drifting by places such as the Dardanelles and recalling parts of history at Ari's urging. At dinner, Winston shared fond stories with Onassis and his own entourage, including Anthony Montague Browne, his last private secretary.

"What did you really think of Lawrence of Arabia?" Montague Browne asked during one voyage.

For a moment, Winston quietly considered T. E. Lawrence, who'd once bragged over dinner that he and Churchill could reshape the Middle East. Lawrence died at age forty-six, in a freak 1935 motorcycle accident—the sort of random accident that had nearly claimed Winston's life in New York a few years before then.

"A very remarkable character and very careful of that fact," Churchill finally surmised.

Onassis and Churchill also discussed contemporary events, including a political scandal involving President Dwight Eisenhower's chief of staff, Sherman Adams. Winston didn't like the way Eisenhower let the scandal go unresolved, eroding his political capital. Churchill said he never vacillated on such matters. "You must either wallop a man or vindicate him," he declared. Later Onassis would underline the value of such Churchill talks to his own son: "One lunch with Sir Winston will teach you more than three years at Oxford."

While recalling historical figures from Churchill's life, Ari wondered about his father, Lord Randolph Churchill. "Your father died young," Onassis said. "If he had lived to your age, you might not have had to struggle so hard. Your life would have been easier and you might not have done what you did."

The comparison of father and son, the intervention of an elder for the good of the next generation in the Churchill family, was not something Winston wished to discuss, which was apparent from his stricken demeanor.

"No, we were very different people," he acknowledged, without elaborating.

Aboard the yacht, the most painful emotional experience, however, soon belonged to Onassis, who'd wind up turning to Winston for comfort and advice.

41

Meetings at Sea

Maria Callas, the raven-haired diva with a heavenly voice, enjoyed worldwide acclaim, though not on the scale of another guest on Aristotle Onassis's yacht. When the *Christina* pulled into port, the paparazzi didn't focus first on Callas but rather on the historic figure in her company. "I like traveling with Winston Churchill," Callas later explained. "It relieves me of some of the burden of my popularity."

In a scene fit for a Fellini movie, Callas and her devoted husband, a rich older businessman named Giovanni Battista Meneghini, met the former prime minister in July 1959, as part of the Greek tycoon's entourage. As if his boat were now a stage, Onassis invited opera's biggest star and the famous statesman–Nobel Prize winner in literature to collaborate in his personal odyssey. With a genius of expression rarely heard before, Callas electrified audiences at opera houses in London, Rome, and New York. Critics marveled at her bravura bel canto soprano as soon as she parted her lips to sing. "Don't talk to me about rules, dear," Callas once explained about her life and art, which often blended into one. "Wherever I stay I make the goddamn rules." On the day of their meeting that July, Winston wore a crème-colored suit and wide-brimmed hat, appearing more like a plantation owner than the familiar 10 Downing Street politician with his dark pinstripe suit and pocket watch. Aboard the ship, Churchill stayed in the Ithaca Suite, the grandest bedroom, reserved for Ari's special guests. Churchill's accompaniment included Clementine, daughter Diana Sandys, granddaughter Celia (who later described Callas as "tall, very dark and striking in a reptilian sort of way"), and Winston's pet bird, Toby. Upon their introduction, Callas stared quizzically at the golden-winged budgerigar on his perch.

"Kiss!" the large parakeet chirped. Winston smiled with bemused satisfaction, as his company laughed heartily.

During the cruise, the Churchills would be confronted with Ari's obvious affair with Callas, the deterioration of his marriage to his beautiful wife, Tina, and the awkward fact that both women were traveling aboard the same ship during this emotional crisis. At Istanbul, Callas and Onassis disappeared off the boat for a while. They returned aflame. "It is all over," Callas told her husband. "I love Ari." The passionate affair between Onassis and Callas consumed the remainder of the trip. "It was as if a fire was devouring them both," recalled Meneghini, watching his wife slip away. Careful not to offend his other well-known guest, Onassis tried to shield Sir Winston from his personal obsession. "All he really wanted was for my grandfather to enjoy himself and for Maria to be happy and for Tina not to make a drama," recalled Celia Sandys. The once seemingly ideal Onassis marriage, producing two children, had been crumbling for years. Tina initiated her own affairs, as had her husband, who bragged he could turn any woman into his mistress. The charm Ari held for women consisted of an attentiveness that overcame his gruff looks, and a generous bank account that could afford the most expensive jewelry as gifts. "Ari's total understanding of women comes out of a Van Cleef and Arpels catalogue," Callas quipped. Before this cruise with the Churchills, Tina and Ari had heard Maria sing in *Medea* at Covent Garden in London, a performance that ignited Ari's spell of infatuation. When Winston asked Callas to sing while they were together on the yacht, however, she declined. Everything would be on this prima donna's terms.

Clementine Churchill, who enjoyed shopping and conversing with Tina, felt heartsick for her friend. Initially reluctant to join Winston on Onassis's yacht, Clementine now firmly resolved never to do so again. Ari worried Sir Winston, too, might condemn his adulterous behavior. There was an almost father-son tone in Ari's admission of failure in his marriage. He confessed to Churchill that his breakup from Tina was "the saddest and I hope greatest misfortune of my life," and thanked Winston for his concern. In reply, Churchill counseled Onassis to proceed slowly before divorce. The former prime minister expressed hope that Tina and Ari would reconcile, suggesting "so many problems in this life change and fade away if only they are given time." Churchill had accepted so much generosity from Onassis (such as a gold cigar box engraved with the names of all their ports of call in the Caribbean) that he weighed his words carefully. "I hope you did not mind my broaching such a personal matter," Winston wrote in a follow-up note.

As she moved toward divorce from Onassis, Tina injured herself skiing and recuperated in a British hospital. When Clementine visited her, she brought along Winston's cousin, the Marquess of Blandford, a handsome blond-haired chap whom Winston called Sonny. To everyone's surprise, Tina and Sonny soon became a couple. When Tina left the hospital, she stayed at Sonny's home at Blenheim Palace, the ancestral place of Winston's birth, and they married within a year. Meanwhile, Ari and Callas would continue their pas de deux courting for years to come without a wedding. Winston could not resist the irony of it all. "So, Ari," he wrote to his Greek tycoon friend, "we are related at last!"

On the Onassis yacht, one of Winston Churchill's least remembered meetings, more fleeting than historic, took place when Senator John F.

Kennedy and his wife, Jacqueline, boarded in 1958. Since a young man, Kennedy had greatly admired the former prime minister. Churchill's views of the world and the use of power and words had so inspired his own. "History was full of heroes for him, and he reveled in the stately cadences of historical prose," biographer Arthur M. Schlesinger Jr. wrote of Kennedy's fondness for Churchill. Schlesinger said that JFK, in recalling Winston's biography of his father, considered Lord Randolph Churchill a "Tory Democrat." Though he'd seen Winston from a distance at various times in London—including at the grand 1939 party at Blenheim Palace just before wartime bombing started—Jack looked forward to a face-to-face meeting with the great man himself.

Several months earlier, Joe Kennedy requested a visit with Churchill in the South of France while vacationing with Lord Beaverbrook. Despite his own loathing for Kennedy, Randolph Churchill informed his father that the former ambassador (whom he called Wicked Papa Joe) had rented a summer house at Cap d'Ail, next to Max's place, and that Beaverbrook wanted to accommodate his American friend. "If Max attaches importance to it, I will go," replied Winston. "But it must not appear in the press." Churchill's personal secretary, Anthony Montague Browne, shared Randolph's distaste for the Wall Streeter–cum–diplomat after they met. "His toothey tendency to smile mirthlessly as a dogfish allowed [is] . . . so unappealingly shark-like," Montague Browne described years later, comparing Joe Kennedy to the convicted financier Ivan Boesky. The discussion between these two friendly antagonists was never revealed publicly, just as Winston wished.

By 1958, Senator Kennedy's much-publicized chance to become the next president had stirred Churchill's interest. Not only had he followed American politics for a long time, but there seemed a natural curiosity about the son of his onetime critic now rising to the top. When he heard that the young senator and his wife were visiting Joe and Rose on vacation along the Mediterranean, Winston decided to extend an invitation.

"They tell me he is presidential timber," Churchill explained to his host, Onassis. "I'd like to meet this presidential timber."

William Douglas-Home, another of Jack's British friends from his London days, accompanied the Kennedys as they anxiously entered Onassis's yacht to join an awaiting Churchill. "He admired Churchill and wanted to meet him," recalled Jacqueline of her husband's anticipation. "He never had a hero worship of any contemporary—it was more in the past." Jackie shared her husband's enthusiasm. Ten years earlier, while on a European trip as a Vassar student, she was invited to a garden party at Buckingham Palace, and shook Churchill's hand— twice: like a schoolgirl, she ran back to the end of the reception line after her first handshake so she could shake his hand again.

Once aboard, Jack was ushered on a path to Churchill, while the magnanimous host, Onassis, showed Jackie around his massive yacht. When she inspected one of the rooms with a huge kidney-shaped bathtub, Jackie seemed delighted. "Why, it's large enough for a carrier of the Forrestal class!" she exclaimed, displaying her own nautical knowledge. On this evening, Jackie wore a white Yves St. Laurent outfit, very simple but very expensive, with the balmy sea breezes flowing through her dark hair. Although Onassis was preoccupied with Maria Callas, the young senator's wife clearly made an impression on him. "She had a withdrawn quality," recalled Onassis, who later claimed he detected her "carnal soul" during this brief tour. "She wasn't conspicuously friendly, but she had a way of making you look at her."

Senator Kennedy didn't give much mind to Onassis. He'd met him a few times before, at social events in New York and Washington, though they'd never exchanged more than a few pleasant words. He thanked Onassis for sending a courier bearing the invitation and focused his attention on impressing Sir Winston. By late that day, however, Churchill seemed fatigued and unable to focus. Along with Douglas-Home, Kennedy had come with another guest, Gianni Agnelli, the wealthy Italian automaker and a friend of Pamela Churchill. Looking at this assemblage, Winston couldn't tell at first who might be Joe Kennedy's son, somewhat to Jack's consternation.

"I knew your father so well," Winston said, addressing the wrong fellow in the group, until Kennedy was clearly identified to him.

Eventually, Churchill asked Jack to assess his chances in the upcoming presidential race.

"I am a Catholic, you know," Kennedy replied. It was an odd but accurate response to the difficulty he faced at home.

"If that's the only difficulty, you can change your religion and still remain a good Christian," Winston offered.

The two men discussed politics for a time, until Onassis returned from his boat tour with the senator's wife. Realizing that Winston seemed tired, Onassis became protective. He politely suggested that the Kennedys leave. The bold and assertive Greek tycoon wasn't impressed with the boyish-looking American with the painfully thin physique and squeaky New England voice. In his eyes, Kennedy wasn't presidential timber. "He believed he could see below the surface of most men, and Kennedy did not seem to him to be a man headed for the White House," wrote Peter Evans, an Onassis biographer. Nevertheless, Onassis would send the Kennedys a detailed bronze model of a whaling ship he'd once owned. Jack and Jackie, both delighted with the gift, kept it in their home.

In departing, Jack Kennedy knew he'd failed to impress Churchill, barely registering a significant comment from the renowned leader he so admired. "He was his hero, and it was rather sad to think that that was the first time he'd ever met him," Douglas-Home remembered.

Jackie, who'd left her own mark aboard the yacht, listened to her husband's disappointment as he described Churchill's confusion. She recognized the huge missed opportunity it meant for him.

"I felt sorry for Jack that evening because he was meeting his hero, only he met him too late," Jackie later recalled. "Think of all he could have—he was so hungry to talk with Churchill at last, or meet him and he just met Churchill when Churchill couldn't really say anything."

That night, Jackie tried to make light of the situation and ease her husband's pain. "Maybe he thought you were the waiter, Jack," she teased.

42

In Their Own Image

"Men make gods in their own image."
—XENOPHANES

The massive seaside mansion called Aitken House in Nassau, the Bahamas (particularly when its owner, Lord Beaverbrook, was in residence), served as a haven for friends seeking respite from their endeavors up north. Beaverbrook had built his expansive two-story winter home on a strip of coastal land known as Gun Point, once a Caribbean hideout for pirates. Surrounded by white sand beaches and azure saltwater lighter than the sky's blue, the land had been granted to Beaverbrook by the Crown for his extraordinary service in World War II.

When not touring the Mediterranean with Onassis, Winston Churchill was invited to enjoy Aitken House's charms. His son, Randolph, despite his protestations against Max, did accept an invitation, and left his burned cigarettes on the parquet floors. On a short jaunt from Florida, Joe Kennedy brought along his most recent mistress when he visited Beaverbrook's sunny resort-like place so far away from the rest of the world. "The whiskey is in Nassau. A whole case of it," Beaverbrook wrote jauntily to Kennedy in 1955, after receiving Joe's trademark holiday gift, a leftover from his distillery days. "Twelve year old whiskey is magnificent. And it will soon be dissolved to nothing by a seventy-six year old man. Come help me."

Joe would insist that his youngest son, Teddy, and his newlywed wife, Joan, spend their honeymoon at Aitken House. In December 1957, Bobby and Ethel Kennedy vacationed there when the much-traveled press titan happened to be in residence. Max provided swimming, fishing boat trips, and elaborate meals with champagne for the visiting Kennedys—as well as long chats about presidential politics. Bobby joked about calling Max "Your Lordship." Max noticed that Bobby's analytical mind worked much like his father's. "I find Bobby a most lively character, with an exceedingly aggressive mind, well-balanced, clear in statement, powerful in argument, well-read and bound to do a great deal in life," Beaverbrook enthused to Joe. "Possibly much mischief if he becomes President. For my part I expect the Kennedys to equal the record of the Adams family." After the young couple departed, Beaverbrook forwarded Ethel a copy of Churchill's book *My Early Life*. Along with his thank-you note, Bobby sent his host a copy of *Men and Power*, Beaverbrook's recently published memoir about World War I, and asked him to inscribe it. The aptly named book described Churchill during the Great War as "bold and imaginative in the sweep of his conceptions, prolific of new ideas, like a machine gun of bullets and expelling his notions in much the same manner." As with Winston, Beaverbrook understood the instinctive needs of his friend Joe Kennedy—from his driving zeal and private avarice to his desire to be known publicly as a faithful family man with a churchgoing wife. In one note to Joe, Max passed along a compliment from an acquaintance who declared, "Rose Kennedy is an uncanonized saint in a Dior dress." Although he rarely alluded to his own family, Beaverbrook seemed to know everything about the Kennedys. "Strange as it may seem, since our first few meetings when I was Ambassador, I have always had the feeling that if ever I needed help or needed a friend, I would have one in you—without asking," Joe wrote Max.

. . .

With an eye toward the 1960 election, Joe Kennedy did everything he could to bolster his son Jack, especially behind the scenes. Money was his biggest offering, just as he helped organize financial contributors to Franklin Roosevelt's first effort in 1932. Jack became the amiable face of his father's ambitions. At the 1958 Gridiron Club dinner in Washington, Jack deftly used humor to defuse his father's reputation as the campaign's hidden hand. "I just received the following wire from my generous daddy—'Dear Jack, Don't buy a single vote more than is necessary,'" Jack kidded, as the crowd laughed along. "I'll be damned if I'm going to pay for a landslide!" Without a hint of rancor or rivalry, Jack even teased about his father's contentious time as ambassador. "On this matter of experience, I had announced earlier this year that if successful I would not consider campaign contributions as a substitute for experience in appointing Ambassadors," he said in late 1960. "Ever since I made that comment I have not received a single cent from my Father."

Joe Kennedy knew that certain alliances and tests of loyalty could make a significant difference for Jack in a tight White House race against Vice President Richard M. Nixon, the certain Republican nominee in 1960. Beaverbrook could influence other businessmen and newspaper owners, but another friendship, with Vatican administrator Count Enrico Galeazzi, could push the hierarchy to convince thousands of American Catholics in critical swing states to support his son. A long-time top aide to Pope Pius XII, Galeazzi remained influential in Rome after the pontiff's death in October 1958. Along with his ecclesiastical ties, Galeazzi also was a key link with the Knights of Columbus, the American Catholic service organization run by laymen.

With his two old friends in distant places, Count Galeazzi and Lord Beaverbrook, Joe Kennedy shared some of his deepest hopes. "By the 1950s, he corresponded regularly and extensively, for the most part, only with his friends Max Beaverbrook in London and Enrico Galeazzi at the Vatican," observed granddaughter Amanda Smith in compiling his letters. In 1955, after a private audience with the Pope in Rome arranged by Galeazzi, Kennedy wrote to Beaverbrook about the implicit Vatican endorsement. "The Holy Father did me the great honor, which I think rarely, if ever, has been accorded anyone, by having his picture taken with me," Joe recalled. "I am sure that this means he approves the life you and I lead."

Joe kept Beaverbrook abreast of the international intrigue surrounding the Vatican, just as he had in the past. They both knew that Galeazzi had acted as the Pope's secret envoy during World War II, pushing Roosevelt and Churchill to spare Rome from Allied bombing. After the war, Galeazzi pursued his own interests with Kennedy, on behalf of the Church and himself. He accepted monetary gifts from the American multimillionaire, but mostly they traded favors and information. Joe offered himself as the Pope's faithful servant. "I don't know what I can continue to do to be of any assistance to him, but you know all you have to do is command me and, if it is humanly possible, I shall do it," Kennedy promised Galeazzi.

One of the biggest Vatican favors for the Kennedys was arranging for American taxpayers to fund repairs on the Pope's summer home. After the conflict, Galeazzi lobbied Joe Kennedy to seek reparations from the U.S. government for bombing damage done to the Pope's residence outside Rome, called Castel Gandolfo. In the late 1940s, Truman refused Joe's request for repair money. But in 1956, Senator John F. Kennedy helped shepherd one million dollars in taxpayer funds for the Pope's summer residence through a larger appropriations measure. "As you know, the authorization for the Vatican bill passed the Senate unanimously yesterday," Jack informed his father in a private note. "I think the appropriation bill will be all right too." Galeazzi's good friend in the American hierarchy, New York's cardinal, Francis J. Spellman, later thanked Senator Kennedy for his discreet intervention. "You have been wonderfully cooperative and wonderfully successful both in obtaining reimbursement to the Vatican for the damages caused during the war and also in obtaining funds to help pay for the damages to the institutions in the Philippines," Spellman wrote. While Jack showed himself a master of outside political theater, his father continued to influence events through his own insider connections. For nearly three decades, Joe Kennedy, Galeazzi, and Spellman had worked privately together to promote the interests of the Church in America, an investment that Joe expected would pay off handsomely now that his son was running for president. "What a wonderful gift it has been to have been so close to the Holy See during the past 20 years, a privilege not given to any other family in the world and it is all due to you," Joe wrote warmly to Galeazzi in February 1958. "You can imagine how grateful the Kennedy family feels towards you."

Joe Kennedy understood the impact of secret intelligence upon history's outcome. Like undercover assets, powerful friends were enlisted in his cause—such as Galeazzi, the gatekeeper of the Vatican's inner sanctum political information, and Beaverbrook, with his network of astute journalists, including Churchill's son. To Galeazzi, Kennedy offered to act as a discreet liaison between the Vatican and CIA director Allen Dulles if his son Jack were elected president. Months before the 1960 campaign, Dulles visited Joe in Florida and indicated that he'd like to remain America's top spymaster. Joe immediately let Galeazzi know he had another bargaining chip to play. "I think that if there is anything that you want me to do, you could let me know at once and I will contact him," Kennedy wrote to his Vatican ally in 1958 about the CIA chief. "He [Dulles] is very aware of the fact that Jack may be the next President and while he has always been very friendly to me, I think that he is more than ever anxious to please." Spying fascinated more than one Kennedy. While in Florida, Dulles chatted at a party with the senator's wife, Jacqueline, who mentioned the James Bond spy novels written by Ian Fleming, a product of Churchill's wartime intelligence machine. Jackie later sent the CIA director his first copy, *To Russia with Love*. "I got so much interested in them that I bought up the next two or three that he got out," Dulles recalled of the novels based on the fictional British spy. "I sent them to Senator Kennedy and [then] President Kennedy and we often talked about James Bond."

Neither Churchill nor Joe Kennedy thought much of the Dulles brothers, however. Winston described John Foster Dulles, Eisenhower's secretary of state and Allen's older sibling, as "the only bull I know who carries his china shop around with him," adding, "That man makes a beautiful declension: 'Dull, Duller, Dulles.'" Though Jack decided to keep Allen Dulles at the CIA for the time being, his father knew Allen could be easily manipulated, and Joe didn't think much of his worldly awareness. After Allen Dulles came to Palm Beach for lunch in 1957, Joe jocularly mentioned part of their conversation in a letter to another source of his inside information, FBI director J. Edgar Hoover. "I asked him what he thought of Marilyn Monroe, Jayne Mansfield and Anita Ekberg," said Kennedy, a friendly informant for the agency. "He said that he had never heard of the last two and then I asked him how he liked Perry Como and he asked me what he did." Hoover, a man not known for his sense of humor or interest in female pulchritude, jotted "no reply necessary" on the margin of Kennedy's letter.

As always, Beaverbrook proved a wonderful informant for Joe, someone who always seemed to act in Kennedy's interest. In November 1958, when Jock Whitney, the publisher of the *New York Herald Tribune*, invited Max to a private meeting with Vice President Richard Nixon, ostensibly to discuss foreign policy, Beaverbrook immediately alerted his friend in America. He humorously compared Whitney, this straightlaced Brahmin operative, to Joe's much cruder Irish-Catholic intermediary Francis X. Morrissey—a "judge" with suspect law credentials who was essentially a gofer for Joe and his sons. "He [Nixon] better get another Judge Morrissey to look after him," Max joked.

Behind the scenes, Joe Kennedy knew he'd done everything possible to help his son with a presidential goal that had once appeared so impossible, both for him and other Irish Catholics. "If I were betting, I would bet that Jack will get the nomination and will have no great difficulty with Nixon," Joe wrote to Beaverbrook in May 1960. As a savvy calculator of political fortune, Max agreed. He had watched the impressive grooming and development of Joe's son ever since visiting Massachusetts to see Jack win his first U.S. Senate campaign. As young Kennedy emerged as the Democratic Party front-runner during the 1960 primary season, Beaverbrook shared his gut assessment with another old friend, Winston Churchill.

"It seemed to me that America regards Kennedy with similar hysteria shown for Lindbergh half a century ago," Max cabled Churchill, "and he will win."

Although a skillful writer, Randolph Churchill found that his effort to establish a public life in his father's image remained a losing cause. In 1959 he tried unsuccessfully to gain the nomination for a safe Conservative seat in Parliament, though his father's party wouldn't have him. He also attempted in vain to stop the rival Labour Party from using a portion of his stinging book about Anthony Eden for a pamphlet called "The Tory Swindle." Fellow journalists tended to describe Randolph as more a buffoon "throwing his battered hat into the ring" than as a potential prime minister. Embarrassingly, Randolph even lost as an "English language expert" on American television's *The $64,000 Question* quiz program, which turned out to be rigged by the producers.

In his private life, Randolph moved to divorce his second wife, June, an emotionally vulnerable woman whom he treated poorly. The couple had lived with their young daughter, Arabella, in a country home outside London called Stour House, similar to Chartwell, until they separated in 1956. June moved out, alleging adultery, but the larger question seemed whether Randolph had ever loved her at all. His longtime infatuation with Laura Charteris remained unrequited, though their friendship would last for years. (Oddly enough, Laura's marital life had its own Churchill-Kennedy connection. Divorced in 1954 from the Earl of Dudley, Laura would soon wed writer Michael Canfield, previously married to Jackie Kennedy's sister, Lee Radziwill. Laura later married Randolph's cousin John Spencer-Churchill, the Tenth Duke of Marlborough, in 1972.) For June, life with Randolph had proved unbearable. "She realized that no woman on earth was cut out to be Randolph's wife—girlfriend maybe, for he was loving and generous and pathetically eager for attention," wrote another cousin, Anita Leslie. "But wife, no!"

During a family visit to Chartwell, long after June had gone to bed for the night, Randolph upset his father once again by raging against Anthony Eden. Drunk and loud, he left Winston in a huff and marched off to his guest room. Randolph awoke his wife, asleep beneath the sheets, and pulled her out of bed.

"You have got to dress and pack," Randolph shouted. "We are leaving this house forever."

June argued with her husband, who was stupefied and in full fury. Their yelling could be heard throughout Chartwell, reverberating through the walls. Finally, a knock sounded at their bedroom door. When it was opened, Winston was standing there in his dressing gown, begging for some peace. "I'm going to die soon," he pleaded at this late hour. "One must *not* have family rows. Let's kiss and forget it."

Exhausted, Randolph and his wife went to bed, though matters between them only intensified until it was clear they couldn't stay together.

Aware that his own aspirations for higher office might never be realized, Randolph focused with intensity on gaining his father's approval for what he called "the great book"—as the official biographer of Winston Churchill. By 1960 this unresolved debate between father and son had existed for more than a decade, stalled between Randolph's desire to show his worthiness and Winston's lingering doubts about his son. During the 1950s, Randolph's tryout credentials involved helping to put together a published study of Blenheim Palace, the family's ancestral home, and writing the life of Lord Derby, an exercise he began in 1956. Randolph considered it the "perfect training for the book he regards as his life work—a biography of his father," observed his friend, journalist C. L Sulzberger. "He won't start until the old man has died. But he wants to prepare himself in the technique."

After much effort, Randolph published his well-received biography *Lord Derby: King of Lancashire,* based on the life of one of his father's contemporaries, Edward, the Seventeenth Earl of Derby. Though not as internationally famous as Winston, Derby shared many of the same characteristics—he was a masterful, flamboyant figure in Conservative Party politics, with a wide range of experiences and a love of thoroughbred horses. Winston seemed particularly impressed with the book's endorsement by Prime Minister Harold Macmillan, the Conservative Party replacement for Eden, during a dinner together.

Finally, Winston agreed to let his son tell his story. The news came in the form of a telegram.

"He's asked me!" Randolph exulted, racing down the driveway at Stour House to tell Natalie Bevan, the newest woman in his life. "He's asked me, at last."

To his father, Randolph expressed his gratitude in writing. "Dearest Papa," he began, "your letter has made me proud and happy. Since I first read your life of your father, 35 years ago when I was a boy of 14 at Eton, it has always been my greatest ambition to write your life. And each year that has passed since this ambition first started in my mind, has nurtured it as your heroic career has burgeoned ... Thank you again from the bottom of my heart for a decision which, apart from what I have already said, adds a good deal to my self-esteem and will, I trust, enable me to do honour in filial fashion, to your extraordinarily noble and wonderful life."

Those who knew the tensions between the two were glad that Winston finally gave this approval to his son. "I had long been convinced that he [Randolph] was the right man for the job," observed Anthony Montague Browne, Winston's personal secretary. "He would have been bitter and permanently hurt if he had not been chosen, and it seemed imperative that the lives of father and son should be brought closer while there was still time."

If Randolph, at age forty-nine, was not to have his own life in politics, at least he could re-create his father's in his own image, employing Winston's splendid words. With full access to his father's papers at Chartwell and to the Royal Archives, Randolph would once again become his father's public defender and most faithful advocate. The curses and remonstrations between them seemed to have ended. Rather than the acid rapier tongue for which his journalism was known, he now set out with earnestness on the center stage of history. In telling the full-bodied version of his father's life, Randolph explained, he planned to follow the advice of John G. Lockhart, the biographer of Sir Walter Scott: "He shall be his own biographer."

Over the next several months, Randolph worked studiously at Stour House and met occasionally with his father at Chartwell to discuss aspects of the book. He scrupulously recorded notes of their sessions.

"Do you realize I have now been out of office for five years?" Winston mentioned at one lunch together.

"Well, that's a very dreadful thing, but don't forget that between the wars you were out of office for ten years," Randolph reminded him, "so there is nothing to worry about."

The familiar rivalry of their wordplay—a reminder of those happier times together when they journeyed to such faraway places as the West Coast of North America—made Winston grin. At this lunch, they chatted some more about the great work, including the research and travel involved.

"You will make quite a fine show for yourself about the book," Winston eventually concluded, "but don't give up about politics."

They both knew the chances for Randolph's resurrection in politics were remote.

"Well, I am happy with the book and my garden, and we might let politics skip a generation," Randolph offered humbly. "Perhaps Winston might get interested."

Little Winston, Randolph's son with Pamela, was now a young man himself, with a big head of golden hair and winning smile. During the summer leading up to the 1960 campaign, young Winston spent time in Washington and considered becoming a volunteer in the presidential campaign headquarters of John F. Kennedy. Young Winston was "filled with excitement" about working for Kennedy and cabled his father to ask his advice. Randolph soon sent back a disapproving telegram.

ASK JACK WHAT HAPPENED TO BRITISH AMBASSADOR SACKVILLE-WEST 1886, Randolph wrote cryptically to his son, referring to Kennedy. SUGGEST YOU FIND SOMETHING LESS POLITICALLY AND CLIMATICALLY HOT THAN WASHINGTON. LET ME KNOW IF I CAN HELP. LOVE = FATHER.

After a little research, young Winston learned that Sir Lionel Sackville-West, the British ambassador, inadvertently butted into the 1888 American presidential race. In a letter that became public, Sackville-West revealed his personal favorite (Grover Cleveland, who lost in the Electoral College), and wound up being sacked for his indiscretion. It was a warning from Randolph to his son about the dangers for Englishmen who dabbled in U.S. domestic politics. "It was a crushing reply but this advice, which I accepted, was entirely right," young Winston recalled about Randolph's telegram. "As several of my father's friends have told me, his advice to them, about their problems or a course of action, was often both dispassionate and wise."

43

Arms to Parley

At the Biltmore Hotel in Los Angeles, where John F. Kennedy's presidential campaign team ran their operation from Suite 8315, a group of hymn-signing protesters outside wore sandwich boards painted with a message: "Pray Much, Christians, We Want a God-Fearing Man, Not a Man Ruled from Rome or from Moscow."

Kennedy arrived at the 1960 Democratic Convention in mid-July as the front-runner. During a successful primary season, he proved in places such as West Virginia that America might be ready to elect a Catholic to the White House—at least a Harvard-educated millionaire's son who preached a strict policy of church and state separation. The Biltmore signs were a reminder of how religion still existed as a major obstacle for Kennedy, and that his nomination was far from assured.

The last gasp of opposition came from Lyndon Johnson, the Senate majority leader from Texas, who thought he might still be able to strong-arm enough delegates away from Kennedy. Behind his back, Johnson's camp referred to the forty-three-year-old junior senator as "Daddy's Boy" and "The Kid." Bobby Kennedy, his brother's campaign manager, showed himself every bit as capable as Johnson of cajoling, twisting arms, and counting heads. Like junkyard dogs, the two men, Bobby and Lyndon, displayed a visceral dislike for each other.

At a pivotal "debate" among some delegates, Johnson suggested John Kennedy wasn't ready for the awesome duties of the presidency. The amiably polite senator from Massachusetts—once willowy thin but now fuller in the face from his testosterone injections to fight off his undisclosed Addison's disease—rose to address these delegates. He promptly put Johnson away with a few rhetorical swings. "The young man hauled off and belted the Texan between the horns with a closing admonition," recounted political writer Jim Bishop. Kennedy's feistiness convinced these delegates he could stand up to any challenge from Republican nominee Richard Nixon. "Who the hell knew Kennedy could fight?" a surprised delegate told Bishop.

At this convention, another journalist impressed with Kennedy's "guts, charm, intelligence and political horse sense" was Randolph Churchill. He covered U.S. presidential campaigns no longer for Beaverbrook's newspaper but for *News of the World*. The huge tabloid picked up Randolph's sizeable tab in his job as roving correspondent in Los Angeles, where this British Tory mingled, drink in hand, with the Democrats. "Randolph was red-faced and exultant, rejoicing over the nomination of Jack Kennedy, whom he adored as extravagantly as he despised Jack's father," recalled Arthur M. Schlesinger Jr., who himself had migrated from the Stevenson camp to Kennedy's. Like most British men of his generation, Churchill's son could not forgive the former ambassador's defeatism during the war. While Schlesinger and his wife, Marian, waited for a cab, he recalled, Randolph poured out his wrath "at length how much he hated Joe Kennedy (and for good reason too)." Though on the Onassis yacht he discouraged any rapprochement by his father with the Kennedys, Randolph had warmed to Jack. He admired the style that young Kennedy projected as a statesman-writer, perhaps as an ideal he wished for himself. Randolph knew enough not to visit the sins of the father on the son.

That night, Schlesinger was dismayed to learn that Jack Kennedy had decided to pick Lyndon Johnson as his vice-presidential running mate. No one was unhappier, though, than Robert Kennedy. In Bobby's estimate, the crude Texas pol had committed a cardinal sin. During his last-minute scramble to round up delegates at the convention, Johnson had personally attacked Joe Kennedy. "I wasn't any Chamberlain umbrella-policy man," Johnson said, reminding delegates of the ambassador's appeasement past. "I never thought Hitler was right." Bobby, dominated by a wish to please his father, far more so than Jack, was furious. With a clenched fist, he vowed to Bobby Baker, LBJ's aide, "You'll get yours."

But Joe Kennedy urged Jack to take on the Texan as his running mate and never let Johnson's personal attack get in the way of his advice. Now that his family's long-awaited moment was at hand, the senior Kennedy, aware of his negative image among liberals, didn't gloat publicly or bathe himself in the glory of Jack's nomination for president. He made the trip to the West Coast for the convention, though stayed out of sight by renting the mansion of Marion Davies—the same hostess with whom the Kennedys and Churchills had stayed during different Los Angeles visits in the 1930s. Despite Bobby's rage at Johnson, which seemed to blind him, Joe never lost sight of a political reality: Johnson could deliver Texas and much of the Bible Belt South in the general election, an important factor with Kennedy's Catholicism still looming as the biggest hurdle of the campaign. JFK reluctantly agreed with his father to choose Johnson, over Bobby's severe objections.

"Don't worry, Jack," Joe told his older son. "In two weeks, they'll be saying it's the smartest thing you ever did."

. . .

During his acceptance speech in Los Angeles, Jack Kennedy referred to the same familiar figure who'd once influenced his political future when he was a sickly teenager reading *The World Crisis* in a Boston hospital. JFK looked to Churchill's example for "his courage, bold pronouncements, and his brilliant oratory," speechwriter Theodore Sorensen later recalled. If Kennedy's own father provided the necessary practical advice, Winston had been a sort of spiritual godfather providing inspiration. "We are not here to curse the darkness, but to light the candle that can guide us through that darkness to a safe and sane future," Kennedy told the crowd, reprising the imagery of Churchill's 1940 "Their Finest Hour" speech. "As Winston Churchill said on taking office some twenty years ago: If we open a quarrel between the present and the past, we shall be in danger of losing the future."

Kennedy relied on the past to critique the GOP's Nixon during the general election campaign. He likened the incumbent vice president to former British prime minister Stanley Baldwin, who ignored Churchill's 1930s warning of a German military buildup. "I spent some months in England in the 1930's, and I heard Winston Churchill speak again and again about the perils that England faced," Kennedy told a Michigan audience. "And I heard Stanley Baldwin and Chamberlain run on programs of 'Never had it so good,' that everything was being done in its proper time and in its proper place. I believe that those who serve freedom in 1960 should tell the American people that this is the best of times, but it is also then a time of hazard, that the United States is not meeting its responsibility, that the tide is not moving in our favor, that the power of the Communists relative to ours is mounting, and that we cannot afford to lose more time in the fight for freedom around the globe."

Though he likely knew better, Kennedy claimed the United States suffered from a "missile gap" with the Soviet Union, suggesting the nation's defenses were secondary and somehow vulnerable to attack. With

Churchill-like pronouncements, Jack moved to awaken his nation from its "locust years" under Eisenhower, just as Winston had warned of Baldwin's policies. "Twenty three years ago, in a bitter debate in the House of Commons, Winston Churchill charged the British Government with acute blindness to the menace of Nazi Germany, with gross negligence in the maintenance of the island's defenses, and with indifferent, indecisive leadership of British foreign policy and British public opinion," Kennedy stated. "The preceding years of drift and impotence, he said, were 'the years the locusts have eaten.' And it seems to me tonight that this nation has, since January 1953, passed through a similar period. When we should have sailed hard into the wind, we, too, drifted."

In this campaign, Kennedy would repeat the same lessons of his book *Why England Slept*—only this time with different players and with himself in a starring role. Kennedy's warnings echoed similar points about Baldwin that Randolph Churchill had emphasized in his introduction to *Arms and the Covenant*, the collection of Winston's 1930s speeches published in America as *While England Slept*. Now in 1960, Kennedy argued before millions that only by building up America's military could the United States avoid a future conflict. "We all saw it as a prelude not to war but to negotiation," Schlesinger later recalled. "Kennedy never tired of quoting Winston Churchill: 'We arm to parley.'"

The "arm to parley" phrase—invoked by Churchill as the Cold War took hold in 1949—was wielded as a rhetorical weapon by Kennedy against Nixon and the administration of Eisenhower, the consummate military leader of their age. Though the United States far outpaced the Soviets in nuclear armaments, the lingering anticommunist scare of the McCarthy era and the successful October 1957 launch of *Sputnik*, the world's first satellite, provided a strategic, if unjustified, political opportunity for Kennedy. "We cannot parley on the basis of equality with the Soviet unless we maintain a military position of equality with them, and that goes in the traditional weapons and in missiles and in outer space," Kennedy proclaimed. "One of the reasons why we have never been able to get an agreement on the disarmament of outer space is because we are second in outer space, and the Soviet Union will not give way their advantage. We arm to parley, and we must be strong if we are going to disarm and maintain our security."

The Churchill allusions and quotes kept flowing during Kennedy's campaign. "The legislative process in a democracy is a slow process, and it always will be," Kennedy reminded the electorate. "For as Winston Churchill once said: 'Democracy is the worst form of government— except all those other forms that have been tried from time to time.'" In the coal country of West Virginia, Kennedy used Churchill to comment about improving health care for the elderly and to compare his proposals to FDR's New Deal program: "When Winston Churchill called at the start of World War II for our arms and destroyers, he pleaded: 'Give us the tools—and we will finish the job.' The people of West Virginia do not want the Federal government to do everything for them. They do not want charity and handouts. They are saying instead, with one voice, 'Give us the tools—and we will finish the job.'"

After the convention, Joe and Rose Kennedy vacationed in the South of France, out of sight from the press. Joe made sure to visit Lord Beaverbrook, who spoke excitedly of his son's historic moment. Using an old Churchill comparison, Max predicted that Jack's winning the presidency at such a young age would be "paralleled only by the triumph of the younger Pitt." It was the kind of reference—of the fabled father-and-son tandem who became eighteenth-century British prime ministers—once envisioned as the destiny of Randolph Churchill.

In Paris, Joe and Rose were hounded by international reporters and paparazzi, and managed to slip away from the Ritz to Monte Carlo. One night at a casino restaurant, Rose emerged with friends from a Mercedes and was greeted by an unexpected host. "Who should be clasping my hand and welcoming me, but [Aristotle] Onassis," she recalled to her children back in the States. "Onassis was so profuse in his greeting and so solicitous about my welfare that I got an idea, he had made plans of his own to have me at his table and be photographed just like that." Ari used the same ploy upon first meeting Winston Churchill—tipping off the paparazzi so the world would see him with a famous or powerful person. When Rose declined his invitation, Onassis seemed quite flustered, and a "grand upheaval" ensued until she wound up at a small table away from the tycoon. A few days later, Onassis tried to make amends with the mother of America's future president. "Onassis sent me four dozen roses with a note regretting any embarrassment which he caused me—so what will he do next year?" Rose recounted to her family, more amused than upset. While the Kennedys were in Monte Carlo, Count Galeazzi "came up from Rome for a day" to visit and talked of their son's impending campaign to become the first Catholic in the White House. "Jack's victory will mean a great service rendered to his community and the Church by freeing his countrymen from bigotry, darkness and ignorance," the Vatican administrator assured. But Beaverbrook also knew what a Kennedy victory would mean for Joe personally. "May your seventy-third year bring you the reward you so richly deserve—your son in the White House," he wrote on September 3, 1960. "Looking back on your own career, I am convinced that, had you not had to strive so hard in your early days for money to pay living expenses, you would have devoted yourself to politics. In that case, you would have had a term or two in the White House yourself."

When Joe arrived back in America, he found the campaign's most vexing political issue, the Kennedys' Catholicism, had not gone away. "I came home to find the campaign not between a Democrat and a Republican, but between a Catholic and a Protestant," he told Beaverbrook. "How effectively we can work against it, I do not know. Jack gave it a bad licking in West Virginia and we are confident that we can lick it now. But with the Baptist ministers working in the pulpit every Sunday, it is going to be tough." That same week, Jack appeared before a group of Protestant ministers in Houston to assure them of his independence in an eloquent speech about church and state that would be studied for decades. "For contrary to common newspaper usage, I am not the Catholic candidate for president," the senator proclaimed. "I am the Democratic Party's candidate for president, who happens also to be a Catholic. I do not speak for my church on public matters, and the church does not speak for me. Whatever issue may come before me as president—on birth control, divorce, censorship, gambling or any other subject—I will make my decision in accordance with these views, in accordance with what my conscience tells me to be the national interest, and without regard to outside religious pressures or dictates. And no power or threat of punishment could cause me to decide otherwise."

Like Churchill, Jack knew humor could disarm critics as well as bolster his dubious supporters. When Kennedy learned that Martin Luther King Jr.'s father, a Baptist minister, initially opposed him because of his religion, he quipped, "Well, we all have fathers, don't we?" After former president Harry S. Truman reluctantly endorsed Kennedy— "It's not the pope I'm afraid of, it's the pop," explained the plainspoken Missourian—he earned Nixon's ire for saying Republicans could go to hell. "While I understand and sympathize with your deep motivation," Jack joked in response to Truman, "I think it is important that our side try to refrain from raising the religious issue." Though Al Smith became embittered by the bigotry he faced in 1928, Kennedy consistently deflected opposition with his charm steeped in Churchillian humor. Nixon, with his tiresome intensity, could be a convenient foil. "Mr. Nixon, in the last seven days, has called me an economic ignoramus, a Pied Piper, and all the rest," Kennedy informed a New York crowd just before Election Day. "I just confined myself to calling him a Republican, but he says that is getting low." Among his staffers, Jack joked when the early poll numbers didn't look very good, "Do you realize the responsibility I carry? I'm the only person standing between Nixon and the White House."

Religion remained Kennedy's biggest barrier, however, the number one issue of the 1960 campaign, the *New York Times* Week in Review editors determined before Election Day. They found that Kennedy's Catholicism exceeded the economy, race relations, and even nuclear war. Throughout his campaign, in a way that might have provoked a lesser man, JFK repeatedly confronted this ugliness with wit, grace, and remarkable coolness. The most alarming blow occurred in New York in September 1960, when a group of 150 ministers, led by the Reverend Dr. Norman Vincent Peale, author of the bestseller *The Power of Positive Thinking* and a Nixon backer, openly questioned whether a Catholic was fit to be president. They doubted whether Kennedy could resist "extreme pressure from the hierarchy of his church" to formulate U.S. foreign policy according to Vatican dictates. "Last week a noted clergyman was quoted as saying that our society may survive in the event of my election, but it certainly won't be what it was," Kennedy remarked, with deprecating humor. "I would like to think he was complimenting me, but I'm not sure he was."

In Los Angeles, one wiseacre reporter flipped the usual religion question on its head. "Do you think a Protestant can be elected president in 1960?" the journalistic rascal asked.

Kennedy didn't miss a beat. "If he's prepared to answer how he stands on the issue of separation of church and state, I see no reason why we should discriminate against him," Kennedy said straight-faced—a Churchillian riposte if ever there was one.

In contrast to Jack's affable posture, Joe Kennedy fumed privately about the bigotry hurled at his son, with little sense of irony about his own prejudices. Yet Joe aimed his greatest outrage at Catholic clergymen such as New York's cardinal, Francis Spellman, for not being more loyal. Ever the politician, Spellman not so secretly supported Nixon, afraid that Kennedy would be too handcuffed to help the Church. The cardinal's sentiments were evident when Jack shared the same stage with Nixon at the annual Al Smith fund-raising dinner in New York. "It all goes to show that, when the chips are down, money counts more than religion," Jack grumbled to Schlesinger. Spellman had married Joe Kennedy's children and baptized his grandchildren. He and Joe had worked together with Galeazzi in arranging FDR's historic 1936 meeting in Hyde Park with the future Pope, Cardinal Pacelli, and on other Spellman pet projects funded with Joe's charitable contributions. Now, at the moment Joe needed Spellman the most—to help sway thousands of Catholic voters toward his son—their friendship had collapsed. "As far as I am concerned, I am disgusted, and I would prefer not to have any further contacts [with Spellman]," Joe advised his other Church pal, Galeazzi. Not only was nominee John F. Kennedy's father upset with Spellman, but so was his wife, Jacqueline. "He so obviously was against Jack. How could you like him? And his little mincing ways," Jackie recalled of the cardinal. "You know, he really was trying to just slit Jack's throat all the time and wouldn't be a help." Not much for churchgoing herself, Jackie always felt it ironic that Jack's bid for the presidency would hinge so much on his religion. Her husband attended Mass regularly but didn't exhibit the religious fervor of his mother, Rose, or even of his brother Bobby. On the question of whether there was a heaven or a hell, Jack, as in life, hedged his bets, saying his prayers every night like a little boy. "I mean he wasn't quite sure, but if it was that way, he wanted to have that on his side," Jackie said of her husband's ideas about heavenly salvation.

After navigating through a world dominated by Protestants in Boston, London, and Washington, the Kennedys had learned that their Irish-Catholic identity was more than a matter of faith or culture, but almost a tribal emblem. Even Jackie, who favored her father's French roots rather than her mother's Irish, recognized the clannishness among Kennedys such as Rose, who constantly asked in private if someone was Catholic. "They always seem to have a sort of persecution thing about them, don't they?" Jackie confided to Schlesinger.

In one of the closest presidential elections in U.S. history, John F. Kennedy beat Richard M. Nixon by a whisper—a 100,000-margin among 68 million votes cast. Although old-style politicking, particularly blocs of ethnic and minority votes from America's cities, helped carry several key states, the first-of-its kind television debate between the two candidates proved decisive. Unlike Nixon, Kennedy carefully prepared for this moment, championing techniques of the new medium, just as his father urged. "John Kennedy walked out of the studio that night the next president of the United States," remembered Don Hewitt, the CBS News producer for the debate. More than a television candidate, JFK became known as a barrier breaker. For decades to come, his would be the touchstone mentioned by every candidate from a minority background seeking national office, including Barack Obama, who later broke through another cultural barrier on race. "I heard too many people saying that he [Obama] had lost his chance to be president the day he was born black in America, just as in 1960 they were saying John F. Kennedy had lost his chance to be president the day he was baptized Catholic in America," Ted Sorensen remembered.

Before the 1960 voting, Randolph Churchill interviewed both candidates, consulted with pollster George Gallup, and boldly predicted for his newspaper column who would win. "I am not sure that I know the answer, but I will be braver than [Gallup]," Randolph told his readers in London. "I think Kennedy will be the next President of the United States."

Though no longer prime minister, Winston felt compelled by duty to send a note of congratulations to young Kennedy upon his victory.

"I salute you," Churchill wrote. "The thoughts and support of the free world will be with you in the challenging tasks that lie ahead."

Kennedy called upon history in his response to Churchill. "The people of the United States and of the world will never forget your valiant leadership in their darkest hours in the fight against tyranny," saluted the new president-elect. "May your unconquerable spirit be with us for years to come." Winston seemed to have no idea how much he'd affected the outlook of the former ambassador's son. "Kennedy certainly has tremendous tasks before him," Winston wrote to a family in-law about the new American president. "I had a friendly exchange of messages with him after his election."

Randolph harbored a personal sympathy for losers. After the 1960 campaign, he dropped a kind note to Nixon, praising "the manful and effective way in which you fought." Randolph said he had tears in his eyes as he watched Nixon's concession speech on television. Recalling his own experience, Churchill wrote that "I, on a tiny scale, have had several election defeats. I admired more than I can say the courageous and dignified way in which you accepted yours." Nixon and his wife seemed genuinely touched by the Churchill gesture. "A message of congratulations after winning an election is of course always appreciated although not unexpected," the Nixons responded to Randolph. "But nothing could have meant more to us than to receive such a warm and thoughtful message after losing."

44

Mending Fences

For nearly two decades, the Churchills and the Kennedys kept a respectful distance, wary of the World War II acrimony between the patriarchs, but also mindful of the many connections they shared. In 1961, with the presidential inauguration of John F. Kennedy, one of their mutual friends, Kay Halle, tried to bridge this gap.

The inauguration of an American president—a ceremony far more public than, say, a British monarch's "Speech from the Throne" at the opening of Parliament—has always been a mix of high and low culture. For this inaugural's nighttime gala, popular singer and Hollywood star Frank Sinatra put together a smorgasbord of entertainers, who serenaded the president. Kennedy had become friendly with Sinatra, the satyr of Las Vegas casinos with his "Rat Pack" pals, through his brother-in-law Peter Lawford, the British actor married to Kennedy's sister Patricia.

For the solemn daytime swearing-in, however, the Kennedys adopted advice from another family friend, Halle, who suggested that dozens of artists, poets, composers, and intellectuals be invited to sit among the honored guests. Robert Frost read a poem as part of the ceremony. "It is the first time that the creative Americans have been considered the equal of the politicians," Halle contended. Winston Churchill, though, was Kennedy's greatest influence that day. "He told me, I remember, that he had read every single thing Churchill had ever written," said Halle.

Kennedy's stirring inaugural speech—an idealistic plea for all Americans to "ask not what your country can do for you, ask what you can do for your country"—reverberated with Churchill's literate thoughts and cadences. For inspiration, Kennedy had listened to recordings of Churchill and shared his vision of Anglo-American unity, almost word for word. "To those old allies whose cultural and spiritual origins we share, we pledge the loyalty of faithful friends," the new president proclaimed. "United, there is little we cannot do in a host of cooperative ventures. Divided, there is little we can do—for we dare not meet a powerful challenge at odds and split asunder."

Kennedy's description of the Cold War's "long twilight struggle" sounded like Churchill during Britain's dark days in World War II. When Jack reminded the crowd of "the graces of young Americans who answered the call to service surround the globe," it undoubtedly brought to mind Joe Jr., lost in battle defending England. Kennedy's rhetoric called for the United States to "pay any price, bear any burden, meet any hardship" to defend liberty against communism. It echoed Churchill's 1940 speech against Nazi totalitarianism, when he vowed that "we shall never surrender." With the new U.S. sphere of influence now more like an empire than Great Britain, Kennedy's speech underlined his intentions to become the heir to Churchill's legacy. "In the long history of the world, only a few generations have been granted the role of defending freedom in its hour of maximum danger," he concluded. "I do not shrink from this responsibility—I welcome it."

. . .

As a keepsake of this special day, Kay Halle put together a private book for Jack with well-wishes from inaugural guests such as Ernest Hemingway, John Steinbeck, W. H. Auden, and Tennessee Williams. Jackie Kennedy and the president's mother, Rose, were particularly appreciative of Halle. "I just had to tell you how absolutely overwhelmed we were by the book you did for Jack," Jacqueline gushed in a note on White House stationery. "He had told you but I couldn't believe my eyes. One is in awe when one turns the pages and sees the treasures there—Hemingway, Sandburg, Tennessee's favorite lines and so many others. I'll never forget." Weeks before the inaugural, Rose Kennedy went to lunch with Halle. With her blonde hair faded to silver, Kay was now a grande dame of Washington society rather than the free-spirited amour of the 1930s involved with Randolph Churchill and Joe Kennedy. Rose fondly recalled their boat trip together to London, when their party visited the Churchills at Chartwell—a time when the two families were friendly before the war redefined their relationship. Rose treated Kay like so many other women in her husband's life, as nothing more than a friend. When Kay asked about the women swooning at Jack's rallies, Rose expressed surprise at how her once-sickly son had become such a charismatic figure. "When he was growing up in our house I never noticed the girls swarming around our door!" Rose confided.

Unsure of herself in Washington, Jackie Kennedy turned to Halle for advice, notably about bringing artists to the White House. "One thing I wish you could help me with," Jackie penned in her fragmented longhand sentences. "Is it enough to just keep doing things in a private way—as one would do if not President—Go to the theatres, symphonies, etc. and try to have the entertainment at the W[hite] House be substantial— ... But that is so little—Do you think we should have an enormous reception at the W. House for artists—that seems rather treating them like freaks—I try to work some into every State dinner— but that's a tiny drop in the bucket—If you have a brainstorm do tell me." Jackie let Kay know how to send notes to her social secretary's attention so that she'd read them personally. "Put your name on the letter and SPECIAL—(my code for getting my own mail!)" she instructed. Kay's advice seemed reflected in a White House state dinner at which Pablo Casals, the famous cellist, entertained while Leonard Bernstein and Aaron Copland listened in the audience. Kay sat at a table with her friend Janet Auchincloss, Jackie's mother. "I think it is tremendously important that we regard music not just as a part of our arsenal in the cold war but an integral part of a free society," President Kennedy impressed upon the crowd.

Months after the inaugural, President Kennedy invited Kay to the White House and they chatted about how beautiful Jackie looked that day. Then their conversation turned to Churchill and a favorite description from his book *The River War.* Halle suggested something more should be done to recognize Winston's greatness.

"What have you got on your mind?" the president asked.

"It's about time we made Churchill an honorary citizen," Halle said.

When Halle first brought up the idea with President Eisenhower, "Churchill indicated that he felt, quite rightly, that it was probably not the time[,] after the Suez crisis," she later recalled. But now seemed the perfect time for Jack to recognize the man he'd so admired throughout his life—an extraordinary gift while both Winston and his father were still alive, ending whatever rancor between the families still remained.

"It's exactly what I'm for," Kennedy promised about the Churchill honor, "and I'm going to get my team on it."

Winston Churchill initially appeared uneasy with the idea of honorary American citizenship. In the past, British political opponents, aware of his mother's Brooklyn birthplace, called him "a Yankee mongrel" behind his back. At age eighty-six, Churchill seemed to misunderstand this effort on his behalf. "He thought the intention was, as it were, to hijack him and change his nationality," recalled Jock Colville. " 'I am,' he said to me, 'a British subject and as that I intend to die.' " However, once the "true and touching intention was made plain," Colville recalled, "he then accepted the honor with the pleasure which the promoters of the plan hoped to give him."

Kay Halle's visit to Chartwell in August 1961 helped settle things. She arrived with Randolph and his lover, Natalie Bevan, the beautiful painter married to one of his neighbors, and Randolph's son, Winston. Clementine Churchill, dressed in a pale yellow dress, sweater, and pearls, greeted them at the gate. On the terrace, Winston could be seen relaxing in a bamboo chair with a beige African campaign hat on his head. The Churchills first chatted privately with Randolph and his son, while Kay and Natalie were taken on a tour of the grounds by Clementine's secretary. Walking past the water gardens, Halle remembered how Winston stocked his man-made lake with swans, surrounded by golden roses, ivy geraniums, and wisteria trees all around the Weald.

Once inside the house, the guests prepared for lunch. Halle stared at some of the artwork on the walls, including a black-and-white portrait drawing of Winston's beautiful mother, Jennie Churchill, by the American artist John Singer Sargent.

"You remember Kay Halle, Winston, Randolph's friend from America," Clementine said, her voice turned up loud so her husband could hear.

Halle sat next to Churchill at the table, across from Clementine and Randolph. To Winston, Halle virtually shouted that she'd recently seen his old friend Bernard Baruch, who was visiting the White House the same day she saw Kennedy. Winston seemed particularly pleased, she recalled, when "I told him I brought the warmest greetings of the President of the United States."

In the most rousing moment of the visit, Churchill lifted his glass off the table and turned to Halle.

"Kay, let us drink to your great President and—and ours," Winston toasted, emphasizing the special relationship between the two nations.

Kennedy was very much on Winston's mind. Three months earlier, Winston had cruised up the East Coast of the United States aboard Onassis's yacht, where they docked in New York and rode out a storm. Sir Winston's arrival caused a sensation, with fireboats and helicopters escorting him to port. Soon the White House called with an invitation. Winston's personal secretary, Ashley Montague Browne, recalled President Kennedy was "markedly friendly" and offered to send a presidential aircraft to pick up Churchill so they could confer "for a day or two in Washington." While in New York, Winston had eaten dinner with Baruch and received visitors such as Adlai Stevenson. But Montague Browne explained that Winston's memory was now faulty, and he wasn't prepared for a discussion about world events with the leader of the free world. "I understand your reasons, and I feared this would be the case," Kennedy replied.

During their fantastical jaunts on Onassis's yacht, Churchill seemed unaware of the surrounding world and increasingly showed "the accumulated damage of his years," Montague Browne wrote. During a stop in Monte Carlo, Winston waited for his car to pick him up outside a casino when singer Frank Sinatra suddenly appeared unannounced. Briskly, the crooner went up to Churchill and shook his hand.

"I've wanted to do that for twenty years," Sinatra said proudly.

As the pop singer walked away, Churchill "who didn't like to be touched, bellowed: 'Who the hell was that?' I told him but he said he was none the wiser," Montague Browne recalled.

During her trip to Chartwell, Halle also noticed Winston's physical decline but was touched by his efforts to keep up with the rest of his guests. "In spite of 5 strokes and not being able to hear, he followed a good bit of the conversation," she wrote in her notes. Winston asked Kay if there was a picture of him in the White House. She said she didn't know but would return with one to give to Kennedy if he liked. Winston grinned gently while considering the offer. When she left Chartwell with the other guests, Halle felt moved enough to give Churchill a slight embrace. By then, he'd settled down next to an unlit fireplace, reading *Tess of the D'Urbervilles*, with his half-glasses balanced on the end of his nose. "I could not resist leaning down—putting my arms around him and kissing him," Halle recalled. "He put his fingers to his lips and blew me a kiss and smiled his Jack o Lantern smile."

At the time of her visit, Halle was preparing a collection of Winston's witticisms for a future book. Her unbounded admiration for Churchill tended toward hagiography. In reporting back to her president, though, Halle was more sober and realistic. "I fear, Mr. President, that if the Honorary American Citizenship we discussed, is not bestowed on Sir Winston soon, even his 'mighty central mass' will have crumbled," she warned. "Though his cheek was warm when I kissed him farewell, both hands were cold."

During the Kennedy administration, the connections between the two families multiplied and became more complex as Churchill's seminal influence on the new president became clearer. When *Life* magazine listed the new president's ten favorites books in March 1961, Kennedy included Churchill's *Marlborough*, calling the biography of Winston's ancestor "the best thing he has done." Within his own bureaucracy, Kennedy argued that persuasive memo writing was an important part of effective governing, pointing to Churchill's wartime missives as proof. "Churchill is very graceful at this," Kennedy instructed. Although a liberal at heart, Kennedy showed Churchill's ability to combine both progressive and conservative ideas into practical solutions. In calling for tax cuts, Kennedy seemed to heed the warning of Churchill in 1951 when he said "all the boastings of the Welfare State have to be set against the fact that more than what they have given with one hand has been filched back by the other." At press conferences, Kennedy's witty impromptu answers reminded many of Churchill's quick repartee in the House and his amusing wordplay amid the most dire circumstances. Even his political opponents were roasted gently. At a July 1963 press conference, a reporter asked his reaction to a recent Republican National Committee resolution "saying you were pretty much a failure—how do you feel about that?" With his disarming smile, Kennedy replied, "I assume it passed unanimously."

No longer detesting the Kennedys, Randolph Churchill became part of their extended social circle once again. He was invited to a private party with the president and First Lady when they flew to London in June 1961 to stand as godparents at the baptism for the baby daughter of Jackie's younger sister, Lee, and her husband Prince Stanislas Radziwill, a London businessman born of Polish nobility. Outside, a crowd chanted, "We want Jackie!" Beaverbrook's newspaper ran a cartoon of the Statue of Liberty with Jackie's face holding the torch of freedom in one hand and *Vogue* magazine in the other. After the christening, Randolph joined other Kennedy family intimates, including the Duke and Duchess of Devonshire, for the party at the Radziwill residence, followed by a black-tie dinner with the queen.

Three months later, Randolph landed an exclusive interview with JFK at the White House, where they discussed the state of the world and the president briefly escorted him around. When Randolph inquired about Jackie, Kennedy showed him a little watercolor sketch done by his wife depicting the White House around 1800. ("I suppose shortly before we Limeys burnt it down in 1812," Randolph joked to himself in his notes.) Kennedy stared at the painting for a moment. "Look at that splendid lawn—it looks rather like Chatsworth," the president said, remembering the mansion where his sister Kick had once stayed with her in-laws. During Randolph's short interview, Kennedy put his feet up on his desk and kept quoting Sir Winston. "He had read all his works and seems to know them better than I do," Randolph noted.

During their talk, Randolph asked about Kennedy's attempt to contain the Communist threat in Berlin, Cuba, and the emerging hotspot in Southeast Asia known as Vietnam. "Kennedy said he was more worried about Vietnam than he was about West Berlin," wrote Randolph. "The President said, in effect, that it was quite clear-cut in Berlin[,] and Russia knew what we were going to do, but in Vietnam it was a tiresome gorilla [*sic*] war which was not the sort of war that the American troops were very good at and it was very hard indeed to know what to do."

Although JFK revealed little of himself in their first Oval Office meeting, Randolph gained a better sense of Kennedy when he returned many months later. They were chatting about the British Labour Party when Kennedy's toddler son, John F. Kennedy Jr., came bounding in.

"I'm a big bear and I'm hungry!" the little boy yelled with glee, jumping out from under the president's desk. "I'm going to eat you up in one bite."

The president's face brightened before offering an explanation to Churchill's son.

"You may think this is strange behavior in the office of the President of the United States," Kennedy explained, "but in addition to being the President, I also happen to be a father."

Several who knew Randolph in London were part of the widening circle of Kennedy friends and political associates. Along with the Devonshires, the inauguration guests had included Pamela Hayward, Randolph's former wife, then married to American theatrical producer Leland Hayward. She also attended a private inaugural party thrown by Jack's father. "Joe Kennedy had a whole thing waiting for us," Pamela recalled. "That's where the family was so great—once a friend, always a friend."

Another Churchill confidant from the war, former New York governor Averell Harriman, gained a new political life with the Kennedys, after serving one term in Albany before losing to Republican Nelson Rockefeller in 1958. Harriman was known as a Stevenson supporter who didn't favor Jack because of his dislike for his father, Joe. "As a diplomat, he found Kennedy's London performance during the early days of Britain's war against Hitler indefensible, and his disloyalty to Roosevelt shameful," observed Harriman biographer Rudy Abramson. But Jack and Bobby Kennedy appreciated Harriman's talents and good advice on foreign policy. They soon forgave any previous family trespasses. At a party for Averell in October 1961, Bobby recalled the older man's time with Churchill. "There was a special touch of historic irony here: Joe Kennedy's boy, the boy Joe thought most like him, giving a party in honor of Harriman, the man whom Roosevelt had sent to England at the beginning of the war almost to counteract the pessimistic impressions and appraisals of Joe as ambassador," recounted historian David Halberstam.

David Ormsby-Gore, the British ambassador known as Lord Harlech, was another longtime friend from London who benefitted from Kennedy's ascension to the presidency. When first elected, Kennedy suggested to Harold Macmillan, the British prime minister, that he send Ormsby-Gore to Washington. "I trust David as I would my own cabinet," said Kennedy. Between the two nations, Macmillan was eager to maintain "the special relationship," as Churchill so often described it. He worried that JFK might prove anti-British, like his father, though his fears quickly dissipated. As both sides realized, Prime Minister Macmillan was an in-law of the Devonshires (Jack jokingly called him "Uncle Harold" in private). Ormsby-Gore was treated like a family member by Bobby Kennedy, who invited him to play touch football on weekends with the rest of the clan. During each crisis, Ormsby-Gore was kept abreast of U.S. plans and later provided Jack with encouragement toward reaching a nuclear test ban treaty with the Soviets. Ormsby-Gore, who married a Catholic, had a better understanding of the personal dynamics and ethnic pride that drove the Kennedys. Macmillan privately viewed the new president as having "some old prejudices (perhaps a little of the Irish tradition) about us—but he lives in the modern world." The president's brother, though, carried the same tribal resentments as his parents and Irish immigrant ancestors. "Why are we, the Kennedys, in America; why are we here at all?" Bobby erupted at a 1961 dinner party with Sir Harold Caccia, the predecessor to Ormsby-Gore. "It is because you, the British, drove us out of Ireland!" Jack's own ethnic identity was usually masked in humor and deflection. At a Washington cocktail party early in the administration, Sissy Ormsby-Gore, the British ambassador's wife, about to leave for the evening, came up to the president looking perplexed.

"I don't know whether to kiss you—or say 'Goodbye, Mr. President,'" kidded Sissy, who had known Jack since 1938, when the Kennedys allowed her to live for a time at the embassy residence following her father's sudden death. Sissy was one of Kick Kennedy's best friends and someone whose own marital example gave Kick the most comfort when she was deciding whether to wed Billy Hartington.

With several journalists encircling them, the president smiled mischievously at the British ambassador's wife.

"You're a good Catholic, Sissy," he replied. "You can kiss my ring."

From the outset, Kennedy believed in the "great man" theory of history, much as Churchill exhibited in his books about war in the twentieth century, where personal actions and decision making were often key determinants in crucial battles or turning-point events. Although Kennedy venerated Churchill, friends of this American president felt that he, too, had displayed greatness in dealing with the Cold War, particularly the 1962 Cuban missile showdown with the Soviets. The prospect of nuclear annihilation faced by Kennedy—of a global war that would rain down lethal contamination on the whole human race—was a world crisis Churchill never faced in World War II. No Caesar had ever confronted such awful choices. "It was quite clear that he [Kennedy] thought in terms of great men and what they were able to do, not at all of impersonal forces—I could see that he was a natural leader," said Isaiah Berlin, the British political historian who knew both men. "I met Mr. Churchill late in life, and he was by this time a famous sacred monster. He behaved exactly like a person permanently on the stage, saying these marvelous things in a splendid voice and delighting the company with it. They weren't the natural utterances of a normal human being. They were the grand utterances of somebody on the great historic stage. Whereas, with Kennedy, you felt that words cost him some effort."

Following the Cuban Missile Crisis that shook the world, Kennedy met in a late 1962 emergency conference with Macmillan in Nassau, the Bahamas, concerning the Skybolt dispute. The British, who had once taken solace in Churchill's alliance with America, were upset when the Kennedy administration canceled development of the antiballistic Skybolt missile with nuclear warheads. Macmillan's government planned to rely upon Skybolt as its main deterrent against the Soviets. Instead, the United States had proposed a submarine-based missile system, which could be controlled more easily. Critics in the House of Commons complained that the switch meant Great Britain would not be a master of its own fate and underlined the once-great empire's reliance on the United States in the nuclear age. The Nassau conference, quickly put together by Kennedy and Macmillan, resulted in a deal that mended fences. Randolph Churchill, who attended the conference, was one of the few British journalists who favored the agreement—a fact noted by

Kennedy. "By the way, over New Year's, the President told me that you had done by far the best and fairest reporting job on the Nassau Conference," Pamela wrote to her ex-husband after she and Leland attended a dinner party at the White House.

Randolph's fidelity to Jack Kennedy, the son of his father's once-reviled critic, continued to grow over the next year. In July 1963, he spent a few days at Kay Halle's ten-bedroom Georgetown mansion, hoping for an interview with the president. Eventually, Randolph received a telephone call from Evelyn Lincoln, the president's secretary, who said he'd be happy to see him the next day in the Oval Office. Unofficially, Randolph had just learned that Macmillan had prostate cancer and would resign soon as prime minister. Virtually no one knew except a small circle of Macmillan's Conservative Party loyalists, one of whom had leaked the news to Churchill's son.

Randolph urged the president's secretary to put the president on the line immediately because of a very pressing matter that he must share. When Kennedy picked up the phone, Randolph informed him about the stricken British leader's condition. The two men expressed their mutual sympathy for Macmillan.

Within moments, Randolph wondered aloud about the opposition Labour Party, led by Harold Wilson, coming to power. In his pointed fashion, he asked Kennedy if he could "face the thought of having to deal with that little shit Harold Wilson?"

Kennedy laughed but didn't say whether he thought of Wilson in such a way. Instead he assured Churchill that "this Government can work with anybody the British voted in as Prime Minister."

45

The Enemy Within

Robert Kennedy, like his father, knew how to drive a hard bargain. His tough-guy image had begun when he was chief counsel for the Senate Select Committee on Improper Activities in the Labor or Management Field (or "Rackets Committee") in the late 1950s. It featured brother Jack as a prominent panel member and became a springboard for his 1960 presidential campaign. The differing good cop, bad cop styles of the two brothers would carry through to the White House. With both courage and zeal, Bobby ferreted out union corruption and exposed the Mafia's pervasive grip in many American cities. The crime panel's 1959 hearings introduced America to such organized crime figures as Chicago's don Sam Giancana, probed by Bobby Kennedy about murder and other foul deeds.

Under hot television lights, Giancana wore dark glasses, a meticulously tailored suit, and his toupee of black hair. He fidgeted nervously.

"Would you tell us—if you have opposition from anybody, that you dispose of them by having them stuffed in a trunk?" asked Bobby, in his best avenging angel, Eliot-Ness-in-*The-Untouchables* voice. "Is that what you do, Mr. Giancana?"

Invoking his Fifth Amendment right against self-incrimination,

Giancana smiled defiantly. He refused to answer more than three dozen times. Under his breath, Sam clucked at the impudence of Joe Kennedy's son. How dare this rich kid—wealthy from a father whose own questionable methods were never investigated like this—interrogate him, Giancana's sneer seemed to say.

"Would you tell us anything about any of your operations or will you just giggle every time I ask you a question?" Bobby Kennedy demanded with his raspy, clipped voice. "I thought only little girls giggled, Mr. Giancana." Usually those in Chicago who dared challenge Giancana this way ended up dead.

Robert Kennedy's crime-busting adventures became a best-selling 1960 book, *The Enemy Within*. Hollywood announced plans for a movie about the book, which many viewed as a blueprint for what Bobby would do as attorney general. "I feel rather like one who has been sent an account of the Crusade written by Richard the Lionheart himself," said Lord Beaverbrook after reading his copy. "But the battle has not ended. You will in due course expose the wicked and bring them to justice as well!"

As a 1960 Christmas gift, the president-elect and Jacqueline Kennedy gave Bobby a specially bound copy in red leather with their own inscriptions. Jackie wrote "To Bobby—who made the impossible possible and changed all our lives," while Jack teased, "For Bobby—The Brother Within—who made the easy difficult. Merry Christmas, Jack."

FBI director J. Edgar Hoover wasn't amused by the Kennedys. He didn't appreciate the publicity given to Jack and Bobby for their Rackets Committee disclosures, which, in effect, highlighted the FBI's shortcomings. During the 1950s, the FBI had done little to investigate the Mob, instead following Hoover's obsession with possible domestic Communists in their midst. Bobby's call for a national crime commission threatened the director's turf and earned Hoover's contempt.

By early 1961, Kennedy's Justice Department pushed Hoover to launch a war against the Mafia, unleashing an army of electronic bugs, wiretaps, and surveillance equipment—some legal, some not—that would be the envy of British intelligence. This snooping provided Hoover's agents with an arsenal of compromising information about the Mob and its activities. But Bobby also made another out-of-the-ordinary request. He asked the director about a spying matter dating back to World War II. "The Attorney General wondered if we had anything in our files regarding Tyler Kent," Hoover wrote in a March 24, 1961, memo to his top investigators. "I told the Attorney General I would have our files checked right away."

Twenty years after he left London as a political pariah, Joe Kennedy and his protective son were unusually anxious about what could be revealed from the 1940 Tyler Kent espionage case. After all, it wasn't Kent's conviction for violating the British Official Secrets Act that had forced Joe Kennedy from office, but rather his own outlandish statements and disloyalty to Roosevelt. Still, years after Kent was released from jail, Joe pressed Beaverbrook in the 1950s for any information he might learn from British government files. And now one of his son's first acts as attorney general (a job Joe had personally arranged upon Jack's election) involved inquiring about a long-ago spy case best forgotten. In his telephone call to Hoover, Bobby indicated that Kent was running a racist, reactionary "hate sheet" in Florida and that the *Miami Herald* was checking out Kent's claims. Kennedy learned that the paper planned to interview the ambassador soon. He told Hoover "his father was going to tell only his own experience."

Aware of the sensitivity, the director provided a report on Tyler Kent in a matter of days. In a memo addressed to the attorney general, Hoover listed the basics of Kent's early life, his education, and that Kent had denied to FBI agents any involvement with espionage either in England or in the United States when he returned from a British prison at the war's end. The director was wise enough not to rehash the heart of the controversy—that Kent's copies of key memos between Roosevelt and Churchill wound up in the hands of Nazi agents and that this lowly clerk's strident opposition to U.S. entry to the war mirrored Ambassador Kennedy's appeasement views at the time. However, Hoover's memo did mention that the Justice Department in 1951 considered bringing Kent before a federal grand jury to testify about his activities in London but that the U.S. attorney in Maryland decided no more could be learned.

Eventually, Joe Kennedy decided to talk to the *Miami Herald* about Kent's arrest by Scotland Yard agents in 1940. "They found in his pocket a message I had received from Winston Churchill just three hours earlier," the senior Kennedy recalled. "The prison sentence was mild to what he deserved." A few months after Joe's published comments, Kent filed a libel lawsuit against him for allegedly derogatory statements. Kent pushed the State Department to make available to him certain documents still kept confidential. A State Department legal adviser began a review and noted that "because of the possible high-level interest in this matter, it is requested that this matter be acted upon as soon as possible." Kent's lawsuit was later dropped. But Hoover's agents continued monitoring him for two years and let the attorney general know of their progress. An April 1963 FBI memo said that Bobby "was very appreciative of being informed."

During the early 1960s, Bobby Kennedy often acted as guardian of the Kennedy family reputation, preventing embarrassing disclosures. Up until this point in life, Joe's ability to avoid serious accounting for his actions was almost as golden as his touch in making money. Though subjected to plenty of public criticism in the past, Joe always managed to stay one step ahead of any consequences. None of his Wall Street deals faced the kind of scrutiny he later enforced as SEC chief; nor did his earlier actions in Hollywood. His secret arrangements after Prohibition to reap millions from the British liquor rights with the help of the president's son had barely caused a ripple for him. Testimony at a 1950 Senate hearing naming Joe as the boss of mobster Thomas Cassara, a Somerset Importers official nearly killed when shot in the head in Chicago, was never pursued with the same vigor as when his sons investigated other Mafia activities. Although he once sought the limelight, Joe had learned to work best in the shadows. Few knew of his private meetings with Winston Churchill, with CIA director Allen Dulles during Florida getaways, or with the Pope's right-hand man in the Vatican. He revealed himself only to his family and a close circle of cronies and hangers-on, men such as Arthur Houghton and Francis X. Morrissey, who could be depended upon for their loyalty if not their good judgment. "The real measure of success," Joe said, "is to get a family that does as well as mine. I don't know what you can throw on the table that is better than that."

In the outer orbit of Joe Kennedy's life were friends and acquaintances more his equal, men of action such as Bernard Baruch and Lord Beaverbrook, a peerage of achieving outsiders who had acted as confidants in the same way with Winston Churchill. "It is my hope that you may have many years of joy and good companions with one son in the White House and another in the Senate," Max wrote for Joe's birthday in September 1961. Joe greatly admired Beaverbrook's industry and what he'd meant for Winston and Great Britain during the war. He wrote the foreword to Beaverbrook's 1954 book, *Don't Trust to Luck*, which advised the young to follow the example of Churchill in pursuing worldly success. Joe made sure his sons got a copy. Joe himself was grateful for Beaverbrook's advice. "You lived today as if you were going to live forever," Joe wrote his friend. "It far transcends anything any doctor has ever been able to tell me that did me any good."

The aura of invincibility surrounding Joe Kennedy burst in December 1961, when the seventy-three-year-old tycoon suffered a severe and debilitating stroke. He could no longer speak, except for an incoherent moan of "No." His body seemed drained of its familiar energy. Kennedy's sheer force of will, which had overcome so many obstacles in life, now couldn't help him.

As Kennedy went for physical therapy, mostly in vain, Beaverbrook and Baruch kept in contact with his sons. "I appreciated more than I can tell you your offer to visit my father," Bobby told Baruch. "He is not too well right now." Ted Kennedy let Beaverbrook know that "Dad's progress is slow but constant." Rose remained hopeful for some recovery, but in her letter to Beaverbrook, she realistically told Max that the active life of her husband, now confined to a wheelchair, was essentially over. She asked Beaverbrook to support Ted's 1962 bid for the U.S. Senate, the same seat from Massachusetts once held by Jack. "We all are trying to help Ted, but we certainly miss Joe's wisdom and judgment, which seemed to me almost infallible," she conceded.

What remained most enigmatic about Joe Kennedy was his success as a father, as noted by historian and White House aide Arthur Schlesinger Jr., perhaps the most astute observer of the family among their contemporaries. At a party Schlesinger attended at Averell Harriman's house in April 1963, the sons of famous men—Bobby Kennedy, Randolph Churchill, and Franklin D. Roosevelt Jr.—all gathered in the same room. "An unusual representation of the great dynasties of the 20th Century," Schlesinger recorded in his diary. "Winston Churchill and Franklin D. Roosevelt were incomparably greater public men than Joseph P. Kennedy. Yet Randolph Churchill and Franklin D. Roosevelt Jr., youth of ability and ambition, never fulfilled their potentialities. The Kennedy sons, for whatever reason, pursued their capacities to the uttermost limits. Had the parents no part in this result?"

Undoubtedly, Rose's intelligence, discipline, and religious faith influenced her children, yet most remarkable were the genuine love and regard that their children held for Joe. He had prepared, steered, and sometimes dictated their course in life, though never in a soul-crushing manner, always with the engagement of a parent who cared about them deeply. Some of his own goals were stunted or kept at bay by both his avarice and his circumstances, yet unselfishly he devoted himself to his family's advancement, overcoming obstacles that had once seemed insurmountable. Schlesinger witnessed firsthand the emotional and personal sway that Joe still had on the president and the attorney general. "It was due to my father," the president told Schlesinger when asked about the Kennedy family's success. "He wasn't around as much as some fathers; but . . . he made his children feel that they were the most important things in the world to him."

At this party, Schlesinger watched Bobby Kennedy chat with Randolph and Franklin Jr., who had become friendly acquaintances with an intertwined past. The attorney general kidded these scions of great men "mercilessly," observed Schlesinger. "He had, of course, the moral advantage of being on the way up while both of them had a consciousness of spoiled and wasted lives."

In January 1963, Randolph Churchill's book publisher announced he would write the official story of his father's life. It would be a book of at least five volumes that would not appear until after Sir Winston's death. With characteristic passion and abandon, Randolph had been working on it for more than a year before this announcement, wading through thousands of documents with a group of researchers. "In this biography, he had clearly found himself," recalled Randolph's friend Christopher Sykes. "He was armed with the merit without which no biographer should undertake his task, an unswerving determination to tell the truth. He faced the facts with all his natural courage and never feared to set them down." When a fellow journalist, Marquis Childs, questioned whether he could be objective, Randolph replied, "You are entitled to your doubt. I am entitled to my faith."

With this endorsement from his father, Randolph looked like he might seize control of his restless, unmoored life. He seemed publicly to have wrestled his self-destructive demons to the ground. Lord Beaverbrook invited Randolph to speak to a standing-room-only Canadian crowd in New Brunswick, just as he had Jack Kennedy a few years earlier. Afterward, Beaverbrook cabled Winston's son: YOU HAVE MADE A TREMENDOUS IMPRESSION. Randolph also gave a well-received speech at Dublin's Trinity College, before the same historical society his father and grandfather, Sir Winston and Lord Randolph, once addressed generations earlier. To many in the United States who knew his name better than his reputation, Randolph's outbursts and impertinence were merely the charming expression of an iconoclast, a brilliant mind that didn't tolerate fools gladly. At one ceremony, unveiling a statue of Sir Winston outside the British embassy in Washington, Randolph suggested that Americans instead should be honoring Lord North and King George III, who provoked the Revolutionary War. "Those, of course, are the men to whom you should be erecting statues," he quipped. "It was on account of their stupidity that you won your independence!"

In preparing the "great work" of his father's life, Randolph also confronted some truths in his own, especially his relationship with his father. "Struggling to establish my own individuality and personality, I often said and wrote some rather reckless things, which I suppose if I hadn't felt this frustration I would have tempered down," he admitted. "Substantially, I went along with my father all the way, but I was always looking for opportunities to establish an individual position, and it's very hard to do so, obviously, when you're living under the shadow of the great oak—the small sapling, so close to the parent tree, doesn't perhaps receive enough sunshine."

This self-perception was starkly different from the similar press interviews he gave as a young man in the early 1930s, when many expected he'd be prime minister someday. Then, Randolph was full of self-confidence. He viewed his father's fame as only a good omen, not a handicap in pursuing his own future. But years of hard drinking and long nights in far-flung places seemed to have taken their toll on him. His once-luxuriant blond hair was now sparse on his head; his face appeared worn, his eyes sullen and bagged; and he had a protruding belly that made him look more like a wrestler than a warrior. In this self-assessment, Randolph didn't mention alcohol as an accelerant in his behavior. But as he lashed out at the world, he seemed to acknowledge the uncontrollable nature of his temperament. "I became bloody-minded, I suppose, and wanted to strike out on my own and adopted possibly rather an arrogant attitude towards people and institutions at a time when I really didn't have the ammunition or the skill to hit the target," he admitted. "I think anyone can see that there were difficulties naturally inherent in the situation."

Kay Halle, a staunch defender of his father's reputation, had grown accustomed to Randolph's jeremiads and his lightning-fast mood swings. At a 1961 dinner party at her house with some national Democratic Party figures, Randolph became upset when a female guest seated beside him uttered the dreaded name of Averell Harriman.

"Averell Harriman is the man who cuckolded me when I was away in the Army," Randolph protested loudly. "Cuckolded me in the Prime Minister's very house."

Kay rolled her eyes. Harriman's affair with Pamela Churchill was still treated by Randolph as one of the great atrocities of the war. As Schlesinger wrote knowingly, Halle was "quite familiar with both Randolph's tiresome complaint and with Harriman's personal magnetism" because she, too, had been his lover. Although table etiquette generally didn't prescribe how to handle such comments, Kay attempted to defuse the situation with a sprinkling of humor.

"But Randolph, how many men did you cuckold when *you* were away in the Army?" she asked, ever so sweetly.

"Perhaps," he conceded with a pause, "but never in the house of a Prime Minister!"

Indeed, Kay had a point about Randolph and adultery. In recent months, he seemed desperate to renew his affair with an old wartime flame, Clare Boothe Luce. Clare gingerly responded to Randolph's odd telegrams and letters, which sought her attention and derided her husband, Henry Luce, whom he referred to as "Robinson," his middle name. "You know that my personal feelings for you are unchanged from when we met at Chartwell and the Ritz Hotel, Paris, and before you had the misfortune to meet Robinson," Randolph wrote. When Clare tried gently to offer some advice, suggesting he might still launch a successful political career outside the shadow of his father, just like the husbands of his sisters Mary and Diana, Randolph became only more agitated. "I think your analysis of my relations with my father is fundamentally wrong-headed," he dismissed with disdain. "I have made immense efforts to stand on my own feet and make a life and career of my own. I suppose I could have been a 'good boy' and gone along with my brothers' in law? Ho!"

Winston's eighth and final voyage aboard Aristotle Onassis's giant yacht began in June 1963, as always a journey of perceptions and self-deceptions. The guests included Prince Stanislas Radziwill and his wife, Lee, Jackie Kennedy's sister. The Radziwills presented themselves as a happily married royal couple, but in reality, Lee already had confided to friends that she wanted a divorce and was looking for a richer and better-known man. "My God, how jealous she is of Jackie. I never knew," Lee's confidant Truman Capote told Cecil Beaton, the famed British photographer. "Understand her marriage is all but finito [*sic*]." As if asking for more trouble, Onassis also invited his lover, Maria Callas, on the cruise, adding to the likelihood of some emotional drama.

Winston's stately presence on board seemed a deterrent to anything getting out of hand. The former prime minister was joined by son Randolph; grandson Winston; his personal secretary during the war, Jock

Colville; Jock's wife, Meg; and Winston's current aide, Anthony Montague Browne and his wife, Nonie. For a time, everyone in the Churchill party enjoyed the ride on Onassis's yacht. Ari appeared lighthearted and content as a king of the high seas.

Then one night, over dinner and drinks, something inside Randolph erupted, upsetting the whole evening. His brooding obsession about Pamela's infidelity with Averell Harriman, his outrage at being a "cuckold," and most of all his anger at his father for not preventing this affair—all these rose again to the surface, upsetting him beyond control. "For no apparent reason his rage was directed at his father, but then he began to particularize with violent reproaches relating to his wartime marriage," recalled Montague Browne.

Long ago, both Pamela and Harriman had moved on with their lives and were now part of the Kennedys' glittering circle of friends and political associates. But Randolph couldn't stop thinking of this ancient betrayal, as if it somehow upset the chain of being in his life, with things never again the same. (His second marriage to June Osborne, which dissolved quickly, finally ended in divorce in 1962. Deeply troubled herself, June later committed suicide.) On the yacht, Randolph suggested his world-famous father had subtly but deliberately sabotaged him, that Winston didn't really want to see his son succeed or outshine him. For his father's perceived disloyalty, Randolph tortured and embarrassed Winston for years with accusations and drunkenness and, perhaps most hurtful, mocked the ambitions his father had once held for him with erratic behavior that made high public office unthinkable. Now, at their table, Randolph scowled at his father and claimed he was to blame. Anthony and Nonie Montague Browne and then Onassis tried to intervene, but Randolph continued his tirade. "Short of hitting him on the head with a bottle, nothing could have stopped him," Montague Browne recalled. "It was one of the most painful scenes I have witnessed."

Those at the dinner—several unacquainted with the Churchill

family's tensions—appeared shell-shocked and speechless. Randolph's own adult son, Winston, eventually called the incident "a desperately sad one and [one that] showed that, even more than twenty years later, Randolph could neither forgive nor forget the fact that his father appeared, at least in his eyes, to have condoned Harriman's wartime affair with his wife, prompting him to unleash a torrent of abuse upon the head of his defenceless 88-year-old father."

The former prime minister rose from the table without saying a word. As Montague Browne recalled, the great man "stared at his son with an expression of brooding rage." (Winston always possessed a pugilist's glare as well as an ebullient smile.) Then he walked silently to his cabin alone. Montague Browne followed him and found Winston "shaking all over." He worried that another stroke might attack the former prime minister. He poured a whiskey and soda and gave it to Winston, stiff and frail, to settle his nerves. Before Montague Brown departed the cabin, Winston instructed that his son leave Ari's yacht as soon as possible, for the good of all.

Montague Browne realized he'd made a terrible mistake. In arranging this trip, there had been some debate over whether Churchill's son should be invited, but he had urged Randolph's inclusion. After all, Randolph had introduced his father to Onassis, and this cruise would be Winston's last. Moreover, Randolph appeared very grateful to be his father's appointed biographer, and he sometimes stood proudly as a surrogate for his father at events honoring him as a legendary figure. Montague Browne knew of past troubles between father and son, though he'd never seen them fight up close.

The next morning, Randolph was delighted to receive a surprise notice from Greece's king, agreeing to the newspaper interview he'd sought for the past several days. The note instructed Randolph to come to Athens immediately. To save face, Onassis had arranged surreptitiously for Randolph's interview so his embattled father could rest and have some peace.

In departing the yacht and as they traveled to the shore, Randolph displayed his up-and-down temperament to Montague Browne in cascading stages, with various masks of emotion. At first he acted joyous about having gotten his exclusive interview with the Greek king, and hummed the musical verse "Get Me to the Church on Time" like a groom joining his bride. Then his mood changed, and he turned sullen. He let Montague Browne know he hadn't been fooled by the interview's approval.

"Anthony, you didn't think that I was taken in by that plan of Ari's and yours, do you?" he asked, with more resignation than suspicion. Randolph's face tightened into a reddened ball of grief and regret. The staggering consequence of his ugly display had led to his banishment from the ship, and once again from his father's life. He began to cry.

"I do so very much love that man," he moaned, "but something always goes wrong between us."

46

After the Ball

Randolph Churchill's behavior toward his father on the Onassis yacht was particularly bewildering because he had acted so loyally a few months earlier, at the Kennedy White House. In an April 1963 Rose Garden ceremony, Winston Churchill's only son filled in admirably for his ailing father, then home in England, as President John F. Kennedy awarded honorary U.S. citizenship to the British wartime leader. The event would be filled with meaning for both the Churchill and Kennedy families, far more than the press or most of the attendees realized.

Jacqueline Kennedy, well aware of its significance, watched emotionally as her husband and Randolph, these two famous sons, paid tribute to the past.

"We were so proud of him and for him—knowing he had failed no one, and had moved many," Jackie later wrote to Kay Halle about Randolph's performance. "I will forever remember that as Randolph's day."

For a time, it had seemed as if this special day wouldn't happen.

· · ·

Honorary citizenship for Winston Churchill presented more difficulties than JFK had ever imagined. Two years after Kay Halle pushed
for recognition—a frustratingly long delay after her enthusiastic 1961
response from the president—part of Kennedy's problem came from
his Irish-Catholic base within the Democratic Party. Many still remembered the Black and Tans' brutalities during the 1920s Irish War of
Independence and objected to any honor given to Churchill. Worried
about the slow progress, Halle enlisted support from former presidents
Truman, Eisenhower, and Herbert Hoover; from James Roosevelt, by
then a congressman from California; and from Bernard Baruch, Winston's best friend in America. By then a man of ninety-two with a large
hearing aid dangling from his ear, Baruch still considered himself an or-
acle of wisdom, though the Kennedy and Churchill camps didn't always
listen. "Baruch thought highly enough of his own political acumen to
send long and rambling letters which Churchill did not often have time
to read," admitted Jock Colville, Winston's former personal secretary.
JFK's New Frontier officials, such as John Kenneth Galbraith, regarded
Baruch with humorous contempt. "I trust your life was suitably enriched by your visit with Baruch," Galbraith kidded the president. "I
appreciate your seeing the old fraud and it liquidates a campaign promise. However, he should not be allowed to think that the best things in
life, including visits to the White House, are free. He never used to."

Nevertheless, Jack Kennedy realized that his own intellectual debt
to Winston Churchill should be properly repaid. The way Churchill
viewed the world, the broad vision that a statesman-writer steeped in
history could bring to the diplomatic table or to discussion in the public square, had never left Jack. He learned that words could be every
bit as effective as explosives in winning a war, especially a cold one.
Kennedy took care to surround himself with learned men who knew
the limits and consequences of power by studying those who preceded
him. They were part of his multidimensional persona. If one side of

his enigmatic circle of friends and political associates included the quick-witted "Boston Mafia" of Irish-Catholic aides such as Dave Powers and Kenny O'Donnell, another, more deliberate side was reflected by speechwriter Theodore Sorensen and Schlesinger, men who carried with them Churchill's long view of history. "Some of us will think it wise to associate as much as possible with historians and cultivate their good will," Kennedy told a group of academics in 1961, "though we always have the remedy which Winston Churchill once suggested when he prophesized during World War II that history would deal gently with us 'because,' Mr. Churchill said, 'I intend to write it!'"

In effect, Kennedy would rewrite his own family history by venerating a man whom his father once condemned as responsible for leading Joe Jr. and countless other Americans to their deaths in an avoidable war. Jack's admiration for Churchill's actions surely rankled his father. Yet, in retrospect, Jack didn't see the death of his older brother and others as senseless, but rather as the price for liberty against tyranny, and the dead as martyrs for good over evil. Winston helped young Kennedy see this distinction far more than Jack's father ever did. On the twentieth anniversary of 1941's Atlantic Charter, the guiding statement for the special relationship between America and Great Britain during World War II, President Kennedy assured its architect Churchill that "[y]our own name will endure as long as free men survive to recall."

Eventually, Congress shared this exceptional feeling for Churchill and overwhelmingly approved the bill proclaiming his special citizenship. A week later, on April 9, 1963, President Kennedy signed it in the Oval Office and gave one of the pens to Randolph Churchill. Then the two walked through a double doorway and stepped into the Rose Garden, where two hundred and fifty onlookers, and a worldwide television audience, waited for them to speak. In this mixed Anglo-American audience were Baruch, Jimmy Roosevelt, Averell Harriman, and Jack's longtime friend David Ormsby-Gore, the British ambassador to the

United States. Fittingly, the Marine Corps band played both "God Save the Queen" and "The Star-Spangled Banner."

The president began by reminding everyone of Winston's finest hour, when the gathering storm of Nazi terror enveloped the free world. "In the dark days and darker nights when Britain stood alone—and most men save Englishmen despaired of England's life—he mobilized the English language and sent it into battle," Kennedy said, speaking in a tone noticeably staccato, more Churchillian than ever. "The incandescent quality of his words illuminated the courage of his countrymen."

Now, with America immersed in the Cold War, Kennedy's description of Churchill resembled his own challenge against the Soviet Union and Communist Bloc nations. The speech was delivered at a time when the U.S. military presence, already in outposts around the world, was spreading into the jungles of Vietnam. "Whenever and wherever tyranny threatened, he has always championed liberty," said Kennedy, reading aloud with head down. "His life has shown that no adversary can overcome, and no fear deter, free men in the defense of their freedom." Kennedy's brief address about Churchill was filled with the same themes he'd underlined at his inaugural.

Then, looking up, Kennedy grinned and motioned toward his guest.

"I would ask Mr. Randolph Churchill—Sir Winston's son who's accompanied by Sir Winston's grandson, Winston Churchill—to read the letter," the president said. The gestures between the two showed that the acrimony from their nasty 1952 exchange in *Time* magazine had long been forgotten.

Randolph thanked the president and began reading his father's prepared statement. Young Winston stood beside him. Jackie Kennedy, her unannounced pregnancy imperceptible in her silk outfit of navy blue, smiled on the stairs behind Randolph. Wearing a three-piece suit, his black horn-rim glasses perched on the tip of his nose, his eyes cocked and glaring, he looked uncannily like his father. With gravitas and great authority, he gave voice to his father's words. "I am, as you know, half American by blood," Winston said through his son, "and the story of my association with that mighty and benevolent nation goes back nearly ninety years to the day of my father's marriage."

Once again, Winston reprised his lifelong themes of English-speaking peoples sharing a common democratic heritage, and the "special relationship" between the U.S. government and Great Britain. Though the British Empire now appeared in eclipse, Churchill refused to admit that its best days were gone. "I reject the view that Britain and the Commonwealth should now be relegated to a tame and minor role in the world," Churchill insisted. "Our past is the key to our future, which I firmly trust and believe will be no less fertile and glorious. Let no man underrate our energies, our potentialities and our abiding power for good."

When finished, Randolph seemed pleased by his performance. At a moment of high ritual, he'd not let his father down. His powerful oration hinted at the glory and achievement that might have been his had he become a "great man" as predicted upon his twenty-first birthday. The First Lady, aware of the gnawing tensions in family dynasties, knew Churchill's son had far exceeded his critics, those who dismissed him as a failure. "I was so happy for Randolph," Jackie later said. "I wished that moment to last forever for him."

Sir Winston watched from home, seeing the black-and-white images of his son and the U.S. president via the brand-new wizardry of satellite television. He sat in his London town house with Clementine. She considered her husband "a child of both worlds," between England and America, never more so than on this day. By then, the sun had fallen in the British capital. Winston soon went to sleep.

Another shadowy figure, virtually unnoticed, watched the Churchill ceremony from a distance. Up on the second floor of the White House, staring through a window, Joe Kennedy silently took in the spectacle of his son praising Churchill as a savior of civilization, a man of the century. Few in the crowd saw Joe peering with his five-year-old granddaughter Caroline through the window at the action below. Though the president intended sincerely to honor his hero, the occasion was "seen by many as filial atonement for Ambassador Kennedy's record back in 1940," observed historian Christopher Catherwood.

Whatever thoughts raced through the mind of Joe Kennedy—the rancor of the past, the lost opportunities of his own political goals, and the tragic forgotten dreams he had once had for his oldest son—could not be expressed. His weak, withered body, with its disfigured mouth, no longer served him. This master of mass communication, a Hollywood producer who early on recognized the power of television in politics and helped JFK become its exemplar, could say nothing in his own defense.

At a small White House party after the ceremony, it would be left to others to figure out what Joe Kennedy might be thinking. "I found Joe in a wheelchair, still handsome and clad in a larkspur blue dressing gown but paralyzed and struck almost mute from a series of strokes," recalled Kay Halle. "Around him were Jack who had attained the Presidency of the United States, Bobby the office of Attorney general and Teddy a US Senate seat from Massachusetts. Caroline and little John were playing happily at his feet. Jo[e] had indeed been dreaming true. His shining eyes, dominating his paralyzed face seem to be saying, 'You see, Kay, it all happened just as I'd planned it.'" Journalist Benjamin C. Bradlee, a friend and neighbor of Jack's before he became president, also spotted Joe Kennedy sitting near the window. "Kennedy senior had apparently caught a glimpse of it," Bradlee wrote about the Churchill ceremony. "The president teased his father about how 'All your old friends showed up, didn't they, Dad?' It was obvious that by 'all your old friends,' Kennedy meant people who were high on the ambassador's enemies list."

Jack treated his father without any deference or condescension to his handicap.

"Bernard Baruch," Jack said, as if reeling off bête noires in a cast from one of his father's Hollywood B-movies. "Dean Acheson, he's on both the offense and the defense, isn't he, Dad?"

Jack and Bobby interacted with their father as they always did, as if he might suddenly talk back to them. The Kennedy grandchildren ran about, "roaring around the living room oblivious to their grandfather," Bradlee recalled, while Joe Kennedy still commanded attention, respect, and ultimately a deep love from his sons. "Here was this powerhouse of a father reduced to a shell," Bradlee recalled. "The Kennedys were at their very best, it seems to me now, when the males were alone together, and united."

On this special day, there seemed no need to explain away Jack's devotion to Winston Churchill, to enter into an old debate about the causes and merits of the war, or whether Joe's views about appeasement could ever be justified. The Kennedy brothers had agreed long ago to disagree with their father on politics and foreign policy. On this day, however, none of this mattered. With the lofty goals and competitiveness Joe Kennedy had set out for his family, there was no doubt who had prevailed. As Jack often said, "My Father's interest is constant."

At a party later held at the British embassy, Bobby Kennedy found himself amused by Randolph's bombast, an enjoyment that quickly became mutual. "[We] had a most amusing and high-spirited conversation," Randolph wrote of the son of the reviled former ambassador. "He has a wonderful gift of quick repartee, a delightful smile and a most engaging personality." As his father's fiercest partisan, Bobby took delight in Randolph's searing but funny assessment of Franklin Roosevelt as "rather a 'feminine' figure with visible prima-donna traits of jealousy." Armed with a rapier Fleet Street quality to his wit, similar to that of his friend and provocateur Evelyn Waugh, Randolph also displayed his father's sense of diplomacy by finding something good to say about Roosevelt. "But his voice—a great voice—instinct with courage," Randolph summarized FDR. "Even more so than my father's."

Bobby invited Randolph and his son to visit his Hickory Hill home in Maryland, and they shared a delightful time with Ethel and the rest of his clan. "There was no question of any formality," young Winston recalled. "Children of all ages would spill out of cupboards and rampage through the house which was filled with shrieks of laughter."

During his April stay in Washington, Randolph socialized with Kay's friend Janet Auchincloss, the mother of Jackie Kennedy. He wound up being invited that August to a spectacular Newport debutante ball featuring Jackie's beautiful younger half-sister, also named Janet. The Auchincloss family transformed their Hammersmith Farm in Rhode Island—the scene of Jack and Jackie's 1953 wedding reception—to make it seem like a Venetian garden. They invited more than a thousand guests: "Everybody who is anybody in Newport," the *New York Times* reported. "It was the most lavish event held here this season." Young Janet carried a bouquet sent by her brother-in-law President Kennedy. Flying in from London, Randolph brought along an eight-week-old pug puppy he'd promised to give to Jackie's mother. Throughout the evening at that Newport ball, young Janet danced and even sang, accompanied by the night's pianist. When nearly everyone had left, Randolph got up and followed with "a rich barroom version" of a favorite turn-of-the-century song, "After the Ball." It was an older man's lament about his faithless sweetheart who'd left him many years ago.

After the Newport ball, the Kennedys invited Randolph and his son to spend a weekend at the compound in Hyannis Port, where the Churchill men soon felt like part of the family. "Randolph was in love with the Kennedys," recalled Frank Gannon, an American researcher then helping Randolph prepare the biography of his father.

Bobby and his wife, Ethel, took Randolph and his son out for a day trip on a cabin cruiser called the *Honey Fitz*, and headed to Martha's Vineyard, meeting other friends for a barbeque along the beach. During the weekend, Randolph bumped into one of the Kennedys' many other guests—his beloved Laura Charteris, no longer Lady Dudley but now married to Michael Temple Canfield, the former husband of Lee Radziwill. Once again, the overlapping circle of friends between the Kennedy and Churchill families now included the woman Randolph had lamented he always wanted to marry. "Remaining a good loser and in this case unshakably devoted, Randolph whisked her off on the evening picnics given by Bobby Kennedy, the President's brother," recalled biographer Anita Leslie, though nothing ever came of this encounter. On the boat ride back to Hyannis Port, as the weather and high winds worsened, Randolph and the Kennedys kept themselves merrily entertained. "Father, who could not sing to save his life, was somewhat implausibly leading Bobby and Ethel in choruses of 'Lloyd George knew my Father . . .' to the tune of 'Onward Christian Soldiers,' as the waves crashed over the boat, drenching us all," recalled Randolph's son, Winston.

Near midnight, the wandering partygoers arrived at the Kennedy compound, where the lights were out and everyone else seemed fast asleep. Suddenly realizing that his own place there was full, Bobby ushered Randolph and his son to another family residence nearby, where Ted Kennedy and his wife, Joan, were sleeping. The previous year, Ted had won his race to become the U.S. senator from Massachusetts, taking over Jack's old seat. "Don't worry Randolph," said the attorney general. "I'll sneak you and Winston into Teddy and Joan's house. They have a spare room. But be sure not to make any noise otherwise you'll wake everyone up!" Bobby countermanded his own order when he stepped accidentally into a rosebush in the dark and started cursing loudly.

The Churchill men were put up in a small room with twin beds.

During the night, Randolph's snores woke up his son, so young Winston slept on the living room couch. The next morning, he awoke to find Joan Kennedy staring at him, wondering who he might be. He identified himself as Winston Churchill, son of Randolph. Joan "seemed not in the least surprised to find a strange man sleeping in her living-room," recalled young Winston. "Evidently it was all part and parcel of life at Hyannis with the Kennedys, to which she had long since become accustomed."

After breakfast, the Churchills and Ted Kennedy walked over to the Kennedy family's main house, the same white clapboard building where so many summers had been spent. It didn't resemble the old red-brick Tudor style of Chartwell, but rather a modest seaside hotel swept by ocean breezes. On the front lawn, two helicopters warmed up with their blades twirling, waiting to take the president and his two brothers back to Washington. Young Winston later wrote that JFK knew that the spectacle of such a sight "would give pleasure to his old and infirm father" as he watched his powerful sons leave for the White House.

At around 9:00 a.m., the president appeared from his residence and started saying good-bye to their weekend guests, now gathered excitedly in the near-deafening noise of the helicopters. The gaiety of the Newport ball and the weekend at Hyannis Port had been muted by the tragedy Jack and Jackie Kennedy had suffered a few weeks earlier. Their newborn son, Patrick, born prematurely, had lived only two days and died August 9. After a funeral Mass the next day, Patrick was buried beside his stillborn sister, Arabella, who died in 1956. The death of Patrick Kennedy, bearing the same name as his ancestor who first arrived from Ireland, left the marriage between the president and his wife more strained than ever before, in ways that would become particularly evident in the weeks ahead. A slight trace of that sadness showed when the president walked toward the Churchills, standing in the driveway, before boarding his helicopter.

Jack greeted Randolph and his son, and wished them well. Then, as he turned toward the helicopter, he paused for a moment, as if realizing how his wife felt about the Churchills. He made one last request.

"Be sure and visit Jackie," the president asked Randolph. "It will cheer her up."

47

The Best and Worst of Days

The summer of 1963, John Fitzgerald Kennedy's last full season on earth, began with a sentimental journey to Ireland, which he called "the best four days of my life."

At the president's insistence, White House aides added Eire to a European tour whose political highlight would be his stirring speech near the Berlin Wall. Before a huge West German crowd, Kennedy reminded the world of the stark contrasts between democracy and Soviet Communist oppression. Churchill himself could not have made the point any better. "There are many people in the world who really don't understand, or say they don't, what is the great issue between the Free World and the Communist world—*let them come to Berlin*!" Kennedy roared, in a landmark Cold War speech every bit as important as Churchill's 1946 address at Fulton, Missouri, and far more moving emotionally. "Today, in the world of freedom, the proudest boast is *'Ich bin ein Berliner.'*"

Riding a crest of excitement, President Kennedy arrived in Ireland with his two sisters Jean and Eunice, who joined him because his then-pregnant wife, Jacqueline, couldn't travel. In Dublin, Jack Kennedy enjoyed a homecoming not only for himself, but for all Americans whose ancestors had left during the famine. Standing in an open car, he glided down boulevards lined with crowds. Deliriously, they cheered and waved the flags of both nations. "In Dublin Kennedy had nothing to bring the Irish people except himself, and himself as profoundly Irish, in all respects one of them," recalled Lord Longford, the British Labour politician and an expert in Irish history. "He felt it; they felt it . . . the *rapport* was total and beyond comprehension."

The trip illuminated Kennedy's Daedalian makeup, another side of his complicated nature often undetected or unappreciated by the press. Here in Ireland, the American president put his own roots proudly on display, as if in a coming-out party for a man whose electoral success had depended on his ability to appear unlike any stereotypical Irish-Catholic politician of the past. The trip tempered the opinions of, and confused, those who insisted Jack Kennedy was a confirmed Anglophile without recognizing the deeper layers of cultural background in his personality. It underlined the enigma of America's first president from a minority group, a politician whose advisers had warned him not to have his photograph taken with nuns during the 1960 campaign lest his Catholicism alarm wary voters. Although Jack admired Churchill's leadership, and while his personal style and sense of history were greatly influenced by the British, close observers said Kennedy's inner soul and the foundation of his politics remained based in his family's Boston Irish-Catholic experience, as an outsider looking in. "The Irish visit was, in Kennedy's case, an exercise of the heart," recalled *Time* magazine columnist Hugh Sidey. "He was rooted there forever."

Kennedy's helicopter tour to his muddy ancestral home in County Wexford reinforced this personal side. It was the same small farm Jack had visited with Pamela Churchill during a 1947 car ride. His father, while U.S. ambassador in London, also visited the family homestead with Joe Jr. in 1938, as if drawn by blood to see where the Kennedys started on their long journey. On this much-photographed day in 1963, Jack shared a cup of tea with his distant Irish cousin Mary Kennedy

Ryan, a hearty older woman who ran the farm. Unbeknownst to the president, she'd been an Irish patriot who, during the 1920s War of Independence, smuggled weapons under her skirt to avoid detection by the British Black and Tans. Much had changed in Ireland since World War II, when Churchill bitterly resented its neutrality and steadfast refusal to join the Allied fight against the Nazis. Although greeted at the Dublin airport like a lost cousin by Ireland's eighty-one-year-old president, Éamon de Valera, Kennedy stressed the old ways would no longer do. "Self-determination can no longer mean isolation," he urged during an address to the Irish Parliament. "New nations can build with their former governing powers the same kind of fruitful relationship which Ireland has established with Great Britain—a relationship founded on equality and mutual interest." The president's view differed markedly from his earlier sympathetic explanation of de Valera's wartime neutrality to a group of Boston Irish in 1946, at the start of his political career.

Yet before leaving on the presidential jet, Kennedy let all of Ireland know how much this trip meant to him by reprising a song about the Irish who moved away during the famine years. He'd first heard it in Limerick, the place where Rose's ancestors lived before heading to Boston a century earlier. "Come back to Erin, Mavourneen, Mavourneen, come back around to the land of thy birth," Kennedy repeated from a verse. "Come with the Shamrock in the springtime, Mavourneen." Aware of how much the Irish diaspora had come full circle with his visit as America's president, Kennedy ended with a promise. "This is not the land of my birth but it is the land for which I hold the greatest affection," he said, "and I certainly will come back in the springtime."

During Kennedy's 1963 trip, the most personal aspect took place in England, however, far from the sight of reporters and photographers.

On the way to see Prime Minister Harold Macmillan, he stopped at the grave of his sister Kathleen, located atop a hill near the Chatsworth mansion, home to the Duke of Devonshire. Kick was once such a vibrant force in his life, and now barely mentioned in Kennedy family history. For several minutes, Jack stared at the stone commemorating Kick's memory, just as his grief-stricken father had done in 1948 after her fatal airplane crash.

The special Anglo-American relationship—which Winston Churchill idealized but never realized with U.S. presidents—was personified in JFK's warm and friendly conversations with "Uncle Harold," his nickname for Prime Minister Harold Macmillan. Their talks usually covered substantial issues, including nuclear arms and the Soviet Union's spread of communism. But this 1963 trip was overshadowed by a sex scandal that threatened to pull apart the Conservative Party's hold on British government. The so-called Profumo affair erupted when Macmillan's secretary of state for war, John Profumo, acknowledged his indiscretion with a showgirl, Christine Keeler. Tabloid newspapers on Fleet Street flashed fleshy photos of Keeler and trumpeted the brunette beauty's notorious links to a Soviet embassy official. Macmillan's political opponents seized upon every sordid detail. Labour Party ministers suggested JFK's stopover at Macmillan's country home was meant to deflect attention away from *l'affaire* Profumo.

In one of his finest hours as a friend, Randolph Churchill rallied to Profumo's defense. During the war, Profumo had been one of his father's strongest supporters. Randolph believed Profumo would never reveal any state secrets and shouldn't be drummed out of government for merely going to bed with a pretty girl, regardless of her occupation. With paparazzi unmercifully chasing Profumo and his embattled family, Randolph offered his sizeable house at Stour as a hideaway. He instructed his house staff to remain quiet about Profumo's presence as he left for Onassis's yacht (on the fateful Mediterranean cruise during which Randolph accused his father of "cuckold" disloyalty). Using the wartime lingo of his old commando unit, Randolph called his giving Profumo refuge "Operation Sanctuary." The favor was never forgotten. Years later, Profumo's son described Randolph as "a man who loved a good crisis, and, however unpopular himself, knew what friendship ought to be."

The political fallout of this sex scandal eventually convinced Macmillan to leave office, ostensibly for health reasons. But Kennedy didn't seem to heed the scandal's cautionary lessons, ignoring how such an incident could expose a disturbing aspect of his own character. In America, the press hinted at a similar sex fiasco brewing within the Kennedy administration. Syndicated columnist Drew Pearson said Republican opponents, preparing for Kennedy's 1964 reelection bid, were hoping "civil rights infighting among Democrats and a possible Washington Profumo scandal will do their best to knock the Democrats for a loop." Although Macmillan generally held Kennedy in high regard, he wasn't above passing along gossip. During a stop in Spain to see Sir Winston on Onassis's yacht, the prime minister made an extraordinary comment, recalled Churchill's aide Anthony Montague Browne. "MacMillan at that time had just returned from a brief visit to President Kennedy and he told, not for the last time, of the President informing him that he had to have a woman every day or else he developed appalling headaches." Browne's memoir doesn't say if he informed his boss of the tidbit, but the prime minister certainly seemed taken aback by it: "A very strange comment to make to a man of my age," Macmillan exclaimed.

Jack Kennedy's philandering posed more political risk than the public realized. During the 1960 campaign, Lord Beaverbrook alerted his friend Joe Kennedy when he learned that Hearst newspapers were investigating adultery rumors, never proven, that Jack was being named

in an English divorce case concerning a woman named Pulham sometime in the past twenty years. "I think this story is pure imagination
and that it is not worth looking into," Max assured in a note without
detail. Usually the Kennedy bersagliere shot down any rumors of sexual escapades by the president, and the mostly all-male press corps jocularly went along. But in February 1962, FBI director J. Edgar Hoover
presented compelling evidence to Attorney General Robert Kennedy
of his older brother's recklessness. Wiretaps and other FBI surveillance
showed that JFK was sharing a girlfriend, Judith Campbell, a divorced
actress introduced to Kennedy by Frank Sinatra, with Chicago mobster
Sam Giancana. Eventually, White House operators logged more than
seventy Campbell phone calls over a two-year period. A few years earlier, during their televised Senate rackets investigation, the Kennedys
labeled Giancana as a Mafia killer. Hoover's dossier placed Bobby Kennedy in an incredibly compromised position. With both the spy files
of Tyler Kent, and now the allegations of extramarital sex and ties to
organized crime figures such as Giancana, Bobby faithfully guarded the
reputations of his father and brother from any public scandal.

Sex for the Kennedy men seemed far different from that in
Churchill's own life—far more complicated and, as some historians
suggest, far more British. Writer Garry Wills described the president
as greatly influenced by one of his favorite books, David Cecil's *Young
Melbourne*, which giddily romanticized the young lords he met in prewar London. "The 'English attitude' towards politics was, for young
Kennedy, the English attitude towards sex," Wills observed. "From Cecil's *Melbourne* he seems to have derived his impression that English
aristocrats have naked women emerge from silver dishes at their ban-
quets . . . The Melbourne described by Cecil, a doting descendant, was
all the things Kennedy wanted to be—secular, combining the bookish
and the active life, supported by a family that defied outsiders."

JFK's political hero, Churchill, generally avoided talk about the subject, except in jest. To be sure, both Winston's father and son engaged

in licentiousness, and Winston's lusty mother, Jennie, used sex transactionally in her social climbing, in a lifetime filled with dozens of lovers, reputedly including the Prince of Wales, the future Edward VII. By contrast, biographers described Winston as "weakly sexed," more caught up in his work than sexual conquest. Virtually no evidence exists of the British leader's eye wandering beyond his beloved wife, Clementine. The Churchill marriage seemed molded by the desire not to repeat the sexual explosiveness of their parents' lives. "It makes no difference," Churchill once quipped to another Parliament member when informed that his fly was open, "the dead bird doesn't leave the nest."

More so than in politics, Jack Kennedy followed his father's example in dealing with the opposite sex. Before felled by a stroke, Joe Kennedy carried on an active sex life with a recklessness that went far beyond the safe and familiar company of intimates such as Kay Halle and Clare Boothe Luce, whom Rose considered family friends. Joe Kennedy's Olympian womanizing, claimed biographer David Nasaw, extended to "hundreds of them over his lifetime: actresses, waitresses, secretaries, stenographers, caddies, models, stewardesses, and others." JFK seemed determined to break his father's brazen record, fueled as he was by daily testosterone shots and a sense of sexual noblesse oblige, regardless of his wife's feelings. "His daddy liked girls—he was a great chaser," recalled JFK's pal, former U.S. senator George Smathers of Florida. "Jack liked girls and girls liked him. He had just a great way with women."

While Bobby seemed defined by his mother's Catholic moral training, Jack reflected his father's risk-taking ethos. Friends in Britain such as Sir Alastair Forbes, who observed the Kennedy men from the ambassador's time in 1930s London to Jack's 1960 American presidency, noticed the paradox. "I'd say that Joe [Joseph P. Kennedy, Jr.] and Jack [John F. Kennedy] and Teddy [Edward M. Kennedy] arranged their mores after the fashion of the ordinary Italian bourgeois in their relations to the Church," Forbes theorized. "The girls and Bobby followed the more traditional Irish pattern. The young Irishman, faced with the problem of being highly sexed, is able because of the economy to resolve it in one of two ways: He can marry very young and have a very large number of children, or he can be promiscuous with ignorant heathens like the English."

Throughout his presidency, Kennedy remained a sexual provocateur like his father, a persona masked behind his public image as a family man. One Englishwoman with whom JFK had an affair in 1963 was Jeanne Campbell, a high-flying, vivacious writer based in Washington who happened to be the granddaughter of Lord Beaverbrook, the long-time friend of both Winston Churchill and Kennedy's father, Joe. Forty years later, to the *New York Times,* Lady Jeanne's two daughters confirmed their mother's intimate relationship with the president. "Powerful men were interested in her because she was intelligent," explained one daughter, Cusi Cram. That was an understatement in Lady Jeanne's case.

Jeanne Campbell grew up in her grandfather's home after her parents divorced. Lord Beaverbrook lavished her with money and attention. In the late 1950s, Jeanne was vacationing in the French Riviera with Beaverbrook when she met his friend, *Time* magazine publisher Henry Luce. In her twenties, Jeanne soon began an intense affair with Luce (a man three decades older), one that nearly broke up his marriage to Clare Boothe Luce. Accidently, Clare found out overhearing a telephone conversation between Luce and his young infatuation. When Clare confronted him, Henry asked for a divorce. Stunned, Clare confided in her old friend and lover Bernard Baruch, who advised, "Don't you budge for less than $17 million." With her own playwriting skills, Clare tried to cover her hurt with a good quip. "If I divorced Harry, and married the Beaver, I would become Harry's grandmother," she joked.

Eventually, Jeanne's affair with Luce dissipated, and she took a job as an American-based correspondent for Britain's *Evening Standard.* In 1960 her writing earned praise from another admirer, Randolph Churchill—who applauded the "brilliant grown-up piece by you in

tonight's Standard. Congratulations. Love Randolph." Jeanne understood Randolph's difficulty as the son of Sir Winston. She admired his
Herculean efforts to compile a multivolume work on his father's life.
"Randolph is built on the heroic scale," she'd later write. "He does not
possess one small fault or one small virtue. Loving, imperious, loyal,
tormented and tempestuous, he is too truthful for his friends' comfort."
Jeanne learned this hard lesson in 1961, when she upset Randolph by
reporting incorrectly about his book efforts. "Apart from the disloyalty
to me in writing about my private affairs, which I had made the mistake of confiding in you, it is pretty sloppy reporting to make so many
mistakes when you had the opportunity of getting it correct," Randolph
chastised.

That same year, Jeanne met another famous man, novelist Norman
Mailer, with whom she became pregnant before deciding to marry
him. Like many in the early 1960s, Mailer was swept up by Kennedy's glamorous image and promise of change after the somnambulistic
Eisenhower era. Attending the 1960 Democratic Convention, Mailer
wrote about JFK's potential for greatness, and the cultural dividing line
Kennedy represented, in a magazine piece entitled "Superman Goes to
the Supermarket." "With such a man in office the myth of the nation
would again be engaged, and the fact that he was Catholic would shiver
a first existential vibration of consciousness into the mind of the White
Protestant," Mailer posed. "For the first time in our history, the Protestant would have the pain and creative luxury of feeling himself in
some tiny degree part of a minority, and that was an experience which
might be incommensurable in its value to the best of them."

Before they wed, Jeanne convinced Mailer to visit Lord Beaverbrook with her at his villa on the Riviera. Beaverbrook, who previously
endured fights with the strong-willed Jeanne as he had with most of
his family, chose not to get angry. At age eighty-two, after witnessing
so much wartime death and only three years away from his own, he
seemed prosaic at the prospect of a new baby.

"Well, sir, under the circumstances you've been gracious," Mailer said, as the couple departed.

"Under the circumstances," the press lord replied. His granddaughter's doomed marriage to Mailer fell apart within a year.

By 1963, Jeanne returned to the good graces of Randolph Churchill, thanks to her friendship with Kay Halle, by then a doyenne of the Washington social scene. Jeanne pleaded with Winston's son to give one of his father's paintings to Halle. "She [Kay Halle] told me that there is nothing on earth that she desires more but she dare not ask!" Jeanne wrote Randolph. "Do find one—you can imagine the pride she would have in it."

After the White House ceremony for Sir Winston that April, Jeanne Campbell joined Kay and Randolph at a table with Jackie Kennedy. They sat inside the Green Room, sipping glasses of warm champagne together. "As you would say, I think we Yankees and Limies are 'pretty steady on parade' these days," Halle later told Randolph. Around this time, Jeanne had a sexual encounter with JFK inside her Georgetown apartment, her daughters attested, though it was "mostly a friendship."

Jackie Kennedy's awareness of her husband's infidelities, and the death of their baby Patrick in August, placed unbearable stress on the Kennedy marriage, compelling the First Lady to stay away from Washington for the rest of summer of 1963. In September, she accepted an invitation to relax with her sister, Lee, aboard Aristotle Onassis's yacht, cruising along the Mediterranean and Aegean Sea—just as Sir Winston Churchill had been enlisted. "The ship will go wherever Mrs. Kennedy wants it to go," Onassis insisted. "She is the captain."

Onassis's generosity with Jacqueline Kennedy, as with the Churchills, was more manipulative than it appeared on the surface. His invitation came with the price of access to both the First Lady and, by extension, the president of the United States. Onassis seized this opportunity when Lee Radziwill stayed on the yacht *Christina* with her husband, Prince Stanislas Radziwill. During their visit, an urgent call came from the Kennedys about the death of their premature baby, Patrick. Though at times rivalrous, the two sisters depended on each other emotionally when in need. At Ari's urging, Lee relayed his offer to make the giant yacht available to Jackie for a relaxing escape. "You can't imagine how terrific Ari's yacht is, and he says we can go anywhere we want," Lee explained. "It will do you so much good to get away for a while." Realizing the political sensitivities involved, Onassis volunteered to stay away from the yacht while the First Lady was aboard. Jackie wouldn't have it. In agreeing to the voyage, she insisted Onassis join them. Jackie told her sister that she "could not accept his generous hospitality and then not let him come along." Uncharacteristically, Onassis remained belowdecks, to avoid the chance of being photographed with the First Lady.

In recounting her Greek getaway, Jackie Kennedy later claimed the president encouraged her to take a trip, to lift her depressed mood after their baby died. "Why don't you go to New York, or go see your sister in Italy?" Jack told her, as she later recounted to Arthur Schlesinger. But other accounts say the president reacted strongly against the idea—"looking like thunder," as his personal secretary, Evelyn Lincoln, recalled.

"For Christ's sake, Jackie!" the president protested to his wife. "Onassis is an international pirate!" Of course, Onassis's checkered past didn't stop JFK himself from previously boarding the yacht to see Winston Churchill. However, the president wasn't in a bargaining position to veto his wife's invitation. "Jackie had made up her mind," Lincoln recalled about the Onassis trip, "and that was that." Nevertheless, the president took steps to ensure that his wife's recovery didn't become a political weapon. He arranged for Franklin D. Roosevelt Jr., then undersecretary of commerce, and Roosevelt's wife to accompany the First

Lady, lending the trip an air of official business. "Your presence will add a little respectability to the whole thing," Jack assured FDR's son.

For the Kennedys, Lee Radziwill also posed a problem, accustomed as she was to getting her own way with men. "She is quite as beautiful as you say," Lord Beaverbrook enthused to his pal Joe Kennedy after meeting Lee with her first husband, Michael Canfield, a few years earlier. "You have not overstated her charm and splendour." Lee's second marriage, to Prince Radziwill, was falling apart by the time Jackie left for Greece. Newspaper columnists speculated about her alleged affair with Onassis. "Does the ambitious Greek tycoon hope to become the brother-in-law of the American President?" asked syndicated columnist Drew Pearson. The Kennedys feared a wider scandal with their Catholic supporters if the First Lady's sister became embroiled in a public spectacle with Onassis. "Just tell her to cool it, will you?" Bobby pleaded with Jackie.

Instead, Jackie turned on her own charm during her Greek odyssey. With each passing moment on the yacht, her spirits improved and she revived, looking ever more radiant. The *Christina*'s luxury proved everything she'd heard, all that Lee had promised—a Shangri-La on the sea. By day, they sunned themselves and relaxed on the ship, with a staff that included two hairdressers and a Swedish masseur. At night, Ari's waiters served vintage wines, caviar, and exotic foods, while a small orchestra provided dancing music. Well past midnight, Jackie chatted with her engaging host in French as well as English. Onassis was much different from her husband: a self-made creation, more of a rogue like Joe Kennedy than like his son. Most significant, Ari, a virtuoso of seduction, seemed totally focused on Jackie's needs and not his own. The Greek tycoon, already linked to Maria Callas and the president's sister-in-law, now found himself deeply attracted to the most elusive prize of all. "What was really happening on the cruise was that Aristotle Onassis was falling in love with the First Lady of the United States," explained his biographer Frank Brady. Though Ari stayed out of sight at first, he joined his guests when the yacht docked in Turkey, and the paparazzi took photos of the happy partiers. Eventually, a long-lens photo of Jackie in a bikini, sunning herself aboard the *Christina*, appeared in newspapers around the world.

Back in the United States, a Republican congressman complained about the public expense surrounding the First Lady's luxury trip aboard a yacht owned by a foreigner who'd defrauded the government. Under a headline "First Lady's Cruise Causes Stir," columnist Drew Pearson in the *Washington Post* sniffed around Onassis's shipping deals. Jack and his attorney general brother were furious. Bobby ordered Secret Service agents to place a security blackout around Jackie, to avoid further publicity. Hoover's FBI reviewed its files on Onassis. In a perturbed call to the yacht, the president asked his wife to return home. Jackie decided to stay a bit longer. It was the kind of ploy (the distant trip) that other wives of famous men, including Clementine Churchill and Jackie's mother-in-law, Rose, employed to make an implicit point with their husbands and establish some equilibrium for themselves. When she finally returned to America, the First Lady received expensive jewelry from Onassis, a diamond-and-ruby necklace—far better than Lee's parting gift: afterward, as if to underline the sisters' rivalry, Lee jokingly complained to Jack "that while Jackie has been laden with presents I only received three dinky little bracelets that Caroline wouldn't wear to her own birthday party."

Jackie raved about her trip, telling the president how refreshed she felt. She sent Ari a cigarette box as a gift of thanks. Gradually, the First Lady realized the political damage she'd caused. "I was melancholy after the death of our baby and I stayed away . . . longer than I needed to," Jackie later confided to a family priest, Rev. Richard McSorley, a Georgetown Jesuit. "I could have made life so much happier, especially for the last few weeks. I could have tried harder to get over my melancholy." She particularly felt bad about the barbs Franklin D. Roosevelt Jr. received from the press, who implied Onassis was trying to unduly influence his Commerce Department's maritime interests. "Poor Franklin didn't want to go along at all," Jackie explained to Ben Bradlee, her husband's journalist friend. Bradlee and his wife had accompanied the Kennedys to view a new James Bond movie when the subject of their discussion wandered onto who might succeed Jack as president someday. Assuming his brothers weren't ready yet, Jack reeled off names of people he couldn't support, including Vice President Lyndon Johnson.

"Well, then who?" Jackie finally asked.

"It was going to be Franklin, until you and Onassis fixed that," Jack teased.

Bradlee recalled how the president later used "Jackie's guilt feelings" about Onassis to convince her to accompany him on his next political trip, this time to Dallas, something she was loath to do.

"Maybe now you'll come with us to Texas next month," Jack said, beaming his all-American smile. His wife wouldn't resist.

"Sure I will, Jack," she agreed.

The 1964 presidential campaign was expected to be Jack Kennedy's last. Unlike in England, he couldn't become his nation's leader again, as Winston Churchill did in 1951, six years after last leaving the prime ministership. "It has recently been suggested that whether I serve one or two terms in the Presidency, I will find myself at the end of that period at what might be called an awkward age—too old to begin a new career, and too young to write my memoirs," Kennedy said, alluding once more to his hero.

At his London home on November 22, 1963, Winston Churchill stared in horror at the video images from America, trying to absorb the news. His old, frail body seemed racked by what was being said. "Tears streamed down his face as he watched the news reports on the television in the dining room," recalled his granddaughter Celia Sandys. In his long life, Winston had witnessed much savagery among men, yet the killing of this singular man moved him deeply.

"Never have I been so filled with revulsion, anger and sorrow, as when I heard of your husband's death," Churchill wrote to Kennedy's widow, Jacqueline, the day after the president's assassination in Dallas. "On this great and good man were set the hopes of humanity ... Nothing can be of consolation to you at this time. But I would like you to know that throughout the world, and in England especially, all men who prize Freedom and hope for Peace share your loss and partake of your grief."

Randolph Churchill also felt shattered, numbed by the news, perhaps because he'd known the slain president so much better than his father had. "For a few moments I could hardly believe it and my mind was half-paralysed by shock," he'd recall. Much of Randolph's life as a Churchill had been spent in a parallel course with Kennedys, with Jack as the best of their generation. Among their many mutual friends and acquaintances, there were always bound to be comparisons between him, as heir to the Churchill name, and the sons of Joe Kennedy. Their association dated back to before the war. With good intentions, Randolph had greeted Jack and Kick when they first came to London in 1938, before he learned to despise their father for his favoring appeasement of Hitler. But in recent years, Randolph's view changed by watching Jack emerge as a politician and realizing how much he had emulated his father, Winston. He had gotten to know Jack's wife and brothers and sisters. Randolph recognized that their hopes and ambitions went far beyond the parochial hatreds and self-centered demands of Joe Kennedy. Jack had learned to emerge from his father's shadow and create his own sterling reputation. He'd become his own man in a way Randolph still hoped to be. In the past year, Randolph had visited with Jack three times and talked to him over the phone like a longtime friend with a shared history. Never had the world seen Randolph Churchill live up to the expectations of greatness as that afternoon in April 1963 when Jack stood next to him while Randolph gave voice to Sir Winston's words, as the heir to his legacy. Randolph's relationship with this extraordinary American family had run through many difficult times and emotions, only to come full circle in friendship. "Perhaps the only thing he bitterly held against America was the murder of J.F.K.," recalled his aide, Frank Gannon. "He could never speak of him without tears."

On deadline, Randolph paid tribute to Kennedy in the *Evening Standard* in the best way he knew how: as a writer rather than as a politician. "If it is not presumptuous to say so, I not only admired him as a statesman, but loved him as a brother," Randolph wrote in his column. He had learned enough about Jack to understand this fraternal significance among the Kennedys, with the Shakespearean allusion to the St. Crispin's Day speech in *Henry V.* During his career, Kennedy quoted his favorite, memorable line from the play ("We few, we happy few, we band of brothers; For he today that sheds his blood with me, shall be my brother") just as Winston Churchill had played upon its familiar chords in rallying his nation during World War II.

Now Randolph eulogized in print this unexpected friend whom he came to admire. "He was the best emblem of hope and leader of our generation in the free world," he said, well aware of who had been the leader for the previous generation. "He had served gallantly, indeed heroically, in the Second World War; he knew the hell of war. He was the surest guarantee that there would not be another war, and that mankind, somehow, would move forward into a sunlit age."

Lord Beaverbrook's sharp news instinct prompted a less glorious response when he learned of the presidential assassination. While having dinner, his *Sunday Express* city editor, William Davis, received a call from Max telling him JFK's murder would mean a Wall Street boom and to get down to the newsroom immediately. Beaverbrook's journalist granddaughter, Jeanne Campbell, rushed to Dallas to cover the strange aftermath of JFK's killing. "She is convinced that there is something very fishy about the assassination which has not come out," Beaverbrook told his top editor, Charles Wintour. "Of course the atmosphere in Dallas is still very strange and it is hard to judge at this distance, but there are certainly an awful lot of unanswered questions." As a friend, though, Beaverbrook understood what it meant for Joe Kennedy. Max framed his response to the tragedy in terms of legacy. In a cable expressing sympathy to Rose, he added, MAY JOE FIND SOLACE IN THE UN-EXAMPLED TRIUMPHS OF HIS SON IN THE ASSURANCE THAT BOBBY WILL REPEAT JACK'S CAREER.

As the world mourned, Aristotle Onassis called Lee Radziwill in London. She asked him to accompany her and husband Stas to the president's funeral. A formal invitation allowed Onassis to stay at the White House, one of a small group there of nonfamily members. A month earlier, Jack and Bobby had talked of banning the Greek shipping magnate from the United States, at least until the 1964 election. Now neither Lee nor her bereaved sister thought of keeping him away. Ari was among the few who paid his respects to the widowed First Lady in her private suite.

On Sunday, November 24, the Greek tycoon attended an informal White House dinner that resembled an Irish wake. Kennedy's brothers, Bobby and Teddy, and many of their closest friends shared drinks and humorous stories about Jack. The party felt as if Jack had never died, that his body wasn't lying in state in the Capitol. Surprised by this strange Irish custom, Onassis played along as best he could. "Ari quickly discovered his role as a kind of court jester," his biographer Peter Evans explained. "It was a part he had played often for Churchill, and he was prepared to play it again for the Kennedys." Perhaps desperate for diversion from his grief, Bobby asked Ari about his colorful past, about his famous yacht, and wondered aloud if the stools on board were really covered with the genitalia of whales. Later, Bobby waved around a fake document and asked Onassis to sign it. The paper bequeathed half his money to the poor in Latin America. "I have never made the mistake of thinking it is a sin to make money," Ari said, somewhat in jest, the kind of comment Jack Kennedy's father might have employed.

Bobby Kennedy's excess on this night could surely be forgiven. Since learning of his brother's death, he had found his life a whirl of agony, pain, and recriminations while trying to comfort Jackie and his family. Another guest in the White House heard him crying alone in the Lincoln Bedroom, "Why God, why?" While the nation's top investigator searched in his mind for answers to a senseless crime, Bobby attended to funeral arrangements and the personal care of Jack's widow and family. In their extraordinary climb through politics together, the two brothers had become inseparable. Perhaps because of their eight-year age difference and complementing natures, Jack never felt a rivalry with Bobby, as he had with Joe Jr. Virtually Robert Kennedy's entire career had been spent in service to his older brother and his family's dream of achieving political greatness. Now, in an awful instant, everything but memories of Jack seemed gone. Bobby's grief "veered close to being a tragedy within a tragedy," recalled Teddy Kennedy, who buried his own feelings in Senate work and drink. "Hope seemed to have died within him, and there followed months of unrelenting melancholia. He went through the motions of everyday life, but he carried the burden of his grief with him always."

One of those who helped the Kennedys through their grief was Averell Harriman. The president's special diplomat and his wife, Marie, allowed Jacqueline Kennedy and her two small children to use their Washington home for several weeks after they left the White House. Harriman also encouraged Bobby, after he resigned as attorney general, to return to public life by running successfully in 1964 for the U.S. Senate in New York, where Harriman had been governor. Ethel Kennedy told Marie Harriman that her husband was "so extraordinarily helpful in getting Bobby over the hump," in those darkest days after the assassination. "Without the advice and encouragement of Averell, Bob would never have thought of being a candidate for the Senate in New York," Rose Kennedy agreed, in another note of thanks. Her husband's derisive personal comments in the past—Joe counted Harriman, with "a Jew wife," among those he hated for influencing FDR on wartime policy after he was replaced as London ambassador—were now forgotten. As the family's matriarch, Rose expressed her gratitude for "your unquestioned loyalty throughout the years—dear Averell, towards two generations of Kennedys."

The widowed former First Lady would stay at the Harrimans' home until she moved to a high-rise apartment in New York, unable to bear the Washington crowds pointing at her and staring through her windows. By her own extraordinary example, with unforgettable grace, she led the nation through the painful ordeal of her husband's funeral. Thousands touched by her husband's memory sent heartfelt letters of sympathy and support. She attempted to reply to each one. But she found it too painful to stay in the capital city where she'd first met Jack Kennedy and shared a life with him for a decade.

Jacqueline Kennedy did remain in touch with a few old friends from her White House years, including Kay Halle, with whom she'd shared advice. In an April 1964 note to Halle, she mentioned an upcoming Easter trip with Caroline and John Jr. and their plans for the future. "I hope it will give me via fresh air some new energy—as I just have had none lately & cannot even touch the ever growing piles on my desk," she wrote to Kay. "But this spring maybe everything will be better— Love Jackie."

48

Thoughts That Lie Too Deep

"Clouds and darkness

Closed upon Camelot;

Arthur had vanish'd

I knew not whither,

The king who loved me,

And cannot die."

—ALFRED LORD TENNYSON, 1889

"Mythology distracts us everywhere."

—JOHN F. KENNEDY, 1962 SPEECH AT YALE UNIVERSITY

Exiting a limousine at Runnymede, the hallowed place outside London where King John signed the Magna Carta seven hundred and fifty years earlier, an otherwise somber Robert Kennedy smiled when he spotted Randolph Churchill wearing his magnificent royal uniform. Bobby shook Churchill's hand, followed by his brother's widow, Jacqueline, and her two small children, who bowed as taught by their English nanny.

On this sunny but sad day in May 1965, the British people dedicated an acre of Runnymede in memoriam to John F. Kennedy—as a champion of democracy and the kind of Anglo-American unity always sought by Winston Churchill. Clad in full Queen's Own Hussars military regalia, complete with hat and sword, Randolph sat in a place of honor along with the Kennedys and other dignitaries. Now left to history, the legacy of these two leaders, Kennedy and Churchill, would be cultivated at events such as this by their families and friends.

A seven-ton white stone bearing Kennedy's name and his inaugural words reminded Runnymede visitors of the fallen American president. "He, together with his family, had many ties with our country," said Queen Elizabeth II at the ceremony. "His elder brother, flying from these shores on a hazardous mission, was killed in our common struggle against the evil forces of a cruel tyranny. A dearly loved sister lies buried in an English churchyard. Bonds like these cannot be broken."

Jacqueline Kennedy intended to speak to the thousands gathered along the Thames, but she became too overcome with emotion when former prime minister Harold Macmillan recalled the shock of her husband's killing. "To all of you who have created this memorial," she acknowledged in a statement, drawing from Wordsworth's verse, "I can only say that it is the deepest comfort to me to know that you share with me thoughts that lie too deep."

After the assassination, Randolph's friendship with the Kennedys grew, as if the president's death re-enforced their personal bonds and common experiences as dynastic families. He stayed in contact with Bobby Kennedy as well as Jackie and her sister, Lee. Whenever in America, he visited the president's widow. "His devotion to Mrs. Jacqueline Kennedy was romantic in the chivalrous sense of the word," remembered Frank Gannon, Randolph's assistant on the impending biography of his father. A few months after the ceremony, when Jackie went skiing at Gstaad, Switzerland, with her children, Randolph flew over the Alps in a chartered helicopter to have lunch with her as if in "a knightly quest," Gannon recalled.

The wrapping of Kennedy's legacy in the British myth of Camelot sprang from Jacqueline Kennedy's memories of her husband listening to recordings of the Broadway show based on the tales of King Arthur and his Knights of the Round Table. "I always keep thinking of Camelot—which is overly sentimental—but I know I am right—for one brief shining moment there was Camelot—and it will never be that way again," she wrote Harold Macmillan in January 1964. Many journalists and historians jumped on the Anglophile imagery in subsequent magazine and books, though others realized JFK was far more complex to explain. Writer Garry Wills described the president as "semi-English" and "semi-Irish" in his makeup. CBS newsman Edward R. Murrow, who worked for the Kennedy administration after quitting the network, felt Jack always remained an enigma. "I saw him at fairly close range under a variety of circumstances, and there remains for me a considerable element of mystery—and maybe that is good," explained Murrow. "I always knew where his mind was. But I was not always sure where his heart was."

In his own grief, Robert Kennedy read the Greeks, and existentialists such as Camus, but reverted to his Irish-Catholic roots to explain his brother's tragedy. In March 1964, in his first public appearance after the assassination, Bobby delivered an agonizing St. Patrick's Day speech that quoted from a favorite poem Jack had recited during his Irish trip the previous year. Bobby repeated the verses telling of a long-ago Irish leader, Owen Roe O'Neill, suddenly struck down in his prime. The poem ends with a lament: "Oh! Why did you leave us, Owen? Why did you die?" Historically, JFK symbolized the Irish-Catholic experience—indeed, the rise of all immigrants and minority groups in the United States—showing that they, too, could reach the very top, that the dream of social ascendancy could become reality. But Americans, accustomed to the Brahmin style of their dead president in TV images repeated constantly after his death, didn't accept such a history, no matter how true. Memories of JFK would soon become captive to the family's mythmaking. While Joe Kennedy's understanding of television's power was central to his son's electoral success in life, Jackie's Camelot narrative shaped his legend in death.

. . .

By the time of his assassination, President Kennedy had moved away from some of Winston Churchill's views, just as a younger Jack learned to distance himself from his father's politics. While he never failed to express his and Churchill's shared belief in liberty and human dignity, Kennedy began to show doubts about America's assumption of the old British Empire's place in the world. He became uneasy with costly responsibilities in places such as Asia, Africa, and the Middle East, which Churchill deftly transferred to previous U.S. presidents. "Arguably, the achievement of Churchill's final years was to cover a necessary and pragmatic retreat from Empire with a mixture of 'no surrender' bluster and sentimental appeal to Anglo-American unity," historian Richard Toye observed. Unlike Churchill, though, Kennedy never embraced the idea of an American empire, in tune with his country's Colonial and Revolutionary past and traditional reluctance to engage in nation building. As he made clear during his Irish visit and elsewhere, Kennedy understood what a policy of imperial oppression can do to a people after so many years under a giant's thumb. "We can no longer afford policies which refuse to accept the inevitable triumph of nationalism in Africa—the inevitable end of colonialism—or the unyielding determination of the new African states to lift their people from their age-old poverty and hunger and ignorance," he proclaimed in 1962.

Yet regarding Vietnam, the pivotal foreign policy question of the 1960s, JFK took a tough Churchillian line, one that his successors expanded after his death into a full-fledged war resulting in fifty-seven thousand American deaths. Spurred by the strong anticommunist stance of both his nation and his Church, Kennedy supported President Ngo Dinh Diem in South Vietnam, a minority Catholic in an overwhelmingly Buddhist nation. In his first year in office, JFK dubbed Diem the "Winston Churchill" of Southeast Asia, in his resisting the onslaught of Communist guerrillas. His friends and his brother Senator Edward Kennedy later argued that JFK never wanted to escalate the conflict, though there is little convincing evidence to support their claim. Kennedy's emulation of Churchill rubbed off on his successor, Lyndon Johnson, who ordered his speechwriters "to read everything about Churchill, to help give Johnson a Churchillian twist," historian David Halberstam observed. With more swagger and less wit than Winston, LBJ spread his approach to places such as the Dominican Republic, where U.S. troops in 1965 invaded to resist the Communists. He instructed his national security adviser, McGeorge Bundy, a carry-over from Kennedy, to relay to the rebel leader, Col. Francisco Caamaño Deñó, a cowboy-like warning: "Tell that son of a bitch that unlike the young man who came before me I am not afraid to use what's on my hip."

Despite the best efforts of Kennedy loyalists, many still consider Vietnam his darkest legacy. "His Churchillian rhetoric ('pay any price, bear any burden . . .') provided the war's rhetorical frame as surely as George W. Bush's post-9/11 speeches did for our intervention in Iraq," wrote *New York Times* columnist Ross Douthat in 2011. "His slow-motion military escalation established the strategic template that Lyndon Johnson followed so disastrously. And the war's architects were all Kennedy people: It was the Whiz Kids' mix of messianism and technocratic confidence, not Oswald's fatal bullet, that sent so many Americans to die in Indochina."

Historically, Kennedy understood that Churchill's record wasn't comprised of military adventurism as much as the military strength needed to maintain British interests abroad and, if necessary, deter or fight off a larger enemy. After World War II, Churchill urged the United States to consider using the atom bomb to stop Soviet expansionism, and his 1946 Fulton speech provided the philosophical underpinnings for the Cold War. However, with the advent of the hydrogen bomb, both Churchill and Kennedy changed their views about nuclear armament. They realized there was something worse than conventional war as they had known it as young men.

For most of his career, Kennedy echoed Churchill's old bellicose rhetoric, especially in his 1960 presidential campaign and inaugural speech. Yet in the White House, he struck a different, more conciliatory tone. He read Barbara Tuchman's 1962 Pulitzer Prize–winning book *The Guns of August,* which examines how leaders (including a young Winston Churchill) stumbled into World War I almost by accident. He also knew that Churchill, in his book about World War II, called it "the unnecessary war." Facing a potential World War III, Kennedy resolved not to cause a nuclear Armageddon by refusing to talk with the Communists. "No country has done more than the United States in the last twelve months to strengthen our military forces in order to protect our commitments," Kennedy explained at a May 1962 press conference. "But we hope, in calling up 160,000 men, adding billions of dollars to our defense budget—I would feel that the purpose of it, we hope, is not to fight a nuclear war, but to establish an environment which permits us to have a useful exchange. Winston Churchill said, 'It is better to jaw, jaw than war, war,' and we shall continue to jaw, jaw, and see if we can produce a useful result. We may fail, but in my opinion, the effort is worth it when we are dealing with such dangerous matters, and when we have seen the history of this century, when statesmen and leaders and others have brought about failure and brought about war as a result."

Later that October, the Cuban Missile Crisis changed Kennedy's willingness to risk a war with thermonuclear weapons. In a June 1963 American University speech, he announced plans for a nuclear test-ban treaty and a stop to atmospheric testing, and he spoke of preparing for peace with the same urgency he'd once spoken of war. "First examine our attitude towards peace itself," Kennedy said. "Too many of us think it is impossible. Too many think it is unreal. But that is a dangerous, defeatist belief. It leads to the conclusion that war is inevitable, that mankind is doomed, that we are gripped by forces we cannot control. We need not accept that view. Our problems are man-made; therefore, they can be solved by man. And man can be as big as he wants. No problem of human destiny is beyond human beings."

Old friends such as William Douglas-Home, whose brother later served as prime minister, noticed how JFK had grown past the combativeness of his Churchill example, finding the courage to make peace. "Whereas, Sir Winston you might think of having a good fight with somebody and then being magnanimous afterwards," explained Douglas-Home. "But Kennedy went one stage further, and he was prepared to be magnanimous without having the fight, which was a great advance in politics. Nobody could really go back after what he did in Cuba." Even political opponent Richard Nixon, who shared Kennedy's admiration for Churchill, called the president's effort at removal of missiles from Cuba "his finest hour."

In the decades after his assassination, the "what if" questions of Kennedy's public legacy and claims to greatness were mixed in with a series of revelations about his personal life, especially his philandering and its potential for political disgrace had he lived. America's most insightful writers and editors seemed taken aback by this unknown portion of his personality, so much at odds with the knightly Camelot myth. One of his best friends, journalist Ben Bradlee, seemed dumbfounded upon learning posthumously of JFK's affair with Bradlee's own sister-in-law. "I can only repeat my ignorance of Kennedy's sex life, and state that I am appalled by the details that have emerged, appalled by the recklessness, by the subterfuge that must have been involved," Bradlee wrote in his memoir. Author Norman Mailer remained enchanted by the president's charisma, even though he'd been apparently cuckolded by him with his estranged wife Lady Jeanne Campbell, the granddaughter of Lord Beaverbrook. "I realized he was a man of many faces," Mailer said thirty years later, recalling an interview with JFK. "At one point he looked like a professor—he was comfortable; he looked like a man of 45, even of 50; he was gray at the edges; he had a gentle, intellectual face. Ten minutes later he could look like a movie star under the sun speaking to a press conference. His face kept changing."

While the Kennedys debated who should be the authorized biographer of the assassinated president, Randolph Churchill, already granted that honor with Sir Winston, struggled to deal with his father's legacy while he was still alive.

Now in his ninetieth year, the former prime minister found his health flagging and his mind wandering. Winston was waiting to die. Although the press called him the great man of the century, he considered himself a failure. "He felt that everything that he had done had ended in disaster," explained Anthony Montague Browne. "He had won the war but lost the Empire, communism had swallowed up half of Europe, and socialism was threatening the world he loved at home." In 1964, his Conservative Party lost power to the Labour Party leaders who fashioned themselves, ironically, on Kennedy's 1960 campaign pledge to get the country moving again. Throughout that year, Winston lingered, and barely rallied when his son came to call. At the end of one visit, as Randolph was about to leave, Winston still flashed the old spirit.

"The Dark Angel beckons—but I still say no!" the old man vowed with barely a whisper.

In researching his father's life, combing through documents with his team, Randolph Churchill found a bit of his own history and the dreams that Winston once had for him. Amid the trove, he discovered one particular letter, written as Winston was going off to the front during World War I, in which he said to Clementine, "If anything should happen to me, Randolph will carry the torch." (The Kennedys would also employ this metaphor in heroic terms.) For Winston's aging son, the phrase only invoked sobering disappointment.

In January 1964, Randolph suffered a respiratory illness and was hospitalized. Aware that he smoked eighty to one hundred cigarettes a day, many feared the worst when doctors removed part of his lung. Bobby Kennedy sent his British friend a cheery get-well message. "England needs you but we also need you back here to straighten us out. Regards Bobby." To his own surprise and delight, Randolph learned that the excised tissue wasn't cancerous. He recovered and soon returned to work on his father's biography. "A typical triumph of modern science to find the only part of Randolph that was not malignant and remove it!" quipped Evelyn Waugh, whose uneasy friendship with Randolph had waned in recent years after a quarrel. Yet when Randolph heard Waugh's droll remark, he was amused enough to send a retort while still in the hospital during Easter. ENCHANTED BY YOUR BENIGNANT THOUGHTS ABOUT ME IN HOLY WEEK, he cabled. HAPPY FEAST OF RESURRECTION.

Randolph tried once more to gain Waugh's endorsement of his father's abilities, as if a Nobel Prize for Literature wouldn't suffice without Evelyn's petulant approval. During the war, the two former comrades in arms had argued about Winston's writerly abilities, and now Randolph sought to resume the debate. He urged Waugh to reconsider the biography of Marlborough, his father's masterwork. After delving into the book, Waugh had walked away unimpressed. "The author has no specifically literary talent but a gift of lucid self-expression in words— lost when least excited," he wrote Randolph. To Waugh, Winston was merely a politician with a pen, not an artist as he strived to be. "I was everywhere outraged by his partisanship & naïve assumption of superior virtue," Waugh condemned. "It is a shifty barrister's case, not a work of literature."

Randolph, hearing echoes of their old dispiriting debate, finally realized he couldn't convert Waugh.

"Incidentally, why did you scrap your phrase about my father's 'sham Augustan style'?" Randolph retorted in disgust.

Randolph's final bitter exchanges with Waugh would be about his father rather than the two of them, cutting jabs that had so often defined their whole relationship. "He is not a man for whom I ever had esteem," Waugh concluded about Winston. "Always in the wrong . . . simply a 'Radio Personality' who outlived his prime. *'Rallied the nation'* indeed! I was a serving soldier in 1940. How we despised his orations."

Randolph realized that his father's long-held doubts about Waugh's friendship were correct. Still, Waugh's disloyalty seemed trivial compared to the treachery of his father's friend Lord Beaverbrook. "You know, when the Devil comes to earth, he needs some sort of human habitation," Randolph explained to Montague Browne, his father's aide. "If he is intent on major mischief, then he puts up in Max Beaverbrook. If on minor, then he chooses Evelyn Waugh."

In June 1964, Lord Beaverbrook died at age eighty-five. For three decades, Max had been a trusted confidant to Joe Kennedy, both men so much alike in their business acumen and cunning. Beaverbrook was one of the few people with whom this patriarch of America's leading political family could relax and reveal his innermost thoughts. During World War II, Max wanted to give his fortune to Kennedy for safekeeping if the Nazis invaded England. Beaverbrook had always been a nexus between the two great families, Kennedys and Churchills, and their world of friends and associates. When Beaverbrook died, Joe Kennedy could no longer speak for himself, but Winston Churchill, in a public message prepared for him by Montague Browne, called Max "my oldest and closest friend." In World War II, Churchill had relied intensely on Max's brilliance and ingenuity. "Sir Winston told me several times that if Britain had been invaded in 1940 and we had had to fall back north to the Thames, he would have ruled Britain with a triumvirate of himself, Beaverbrook and [Minister of Labor] Ernest Bevin," wrote Montague Browne. "He confided in him [Beaverbrook] as much as anyone both on personal and political matters."

Winston soon followed his friend in death. Another stroke and the toll of old age had drained him, enough for his family to be called to his bedside in January 1965. Clementine Churchill watched her husband lie silently, each of his breaths growing fainter. Like Rose Kennedy, she had been supportive and steadfast about her family's life in politics, though she'd learned to set a separate course for herself, often with long trips away, if only to give herself some distance from her husband's overwhelming public demands. "What a burden you have borne over so many years—and with what charm & dignity," Beaverbrook wrote to "dear Clemmie" in one his last letters, marking Winston's birthday. "How much the Nation & the World owe to you for all your labours."

At the bedside, Randolph asked to spend some remaining time alone with his father. There was so much to remember between them, so much to forget. Whatever warring impulses remained in him had now found some measure of peace. "As I closed the door, I saw him lift his father's hand to his lips," recalled Winston's physician, Lord Moran. In his final moments, Winston Churchill's wife and surviving adult children surrounded him, hoping for some reprieve from mortality. Then all was still. "He's gone," said Moran.

The family followed Clementine into her sitting room inside their Hyde Park Gate town house, including young Winston, Randolph's son, who had married and named his newborn son Randolph. There had been talk of burying the former prime minister near his beloved Chartwell, but in death as in his life, tradition ruled. Winston's remains would be interred near Blenheim Palace, the ancestral home of John Churchill, the First Duke of Marlborough.

With the rest of the family still in the sitting room, Randolph wandered toward a bookcase and returned holding aloft a book about Lord Randolph Churchill.

"Would you believe it, he has died on the same day, and at almost the same hour that his father died," Randolph marveled, as if discovering his father's last miracle on this earthly domain. Indeed, seventy years earlier in London, on January 24, 1895, Lord Randolph Churchill died—the emotionally searing event that so defined his son Winston's life as a young man in a hurry, afraid that he might not live long enough to reach old age.

"Mine eyes have seen the glory of the coming of the Lord."

"The Battle Hymn of the Republic" filled St. Paul's Cathedral during the state funeral for Winston Churchill, a tribute to the British Empire's greatest defender and a lifelong admirer of the United States. "I want it in memory of my American mother," Winston instructed about the song to be played after his death. Nearly one million mourners filled the London streets near the cathedral to pay their last respects to "Winnie," the fatherly figure who shepherded them through war.

In one of the pews, former president Dwight Eisenhower sat with tears in his eyes, recalling the "soldier, statesman and leader whom two great countries were proud to honor as their own." Part of the American entourage that joined Eisenhower at the funeral included Undersecretary of State Averell Harriman, the roving diplomat for both FDR and JFK (and a fill-in for President Lyndon Johnson, sick at home with the flu), and Kay Halle, the longtime friend of both families. "Poor Randolph Churchill called me from London today—all choked up about his father," Halle wrote to Bobby Kennedy before she left for London. "What a titan is Sir Winston. An eternal flame he is too."

Many commentators recalled Churchill's honorary citizenship

awarded by President Kennedy less than two years earlier and expressed sorrow that two of the twentieth century's most revered leaders had passed from the scene. Watching on television from Washington, *New York Times* columnist James Reston said that Churchill's funeral impacted the capital "more than any other event since the assassination of President Kennedy." Winston's remarkable example underlined "the imponderables of life," Reston said, and "suggested that sentiment and history, that ideas and philosophy, are also powerful, and that the 'special relationship' between London and Washington was not merely a source of contention with Paris, but by itself something highly important."

As Winston's coffin floated down the Thames on its way to burial, his friends and family struggled to consider life without him. At the cathedral, Aristotle Onassis wept inconsolably—"sobbing like a baby" said one observer—at the loss of his friend and the most famous guest aboard his yacht. Yet Ari kept enough composure to insist that his former wife, Tina, now married to Winston's cousin John Spencer-Churchill, the Eleventh Duke of Marlborough, be seated far away from him in the pews.

On the flight back to America, Kay Halle flew with Eisenhower and Averell Harriman and talked about old times. Both she and Pamela Hayward, the ex-wife of Randolph Churchill, had been invited by the former president to join him on the returning air force plane, with officers in white jackets serving caviar and champagne. Halle recalled how Winston always credited Eisenhower with putting the Allied cause in World War II above nationalism and his being the "architect" of victory against the Nazi war machine. Ike described the painting Winston gave him as a gift. He joked about the gray-haired appearance of their wartime British contemporaries, such as former prime minister Anthony Eden. "Averell, they look older than we do, though they're younger," Ike teased, putting aside his and Harriman's past political differences.

For most of the long flight, Harriman chatted with Pamela, his former lover, whom he'd not seen in nearly fifteen years. The last time they'd spoken, she resented Averell's fitful warning about her reputation after divorcing Randolph, as if she needed a morality lecture from a rich married man who'd cheated on his own wife with her. But this trip to attend Winston's funeral became a sentimental journey for Pamela. Now living in New York, she felt pleased to see her son, Winston, and new grandchild, and still be treated by Clementine as a member of the Churchill extended family. At age forty-four, Pamela hardly looked dowdy, appearing just as attractive, with her light auburn hair and come-hither eyes, as when she and Harriman conducted their affair while Randolph was away at war. "It had been a memorable moment in Harriman's life, saying good-bye to the leader he idolized, and seeing the woman who still possessed him and talking with her for hours as they crossed the Atlantic," described his biographer Rudy Abramson. Both Ave and Pamela were still married during that plane ride, but six years later, when both their spouses had died, they met again, at a Georgetown dinner party hosted by publisher Katharine Graham (whose other guests included Kay Halle). "Since we were both suddenly free and alone, it just seemed the most natural thing in the world to kind of get together again," explained Pamela. One of the witnesses at their wedding was Ethel Kennedy. When young Winston told Clementine about his mother's intentions to marry Harriman, Churchill's widow seemed pleased. "My dear," replied Clemmie, "it's an old flame rekindled."

After Winston's death, both his magnificent achievements and glaring shortcomings were explored by biographers, equaled in number only by those chronicling JFK and his family. "That he was a great man cannot be doubted, but his flaws too were on the same heroic scale as the rest of the man," concluded Churchill revisionist biographer John Charmley in 1993. The troubles of Churchill's family life—suicide, addiction, divorce, and depression—were particularly at odds with his famous profile as a father figure to his nation, a fact unforgettably displayed by the crowds at his funeral. Unlike Joseph Kennedy, whose colossal failure in politics allowed him to pour his unrequited ambitions into his sons' careers, Winston never really left the public stage, never stepped aside for the next generation of Churchills. His daughters, such as actress Sarah Churchill, played minor cameos in his life's drama, while his only son, Randolph, despite his once-golden promise, felt ultimately overwhelmed by his father's legacy. Unlike his masterful behavior in the House of Commons, Winston seemed unable to calibrate his feelings at home, which ranged from indulgence to sharp rebukes, and he left an inchoate imprint as a parent. "He never wavered in his affection and help for them," observed Pamela, "but he was often saddened by many of us."

Sarah Churchill, the pretty redheaded actress often by her father's side during the war, never gained Winston's acceptance for her second marriage, to photographer Anthony Beauchamp in 1949, just as she never had for her choice of first husband, Vic Oliver, in the 1930s. By the late 1950s, Sarah's career and marriage had fallen apart, due in no small measure to her constant drinking. Beauchamp, a talented lensman who captured such beauties on film as Marilyn Monroe and Elizabeth Taylor, proved an unfaithful husband. "Anthony's wild and frequent infidelities were well-known to others and finally actually discovered by me," Sarah later wrote in a memoir. "In solemn desperation I embarked on a few flirtations, but they could not fill my sense of loneliness and defeat." In 1957, she had resolved to divorce Beauchamp—giving up the pretense that they would wait until Sir Winston passed away before taking action—when she got word that her estranged husband had taken his life with sleeping pills. Clementine broke the news to her daughter over the telephone. The death of Sarah's husband was "a tremendous shock to her," recalled Mary Soames, the Churchills' youngest daughter, "and suicide leaves such a cruel legacy of unanswered and unanswerable questions."

Shortly afterward, Sarah was arrested for public drunkenness in Malibu, California, while there for some television appearances. Photos of Churchill's daughter grappling with police filled the world's newspapers and triggered a backlash in England, where Fleet Street newspapers accused the American constables of being too rough with her. Randolph flew in from New York and urged his sister to dispose of the case as quickly as possible. "When I saw him, he said that I must plead guilty," Sarah recalled. "I could not upset America, or Anglo-American relations." Nonetheless, when an American television interviewer asked about his sister's arrest, Randolph threw discretion to the wind, erupting in protective fury. "I never discuss matters affecting members of my family with total strangers," he snapped. "I didn't bother to look up what your sisters had done or who your father was. I don't even know if you had a father or if you know who your father was."

Of Churchill's children, Diana may have been the most troubled, and certainly the saddest. Her second marriage, to Duncan Sandys, provided her ambitious, elegantly tailored husband with an important post in her father's wartime government and earned Sir Winston's approval, sometimes to Randolph's envious rage. But the marriage also brought heartbreak years later, as Diana learned of Duncan's infidelities. She suffered a nervous breakdown. As her life spiraled downward, her parents weren't much help. "Diana had not, at least for many years, meant nearly as much to her father as her two sisters, and Clementine had little personal regard for Duncan Sandys," observed Winston's former aide, Jock Colville. Her father tried to understand Diana's problems with distress, recalled Mary Soames, "although Winston found psychological troubles and their explanation quite beyond his ken." Mary's marriage, to Christopher Soames, was the only initial one to survive among those of the Churchill siblings. The British public and her parents' circle of friends often viewed Mary as the only stable one as well, thanks to the household help. "My mother had a very wonderful nanny called Madeleine White, who was a distant cousin and who brought my mother up incredibly strictly," recalled Mary's daughter Emma Soames in 2010. "And she always stayed on the rails, when rather spectacularly her brother and sisters all came off."

After Duncan Sandys divorced her to marry a much younger woman, Diana legally changed her name back to Churchill. She remained deeply depressed and inclined to excessive drinking and prescription drug abuse. In October 1963, she took her own life, found dead of a barbiturate overdose inside her bathroom. It fell to Mary, the youngest, to tell her parents. By then, Winston seemed inured to family tragedy. "As he grew older, he seemed to acquire a degree of insulation from sad and unpleasant news about those he loved," Mary explained.

Randolph Churchill was still distraught about the circumstances surrounding his older sister's death when, a month later, he wrote about the death of JFK, again unable to fathom the reasons for it. When a distant cousin familiar with their childhood suggested that Winston and Clementine's emotionally distant parenting might be blamed for Diana's demise, Randolph spewed with disgust. "You non-entity," he burst. "I refuse to discuss your crack-pot ideas."

Sir Winston's passing in early 1965 seemed to energize Randolph to complete the first volume of his multipart biography. Old family friends such as Bernard Baruch reminded Randolph it was now his duty to be his father's Boswell. "I fully agree with what you write about the responsibilities which now are mine, and I hope by my book to erect an enduring memorial to my father," he replied quite earnestly. Though he looked gaunt and much older than his fifty-five years, Randolph seemed to recognize that this upcoming book might be his best chance for glory, perhaps even political rehabilitation, especially now that his father's towering presence was gone. "Randolph really had all the right instincts," Pamela recalled, "and the one thing he wanted his father to do was to be proud of him."

Randolph's first volume of his father's life appeared to acclaim and commercial success in Great Britain and the United States. Historians and critics, including his onetime political opponent Michael Foot, praised Randolph's thoroughness and writing skill. "It could hardly be done better," adjudged historian A. J. P. Taylor. The book focused on Winston's early years and explained his journey in overcoming the shadow of Lord Randolph after his death on January 24, 1895. "There was now no one to help him—or stand in his way; for if Lord Randolph had lived, even in better health, he would have been an obstacle to Winston's career and prospects," Randolph wrote, as if an apologia for himself.

When she read the favorable reviews, ex-wife Pamela sent her congratulations to Randolph. She understood the book's deep significance for this wayward son, not so much in literary terms but in personal amends. "Please know how happy it makes me, for you," she wrote. "It is truly a just reward."

To his fellow journalists, Randolph promised more volumes to come, more opportunities to shed light on modern British history, and to try his best to make the world understand the extraordinary brilliance of Sir Winston's life. "Of course, I have thousands of anecdotes about my father," he explained to the *New York Times*. "But I could never hope to recapture the subtleties of his conversation—the skill and timing with which he would build up some magnificent bubble of imagination and then, with a word or gesture, explode it."

49

The Once and Future King

"The praises of so great and good a king;
Shall Churchill reign, and shall not Gotham sing?"
—CHARLES CHURCHILL, 1776

"Only fools want to be great."
—T. H. WHITE, *The Once and Future King*

Attorney General Robert Kennedy kept a bust in his office of Winston Churchill, along with his stirring words from the wartime "Never Surrender" speech. Over time, Bobby had grown to admire his father's nemesis like his brother Jack had. As the newly elected U.S. senator from New York, Bobby could be seen reading a Churchill book during his 1965 plane ride to climb Mount Kennedy, the snowcapped Canadian peak named for the slain president. And the next year, when Randolph Churchill's version of his father's life was published, Kennedy bought a hundred copies. He asked the great man's son to sign each, and gave them out as Christmas gifts.

Recriminations toward Winston Churchill once voiced by Joe Kennedy about World War II—as well as the memories of Honey Fitz's generation, of Boston Irish who blamed Churchill for the British Black and Tans' brutalities during the 1920 Irish War of Independence—now all seemed in the distant past, if not forgotten. From one generation to the next, the animosity between the Kennedys and Churchills faded, replaced with a surprising personal regard between the sons. This union became particularly evident with "Project K."

In 1966, in the glow of public praise for the initial volume of Winston's life, Randolph Churchill received a stunning offer from Bobby: to write the official biography of President John F. Kennedy. Bobby promised full access to JFK's papers and the cooperation of his widow, Jacqueline.

"This is the greatest compliment I have ever been paid," Randolph said about RFK's offer, which he relayed excitedly to Martin Gilbert, part of the team preparing his father's biography. Randolph dubbed this second massive endeavor Project K—a cryptic title like some James Bond plot or CIA code name—lest the news get out prematurely. Late nights at Stour House, while sitting around the fire with his band of researchers, Randolph shared his plans for the Kennedy book, to begin sometime in 1970, after the full multivolume study of Sir Winston was completed. "Randolph envisaged a two-volume work, the first on Kennedy's rise to power, the second on his Presidency," recalled Gilbert.

Churchill's son would write the story not only of his father's life, but with the blessing of the Kennedy family, also the official version of the life of JFK, arguably Winston's political heir on the world stage. The linkage between the two dynastic families would become immortalized, embedded in the pages of history.

"It was like being given three Nobel prizes for Literature piled on top of each other," wrote Randolph to Natalie Bevan, his friendly neighbor and lover. He instructed her to keep his upcoming project "top secret" and to refer to its code name when writing to him.

The offer to Randolph had resulted from the controversy surrounding William Manchester's planned biography of JFK's assassination, *The Death of a President*. Manchester originally gained the Kennedy family's approval. But when the huge manuscript was given to Bobby and Jackie for their review, their aides found enough unflattering detail—including Jackie's smoking in private, a fact she had kept from the press—to prompt the president's widow to file a lawsuit to stop its publication. Manchester's book eventually appeared, but Bobby Kennedy was still upset about it when Randolph came for a visit to his Hickory Hill house in December 1966.

After a half hour discussing Manchester, Bobby asked Randolph when he planned to finish his "great work" on Sir Winston's life. When Randolph said 1970, Bobby seemed pleased. "By then we will have all President Kennedy's papers sorted," he said, referring to the ongoing work by the National Archives. "Would you like to edit them?"

Randolph couldn't believe his good fortune. "Yes, of course," Churchill said, "and should I write his Life too?"

"Certainly," Kennedy replied. Bobby had read the positive reviews of Randolph's volume on his father's life. They both agreed that his version of John Kennedy's life would be "done in the same objective manner as my book on my father," Randolph recalled.

In typical bombastic fashion, Randolph had jumped into the fray surrounding the Manchester book without revealing his own interest in writing JFK's life with the Kennedy family's approval. Like a chivalrous knight, he publicly defended the honor of Jackie Kennedy, by then criticized in the press for attempting to quash Manchester's book and promulgating her own Camelot myth. "I have known Mrs. Kennedy for ten years and have never noticed anything remotely regal in her manner," Randolph said, coming to the rescue against her critics. "But this seems to be the mood of the moment—create the legend of a queen and then decapitate her."

By entrusting Randolph with the official Kennedy biography, Bobby and Jackie hoped to avoid publicity problems, unlike the previous fiasco, which had occurred even though Manchester's publishing house, Harper and Row, had also put out JFK's *Profiles in Courage* and RFK's *The Enemy Within*. (Harper's chief was the father of Michael Canfield, the former first husband of Lee Radziwill.) When Jackie realized the

Manchester publicity was hurting Bobby's political reputation, the Kennedys and the publisher settled out of court. "You can't go through life without trusting anybody," Bobby explained to Randolph as they discussed the Manchester book. "Sometimes you and your family are bound to be let down."

As she moved on with her life, Jacqueline Kennedy consistently topped the national polls as most admired woman in the United States, a status inspired by her unforgettable dignity and courage in the aftermath of her husband's assassination. By 1967, Americans were eager to see their widowed former First Lady find happiness once again. Photographers and gossip columns reported on Jackie's arrival at social events with various male escorts, composed mainly of ex–Kennedy administration figures and family friends, including Randolph Churchill. Romantic speculation centered on David Ormsby-Gore, named Lord Harlech in 1964, who had served as Great Britain's ambassador to the United States during JFK's presidency. Ormsby-Gore had been Jack's best friend in England, reaching back to their prewar days in London. A convert to Catholicism, he had introduced Kick Kennedy to her future husband, Billy Hartington. In mourning President Kennedy "as though he were my own brother," Ormsby-Gore sent a note to Bobby calling Jack "the most charming, considerate and loyal friend I have ever had." On the night JFK's body was returned from Dallas, Jackie tearfully confided at the White House to David and his wife, Sissy, that she and Jack had planned to ask them to be the godparents to Patrick Kennedy, if their newborn son had survived. Lord Harlech later endured a horrific event of his own. In May 1966, Sissy lost her life in a car accident. Jackie flew to England for the funeral with Bobby and his sisters Eunice and Jean. Following that tragedy, Lord Harlech visited with Jackie and her children during a June trip to Ireland and then accompanied her on a November 1967 trip to Cambodia. By February 1968, rumors swirled about Jackie marrying the British widower, an idea that pleased even Jack's mother, Rose. "David Harlech seemed to be an almost ideal choice due to the fact that he was very close to the family and very compatible intellectually and we all knew him as a man of integrity and charm," Rose wrote in her diary.

But in reality, Jackie had decided to marry Aristotle Onassis, whom she'd met a decade earlier when her husband visited Churchill aboard the Greek magnate's boat. Few knew of her intentions, including Rose. Onassis had been the self-described "invisible man" in Jackie's life. He visited her regularly after she moved from Washington to her Fifth Avenue apartment in Manhattan with her two children. When Bobby learned of Jackie's impending marriage to Onassis, he tried to dissuade her. Failing that, he urged her not to mention her plans publicly while he was running for president in 1968.

Robert Kennedy decided to challenge his brother's successor, Lyndon Johnson, ostensibly because of the poorly run war in Vietnam, but also because of his deep contempt for the president, as if a pretender to the throne. Johnson avoided a grudge match by soon dropping out of the race in a surprise announcement. After losing in Oregon, Bobby won primaries against the other Democratic challenger, Sen. Eugene McCarthy of Minnesota, and hoped to gain the party's presidential nomination that summer in Chicago. His brother, Sen. Edward "Ted" Kennedy, advised his campaign just as Bobby and their father Joe had helped Jack. And just as Bobby had managed to keep his father away from the press in the 1960 race, Jacqueline Kennedy agreed to keep her relationship with Ari out of the public's glare. "I know this is what the Ambassador would want me to do," she told friends about the Onassis subterfuge. Yet she couldn't hide her dread. "Do you know what I think will happen to Bobby?" she told Arthur M. Schlesinger Jr. "The same thing that happened to Jack. I've told Bobby this, but he isn't fatalistic, like me."

On the night of the June 4 California primary, after weeks of endless travel seeking votes, Bobby Kennedy waited in his hotel campaign headquarters for the final returns. By 9:00 p.m., he engaged in some joyous back-and-forth banter with reporters in a hallway. One friendly reporter suggested that McCarthy, who had fashioned his high-minded appeal around liberals and the Democratic intelligentsia, was sounding these days more like a demagogic politician.

"I like politicians," Bobby replied, almost meekly, surrounded by microphones and camera lights. "I like politics. It's an honorable adventure."

When someone in the crowd expressed a vague familiarity with the phrase, Bobby asked the press to identify the author who had described politics as "an honorable adventure." None of the two dozen political reporters knew the answer. As journalist Jack Newfield later recalled, for a moment Kennedy stood beaming with a toothy smile, like a proud schoolboy who'd mastered his homework assignment.

"That was Lord Tweedsmuir—does anybody here know who he was?" asked RFK, as the headline writers now called him.

When the flock of reporters again disappointed, Bobby explained Lord Tweedsmuir was the peerage name and title for Scottish writer John Buchan, best known for *The Thirty-Nine Steps*, the novel made into a Hitchcock film. Bobby didn't mention that Buchan also wrote *Pilgrim's Way*, his brother Jack's favorite, which contained that memorable description of politics as "an honorable adventure." *Pilgrim's Way* recalled the debonair style and undaunted bravery of Raymond Asquith, the noble son of the prime minster killed in the Great War—the same life lionized by Winston Churchill in his *Great Contemporaries* collection of profiles. Both Bobby and his late brother credited Buchan's inspiration for their own adventure in politics.

Two hours later, surrounded by family and friends in the ballroom of the Ambassador Hotel, Bobby flashed the *V* symbol with his fingers, just as Churchill did famously in claiming victory. The California primary would prove to be Robert Kennedy's greatest personal triumph in politics. His victory didn't depend on his father's money or his brother's legacy as much as on a patchwork of labor, students, minority supporters (especially blacks and Latinos), and the strength of his own reputation.

"Now it's on to Chicago and let's win there," said Kennedy, pushing his now longer, unruly hair from his eyes. Then RFK exited through a backdoor kitchen where he was fatally shot by an assassin.

News of Robert Kennedy's murder reached his friend Randolph Churchill as his own life was ebbing way. "And now Bobby," he reacted in a weak voice. The violence in America filled him with revulsion. "What stupid people," Randolph said at Stour, the country home where work on his father's biography had momentarily ceased because of his poor health.

The damage to Randolph's body was largely self-inflicted. Years of excessive drinking and smoking had taken their toll. He'd suffered minor strokes, and had shortened breath and cirrhosis of the liver, which had wasted him. He died at the same age and condition as his godfather, F. E. "Freddie" Smith, Lord Birkenhead, Winston's best friend. At fifty-seven, the great man's son, no longer an enfant terrible, had become an object of pity among those who knew him. "I have become reconciled to Randolph," wrote Evelyn Waugh in 1964, signaling a cease-fire in his perennial feuds with his friend. "He looked so pathetically thin and feeble and when he tried to shout a whisper came. So 12 years of enmity are expunged."

Randolph was himself aware of his faded good looks. His once-princely blond hair was white and sparse. He'd even lost his middle-age pot belly and jowls, the visible signs of his indulgences; they'd given way to a haggardly thin physique and a washed-out look to his face. A friend who stopped by his study earlier in 1968 noticed hanging on his wall an old portrait of Randolph as a young, handsome, and supremely confident man. "Yes, it is hard to believe that was me, isn't it?" Randolph chuckled, in a melancholy way, at the oil painting that seemed to mock him. "I was a jolly garçon in those days."

On June 6, the same day the world watched in horror as a comatose Robert Kennedy passed away from his wounds, Randolph went to bed alone and died in his sleep. There were no dramatic gunshots, no crying followers. His secretary didn't notice he was dead until the next morning. "A doctor has to write the cause of death and with Randolph the answer is everything," explained his cousin Anita Leslie in her slim biography of him. "His liver and kidneys and lungs and guts have all packed up. He's worn out every organ in his body at the same time."

Without fanfare, Randolph's remains were buried in the church graveyard near his family's ancestral home at Blenheim Palace, resting at the side of his father and grandfather Lord Randolph. Obituaries of the former prime minister's son were carried in newspapers around the world. They appeared almost inconsequential compared to the widespread coverage devoted to Robert Kennedy's assassination and the public mourning surrounding his quest for the American presidency. In death, Randolph had been overshadowed by a great man he befriended just as he had been by a father whom he loved in life. "Poor Randolph Churchill died today," his friend C. L. Sulzberger noted in his diary, "as always, a footnote."

Tending to their legacy of greatness remained a solemn obligation for the Churchill and Kennedy families in the ensuing years, as both a source of pride and a way of defining their remaining ambitions. Millions visited St. Martin's cemetery near Blenheim Palace or Arlington National Cemetery in Virginia, where Bobby Kennedy lay buried thirty yards from his brother Jack. When Joseph Kennedy died in November 1969, at age eighty-one, crippled and silent for the last eight years of his life, Americans recalled his legacy as a successful father rather than a failed politician. "With single-minded perseverance Joseph Patrick Kennedy devoted himself to founding a family political dynasty," began his obituary in the *New York Times*. "To this purpose he committed his extraordinary skill for making money, his far-reaching business and political friendships and his unquestioned position as a paterfamilias." The headline was even more succinct, declaring of the senior Kennedy, the father of a president and two senators: "Built Fortune to Gain Real Goal, Fame for His Sons."

Throughout Great Britain, Joe Kennedy was still remembered as Winston Churchill had defined him: an appeaser who sought to accommodate Hitler rather than fight him at a critical moment in history. Critics called Joe a coward who left London during the bombing, a shortsighted Irish Catholic who harbored ancient hatreds. They said his lies and diplomatic obfuscation prevented America from joining the Allies in Europe until 1941—a delay that led to a prolonged conflict and thousands of unnecessary deaths, including that of his own beloved son Joe Jr., lost during the last days of the war.

Clementine Churchill expressed this bitter vehemence toward Joe Kennedy when she encountered his wife, Rose, at a 1970 formal dinner in Paris. Her acid tone was much different from her comportment during their first convivial meeting at Chartwell in the 1930s, when Rose described Winston's spouse as smart, refined, and "one of the most attractive women I have ever met." Clementine and Rose, as matriarchs of two large political families, appeared to have much in common, including the burden and excitement of being married to a famous man who dominated her life. Each was fiercely loyal to her husband's name. "His cause was her cause, his enemies were her enemies," Churchill biographer Violet Bonham Carter observed of Winston's wife, a credo that applied to the ambassador's wife as well. Their daughters and granddaughters would run their own careers and independent lives, but Clementine and Rose, like most women of their generation, were solely devoted to their families, regardless of how much time those families were apart. Now that both husbands were deceased, they spent the remainder of their lives guarding and commemorating their family's reputation. Several months after the deaths of Bobby and Randolph, who became friends late in life, the two matriarchs agreed to meet at the formal dinner in Paris at the suggestion of Mary Soames, Churchill's youngest daughter. Her husband, Christopher Soames, was appointed British ambassador to France in 1968. Virtually at the same time, R. Sargent Shriver, married to JFK's sister Eunice, was sent to Paris as the American ambassador. Once again, the fate of the Churchills and Kennedys seemed destined to intertwine. After a few pleasantries at this dinner, however, Clementine dropped her façade and dredged up the grave issue that had haunted the Kennedys for so long.

"I hear your husband thought we could not win the war," said Clementine coldly. Her main source for this information, obviously, had been her own late husband, Winston. Rose recalled her encounter with Churchill's widow in typewritten notes for her 1974 memoir, *Times to Remember*, but never included it in her book. According to Rose's gilded account, she didn't deny Clementine's claim. Instead, she took the high road, arguing intellectually rather than emotionally. "A great many Englishmen thought so, too," Rose replied. "Have you read Harold Nicolson's book?"

Rose referred to the wartime diaries of Sir Harold Nicolson, a writer and former Tory official in Winston's Ministry of Information, published in 1968 by his son. The diaries revealed that Nicolson, like many other Englishmen, had feared a German invasion enough that he kept a poison suicide pill at the ready. (Apparently Rose didn't mention that Nicolson's diaries also said that Ambassador "Kennedy has been spreading it abroad in the USA that we shall certainly be beaten and he will use his influence here to press for a negotiated peace.") If Rose's account is accurate, Clementine's comments, to a woman who had one son killed during the war and two other sons recently assassinated, were not only impolitic but cruel. Nevertheless, even though Churchill's widow treated Joe's memory with contempt, Rose Kennedy praised the greatness of Winston Churchill to her.

"But through your husband's great courage, determination, and gift of oratory he brought forth new resolution to the people and raised them to new heights of zeal and dedication," Rose claimed to have told Clementine. "You and all the British must be very proud of him, as we all are in America. Good night, Lady Churchill."

Legacy weighed heavily on Ted Kennedy, the last brother and son. At age thirty-six, he became the patriarch of a large extended family ravished by violence and misfortune. Despite his own personal disasters and defeats, Ted honored his family's commitments as best he could.

Historians credited the John F. Kennedy administration with many progressive achievements—in civil rights, arms reduction, the creation of the Peace Corps, the space program's dazzling race to the moon—which his brother carried on in the Senate. But other achievements in the Kennedy legacy became apparent only after many years had passed. In JFK's memory, Ted and Bobby Kennedy pushed through a 1965 immigration reform act that ended the nation's traditional racial and ethnic barriers. It was rooted in Jack's 1958 book, *A Nation of Immigrants*, and proposed by the president shortly before his death in 1963. This single unheralded law not only reflected the Kennedy family's ascendancy as an Irish-Catholic minority in a predominately white Anglo-Saxon Protestant nation, but it literally changed the demographic face of today's America. This most lasting of Kennedy legacies wound up opening the door to millions of new arrivals from Latin America, Asia, Africa, and other nonwhite countries previously restricted. History showed that the Kennedys—outsiders who became the ultimate insiders in America—championed a far more equalitarian society than Winston Churchill, with his emphasis on empire and restricting freedoms for native inhabitants, could ever have allowed.

Despite the yearnings of his family's supporters, Ted Kennedy never reached the White House. The year after Bobby's assassination, he drove off a Chappaquiddick Island bridge coming from a summer party, causing the drowning of a young former RFK campaign aide who was asleep in the backseat of his car. The scandal surrounding the fatal 1969 accident effectively ended Ted's chance of becoming president. His misguided attempt in 1980 to challenge an incumbent Democratic president, Jimmy Carter, led to the election of Republican Ronald Reagan, just as RFK's insurgency had undermined Lyndon Johnson and helped revive the presidential chances of Richard Nixon in 1968. Yet Ted Kennedy became one of the twentieth century's most effective legislators, with a distinguished Senate career that resembled Winston's in the House of Commons far more closely than those of his brothers. He served as his party's clarion of conscience, especially when out of power during the political wilderness of the Reagan era. Embracing his family's legacy more than being imprisoned by it, Kennedy, with his good works and political skill, had earned the sobriquet the Last Lion when he died in 2009.

Ted's memoir, published posthumously, delved greatly into the relationship between fathers and sons. It was more candid, more reflective than his two brothers ever were in public. "My thoughts turned often to my dad," he wrote about his troubled times. "What had I left unsaid to this great man? So many things." With an eye toward history, he loyally defended his father's actions in England opposing America's entry into the war, and explained how the former ambassador's lifetime chip on his shoulder as an Irish Catholic informed so many of his actions. "Even as he marched through one invisible barricade after another, Dad always understood that he was never completely accepted as an equal by the old Yankee stock," Ted attested. "He would always be an 'Irish Catholic' first, and an individual second." More revealingly, Ted's anecdotes underlined the demands Joe Kennedy placed on his children, especially his sons. After some frivolous infraction when he was about age thirteen, Ted was beckoned to his father's room and issued a matter-of-fact warning forever imprinted in his mind.

"You can have a serious life or a nonserious life, Teddy," Joe Kennedy said in a concise and vivid voice. "I'll still love you whichever choice you make. But if you decide to have a nonserious life, I won't have much time for you. You make up your mind. There are too many children here who are doing things that are interesting for me to do much with you." These words sounded very similar to the warning Joe gave his son Jack after his near-expulsion from Choate, when the future president exhibited far less seriousness and vigor than his older brother, Joe Jr., his parents' sterling example.

This alchemy of love and discipline between the senior Kennedy and his sons somehow seemed far more effective than the overegging by Winston Churchill. Winston had indulged his only son—demonstrably more talented at age twenty-one than any of the Kennedy boys—and threw him a "sons of great men" party at Claridge's in London, with Randolph as its star. Greatness in this hidebound system would be bequeathed through bloodlines rather than earned by sweat or toil. This paradox left Randolph desperate at times to be more heroic in war than Winston, wittier than his erudite father, more ambitious in politics and prose, and more capable of drinking alcohol in a way that was never quite enough. Somehow, the relationship of Winston, the great man of the century, to his fair-haired son seemed more rivalrous and raw than any demands Joe Kennedy, the frustrated diplomat in disrepute, ever imposed. Whether out of indulgence or an attempt to make up for the cold condemnations of his own father, Winston saddled Randolph with a set of lofty expectations destined for disappointment. By 1964, when Randolph published a short memoir of his youth called *Twenty-One Years*, he seemed to recognize he'd been a failure by Churchillian standards. For Randolph, there would be no recovery, no second act, no emergence from the "wilderness" that his father pulled off so admirably again and again in his career. An interviewer for London's *Sunday Times*, Clive Irving, posed the question that turned out to be Randolph's epitaph.

"You started out with these enormous political ambitions," Irving said. "Why do you think that they never came to anything?"

Even personal failure was measured in terms of his father.

"I think my father was big enough and sufficiently well known with his immense genius and power of self-expression—he was able to weather the storm and survive in those difficult and unhappy years in the thirties, when he was immensely isolated," Randolph explained. "But in the nature of things there wasn't room for me. I'm not making excuses—it was largely my own fault, but I think it was a handicap for me. And, of course, I'm not very good at kissing babies and I don't tolerate fools very gladly."

The difference between the Kennedys and other dynasties, the Churchills and the Roosevelts, remained a constant source of fascination for historian Arthur M. Schlesinger Jr., one without easy resolve. When he interviewed Jacqueline Kennedy shortly after the assassination (for a 1964 oral history kept under seal by the Kennedy Library until 2011), the Harvard-trained academic posed the key question he'd wondered about in his own diaries and discussed among friends.

> SCHLESINGER: Now it always seemed to me quite extraordinary. Here are three men who lived about the same time—Winston Churchill, Franklin Roosevelt, and Joseph P. Kennedy, of whom the first two were in one sense or another great men and the third was a very successful man, a very talented man, but not a great man. And yet the children of Churchill and the children of Roosevelt have all been—in many cases, bright and talented, but somehow it all missed fire. And the Kennedy children have this extraordinary discipline.

JACKIE KENNEDY: I really think you have to give a lot of that credit to Mr. [Joe] Kennedy, because Jack used to talk about that a lot. You know, he bent over backwards. When his children were doing something, he wrote them letters endlessly. Whenever they were doing anything important at school, he'd be there for it. The way he'd talk at the table. If you just go on being a great man, and your children are sort of shunted aside, you know—he watched—I always thought he was the tiger mother. And Mrs. Kennedy, poor little thing, was running around, trying to keep up with this demon of energy, seeing if she had enough placemats in Palm Beach, or should she send the ones from Bronxville, or had she put the London ones in storage. You know, that's what—her little mind went to pieces, and it's Mr. Kennedy who ... He did all—he made this conscious effort about the family, and I don't think those other two men [Winston Churchill and FDR] did.

In her grief, Jacqueline Kennedy focused on her husband's postmortem public image with the same obsessive care that Jack's father had in life. She worried America might forget him. "In newspapers she read that he had not been in office long enough to achieve greatness," William Manchester observed. "There was no way of knowing that the very brevity of his Presidency would add poignancy to his story. Therefore she made certain it would be pondered by future presidents."

Her marriage to Onassis in 1968, soon after Bobby's killing, upset that image. The American public seemed repulsed by the Greek tycoon so different in style from JFK. The Vatican condemned Jackie as a "public sinner" for wedding a divorced man. Many believed her motivation was money rather than love. "Mr. and Mrs. Onassis are certainly spending more money this year than anyone in international society by far," sniffed Lady Sarah Spencer-Churchill, whose brother, the Duke of

Marlborough, had married Tina Livanos Onassis, Ari's first wife. Sarah had known the Kennedys for years, since they attended her debutante ball in 1939 at Blenheim Palace along with Winston and his side of the Churchill family. "I have seen them [Jackie and Aristotle] in Paris, London, New York, Nassau, and Athens, during the course of the year, and, believe me, the sky is the limit."

Jackie's marriage to Onassis never worked out, as their differences only widened. When she changed the interior of his giant yacht, he waited for her to leave before reverting back to the original design. They even differed in their estimate of Winston Churchill. Onassis venerated the great man, while Jackie, perhaps competitively with her late husband's legacy, noticed his human flaws. To Schlesinger, Jackie repeated the observation of Churchill's portrait painter Graham Sutherland, who confided that "power made him [JFK] a better man," but with Winston, he "became less nice." Nevertheless, Jackie and Aristotle Onassis did share the same regard for Randolph. Both agreed to contribute when Kay Halle published a 1971 book of remembrances dedicated to his memory.

Over four decades, Halle had known three separate generations of Kennedys and Churchills, becoming a friend and unofficial chronicler of both families. Soon after Randolph died in 1968, Kay started collecting written recollections about him from friends and relatives. The tributes to Randolph contained references to both the best and worst aspects of his character but were always, like Churchill himself, bold and brutally honest. They were assembled into a book edited by Halle (called *The Young Unpretender* in Britain, where he was far better known; the American version dressed up the title to a rosier *The Grand Original*). This small book was similar to Kay's efforts to commemorate JFK's inaugural and Sir Winston's citizenship ceremony in April 1963.

Aristotle Onassis (like Arthur Schlesinger, Sir Fitzroy Maclean, Lady Jeanne Campbell, Harold Macmillan, and several other contributors) reflected on Randolph's legacy as the son of Winston Churchill and on the great potential he once possessed. "His was such an exuberance of talents," wrote Onassis. "Without exaggeration, I believe that the brilliance, the nobility of feature, the rhetoric, the voice, all such vital generators of public appeal—Randolph had these in excess of his father."

The waste of these talents, several contributors suggested, was the tragedy of Randolph's life, though most preferred to portray him as just a colorful British eccentric. In amusing anecdotes, they recalled Randolph's outrageous behavior in war, politics, and journalism, with only polite hints of his emotional high and low extremes, his chronic alcohol abuse, and the hidden psychological demons that plagued his life. "He was the heir to an enormous and excessively awkward inheritance," wrote Christopher Sykes, a friend of forty years from Oxford. "Small wonder that some of the results were destructive to himself. But in this connection one thing must always be remembered to his immense credit. Most men who are overshadowed by greatness in a father tend to denigrate the father. If it is a mean reaction, it is a most natural one. Nothing of this was ever found in Randolph. Throughout life he gave his father respect, honour, loyalty and love in abundance."

Jacqueline Kennedy Onassis provided the most remarkable contribution to Kay's book of remembrances. The president's widow recalled her family's close relations with the Churchills, in both small gestures and grand visions. With the intimacy of an eyewitness, Jackie recounted the anxiety of Randolph and JFK during the 1963 White House citizenship ceremony for Sir Winston ("they are both so nervous it will be a disaster") and her elation at the outcome. Before the ceremony, inside the Oval Office, Randolph "was ashen, his voice a whisper." Outside, on the Lawn, in front of the crowd, Jackie tried to listen to her husband's introduction but couldn't because of her own worry that "every second was ticking closer to Randolph." With the whole world watching, Jackie recalled, Churchill's son didn't stumble or fall. "His voice was strong," she wrote. "He spoke on, with almost the voice of Winston

Churchill, but while others could imitate Sir Winston, Randolph's voice was finer."

Jackie was particularly grateful for Randolph's personal kindness in the years after Jack's assassination. More than most, he understood the dynastic pressures on her family. She appreciated Randolph also for his uncensored honesty and undying loyalty, as if he'd grown free of the constraints imposed by his famous name.

"You know how Jack and Bobby loved him—but did you know how my son John loved him?" she asked. Around her children, Jackie wrote, Randolph "was completely himself—and never changed gears for them." She said little John Jr. was particularly fascinated by Randolph's English accent and gregarious manner.

At the 1965 Runnymede memorial ceremony, she recalled, Randolph told her that he planned to have all the first editions of Winston Churchill's books beautifully bound and to donate them to the new Kennedy presidential library in Boston. But later he changed his mind, saying he hated to give things to institutions. Better to send Sir Winston's writings to little John, the son of a great man, so he could learn from them.

In front of the Kennedys' Fifth Avenue apartment in Manhattan, a painted tin truck soon rolled up and delivered the books—all forty-nine volumes of Winston S. Churchill's writings. "They are in the bookshelves in the dining room, beside Jack's *Marlborough*, which he read when he had scarlet fever as a boy, and the Churchill books he had at Harvard," Jackie recalled.

At supper some nights, John Jr. and Caroline played a guessing game based on what they had read from the Churchill books. Occasionally they even stumped their uncle Bobby with it, Jackie wrote. In particular, John Jr. cared about the books because they reminded him of his fondness for Randolph.

Uncertain of what her son's future might bring, Jackie hoped President Kennedy's heir might discover lessons about greatness from these

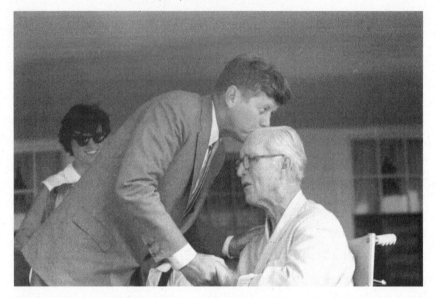

The house of Kennedy. At Hyannis Port in 1963, President Kennedy kissed his father, crippled by a stroke, before leaving for the White House. Painfully aware of Irish Catholic bigotry in his own life, patriarch Joseph P. Kennedy orchestrated his son's barrier-breaking rise to the American presidency as the first person elected from a minority group. JFK LIBRARY

bound volumes, just as other men had. "If, when he is older, he finds in them what his father found in them—that would be this strange, touching legacy of Randolph's," Jackie concluded. "Winston Churchill and Randolph outlived Jack—but maybe Randolph will be the one to draw John to the books that shaped John's father."

This legacy between fathers and sons, mothers and daughters, the eternal questions about families and fate, and our lasting impression of greatness, were all part of the shared experience between the Churchills and the Kennedys. In the twentieth century, no two families existed on a bigger world stage, epitomizing the Anglo-American "special relationship" over four decades. With courage, wit, and unforgettable determination, both Winston S. Churchill and John F. Kennedy helped define and save the world as we know it today. Yet so many of the private and political dealings between the two families remained unexplored or misunderstood by history. What started out as friendly in the early 1930s, full of promise and fortune, had devolved into bitterness

Three generations of Churchills. Dating back to historic Blenheim Palace, the Churchill name provided a daunting legacy for Winston Churchill, his son, Randolph, and namesake grandson, Winston. "It's very hard," explained Randolph, "when you're living under the shadow of the great oak." LIBRARY OF CONGRESS

and death by World War II, only to be followed now in the 1960s by this surprising rapprochement. Regardless of how far they drifted apart, the Kennedys and Churchills never seemed to lose their awareness of each other. This gift of books from the son of Winston to the son of Jack was only one more example in this saga, a small but meaningful gesture between them. Little was known publicly about these private exchanges, because those involved wanted it kept that way—as if only they could understand one another, lifelong participants born into the political arena, with all the blood, brains, and passion that drives family dynasties from one generation to the next.

Notes

Research for this book about the Churchills and Kennedys, like the transatlantic story it depicts from 1930 to 1970, took place in many locales—from London, Blenheim Palace, and Chartwell Manor in the United Kingdom to archives in Boston; Washington, DC; Princeton, NJ; and Hyde Park, NY. Pieced together, the documentation cited here illuminates the relationship between these two dynasties, a tale often hiding in plain sight.

Staffers at the Churchill Archives Centre in Cambridge—where the papers of Sir Winston are stored along with those of his family—were unflaggingly gracious, as were archivists at the National Archives in London and at the John F. Kennedy Presidential Library in Boston, where the personal papers of his father, former U.S. ambassador Joseph P. Kennedy, and dozens of others are also housed.

Many documents in this book are cited for the first time, including the Kay Halle Personal Papers, which became available at the JFK Library during my research. Halle's friends and family provided me with other documents, and with their recollections. Remarkably, Halle's love and friendships with the Churchills and Kennedys extended throughout the four decades covered in this book. Other collections provided little-known documents that informed this narrative. The digitalization of the Churchill archival records allowed me to identify the stock transactions involving Winston Churchill and the American companies connected to Joe

Kennedy and to gain further details that transform our understanding of their initial relationship. In the James Roosevelt Papers, I discovered President Roosevelt's concerns about his oldest son's secret business arrangements involving Joe Kennedy and their possible political impact. In the Bernard M. Baruch Papers at Princeton University, Winston Churchill's telegrams underlined his concern about the fate of his investments in a New York subway firm, then controlled by Kennedy and their mutual pal Baruch. At the United Kingdom's National Archives, Lord Beaverbrook's papers detailed his close friendship with both families and why Max was so feared and beloved. The British archives also provided the government dossier on Joseph Kennedy's activities in America, showing the extent of its concerns with the U.S. ambassador who favored appeasement of Hitler. Winston Churchill's FBI file casts new light on his postwar views about using the atom bomb against the Soviet Union. And obscure files marked "Tyler Kent" in the FDR Library revealed Attorney General Robert Kennedy's deep concerns in the early 1960s about the twenty-year-old British spy case against Kent, an American convicted in wartime London of providing top-secret papers to the Nazis while working for Ambassador Kennedy.

Perhaps most significant, many letters, cables, and cards provided insight about the emotions, yearnings, and private lives of the Churchills and Kennedys, including some of Pamela Churchill Harriman's unpublished comments about her family to author William Manchester, in Wesleyan University's archives, and the rather bitter exchange between Clementine Churchill and Rose Kennedy after both their husbands were dead, found in Rose's papers at the JFK Library.

In a sense, this journey began with my 2003 book, *The Kennedys: America's Emerald Kings,* which examined how the family's Irish-Catholic immigrant background influenced their public and personal lives. My previous research in Ireland and at the Vatican Secret Archives in Rome, and numerous interviews with Kennedy family and friends—including the late senator Edward M. Kennedy, former lieutenant governor Kathleen Kennedy Townsend, and Theodore C. Sorensen—helped inform this new work and piqued my interest in the complex relationship between the Churchills and Kennedys. While most in this cast of characters are long since deceased, I thank the following friends and survivors for their personal recollections: Adrian Berry, Ann Crile Esselstyn, Sam Little, Susan Lyne, Stephen Schlesinger, Marian Schlesinger, Lady Juliet Townsend, Dolores Velez, Barbara Rodman Wilson, and Page Huidekoper Wilson. Researchers Fred Winston and Suzanne McGuire of the Commack, NY, Public Library also graciously helped.

On some research trips, my wife, Joyce, and three sons, Andrew, Taylor, and Reade, joined me. As always, they provided invaluable love, support, and insights throughout the preparation of this book. Many thanks also go to Sean Desmond, Claire Potter, Miriam Chotiner-Gardner, Jenna Dolan, and especially Vanessa Mobley at Crown, as well as to my literary agent, John W. Wright, for all their wisdom and confidence.

—Thomas Maier,
Long Island, New York
November 2014

In this narrative's notes, the following abbreviations indicate the archives, individual collections, and major reference sources where citations can be found:

BBK Papers of Sir William Maxwell Aitken (1879–1964), Lord Beaverbrook, First Baron. Parliamentary Archives, London, UK.

BMB Bernard M. Baruch Papers. Princeton University Library, Department of Rare Books and Special Collections, Seeley G. Mudd Manuscript Library, Princeton, NJ.

CBL Clare Boothe Luce Papers. Library of Congress, Washington, DC.

CHUR The Papers of Sir Winston Churchill. Churchill Archives Centre, Cambridge, UK.

FDR Franklin D. Roosevelt Papers. Franklin D. Roosevelt Presidential Library and Museum, Hyde Park, NY.

HLH The Harry L. Hopkins Papers. Special Collections Research Center, Georgetown University Library, Washington DC.

HTF Smith, Amanda. *Hostage to Fortune: The Letters of Joseph P. Kennedy.* New York: Viking, 2001.

JFK Papers of John F. Kennedy. Pre-Presidential Papers. John F. Kennedy Presidential Library and Museum, Boston, MA.

JIM James Roosevelt Papers. Franklin D. Roosevelt Presidential Library and Museum, Hyde Park, NY.

JPK Joseph P. Kennedy Personal Papers. John F. Kennedy Presidential Library and Museum, Boston, MA.

KMH Kay Halle Personal Papers and Oral History. John F. Kennedy Presidential Library and Museum, Boston, MA.

NYT *New York Times.*

PAM Pamela Harriman Papers. Manuscript Division, Library of Congress, Washington, DC.

RDCH Papers of Randolph Churchill. Churchill Archives Centre, Cambridge, UK.

RKT Schlesinger, Arthur M. Jr. *Robert Kennedy and His Times.* Boston: Houghton Mifflin, 1978.

ROSE Rose Fitzgerald Kennedy Personal Papers. John F. Kennedy Presidential Library and Museum, Boston, MA.

WAH W. Averell Harriman Papers. Manuscript Division, Library of Congress, Washington, DC.

WMP William Manchester Papers. Special Collections and Archives, Olin Library, Wesleyan University, Middletown, CT.

FRONTISPIECE

Opening quotes from William Shakespeare's *The Taming of the Shrew,* **and from Winston Churchill:** Carlo D'Este, *Warlord: A Life of Winston Churchill at War, 1874–1945,* p. 375. **T. E. Lawrence quote:** *The Seven Pillars of Wisdom: A Triumph,* p. 24. John Buchan's quote: *Pilgrim's Way,* p. 232.

CHAPTER 1: OVERTURE: "THE SPECIAL RELATIONSHIP"

Rose Kennedy's written recollections of Churchill visit: Document dated 1933, ROSE. (Archivists question this date, and suggest 1935 or 1936.) Further details from Charles Higham, *Rose: The Life and Times of Rose Fitzgerald Kennedy,* p. 157; and *RKT,* p. 10. **Winston**

Churchill at Chartwell home: Kay Halle, *The Irrepressible Churchill: Winston's World, Wars, and Wit,* p. 3. **Overall descriptions about Winston Churchill:** Sarah Churchill, *A Thread in the Tapestry,* pp. 23–24, 26–28; Stefan Buczacki, *Churchill and Chartwell: The Untold Story of Churchill's Houses and Gardens,* p. 105; Geoffrey Best, *Churchill: A Study in Greatness,* pp. 144–46; Mary Soames, *Winston and Clementine: The Personal Letters of the Churchills,* p. 273; Norman Rose, *Churchill: The Unruly Giant,* p. 258; William Manchester, *The Last Lion: Winston Spencer Churchill, Visions of Glory, 1874–1932,* p. 567; William Manchester, *The Last Lion: Winston Spencer Churchill: Alone, 1932–1940,* p. 22; Veronica Maclean, *Past Forgetting: A Memoir of Heroes, Adventure, and Love,* p. 250; Martin Gilbert, *Churchill: A Life,* p. 486; Lady Diana Cooper, "The Lion's Heart," p. 59; and Kathleen Woodward, "The Incredible Mr. Winston Churchill," p. 4. Further description of Chartwell is based on author's October 2012 visit. **Churchill's quote about being "shot at":** Winston Churchill, *The Story of the Malakand Field Force: An Episode of the Frontier War,* p. 172. **"Chartwell is to be our home":** Mary Soames, *Clementine Churchill: The Biography of a Marriage,* p. 252. **Winston's "Anyone can rat" and "here I am":** Halle, *The Irrepressible Churchill,* pp. 45 and 3. **"Happy-go-lucky":** *HTF,* p.120. **"Don't let me lose confidence":** *RKT,* p. 15. **FDR's "set a thief":** Conrad Black, *Franklin Delano Roosevelt: Champion of Freedom,* p. 320. **JPK's "leaving public life":** September 23, 1935, letter to Arthur Hays Sulzberger, Securities and Exchange Commission Historical Society. **Both Baruch September 25, 1935, cables to Churchill and Kennedy:** BMB. **Churchill's "too many Irish haters":** *RKT,* p. 10. **October 1935 "Rose and I" cable to Baruch:** BMB. **October 6, 1934, cable to Rose about "Jack's blood count":** JPK. **November 11, 1935, cable to Robert Worth Bingham that "Jack is far from being a well boy":** JPK. **Churchill cable to Kennedy "about your son":** *RKT,* p. 10.

CHAPTER 2: A TROUBLESOME BOY

"Malborough *s'en va-t-en guerre*": Leo Tolstoy, *War and Peace,* p. 101. **Mark Twain and Churchill meeting:** Described in Winston Churchill, *My Early Life,* p. 357; Randolph S. Churchill, *Winston S. Churchill: Volume 1: Youth, 1874–1900,* p. 525; and "How Lieut. Churchill Escaped from Boers," *NYT*, December 13, 1900. **"I have so much need for money"**: Randolph S. Churchill, *Winston S. Churchill: Volume 1*, pp. 523, 527. **"Picture to yourself"**: Kay Halle, ed., *Winston Churchill on America and Britain: A Selection of His Thoughts on Anglo-American Relations*, p. 9. **"You are indeed an orator"**: Martin Gilbert, *Churchill and America*, p. 22. **"A child of both worlds"**: Halle, ed., *Winston Churchill on America and Britain*, p. 1. **"We are all worms"**: Violet Bonham Carter, *Winston Churchill as I Knew Him*, pp. 3–4. **"The strength of the two natures"**: Alfred Leslie Rowse, *The Later Churchills*, p. 455. **"It certainly is inspiring"**: Gilbert, *Churchill and America*, pp. 153–54. **"She shone for me like the Evening Star"**: Bonham Carter, *Winston Churchill as I Knew Him*, p. 12. **"There was a touch of Joseph P. Kennedy"**: Roy Jenkins, *Churchill: A Biography*, p. 6. **"I was a child of the Victorian era" and recollection of Ireland**: Winston Churchill, *My Early Life*, pp. ix, 1–3. **Fitzgerald's "a Catholic monument" description**: Peter Collier and David Horowitz, *The Kennedys: An American Drama*, p. 74. **Lord Randolph's comment on Fenians**: *Quebec Saturday Budget*, May 13, 1882, p. 2. **Mrs. Everett's view of Catholics**: Winston Churchill, *My Early Life*, pp. 12–14. **"Play the Orange card"**: Randolph Churchill and Martin Gilbert, *Winston S. Churchill, Volume 2: Young Statesman, 1901–1914*, p. 440. **"No man is so entirely alone"**: Robert Rhodes James, *Churchill: A Study in Failure, 1900–1939*, pp. 9–10. **"A veil of the incalculable"**: R. F. Foster, *Lord Randolph Churchill: A Political Life*, p. 390. **"A troublesome boy"**: Winston Churchill, *My Early Life*, p. 8. **"I cannot think"**: Martin Gilbert, *Churchill: A Life*, pp. 9, 38. **"If ever I began"**: William Manchester, *The Last Lion: Winston Spencer Churchill, Visions of Glory, 1874–1932*, p. 187. **"You must be happy without me"**: Randolph S. Churchill, *Winston S. Churchill: Volume 1*, p. 101. **"A diamond star"**: Ibid., p. 35. **"He has a future"**: Anita Leslie, *Lady Randolph Churchill: The Story of Jennie Jerome*, p. 373. **"In my interest"**: Norman Rose, *Churchill: The Unruly Giant*, p. 37. **"The dunce of the family will take revenge"**: Rene Kraus, *Winston Churchill: A Biography*, p. 42. **"Possessed by the spirit of his father"**: Foster, *Lord Randolph Churchill*, p. 385. **"All my dreams of comradeship"**: Manchester, *The Last Lion: Winston Spencer Churchill, Visions of Glory*, p. 209. **Theodore Roosevelt's "clever, forceful, rather** cheap": David Cannadine, *Aspects of Aristocracy: Grandeur and Decline in Modern Britain*, p. 155. **"For what can be more glorious"**: Robert Rhodes James, *Churchill: A Study in Failure, 1900–1939*, p. 334. **"My business and my toys"**: Mary Soames, *Winston and Clementine: The Personal Letters of the Churchills*, p. 679. **A "young man in a hurry"**: John Ramsden, *Man of the Century: Winston Churchill and His Legend since 1945*, p. 38. **"I believe I am"**: Gilbert, *Churchill: A Life*, p. 107. **"These were as brave men"**: Bonham Carter, *Winston Churchill as I Knew Him*, pp. 195 and 27. **"And what are they?"**: Kay Halle, *The Irrepressible Churchill: Winston's World, Wars, and Wit*, p. 64. **"It was natural"**: Winston Churchill, *The World Crisis, 1911–1918*, p. 692. **"He acted like a stinker"**: *HTF*, p. 5. **"He came, he saw, he capitulated"**: John Lukacs, *Churchill: Visionary. Statesman. Historian*, p. 126. **"I had long hours"**: Bonham Carter, *Winston Churchill as I Knew Him*, p. 464. **"It's no damn use ducking"**: Carlo D'Este, *Warlord: A Life of Winston Churchill at War, 1874–1945*, p. 279. **"When it is all over"**: Mary Soames, *Clementine Churchill: The Biography of a Marriage*, p. 180. **Churchill's comment about Asquith and impact on JFK**: Arthur M. Schlesinger Jr., *A Thousand Days: John F. Kennedy in the White House*, p. 87. **"If anything should happen to me"**: Clive Irving, "The Shade of Churchill: Randolph in Retrospect," *Sunday Times* (undated but clearly June 1968), KMH. **Bracken's "Nature has made you"**: "Long Friendship with Churchill Began at '19 Peace Conference," *NYT*, June 21, 1965. **"I now became the Nitrate King"**: Winston Churchill, *The World Crisis, 1911–1918*, p. 199. **Balfour on "Winston's brilliant autobiography"**: Olivia E. Coolidge, *Winston Churchill and the Story of Two World Wars*, p. 88. **"Politics are almost as exciting"**: Steven F. Hayward, *Churchill on Leadership: Executive Success in the Face of Adversity*, p. 29. **"He looked what he was"**: Richard Toye, *Churchill's Empire*, p. 143. **"The causes of war"**: Martin Gilbert, *Churchill: The Power of Words*, p. 175. **"I've had a number of threatening letters"**: Manchester, *The Last Lion: Winston Spencer Churchill, Visions of Glory*, p. 731. **"Winston was very unpopular"**: Lynne Olson, *Troublesome Young Men: The Rebels Who Brought Churchill to Power and Helped Save England*, p. 257. **"I have made up my mind"**: Paul Addison, *Churchill: On the Home Front, 1900–1955*, p. 292.

CHAPTER 3: SPEAKING ENGAGEMENTS

The 1929 Churchill trip to Hollywood and North America: Described in Martin Gilbert, *Winston Churchill: The Wilderness Years*, pp. 24–25; Ben H. Procter, *William Randolph Hearst: Final Edition, 1911–1951*, p. 152; Martin Gilbert, *Churchill and America*, p. 116; David T. Leary, "Winston S. Churchill in California," pp. 1–15; David Wallace, *Lost Hollywood*, p. 88–89; and Marion Davies, *The Times We Had: Life with William Randolph Hearst*, p. 187. **Description of Randolph Churchill next to Hearst:** Based on photo at the Hollywood dinner later appearing in *Life*, August 27, 1951. **"I got to like him":** Mary Soames, *Winston and Clementine: The Personal Letters of the Churchills*, p. 346. **"Jesus Christ" anecdote:** Sarah Churchill, *A Thread in the Tapestry*, p. 35. **"With her—a lovely green-eye faun":** Anita Leslie, *Randolph: The Biography of Winston Churchill's Son*, pp. 17–18. **"It is a pleasure to me to show the world," "logical strength," and other Winston comments about young Randolph:** Soames, *Winston and Clementine*, pp. 305, 320, 336–37, 341. **"This is most unfair":** Brian Roberts, *Randolph: A Study of Churchill's Son*, pp. 35–36. **" 'Tis better to have hooked and lost":** Gilbert, *Winston Churchill: The Wilderness Years*, pp. 21–23. **" 'The meteor flag,' " "soon we are going," "we must have been horrible children," and "my father said to me":** Randolph S. Churchill, *Twenty-One Years*, pp. 11, 9, 4, 18–19. **"It would have been difficult for any son":** Leslie, *Randolph*, p. 34. **"A foolish cleric with Socialist leanings":** Soames, *Winston and Clementine*, p. 344. **"Proceeded to very mildly twit the dean":** Randolph S. Churchill, *Twenty-One Years*, p. 80. **Winston accepting Schwab offer of railway carriage for North America trip:** CHUR, several documents dated August 1929. **"Prof seems anxious":** Randolph Churchill and Martin Gilbert, *Winston S. Churchill, Volume 5: The Wilderness Years, 1929–1935*, p. 80. **"It was far less laborious":** Winston S. Churchill, *His Father's Son: The Life of Randolph Churchill*, p. 64. **"Your idle & lazy life":** Ibid., pp. 64–65. **"A fair-haired handsome youth":** "Young Churchill Impresses Oxford Union Using Father's Rhetoric in Maiden Speech," *NYT*, February 21, 1930. **Randolph's "she slapped my face" and Clementine's "it was very effective":** Pamela Harriman interview, PAM. **"Everyone, except Winston":** Soames, *Clementine Churchill*, p. 271. **"Papa is**

amused & rather outraged": Soames, *Winston and Clementine*, p. 350.
"High hopes": Winston S. Churchill, *His Father's Son*, p. 88. "I thought
it was more blessed to teach": Leslie, *Randolph*, p. 19.

CHAPTER 4: LOVE AND FRIENDSHIPS
"A young Apollo, golden haired": Kay Halle, *The Grand Original: Portraits of Randolph Churchill by His Friends*, pp. 1–3. Halle's early relationship with Randolph: In other letters, documents, and photographs,
KMH. "His share of the fiery temperament": "Son of Churchill Is
Here to Lecture," *NYT*, October 8, 1930. "Creating a sensation wherever he speaks": *Berkeley* (Calif.) *Daily Gazette*, p. 4. Baruch's October
24, 1930, letter "all of which seemed to have been great successes":
BMB. "Half-Irish, half-American": Anita Leslie, *Randolph: The Biography of Winston Churchill's Son*, p. 19. "He intends to marry her":
Mary Soames, *Winston and Clementine: The Personal Letters of the
Churchills*, p. 352. "Come home, dear Randolph": Kay Halle, *The Ir-
repressible Churchill: Winston's World, Wars, and Wit*, p. 264. "It will
be an intense grief to me": Winston S. Churchill, *His Father's Son:
The Life of Randolph Churchill*, pp. 77–78. "Utter honesty": Halle, *The
Grand Original*, p. 3. "She would be Randolph's greatest friend": Les-
lie, *Randolph*, p. 20. "The Rabbit": Soames, *Winston and Clementine*,
p. 355. Baruch's affair with Clare Boothe: Detailed in Sylvia Jukes
Morris, *Rage for Fame: The Ascent of Clare Boothe Luce*, pp. 198–208.
"Drenchingly beautiful": "The Londoner's Diary: Fifty Thousand
Pounds from Play," *Evening Standard*, May 18, 1938, CHUR. "A man
has only one escape": Clare Boothe Luce, *The Women*, p. 25. "It was
Bernie Baruch": Jukes Morris, *Rage for Fame*, p. 238. "She had been
very indiscreet": Soames, *Winston and Clementine*, p. 355. "It is really
a pleasure for me": Jordan A. Schwarz, *The Speculator: Bernard Baruch
in Washington, 1917–1965*, p. 34. "Baruch is the greatest speculator":
Randolph S. Churchill, *Twenty-One Years*, p. 91. "He knew nothing":
John Colville, *Winston Churchill and His Inner Circle*, pp. 114–15. "I
believe that": Halle, *The Grand Original*, pp. 30–31. "I sensed his way
he had of looking at and through you": Kay Halle, August 6, 1980,
interview, WMP. "My dear Mrs. Halle": "Remembering Katherine
Murphy Halle," pp. 5–6. "A long dark car rushing": Jack Fishman,

"My Darling Clementine": The Story of Lady Churchill, pp. 73–75. **"I do not understand why I was not broken like an eggshell"**: William Manchester, *The Last Lion: Winston Spencer Churchill, Visions of Glory, 1874–1932*, pp. 878–81. **"Tell me, Baruch"**: Kay Halle, ed., *Winston Churchill on America and Britain: A Selection of His Thoughts on Anglo-American Relations*, p. 247. **"You will find me"**: Martin Gilbert, *Winston Churchill: The Wilderness Years*, pp. 41–43. **"The loss of all that money"**: Manchester, *The Last Lion: Winston Spencer Churchill, Visions of Glory*, p. 880. **"We think there is a certain appropriateness"**: Bracken, January 14, 1932, correspondence about plans to buy Rolls-Royce gift for Winston after accident, BMB. **"I have been treated so splendidly"**: Martin Gilbert, *Churchill and America*, p. 139. **"Really, there is only one issue"**: Schwarz, *The Speculator*, p. 192. **Winston's reaction atop Empire State Building with former governor Al Smith:** http://www.britishpathe.com/record.php?id=2834.

CHAPTER 5: A MAN ON THE MAKE

"Who is it that" and "a very attractive Irishman": February 7, 1967, KMH, along with details of scenes with Joseph P. Kennedy, James Roosevelt, and his wife, Betsey, and visiting young Jack Kennedy in hospital bed. **"We used to laugh"**: Ted Sorensen, *Kennedy*, p. 41. **"Joe once told me, paraphrasing the German poet Goethe"**: Draft of unpublished "Joseph P. Kennedy: The Motor under the Hood," KMH. **Halle's obituary refers to "intimates who are certain that she had been Joseph Kennedy's favorite mistress"**: Robert McG. Thomas Jr., "Kay Halle, 93, an Intimate of Century's Giants," *NYT*, August 24, 1997. **"A fool ... or a saint"**: Gloria Swanson, *Swanson on Swanson* (New York: Random House, 1980), p. 401. **"I was very romantic and there were no two ways about it"**: Laurence Leamer, *The Kennedy Women*, p. 93. **"Can I be Godfather to the baby?"**: Lester David, *Ted Kennedy, Triumphs and Tragedies* (New York: Grosset and Dunlap, 1972), p. 157. **"The gist of the conversation"**: February 7, 1967, KMH. **Donations to 1932 FDR campaign by Kennedy, Bernard Baruch, National Distillers Products head Seton Porter, and William Randolph Hearst:** "Democrats' Outlay Less Than a Million," *NYT*, November 1, 1932. **"You drew to the purpose"**: Herbert Bayard Swope, November 9, 1932, letter, JPK.

"Man of mystery": " 'Man of Mystery' Here Recognized: J. P. Kennedy, Roosevelt Adviser, Visits Boston," *Boston Globe*, November 3, 1932, including Honey Fitz's "Joe is always in the background." **"There is nothing I want"**: James L. Wright, "Joe Kennedy Sits in Inner Circle of Roosevelt Campaign Train," *Boston Globe*, September. 25, 1932. **Henry Mason Day involvement in Teapot Dome scandal:** "Sinclair, Day Silent When Liberty Denied," *Miami News*, September 1929, p. 6, and in Richard J. Whalen, *The Founding Father: The Story of Joseph P. Kennedy*, pp. 132–33. **James A. Fayne's recollections of Joseph P. Kennedy:** Oral history dated August 8, 1968, for the Herbert Hoover Presidential Library and Museum, West Branch, IA. **"Only solution is for Dad to work harder"**: Evan Thomas, *Robert Kennedy: His Life*, p. 186. **"I have no first hand knowledge of the Depression"**: Hugh Sidey introduction to Kennedy and Henderson, *Prelude to Leadership*, p. xxiv. **Charles M. Schwab's secrecy at Fore River plant where JPK would work:** "Secrecy at Fore River," *The Boston Transcript*, May 31, 1915, p. 1. **"We got on very well"**: Martin Gilbert, *Churchill and America*, p. 56. **"Roosevelt was the hardest trader"**: Jean Edward Smith, *FDR*, p. 144. **"Modern usage"**: "The Merits of Speculation," *Time*, September 22, 1967. **"I never had the least ambition to be Alderman"**: Bernard Mannes Baruch, *Baruch, The Public Years*, p. 172. **"He has foreign friends and associations"**: 1932 memo from Kennedy to FDR, Baruch file, JPK, which also mentions Al Smith. **"More charm"**: ROSE. **"The impact which she made on men"**: Sylvia Jukes Morris, *Rage for Fame*, p. 194. **"You know she was Barney Baruch's girl"**: Jordan A. Schwarz, *The Speculator: Bernard Baruch in Washington, 1917–1965*, pp. 171–72. **"The only effective method"**: September 1, 1932, Brendan Bracken note, BMB. **"Fights so hard in conferences"**: James Kieran, "The 'Cabinet' Mr. Roosevelt Already Has," *NYT*, November 20, 1932. **"The drama of that room"**: "Dearest Mother" letter dated November 11, 1932, KMH. For further background, see David E. Koskoff, *Joseph P. Kennedy: A Life and Times*, p. 48.

CHAPTER 6: ACROSS THE ATLANTIC

Comments about James Roosevelt and his onboard entourage (including Joseph and Rose Kennedy, Halle, Mason Day, and Hough-

ton): "President's Son Off to Travel in Europe," *NYT,* September 27, 1933; also "Roosevelt Hailed by Throngs Here," *NYT,* September 27, 1933, and Charles Higham, *Rose: The Life and Times of Rose Fitzgerald Kennedy,* p. 148. **"Bring a flood of foreign liquors":** "Flood of Liquor from Abroad Seen," *NYT,* July 21, 1933. **Kennedy's 1929 "Prohibition Service" permit:** JPK. **Further detail relating to Kennedy's move for British rights:** "May Allow Rise in Liquor Imports," *NYT,* September 24, 1933. **"Mr. Seton Porter has been very kind":** September 21, 1933, James Roosevelt letter to Marguerite "Missy" LeHand, JIM. **"We understand that you wish before sailing":** September 18, 1933, document by Seton Porter to Kennedy granting exclusivity as sales agent for New England and mentioning meeting with Mason Day, in the National Distillers Products Corp. file, JPK. **"I am now and shall be able to look any man straight in the eye":** Associated Press, "Sinclair's Pal Enters Prison," *Youngstown Vindicator,* June 25, 1929. **Details about Kennedy's repeal stock investment in Libbey-Owens and testimony of Henry Mason Day:** U.S. Senate Banking and Currency Committee hearings on alcohol pools held February 21–26, 1934 (n.b.: identified as Libby-Owens in testimony). **Walker identified as "bankless banker" and his involvement with Baruch and Swope in BMT:** "Business: Personnel," *Time,* August 1, 1932. **"Best of all":** May 13, 1933, James Roosevelt letter to Elisha Walker, JIM. **Kennedy's involvement in BMT with Baruch and others:** "B.M.T. Stockholders at Peace with Dahl," *NYT,* July 16, 1932; Richard J. Whalen, *The Founding Father: The Story of Joseph P. Kennedy,* pp. 132–33; Ronald Kessler, *The Sins of the Father: Joseph P. Kennedy and the Dynasty He Founded,* p. 83; and "In the Matter of Brooklyn Manhattan Transit Corp.," I SEC 147 (1935). **"Which I feel we are qualified":** February 8, 1933, James Roosevelt letter to Elisha Walker, JIM. **"He was altogether different than Jack":** David E. Koskoff, *Joseph P. Kennedy: A Life and Times,* p. 374. **"I never taught the boys":** Whalen, *The Founding Father,* p. 172. **"It is more interesting":** "Dear Dad" letter from Joseph P. Kennedy Jr., dated November 6, 1933, JPK. **"He had his heart set on a political career":** Joe McCarthy, *The Remarkable Kennedys,* p. 108. **"If we live long enough" and "Joe knew what he wanted":** Laurence Leamer, *The Kennedy Women: The Saga of an American Family,* pp. 206–7. "I

think that the Irish in me": Thomas Maier, *The Kennedys: America's Emerald Kings*, p. 299. **"He wanted his sons":** 1967 oral history, p. 12, KMH. **"The golden boy":** Doris Kearns Goodwin, *No Ordinary Time*, p. 178. **"And this is my little boy James":** Frank Burt Freidel, *Franklin D. Roosevelt: A Rendezvous with Destiny*, p. 77. **"Sell him or give him away," "there is one person," and "a very useful man":** Ronald Kessler, *The Sins of the Father: Joseph P. Kennedy and the Dynasty He Founded*, pp. 95–99, and also see May 19, 1933, James Roosevelt note, JPK. **"Clad in overalls and muddy boots":** Kay Halle, *The Irrepressible Churchill: Winston's World, Wars, and Wit*, pp. 1–2. **"They were talking about the origins of the First World War":** Kay Halle's August 6, 1980, interview, WMP. **"Randolph called me yesterday":** April 2, 1932, Halle note, KMH. **"Poor little R——— I do really adore him":** May 1, 1932, Halle note to her mother, KMH. **"The only unplucked blossom in Cleveland":** May 24, 1932, Halle note to her mother, KMH, which includes comments calling Winston a great man. **Halle's description of October 1933 Chartwell visit:** November 11, 1932, letter to her mother, KMH. **Descriptions of Winston Churchill's conversation with James Roosevelt and company:** Martin Gilbert, *Churchill and America*, p. 150; Jon Meacham, *Franklin and Winston: An Intimate Portrait of an Epic Friendship*, p. 37; Kay Halle, *Winston Churchill on America and Britain*, p. 48; and Drew Pearson, "Churchill Realizes an Old Dream in Conferences with Roosevelt," p. 6; William Manchester, *The Last Lion: Winston Spencer Churchill: Alone, 1932–1940*, p. 550; and Warren F. Kimball, "Wheel within a Wheel: Churchill, Roosevelt, and the Special Relationship," in Robert Blake, ed., *Churchill: A Major New Assessment of His Life in Peace and War*, p. 297.

CHAPTER 7: THE DEAL

Chesterton quote "We are past the point": Richard Watson Gilder, *The Century Illustrated Monthly Magazine*, p. 237. **"I admire and dine with him":** Kay Halle, *The Irrepressible Churchill: Winston's World, Wars, and Wit*, p. 5. **"All I can say is that I have taken more out of alcohol":** Charles Eade, *Churchill: By His Contemporaries*, p. 309. **"Whatever else they may say of me as a soldier":** Robert Lewis Taylor, *Winston Churchill: The Biography of a Great Man*, p. 271. **"I must

confess": Richard M. Langworth, *Churchill by Himself: The Definitive Collection of Quotations,* p. 133. **"Prohibition is a complete farce":** Randolph S. Churchill, *Twenty-One Years,* pp. 85–90. **"The United States, far from being dry" and other Churchill comparisons of American and British policies on alcohol:** "Churchill Hits Drys; Tells British Brewers That Prohibition Leads to Corruption," *NYT,* March 16, 1926, and "Churchill Discovers We Export Liquors," *NYT,* August 5, 1932. **"Why don't you tax alcoholic liquor":** Martin Gilbert, *Churchill and America,* p. 144. **Joe Kennedy's creation and investment in Somerset Importers:** Daniel Okrent, *Last Call: The Rise and Fall of Prohibition,* p. 367. **"The very best people":** David E. Koskoff, *Joseph P. Kennedy: A Life and Times,* p. 52; and William V. Shannon, *The Heir Apparent: Robert Kennedy and the Struggle for Power,* p. 61. **"Assure[d] them Prohibition would shortly end":** C. L. Sulzberger, *The Last of the Giants,* pp. 629–30. **Schlesinger account of Randolph's recollection of the 1933 trip by Kennedy to England:** Kay Halle, *The Grand Original: Portraits of Randolph Churchill by His Friends,* p. 281. **"The British distillers were much impressed by Kennedy":** Lord Longford, *Kennedy,* p. 10. **The Kennedy/Roosevelt party conferring with Ramsay MacDonald and Neville Chamberlain:** Charles Higham, *Rose: The Life and Times of Rose Fitzgerald Kennedy,* p. 149. **"If Joe Kennedy wanted to open political doors or commercial ones":** Okrent, *Last Call,* p. 367. **Kennedy meeting with Sir James Calder:** Higham, *Rose,* p. 148. **Calder's trip to Florida:** *HTF,* p.127. **Kennedy selling 150,000 cases of Scotch whiskey in first year:** Ronald B. Weir, *The History of the Distillers Company, 1877–1939: Diversification and Growth in Whisky and Chemicals,* p. 280. **"We have done surprisingly well with the contracts":** *HTF,* p. 135. **Winston's investments in Brooklyn Manhattan Transit Corp. and National Distillers and subsequent sales:** Detailed in stock documents and letters from September 1933 to October 1935, in the Chartwell papers, CHUR. **"I bought seven hundred Brooklyn Manhattan T":** October 15, 1933, note from Winston Churchill to Baruch, BMB. **"In private life it was quite true":** James Grant, *Bernard M. Baruch: The Adventures of a Wall Street Legend,* p. 265. **"The more I study the stocks":** Martin Gilbert, *Churchill and America,* pp. 147–49. **"Do you still like BWT":** November 18, 1933, cable from Win-

ston Churchill to Baruch, BMB. **"Are you still pleased with B.M.T.":**
October 27, 1934, Churchill note to Baruch, BMB; also contained in
Chartwell papers, CHUR. **"I telegraphed Baruch about Brooklyn":**
Winston's October 27, 1934, personal note to brother Jack in Chartwell
papers, CHUR. **"While disappointed delayed transit consolidation":**
Baruch cable to Churchill in Chartwell papers, CHUR; also BMB. **Sir
Ernest Cassel's financial ties to Churchill, including Lord Alfred
Douglas comment "this ambitious and brilliant man":** David Cannadine, *Aspects of Aristocracy: Grandeur and Decline in Modern Britain,*
pp. 144–48. **"If we do not get a good price":** Mary Soames, *Winston
and Clementine: The Personal Letters of the Churchills,* p. 426. **"Without
distraction and anxiety":** Churchill, March 19, 1938, letter to Brendan Bracken, CHUR. **"The exact details of Strakosch's intervention":**
Cannadine, *Aspects of Aristocracy,* p. 146. **"It is almost as difficult for
an Englishman":** February 2, 1934, note from Joe Kennedy to Peter
Dewar, JPK. **"Kennedy put his arm around Jimmy":** Ronald Kessler,
The Sins of the Father: Joseph P. Kennedy and the Dynasty He Founded,
p. 98. **"Oh, I know he was a financial genius":** Ralph G. Martin, *A
Hero for Our Time: An Intimate Story of the Kennedy Years,* p. 22. **"Your
son James":** August 9, 1934, J. Henry Neale letter to FDR, in JIM. **"You
wanted a statement of facts":** August 28, 1934, James Roosevelt letter
to father, JIM. **"I sent your letter":** September 6, 1934, FDR letter to
Neale, JIM. **"Whoever started that is either purposely lying":** Associated Press, *Youngstown Daily Vindicator,* August 12, 1938. **"I did have
the insurance account of the National Distillers":** James Roosevelt
oral history, Regional Oral History Office, University of California,
Berkeley. **"I'm still cutting my teeth in a business way":** 1933 James
Roosevelt note to Joe Kennedy, JPK. **"Greatest friend in Europe":** Oral
History of James A. Fayne, p. 2, Miller Center, University of Virginia.

CHAPTER 8: THE KING OF WALL STREET

"You would be surprised": *HTF,* p. 127. **"I shall remember":** October
1933 note from Rose Kennedy to Enrico Galeazzi, JPK. **"Well—it is the
best I could get out of him":** October 29, 1933, Arthur Houghton note
to Galeazzi, JPK. **"As for Miss Halle":** October 24, 1933, Felix Frankfurter note, JPK. **"Tonight Joe Kennedy called me from N.Y.":** Febru-

ary 7, 1934, Halle note to family, KMH. **"By strange co-incidence":** *HTF,* p. 107. **"He thought it would be a very nice thing":** Ibid., p. 134. **"Lent a quiet, helping hand":** Paul Mallon column, *Miami News,* July 14, 1934. **"I don't believe any appointment":** June 29, 1934, Swope note to Roosevelt, JPK. **"Defied anyone":** Raymond Moley, *After Seven Years,* p. 288. **"Setting a wolf to guard a flock of sheep":** David E. Koskoff, *Joseph P. Kennedy: A Life and Times,* p. 59. **"A credit to the country":** Moley, *After Seven Years,* p. 288. **"He's independently wealthy" and other comments about Kennedy's appointment:** "Business: Four Men & One," *Time,* July 9, 1934. **"The way I handled it":** August 1, 1934, note from Swope, JPK. **"Shooting not only at me":** August 7, 1934, memo to Baruch, BMB. **Swope upset about not getting Somerset stake:** Koskoff, *Joseph P. Kennedy,* p. 53. **"I thought money":** Edward Renehan Jr., *The Kennedys at War: 1937–1945,* p. 19. **Description of Kennedy as "important" American:** September 25, 1935, Baruch cable to Churchill, BMB. **"Look into the question of foreign bonds":** September 23, 1935, Roosevelt letter to Bingham, FDR. **"My trip is most interesting":** October 10, 1935, Kennedy note to Mason Day, JPK.

PART II: FAMILY FORTUNES

"It is a wise father": *Merchant of Venice,* in William Shakespeare, *Plays of William Shakespeare,* p. 183. **"Don't hold your parents up to contempt":** Evelyn Waugh, *The Tablet,* May 9, 1951.

CHAPTER 9: THE SONS OF GREAT MEN

"Two dogs are biting us": "The Stormy Churchills: National Government Attacked," London dispatch in the *West Australian,* February 7, 1935. **"He saw a chance to make trouble":** "A Chip Off the Old Block," *NYT,* February 8, 1935. **"My son has taken this step":** "M.P. Seat Sought by Churchill's Son," *NYT,* January 20, 1935. **"Most rash and unconsidered plunge":** Mary Soames, *Winston and Clementine: The Personal Letters of the Churchills,* p. 374. **"If anybody had disputed my belief":** John Colville, *Winston Churchill and His Inner Circle,* p. 35. **"In most cases the son":** Randolph S. Churchill, "How I Mean to Win Success," *Daily Dispatch,* August 1, 1932. **" 'Great Men' and Their Sons":** Winston S. Churchill, *His Father's Son: The Life of Randolph Churchill,*

p. 88. **"It was a splendid occasion"**: Randolph S. Churchill, *Twenty-One Years*, pp. 119–23. **"A fine machine gun"**: Clive Irving, "The Shade of Churchill: Randolph in Retrospect," *Sunday Times*, June 1968. **"Naturally I have high hopes for Randolph"**: Winston S. Churchill, *His Father's Son*, p. 88. **"Because things came so naturally to him"**: John Charmley, *Churchill: The End of Glory—A Political Biography*, p. 300. **"Work, my boy, work!"**: Randolph S. Churchill, *Twenty-One Years*, p. 120. **"The reason the historical English families"**: Paul K. Alkon, *Winston Churchill's Imagination*, p. 90. **"What a creature of strange mood"**: Virginia Cowles, *Churchill: The Era and the Man*, p. 202. **"The most compelling and consistently fascinating"**: Sarah Churchill, *A Thread of Tapestry*, p. 35. **"You bloody fool!"**: Anne Chisholm and Michael Davie, *Lord Beaverbrook: A Life*, p. 184. **"He had all the canine virtues"**: Violet Bonham Carter, *Winston Churchill as I Knew Him*, p. 147. **"Churchill's tastes are simple"**: Geoffrey Best, *Churchill: A Study in Greatness*, p. 143. **"In all of them there"**: Mary Soames, *Clementine Churchill: The Biography of a Marriage*, p. 282. **"She objected to the thoughtless encouragement"**: John Colville, *Winston Churchill and His Inner Circle*, p. 19. **"Smart bunch"**: Randolph S. Churchill, *Twenty-One Years*, pp. 63–67. **"He smoked matches"**: Paul Johnson, *Churchill*, pp. 68–70. **"I do not know which is the more offensive"**: Anita Leslie, *Randolph: The Biography of Winston Churchill's Son*, p. 31. **"I refused as I think life"**: Martin Gilbert, *Winston Churchill: The Wilderness Years*, p. 143. **"Chuckled with appreciation"** and **"rogue elephant"**: Winston S. Churchill, *His Father's Son*, pp. 148 and 68. **"Six times better"**: Carlos Villar Flor and Robert Murray Davis, eds., *Waugh Without End: New Trends in Evelyn Waugh Studies*, p. 247. **"Utterly loyal to him"** and **"nothing is so piercing"**: Winston S. Churchill, *His Father's Son*, p. 96. **"It is alarming"**: Arthur Herman, *Gandhi and Churchill: The Epic Rivalry That Destroyed an Empire and Forged Our Age*, p. 359. **"Little brown man in the loincloth"**: Brian Roberts, *Randolph: A Study of Churchill's Son*, p. 86. **"Randolph was determined"**: Soames, *Clementine Churchill*, p. 242. **"This was Randolph's first foray"**: Sarah Churchill, *Keep On Dancing*, p. 45. **"My father died"**: Winston S. Churchill, *His Father's Son*, p. 86.

CHAPTER 10: MENACE ON THE HORIZON

Book review of Hitler's *Mein Kampf***:** John Chamberlain, "Books of the Times," *NYT,* October 11, 1933. **"One of the great anachronisms":** Steven F. Hayward, *Greatness: Reagan, Churchill, and the Making of Extraordinary Leaders,* p. 46. **"It was a horrible thing":** April 23, 1934, letter from Joseph P. Kennedy Jr. to his father, JPK. **"He saw the need of a common enemy," "a very keen sense of perception":** *HTF,* pp. 131–33. **Randolph Churchill's visit to Nazi Germany in 1932:** Randolph S. Churchill, *Twenty-One Years,* pp. 124–25; Martin Gilbert, *Winston Churchill: The Wilderness Years,* p. 51; and Robert Rhodes James, *Churchill: A Study in Failure, 1900–1939,* p. 246. **"Hitler produced a thousand excuses":** Jon Meacham, *Franklin and Winston: An Intimate Portrait of an Epic Friendship,* pp. 189–90. **"He criticizes Churchill very strongly":** John Lukacs, *The Duel: The Eighty-Day Struggle between Churchill and Hitler,* p. 37. **"Or whether he will go down in history":** Winston Churchill, *Great Contemporaries,* p. 212. **"The story of the human race is war":** Norman Rose, *Churchill: The Unruly Giant,* pp. 258–62. **"I affected a combination":** Kay Halle, *The Irrepressible Churchill,* p. 254. **"Vindication of Marlborough from neglect and contumely":** Henry Steele Commager introduction to Winston Churchill, *Marlborough: His Life and Times, Volume 1,* p. xxiii. **"A good knowledge of history":** Martin Gilbert, *Churchill: A Life,* p. 81. **"No glittering wheels of royal favour":** Winston Churchill, *Lord Randolph Churchill, Volume 1,* p. xii. **"An imaginative portrayal":** David Cannadine, *Aspects of Aristocracy: Grandeur and Decline in Modern Britain,* p. 152. **"Turned for everything," "biographer of eminent persons," and "conforms closely":** R. F. Foster, *Lord Randolph Churchill: A Political Life,* pp. 395–99. **"Think a little meanwhile":** Martin Gilbert, *Churchill and the Jews: A Lifelong Friendship,* p. 107.

CHAPTER 11: LONDON CALLING

"It was easily the best analysis": November 17, 1936, note from Kennedy to Brendan Bracken, in JPK. **"After the 1936 campaign":** James Roosevelt, *My Parents: A Differing View,* p. 208. **FDR decision to appoint Kennedy as ambassador:** Jean Edward Smith, *FDR,* p. 417; and Conrad Black, *Franklin Delano Roosevelt: Champion of Freedom,* p. 439.

"Intrigued with the idea of twisting the lion's tale a little": Joseph E. Persico, *Roosevelt's Secret War: FDR and World War II Espionage*, p. 28. **"Joe, would you mind stepping back a bit":** James Roosevelt, *My Parents*, p. 209. **"I got the impression that deep down in his heart":** Kennedy's diary at JFK Library, in Thomas Maier, *The Kennedys: America's Emerald Kings*, p. 128. **"Help that Jimmy built up his insurance business":** Ronald Kessler, *The Sins of the Father: Joseph P. Kennedy and the Dynasty He Founded*, p. 97. **"I have made arrangements to have Joe Kennedy watched hourly":** David E. Koskoff, *Joseph P. Kennedy: A Life and Times*, p. 117. **"I don't know what kind of a diplomat I shall be, probably rotten":** January 13, 1938, Joe Kennedy telegram, FDR. **"The most thrilling, exciting and interesting years":** March 1938 note, ROSE. **"Well, Rose, this is a helluva long way":** Richard Whalen, *The Founding Father: The Story of Joseph P. Kennedy*, p. 205. **"Was heightened by the fact that my Irish-American background":** Diplomatic memoir draft, chap. 2, p. 1, JPK. **"You don't understand the Irish":** Kessler, *The Sins of the Father*, p. 136. **"I know you can hit a home run":** December 13, 1937, Bernard Baruch telegram, JPK. **Randolph greeting Kennedys at arrival at Plymouth:** Will Swift, *The Kennedys: Amidst the Gathering Storm*, p. 21. **"Has charged Mr. Kennedy with the mission of advising him":** Randolph Churchill, "Ambassador Brings Vital Speech," *Evening Standard*, March 2, 1938. **Known for "his excellent singing voice":** "Honey Fitz," *Evening Standard*, June 24, 1938, in Randolph Churchill news clippings, CHUR. **Joe's hole in one and the Kennedys' reception in London:** David Nunnerley, *President Kennedy and Britain*, p. 19. **"I hoped it was a good omen":** Diplomatic memoir draft, chap. 2, p. 2, JPK. **"His favorite theme":** Frederick Kuh, "Kennedy Winning British Hearts," United Press, *Bend-Bulletin* (OR), June 16, 1938. **"Pronounced and persistent opposition":** Diplomatic memoir draft, chap. 2, p. 9, JPK. **"One strong young figure":** Winston S. Churchill, *The Second World War, Volume 1: The Gathering Storm*, p. 231. **"It was natural for Churchill":** Diplomatic memoir draft, chap. 2, p. 9, JPK. **"A realistic, practical mind":** Koskoff, *Joseph P. Kennedy*, p. 167. **"My dinner companion was Mrs. Churchill":** HTF, p. 250.

CHAPTER 12: ASTOR PLACE

"Madam, if you were my wife, I'd drink it": Elizabeth Coles Langhorne, *Nancy Astor and Her Friends*, p. 57. **"A kindred soul"**: Will Swift, *The Kennedys: Amidst the Gathering Storm*, p. 43. **"You have no right"**: Nigel Hamilton, *JFK: Reckless Youth*, p. 482. **"My father impressed upon me"**: December 8, 1938, note to Nancy Astor, JPK. **"She is great fun"**: 1939 Diary, p. 35, ROSE. **"I'm glad you are smart enough"**: Edward Renehan Jr., *The Kennedys at War: 1937–1945*, p. 41. **Details of Kennedy and Lindbergh in London together**: Scott A. Berg, *Lindbergh*, pp. 374–75; and Lindbergh letters, JPK. **"A great man"**: Wayne S. Cole, *Charles A. Lindbergh and The Battle Against American Intervention in World War II*, p. 34. **"She is small" and "The Colonel gave us a rude awakening"**: 1938 Diary, p. 52, ROSE. **"Who feeds the crocodile"**: James C. Humes, *Eisenhower and Churchill: The Partnership That Saved the World*, p. 141. **"After two years"**: Adrian Fort, *Nancy: The Story of Lady Astor*, p. 148. **"I have great regard"**: Robert Lewis Taylor, *Winston Churchill: The Biography of a Great Man*, p. 301. **"Nancy, when you entered the House"**: Dominique Enright, *The Wicked Wit of Winston Churchill*, p. 102. **"How many toes"**: Swift, *The Kennedys: Amidst the Gathering Storm*, p. 42. **"Why don't you come sober?"**: Christopher Sykes, *Nancy: The Life of Lady Astor*, p. 195. **"You hardly ever"**: Martin Gilbert, *Churchill and America*, p. 125. **"He represents all that a man"**: Scott A. Berg, *Lindbergh*, p. 149. **"Might be swept up"**: Sarah Churchill, *A Thread in the Tapestry*, p. 45. **"Very much in love" and "greatest friend"**: Randolph S. Churchill, *Twenty-One Years*, p. 27. **"Everyone looked happy"**: Swift, *The Kennedys: Amidst the Gathering Storm*, p. 31. **"Unity Mitford is one of the most unusual"**: HTF, p. 355. **"Disaster of the first magnitude"**: John Lukacs, *The Duel: The Eighty-Day Struggle between Churchill and Hitler*, p. 24. **"We have sustained a defeat without a war"**: Winston S. Churchill, *The Second World War, Volume 1: The Gathering Storm*, p. 294. **"You won't be satisfied" and "our cock won't fight"**: Lord Beaverbrook, *The Abdication of King Edward VIII*, pp. 80–81. **"As I saw Mr. Churchill walk off"**: Duke of Windsor H.R.H. Edward, *A King's Story: The Memoirs of The Duke of Windsor*, pp. 406–7. **"If it had been possible for me"**: "Germany: Herzogin von Windsor," *Time*, November

1, 1937. **Randolph gets an exclusive interview with the king:** Anne Chisholm and Michael Davie, *Lord Beaverbrook: A Life*, p. 343. **"If a king wants to sleep with a whore":** June 1938 diary entry, JPK. **"I know of no job":** Diplomatic memoir draft, chap. 26, p. 8, JPK. **"The British aren't accustomed":** Philip Seib, *Broadcasts from the Blitz: How Edward R. Murrow Helped Lead America into War*, p. 32. **"Had been taken in hand by Lady Astor":** Leonard Mosley, *On Borrowed Time: How World War II Began*, p. 101. **"Who would have thought":** Garry Wills, *The Kennedy Imprisonment: A Meditation on Power*, pp. 76–77. **"There is simply no sense":** Jasper Vanderbilt Garland, *War and the Americas*, p. 84. **"England has been offered":** C. L. Sulzberger, *A Long Row of Candles: Memoirs & Diaries, 1934–1954*, p. 33.

CHAPTER 13: THE KENNEDY WOMEN

Debutante gala at Buckingham Palace: 1938 Diary, p. 38, ROSE; Lynne McTaggart, *Kathleen Kennedy: Her Life and Times*, pp. 35–40; and Will Swift, *The Kennedys: Amidst the Gathering Storm*, p. 38. **"The girls all wore white" and "vital, intelligent and outgoing":** Deborah Devonshire, *Wait for Me!: Memoirs*, pp. 85–90. **"Do speak English again, Kick":** McTaggart, *Kathleen Kennedy*, p. 34. **"Mark my words":** Deborah Mitford, Duchess of Devonshire, *Wait for Me!*, p. 90. **"Child rearing as a profession":** Swift, *The Kennedys*, p. 77. **"The Music Hall joke about Kennedy":** April 9, 1938, diary entry, JPK. **"They were incredibly close":** Author's 2011 interview with Page Huidekoper Wilson. **"Bowel movement":** McTaggart, *Kathleen Kennedy*, p. 36. **"I know one shouldn't say this to a queen":** *HTF*, p. 329. **"She is an uninteresting little body":** Robert Rhodes James, ed., *Chips: The Diaries of Sir Henry Channon*, p. 205. **"Mr. Winston Churchill, who is said to be the most fascinating":** 1938 Diary, p. 59, ROSE. **"If Joe Kennedy's daughters":** David Halberstam, *The Best and the Brightest*, pp. 98–99. **"If Eunice had balls":** Ralph G. Martin, *A Hero for Our Times: An Intimate History of the Kennedy Years*, p. 400. **"That's what all men do":** McTaggart, *Kathleen Kennedy*, p. 62. **"Kick had by now become":** Mitford, *Wait for Me!* p. 94. **"He was fascinated by English political society":** Arthur M. Schlesinger Jr., *A Thousand Days: John F. Kennedy in the White House*, p. 83. **"The big men of Berlin and London":**

JFK, September 19, 1939, note to Claiborne Pell in Swift, *The Kenne-dys: Amidst the Gathering Storm*, p. 194. **"His father thinks he should write a book":** April 7, 1939, diary entry, p. 30, ROSE. **"Bend over backwards":** Swift, *The Kennedys: Amidst the Gathering Storm*, p. 177. **"I can take care of myself":** Richard J. Whalen, *The Founding Father: The Story of Joseph P. Kennedy*, p. 173. **"There is a very definite feeling here":** October 13, 1939, Kennedy note to his sons Joe Jr. and Jack, JPK. **"While I read and hear about you":** January 10, 1938, Kennedy let-ter to Halle, KMH. **"As a bridge figure":** Wilfred Sheed, *Clare Boothe Luce*, p. 159. **"I do not like to go to bed without you"** and **"Clare made no secret":** Sylvia Jukes Morris, *Rage for Fame: The Ascent of Clare Boothe Luce*, pp. 358–59, p. 238-39. **"The most politically ingra-tiating family since Theodore Roosevelt's":** "The Nine Kennedy Kids Delight Great Britain," *Life*, April 11, 1938, pp. 16–17. **"Save me lunch"** and **"You're angel":** June 1939 Luce cables to Kennedy, in CBL. **"We Americans can live quite comfortably":** Clare Boothe, *Europe in the Spring*, p. 198. **"She's the tops"** and **"Now you can take them all off":** Morris, *Rage for Fame*, pp. 520, 238–39.

CHAPTER 14: THE DESIRE TO PLEASE
"I knew her as anyone," about Pamela Digby's first meeting Kick Kennedy at **"coming out balls":** Ogden interview, unprocessed file, Group 2 of 3, p. 152, PAM. **"Rather fat, fast and the butt of many teases":** Deborah Mitford, Duchess of Devonshire, *Wait for Me!: Mem-oirs*, p. 85. **"A redheaded bouncing little thing"** and **"fat, stupid little butterball":** Sally Bedell Smith, *Reflected Glory: The Life of Pamela Churchill Harriman*, p. 46. **"Although we talked endlessly":** Veronica Maclean, *Past Forgetting: A Memoir of Heroes, Adventure, and Love*, p. 91. **"My sister Pamela"** and **"He was a cardboard figure":** Marie Brenner, *Great Dames: What I Learned from Older Women*, pp. 203–5. **"I want to speak to you"** and other parts of Randolph and Pam-ela introduction: Michael Gross, "Mother of the Clinton Court," *New York*, January 18, 1993, p. 28, and in John Pearson, *The Private Lives of Winston Churchill*, pp. 278–79. **"She was always worried":** Ogden interview, unprocessed file, Group 1 of 3, p. 11, PAM. **"Sarah is an oyster, she will not tell us her secrets":** Sarah Churchill, *A Thread in*

the Tapestry, p. 31. **"Girls who danced fairly naked":** William Manchester, *The Last Lion: Winston Spencer Churchill: Alone, 1932–1940,* p. 256. **"Was never to feel alone or strange":** Sarah Churchill, *Keep On Dancing: An Autobiography,* p. 31. **"How much I love you":** Randolph Churchill and Martin Gilbert, *Winston S. Churchill: Finest Hour, 1939– 1941,* p. 206. **"It's very strange"** and **"I like my new son-in-law":** Mary Soames, *Clementine Churchill: The Biography of a Marriage,* p. 275. **"To escape from all the endless talk":** John Pearson, *The Private Lives of Winston Churchill,* p. 233. **"If he does not take American":** Sarah Churchill, *A Thread in the Tapestry,* p. 52. **"I am going to America":** Sarah Churchill, *Keep On Dancing,* p. 71. **"The effect of the letter you wrote to Randolph":** Mary Soames, *Winston and Clementine: The Personal Letters of the Churchills,* p. 404. **"I didn't know anything about this until now":** Brian Roberts, *Randolph: A Study of Churchill's Son,* p. 158. **"If the family is willing":** Associated Press, "Sarah Churchill's Romance Not Yet Described as Such," September 22, 1936. **"That's a good joke":** "Sarah Churchill and Oliver Wed," *NYT,* December 25, 1936. **"Winston was more relaxed and indulgent":** Soames, *Clementine Churchill ,* p. 267. **"She said 'So tired' and closed her eyes":** Anthony Montague Browne, *Long Sunset: Memoirs of Winston Churchill's Last Private Secretary,* p. 147. **"I wish you could have come":** Soames, *Winston and Clementine,* p. 241. **"As children, we soon became aware":** Soames, *Clementine Churchill,* p. 238. **"Mrs. C. considers it one of her missions":** John Colville, *The Fringes of Power: The Incredible Inside Story of Winston Churchill During World War II,* p. 273. **"Had no real understanding of the childish mind":** Soames, *Clementine Churchill,* p. 237. **"Modern young people will do what they like":** Jack Fishman, *"My Darling Clementine": The Story of Lady Churchill,* p. 112. **"Winston never backed Clementine up":** Smith, *Reflected Glory,* p. 55. **"This lively boy manifestly needed a father's hand":** Soames, *Clementine Churchill,* p. 241. **A more casual and contemporary style:** John Charmley, *Churchill: The End of Glory—A Political Biography,* p. 339. **"An occasional blast":** Anne Chisholm and Michael Davie, *Lord Beaverbrook: A Life,* p. 368. **"You're all a lot of quislings":** Ogden interview, Group 2 of 3, p. 155, PAM. **"Dubious about the hole in one":** Doris Kearns Goodwin, *The Fitzgeralds and The Kennedys: An Ameri-*

can Saga, p. 516. **"Singularly unkind":** Manchester, *The Last Lion: Winston Spencer Churchill: Alone,* p. 255. **"When I was thirteen and fourteen years old":** Anita Leslie, *Randolph: The Biography of Winston Churchill's Son,* p. 40. **"It was grossly rude, & as such wounded me deeply":** Randolph Churchill and Martin Gilbert, *Winston S. Churchill, Volume 5: The Prophet of Truth, 1922–1939,* p. 899. **"That was what was terrible"** and **"What had really happened":** Leslie, *Randolph: The Biography of Winston Churchill's Son,* p. 40. **"One of the reasons I fell for him originally":** Ogden interview, Group 1 of 3, p. 19, PAM. **"I was getting so upset"** and **"rather egged me on":** Michael Gross, "Mother of the Clinton Court," p. 28. **"What you need is a double bed":** August 22, 1980, Pamela Harriman interview, p. 29, WMP. **"Are you Catholic?":** Ibid. **"Yes, you had your heads chopped off in the Gunpowder Plot":** Pamela Harriman interview, p. 1, transcript of interview for *Churchill* documentary, CHUR. **"That being out of the way":** August 22, 1980, Pamela Harriman interview, p. 29, WMP. **"Since the age of 19":** "Pamela Digby Wed to Churchill's Son," *NYT,* September 26, 1939. **"Would have done so but for the refusal of the Archbishop":** May 26, 1950, document, PAM, which details how Pamela Churchill sought annulment in order to convert to Catholicism and explains Joseph Kennedy's interaction with her former husband Randolph, who sought the intervention of the Archbishop of Canterbury. **"In middle age he began":** *HTF,* p. xxiv. **"Rather liked":** Ogden interview, Group 2 of 3, pp. 157–58, PAM. **"Nuts! I call it":** *HTF,* pp. xxiv–xxv. **"I made that speech straight at Churchill":** Ibid., p. 353.

CHAPTER 15: BREACH OF FAITH

"All the interesting and stimulating experiences": January 1939 note from Rose Kennedy, FDR. **"If I had my eye on another job":** David E. Koskoff, *Joseph P. Kennedy: A Life and Times,* p. 141. **"It was a terrible blow to him":** Doris Kearns Goodwin, *The Fitzgeralds and the Kennedys: An American Saga,* p. 534. **"Can you imagine Joe Kennedy declining":** Richard J. Whalen, *The Founding Father: The Story of Joseph P. Kennedy,* p. 229. **"He'd put them in an orphanage":** *HTF,* p. 268. **"It was a true Irish anger that swept me":** Goodwin, *The Fitzgeralds and The Kennedys,* p. 536. **"The man is almost paralyzed":**

Diplomatic memoir draft, chap. 5, p. 6D, JPK. **"The premier Scotch whisky salesman in America"**: "Kennedy Denies Son Jim Helped Secure Job," Associated Press, *Sarasota Herald-Tribune*, June 29, 1938. **"Being the President's son"**: "Roosevelt Son Answers Claim on His Income," International News Service, *Milwaukee Sentinel*, August 12, 1938. **"Complete unadulterated lie" and "I admit I am the ambassador"**: "Kennedy Labels Article a 'Lie,'" Associated Press, *Ludington Daily News*, June 29, 1938. **"Cradled his head"**: Jean Edward Smith, *FDR*, p. 403. **"Washington gossips"**: Steve Early February 27, 1934, note to James Roosevelt, FDR. **"Well here is your old pal"**: April 10, 1938, Kennedy note to Jimmy's wife, Betsey, FDR. **"Good deal upset"**: Ronald Kessler, *The Sins of the Father: Joseph P. Kennedy and the Dynasty He Founded*, p. 96, 56–57. **Boettiger sent Joe notes**: June 5, 1937, cables from Boettiger, JPK. **"The great 'war-buster'"**: October 26, 1938, Boettiger note, FDR. **"I am *persona non grata*"**: November 25, 1938, Joe Kennedy note to John Boettiger, FDR. **"All you have done for my children"**: Eleanor Roosevelt note to Joseph Kennedy, marked May 24 (but with undated year), JPK. **"I realize more and more that FDR is a great man"**: Smith, *FDR*, p. 144. **"My brother is just a different human being"**: Three Missy LeHand letters to Joe Kennedy, from 1935 to 1936, FDR. **"Our Ambassador to the Court of Haig & Haig"**: Lord Longford, *Kennedy*, p. 10. **"I don't intend to see this lost to the family"**: September 6, 1938, letter to Ted O'Leary, JPK. **"The fact that you were in the liquor business"**: March 1, 1938, letter from Ted O'Leary, JPK. **"It got so bad"**: Seymour Hersh, *The Dark Side of Camelot*, pp. 65–67. **"Capitalist Kennedy"**: William Stevenson, *A Man Called Intrepid*, p. 148. **"Made a very profitable deal"**: April 1942 FBI memo of Joseph P. Kennedy, File 8 of 8, detailing rumors about Somerset's 1933 creation and deals with British distillers. **"Bernard Baruch is planning to sail to England"**: Margaret L. Coit, *Mr. Baruch*, p. 466; also see Edward J. Renehan Jr., *The Kennedys at War: 1937–1945*, p. 34. **"War is coming very soon," "friendship with the American Jewish millionaire Baruch," and "Many thanks, but Diana is air-raid"**: Martin Gilbert, *Churchill and America*, p. 166, 103, and 168–70. **"I said there wasn't a word of truth in the whole story"**: *HTF*, p. 307. **"He knew the way I felt about him"**: February 9, 1939, diary entry, JPK.

"He did not believe that it was ethical": Alfred Allan Lewis, *Man of the World, Herbert Bayard Swope: A Charmed Life of Pulitzer Prizes, Poker and Politics*, p. 218–19. "Baruch is trying to get an appointment," "democracy as we now conceive it," and "I hate to think": *HTF*, p. 377, 386, and 231. "The democratic and dictator countries": Barbara Leaming, *Jack Kennedy: The Education of a Statesman*, p. 71. "Understanding and sympathy" and von Dirksen's comment: Ray Bearse and Anthony Read, *Conspirator: The Untold Story of Tyler Kent*, p. 74. "While it seemed to be unpopular with the Jews": James MacGregor Burns, *John Kennedy: A Political Profile*, p. 52. "Word was passed around": C. L. Sulzberger, *The Last of the Giants*, p. 629. "Be licked," as reported by Lippmann and Churchill's reply: Martin Gilbert, *Churchill: A Life*, p. 615; and John Charmley, *Churchill: The End of Glory—A Political Biography*, p. 363.

CHAPTER 16: THE CROSS AND DOUBLE-CROSS

"The 'cousinhood' of intelligence": Christopher Hitchens, *Blood, Class and Empire: The Enduring Anglo-American Relationship*, p. 298. "Our intelligence service has won": Winston S. Churchill, *The World Crisis*, p. 254. "The geese who laid the golden eggs and never cackled": Norman Rose, *Churchill: The Unruly Giant*, p. 345. "In the higher ranges of Secret Service work": Winston S. Churchill, *Amid These Storms: Thoughts and Adventures*, p. 87. "The best information service in Europe": David J. Alvarez, *Spies in the Vatican: Espionage and Intrigue from Napoleon to the Holocaust*, p. 269. "Experiences in London": Diplomatic memoir draft, chap. 39, pp. 1–2, JPK. "A strictly confidential memorandum": April 19, 1938, note to James Roosevelt, JPK. "A convinced pro-German": Christopher Andrew, *Defend the Realm: The Authorized History of MI5*, p. 104. "At times powerless": Pacelli memo attached to April 19, 1938, note to James Roosevelt, JPK. "He thought the Communists": Author's 2011 interview with Page Huidekoper Wilson. **Joe Kennedy's longtime friendship with Vatican administrator Count Enrico Galeazzi and their behind-the-scenes interactions with Cardinal Spellman, various U.S. leaders, and the 1960 presidential campaign of John F. Kennedy:** Thomas Maier, *The Kennedys: America's Emerald Kings*, pp. 124–28, 293–312, 400–401,

506, 555, 570; also in David Nasaw, *The Patriarch: The Remarkable Life and Turbulent Times of Joseph P. Kennedy.* **"Started out in Galeazzi's car"**: August 7, 1937, diary note, JFK. **"Terribly impressive"**: August 8, 1937, diary note, JFK. **"When the new Pope is elected"**: Galeazzi correspondence and other March 1939 documents and diary notes, JPK. **"I had a great time in Rome"**: March 20, 1939, letter to James Roosevelt, JPK. **"A thorough search"** and **"The Hierarchy, I think"**: Maier, *The Kennedys,* pp. 125–27. **"Please remember that I am yours to command"**: November 3, 1939, letter to Galeazzi, JPK. **"A subconscious prejudice"**: April 5, 1939, Kennedy letter to Sumner Welles, in FDR. **"Had just been approached by the German Government"**: Diplomatic memoir draft, chap. 40, pp. 3–4, JPK. **"Moore proved to be a good spy"**: Charles Higham, *Rose: The Life and Times of Rose Fitzgerald Kennedy,* p. 214. **"What can the Pope do?"**: March 5, 1940, Galeazzi note, JPK. **"The Irish have a genius for conspiracy"**: Martin Gilbert, *Churchill: A Life,* p. 446. **"Rose, De Valera and I talked all the time"**: March 12, 1939, diary notes, JPK. **"How happy I should be"**: Frank Pakenham Longford (Earl of) and Thomas P. O'Neill, *Eamon de Valera,* p. 318. **"I say that the ports may be denied"**: Parliamentary Debates, House of Commons, Official Report, Volume 335, 1938. **"The land of my forefathers"**: Diplomatic memoir draft, chap. 11, p. 1, JPK. **"I must say I enjoyed my trip to Dublin"**: July 20, 1938, Kennedy letter, JPK. **"His deep resentment against Churchill"**: Diplomatic memoir draft, chap. 11, p. 1, JPK. **"Could not forgive those who had been responsible"**: Richard J. Whalen, *The Founding Father: The Story of Joseph P. Kennedy,* p. 231. **"To pacify the East Coast Irish"**: September 3, 1940, British Foreign Office memo, in Tyler Kent file, FDR. **"That murderer and perjurer"**: John Ramsden, *Man of the Century: Winston Churchill and His Legend Since 1945,* p. 243. **"It would seem that money"** and **"What does intelligence say"**: David Stafford, *Roosevelt and Churchill: Men of Secrets,* pp. 66, 22–25. **"Thought she was so lucky to be American"** and **"If the American Ambassador or some of his family were shot"**: April 7, 1939, diary entry, p. 30, ROSE. **"He kept smiling when he talked of 'neutrality'"**: October 5, 1939, diary entry, JPK.

CHAPTER 17: THE LAST DANCE

"To be born, and to marry, and I never regretted either": David Cannadine, "The Pitfalls of Family Piety," in Robert Blake, ed., *Churchill: A Major New Assessment of his Life in Peace and War*, p. 9. **Description of Blenheim Palace gala**: Angela Lambert, *1939: The Last Season of Peace*, pp. 167–71; and in Mary S. Lovell, *The Churchills: In Love and War*, p. 405. **"Shall we ever see the like again?"**: "Obituaries: Lady Sarah Spencer-Churchill," *Daily Telegraph*, October 19, 2000; and in Robert Rhodes James, ed., *Chips: The Diaries of Sir Henry Channon*, p. 477. **"Oh look at that poor old has-been"**: Angela Lambert, *1939: The Last Season of Peace*, pp. 167–71. **"Randolph, you've been drinking"**: John Pearson, *The Private Lives of Winston Churchill*, pp. 274–75. **"In the realization that I had achieved"**: Laurence Leamer, *The Kennedy Women: The Saga of an American Family*, p. 280. **"There is something very English"**: HTF, p. 344. **"Nearly as big as Versailles"**: Will Swift, *The Kennedys: Amidst the Gathering Storm*, p. 175. **"The British to me live in the past"**: 1939 recollection, ROSE. **"You had the feeling of an era ending"**: Hank Searls, *The Lost Prince: Young Joe, the Forgotten Kennedy*, pp. 115–17. **"The boat lurched"**: BBC Archive, "Survivors Recall the Sinking of the SS *Athenia*," http://www.bbc.co.uk/archive/ww2outbreak/7924.shtml. **"Everything that I have worked for"**: John Ruggiero, *Neville Chamberlain and the British Rearmament: Pride, Prejudice and Politics* (Westport, CT: Greenwood Press, 1999), p. 221. **"We are fighting to save the whole world"**: Martin Gilbert, *Churchill: The Power of Words*, p. 224. **"Felt no wish to cheer"**: Nigel Hamilton, *JFK: Reckless Youth*, p. 281. **"Winston is back" and "It was a strange experience"**: Carlo D'Este, *Warlord: A Life of Winston Churchill at War, 1874–1945*, pp. 744, 335. **"The occurrence should have a helpful effect"**: Martin Gilbert, *Churchill and America*, p. 175. **"Your impudent lies, Herr Churchill"**: William L. Shirer, *Berlin Diary: The Journal of a Foreign Correspondent, 1934–1941*, p. 40. **JFK dealing with *Athenia* survivors**: "At Sea: Angry Athenians," *Time*, September 28, 1939. **"He was the son of the Ambassador"**: Author's interview with Barbara Rodman Wilson in 2011. **"You can't trust the Germany Navy!" and "It is much better to be on an American boat" with other angry passengers' comments to JFK**: "At Sea: Angry Athenians," *Time*,

September 28, 1939. **"A wisdom and sympathy of a man twice his age"**: Hamilton, *JFK: Reckless Youth*, p. 285. **"It is an eerie experience"**: *HTF*, p. 371. **"Oh, we must get back to school"**: Hamilton, *JFK: Reckless Youth*, p. 282. **"Thanks a lot Daddy"**: Doris Kearns Goodwin, *The Fitzgeralds and the Kennedys: An American Saga*, p. 606. **"Joe was determined"**: Author's 2011 interview with Page Huidekoper Wilson. **"Of course they all wanted to know"** and **"Churchill has energy and brains but no judgment"**: *HTF*, p. 391. **"The Astors surprisingly enough"**: Robert Rhodes James, ed., *Chips: The Diaries of Sir Henry Channon*, p. 204. **"Had to believe in the Devil"**: Evelyn Waugh quote from Alan Brien's *Sunday Times* undated column, KMH. **"A treacherous little bastard"**: *RKT*, p. 48. ("But then," Schlesinger amiably noted, "all of Beaverbrook's best friends thought this about him at one time or another.") **"There would be a great deal to be said"**: John Lukacs, *Churchill: Visionary. Statesman. Historian*, p. 90. **"He is strictly honest and truthful"**: Robert Rhodes James, *Churchill: A Study in Failure, 1900–1939*, p. 326. **"He's a great friend of England's"**: Quentin Reynolds, *A London Diary*, pp. 37–38. **"Mr. Kennedy is not to be criticized"**: Anne Chisholm and Michael Davie, *Lord Beaverbrook: A Life*, p. 370. **"All my papers, my money, and everything else I own is yours"**: *HTF*, p. 378. **"I could see he [Chamberlain] bitterly distrusts Churchill"**: Ibid., pp. 395, 399. **"He has developed into a fine two-handed drinker"**: July 20, 1939, correspondence to President Roosevelt, JPK. **"Remember, Churchill has in America"**: Kennedy correspondence to president, November 3, 1939, FDR. **"It is because you and I occupied similar positions in the World War"**: September 11, 1939, letter from Roosevelt to Churchill, FDR. **"One of the most exhilarating experiences"**: Joseph E. Persico, *Roosevelt's Secret War: FDR and World War II Espionage*, p. 20. **"I resented this by-passing of me"** and concerns about United States being drawn into the war: Diplomatic memoir draft, chap. 11, pp. 2–3, and diplomatic memoir draft, chap. 34, pp. 4–9, JPK. **"Whenever you feel they would be of use"**: John Baylis, *Anglo-American Defence Relations, 1939–1984: The Special Relationship*, p. 2. **"Somewhat pasty"** and **"Eunice would like to go to the party"**: *HTF*, 403–4. **"I'm giving him attention now"**: Warren F. Kimball, ed., *Churchill and Roosevelt: The Complete Correspondence*,

Volume 1, p. 7. **"I'm willing to help them all I can"**: Jon Meacham, *Franklin and Winston: An Intimate Portrait of an Epic Friendship*, p. 34. **"Plates to keep spinning on sticks"**: Edward J. Renehan Jr., *The Kennedys at War: 1937–1945*, p. 128. **"I cannot go against the guy"**: *HTF*, p. 283. **"After 1940 I am going to look"**: Diplomatic memoir draft, chap. 22, p. 8, JPK. **"Don't let anything that comes out of any country"** and **"his discontent over returning to London"**: Richard J. Whalen, *The Founding Father: The Story of Joseph P. Kennedy*, pp. 285–87.

CHAPTER 18: WHILE AMERICA SLEPT

Randolph's appearance at Oxford Union and parody of "Onward Conscript Soldiers": Barbara Leaming, *Jack Kennedy: The Education of a Statesman*, p. 82. **"He claims that he would give it up"**: *HTF*, p. 305. **"Joe was received less enthusiastically"**: Lynne McTaggart, *Kathleen Kennedy: Her Life and Times*, pp. 42–43. **"I wouldn't think of telling him what to do"**: James MacGregor Burns, *John Kennedy: A Political Profile*, p. 58. **"Ought to be doing something"**: "Joseph Kennedy Jr. Begins Navy Training," United Press, (Wilmington, DE) *Sunday Morning Star*, July 13, 1941, p. 5. **"Appeasement sentiments were shared by his two sons"**: December 17, 1940, FBI memo in agency's file on Joseph P. Kennedy, part 7 of 8, p. 4. **"Discuss class influence in England"**: Joan Blair and Clay Blair, *The Search for JFK*, p. 77. **"I wouldn't say my father got me interested in it"** and **"represents more work"**: Richard J. Whalen, *The Founding Father: The Story of Joseph P. Kennedy*, p. 294. **"In light of the present-day war, we are able to wonder"**: Herbert S. Parmet, *Jack: The Struggles of John F. Kennedy*, p. 71. **"A singularly dispassionate statement"**: *RKT*, p. 39. **"I read it before he had finished it up"**: *HTF*, p. 410. **"I think that you better go over the material"**: Michael O'Brien, *John F. Kennedy: A Biography*, p. 107. **"If John Kennedy is characteristic of the younger generation"**: Alan Brinkley, *The Publisher: Henry Luce and His American Century*, p. 422. **"For while it is the book of a lad"**: August 21, 1940, letter to Kennedy, in FDR. **"It occurs to me that there is a lesson for America"**: May 10, 1940, note to Brendan Bracken, JPK. **"But in view of the number of your children"**: August 1940 Bracken reply, JPK. **"I told him that young Jack had finished his book"**: *HTF*, p. 460. **"He evinced a great**

interest": Jock Colville note sent on Churchill's behalf and in JPK. **"A defeat of the Allies may simply be one more step"**: John F. Kennedy, *Why England Slept*, p. xxiii. **"You would be surprised how a book"**: Robert Dallek, *An Unfinished Life: John F. Kennedy, 1917–1963*, p. 66.

CHAPTER 19: WE SHALL FIGHT

"Take the workman" and Kennedy's reply: Jay Moffat and Nancy Harvison Hooker, eds., *The Moffat Papers: Selections from the Diplomatic Journals of Jay Pierrepont Moffat, 1919–1943*, p. 303. **"Get across many unpalatable home truths"**: Will Swift, *The Kennedys: Amidst the Gathering Storm*, p. 225. **"I thought this would give me some protection"**: April 1940 entry in diplomatic memoir draft, chap. 40, p. 43, JPK. **"It would just embarrass us"**: Michael R. Beschloss, *Presidential Courage: Brave Leaders and How They Changed America 1789–1989*, p. 160. **"I just won't go for a third term"**: Nigel Hamilton, *JFK: Reckless Youth*, p. 305. **"If we stirred up some action here in July"**: March 1940 entry in diplomatic memoir draft, chap. 41, pp. 3–4, JPK. **"Monster born of hatred"**: April 1940 entry in diplomatic memoir draft, chap. 40, pp. 32–33, JPK. **"For Christ's sakes, stop trying"**: Moffat and Hooker, eds., *The Moffat Papers: Selections from the Diplomatic Journals of Jay Pierrepont Moffat, 1919–1943*, p. 303. **"Cascade of oratory"**: Henry Pelling, *Winston Churchill*, p. 428. **"If Chamberlain had shown more strength"**: Swift, *The Kennedys: Amidst the Gathering Storm*, p. 136. **"He had signed on for the voyage"**: Harold Macmillan, *The Blast of War, 1939–1945*, p. 61. **"I must have had a great many more real talks"**: R. F. Foster, *Lord Randolph Churchill: A Political Life*, p. 387. **"I could not help" and "It's the letter of an old man"**: Diplomatic memoir draft, chap. 43, pp. 6–10, JPK. **"Felt partly responsible for his new job" and "Eunice went to the party"**: Diplomatic memoir draft, chap. 43, p. 12, JPK. **"I felt as if I were walking with destiny"**: Geoffrey Best, *Churchill: A Study in Greatness*, p. 165. **"Oh, I don't know about that"**: Randolph Churchill and Martin Gilbert, *Winston S. Churchill, Volume 6: Finest Hour, 1939–1941*, p. 306. **"I am so delighted"**: May 11, 1940, letter, PAM. **"God alone knows how great it is"**: Brian Moynahan, "Guarding the Bulldog," October 30, 2005, *Sunday Times* (London). **"At last you have the power"**: Martin Gilbert, *Churchill: A Life*,

p. 645. **"Pluck, his courageous energy and magnificent English"**: Robert Rhodes James, ed., *Chips: The Diaries of Sir Henry Channon*, p. 272. **"This war will be won by carnivores"**: John Pearson, *The Private Lives of Winston Churchill*, p. 283. **"Blood, toil, tears and sweat"**: Winston Churchill and David Cannadine, *Blood, Toil, Tears and Sweat: The Speeches of Winston Churchill*, p. 147. **"Go and pray for me" and "You ought to have cried 'Shame'"**: John Colville, *The Fringes of Power: The Incredible Inside Story of Winston Churchill during World War II*, p. 195, 135. **"I suppose you don't know why"**: Winston S. Churchill, *The Second World War, Volume 1: The Gathering Storm*, p. 665. **"Power to inspire and drive," "I was glad," and "I need his vital and vibrant energy"**: Anne Chisholm and Michael Davie, *Lord Beaverbrook: A Life*, pp. 376–78. **"Lord Beaverbrook is producing the goods"**: Colville, *The Fringes of Power*, p. 148. **"He didn't talk like his old self"**: *HTF*, pp. 445–46. **"After all, if we can't think we are going to win"**: June 24, 1940, diary entry, JPK. **"He is really a very peculiar man"**: May 31, 1940, diary entry, JPK. **"Greeted me warmly"**: Diplomatic memoir draft, chap. 44, pp. 8–14, JPK. **"I couldn't help but think"**: *HTF*, pp. 426–27. **"We need the troops in England anyway" and "It isn't fair to ask us"**: Diplomatic memoir draft, chap. 44, pp. 9–13, JPK. **"Regardless of what Germany does," "We have all got to put on a good front," and "It is the view of my friend"**: *HTF*, pp. 425–28. **"I shall drag the United States in"**: Jon Meacham, *Franklin and Winston: An Intimate Portrait of an Epic Friendship*, p. 51.

CHAPTER 20: A SPY IN THEIR MIDST

Bracken's "a pompous lecture": Winston S. Churchill, *His Father's Son: The Life of Randolph Churchill*, p. 177. **"Her gay conversation was a contrast to the greyness"**: Diplomatic memoir draft, chap. 40, p. 1, JPK. **"JPK in bedroom"**: Sylvia Jukes Morris, *Rage for Fame: The Ascent of Clare Boothe Luce*, p. 372. **"He couldn't keep his mouth shut or his pants on"**: James Reston, *Deadline: A Memoir*, p. 71. **"Johnson's language was guarded"**: *HTF*, p. 430. **"He was always very well-dressed"**: Author's 2011 interview with Page Huidekoper Wilson. **"It was a complete lie of course" and "Ambassador Kennedy was having copies"**: Comments in BBC archival documentary, at http://www

.bbc.co.uk/blogs/adamcurtis/2010/12/wicked_leaks.html. **"We had reached the point of bugging"**: Joseph E. Persico, *Roosevelt's Secret War: FDR and World War II Espionage*, p. 30. **"Churchill was exceptional among British statesmen"**: F. H. Hinsley, "Churchill and the Use of Special Intelligence," in Robert Blake, ed., *Churchill: A Major New Assessment of His Life in Peace and War*, p. 407. **"One day you are speaking to one man"**: Anne De Courcy, *Diana Mosley: Mitford Beauty, British Fascist, Hitler's Angel*, p. 152. **"Under Mosley or some such person"**: John Lukacs, *Five Days in London—May 1940*, p. 183. **"If any doubt existed"**: Randolph Churchill and Martin Gilbert, *Winston S Churchill, Volume 6: Finest Hour, 1939–1941*, p. 378. **"In case Kent says his rooms"**: Ray Bearse and Anthony Read, *Conspirator: The Untold Story of Tyler Kent*, p. 146. **"Both were scantily attired"**: Diplomatic Memoir, chap. 44, pp. 16–18, JPK. **"From the way she behaved"**: May 28, 1940, memo from Franklin Gowen, second secretary of the U.S. embassy, Tyler Kent file, FDR. **"Admittedly immoral purposes"**: Bryan Clough, *State Secrets: The Kent-Wolkoff Affair*, p. 239. **"This is quite a serious situation"**: May 20, 1940, interrogation of Tyler Kent by Scotland Yard investigators in Ambassador Kennedy's office according to transcript, FDR. **"If we had to protect"** and **"practically everything"**: Ray Bearse and Anthony Read, *Conspirator: The Untold Story of Tyler Kent*, pp. 147, 129. **"I was naturally distressed"**: *HTF*, pp. 430–32. **"Nothing like this has ever happened"**: Joseph E. Persico, *Roosevelt's Secret War: FDR and World War II Espionage*, p. 31. **"The Germans did not need any secret service in Europe"**: John H. Waller, *The Unseen War in Europe: Espionage and Conspiracy in the Second World War*, p. 139. **"Kennedy begs us to keep this out of the press"**: Nigel Nicolson, ed., *The Harold Nicolson Diaries*, p. 220. **"If America had been at war"**: Bryan Clough, *State Secrets: The Kent-Wolkoff Affair*, p. 83. **"Churchill may well have known"**: David Stafford, *Churchill and the Secret Service*, p. 199–200. **"A traitor as well as thief"**: Bearse and Read, *Conspirator*, p. 199. **"Frankly and honestly"**: *HTF*, p. 463. **"Ever since the Tyler Kent case"**: George M. Elsey, *An Unplanned Life: A Memoir*, p. 25.

CHAPTER 21: GRACE UNDER FIRE

"We could see the fuzz on the pilot's face": "A Nazi Drops In: Plane Narrowly Misses Kennedy's Home," United Press, *Milwaukee Journal,* October 1, 1940, p. 2. **"It is by far the most unsatisfactory method"** and **"The last three nights in London":** *HTF,* pp. 474. 467. **"I trust that Joe Kennedy":** Robert Rhodes James, ed., *Chips: The Diaries of Sir Henry Channon,* p. 23. **"Taking into account":** September 15, 1940, diary entry, JPK. **"I haven't the slightest doubt":** Diplomatic memoir draft, chap. 47, p. 4, JPK. **"I thought my daffodils":** Richard Collier, *The World in Flames: 1940,* p. 64. **"Randolph had poisoned his father against me":** Diplomatic memoir draft, chap. 46, p. 5, JPK. **"In the secrecy of this room":** Diplomatic memoir draft, chap. 50, pp. 3–4, JPK. **"Knows quite well that I have no standing":** Will Swift, *The Kennedys: Amidst the Gathering Storm,* p. 273. **"Our intention is, whatever happens, to fight on to the end":** Winston S. Churchill, *The Second World War, Volume 2: Their Finest Hour,* p. 56. **"It is of course apparent":** *HTF,* p. 474. **"Well, you certainly picked a nice time":** Diplomatic memoir draft, chap. 46, p. 6. **"Let's get along home":** Anne Chisholm and Michael Davie, *Lord Beaverbrook: A Life,* 1993, p 378. **"I believe we shall make them rue":** Winston S. Churchill, *The Second World War, Volume 2: Their Finest Hour,* p. 449. **"We shall fight on the beaches":** Doris Kearns Goodwin, *No Ordinary Time: Franklin and Eleanor Roosevelt, the Home Front in World War II,* p. 63. **"... And if they do come, we shall hit them on the head with beer bottles":** Collier, *The World in Flames: 1940,* p. 91. **"It is refreshing":** John Colville, *The Fringes of Power: The Incredible Inside Story of Winston Churchill During World War II,* p. 135. **"It was the nation and the race":** Tom Hutchinson, *The Battle of Britain: The True Story of Those Dramatic Four Months in 1940,* p. 7. **"If he felt that way about it" citing Bracken:** August 6, 1940, diary entry, JPK. **"Never in the field of human conflict":** David Cannadine, *In Churchill's Shadow: Confronting the Past in Modern Britain,* p. 92. **"Upon this battle":** Robert Rhodes James, ed., *Winston S. Churchill: His Complete Speeches, 1897–1963,* p. 6238. **"I had them all signed for the children":** *HTF,* p. 467. **"While I know there are things":** July 10, 1940, correspondence with Churchill (sent along with a Virginia ham), JPK. **"My God, you make me feel":** David E.

Koskoff, *Joseph P. Kennedy: A Life and Times*, p. 249. **"I made it clear in the presence of all"**: Diplomatic memoir draft, chap. 49, pp. 1–2, JPK. **"Will they be able to come across the ocean" and "Churchill asked me how many people"**: *HTF*, p. 463–65. **"The danger to the world was Germany and not Russia"**: Diplomatic memoir draft, chap. 36, pp. 1–2, JPK. **"You know that I was the only one"**: *HTF*, p. 461.

CHAPTER 22: CRASH LANDING

"I'd rather see you": July 8, 1940, Clare Boothe Luce cable to JPK, in CBL. **Effort to stop FDR third term and Clare Boothe Luce's London visit with Kennedy**: C. L. Sulzberger, *The Last of the Giants*, p. 629. **"Treated Clare cavalierly"**: David Halberstam, *The Powers That Be*, p. 63. **"I think of you constantly" and "a masterpiece"**: July 8, 1940, Clare Boothe Luce cable to JPK, in CBL. **"I've just got the teeniest, weeniest suspicions" and "136 air raids"**: October 1, 1940, JPK correspondence, CBL. **"I know too well your private opinions"**: Michael Beschloss, *Presidential Courage: Brave Leaders and How They Changed America, 1789–1989*, pp. 187–88. **"We read in the paper," "defeatist point of view," and "I know what an increasingly severe strain"**: *HTF*, pp. 474–77. **"I don't want a new man over here"**: Beschloss, *Presidential Courage*, p. 181. **"I reminded him that I was having a row"**: Nigel Hamilton, *JFK: Reckless Youth*, p. 363. **Bracken giving intercepted JPK material to Hopkins**: Sulzberger, *The Last of the Giants*, p. 630. **"These plans depend on keeping the right man"**: Herbert S. Parmet, *Jack: The Struggles of John F. Kennedy*, p. 81. **"When you land tell the press"**: Laurence Leamer, *The Kennedy Men: 1901–1963*, p. 153. **"One may wonder what I thought"**: Lord Longford, *Kennedy*, p. 22. **"The president sent you, a Catholic" and "For a man as busy as you"**: Charles Higham, *Rose: The Life and Times of Rose Fitzgerald Kennedy*, pp. 222–23. **"Joe did most of the talking"**: October 29, 1940, note marked "Visit to Washington," ROSE. **"Since it is not possible for me to see the president alone"**: Beschloss, *Presidential Courage*, p. 184. **"We then discussed the status of the war"**: Diplomatic memoir draft, chap. 51, pp. 4–5, JPK. **"Soft-soap"**: Will Swift, *The Kennedys: Amidst the Gathering Storm*, p. 264. **"Clare tried to get hold of him"**: Leamer, *The Kennedy Men*, p. 156. **"War would stop if it were not for**

Churchill": Charles A. Lindbergh, *The Wartime Journals of Charles A. Lindbergh*, p. 420. **"I have said this before"**: Peter Collier and David Horowitz. *The Kennedys: An American Drama*, p. 88, and James Mac-Gregor Burns, *John Kennedy: A Political Profile*, p. 46. **"My wife and I have given nine hostages to fortune"**: Conrad Black, *Franklin Delano Roosevelt: Champion of Freedom*, p. 593. **"I certainly don't begrudge you"**: November 6, 1940, diary entry, JPK. **"Mr. President, Churchill is keeping this fight going" and "theory that the stomach trouble"**: December 1, 1940, diary entry, JPK. **"Temperamental Irish boy"**: March 3, 1941, correspondence with son-in-law John Boettiger, FDR. **"Well that explodes"**: December 1, 1940, diary entry, JPK. **"The best informed men that I have met"**: December 6, 1940, letter to son John, JPK. **"Democracy is finished in England"**: David Nunnerley, *President Kennedy and Britain*, p. 21. **"While he was here, his suave, monotonous smile"**: December 11, 1940, *NY Journal American* article quoting British columnist A. J. Cummings, JPK. **"I think in that Jack is not doing anything"**: *RKT*, p. 40. **"It must be remembered continually" and "it was felt he was a gloom monger"**: December 6, 1940, John F. Kennedy letter to his father, JFK.

PART III: WARTIME
"And how can man die better / Than facing fearful odds": Thomas Babington Macaulay, *Lays of Ancient Rome*, p. 56. **"Arm yourselves, and be ye men of valour, and be in readiness for the conflict"**: Henning Krabbe, *Voices from Britain: Broadcast History, 1939–45*, p. 35.

CHAPTER 23: THE HOUSE OF CHURCHILL BEARS A SON
"I hope the House will pardon me": *Parliamentary Debates: Official Report*, Volume 367, London: H.M. Stationery Office, 1941, p. 155. **"The sample he has given us"**: Brian Roberts, *Randolph: A Study of Churchill's Son*, p. 195. **"Fancy trying to read me"**: Winston S. Churchill, *His Father's Son: The Life of Randolph Churchill*, p. 174. **"One of the most objectionable people"**: John Colville, *The Fringes of Power: The Incredible Inside Story of Winston Churchill during World War II*, p. 177. **"I am sure y[ou]r best & indeed *only* course"**: Winston S. Churchill, *His Father's Son: The Life of Randolph Churchill*, p.175.

"Of course, Old Winston was very much hoping": Ogden interview, Library of Congress unprocessed file, Group 1 of 3, p. 2, PAM. **"I had to get my sleep"**: August 22, 1980, Pamela Churchill Harriman interview, p. 1, WMP. **"But Papa, what can I do?"**: William Manchester, *The Last Lion: Winston Spencer Churchill, Visions of Glory, 1874–1932*, p. 6. **"The first time you meet Winston"**: Randolph Churchill and Martin Gilbert, *Winston S. Churchill, Volume 2: Young Statesman, 1901–1914*, p. 109. **"His father was furious"**: Ogden interview, Library of Congress unprocessed file, Group 1 of 3, pp. 16–18, PAM. **"They couldn't find him"**: Ibid., pp. 2–3. **Lord Beaverbrook and Brendan Bracken stood as godfathers**: Mary Soames, *Clementine Churchill: The Biography of a Marriage*, p. 300. **"Poor infant"**: Winston S. Churchill, *His Father's Son*, p. 181. **"I've never seen the family look so happy"**: Mary Soames, *A Daughter's Tale: The Memoir of Winston Churchill's Youngest Child*, p. 169.

CHAPTER 24: NEW ALLIANCES

"You should never harness a thoroughbred": Charles Lysaght, *Brendan Bracken*, p. 189. **"An ill-fed horse"**: David Stafford, *Roosevelt and Churchill: Men of Secrets*, p. 33. **"Brendan said that Hopkins"**: John Colville, *The Fringes of Power: The Incredible Inside Story of Winston Churchill during World War II*, pp. 331–33. **"His man Friday"**: Randolph Churchill and Martin Gilbert, *Winston S Churchill, Volume 6: Finest Hour, 1939–41*, p. 981. **"I told him there was a feeling in some quarters"**: Max Hastings, *Winston's War: Churchill 1940–1945*, p. 154. **"Help Britain, but make damn sure"**: Colville, *The Fringes of Power*, p. 347. **"I have never had such an enjoyable time"**: Jon Meacham, *Franklin and Winston: An Intimate Portrait of an Epic Friendship*, pp. 84–87. **"I don't give a damn about the cottages"** and **"This little shriveled creature with a dead cigarette"**: August 22, 1980, Pamela Churchill interview, p. 5, WMP. **"A catalytic agent between two PRIMA DONNAS"**: Robert E. Sherwood, *Roosevelt and Hopkins: An Intimate History, Volume 1*, p. 289. **"Harry had an extraordinary faculty"**: August 22, 1980, Pamela Churchill interview, p. 5, WMP. **"Raeburnesque red curls and freckles"**: Cecil Beaton, *The Years Between: Diaries 1939–1940*, p. 53. **"Great bulldog jaw and penetrating stare"**: "Winston Churchill: He

Inspires an Empire in Its Hour of Need," *Life*, January 27, 1941, p. 59. **"I cannot believe"**: David Stafford, *Roosevelt and Churchill: Men of Secrets*, p. 51. **"Randolph, who had thought he was well-regarded, burst into tears"**: Anita Leslie, *Randolph: The Biography of Winston Churchill's Son*, p. 49. **"All the wives said"**: Winston S. Churchill, *His Father's Son: The Life of Randolph Churchill*, p. 185. **"How wonderful it would be"**: Winston S. Churchill, *The Second World War, Volume 2: Their Finest Hour*, p. 243. **"We seem to have gone different ways"**: Randolph Churchill, "Letters from Evelyn Waugh," *Encounter*, July 1968, p. 3. **"A good commando fighter"**: Evelyn Waugh, "Commando Raid on Bardia," *Life*, November 17, 1941, p. 63. **When Waugh got in trouble for the unauthorized *Life* profile**: Based on Paula Byrne, *Mad World: Evelyn Waugh and the Secrets of Brideshead*, p. 281. **"We have been at sea a week now"**: Martin Stannard, *Evelyn Waugh: The Later Years, 1939–1966*, p. 26. **"Drawn from various famous regiments"**: Kenneth T. Downs essay, in Kay Halle, *The Grand Original: Portraits of Randolph Churchill by His Friends*, p. 112. **"The company's commander's course"**: Randolph Churchill, "Letters from Evelyn Waugh," *Encounter*, July 1968, p. 4. **"He did not care if he was killed"**: Anita Leslie, *Randolph: The Biography of Winston Churchill's Son*, p. 51. **Big bet lost to Peter Fitzwilliam, "You must promise me," "bombshell," and "little Jenny"**: Ogden interview, Library of Congress unprocessed file, Group 1 of 3, p. 5, PAM. **"I thought, 'What the hell do I do?' "**: Ibid., p. 6; Beaverbrook bailout also in Winston S. Churchill, *His Father's Son*, pp. 187–88. **"You must not get under the Beaverbrook spell"**: August 22, 1980, Pamela Churchill interview, pp. 2–3, WMP. **"If you want me to give you a check"**: Ogden interview, Library of Congress unprocessed file, Group 1 of 3, p. 6, PAM. **"Smelled danger" and "Max had to have control"**: Ibid. **"Poor Pamela will have to go to work"**: Sally Bedell Smith, *Reflected Glory: The Life of Pamela Churchill Harriman*, pp. 75, 94. **"That was the first realization in my life"**: Ogden interview, Library of Congress unprocessed file, Group 1 of 3, p. 6, PAM. **"Winston often speaks about you"**: May 15, 1941, Brendan Bracken correspondence, HLH. **"Nothing will be kept from you"**: Rudy Abramson, *Spanning the Century: The Life of W. Averell Harriman, 1891–1986*, p. 280. **"She knows everything in London"**: Charles J. Kelly, *Tex McCrary:*

Wars-Women-Politics, An Adventurous Life across the American Century,
p. 41. **"He [Max] made a great fuss over me":** August 22, 1980, Averell Harriman interview, p. 33, WMP. **"The best-looking man I had
ever seen" and "Tell me about Max Beaverbrook":** Ogden interview,
Library of Congress unprocessed file, Group 1 of 3, pp. 7–9, PAM. Beaverbrook manipulation of Pam and Averell relationship also in Anne
Chisholm and Michael Davie, *Lord Beaverbrook: A Life,* p. 500.

CHAPTER 25: "THE MASTERS OF OUR FATE"

**"Men are not prisoners of fate, but only prisoners of their own
minds":** President Franklin D. Roosevelt's Pan-American Day speech,
April 15, 1939. **"This is a strange Christmas Eve":** Winston Churchill,
The Great Republic: A History of America, p. 336. **"We are all in the
same boat now":** Terry Golway, *Together We Cannot Fail: How FDR
Led the Nation from Darkness to Victory,* p. 199. **"Fought to the last des-
perate inch":** Kay Halle, ed., *Winston Churchill on America and Brit-
ain: A Selection of His Thoughts on Anglo-American Relations,* p. 16. **"I
went to bed":** Mary Soames, *Clementine Churchill: The Biography of a
Marriage,* p. 310. **"They looked like two little boys playing soldier":**
David Stafford, *Roosevelt and Churchill: Men of Secrets,* pp. 125–27.
"Pray enter": Kay Halle, *The Irrepressible Churchill: Winston's World,
Wars and Wit,* p. 181. **"No lover ever studied every whim":** Martin
Gilbert, *Churchill and America,* p. 133. **"I cannot help reflecting that
if my father had been American":** "Churchill's American Ancestors,"
Life, February 27, 1950, p. 73. **"Now we are the masters of our fate":**
Winston Churchill, *The Unrelenting Struggle: War Speeches by the Rt.
Hon. Winston S. Churchill,* p. 356. **"I thought your Washington speech
the best" and "That would mean publishing to the world":** Martin
Gilbert, *Winston S. Churchill, Volume 7: Road to Victory, 1941–45,* pp. 30–
31. **"If we lose Churchill":** Anne Chisholm and Michael Davie, *Lord
Beaverbrook: A Life,* pp. 424–26. **"In this great crisis":** December 7,
1941, cable cited in diplomatic memoir draft, chap. 52, JPK. **"From the
moment we became allies":** Gilbert, *Road to Victory,* p. 53. **"I hate all
those God-damned Englishmen from Churchill on down":** Edward
J. Renehan Jr., *The Kennedys at War: 1937–1945,* p. 180. **"More evidence
of regrettable activities," Kennedy warnings in Hollywood, and**

Cleugh's assessment: January 1941 British Press Services dossier on Kennedy in National Archives, in Kew, Ref: FO371/26217. **"Tattle tale," November 19, 1940, letter by Fairbanks:** FDR; also Louis Pizzitola, *Hearst Over Hollywood: Power, Passion, and Propaganda in the Movies,* p. 385. **"What you say fits in with the general picture":** Roosevelt November 25, 1940, letter to Fairbanks, FDR. **"We should never take such a grave step just because we hate Hitler and love Churchill":** "Demand Facts on War Plans, Says Kennedy," INS, *Milwaukee Sentinel,* May 25, 1941. **"What you are doing is vital" and JFK's $100 contribution:** Justus D. Doenecke, *In Danger Undaunted: The Anti-Interventionist Movement of 1940–41,* pp. 17, 58; also in John Lukacs, *The Duel: The Eighty-Day Struggle between Churchill and Hitler,* p. 201. **"Well, not too much but I would have much more confidence in Beaverbrook":** *HTF,* p. 529. **"We talked about Jimmy":** January 21, 1941, diary entry, JPK. **"Why don't you take over my United Artists contract":** December 3, 1940, Jimmy Roosevelt letter, JPK. **"Offers worse trials":** December 11, 1940, reply to Jimmy Roosevelt, JPK. **"I am still one of those guys":** January 3, 1941, Kennedy letter to Boettiger, in FDR. **"Somehow or other, I feel sure":** January 31, 1941, Boettiger letter to Kennedy, in FDR. **"It is, I think, a little pathetic":** March 3, 1941, presidential letter to son-in-law Boettiger, in FDR. **"With that baby stare of his," "I am convinced that he knew it's Hopkins," and other details of Beaverbrook-Kennedy conversation:** *HTF,* pp. 535–36. **"There is a real feeling here," "I do not intend to be the only one among them wearing coward's tweeds," and "Father does not always know best":** Edward J. Renehan Jr., *The Kennedys at War: 1937–1945,* pp. 183, 191, and 200. **"I haven't heard from him for simply ages":** *HTF,* p. 532. **"The old goat":** Seymour Hersh, *The Dark Side of Camelot,* pp. 83–85. **"He can help me a lot":** Laurence Leamer, *The Kennedy Men: 1901–1963,* p. 174. **"Pa Kennedy no like":** Lynne McTaggart, *Kathleen Kennedy: Her Life and Times,* p. 108. **"Damn it, Jack":** Herbert S. Parmet, *Jack: The Struggles of John F. Kennedy,* p. 90. **"I am not going to try and make you change":** Ronald Kessler, *The Bureau: The Secret History of the FBI,* p. 135. **"He has become disgusted with the desk jobs":** June 20, 1942, letter to son Joseph Jr., JPK. **"If Joe is frank":** "Pearson and Allen's Washington Merry-Go-Round," *Lodi*

News-Sentinel, January 9, 1942, p. 4. **"I don't want to appear"**: March 4, 1942, Kennedy letter to president, in FDR. **"Stepping up the great increase in our shipbuilding"**: March 7, 1942, presidential letter to Kennedy, in JPK. **"Without a definite assignment"**: March 12, 1942, Kennedy letter to president, in JPK. **"I am withstanding all efforts"**: *HTF,* p. 513.

CHAPTER 26: REPLACEMENTS

"The New Hampshire Lincoln": Jack Stinnett, "Envoy Typical of 1941 Spirit," Associated Press, February 15, 1941. **"Send us John Winant"**: Bernard Bellush, *He Walked Alone: A Biography of John Gilbert Winant,* p. 155. **"House agents have an exaggerated notion"**: April 30, 1941, Bracken note to Winant, in FDR. **"You have taught me"**: Undated note (1945?) from Winant to Churchill, in FDR. **"Winant had fallen rather ethereally in love"**: Roy Jenkins, *Churchill: A Biography,* p. 653. **"You cheeky bitch!"**: Sarah Churchill, *Keep On Dancing: An Autobiography,* p. 58. **"Well, at least he had the pleasure of murdering his son-in-law"**: Paul Johnson, *Churchill,* p. 128. **"War is a game played with a smiling face"**: Sarah Churchill, *A Thread in the Tapestry,* p. 63. **"Love affair which my father suspected but about which we did not speak"**: Sarah Churchill, *Keep On Dancing,* p. 159. **"A certain naval person has spent a great deal of time"**: April 3, 1941, Winant note to president, in FDR. **"Almost an appendage of the Prime Minister"**: John Colville, *Winston Churchill and His Inner Circle,* p. 121. **"Averell not only took the glamour out of Winant's job"**: Rudy Abramson, *Spanning the Century: The Life of W. Averell Harriman, 1891–1986,* p. 303. **"I have been by-passed continuously"**: Fraser J. Harbutt, *The Iron Curtain: Churchill, America and the Origins of the Cold War,* p. 22. **"Randolph's wife had no intention of sticking"**: Brian Roberts, *Randolph: A Study of Churchill's Son,* p. 230. **"I think her problem with Randolph"**: August 22, 1980, Pamela Harriman interview, p. 30, WMP. **"A wonderful girl, my age"**: Abramson, *Spanning the Century,* p. 306. **"Of course, I'm not a fool!"**: Ogden interview, Library of Congress unprocessed file, Group 1 of 3, pp. 11–12, PAM. **"Kitten eyes full of innocent fun"**: Michael Gross, "Mother of the Clinton Court," *New York,* January 18, 1993, p. 29. **"Pam is also a bitch"** and **"There's a very**

rich American": Marie Brenner, "To War in Silk Stockings," *Vanity Fair,* November 11, 2011. **"Enjoys my complete confidence"**: Martin Gilbert, *The Churchill War Papers: The Ever-Widening War, 1941,* p. 753. **"Randolph thought him shrewd and wonderful"**: Anita Leslie, *Randolph: The Biography of Winston Churchill's Son,* p. 56. **"Randolph's post as officially described"**: Soames, *Winston and Clementine,* p. 457. **"Good friend" and "The United States are giving us more help every day"**: June 8, 1941, letter from Winston to Randolph, CHUR. **"I have been tremendously impressed by Harriman"**: Abramson, *Spanning the Century,* p. 314. **"I found him absolutely charming"**: John Pearson, *The Private Lives of Winston Churchill,* p. 303. **"I wonder if he will like me?" and "the President is intrigued and likes him enormously"**: John Charmley. *Churchill: The End of Glory—A Political Biography,* p. 459. **"I know Churchill put Harriman in her way"**: Sally Bedell Smith, *Reflected Glory: The Life of Pamela Churchill Harriman,* p. 106. **"He only mentioned it once"**: Arthur M. Schlesinger Jr., *Journals: 1952–2000,* pp. 342–43. **"You know they are saying a lot of things"**: Ogden interview, Library of Congress unprocessed file, Group 3 of 3, p. 519, PAM. **"In retrospect, Pam feels"**: Schlesinger, *Journals: 1952–2000,* p. 343. **"I described Max to him"**: Ogden interview, Library of Congress unprocessed file, Group 1 of 3, pp. 18, 12. **"Even his best friends are scared of him"**: Anne Chisholm and Michael Davie, *Lord Beaverbrook: A Life,* p. 404. **"Just like Max"**: John Colville, *The Fringes of Power: The Incredible Inside Story of Winston Churchill During World War II,* p. 555. **"The PM considers that Beaverbrook"**: Chisholm and Davie, *Lord Beaverbrook,* p. 445. **"1943 will be the best year"**: January 4, 1943, presidential correspondence with Beaverbrook, in FDR. **"It is the general view that Bevan"**: A. J. P. Taylor, *Beaverbrook,* p. 539. **"Favored as I was with a ringside seat"**: Kennedy introduction to Lord Beaverbrook, *The Three Keys to Success,* p. iii. **"Lord Spitfire" and "You will be talked of even more widely"**: Colville, *The Fringes of Power,* pp. 555, 344. **"Never liked or trusted Max"**: Ogden interview, Library of Congress unprocessed file, Group 1 of 3, p. 19, PAM. **"Exorcise this bottle Imp"**: Richard Alexander Hough, *Winston and Clementine: The Triumphs and Tragedies of the Churchills,* p. 459. **"I never thought he was as loyal"**: Harriman August 22, 1980, interview, WMP.

CHAPTER 27: THE CHURCHILL CLUB

"The winds and waves": Edward Gibbon, *The History of the Decline and Fall of the Roman Empire*, volume 5 (London: Longman, Rees, 1826), p. 423. **"I always avoid prophesying beforehand" and "we have to thank the military intuition"**: Robert Rhodes James, ed., *Winston S. Churchill: His Complete Speeches, 1897–1963*, pp. 6738, 6781. **"Never forget that when History looks back"**: Mary Soames, *Winston and Clementine: The Personal Letters of the Churchills*, p. 486. **"He is a candidate for the fourth term" and "We would like to see Roosevelt re-elected"**: *HTF*, pp. 556–57. **"In Washington, Churchill certainly seems"**: Anne Chisholm and Michael Davie, *Lord Beaverbrook: A Life*, p. 445. **"I had two fights" and "I reminded Beaverbrook"**: *HTF*, p. 557. **"Kennedy makes attacks"**: Jon Meacham, *Franklin and Winston: An Intimate Portrait of an Epic Friendship*, p. 290. **"Max is back"**: September 1943 Pamela Churchill letter to Hopkins, HLH. **"Kick is very keen to go over"**: Lynne McTaggart, *Kathleen Kennedy: Her Life and Times*, p. 77. **"I know when she was working"**: Author's 2011 interview with Page Huidekoper Wilson. **"She is heart-whole and fancy-free"**: Undated "Smart Set—Hat's Off" column, JPK. **"Everyone is very surprised"**: Laurence Leamer, *The Kennedy Women*, p. 362. **"He's very good company"**: July 29, 1943, Kathleen Kennedy letter to brother Jack, JPK. **"She is surrounded by her old friends"**: July 7, 1943, Tony Rosslyn correspondence, JPK. **"The steadiest battler"**: Kennedy correspondence with Tony Rosslyn, in JPK. **"London's glamour girl"**: Sally Bedell Smith, *Reflected Glory: The Life of Pamela Churchill Harriman*, p. 115. **"We find that the majority"**: September 1943 Pamela Churchill letter, HLH. **"The cherished heritage of the English-speaking peoples"**: Description of Churchill Club in PAM. **"I must say"**: Mark Amory, ed., *The Letters of Evelyn Waugh*, p. 349. **"The chic ones"**: August 22, 1980, Pamela Harriman interview, p. 32, WMP. **Winston's encounter with composer Irving Berlin**: Kay Halle, *The Irrepressible Churchill: Winston's World, Wars, and Wit*, p. 218; and in Ogden interview, Library of Congress unprocessed file, Group 1 of 3, pp. 15–16, PAM. **"Help Pam straighten herself out"**: Marie Brenner, "To War in Silk Stockings," *Vanity Fair*, November 11, 2011. **"Incidentally the Harriman Mission"**: Letter to Harriman dated September 21

(1944?), PAM. **"The fact that I was in love"**: Ogden interview, Library of Congress unprocessed file, Group 1 of 3, p. 9, PAM. **"This admirer is the combined age"**: Rose Fitzgerald Kennedy, *Times to Remember,* p. 290. **"Of course I know he"**: July 29, 1943, Kathleen Kennedy letter to her brother Jack, in JPK.

CHAPTER 28: "HIS HEART'S DESIRE"

"Courage is the ladder": *Reader's Digest Quotable Quotes*, p. 76. **"He looked very handsome"** and **"Do what you can to see"**: Sylvia Jukes Morris, *Rage for Fame: The Ascent of Clare Boothe Luce*, pp. 444–45. **"Ann always got the feeling"**: C-SPAN *Booknotes* interview with Sylvia Jukes Morris, July 27, 1997; also Morris, *Rage for Fame*, p. 436. **"I look like hell, but my stomach is a thing of beauty"**: Doris Kearns Goodwin, *The Fitzgeralds and the Kennedys: An American Saga*, p. 632. **"The great time I had last evening"**: December 20, 1940, John F. Kennedy letter, CBL. **"A great and prophetic book"**: "Churchill on Lea," *Newburgh Evening News*, December 6, 1961, p. 4. **"spent several hours with her"**: February 16, 1942, Rose Kennedy letter, JPK. **"He has everything a boy needs"** and **"Heavens knows"**: Nigel Hamilton, *JFK: Reckless Youth*, pp. 464–65. **"Has much better than an even chance"**: October 1, 1942, letter to Lord Beaverbrook in JPK. **"You will get there"** and **"Beaverbrook might be the logical successor to Churchill"**: Hamilton, *JFK: Reckless Youth*, pp. 473, 466–68. **"I couldn't have been more pleased"**: September 29, 1943, John F. Kennedy letter, CBL. **"Jack has been sent to the Pacific"**: March 2, 1943, Rose Kennedy letter, CBL. **"Although we had little knowledge"**: Winston S. Churchill, *The Second World War, Volume 5: Closing the Ring*, pp. 17–21. **"Kathleen reports that even a fortune-teller"**: Goodwin, *The Fitzgeralds and the Kennedys*, p. 651. **"This is how it feels to be killed"**: James MacGregor Burns, *John Kennedy: A Political Profile*, p. 62. **"Jack Kennedy, Ambassador's son, was on the same boat"**: John Hersey, "Survival," in A. J. Liebling, ed., *The New Yorker Book of War Pieces*, p. 65. **"You've got to hand it to the British"**: Goodwin, *The Fitzgeralds and the Kennedys*, p. 657. **"Good-luck piece"**: October 20, 1943, John F. Kennedy letter, CBL. **"He is really at home"**: Michael O'Brien, *John F. Kennedy: A Biography,* p. 166. **"I myself am completely"**: *HTF*, p. 568. **"This is a short note to

tell you that I am alive": O'Brien, *John F. Kennedy,* p. 161. **"People get so used to talking about billions of dollars"**: Joan Blair and Clay Blair, *The Search for JFK,* p. 283. **"I wrote within a few days of speaking"**: October 30, 1943, letter to Joseph Kennedy, CBL. **"It was involuntary"**: Arthur M. Schlesinger Jr., *A Thousand Days: John F. Kennedy in the White House,* p. 114. **"What a splendid story"**: November 6, 1943, Lord Beaverbrook letter, JPK. **"I was terribly moved"**: June 26, 1944, letter to Kay Halle, KMH. **"You will wish"**: June 22, 1944, letter to John F. Kennedy, CBL. **"Never again must we succumb"**: "International: The Old Adam," *Time,* July 24, 1944. **"What a wonderful boy Jack"**: June 12, 1944, letter to Joseph Kennedy, CBL. **"I thought that I had become hardened"**: January 11, 1944, John F. Kennedy letter, CBL. **"It just shows how ironic life can be"**: January 12, 1944, Kathleen Kennedy letter, JPK.

CHAPTER 29: STRATAGEMS OF HELL

"The Father knows the Son": John Milton, *The Complete Poetry and Essential Prose of John Milton* (New York: Random House, 2009), p. 640. **"Have the doctors gone to bed?"**: Anita Leslie, *Randolph: The Biography of Winston Churchill's Son,* p. 80. **"I am afraid I shall have to stay"**: Winston S. Churchill, *The Second World War, Volume 5: Closing the Ring,* p. 373. **"Once he opened his eyes"**: Sarah Churchill, *A Thread in the Tapestry,* p. 69. **"I think they [Germany] are now convinced"**: Martin Gilbert, *Winston S. Churchill, Volume 7: Road to Victory, 1941–45,* p. 385. **"This is the Parliament of Munich"**: Associated Press, "Churchill Confidence Vote Today," *Schenectady* (NY) *Gazette,* January 29, 1942, p. 4. **"Before the honorable and gallant Member"**: John Pearson, *The Private Lives of Winston Churchill,* p. 309. **"Do not speak to me"**: John Charmley, *Churchill: The End of Glory—A Political Biography,* pp. 482–83. **"It was maddening for him"**: Leslie, *Randolph,* p. 74. **"I grieve that he has done this"**: Mary Soames, *Clementine Churchill: The Biography of a Marriage,* pp. 314–15. **"Not at all"**: Kay Halle, *The Grand Original: Portraits of Randolph Churchill by His Friends,* pp. 46–47. **"Just in case I hesitate"**: Leslie, *Randolph,* pp. 60–61. **"Thank God the bloody thing opened"**: Virginia Cowles, *The Phantom Major: The Story of David Stirling and His Desert Com-*

mand, p. 124. **"Of course I do not wish to hamper you in any way"**: Winston S. Churchill, *His Father's Son: The Life of Randolph Churchill,* pp. 206–10. **"Why are you going so much faster"**: Leslie, *Randolph,* p. 61. **"The crack of the detonator"** and **"We could hardly have made more noise"**: Fitzroy Maclean, *Eastern Approaches,* pp. 213–14, 223. **"The situation's splendid"**: Cecil Beaton, *The Years Between: Diaries 1939–1940,* p. 183. **"It is very disappointing"**: Gilbert, *Road to Victory,* p. 136. **"And if we're unlucky"**: "Young Churchill Says War Will End in 2 More Years," Associated Press, July 22, 1942. **"One of the most class-conscious and snob-ridden"**: Kenneth Harris, "The Weight of Expectation," *NYT,* August 31, 1997. **"Is a great treasure and blessing to us all"**: Gilbert, *Road to Victory,* p. 101. **"I had absolutely no knowledge"**: Ogden interview, Library of Congress unprocessed file, Group 1 of 3, p. 12, PAM. **"She hates him so much"** and **"I suppose urging her to bear her burden bravely"**: Michael Davie, *The Diaries of Evelyn Waugh, Part 2,* p. 525. **"There was an aura"**: Ann M. Sperber, *Murrow: His Life and Times,* p. 244. **"Pam liked to go around with men"**: Pamela Warrick, "This Girl Just Wanted to Have Fun," *Los Angeles Times,* November 4, 1996. **"That very strong Churchill quality of determination"**: Brian Roberts, *Randolph: A Study of Churchill's Son,* p. 177. **"Randolph is treating our darling Pamela badly"**: Ogden interview, Library of Congress unprocessed file, Group 1 of 3, p. 12, PAM. **"I rather think Randolph is trying"**: Mary Soames, *Winston and Clementine: The Personal Letters of the Churchills,* p. 481. **"Through the years I realized"**: Ogden interview, Library of Congress unprocessed file, Group 1 of 3, p. 12, PAM. **"So many brave young men going to their death tonight"**: Sally Bedell Smith, *Reflected Glory: The Life of Pamela Churchill Harriman,* p. 113. **"They were very, very understanding about that"**: Ogden interview, Library of Congress unprocessed file, Group 3 of 3, p. 515, PAM. **"Harry Hopkins always told me"**: Ibid., p. 517. **"The most beautiful woman in London"**: William Walton April 23, 1945, correspondence, PAM. **"Had condoned adultery beneath their own roof"**: Rudy Abramson, *Spanning the Century: The Life of W. Averell Harriman, 1891–1986,* p. 316. **"It was extremely painful to him"**: Leslie, *Randolph,* p. 71. **"Not only did these events destroy my parents' marriage"**: Winston S. Churchill, *His Father's Son,* pp. 202–3.

"I think the greatest misfortune in R's life": Jon Meacham, *Franklin and Winston: An Intimate Portrait of an Epic Friendship*, p. 173. **"I have made it clear that"** and **"He is a lonely figure"**: Gilbert, *Road to Victory*, pp. 600, 887. **"I grieve so much"**: Martin Gilbert, *Churchill: A Life*, p. 863.

CHAPTER 30: TESTS OF FAITH

"I know that one goes into a war": Selina Hastings, *Evelyn Waugh: A Biography*, p. 407. **"If we are together, nothing is impossible"**: Kay Halle, ed., *Winston Churchill on America and Britain: A Selection of His Thoughts on Anglo-American Relations*, p. 1; also see Martin Gilbert, *Churchill and America*, p. 283. **"Soft underbelly of the crocodile"**: Robin Edmonds, *The Big Three: Churchill, Roosevelt and Stalin in Peace and War*, p. 301. **"We must be careful not to bomb the Pope"**: John Colville, *The Fringes of Power: The Incredible Inside Story of Winston Churchill during World War II*, p. 284. **"I cannot see any reason why"**: Martin Gilbert, *Winston S. Churchill, Volume 7: Road to Victory, 1941–45*, p. 458. **"I am sending the following message"**: Warren F. Kimball, *Churchill and Roosevelt: Alliance Forged, November 1942–February 1944*, p. 319. **"In my long talks"**: Mary Soames, *Speaking for Themselves: The Personal Letters of Winston and Clementine Churchill*, p. 482. **"In my view it is the Germans"**: Gilbert, *Road to Victory*, p. 731. **"Do you realise"**: John Keegan, *Winston Churchill: A Life*, p. 165. **"The Americans could not understand"**: Terry H. Anderson, *The United States, Great Britain, and the Cold War, 1944–1947*, p. 199. **"He [Churchill] began the connection with the highest hopes"**: Richard M. Ketchum, *The Borrowed Years: 1938–1941*, p. 598. **"Forces have been unleashed"**: "Stalin Pictured as Peace Power: Joseph P. Kennedy Urges Smaller Navy," Associated Press, *Toledo Blade*, May 23, 1944. **"Where's Evelyn Waugh?"** and **"I can't go to Croatia"**: Kay Halle, *The Grand Original: Portraits of Randolph Churchill by His Friends*, pp. 46–47; also see Randolph Churchill, "Letters from Evelyn Waugh," *Encounter*, July 1968, p. 2. **"Warrior-ambassador"**: David Pryce-Jones, *Evelyn Waugh and His World*, p. 140. **"On operations I knew him"**: Fitzroy Maclean, *Eastern Approaches*, p. 407. **"I explained to him that the whole trend today"**: June 13, 1944, Randolph letter to WSC, CHAR 20/166, CHUR. "I

thought Captain Waugh's reputation": Ned Sherrin, *Oxford Diction-ary of Humorous Quotations*, p. 137. **"The trouble, you know"**: David Pryce-Jones, *Evelyn Waugh and His World*, pp. 134, 139; also see Paula Byrne, *Mad World: Evelyn Waugh and the Secrets of Brideshead*, p. 291. **"Confused talk"**: Anita Leslie, *Randolph: The Biography of Winston Churchill's Son*, pp. 88–91. **"I am very happy that Randolph has come through"**: Jon Meacham, *Franklin and Winston: An Intimate Portrait of an Epic Friendship*, p. 286. **"Were very close, almost inseparable"**: Halle, *The Grand Original*, p. 95. **"The retelling of memorable say-ings"**: Martin Stannard, *Evelyn Waugh: The Later Years 1939–1966*, p. 122. **"Christ, God is *a shit!*"**: Pryce-Jones, *Evelyn Waugh and His World*, pp. 161–63. **"As history, it is beneath contempt" and "Have you ever noticed"**: David Lebedoff, *The Same Man: George Orwell and Evelyn Waugh in Love and War*, pp. 105–6. **"He is not a good compan-ion"**: Byrne, *Mad World*, p. 294. **"On the fringe of Government"**: Eve-lyn Waugh, *Brideshead Revisited: The Sacred and Profane Memories of Captain Charles Ryder, A Novel*, p. 216. **"Had a way of making you tell all"**: Ogden interview, Library of Congress unprocessed file, Group 1 of 3, p. 4, PAM. **"So fiercely"**: Stannard, *Evelyn Waugh: The Later Years*, p. 58, 114. **"Get up, you fool"**: Leslie, *Randolph*, p. 96. **"Do take care not to be captured"**: Ibid., p. 93. **"You bloody little swine" and "My dear Randolph"**: David Lebedoff, *The Same Man: George Orwell and Evelyn Waugh in Love and War*, p. 106. **"Churchill had many faults"**: Stannard, *Evelyn Waugh: The Later Years*, pp. 122–23. **"If it is thought he is doing no good" and "It is kind of your Generals"**: Gilbert, *Road to Victory*, pp. 802, 808.

CHAPTER 31: LOVE AMONG THE RUINS

"Have you news of my boy Jack?": Rudyard Kipling, *The Collected Poems of Rudyard Kipling*, p. 228. **"I have just heard"**: Thomas Maier, *The Kennedys: America's Emerald Kings*, p. 171. **"Richard really is the soul of honesty," "like so many other British fathers," and "I suppose I really always expected to marry Billy"**: *HTF*, pp. 593, 599, 597. **"I would advise strongly against"**: Barbara Leaming, *Jack Kennedy: The Education of a Statesman*, p. 128. **"Never in history"**: 1943 John F. Ken-nedy letter to his mother, in JFK. **"Billy Hartington wants to know"**:

February 13, 1942, Kathleen Kennedy letter, JFK. **"I doubt it"**: Nigel Hamilton, *JFK: Reckless Youth*, p. 535. **"Mary Churchill wore a light blue crepe dress" and "The best part of the evening"**: January 12, 1944, Kathleen Kennedy letter, JPK. **"Kik [sic] Kennedy's apostasy is a sad thing"**: Mark Amory, ed., *The Letters of Evelyn Waugh*, p. 183. **"I suppose it will [be] practically impossible"**: Doris Kearns Goodwin, *The Fitzgeralds and the Kennedys*, p. 674. **"Parnell's ghost must be smiling sardonically"**: Undated 1944 "Talk of the Town" column in (London) E*vening News*, JPK. **"He will not budge"**: Robert Rhodes James, ed., *Chips: The Diaries of Sir Henry Channon*, p. 221. **"Of course the Dukie is very worried"**: Goodwin, *The Fitzgeralds and the Kennedys*, p. 675. **"Churchill wrote him" and "I don't know what the people want"**: February 22, 1944, Kathleen Kennedy letter, JPK. **"I am going out now to fight"**: "L[or]d Hartington Killed in France," (London) *Evening News*, September 18, 1944, JPK. **"I have loved Kick for a long time"**: *HTF*, p. 584. **"Of course, she still hopes I'll marry Billy"**: Maier, *The Kennedys*, p. 145. **"Because of the family's ambitions"**: Lynne McTaggart, *Kathleen Kennedy: Her Life and Times*, p. 156. **"Galleazzi's [sic] pal said of course"**: Maier, *The Kennedys*, p. 149. **"Almost a saint"**: John Grover, "Lord Halifax Is Unusual," Associated Press, *Prescott Evening Courier,* January 13, 1941. **"His attitude seemed"**: John Cooney, *The American Pope: The Life and Times of Francis Cardinal Spellman*, p. 101. **"Was the first time since 1694"**: "Hartington-Kennedy Union Stunned Society," *Boston Globe*, May 14, 1948. **"Only grief"**: May 7, 1944, Nancy Astor correspondence with Rose Kennedy, in JPK. **"I was very worried about a newspaper report"**: Goodwin, *The Fitzgeralds and the Kennedys*, p. 680. **"When Kathleen feels that strongly"**: June 8, 1944, correspondence to Tony Rosslyn, in JPK. **"Rose and I finally came around"**: June 8, 1944, correspondence to Sir James Calder, in JPK. **"I see now that I've lost one of my daughters"**: May 24, 1944, correspondence to Lord Beaverbrook, in JPK. **"I am much more favorably impressed" and "The power of silence is great"**: *HTF*, pp. 589, 587. **"Jack bought me a miniature Torpedo Boat"**: February 16, 1943, Joseph Kennedy document, JFK. **"In their long brotherly, friendly rivalry"**: Rose Fitzgerald Kennedy, *Times to Remember,* p. 285. **"By God, *I'll* show them"**: Laurence Leamer, *The Kennedy Men: 1901–*

1963, p. 199. "**She had the feeling**": McTaggart, *Kathleen Kennedy*, p. 146. "**We did not know this until afterward**": Winston S. Churchill, *The Second World War, Volume 6: Triumph and Tragedy*, p. 54. "**I hate to see brave men killed**": Martin Gilbert, *Winston S. Churchill, Volume 7: Road to Victory, 1941–45*, p. 1272. "**Elliott has returned to this country**": June 10, 1945, Eleanor Roosevelt correspondence to Rose Kennedy, in JPK. "**Children, your brother Joe has been lost**": Geoffrey Perret, *Jack: A Life Like No Other*, p. 124. "**We must carry on like everyone else**": *HTF*, p. 599. "**He was so keen about politics**": September 4, 1944, Rose Kennedy correspondence, CBL. "**Eventually, we may think of Peter and Joe**": August 1944 correspondence to Governor Salton-stall, in JPK. "**Your great sorrow**": August 27, 1944, presidential correspondence to Joseph Kennedy, in FDR. "**I had always imagined**": August 29, 1944, Joseph Kennedy reply, FDR. "**Of course, it has been a terrible blow**": August 29, 1944, Joseph Kennedy correspondence with Grace Tully, FDR. "**Jack, don't you and your friends**": Nigel Hamilton, *JFK: Reckless Youth*, p. 665. "**I am now shadowboxing in a match**": Robert Dallek, *An Unfinished Life: John F. Kennedy, 1917–1963*, p. 108. "**Why don't you go talk to Daddy**": Laurence Leamer, *The Kennedy Women*, p. 398. "**Come on you fellows, buck up**": Joe McCarthy, *The Remarkable Kennedys*, p. 113. "**Very sad news**": September 1944 correspondence from Pamela Churchill, in JPK. "**It is indeed a cruel blow**": September 23, 1944, Lord Beaverbrook correspondence, BBK. "**I want you never, never to forget**": *HTF*, p. 601. "**I have always been so fond**": September 21, 1944, Jack Kennedy letter, JFK. "**Please tell Kathleen**": September 20, 1944, presidential correspondence to Joseph Kennedy, FDR. "**In speaking about Kathleen's husband**": October 1944 diary entry, JPK. "**Because I was *persona non grata* to the powers that be**": Michael R. Beschloss, *Presidential Courage: Brave Leaders and How They Changed America*, p. 193. "**In fact Elliott was recommended**": *HTF*, p. 609. "**For a fellow**": October 23, 1944, letter to Lord Beaverbrook, in JPK.

CHAPTER 32: VICTORY AND DEFEAT

"**This is your victory**": John Ramsden, *Man of the Century: Winston Churchill and His Legend since 1945*, p. 74. "**All my thoughts are with**"

you": Mary Soames, *Winston and Clementine: The Personal Letters of the Churchills,* p. 531. **"I must say that it was a most moving sight"**: *HTF,* p. 619. **"We roared ourselves hoarse"**: Russell Miller with Renate Miller, *Ten Days in May: The People's Story of VE Day,* p. 256. **"Feels as we all do"**: *HTF,* p. 619. **"A very great man who was also a warm-hearted friend"**: Winston S. Churchill, *The Second World War, Volume 2: Their Finest Hour,* p. 23. **"I don't think it made any very great impression"**: *HTF,* p. 616. **"He wanted to beat me just once"**: February 21, 1945, Kathleen Kennedy letter, JPK. **"The terrific slaughter"**: John F. Kennedy, and Deirdre Henderson, ed., *Prelude to Leadership: The European Diary of John F. Kennedy,* p. 16. **"Everyone here thinks"**: June 20, 1945, Kathleen Kennedy letter, JPK. **"Picking up a pointer or two"**: Veronica Maclean. *Past Forgetting: A Memoir of Heroes, Adventure and Love,* p. 168. **"He had a detachment"**: Nigel Hamilton, *JFK: Reckless Youth,* p. 709. **"Mrs. Wilson's piece on Brother Joe"**: December 22, 1944, Kathleen Kennedy letter to brother Jack, in JPK. **"He went to his fate"**: Churchill quoted about Asquith in Arthur M. Schlesinger Jr., "The First Close Portrait of John Kennedy," *Life,* July 16, 1965, p. 29. **"Letter about the cool and gallant way"**: September 21, 1944, Jack Kennedy letter, JFK. **"A slight detachment from things"**: Hank Searls, *The Lost Prince: Young Joe, The Forgotten Kennedy,* p. 119–20. **"When I think of how much"**: Lord Longford, *Kennedy,* p. 30. **"Of the two, I think that the latter"**: Kennedy and Henderson, ed., *Prelude to Leadership,* p. 7. **"Send us John Winant"**: Bernard Bellush, *He Walked Alone: A Biography of John Gilbert Winant,* p. 155. **"Spoke with great venom"**: Kennedy and Henderson, ed., *Prelude to Leadership,* pp. 23–24. **"Frolic"**: Richard Toye, *Churchill's Empire: The World That Made Him and the World He Made,* p. 289. **"Mr. Churchill's threats do not affect us"**: William Manchester, *The Last Lion: Winston Spencer Churchill, Visions of Glory, 1874–1932,* pp. 729–31. **"Churchill's speech at the end of the war," "You can easily understand," and "gives no hint that Kennedy"**: Kennedy and Henderson, ed., *Prelude to Leadership,* pp. 27, 74, xliii. **"Frightful methods"**: Norman Rose, *Churchill: The Unruly Giant,* p. 270. **"After leading Britain"**: Marquis Childs, "Churchill Confident of Winning," *Miami News,* July 4, 1945, p. 6. **"Churchill is fighting a tide"**: Herbert S. Parmet, *Jack: The Struggles of John F. Kennedy*, p. 133. **"While everyone knows Churchill's strengths"**: Nigel Hamilton, *JFK: Reckless Youth*, p. 704. **"The Conservative Party, fat and happy"**: November 11, 1945, speech at the Crossup-Pishon American Legion Post, JFK. **"Thought themselves undefeatable"**: Anita Leslie, *Randolph: The Biography of Winston Churchill's Son*, p. 105. **"Let him make his point" and "Father and son were taken aback"**: "Churchill Rebukes His Son: Incident in House of Commons," *Indian Express*, June 14, 1945, p. 5. **"Some form of Gestapo"**: Randolph Churchill and Martin Gilbert, *Winston S. Churchill: Never Despair, 1945–1965*, p. 27. **"The Gestapo speech was one of the worst-judged acts"**: John Keegan, *Winston Churchill: A Life*, p. 173. **"As I look at the Europe Hitler has devastated"**: Martin Gilbert, *Churchill and the Jews: A Lifelong Friendship*, p. 219. **"After ripping the Gestapo out of the still bleeding heart"**: Maureen Waller, *London 1945: Life in the Debris of War*, p. 333. **Randolph "approved" of the Gestapo speech**: A. J. P. Taylor, *Beaverbrook*, p. 566. **"But he would not heed her"**: Roy Jenkins, *Churchill: A Biography*, p. 792; also see May 14, 1944, Randolph Churchill correspondence with father, CHUR 1/381/35–37, CHUR. **"Randolph's house"**: Brian Roberts, *Randolph: A Study of Churchill's Son*, pp. 288–89. **"Your guess was better"**: 1945 "Veronica" letter, JFK. **"It hurt more"**: Max Hastings, "Churchill Had Won the War," *Daily Mail*, August 27, 2009. **"It was not so much the loss of power" and "blessing in disguise"**: Sarah Churchill, *A Thread in the Tapestry*, p. 86.

PART IV: MAKING PEACE

"Kennedy never tired of quoting Winston Churchill": *RKT*, p. 427. **"What is the cause of historical events? Power. What is Power?"**: Leo Tolstoy, *War and Peace*, vol. 3, p. 255.

CHAPTER 33: FEELING THE HEAT

"I don't understand why anybody": "Joseph Kennedy Buys Bradley Hialeah Stock, Plans 'Little Activity,'" United Press, *Miami News*, May 15, 1943, p. 9. **"Fine, a little later in the afternoon"**: *HTF*, p. 622. **"Papa has not yet settled down"**: Mary Soames, *Clementine Churchill: The Biography of a Marriage*, p. 441. **"I remember that one of the**

last times": *HTF*, pp. 622–23, based on JPK's memorandum of the encounter dated January 31, 1946. **Kick "was my close friend"**: Pamela Churchill Harriman, August 22, 1980, interview, WMP. **"Quite pale"**: Sally Bedell Smith, *Reflected Glory: The Life of Pamela Churchill Harriman*, p. 129. **"Winston presented a very comical sight" and "Daddy took umbrage"**: *HTF*, p. 624. **"Staying with Goering"**: Christopher Ogden, *Life of the Party: The Biography of Pamela Digby Churchill Hayward Harriman*, p. 180. **"Never forget not only"**: Pamela Churchill Harriman, August 22, 1980, interview, WMP. **"I think it shows there's a lot of life"**: January 12, 1945, Kathleen Kennedy family letter, JPK. **"The sheer ballsy gall of it"**: Truman Capote, *Answered Prayers: The Unfinished Novel*, p. 128. **"The center of power is in Washington"**: Walter Isaacson and Evan Thomas, *The Wise Men: Six Friends and the World They Made* (New York: Simon & Schuster, 1986), p. 377. **"On weeknights, the commerce"**: Rudy Abramson, *Spanning the Century: The Life of W. Averell Harriman, 1891–1986*, p. 431. **"She knew if she married Averell"**: Christopher Ogden, *Life of the Party: The Biography of Pamela Digby Churchill Hayward Harriman*, p. 333. **"Rather sanctimoniously blurted out"**: Abramson, *Spanning the Century*, p. 681. **"While she was actually in a relationship"**: Mary S. Lovell, *The Churchills: In Love and War,* p. 501. **"Mother and I were talking it over"**: *HTF*, pp. 615–16. **"I know it is unfair"**: December 25, 1943, Kathleen Kennedy family letter, JPK. **"Apparently Robin was so impressed"**: January 2, 1943, Kathleen Kennedy letter, JPK. **"Billy and I had been living in sin"**: January 21, 1945, Kathleen Kennedy letter, JPK. **"Dear Max Young Jack"**: *HTF,* p. 626. **"Realized immense profits"**: Richard J. Whalen, *The Founding Father: The Story of Joseph P. Kennedy,* pp. 380–81. **"That anything that has transpired between them"**: September 21, 1945, Arthur Houghton letter quoting James Roosevelt conversation, JPK. **The Justice Department's antitrust division**: September 29, 1954, FBI memo found in agency's Joseph P. Kennedy archival file, Part 4 of 8, p. 11; also see Joseph Fusco testimony, U.S. Senate Hearings Before Special Committee to Investigate Organized Crime in Interstate Commerce, 1950, pp. 595, 607. **"There are lots of odds and ends"**: July 1946 letter to Sir James Calder, in *HTF*, pp. 627–28. **"Harry, what the hell"**: David McCullough, *Truman*, p. 409. **"He never drank Scotch"**:

February 26, 1970, Truman Library Oral History interview, with Judge Oliver J. Carter, former California politician. **"It takes three things to win"**: Ralph G. Martin and Ed Plaut, *Front Runner: Dark Horse*, p. 133. **"He's doing this on his own"**: Leonard Lyons, "The Lyon's Den," *St. Petersburg Times*, September, 29, 1946. **"Your Jack is worth a king's ransom"**: Doris Kearns Goodwin, *The Fitzgeralds and The Kennedys: An American Saga*, p. 708. **"My father's eyes on the back of my neck"** and **"After getting a close look"**: John F. Kennedy and Deirdre Henderson, ed., *Prelude to Leadership: The European Diary of John F. Kennedy*, p. 86. **"The American pope"**: John Cooney, *The American Pope: The Life and Times of Francis Cardinal Spellman*, numerous references to term. **"Let's not forget"**: Thomas Maier, *The Kennedys: America's Emerald Kings*, p. 215. **"Sweet Adeline"**: Kenneth P. O'Donnell and David F. Powers, *Johnny, We Hardly Knew Ye: Memoirs of John Fitzgerald Kennedy*, p. 79. **"I did not know he had it in him"** and **"I'm just filling Joe's shoes"**: David E. Koskoff, *Joseph P. Kennedy: A Life and Times*, pp. 408, 406. **"The folks here think"**: July 13, 1946, Kathleen Kennedy letter to brother Jack, JFK. **"It's rather nice not having to be a Kennedy"**: Peter Collier and David Horowitz, *The Kennedys: An American Drama*, p. 141.

CHAPTER 34.: THE COLDEST WAR

"Conservation of energy": Paul Johnson, *Churchill*, p. 5. **"Mr. President, I think"**: David McCullough, *Truman*, pp. 583–85. **"Listen, this man's oratory"**: December 8, 1999, David Brinkley interview, Archive of American Television. **"But, Boss, *this guy's a pigeon*"**: Raymond H. Geselbracht, "Harry Truman, Poker Player," *Prologue* (National Archives), 35, no. 1 (Spring 2003). **"Even though I deplore some of your customs"**: Martin Gilbert, *Churchill and America*, p. 368. **"An iron curtain has descended"**: Fraser J. Harbutt, *The Iron Curtain: Churchill, America, and the Cold War*, p. 186. **"Unanimous, automatic, unquestioned"**: David McCullough, *Truman*, p. 535. **"Let me know whether it is a flop or a plop"**: John Colville, *The Fringes of Power: The Incredible Inside Story of Winston Churchill during World War II*, p. 610. **"Almost catastrophic blunder"**: McCullough, *Truman*, p. 586. **"Pulled back into his shell"**: "The Presidency: No Cause for Alarm?" *Time*, March

25, 1946. **"The strangling of Bolshevism at its birth"**: Norman Rose, *Churchill: The Unruly Giant*, p. 183. **"At the highest point of majesty"**: Kay Halle, ed., *Winston Churchill on America and Britain: A Selection of His Thoughts on Anglo-American Relations*, p. 55. **"Dominate the world for the next five years" and "a showdown"**: Barbara Leaming, *Jack Kennedy: The Education of a Statesman*, p. 179. **"The argument is now put forward"**: Kay Halle, *The Irrepressible Churchill: Winston's World, Wars, and Wit*, p. 276. **"He [Churchill] pointed out that if an atomic bomb could be dropped"**: December 5, 1947, FBI memo from D. M. Ladd to FBI director J. Edgar Hoover about Sen. Styles Bridges's account of Churchill's comments to him, FBI archival file on Winston Churchill, Part 3 of 3, p. 39; also see "Moral Re-armament in Europe" Styles Bridges report received by Churchill, Public and Political Correspondence, June 1946–December 1947, CHUR. **"We ought not to wait until Russia is ready"**: Martin Gilbert, *Winston S. Churchill, Volume 8: Never Despair, 1945–1965*, p. 258. **"Politically embarrassing statements"**: March 1949 Averell Harriman letter to U.S. secretary of state, in WAH. **"I must not conceal from you the truth as I see it"**: "Only A-Bomb Is Holding Reds at Bay, Churchill Tells Boston Audience," United Press, *St. Petersburg Times*, April 1, 1949, p. 1. **"War has always fascinated him"**: Lord Moran, *Churchill: Taken from the Diaries of Lord Moran: The Struggle for Survival, 1940–1965*, p. 136. **"The greatest living Englishman"**: Margaret L. Coit, *Mr. Baruch*, p. 674. **"Do the Americans have a bad conscience," "the only deterrent to the Soviets," and "I shall defend myself"**: Halle, *The Irrepressible Churchill*, pp. 7–8, 236. **"Do you think that the atomic bomb"**: Randolph Churchill and Martin Gilbert, *Winston S. Churchill, Volume 8: Never Despair*, p. 254. **"Was an almost equal horror"**: Halle, *The Irrepressible Churchill*, pp. 7–8. **"I asked them chaffingly"**: Winston S. Churchill, *His Father's Son: The Life of Randolph Churchill*, p. 281. **"The Dream"**: Martin Gilbert, *Churchill and America*, p. 385. **"Dear Randolph, utterly unspoiled by failure"**: Graham Payn, *My Life with Noel Coward*, p. 251. **"It was perhaps just as well that America existed for Randolph"**: Anita Leslie, *Randolph: The Biography of Winston Churchill's Son*, p. 114. **"Britishly drunk all the time"**: Brian Roberts, *Randolph: A Study of Churchill's Son*, pp. 293–94. **"He could *feel* when-**

ever an illogical tantrum": Leslie, *Randolph*, p. 114. "He certainly was a person who was very up and down": From author's 2012 interview with Lady Juliet Townsend. "Randolph's friendships": Author's 2012 interview with Adrian Berry. "Kay tried to train him to check": Leslie, *Randolph*, p. 114. "One of the safest in the world": "Randolph Churchill Fined $50 by Court in New Canaan for 'Reckless Driving,'" *NYT*, December 10, 1946. "As you know the only career": Churchill and Gilbert, *Winston S. Churchill, Volume 8: Never Despair*, pp. 313–14. "I have had occasion to think of you often": February 13, 1945, Sarah Churchill correspondence with Winant, in FDR. "The former's book is due": *HTF*, p. 633. "That power has to be used": John Gilbert Winant, *Letter from Grosvenor Square: An Account of a Stewardship*, p. 106. "What a waste": Ann M. Sperber, *Murrow, His Life and Times*, p. 298. "Am I not a human being?": Gilbert, *Winston S. Churchill, Volume 8: Never Despair*, p. 451. "The change from the intense executive activities": Mary Soames, *Clementine Churchill: The Biography of a Marriage*, p. 146. "How unfair to accuse you" and "I have thought of you and your gallant father very often since the elections": Clare Boothe Luce October 27, 1945, letter to Randolph Churchill, CBL. "Let us stop our melancholy recriminations": Halle, *The Irrepressible Churchill*, p. 254. "It can be worth the space": Alan Brinkley, *The Publisher*, p. 331. "I read the Fulton speech over": Meyer Berger, "Churchill Arrives Beaming; Backs Pact, Cigar Tells Rest," *NYT*, March 24, 1949. JFK attending dinner honoring WSC: March 25, 1949, dinner invitation, BMB.

CHAPTER 35: CIRCLES OF FRIENDS

"Kick's house is really very cute": October 1, 1946, Eunice Kennedy letter to family, JPK. "Most God awful": Lynne McTaggart, *Kathleen Kennedy: Her Life and Times*, pp. 204–7, along with Kick's personal interest in Seymour Berry and Richard Wood. "The widow Hartington is in love with me": McTaggart, *Kathleen Kennedy*, p. 195. "You know, Frank": "A Shadow Hung over Their Happiness," *Washington Times-Herald*, May 14, 1948. "King dandy and scum": McTaggart, *Kathleen Kennedy*, pp. 206–17. "You don't know him": McTaggart, *Kathleen Kennedy*, p. 217. "Kick was the perfect friend for Pamela": Sally Bedell

Smith, *Reflected Glory: The Life of Pamela Churchill Harriman,* p. 141. **"Really, no one here takes any notice of them":** *HTF,* pp. 631–34. **"After Pam's dinner party":** June 1, 1947, Kathleen Kennedy Hartington letter, ROSE. **"It was certainly":** November 8, 1946, Kathleen Kennedy Hartington letter, ROSE. **"I hope Jack will let me know":** June 22, 1947, Kathleen Kennedy Hartington letter, ROSE. **"Brought in here, dying":** August 8, 1945, Kathleen Kennedy Hartington letter, JPK. **"It is you who have led":** David Dimbleby and David Reynolds, *An Ocean Apart: The Relationship between Britain and America in the Twentieth Century,* p. 172. **"Anthony Eden arrives today":** Robert Dallek, *An Unfinished Life: John F. Kennedy, 1917–1963,* p. 4. **"Sporting around in my morning coat":** Nigel Hamilton, *JFK: Reckless Youth,* p. 257. **"Anthony Eden, who was very easy":** September 18, 1947, Kathleen Kennedy Hartington letter, JPK. **"Anthony, don't you think Kick is pretty?":** *HTF,* p. 630. **"They'll cheer but the blighters won't vote"** and **"She is in America":** June 22, 1947, Kathleen Kennedy Hartington letter, JPK. **"I long to see you":** January 10, 1948, Anthony Eden letter to Kathleen Kennedy Hartington, JPK. **"In England we dated":** Christopher Ogden, *Life of the Party: The Biography of Pamela Digby Churchill Hayward Harriman,* pp. 194–95. **"The hardest and longest move of all":** James MacGregor Burns, *John Kennedy: A Political Profile,* pp. 3–5. **"I'm John Kennedy from Massachusetts":** John Henry Cutler, *Honey Fitz: Three Steps to the White House: The Life and Times of John F. (Honey Fitz) Fitzgerald,* p. 71. **"Jack kept pressing on about his ancestors":** Arthur Mitchell, *JFK and His Irish Heritage,* p. 32. **" 'Wife?' they'd ask. I'd say no":** Doris Kearns Goodwin, *The Fitzgeralds and The Kennedys: An American Saga,* p. 732. **"Left in a flow of nostalgia and sentiment"** and **"That was just like *Tobacco Road!*":** Herbert S. Parmet, *Jack: The Struggles of John F. Kennedy,* p. 190. **"The English lady":** Burns, *John Kennedy,* pp. 3–5. **"I felt like kicking her out":** Kenneth P. O'Donnell and David F. Powers, *Johnny, We Hardly Knew Ye: Memoirs of John Fitzgerald Kennedy,* p. 418. **"Well, did they have a bathroom?":** Laurence Leamer, *The Kennedy Men: 1901–1963,* p. 251. **"That American friend of yours":** Peter Collier and David Horowitz, *The Kennedys: An American Drama,* p. 292. **"Kick was my closest friend in those days"** and **"Basically, I'm a back-**

room girl": Michael Gross, " 'Basically, I'm a Backroom Girl': Of Lovers, Husbands, Wealth and Power," *NYT,* February 16, 1997. **Further details of Pamela Churchill and Kick Kennedy's postwar friendship:** Smith, *Reflected Glory,* p. 145; Ogden, *Life of the Party,* p. 198; Nellie Bly, *The Kennedy Men: Three Generations of Sex, Scandal, and Secrets,* p. 82. **"Terrified":** Barbara Leaming, *Jack Kennedy: The Education of a Statesman,* p. 462. **"Her friends began to suspect":** McTaggart, *Kathleen Kennedy,* pp. 217–19. **"I was overjoyed":** Laurence Leamer, *The Kennedy Women: The Saga of an American Family,* pp. 399–410. **"If you want to commit adultery":** Edward J. Renehan Jr., *The Kennedys at War: 1937–1945,* p. 317. **"Favorite of all the children":** Leaming, *Jack Kennedy,* p. 192. **"The measure of a man's success":** David E. Koskoff, *Joseph P. Kennedy: A Life and Times,* p. 375. **"Put them on the plane together":** Ogden, *Life of the Party,* p. 202. **"No one who ever met her":** Undated 1948 document, JPK. **"He stood alone":** *RKT,* p. 78. **"Pray accept my sincere sympathy":** Undated 1948 Winston Churchill telegram, JPK. **"Rose and I are exceedingly grateful":** June 14, 1948, letter to Churchill, JPK. **"He [Bobby] is just starting off":** March 23, 1948, letter to Beaverbrook, in JPK. **"If something happens to you":** Burns, *John Kennedy,* p. 54. **"We will not mention her again":** McTaggart, *Kathleen Kennedy,* p. 244. **"We have received":** June 29, 1949, Rose Kennedy note, JPK. **"The sudden death":** Koskoff, *Joseph P. Kennedy,* p. 375. **"I am afraid that Palm Beach":** *HTF,* p. 638.

CHAPTER 36: WARRIOR HISTORIANS

"An impalpable crystal sphere": Winston Churchill, *My Early Life: 1874–1904,* p. 212. **"Words are the only things":** Paul Johnson, *Churchill,* p. 147. **"It is sometimes necessary":** Winston S. Churchill, *A History of the English Speaking Peoples,* p. 215. **"On the whole":** Randolph Churchill and Martin Gilbert, *Winston S. Churchill, Volume 8: Never Despair, 1945–1965,* p. 890. **"Unthinkingly talked up the extent":** Peter Clarke, *Mr. Churchill's Profession: The Statesman as Author and the Book That Defined the "Special Relationship,"* p. 292. **"Things in History":** Kay Halle, *The Irrepressible Churchill: Winston's World, Wars, and Wit,* p. 284. **"A historian's mind":** Paul Johnson, *Churchill,* p. 20. **"An unnecessary war":** Christopher M. Bell, *Churchill and Sea Power,*

p. 323. **"Long series of miscalculations"**: Winston S. Churchill, *The Second World War, Volume 1: The Gathering Storm*, p. 326, iv. **"They are replete with serious inaccuracies"**: Joseph P. Kennedy, "The Churchill Memoirs," *NYT*, September 26, 1948; also in David Reynolds, *In Command of History: Churchill Fighting and Writing the Second World War*, p. 136. **"Serious and offensive allegations"**: Randolph S. Churchill, "The Churchill Memoirs: Documents Discussing the Crisis," *NYT*, October 17, 1948. **"The misinformation that surrounds Munich"**: November 4, 1948, Joseph P. Kennedy letter to Neville Chamberlain's widow, JPK. **"Though some of us thought"**: Randolph S. Churchill, "The Myth of Munich," *Time*, June 9, 1952. **"President Roosevelt never sent"**: "Munich: Kennedy v. Churchill," *Time*, July 28, 1952. **"Kennedy had his own proposal"**: "National Affairs: The World and Democracy," *Time*, March 24, 1947. **"To prevent World War III"**: Joseph P. Kennedy, "The U.S. and the World," *Life*, March 18, 1946, p. 106. **"Where are we now?"**: "A Troubled Nation Weighs Its Future," *Life*, January 8, 1951, p. 10. **"As a breezy chronicle"**: *HTF*, p. 226. **"Read like an espionage thriller"**: "State Department Explains Case of Tyler Kent, Jailed for Spying," *NYT*, September 3, 1944. **"Moral right"**: "Kent Denies the Intent to Aid the Axis; Took Papers 'to Inform Senate,'" *NYT*, December 5, 1945. **"He might have kept us out"**: Westbrook Pegler, "American Jailed in Britain to Keep FDR Messages Secret," (Charleston, SC) *News and Courier*, April 18, 1955, p. 3. **"All pure unadulterated bunk"**: *HTF*, p. 621. **"If some parallel British-American actions"**: William S. White, "Republicans Propose Churchill as Pearl Harbor Inquiry Witness," *NYT*, January 18, 1946. **"Were I to become"**: Churchill's alleged quote denied by Kennedy in his unpublished diplomatic memoir draft, p. 671, JPK. **"Has always made something terribly diabolical"**: *HTF*, p. 376. **"Have you been able to dig anything up"**: November 2, 1951, Kennedy letter to Lord Beaverbrook, JPK. **"The Tyler Kent business will have to stand over"**: November 23, 1951, Lord Beaverbrook letter, JPK. **"I cannot accept payment"**: May 7, 1948, Paul Mallon letter, JPK. **"I think it's a great opportunity"**: Undated 1932 Randolph Churchill papers, CHUR. **"I can't afford to give my son motor boats"**: Ogden interview, Library of Congress unprocessed file, Group 2 of 3, pp. 333–34, PAM. **"Knowledge about the religion"**: Christopher Ogden, *Life of the*

Party: The Biography of Pamela Digby Churchill Hayward Harriman, p. 288. **"Your cable was a help on a dark day"**: June 14, 1948, letter to Clare Boothe Luce, JPK. **"I do not know the young lady" and "I have known him for a long time"**: Randolph Churchill, "Letters from Evelyn Waugh," *Encounter,* July 1968, p. 5. **"Randolph, June and little W"**: Mary Soames, *Winston and Clementine: The Personal Letters of the Churchills,* p. 554. **"Thanks to your kind offices"**: Arthur Jones, "Literary Scamp Evelyn Waugh," *Notre Dame Magazine,* Autumn 2003. **"The Duke of Devonshire sent a message"**: Mark Amory, *The Letters of Evelyn Waugh,* p. 243. **"I thought this man was your friend" and "had a naive view about friendship"**: Randolph Churchill, "Letters from Evelyn Waugh," pp. 4–6.

CHAPTER 37: GREAT CONTEMPORARIES

"It was," she liked to say, "the greatest collection of brains": "Remembering Katherine Murphy Halle," privately published document at her memorial provided to author by family friends, pp. 10–11. **"Kay, I wish you would tell Jack"**: David E. Koskoff, *Joseph P. Kennedy: A Life and Times,* p. 393. **"I always believed"**: John Ramsden, *Man of the Century: Winston Churchill and His Legend since 1945,* p. 154. **"Well, Kay, that's why I settled a million dollars"**: Herbert S. Parmet, *Jack: The Struggles of John F. Kennedy,* p. 207. **"Reserved" and "He turned white as a sheet"**: February 7, 1967, KMH. **"He was the golden boy"**: June 1, 1966, Margaret L. Coit oral history, JFK; also see Orville Prescott, "Books of the Times," *NYT,* March 3, 1950. **"I thought up what possible," "He frightened me to death," and other exchanges between Coit and Kennedy, including Arthur Krock's comments**: June 1, 1966, Margaret L. Coit oral history, JFK. **"Heroism, romance and drama"**: Arthur M. Schlesinger Jr., *Jacqueline Kennedy: Historic Conversations on Life with John F. Kennedy,* p. 42. **"Did you ever read anything like that"**: Chris Matthews, *Jack Kennedy: Elusive Hero,* p. 109. **"I don't mean that he decided he'd marry when Churchill did"**: Joan Blair and Clay Blair, *The Search for JFK,* p. 111. **"A substitute for Kick"**: Barbara Leaming, *Mrs. Kennedy: The Missing History of the Kennedy Years,* p. 29. **"Always felt that that time in England"**: June 18, 1964, Joseph A. Alsop oral history, pp. 12–13, JFK. **"The part for**

which he cared most": Jacqueline Kennedy, "The Words JFK Loved Best," *Look*, November 17, 1964. **"Everything seemed easy**": Winston S. Churchill, *Great Contemporaries*, p. 114. **"Mischievous**": Michael Bentley, *Public and Private Doctrine: Essays in British History Presented to Maurice Cowling*, p. 231. **"I can't go on like this," "I always thought of him,"** and **"wonderful sort of seraglio prose**": Schlesinger, *Jacqueline Kennedy: Historic Conversations*, pp. 17–21, 48. **"Courage is rightly esteemed**": Thurston Clarke, *Ask Not: The Inauguration of John F. Kennedy and the Speech That Changed America*, p. 68. **"I cannot let this stand**": Clark M. Clifford and Richard Holbrooke, *Counsel to the President: A Memoir*, p. 307. **"I really saw Jack writing that book**": Schlesinger, *Jacqueline Kennedy: Historic Conversations*, pp. 60–61. **"Remember I've always said he's a child of fate**": Thomas Maier, *The Kennedys: America's Emerald Kings*, p. 265. **"Thanks for thinking of me**": June 7, 1957, letter to Coit, in JFK.

CHAPTER 38: WINNERS AND LOSERS
"I would my father look'd but with my eyes": William Shakespeare, *Shakespeare Complete Works*, p. 891. **"Do be good tonight, dear boy"** and other Churchill-Burton detail, including **"My Lord Hamlet, may I use your lavatory?**": Kay Halle, *The Irrepressible Churchill: Winston's World, Wars, and Wit*, pp. 87–88, as well as Earl Wilson, "Burton, as 'Hamlet,' Had Churchill as Prompter," *Milwaukee Sentinel*, September 6, 1967, p. 6; and in William A. Raidy, "Richard Burton Returns to 'Camelot,'" *NYT* News Service, June 27, 1980. **"To stud?**": Randolph Churchill and Martin Gilbert, *Winston S. Churchill, Volume 8: Never Despair, 1945–1965*, p. 488. **"There are always a lot of bloody rows**": Lord Moran, *Churchill: Taken from the Diaries of Lord Moran: The Struggle for Survival, 1940–1965*, p. 562. **"I always remember**": William Manchester, *The Last Lion: Winston Spencer Churchill, Visions of Glory, 1874–1932*, p. 810. **"He bustled in**": Michael Foot, *Debts of Honour*, p. 149. **"All that is linked with the fortune**": Winston S. Churchill, *His Father's Son: The Life of Randolph Churchill*, pp. 293–94. **"Along with his honesty**": Foot, *Debts of Honour*, p. 165. **"The members of this house**": "Oxford Union 'Regrets Domination' by U.S. in Vote after Fiery Debate," *NYT*, June 2, 1950. **"Your failure and the gener-**

ally wretched outcome": Randolph Churchill, "Letters from Evelyn Waugh," *Encounter*, July 1968, p. 6. **"Winston worshipped his son"**: August 22, 1980, Pamela Harriman interview, p. 29, WMP. **"I realize too that you regard me as a failure," "I believe that a single episode with Anthony Eden," and "It has been a growing sense of grief"**: Churchill and Gilbert, *Winston S. Churchill, Volume 8: Never Despair*, p. 765–68. **"As far removed from the atom bomb"**: John Colville, *Winston Churchill and His Inner Circle*, p. 212. **"I always feared that mass pressure"**: Anthony Montague Browne, *Long Sunset: Memoirs of Winston Churchill's Last Private Secretary*, pp. 156, 316. **"Bloody world"**: Lord Moran, *Churchill: Taken from the Diaries of Lord Moran: The Struggle for Survival, 1940–1965*, p. 559. **"Winston is trying to relive the days of World War II"**: Stephen E. Ambrose,. "Churchill and Eisenhower in the Second World War," in Robert Blake, ed., *Churchill: A Major New Assessment of His Life in Peace and War*, pp. 397–402. **"We English have always needed"**: Halle, *The Irrepressible Churchill*, p. 196. **"Uncivilized tribes"**: Piers Brendon, *The Decline and Fall of the British Empire, 1781–1997*, p. 326. **"After all, you can't take twenty million"**: C. L. Sulzberger, *The Last of the Giants*, p. 304. **"This award says words"**: "The Pen Is Mightier," *NYT*, October 16, 1953. **"I do hope you are right"**: Halle, *The Irrepressible Churchill*, p. 302. **"Winston himself could be maddening"**: Mary Soames, *Winston and Clementine: The Personal Letters of the Churchills*, p. 588. **"I could do nothing while he is alive"**: Sulzberger, *The Last of the Giants*, p. 115. **"Which way shall we turn"**: John Lukacs, *Churchill: Visionary. Statesman. Historian*, p. 18. **"Meanwhile, never flinch, never weary, never despair"**: Geoffrey Best, *Churchill: A Study in Greatness*, pp. 299–300. **"Besides, he said, what good"**: John Colville, *The Fringes of Power: The Incredible Inside Story of Winston Churchill during World War II*, p. 709. **"Power must pass"**: Randolph Churchill and Martin Gilbert, *Winston S. Churchill, Volume 8: Never Despair, 1945–1965*, p. 1366. **"Sometimes lonely"**: John Colville, *Winston Churchill and His Inner Circle*, pp. 264–70. **"I have now retired from literature"**: Martin Gilbert, *Churchill: A Life*, p. 952.

CHAPTER 39: BLACK KNIGHTS ON A CHESSBOARD

"Like the black knight on a chessboard": Nicholas Fraser, Philip Jacobson, Mark Ottaway, and Lewis Chester, *Aristotle Onassis*, pp. 168–69. **"Sitting on the biggest penis in the world" and "They say I have no class"**: Rhoda Koenig, "A Bathtub Odysseus," *New York*, June 16, 1986, p. 64. **"Too earthy, vulgar and ugly"**: Christopher Ogden, *Life of the Party: The Biography of Pamela Digby Churchill Hayward Harriman*, p. 257. **"My cup is filled to overflowing"**: *HTF*, p. 665. **"I don't think there is a man or woman on earth"**: Peter Evans, *Ari: The Life and Times of Aristotle Onassis*, p. 145; also see Jack Ashley, *Journey into Silence*, p. 102. **"He's a Turk"**: Evans, *Ari*, p. 157. **"Randolph has arrived"**: Randolph Churchill and Martin Gilbert, *Winston S. Churchill, Volume 8: Never Despair, 1945–1965*, pp. 1173–75. **"That is a man of mark"**: Nicholas Gage, *Greek Fire: The Story of Maria Callas and Aristotle Onassis*, p. 54. **"Randolph seemed to miss"**: Evans, *Ari*, p. 152. **"The most beautiful structure"**: Mary Soames, *Clementine Churchill: The Biography of a Marriage*, p. 462. **"A little Easter cruise"** and **"somehow I don't want to be beholden"**: Mary Soames, *Winston and Clementine: The Personal Letters of the Churchills*, p. 604. **"A rather unsavory character"**: C. L. Sulzberger, *The Last of the Giants*, p. 117. **"I regard you as my son"**: John Charmley, *Churchill: The End of Glory—A Political Biography*, pp. 490–91. **"Clarissa's apostasy"**: Martin Stannard, *Evelyn Waugh: The Later Years, 1939–1966*, p. 309. **"Winston will probably bury Eden"**: Sulzberger, *The Last of the Giants*, p. 115. **"Told me that Anthony"**: *HTF*, p. 665. **"I don't think Anthony can do it"**: John Colville, The *Fringes of Power: The Incredible Inside Story of Winston Churchill during World War II*, p. 708. **"Eden says he wants," "Anthony told me everything," and "an Anthony man"**: Randolph Churchill and Martin Gilbert, *Winston S. Churchill, Volume 8: Never Despair*, pp. 1201, 1203–4, 1223. **"Readers of this book"**: Robert Rhodes James, *Anthony Eden*, p. 615. **"Randolph's a drunk" and "To my favourite spy"**: Peter Evans, *Nemesis: The True Story of Aristotle Onassis, Jackie O., and the Love Triangle That Brought Down the Kennedys*, p. 37.

CHAPTER 40: FRIENDS IN HIGH PLACES

"The television has come to take its place in the world": Richard M. Langworth, ed., *The Definitive Wit of Winston Churchill*, p. 176. **"What has happened today"**: Ralph G. Martin and Ed Plaut, *Front Runner: Dark Horse*, p. 105. **"The hottest thing we have in America on television"**: September 6, 1952, letter to Lord Beaverbrook, JPK. **"In America, when they elect a President"**: Lord Moran, *Churchill: Taken from the Diaries of Lord Moran: The Struggle for Survival, 1940–1965*, p. 698. **"Who inspired me when I was 19"**: Martin Gilbert, *Churchill and America*, p. 17. **"Quite grown up"**: C. L. Sulzberger, *The Last of the Giants*, p. 325. **"Scores of beautiful models"**: Russell Baker, " 'Great Americans' View to Be First in Conceding Race to Stevenson," *NYT*, August 17, 1956. **"Much obliged"**: Raymond Daniel, "Son of Churchill Raps Beaverbrook," *NYT*, November 20, 1952. **"We never were very far apart on world affairs"**: September 18, 1953, letter to Lord Beaverbrook, in JPK. **"I have always pursued politics as an art"**: June 13, 1956, Lord Beaverbrook letter, JPK. **"Call Dad" and "Whew, is he mad!"**: Kenneth P. O'Donnell and David F. Powers, *Johnny, We Hardly Knew Ye: Memoirs of John Fitzgerald Kennedy*, p. 140. **"That's it, let's go" and "The death of the baby"**: Doris Kearns Goodwin, *The Fitzgeralds and the Kennedys: An American Saga*, pp. 784, 786. **"Learned what not to do"**: Evan Thomas, *Robert Kennedy: His Life*, p. 74. **"Honey, vigor, compassion"**: Gary Edgerton, *The Columbia History of American Television*, p. 222. **"He came out of the convention"**: HTF, p. 677. **"Maybe B.M.B. has the common failing"**: Jordan A. Schwarz, *The Speculator: Bernard Baruch in Washington, 1917–1965*, p. 537. **"Just knowing that someone like you"**: 1954 Jacqueline Kennedy letter, BMB. **"I would say, my dear friend"**: April 1, 1955, Baruch letter, JPK. **"To let you know of my deep interest in your recovery"**: February 9, 1956, Baruch letter, BMB. **"Politics is a fascinating thing"**: April 6, 1956, Baruch letter, CHUR. **"By nature he is, as you know, the kindest of men"**: November 5, 1951, Brendan Bracken letter, BMB. **"You were always on the good side"**: Anita Leslie, *Randolph: The Biography of Winston Churchill's Son*, p. 146. **"I am very glad that you like my companionship"**: Martin Gilbert, *Churchill: A Life*, p. 1274. **"Put in fairy tales about Onassis"**: Martin Gilbert, *Winston S. Churchill, Volume 8:*

Never Despair, 1945–1965, p. 1190. **"Oh, he's an amusing dog"**: Anne Chisholm and Michael Davie, *Lord Beaverbrook: A Life*, pp. 4–5. **"We must remember"**: Nicholas Gage, *Greek Fire: The Story of Maria Callas and Aristotle Onassis*, p. 92. **"As the great man once told me . . ."**: Fraser, Jacobson, Ottaway, and Chester, *Aristotle Onassis*, pp. 214–25. **"What did you really think of Lawrence of Arabia?"**: Gage, *Greek Fire*, pp. 74–78. **"You must either wallop a man"**: Peter Evans, *Ari: The Life and Times of Aristotle Onassis*, p. 182. **"Your father died young"**: Lord Moran, *Churchill: Taken from the Diaries of Lord Moran: The Struggle for Survival, 1940–1965*, p. 818.

CHAPTER 41: MEETINGS AT SEA

"I like traveling with Winston Churchill": Nicholas Gage, *Greek Fire: The Story of Maria Callas and Aristotle Onassis*, pp. 52–53. **"Don't talk to me about rules"**: Jessie Shiers, *The Quotable Bitch: Women Who Tell It Like It Really Is*, p. 6. **"Tall, very dark and striking" and "Kiss!"**: Celia Sandys, *Chasing Churchill: The Travels of Winston Churchill*, p. 5. **"It is all over"**: Nicholas Fraser, Philip Jacobson, Mark Ottaway, and Lewis Chester, *Aristotle Onassis*, pp. 168–69. **"It was as if a fire"**: Arianna Stassinopoulos Huffington, *Maria, Beyond the Callas Legend*, p. 174. **"Ari's total understanding of women"**: Peter Evans, "The Onassis Diamonds," *New York Social Diary*, June 25, 2008. **"The saddest and I hope greatest misfortune" and "I hope you did not mind my broaching"**: October 1959 exchange of letters between Aristotle Onassis and Winston Churchill, CHUR. **"So, Ari . . . we are related at last"**: Martin Gilbert, *Winston S. Churchill, Volume 8: Never Despair, 1945–1965*, p. 1339. **"History was full of heroes for him"**: Arthur M. Schlesinger Jr., *A Thousand Days: John F. Kennedy in the White House*, p. 80. **Wicked Papa Joe**: Winston S. Churchill, *His Father's Son: The Life of Randolph Churchill*, p. 411. **"If Max attaches importance to it"**: Peter Evans, *Nemesis: The True Story of Aristotle Onassis, Jackie O., and the Love Triangle That Brought Down the Kennedys*, p. 42. **"His toothey tendency"**: Anthony Montague Browne, *Long Sunset: Memoirs of Winston Churchill's Last Private Secretary*, pp. 194–95. **"They tell me he is presidential timber"**: Peter Evans, *Ari: The Life and Times of Aristotle Onassis*, p. 160. **"He admired Churchill"**: Arthur M.

Schlesinger Jr., *Jacqueline Kennedy: Historic Conversations on Life with John F. Kennedy*, p. 47. **"Why, it's large enough"**: Fred Sparks, *The $20,000,000 Honeymoon*, p. 169. **"She had a withdrawn quality"** and **"carnal soul"**: Peter Evans, *Ari: The Life and Times of Aristotle Onassis*, pp. 163–64. **"I knew your father so well"**: Schlesinger, *Jacqueline Kennedy: Historic Conversations*, pp. 219–20. **"I am a Catholic, you know"**: Fred Sparks, *The $20,000,000 Honeymoon*, pp. 4–6. **"He believed he could see below the surface"**: Evans, *Ari*, pp. 164–65. **"He was his hero"**: William Douglas-Home Oral History, October 28, 1966, p. 12, JFK. **"I felt sorry for Jack that evening"**: Arthur M. Schlesinger Jr., *A Thousand Days: John F. Kennedy in the White House*, p. 84. **"Maybe he thought you were the waiter"**: William Douglas-Home Oral History, October 28, 1966, p. 12, JFK.

CHAPTER 42: IN THEIR OWN IMAGE

"Men make gods in their own image": Robin Osborne, *Greece in the Making, 1200–479 BC*, p. 299. **"The whiskey is in Nassau"**: December 5, 1955, Lord Beaverbrook letter, JPK. **"I find Bobby a most lively character"**: December 11, 1957, Lord Beaverbrook letter, JPK. *Men and Power*: January 3, 1958, Robert F. Kennedy letter, BBK. **"Bold and imaginative"**: Lord Beaverbrook, *Men and Power, 1917–1918*, pp. 142–43. **"Rose Kennedy is an uncanonized saint"**: October 12, 1957, Lord Beaverbrook letter, BBK. **"Strange as it may seem"**: September 15, 1958, letter to Lord Beaverbrook, JPK. **"I just received the following wire"**: Art Buchwald, A Man with Humor," November 28, 1963, syndicated column in (Charlestown, SC) *News and Courier*, p. 3. **"On this matter of experience"**: Theodore H. White, *The Making of the President 1960*, p. 298. **"By the 1950s"**: *HTF*, p. 520. **"The Holy Father did me the great honor"**: June 24, 1955, Joseph P. Kennedy letter, BBK. **"I don't know what I can continue to do," "As you know, the authorization for the Vatican bill," "You have been wonderfully cooperative,"** and **"What a wonderful gift it has been to have been so close to the Holy See"**: Thomas Maier, *The Kennedys: America's Emerald Kings*, pp. 294, 301–2. **"I think that if there is anything that you want me to do"**: David Nasaw, *The Patriarch*, p. 718; also in Maier, *The Kennedys*, p. 310. **"I got so much interested in them"**: Allen Dulles Oral

History, p. 16, JFK. **"The only bull I know"**: Paul Johnson, *Churchill*, p. 155. **"I asked him what he thought of Marilyn Monroe"**: Joseph P. Kennedy FBI file, Part 4 of 8, p. 359. **"If I were betting"**: *HTF*, p. 688. **"It seemed to me that America regards Kennedy"**: Ibid., p. 13. *The $64,000 Question*: Sarah Churchill, *Keep On Dancing: An Autobiography*, p. 50. **"She realized that no woman on earth," "You have got to dress and pack,"** and **"I'm going to die soon"**: Anita Leslie, *Randolph: The Biography of Winston Churchill's Son*, p. 133. **"Perfect training for the book"**: C. L. Sulzberger, *The Last of the Giants*, p. 296. **"He's asked me!"**: Mary S. Lovell, *The Churchills: In Love and War*, p. 542. **"Dearest Papa"**: John Pearson, *The Private Lives of Winston Churchill*, p. 408. **"I had long been convinced"**: Anthony Montague Browne, *Long Sunset: Memoirs of Winston Churchill's Last Private Secretary*, p. 316. **"He shall be his own biographer"**: Leslie, *Randolph*, p. 156. **"Do you realize"** and **"Well, I am happy with the book"**: Martin Gilbert, *Winston S. Churchill, Volume 8: Never Despair, 1945–1965*, p. 1319. **"Ask Jack what happened"** and **"It was a crushing reply"**: Winston S. Churchill, *His Father's Son: The Life of Randolph Churchill*, p. 377.

CHAPTER 43: ARMS TO PARLEY

"Pray Much, Christians": Theodore H. White, *The Making of the President 1960*, p. 151. **"The young man hauled off"**: Jim Bishop, "Jack Trades Kid Gloves for Boxing Gloves," *Milwaukee Sentinel*, July 14, 1960, p. 23. **"Randolph was red-faced and exultant"**: Arthur M. Schlesinger Jr., *A Life in the Twentieth Century: Innocent Beginnings, 1917–1950*, p. 385. **"I wasn't any Chamberlain umbrella-policy man"** and **"You'll get yours"**: Doris Kearns Goodwin, *The Fitzgeralds and the Kennedys: An American Saga*, p. 800. **"Don't worry, Jack"**: Evan Thomas, *Robert Kennedy: His Life*, p. 99. **"His courage, bold pronouncements"**: Will Swift, *The Kennedys: Amidst the Gathering Storm*, p. 306. **"We are not here to curse the darkness"**: Kennedy Democratic Party nomination acceptance address, July 15, 1960, JFK. **"I spent some months in England"**: Senator Kennedy remarks at Battle Creek, MI, October 14, 1960, JFK. **"Twenty three years ago"**: Kennedy remarks in Nashua, NH, March 5, 1960, JFK. **"We all saw it as a prelude not to war"**: *RKT*, p. 427. **"We cannot parley on the basis"**: Senator Kennedy remarks in

Milwaukee, WI, October 23, 1960, JFK. **"The legislative process in a democracy"**: Senator Kennedy remarks at dinner honoring Herbert Hoover, February 4, 1957, JFK. **"When Winston Churchill called at the start"**: Senator Kennedy's remarks in Fairmont, WV, April 18, 1960, JFK. **"Paralleled only by the triumph of the younger Pitt"**: June 4, 1960, letter to Joe Kennedy, BBK. **"Who should be clasping my hand"** and **"Onassis sent me four dozen roses"**: *HTF*, pp. 690–91. **"May your seventy-third year bring you the reward"**: September 3, 1960, Lord Beaverbrook letter, BBK. **"I came home to find"**: September 9, 1960, Joseph Kennedy letter, BBK. **"For contrary to common newspaper usage"**: White, *The Making of the President 1960*, p. 439. **"Well, we all have fathers"**: *RKT*, p. 218. **"It's not the pope I'm afraid of"**: David McCullough, *Truman*, p. 1147. **"While I understand and sympathize"**: Art Buchwald, "A Man with Humor," November 28, 1963, syndicated column in Charlestown, SC, *News and Courier*, p. 3. **"Mr. Nixon, in the last seven days"**: "Freedom of Communications: The Speeches, Remarks, Press Conferences, and Statements of Senator John F. Kennedy, August 1 through November 7, 1960," U.S. Government Printing Office, 1961, p. 900. **"Do you realize the responsibility I carry?"**: Arthur M. Schlesinger Jr., *A Thousand Days: John F. Kennedy in the White House*, p. 72. **"Extreme pressure from the hierarchy of his church"**: Thomas Maier, *The Kennedys: America's Emerald Kings*, p. 342. **"Last week a noted clergyman"**: Bill Adler, *The Kennedy Wit*, p. 21. **"Do you think a Protestant can be elected president in 1960?"**: James MacGregor Burns, *John Kennedy: A Political Profile*, p. 225. **"It all goes to show that, when the chips are down"**: Schlesinger, "A Thousand Days," excerpt in *Life*, July 16, 1965, p. 36. **"As far as I am concerned"**: David Nasaw, *The Patriarch: The Remarkable Life and Turbulent Times of Joseph P. Kennedy*, p. 754; also in Maier, *The Kennedys*, p. 400. **"He so obviously was against Jack"** and **"I mean he wasn't quite sure"**: Arthur M. Schlesinger Jr., *Jacqueline Kennedy: Historic Conversations on Life with John F. Kennedy*, pp. 101–5. **"They always seem to have a sort of persecution thing"**: Ibid., p. 76. **"John Kennedy walked out of the studio that night"**: Kerwin Swint, *Dark Genius: The Influential Career of Legendary Political Operative and Fox News Founder Roger Ailes*, p. 9. **"I heard too many people"**: January 31, 2008, Theodore

Sorensen video interview, www.bigthink.com. **"I am not sure that I know the answer"**: Winston S. Churchill, *His Father's Son: The Life of Randolph Churchill,* pp. 402–3. **"I salute you"**: *RKT,* p. 221. **"The people of the United States"**: November 27, 1963, John F. Kennedy cable to Churchill, BBK. (Beaverbrook was asked by Joe Kennedy to get the original cable received by Churchill.) **"Kennedy certainly has tremendous tasks before him"**: Randolph Churchill and Martin Gilbert, *Winston S. Churchill, Volume 8: Never Despair, 1945–1965,* p. 1318. **"The manful and effective way"**: Winston S. Churchill, *His Father's Son,* pp. 402–3.

CHAPTER 44: MENDING FENCES

"It is the first time that the creative Americans": L. Boyd Finch, *Legacies of Camelot: Stewart and Lee Udall, American Culture, and the Arts,* p. 24. **"To those old allies" and "I do not shrink"**: John F. Kennedy's Inaugural Address, JFK. **"I just had to tell you how absolutely overwhelmed"**: "Remembering Katherine Murphy Halle," privately published brochure, p. 14. **"When he was growing up in our house"**: Kay Halle, "In This Neighborhood People Keep Up with the Kennedys," *Cleveland Plain Dealer,* November 30, 1960, KMH. **"One thing I wish you"**: July 31, 1961, Jacqueline Kennedy letter, KMH. **"I think it is tremendously important"**: Kay Halle, "Thrill of a Lifetime: White House Dinner," *Cleveland Plain Dealer,* November 18, 1961, KMH. **"What have you got on your mind?" and "It's exactly what I'm for"**: February 7, 1967, p. 11, KMH. **"A Yankee mongrel" and "He thought the intention was"**: John Colville, *Winston Churchill and His Inner Circle,* pp. 112–13. **"Kay, let us drink to your great President"**: Martin Gilbert, *Winston S. Churchill, Volume 8: Never Despair, 1945–1965,* p. 1327. **"I understand your reasons" and "I've wanted to do that for twenty years"**: Anthony Montague Browne, *Long Sunset: Memoirs of Winston Churchill's Last Private Secretary,* pp. 290, 220. **Further details of Halle visit**: "Day at Chartwell" memo from circa 1961, KMH. **"In spite of 5 strokes" and "He put his fingers to his lips"**: "Day at Chartwell" memo from circa 1961, KMH. **"I fear, Mr. President"**: August 19, 1961, Halle letter to President Kennedy, BMB. **"The best thing he has done" and "Churchill is very graceful at this"**: Hugh Sidey,

"The President's Voracious Reading Habits," *Life*, March 17, 1961, p. 55. **"All the boastings of the Welfare State"**: Robert Rhodes James, ed., *Winston S. Churchill: His Complete Speeches, 1897–1963*, p. 8226. **"I assume it passed unanimously"**: Bill Adler, *The Kennedy Wit*, p. 81. **"I suppose shortly before we Limeys"** and **"Kennedy said he was more worried about Vietnam"**: October 1961 Randolph Churchill interview with President Kennedy, pp. 2–3, 10, CHUR. **"I'm a big bear"** and **"You may think this is strange"**: Elaine Landau, *John F. Kennedy Jr.*, p. 34. **"Joe Kennedy had a whole thing"**: Ogden interview, Library of Congress unprocessed file, Group 3 of 3, p. 252, PAM. **"As a diplomat"**: Rudy Abramson, *Spanning the Century: The Life of W. Averell Harriman, 1891–1986*, p. 577. **"There was a special touch of historic irony here"**: David Halberstam, *The Best and the Brightest*, p. 191. **"I trust David"**: Anthony Sampson, *Macmillan: A Study in Ambiguity*, p. 226. **"Some old prejudices"**: Nigel Ashton, *Kennedy, Macmillan and the Cold War: The Irony of Interdependence*, p. 55. **"Why are we, the Kennedys, in America"**: Lord Longford, *Kennedy*, p. 8. **"I don't know whether to kiss you"** and **"You're a good Catholic, Sissy"**: William Douglas-Home Oral History, October 28, 1966, p. 12, JFK. **"It was quite clear"**: Isaiah Berlin Oral History, April 12, 1965, pp. 7–10. **"By the way, over New Year's"**: Winston S. Churchill, *His Father's Son: The Life of Randolph Churchill*, p. 429. **"Face the thought of having to deal"**: February 7, 1967, p. 11, KMH; as well as Jonathan Aitken, *Heroes and Contemporaries*, p. 42.

CHAPTER 45: THE ENEMY WITHIN

"Would you tell us" and **"I thought only little girls giggled"**: *RKT*, p. 165. **"I feel rather like one"**: May 11, 1962, Lord Beaverbrook letter to Attorney General Robert Kennedy, BBK. **"To Bobby—who made the impossible possible"**: Ronald Goldfarb, *Perfect Villains, Imperfect Heroes: Robert F. Kennedy's War against Organized Crime*, p. 3. **"The Attorney General wondered if we had anything"**: March 24, 1961, FBI director J. Edgar Hoover memo in Tyler Kent file, FDR. **"They found in his pocket"**: JPK quotation in Stephen Trumbull and David Kraslow, "Convicted Embassy Official Reported Smearing Kennedy," *Charlotte Observer*, April 9, 1961, p. 11A, contained in Tyler Kent file,

FDR. **"Because of the possible high-level interest"**: June 10, 1963, State Department memo in Tyler Kent file, FDR. **"Was very appreciative of being informed"**: April 7, 1963, FBI memo in Tyler Kent file, FDR. **"The real measure of success"**: "The Presidency: Dad's Gotten Sick," *Time*, December 29, 1961. **"It is my hope"**: Undated Lord Beaverbrook cable, BBK. **"You lived today"**: Undated May 1959 Joseph P. Kennedy cable to Lord Beaverbrook, BBK. **"I appreciated more than I can tell you"**: March 21, 1963, Robert Kennedy letter to Baruch, in BMB. **"Dad's progress is slow"**: April 12, 1962, Edward M. Kennedy letter, BBK. **"We all are trying to help Ted"**: August 1, 1962, Rose Kennedy letter, BBK. **"An unusual representation of the great dynasties"** and **"It was due to my father"**: Arthur M. Schlesinger Jr., *Journals: 1952–2000*, pp. 188, 150. **"In this biography, he had clearly found himself"** and **"You are entitled to your doubt"**: Christopher Sykes essay, in Kay Halle, *The Grand Original: Portraits of Randolph Churchill by His Friends*, pp. 46–48. **"You have made a tremendous impression"**: October 5, 1963, Lord Beaverbrook cable, BBK. **"Those, of course, are the men"**: Halle, *The Grand Original*, pp. 10–11. **"Struggling to establish my own individuality"**: Sally Bedell Smith, *Reflected Glory: The Life of Pamela Churchill Harriman*, p. 56. **"I became bloody-minded"**: Randolph Churchill, *Twenty-One Years*, p. 136. **"Averell Harriman is the man who cuckolded me"**: Schlesinger, *Journals: 1952–2000*, p. 139. **"You know that my personal feelings"**: January 6, 1963, Randolph Churchill letter, CBL. **"I think your analysis of my relations"**: August 1960 Randolph Churchill letter, CBL. **"My God, how jealous"**: Anne Edwards, *Maria Callas: An Intimate Biography*, p. 258. **"For no apparent reason"** and **"Short of hitting him"**: Anthony Montague Browne, *Long Sunset: Memoirs of Winston Churchill's Last Private Secretary*, pp. 299–301. **"A desperately sad one"**: Winston S. Churchill, *His Father's Son: The Life of Randolph Churchill*, p. 439. **"Anthony, you didn't think"**: Montague Browne, *Long Sunset*, pp. 300–301. **"I do so very much love that man"**: Winston S. Churchill, *His Father's Son*, p. 439.

CHAPTER 46: AFTER THE BALL

"We were so proud of him": Jacqueline Kennedy essay in Kay Halle, *The Grand Original: Portraits of Randolph Churchill by His Friends*,

p. 285. **"Baruch thought highly enough"**: John Colville, *Winston Churchill and His Inner Circle*, p. 115. **"I trust your life was suitably enriched" and comment about "the old fraud"**: August 15, 1961, John Kenneth Galbraith letter in John Kenneth Galbraith, *Letters to Kennedy*, p. 79. **"Some of us will think it wise"**: Christina Koning, *The Wicked Wit of John F. Kennedy*, p. 43. **"Your own name will endure as long as free men survive to recall"**: John Ramsden, *Man of the Century: Winston Churchill and His Legend since 1945*, p. 112. **"In the dark days and darker nights"**: Reader's Digest Association, *Man of the Century: A Churchill Cavalcade*, p. 295. **"I would ask Mr. Randolph Churchill" and "I am, as you know, half American"**: Kay Halle, ed., *Winston Churchill on America and Britain: A Selection of His Thoughts on Anglo-American Relations*, pp. 41–43, supplemented with filmed account of the ceremony. **"I reject the view that Britain and the Commonwealth"**: Douglas B. Cornell, Associated Press, "Churchill Given U.S. Citizenship in Unique Honor," *Schenectady* (NY) *Gazette*, April 10, 1963, p. 1. **"I was so happy for Randolph"**: Jacqueline Kennedy quoted in Winston S. Churchill, *His Father's Son: The Life of Randolph Churchill*, p. 431. **"A child of both worlds"**: Clementine Churchill quoted in Halle, ed., *Winston Churchill on America and Britain*, p. 1. **Up on the second floor of the White House, staring through a window:** Based on mention of Joe Kennedy in Douglas B. Cornell, Associated Press, "Churchill Given U.S. Citizenship in Unique Honor," *Schenectady* (NY) *Gazette*, April 10, 1963, p. 1. **"Seen by many as filial atonement"**: Christopher Catherwood, *Winston Churchill: The Flawed Genius of World War II*, p. 23. **"I found Joe in a wheelchair"**: Unpublished draft of "Joseph P. Kennedy: The Motor under the Hood," an article by Kay Halle, p. 4, KMH. **"Kennedy senior had apparently caught a glimpse of it"**: Benjamin C. Bradlee, *Conversations with Kennedy*, p. 168. **"Here was this powerhouse of a father"**: Ben Bradlee, *A Good Life*, p. 246. **"My Father's interest is constant"**: Unpublished draft of "Joseph P. Kennedy: The Motor under the Hood," an article by Kay Halle, p. 3, KMH. **"[We] had a most amusing and high-spirited conversation"**: Brian Roberts, *Randolph: A Study of Churchill's Son*, p. 349. **"Rather a 'feminine' figure with visible prima-donna traits of jealousy"**: Jon Meacham, *Franklin and Winston: An Intimate Por-*

trait of an Epic Friendship, p. 368. **"Children of all ages"**: Winston S. Churchill, *His Father's Son*, pp. 432–34. **"Everybody who is anybody in Newport"**: Charlotte Curtis, "Janet Jennings Auchincloss Presented in Newport," *NYT*, August 18, 1963, p. 90. **"A rich barroom version"**: "Society: The Big Weekend," *Time*, August 30, 1963. **"Randolph was in love with the Kennedys"**: Winston S. Churchill, *His Father's Son*, pp. 432–34. **"Remaining a good loser"**: Anita Leslie, *Randolph: The Biography of Winston Churchill's Son*, p. 172. **"Father, who could not sing," "Don't worry Randolph," and "Be sure and visit Jackie"**: Ibid., pp. 433–34.

CHAPTER 47: THE BEST AND WORST OF DAYS
"The best four days of my life": Ryan Tubridy, *JFK in Ireland: Four Days That Changed a President*, p. 302. **"There are many people in the world"**: William Safire, *Lend Me Your Ears: Great Speeches in History*, p. 559. **"In Dublin Kennedy had nothing to bring"**: Lord Longford, *Kennedy*, p. 152. **"The Irish visit"**: Hugh Sidey essay in Deirdre Henderson, ed., *Prelude to Leadership: The European Diary of John F. Kennedy*, p. xl. **"Come back"**: Arthur M. Schlesinger Jr., *A Thousand Days*, p. 886. **"This is not the land of my birth"**: Pete Hamill, "JFK: The Real Thing," *New York*, November 28, 1988, p. 46. **"Uncle Harold"**: David Nunnerley, *President Kennedy and Britain*, p. 34–35. **"Operation Sanctuary" and "A man who loved a good crisis"**: David Profumo, *Bringing the House Down: A Family Memoir*, p. 211. **"Civil rights infighting"**: Drew Pearson, "Merry-Go-Round: Tuesday Elections Barometer for JFK," syndicated column, in *St. Petersburg Times*, November 4, 1963, p. 10. **"MacMillan at that time"**: Anthony Montague Browne, *Long Sunset: Memoirs of Winston Churchill's Last Private Secretary*, p. 287. **"I think this story is pure imagination"**: July 27, 1960, Lord Beaverbrook letter to Joseph Kennedy, BBK. **More than seventy Campbell phone calls**: Evan Thomas, *Robert Kennedy: His Life*, p. 167. **"The 'English attitude' towards politics"**: Garry Wills, *The Kennedy Imprisonment: A Meditation on Power*, pp. 73, 82. **"Weakly sexed" and "It makes no difference"**: Barton Biggs, *Wealth, War and Wisdom*, p. 62. **"Hundreds of them over his lifetime"**: David Nasaw, *The Patriarch: The Remarkable Life and Turbulent Times of Joseph P. Kennedy*,

p. 48. **"His daddy liked girls"**: Robert Dallek, *An Unfinished Life: John F. Kennedy, 1917–1963*, p. 151. **"I'd say that Joe"**: Alastair Granville Forbes oral history interview, October 31, 1966, JFK. **"Powerful men were interested in her"**: Rosemary Mahoney, "Powerful Attractions: Lady Jeanne Campbell," *New York Times Magazine*, December 30, 2007. **"Don't you budge for less than $17 million"**: Helen Lawrenson, *Stranger at the Party*, p. 108. **"If I divorced Harry"**: Alan Brinkley, *The Publisher: Henry Luce and His American Century*, p. 432. **"Brilliant grown-up piece"**: October 17, 1960, Randolph Churchill letter to Jeanne Campbell, CHUR. **"Randolph is built on the heroic scale"**: Lady Jean Campbell essay in Kay Halle, *The Grand Original: Portraits of Randolph Churchill by His Friends*, p. 160. **"Apart from the disloyalty to me"**: January 1, 1961, Randolph Churchill letter, CHUR. **"With such a man in office"**: Norman Mailer, "Superman Comes to the Supermarket," *Esquire*, November 1960. **"Well, sir, under the circumstances"**: Anne Chisholm and Michael Davie, *Lord Beaverbrook: A Life*, p. 488. **"As you would say"**: July 29, 1963, Kay Halle letter to Randolph Churchill, KMH. **"The ship will go wherever"**: Frank Brady, *Onassis: An Extravagant Life*, pp. 162–66. **"You can't imagine how terrific"**: Arianna Huffington, *Maria, Beyond the Callas Legend*, p. 217. **"Could not accept his generous hospitality"**: Nicholas Gage, *Greek Fire: The Story of Maria Callas and Aristotle Onassis*, p. 235. **"Why don't you go to New York"**: Arthur M. Schlesinger Jr., *Jacqueline Kennedy: Historic Conversations on Life with John F. Kennedy*, p. 25. **"Looking like thunder"**: Peter Evans, *Nemesis: The True Story of Aristotle Onassis, Jackie O., and the Love Triangle That Brought Down the Kennedys*, p. 76. **"For Christ's sake, Jackie"**: Gage, *Greek Fire*, p. 235. **"Jackie had made up her mind"**: Evans, *Nemesis*, p. 76. **"Your presence"**: Peter Evans, *Ari: The Life and Times of Aristotle Onassis*, pp. 195–96. **"She is quite as beautiful as you say"**: March 29, 1955, Lord Beaverbrook letter to Joseph P. Kennedy, in BBK. **"Does the ambitious Greek tycoon"**: Arianna Huffington, *Maria, Beyond the Callas Legend*, p. 252. **"Just tell her to cool it"**: Evans, *Ari*, pp. 195–97. **"What was really happening on the cruise"**: Frank Brady, *Onassis: An Extravagant Life*, p. 164. **"First Lady's Cruise Causes Stir"**: Headline in Drew Pearson column, *Washington Post*, October 17, 1963, contained in FBI file on Aristotle Onassis,

Part 1 of 10, p. 51. **"That while Jackie has been laden with presents"**: Fred Sparks, *The $20,000,000 Honeymoon*, p. 11. **"I was melancholy after the death of our baby"**: Based on author's interview with Father Richard McSorley and his personal papers housed at the Georgetown University Library, which first appeared in *The Kennedys: America's Emerald Kings*, p. 474. (N.B.: After the book's publication, Georgetown held a press conference to mark the historical nature of the McSorley papers, but soon ended access to these papers at the request of the Kennedy family to the Jesuits, detailed in "Will Scholars Regain Access to Georgetown's JFK Material?" *Library Journal* [December 17, 2003].) **"Poor Franklin" and "Maybe now you'll come to Texas"**: Benjamin C. Bradlee, *Conversations with Kennedy*, pp. 219–20. **"It has recently been suggested"**: Art Buchwald, "A Man with Humor," November 28, 1963, syndicated column, in KMH. **"Tears streamed down his face"**: Robin Weaver, "Celia Sandys—Chasing Churchill," November 15, 2010, www.womanaroundtown.com. **"Never have I been so filled with revulsion"**: November 24, 1963, Winston Churchill letter to Jacqueline Kennedy (copy), KMH. **"For a few moments"**: Winston S. Churchill, *His Father's Son: The Life of Randolph Churchill*, p. 434. **"Perhaps the only thing he bitterly"**: Frank Gannon essay in Halle, *The Grand Original*, p. 247. **"We few, we happy few"**: Laurence Leamer, *The Kennedy Men, 1901–1963*, p. 479. **"He was the best emblem"**: Winston S. Churchill, *His Father's Son*, p. 434. **"She is convinced that there is something very fishy"**: November 28, 1963, Lord Beaverbrook memo in BBK. **"May Joe find solace"**: Ralph Martin, *Seeds of Destruction: Joe Kennedy and His Sons*, p. 487. **"Ari quickly discovered his role"** and **"I have never made the mistake"**: Evans, *Ari*, pp. 197–98. **"Why God, why?"**: Charles Spaulding oral history, March 14, 1968, JFK. **"Veered close to being a tragedy"**: Edward M. Kennedy, *True Compass: A Memoir*, p. 210. **"So extraordinarily helpful"**: August 1964, Ethel Kennedy letter to Marie Harriman, WAH. **"A Jew wife"**: *HTF*, p. 531. **"Your unquestioned loyalty"**: July 22, 1966, Rose Kennedy letter, Averell Harriman Papers, Library of Congress, Washington, DC. **"I hope it will give me"**: April 1964 Jacqueline Kennedy letter, KMH.

CHAPTER 48: THOUGHTS THAT LIE TOO DEEP

"Clouds and darkness": Alfred Lord Tennyson's "Merlin and the Gleam," collected in Curtis Hidden Page, ed., *British Poets of the Nineteenth Century*, p. 552. **"Mythology distracts us everywhere":** Ted Widmer, *Listening In: The Secret White House Recordings of John F. Kennedy*, p. 1. **"He, together with his family," "To all of you," and details of Runnymede ceremony:** Anthony Lewis, "British Shrine Honors Kennedy," *NYT*, May 15, 1965, p. 1, supplemented by other newspaper coverage and Internet footage of Queen Elizabeth's comments at ceremony. **"His devotion to Mrs. Jacqueline Kennedy":** Frank Gannon essay in Kay Halle, *The Grand Original: Portraits of Randolph Churchill by His Friends*, p. 248. **"I always keep thinking of Camelot":** Alistair Horne, *Harold Macmillan, Volume 2: 1957–1986*, p. 577. **"I saw him at fairly close range":** Ann M. Sperber, *Murrow, His Life and Times*, p. 694. **"Oh! Why did you leave us, Owen":** Evan Thomas, *Robert Kennedy: His Life*, p. 289. **"Arguably, the achievement of Churchill's final years":** Richard Toye, *Churchill's Empire: The World That Made Him and the World He Made*, p. 316. **"We can no longer afford":** David Nunnerley, *President Kennedy and Britain*, p. 197. **JFK dubbed Diem the "Winston Churchill" of Southeast Asia:** *RKT*, p. 725. **"To read everything about Churchill" and "Tell that son of a bitch":** David Halberstam, *The Best and the Brightest*, pp. 431, 531. **"His Churchillian rhetoric":** Ross Douthat, "The Enduring Cult of Kennedy," *NYT*, November 26, 2011. **"Unnecessary war":** David Reynolds, *In Command of History: Churchill Fighting and Writing the Second World War*, p. 90. **"No country has done more":** Transcript of President Kennedy press conference, May 9, 1962, JFK. **"First examine our attitude towards peace itself":** Jeffrey D. Sachs, *To Move the World: JFK's Quest for Peace*, p. 76. **"Whereas, Sir Winston":** William Douglas-Home oral history, October 28, 1966, p. 12, JFK. **"His finest hour":** April 30, 1970, President Richard M. Nixon address about Southeast Asia; and Hal Bochin, *Richard Nixon: Rhetorical Strategist*, p. 135. **"I can only repeat my ignorance":** Ben Bradlee, *A Good Life*, p. 217. **"I realized he was a man of many faces":** June 25, 1995, Norman Mailer interview with *Booknotes* host Brian Lamb, www.booknotes. org. **"He felt that everything" and "The Dark Angel beckons":** John

Pearson, *The Private Lives of Winston Churchill*, p. 421. **"If anything should happen to me"**: Clive Irving, "The Shade of Churchill: Randolph in Retrospect," *Sunday Times* (undated but clearly June 1968), KMH. **"England needs you"**: Winston S. Churchill, *His Father's Son: The Life of Randolph Churchill*, p. 447. **"A typical triumph of modern science"**: R. Z. Sheppard, "Books: An Establishment of One," *Time*, October 17, 1977, in review of Michael Davie, ed., *The Diaries of Evelyn Waugh* (New York: Little, Brown, 1977). **"Enchanted by your benignant thoughts"**: Halle, *The Grand Original*, p. 12. **"The author has no specifically literary talent"** and **"incidentally, why did you scrap your phrase"**: "Letters from Evelyn Waugh," *Encounter*, July 1968, p. 14. **"He is not a man"**: Jon Meacham, *Franklin and Winston: An Intimate Portrait of an Epic Friendship*, p. 41. **"You know, when the Devil comes to earth"**: Anthony Montague Browne, *Long Sunset: Memoirs of Winston Churchill's Last Private Secretary*, p. 150. **"My oldest and closest friend"** and **"Sir Winston told me several times"**: Randolph Churchill and Martin Gilbert, *Winston S. Churchill, Volume 8: Never Despair, 1945–1965*, p. 1353. **"What a burden you have borne"**: Mary Soames, *Clementine Churchill: The Biography of a Marriage*, p. 532. **"As I closed the door"**: Lord Moran, *Churchill: Taken from the Diaries of Lord Moran: The Struggle for Survival, 1940–1965*, p. 136. **"Would you believe it"**: Sarah Churchill, *Keep On Dancing*, pp. 336–37. **"I want it in memory of my American mother"** and **"soldier, statesman and leader"**: Eddy Gilmore, "World Pauses to Honor Sir Winston Churchill at Momentous Funeral," Associated Press, *The Day*, January 30, 1965, p. 1. **"Poor Randolph Churchill called me"**: January 22, 1965, Kay Halle letter to Robert Kennedy, KMH. **"More than any other event since the assassination"**: James Reston, "Capital Impressed: Capital Is Moved by London Scenes," *NYT*, January 31, 1965, p. 1. **"Sobbing like a baby"**: Peter Evans, *Ari: The Life and Times of Aristotle Onassis*, p. 203. **"Averell, they look older"**: "Kay Halle Recalls Flight with Ike," essay, KMH. **"It had been a memorable moment"**: Rudy Abramson, *Spanning the Century: The Life of W. Averell Harriman, 1891–1986*, p. 682. **"Since we were both suddenly free and alone"** and **"My dear,"** replied Clemmie, **"it's an old flame rekindled"**: Ogden interview, Library of Congress unprocessed file, Group 3 of 3, p. 520, PAM. **"That he was a great man cannot be doubted": John Charmley, *Churchill: The End of Glory—A Political Biography,* p. 648. "He never wavered": Pamela Harriman interview, CHUR. "Anthony's wild and frequent infidelities": Sarah Churchill, *Keep On Dancing,* p. 256. "A tremendous shock to her": Gilbert, *Winston S. Churchill, Volume 8: Never Despair,* p. 1249. "When I saw him": Sarah Churchill, *Keep On Dancing,* p. 166. "I never discuss": Brian Roberts, *Randolph: A Study of Churchill's Son,* p. 310. "Diana had not, at least for many years": John Colville, *Winston Churchill and His Inner Circle,* p. 39. "Although Winston found psychological troubles": Soames, *Clementine Churchill,* pp. 443–44. "My mother had a very wonderful nanny": Justine Picardie, "The Soames Saga," (London) *Telegraph,* June 6, 2010. "As he grew older": John Pearson, *The Private Lives of Winston Churchill,* p. 414. "You non-entity": Rupert Strong recollections, KMH. "I fully agree with what you write": April 15, 1965, Randolph Churchill letter to Baruch, BMB. "Randolph really had all the right instincts": Ogden interview, Library of Congress unprocessed file, Group 1 of 3, p. 14, PAM. "It could hardly be done better" and "there was now no one to help him": Associated Press, "Randolph Churchill's Biography of Father Acclaimed," *Sarasota* (FL) *Herald Tribune,* November 28, 1966, p. 12. "Please know how happy": Winston S. Churchill, *His Father's Son,* p. 479. "Of course, I have thousands of anecdotes": "Churchill's Muse Pursued by Son," *NYT,* November 27, 1966.

CHAPTER 49: THE ONCE AND FUTURE KING
"The praises of so good and great a king": Charles Churchill, *Poems,* p. 97. "Only fools want to be great": T. H. White, *The Once and Future King,* p. 180. A bust in his office of Winston Churchill: Evan Thomas, *Robert Kennedy: His Life,* p. 114. "This is the greatest compliment": Winston S. Churchill, *His Father's Son: The Life of Randolph Churchill,* pp. 483–85. "Randolph envisaged a two-volume work" and "It was like being given three Nobel prizes": Martin Gilbert's essay, in Kay Halle, *The Grand Original: Portraits of Randolph Churchill by His Friends,* p. 240. "By then we will": Winston S. Churchill, *His Father's Son,* pp. 483–85. "I have known Mrs. Kennedy": Randolph Churchill essay, "The Manchester Book," CHUR. "You can't go through life":

Randolph S. Churchill, "Why Mrs. Kennedy Went to Law," undated published article, CHUR. **"As though he were my own brother"**: William Manchester, *The Death of a President, November 20–November 25, 1963*, p. 260. **"David Harlech seemed to be an almost ideal choice"**: Kevin Cullen, "Finding Her Way in the Clan," *Boston Globe*, May 13, 2007. **"Invisible man" and "I know this is what the Ambassador"**: Fred Sparks, *The $20,000,000 Honeymoon*, pp. 14, 225. **"Do you know what I think"**: *RKT*, p. 895. **"I like politicians" and "That was Lord Tweedsmuir"**: Jack Newfield, *RFK: A Memoir*, p. 291. **"Now it's on to Chicago"**: Mark Kurlansky, *1968: The Year That Rocked the World*, p. 262. **"And now Bobby"**: Fernand Auberjonois, "The European Diary: Churchills' Fate Compared to Kennedys'," *Toledo Blade*, June 10, 1968, p. 8. **"What stupid people"**: Anita Leslie, *Randolph: The Biography of Winston Churchill's Son*, p. 207. **"I have become reconciled"**: David Lebedoff, *The Same Man: George Orwell and Evelyn Waugh in Love and War*, p. 110. **"Yes, it is hard to believe"**: Alan Brien, "Great Contemporary," *The New Statesman*, June 14, 1968, KMH. **"A doctor has to write"**: Leslie, *Randolph*, p. 207. **"Poor Randolph Churchill"**: Brian Roberts, *Randolph: A Study of Churchill's Son*, p. 364. **"With single-minded perseverance"**: Alden Whitman, *Come to Judgment*, p. 126. **"His cause was her cause"**: Mary Soames, *Clementine Churchill: The Biography of a Marriage*, p. 279. **"I hear your husband thought" and "But through your husband's great courage"**: June 9, 1971, Rose Kennedy memo, ROSE. **The Last Lion:** Peter S. Canellos, ed., *The Last Lion: The Fall and Rise of Ted Kennedy*, p. 5. **"My thoughts turned often to my dad," "Even as he marched through one invisible barricade," and "You can have a serious life"**: Edward M. Kennedy, *True Compass: A Memoir*, pp. 40–47. **"You started out"**: Clive Irving interview in Randolph S. Churchill, *Twenty-One Years*, p. 135. **"Now it always seemed to me"**: Arthur M. Schlesinger Jr., *Jacqueline Kennedy: Historic Conversations on Life with John F. Kennedy*, pp. 50–51. **"In newspapers she read"**: Manchester, *The Death of a President*, p. 628. **"Mr. and Mrs. Onassis are certainly spending"**: Sparks, *The $20,000,000 Honeymoon*, p. 50. **"Power made him [JFK] a better man"**: Schlesinger, *Jacqueline Kennedy: Historic Conversations*, p. 248. **"His was such an exuberance"**: Aristotle Onassis essay, in Halle, *The Grand Original*, p.

286. **"He was the heir to an enormous"**: Christopher Sykes essay, in Halle, *The Grand Original*, p. 44. **"They are both so nervous"**: Halle, *The Grand Original*, p. 284. **"You know how Jack and Bobby loved him"**: May 12, 1969, Jacqueline Kennedy Onassis letter to Kay Halle, KMH. **"If, when he is older"**: Halle, *The Grand Original*, p. 284.

Selected Bibliography

Abramson, Rudy. *Spanning the Century: The Life of W. Averell Harriman, 1891–1986.* New York: William Morrow, 1992.

Addison, Paul. *Churchill: On the Home Front 1900–1955.* London: Pimlico, 1993.

Adler, Bill. *The Kennedy Wit.* New York: Grammercy, 1964.

Aitken, Jonathan. *Heroes and Contemporaries.* London: Continuum, 2006.

Alkon, Paul K. *Winston Churchill's Imagination.* Cranbury, NJ: Associated University Presses, 2006.

Alvarez, David J. *Spies in the Vatican: Espionage and Intrigue from Napoleon to the Holocaust.* Lawrence: University Press of Kansas, 2002.

Amory, Mark, ed. *The Letters of Evelyn Waugh.* London: Weidenfeld and Nicolson, 1980.

Anderson, Terry H. *The United States, Great Britain, and the Cold War, 1944–1947.* Columbia: University of Missouri Press, 1981.

Andrew, Christopher. *Defend the Realm: The Authorized History of MI5.* New York: Random House, 2009.

Ashley, Jack. *Journey into Silence.* London: Bodley Head, 1973.

Ashton, Nigel. *Kennedy, Macmillan and the Cold War: The Irony of Interdependence.* New York: Palgrave Macmillan, 2002.

Baruch, Bernard Mannes. *Baruch: The Public Years.* New York: Holt, Rinehart and Winston, 1960.

Baylis, John. *Anglo-American Defence Relations, 1939–1984: The Special Relationship.* New York: Macmillan, 1984.

Bearse, Ray, and Anthony Read. *Conspirator: The Untold Story of Tyler Kent.* New York: Nan A. Talese/Doubleday, 1991.

Beaton, Cecil. *The Years Between: Diaries 1939–1940.* New York: Holt, Rinehart and Winston, 1965.

Beaverbrook, Lord. *The Abdication of King Edward VIII.* New York: Atheneum, 1966.

———— (Max Aitken). *Men and Power, 1917–1918.* London: Archon Books, 1968.

————. *The Three Keys to Success,* New York: Duell, Sloan & Pearce, 1956.

Bell, Christopher M. *Churchill and Sea Power.* Oxford, UK: Oxford University Press, 2012.

Bellush, Bernard. *He Walked Alone: A Biography of John Gilbert Winant.* The Hague: Mouton, 1968.

Bentley, Michael. *Public and Private Doctrine: Essays in British History Presented to Maurice Cowling.* Cambridge, UK: Cambridge University Press, 2002.

Berg, Scott A. *Lindbergh.* New York: G. P. Putnam's Sons, 1998.

Beschloss, Michael R. *Presidential Courage: Brave Leaders and How They Changed America 1789–1989.* New York: Simon & Schuster, 2008.

Best, Geoffrey. *Churchill: A Study in Greatness.* London: Hambledon and London, 2001.

Biggs, Barton. *Wealth, War, and Wisdom.* New York: John Wiley and Sons, 2008.

Black, Conrad. *Franklin Delano Roosevelt: Champion of Freedom.* New York: PublicAffairs, 2005.

Blair, Joan, and Clay Blair. *The Search for JFK.* New York: Berkley Publishing, 1976.

Blake, Robert, ed. *Churchill: A Major New Assessment of his Life in Peace and War.* New York: W. W. Norton and Company, 1993.

Bly, Nellie. *The Kennedy Men: Three Generations of Sex, Scandal, and Secrets.* New York: Kensington Books, 1996.

Bochin, Hal. *Richard Nixon: Rhetorical Strategist.* New York: Greenwood Press, 1990.

Boothe, Clare. *Europe in the Spring.* New York: Alfred A. Knopf, 1940.

Bradford, Sarah. *America's Queen: The Life of Jacqueline Kennedy Onassis.* New York: Viking, 2000.

Bradlee, Ben. *A Good Life.* New York: Simon & Schuster, 1996.

———. *Conversations with Kennedy.* New York: W. W. Norton, 1984.

Brady, Frank. *Onassis: An Extravagant Life.* Englewood Cliffs, NJ: Prentice-Hall, 1977.

Brendon, Piers. *The Decline and Fall of the British Empire, 1781–1997.* New York: Alfred A. Knopf, 2008.

Brenner, Marie. *Great Dames: What I Learned from Older Women.* New York: Crown, 2001.

Brinkley, Alan. *The Publisher: Henry Luce and His American Century.* New York: Alfred A. Knopf, 2010.

Buchan, John. *Pilgrim's Way.* Boston: Houghton Mifflin, 1940.

Buczacki, Stefan. *Churchill and Chartwell: The Untold Story of Churchill's Houses and Gardens.* London: Frances Lincoln, 2007.

Burns, James MacGregor. *John Kennedy: A Political Profile.* New York: Harcourt, Brace and World, 1961.

Byrne, Paula. *Mad World: Evelyn Waugh and the Secrets of Brideshead.* New York: HarperCollins, 2010.

Canellos, Peter S., ed. *The Last Lion: The Fall and Rise of Ted Kennedy.* New York: Simon & Schuster, 2009.

Cannadine, David. *Aspects of Aristocracy: Grandeur and Decline in Modern Britain.* New Haven, CT: Yale University Press, 1994.

———. *In Churchill's Shadow: Confronting the Past in Modern Britain.* New York: Penguin, 2002.

Capote, Truman. *Answered Prayers: The Unfinished Novel.* New York: Random House, 1987.

Carter, Violet Bonham. *Winston Churchill as I Knew Him.* New York: Harcourt Brace and World, 1965 (published in the United States as *Winston Churchill: An Intimate Portrait*).

Catherwood, Christopher. *Winston Churchill: The Flawed Genius of World War II.* New York: Berkley, 2009.

Charmley, John. *Churchill: The End of Glory—A Political Biography.* New York: Harcourt, Brace, 1993.

Chisholm, Anne, and Michael Davie. *Lord Beaverbrook: A Life.* New York: Alfred A. Knopf, 1993.

Churchill, Charles. *Poems*. London: J. Wilkes, 1776.

Churchill, Randolph S. *Twenty-One Years*. Boston: Houghton Mifflin, 1965.

———. *Winston S. Churchill, Volume I: Youth, 1874–1900*. Boston, Houghton Mifflin, 1966.

Churchill, Randolph, and Martin Gilbert. *Winston S. Churchill: The Wilderness Years, 1929–1935*. London: Heinemann, 1967.

———. *Winston S. Churchill, Volume 2: Young Statesman, 1901–1914*. London: Heinemann, 1967.

———. *Winston S. Churchill, Volume 5: The Prophet of Truth, 1922–1939*. Boston: Houghton Mifflin, 1976.

———. *Winston S. Churchill, Volume 6: Finest Hour, 1939–41*. Boston: Houghton Mifflin, 1983.

———. *Winston S. Churchill, Volume 8: Never Despair, 1945–1965*. London: Heinemann, 1966.

Churchill, Sarah. *Keep On Dancing: An Autobiography*. New York: Coward, McCann and Geoghegan, 1981.

———. *A Thread in the Tapestry*. London: Andre Deutsch, 1967.

Churchill, Winston. *Amid These Storms: Thoughts and Adventures*. New York: Scribner, 1932.

———. *Great Contemporaries*. London: Collins, 1959.

———. *The Great Republic: A History of America*. New York: Random House, 1999.

———. *A History of the English Speaking Peoples, Volume 4*. New York: Dodd, Mead & Co., 1966.

———. *Lord Randolph Churchill, Volume 1*. London: Macmillan, 1906.

———. *Marlborough: His Life and Times, Volume 1*. New York: Scribner, 1968.

———. *My Early Life*. London: Eland, 1930.

———. *The Second World War, Volume 1: The Gathering Storm*. Boston: Houghton Mifflin, 1948.

———. *The Second World War, Volume 2: Their Finest Hour*. Boston: Houghton Mifflin, 1949.

———. *The Second World War, Volume 5: Closing the Ring*. London: Cassell, 1952.

————. *The Second World War, Volume 6: Triumph and Tragedy*. London: Cassell, 1954.

————. *The Story of the Malakand Field Force: An Episode of the Frontier War*. London: Longmans, Green, 1901.

————. *The Unrelenting Struggle: War Speeches by the Rt. Hon. Winston S. Churchill*. Boston: Little, Brown, 1942.

————. *The World Crisis, 1911–1918*. New York: Scribner, 1931.

Churchill, Winston, and David Cannadine. *Blood, Toil, Tears, and Sweat: The Speeches of Winston Churchill*. Boston: Houghton Mifflin, 1989.

Churchill, Winston S. *His Father's Son: The Life of Randolph Churchill*. London: Weidenfeld and Nicolson, 1996.

Clarke, Peter. *Mr. Churchill's Profession: The Statesman as Author and the Book That Defined the "Special Relationship."* New York: Bloomsbury, 2012.

Clarke, Thurston. *Ask Not: The Inauguration of John F. Kennedy and the Speech That Changed America*. New York: Henry Holt, 2004.

Clifford, Clark M., and Richard Holbrooke. *Counsel to the President: A Memoir*. New York: Anchor, 1992.

Clough, Bryan. *State Secrets: The Kent-Wolkoff Affair*. Hove, UK: Hideaway Publications, 2005.

Coit, Margaret L. *Mr. Baruch*. Boston: Houghton Mifflin, 1957.

Cole, Wayne S. *Charles A. Lindbergh and the Battle against American Intervention in World War II*. New York: Harcourt Brace Jovanovich, 1974.

Collier, Peter, and David Horowitz. *The Kennedys: An American Drama*. New York: Summit Books, 1984.

Collier, Richard. *The World in Flames: 1940*. London: Hamish Hamilton, 1979.

Colville, John. *The Fringes of Power: The Incredible Inside Story of Winston Churchill during World War II*. Guilford, CT: Lyons Press, 2002.

————. *Winston Churchill and His Inner Circle*. New York: Wyndam Books, 1981.

Coolidge, Olivia E. *Winston Churchill and the Story of Two World Wars*. Boston: Houghton Mifflin, 1960.

Cooney, John. *The American Pope: The Life and Times of Francis Cardinal Spellman*. New York; Times Books, 1984.

Cowles, Virginia. *Churchill: The Era and the Man*. London: Hamish Hamilton, 1953.

———. *The Phantom Major: The Story of David Stirling and His Desert Command*. New York: Harper, 1958.

Cutler, John Henry. *Honey Fitz: Three Steps to the White House: The Life and Times of John F. (Honey Fitz) Fitzgerald*. Indianapolis: Bobbs-Merrill, 1962.

Dallek, Robert. *An Unfinished Life: John F. Kennedy, 1917–1963*. Boston: Little, Brown, 2003.

David, Lester. *Ted Kennedy: Triumphs and Tragedies*. New York: Grosset and Dunlap, 1972.

Davie, Michael. *The Diaries of Evelyn Waugh, Part 2*. London: Weidenfeld and Nicolson, 1976.

Davies, Marion. *The Times We Had: Life with William Randolph Hearst*. Indianapolis: Bobbs-Merrill, 1975.

De Courcy, Anne. *Diana Mosley: Mitford Beauty, British Fascist, Hitler's Angel*. New York: HarperCollins, 2003.

D'Este, Carlo. *Warlord: A Life of Winston Churchill at War, 1874–1945*. New York: HarperCollins, 2008.

Dimbleby, David, and David Reynolds. *An Ocean Apart: The Relationship between Britain and America in the Twentieth Century*. New York: Random House, 1988.

Doenecke, Justus D. *In Danger Undaunted: The Anti-Interventionist Movement of 1940–1941 as Revealed in the Papers of the America First Committee*. Stanford, CA: Hoover Institution Press, 1990.

Eade, Charles. *Churchill: By His Contemporaries*. New York: Simon & Schuster, 1954.

Edgerton, Gary. *The Columbia History of American Television*. New York: Columbia University Press, 2010.

Edmonds, Robin. *The Big Three: Churchill, Roosevelt, and Stalin in Peace and War*. London: Hamish Hamilton, 1991.

Edwards, Anne. *Maria Callas: An Intimate Biography*. New York: Macmillan, 2001.

Elsey, George M. *An Unplanned Life: A Memoir*. Columbia: University of Missouri Press, 2005.

Enright, Dominique. *The Wicked Wit of Winston Churchill.* London: Michael O'Mara Books, 2001.

Evans, Peter. *Ari: The Life and Times of Aristotle Onassis.* New York: Summit Books, 1986.

———. *Nemesis: The True Story of Aristotle Onassis, Jackie O, and the Love Triangle That Brought Down the Kennedys.* New York: ReganBooks/HarperCollins, 2004.

Finch, L. Boyd. *Legacies of Camelot: Stewart and Lee Udall, American Culture, and the Arts.* Norman: University of Oklahoma Press, 2008.

Fishman, Jack. *"My Darling Clementine": The Story of Lady Churchill.* New York: David McKay, 1963.

Flor, Carlos Villar, and Robert Murray Davis, eds. *Waugh Without End: New Trends in Evelyn Waugh Studies.* Bern: Peter Lang, 2005.

Foot, Michael. *Debts of Honour.* New York: HarperCollins, 1981.

Fort, Adrian. *Nancy: The Story of Lady Astor.* New York: St. Martin's Press, 2013.

Foster, R. F. *Lord Randolph Churchill: A Political Life.* Oxford, UK: Clarendon Press, 1981.

Fraser, Nicholas, Philip Jacobson, Mark Ottaway, and Lewis Chester. *Aristotle Onassis.* Philadelphia: J. B. Lippincott Company, 1977.

Freidel, Frank Burt. *Franklin D. Roosevelt: A Rendezvous with Destiny.* Boston: Little, Brown, 1990.

Gage, Nicholas. *Greek Fire: The Story of Maria Callas and Aristotle Onassis.* New York: Alfred A. Knopf, 2000.

Galbraith, John Kenneth. *Letters to Kennedy.* Cambridge, MA: Harvard University Press, 1998.

Garland, Jasper Vanderbilt. *War and the Americas.* New York: H. W. Wilson, 1941.

Gilbert, Martin. *Churchill: A Life.* New York: Henry Holt, 1991.

———. *Churchill and America.* New York: Simon & Schuster, 2008.

———. *Churchill and the Jews: A Lifelong Friendship.* New York: Macmillan, 2008.

———. *Churchill: The Power of Words.* New York: DaCapo Press, 2012.

———. *The Churchill War Papers: The Ever-Widening War, 1941.* New York: W. W. Norton, 2001.

———. *Winston Churchill: The Wilderness Years.* London: Book Club Associates/Macmillan, 1981.

———. *Winston S. Churchill, Volume 7: Road to Victory, 1941–1945.* London: Heinemann, 1986.

Gilder, Richard Watson. *The Century Illustrated Monthly Magazine.* New York: Scribner, 1913.

Goldfarb, Ronald. *Perfect Villains, Imperfect Heroes: Robert F. Kennedy's War against Organized Crime.* New York: Random House, 1995.

Golway, Terry. *Together We Cannot Fail: How FDR Led the Nation from Darkness to Victory.* Naperville, IL: SourceBooks, 2009.

Goodwin, Doris Kearns. *The Fitzgeralds and the Kennedys: An American Saga.* New York: Simon & Schuster, 1987.

———. *No Ordinary Time: Franklin and Eleanor Roosevelt, the Home Front in World War II.* New York: Simon & Schuster, 1995.

Grant, James. *Bernard M. Baruch: The Adventures of a Wall Street Legend.* New York: Simon & Schuster, 1983.

Halberstam, David. *The Best and the Brightest.* New York: Random House, 1972.

———. *The Powers That Be.* New York: Alfred A. Knopf, 1979.

Halle, Kay. *The Grand Original: Portraits of Randolph Churchill by His Friends.* Boston: Houghton Mifflin, 1971.

———. *The Irrepressible Churchill: Winston's World, Wars and Wit.* London: Conway, 1985.

———, ed. *Winston Churchill on America and Britain: A Selection of His Thoughts on Anglo-American Relations.* New York: Walker and Company, 1970.

Hamilton, Nigel. *JFK: Reckless Youth.* New York: Random House, 1993.

Harbutt, Fraser J. *The Iron Curtain: Churchill, America, and the Origins of the Cold War.* New York: Oxford University Press, 1986.

Hargrove, Julia. *John F. Kennedy's Inaugural Address.* Dayton, OH: Lorenz, 2000.

Hastings, Max. *Winston's War: Churchill, 1940–1945.* New York: Alfred A. Knopf, 2010.

Hastings, Selina. *Evelyn Waugh: A Biography.* New York: Random House, 1995.

Hayward, Steven F. *Churchill on Leadership: Executive Success in the Face of Adversity.* New York: Random House, 2010.

————. *Greatness: Reagan, Churchill, and the Making of Extraordinary Leaders.* New York: Crown Forum, 2005.

Herman, Arthur. *Gandhi and Churchill: The Epic Rivalry That Destroyed an Empire and Forged Our Age.* New York: Bantam Dell, 2008.

Hersey, John. "Survival." In A. J. Liebling, ed. *The New Yorker Book of War Pieces: London, 1939–Hiroshima, 1945.* New York: Reynal and Hitchcock, 1947.

Hersh, Seymour. *The Dark Side of Camelot.* Boston: Little, Brown, 1997.

Higham, Charles. *Rose: The Life and Times of Rose Fitzgerald Kennedy.* New York: Pocket, 1995.

Hitchens, Christopher. *Blood, Class, and Empire: The Enduring Anglo-American Relationship.* New York: Nation Books, 2004.

Horne, Alistair. *Harold Macmillan, Volume 2: 1957–1986.* New York: Viking, 1989.

Hough, Richard Alexander. *Winston and Clementine: The Triumphs and Tragedies of the Churchills.* New York: Bantam, 1981.

Huffington, Arianna Stassinopoulos. *Maria: Beyond the Callas Legend.* London: Weidenfeld and Nicolson, 1980.

Humes, James C. *Eisenhower and Churchill: The Partnership That Saved the World.* New York: Broadway Press, 2001.

Hutchinson, Tom. *The Battle of Britain: The True Story of Those Dramatic Four Months in 1940.* London: Purnell, 1969.

James, Robert Rhodes. *Anthony Eden.* New York: McGraw-Hill, 1987.

————, ed. *Chips: The Diaries of Sir Henry Channon.* London: Weidenfeld and Nicolson, 1967.

————. *Churchill: A Study in Failure, 1900–1939.* New York: World Publishing, 1970.

————, ed. *Winston S. Churchill: His Complete Speeches, 1897–1963.* London: Chelsea House, 1974.

Jenkins, Roy. *Churchill: A Biography.* New York: Farrar, Straus and Giroux, 2001.

Johnson, Paul. *Churchill.* New York: Viking, 2009.

Keegan, John. *Winston Churchill: A Life.* New York: Penguin, 2007.

Kelly, Charles J. *Tex McCrary: Wars-Women-Politics, An Adventurous Life Across The American Century.* Lanham, MD: Hamilton Books/ Rowman and Littlefield, 2009.

Kennedy, Edward M. *True Compass: A Memoir.* New York: Twelve, 2009.

Kennedy, John F. *Why England Slept.* London: Hutchinson, 1940.

Kennedy, John F., and Deirdre Henderson, ed., with an introduction by Hugh Sidey. *Prelude to Leadership: The European Diary of John F. Kennedy: Summer 1945.* Washington, DC: Regnery Publishing, 1995.

Kennedy, Rose Fitzgerald. *Times to Remember.* New York: Harper, 1974.

Kessler, Ronald. *The Bureau: The Secret History of the FBI.* New York: Macmillan, 2003.

―――. *The Sins of the Father: Joseph P. Kennedy and the Dynasty He Founded.* New York: Warner Books, 1997.

Ketchum, Richard M. *The Borrowed Years: 1938–1941.* New York: Anchor, 1989.

Kimball, Warren F. *Churchill and Roosevelt: Alliance Forged, November 1942–February 1944.* Princeton, NJ: Princeton University Press, 1984.

―――, ed. *Churchill and Roosevelt: The Complete Correspondence, Vol. 1.* Princeton, NJ: Princeton University Press, 1984.

Kipling, Rudyard. *The Collected Poems of Rudyard Kipling.* Ware, UK: Wordsworth, 1994.

Koning, Christina. *The Wicked Wit of John F. Kennedy.* London: Michael O'Mara, 2003.

Koskoff, David E. *Joseph P. Kennedy: A Life and Times.* Englewood Cliffs, NJ: Prentice-Hall, 1974.

Krabbe, Henning. *Voices from Britain: Broadcast History, 1939–45.* Crows Nest, Australia: George Allen and Unwin, 1947.

Kraus, Rene. *Winston Churchill: A Biography.* New York: J. B. Lippincott Company, 1940.

Kurlansky, Mark. *1968: The Year That Rocked the World.* New York: Random House, 2005.

Lambert, Angela. *1939: The Last Season of Peace.* New York: Weidenfeld and Nicolson, 1989.

Landau, Elaine. *John F. Kennedy Jr.* Brookfield, CT: Twenty-First Century Books, 2000.

Langhorne, Elizabeth Coles. *Nancy Astor and Her Friends*. New York: Praeger, 1974.

Langworth, Richard M. *Churchill by Himself: The Definitive Collection of Quotations*. New York: Public Affairs, 2008.

———. *The Definitive Wit of Winston Churchill*. New York: Public Affairs, 2009.

Lawrence, T. E. *The Seven Pillars of Wisdom: A Triumph*. New York: Anchor Books, 1935.

Lawrenson, Helen. *Stranger at the Party*. New York: Random House, 1975.

Leamer, Laurence. *The Kennedy Men: 1901–1963*. New York: HarperCollins, 2002.

———. *The Kennedy Women: The Saga of an American Family*. New York: Villard, 1994.

Leaming, Barbara. *Jack Kennedy: The Education of a Statesman*. New York: W. W. Norton, 2006.

———. *Mrs. Kennedy: The Missing History of the Kennedy Years*. New York: Simon & Schuster, 2002.

Lebedoff, David. *The Same Man: George Orwell and Evelyn Waugh in Love and War*. New York: Random House, 2008.

Leslie, Anita. *Lady Randolph Churchill: The Story of Jennie Jerome*. New York: Scribner, 1969.

———. *Randolph: The Biography of Winston Churchill's Son*. New York: Beaufort Books, 1985.

Lewis, Alfred Allan. *Man of the World, Herbert Bayard Swope: A Charmed Life of Pulitzer Prizes, Poker, and Politics*. Indianapolis, IN: Bobbs-Merrill, 1978.

Lindbergh, Charles A. *The Wartime Journals of Charles A. Lindbergh*. New York: Harcourt Brace Jovanovich, 1970.

Longford, Frank Pakenham (Earl of), and Thomas P. O'Neill. *Éamon de Valera*. Boston: Houghton Mifflin, 1971.

Longford, Lord. *Kennedy*. London: Weidenfeld and Nicolson, 1976.

Lovell, Mary S. *The Churchills: In Love and War*. New York: W. W. Norton, 2011.

Luce, Clare Boothe. *Margin of Error: A Satirical Melodrama*. New York: Random House, 1940.

————. *The Women*. New York: Random House, 1937.

Lukacs, John. *Churchill: Visionary. Statesman. Historian*. New Haven, CT: Yale University Press, 2002.

————. *The Duel: The Eighty-Day Struggle between Churchill and Hitler*. New Haven, CT: Yale University Press, 2001.

————. *Five Days in London—May 1940*. New Haven, CT: Yale University Press, 1999.

Lysaght, Charles. *Brendan Bracken*. London: Allen Lane, 1979.

Maclean, Fitzroy. *Eastern Approaches*. New York: Penguin, 1949.

Maclean, Lady Veronica. *Past Forgetting: A Memoir of Heroes, Adventure and Love*. London: Review, 2002.

Macmillan, Harold. *The Blast of War, 1939–1945*. New York: Harper and Row, 1968.

Maier, Thomas. *The Kennedys: America's Emerald Kings*. New York: Basic Books, 2003.

Manchester, William. *The Death of a President*. New York, Harper and Row, 1967.

————. *The Last Lion: Winston Spencer Churchill: Alone, 1932–1940*. Boston: Little, Brown, 1988.

————. *The Last Lion: Winston Spencer Churchill: Visions of Glory, 1874–1932*. Boston: Little, Brown, 1983.

Manso, Peter. *Mailer: His Life and Times*. New York: Simon & Schuster, 1985.

Martin, Ralph G. *A Hero for Our Time: An Intimate Story of the Kennedy Years*. New York: Random House, 1984.

————. *Seeds of Destruction: Joe Kennedy and His Sons*. New York: G. P. Putnam, 1995.

Martin, Ralph G., and Ed Plaut. *Front Runner: Dark Horse*. New York: Doubleday, 1960.

Matthews, Chris. *Jack Kennedy: Elusive Hero*. New York: Simon & Schuster, 2012.

McCarthy, Joe. *The Remarkable Kennedys*. New York: Dial Press, 1960.

McCullough, David. *Truman*. New York: Simon & Schuster, 2003.

McTaggart, Lynne. *Kathleen Kennedy: Her Life and Times*. Garden City, NY: Dial Press, 1983.

Meacham, Jon. *Franklin and Winston: An Intimate Portrait of an Epic Friendship.* New York: Random House, 2003.

Miller, Russell, with Renate Miller. *Ten Days in May: The People's Story of VE Day.* London: Bloomsbury, 2011.

Mitchell, Arthur. *JFK and His Irish Heritage.* Dublin: Moytura Press, 1993.

Mitford, Deborah, Duchess of Devonshire. *Wait for Me! Memoirs.* New York: Farrar, Straus and Giroux, 2010.

Moffat, Jay, and Nancy Harvison Hooker, ed. *The Moffat Papers: Selections from the Diplomatic Journals of Jay Pierrepont Moffat, 1919–1943.* Cambridge, MA: Harvard University Press, 1956.

Moley, Raymond. *After Seven Years.* New York: Harper and Brothers, 1939.

Montague Browne, Anthony. *Long Sunset: Memoirs of Winston Churchill's Last Private Secretary.* London: Cassell Publishers, 1995.

Moran, Lord. *Churchill: Taken from the Diaries of Lord Moran: The Struggle for Survival, 1940–1965.* Boston: Houghton Mifflin, 1966.

Morin, Relman. *Dwight D. Eisenhower: A Gauge of Greatness.* New York: Simon & Schuster, 1969.

Morris, Sylvia Jukes. *Rage for Fame: The Ascent of Clare Boothe Luce.* New York: Random House, 1997.

Mosley, Leonard. *On Borrowed Time: How World War II Began.* New York: Random House, 1969.

Nasaw, David. *The Patriarch: The Remarkable Life and Turbulent Times of Joseph P. Kennedy.* New York: Penguin, 2012.

Nevins, Allan. *The Burden and the Glory.* New York: Harper and Row, 1964.

Newfield, Jack. *RFK: A Memoir.* New York: E. P. Dutton, 1969.

Nicolson, Nigel, ed. *The Harold Nicolson Diaries.* London: Orion Publishing, 2004.

Nixon, Richard. *Six Crises.* New York: Doubleday, 1962.

Nunnerley, David. *President Kennedy and Britain.* New York: St. Martin's Press, 1972.

O'Brien, Michael. *John F. Kennedy: A Biography.* New York: Macmillan, 2006.

O'Donnell, Kenneth P., and David F. Powers. *Johnny, We Hardly Knew Ye: Memoirs of John Fitzgerald Kennedy.* Boston: Little, Brown, 1970.

Ogden, Christopher. *Life of the Party: The Biography of Pamela Digby Churchill Hayward Harriman.* Boston: Little, Brown, 1994.

Okrent, Daniel. *Last Call: The Rise and Fall of Prohibition.* New York: Scribner, 2010.

Olson, Lynne. *Troublesome Young Men: The Rebels Who Brought Churchill to Power and Helped Save England.* New York: Farrar, Straus and Giroux, 2007.

Osborne, Robin. *Greece in the Making, 1200–479 BC.* New York: Routledge, 2009.

Page, Curtis Hidden. *British Poets of the Nineteenth Century.* Chicago: B. H. Sanborn, 1918.

Parmet, Herbert S. *Jack: The Struggles of John F. Kennedy.* New York: Doubleday, 1980.

Payn, Graham. *My Life with Noel Coward.* New York: Applause Books, 1996.

Pearson, John. *The Private Lives of Winston Churchill.* New York: Simon & Schuster, 1991.

Pelling, Henry. *Winston Churchill.* New York: Dutton, 1974.

Perret, Geoffrey. *Jack: A Life Like No Other.* New York: Random House, 2001.

Persico, Joseph E. *Roosevelt's Secret War: FDR and World War II Espionage.* New York: Random House, 2002.

Pizzitola, Louis. *Hearst Over Hollywood: Power, Passion, and Propaganda in the Movies.* New York: Columbia University Press, 2002.

Procter, Ben H. *William Randolph Hearst: Final Edition, 1911–1951.* New York: Oxford University Press, 2007.

Profumo, David. *Bringing the House Down: A Family Memoir.* London: John Murray, 2006.

Pryce-Jones, David, ed. *Evelyn Waugh and His World.* Boston: Little, Brown, 1973.

Ramsden, John. *Man of the Century: Winston Churchill and His Legend since 1945.* New York: Columbia University Press, 2002.

Reader's Digest Association. *Man of the Century: A Churchill Cavalcade.* Boston: Little, Brown, 1965.

Renehan, Edward Jr. *The Kennedys at War: 1937–1945*. New York: Doubleday, 2002.

Reston, James. *Deadline: A Memoir*. New York: Times Books, 1992.

Reynolds, David. *In Command of History: Churchill Fighting and Writing the Second World War*. New York: Basic Books, 2007.

Reynolds, Quentin. *A London Diary*. New York: Random House, 1941.

Roberts, Brian. *Randolph: A Study of Churchill's Son*. London: Hamish Hamilton, 1984.

Roosevelt, James. *My Parents: A Differing View*. Chicago: Playboy Press, 1976.

Rose, Norman. *Churchill: The Unruly Giant*. New York: Free Press, 1995.

Rowse, Alfred Leslie. *The Later Churchills*. New York: Macmillan, 1958.

Sachs, Jeffrey D. *To Move the World: JFK's Quest for Peace*. New York: Random House, 2013.

Safire, William. *Lend Me Your Ears: Great Speeches in History*. New York: W. W. Norton, 2004.

Sampson, Anthony. *Macmillan: A Study in Ambiguity*. London: Allen Lane/Penguin Press, 1967.

Sandys, Celia. *Chasing Churchill: The Travels of Winston Churchill*. New York: Carroll & Graf, 2003.

Schlesinger, Arthur M. Jr. *Jacqueline Kennedy: Historic Conversations on Life with John F. Kennedy, Based on 1964 Interviews with Arthur M. Schlesinger Jr*. New York: Hyperion, 2011.

———. *Journals: 1952–2000*. New York: Penguin, 2008.

———. *A Life in the Twentieth Century: Innocent Beginnings, 1917–1950*. Houghton Mifflin Harcourt, 2002.

———. *Robert Kennedy and His Times*. Boston: Houghton Mifflin, 1978.

———. *A Thousand Days: John F. Kennedy in the White House*. New York: Houghton Mifflin Harcourt, 2002.

Schwarz, Jordan A. *The Speculator: Bernard Baruch in Washington, 1917–1965*. Chapel Hill, NC: University of North Carolina Press, 1981.

Searls, Hank. *The Lost Prince: Young Joe, the Forgotten Kennedy*. New York: New American Library, 1969.

Seib, Philip. *Broadcasts from the Blitz: How Edward R. Murrow Helped Lead America into War*. Sterling, VA: Potomac Books, 2006.

Shakespeare, William. *Plays of William Shakespeare*. London: C. J. Rivington, 1826.

———. *Shakespeare's Dramatic Works*. London: J. Stockdale, 1790.

Shannon, William V. *The Heir Apparent: Robert Kennedy and the Struggle for Power*. New York: Macmillan, 1967.

Sheed, Wilfred. *Clare Boothe Luce*. New York: Dutton, 1982.

Sherrin, Ned. *Oxford Dictionary of Humorous Quotations*. New York: Oxford University Press, 2008.

Sherwood, Robert E. *Roosevelt and Hopkins: An Intimate History, Volume 1*. New York: Harper and Row, 1948.

Shiers, Jessie. *The Quotable Bitch: Women Who Tell It Like It Really Is*. Guilford, CT: Globe Pequot, 2007.

Shirer, William L. *Berlin Diary: The Journal of a Foreign Correspondent, 1934–1941*. New York: Alfred A. Knopf, 1941.

Smith, Amanda. *Hostage to Fortune: The Letters of Joseph P. Kennedy*. New York: Viking, 2001.

Smith, Jean Edward. *FDR*. New York: Random House, 2007.

Smith, Sally Bedell. *Reflected Glory: The Life of Pamela Churchill Harriman*. New York: Simon & Schuster, 1996.

Soames, Mary. *Clementine Churchill: The Biography of a Marriage*. London: Cassell, 1979.

———. *Clementine Churchill: The Biography of a Marriage*. New York: Houghton Mifflin Harcourt, 2003.

———. *A Daughter's Tale: The Memoir of Winston Churchill's Youngest Child*. New York: Random House, 2012.

———. *Speaking for Themselves: The Personal Letters of Winston and Clementine Churchill*. New York: Doubleday, 1998.

———. *Winston and Clementine: The Personal Letters of the Churchills*. New York: Houghton Mifflin, 1998.

Sorensen, Ted. *Kennedy*. New York: Harper and Row, 1965.

Sparks, Fred. *The $20,000,000 Honeymoon*. New York: Dell, 1970.

Sperber, Ann M. *Murrow: His Life and Times*. New York: Fordham University Press, 1986.

Stafford, David. *Churchill and the Secret Service*. London: Murray, 1997.

———. *Roosevelt and Churchill: Men of Secrets*. New York: Overlook Press, 2000.

Stannard, Martin. *Evelyn Waugh: The Later Years 1939–1966.* New York: W. W. Norton, 1992.

Stevenson, William. *A Man Called Intrepid.* New York: Harcourt, 1976.

Sulzberger, C. L. *The Last of the Giants.* New York, Macmillan, 1970.

———. *A Long Row of Candles: Memoirs and Diaries, 1934–1954.* New York: Macmillan, 1969.

Summers, Anthony, and Robbyn Swan. *Sinatra: The Life.* New York: Random House, 2006.

Swanson, Gloria. *Swanson on Swanson.* New York: Random House, 1980.

Swift, Will. *The Kennedys: Amidst the Gathering Storm.* New York: Smithsonian/HarperCollins, 2008.

Swint, Kerwin. *Dark Genius: The Influential Career of Legendary Political Operative and Fox News Founder Roger Ailes.* New York: Union Square Press, 2008.

Sykes, Christopher. *Nancy: The Life of Lady Astor.* London: Collins, 1972.

Taylor, A. J. P. *Beaverbrook.* New York: Simon & Schuster, 1972.

Taylor, Robert Lewis. *Winston Churchill: The Biography of a Great Man.* New York: Pocket Books, 1952.

Thomas, Evan. *Robert Kennedy: His Life.* New York: Simon & Schuster, 2002.

Tolstoy, Leo. *War and Peace.* New York: Thomas Cromwell, 1899.

Toye, Richard. *Churchill's Empire: The World That Made Him and the World He Made.* New York: Henry Holt, 2010.

Tubridy, Ryan. *JFK in Ireland: Four Days That Changed a President.* New York: HarperCollins, 2012.

Volkan, Vamik D., Norman Itzkowitz, and Andrew W. Dod. *Richard Nixon: A Psychobiography.* New York: Columbia University Press, 1997.

Wallace, David. *Lost Hollywood.* New York: Macmillan, 2001.

Waller, John H. *The Unseen War in Europe: Espionage and Conspiracy in the Second World War.* London: I. S. Tauris, 1996.

Waller, Maureen. *London 1945: Life in the Debris of War.* New York: Macmillan, 2005.

Waugh, Evelyn. *Brideshead Revisited: The Sacred and Profane Memories of Captain Charles Ryder, A Novel.* Boston: Little, Brown, 1945.

Weir, Ronald B. *The History of the Distillers Company, 1877–1939: Diver-*

sification and Growth in Whisky and Chemicals. New York: Oxford University Press, 1995.

Whalen, Richard J. *The Founding Father: The Story of Joseph P. Kennedy.* New York: New American Library, 1964.

White, Theodore H. *The Making of the President 1960.* New York: Atheneum, 1961.

Whitman, Alden. *Come to Judgment.* New York: Penguin Books, 1981.

Widmer, Ted. *Listening In: The Secret White House Recordings of John F. Kennedy.* New York: Hyperion, 2002.

Wills, Garry. *The Kennedy Imprisonment: A Meditation on Power.* Boston: Little, Brown, 1985.

Winant, John Gilbert. *Letter from Grosvenor Square: An Account of a Stewardship.* Boston: Houghton Mifflin, 1947.

Windsor, Duke of, H.R.H. Edward. *A King's Story: The Memoirs of The Duke of Windsor.* New York: G.P. Putnam's Sons, 1951.

BYLINED ARTICLES IN PERIODICALS AND NEWSPAPERS

Associated Press. "Churchill Confidence Vote Today." *Schenectady* (NY) *Gazette,* January 29, 1942.

Associated Press. "Randolph Churchill's Biography of Father Acclaimed." *Sarasota* (FL) *Herald Tribune,* November 28, 1966.

Auberjonois, Fernand. "The European Diary: Churchills' Fate Compared to Kennedys.'" *Toledo Blade,* June 10, 1968.

Baker, Russell. "'Great Americans' View to Be First in Conceding Race to Stevenson." *New York Times,* August 17, 1956.

Berger, Meyer. "Churchill Arrives Beaming; Backs Pact, Cigar Tells Rest." *New York Times,* March 24, 1949.

Bishop, Jim. "Jack Trades Kid Gloves for Boxing Gloves." *Milwaukee Sentinel,* July 14, 1960.

Brenner, Marie. "To War in Silk Stockings." *Vanity Fair,* November 11, 2011.

Buchwald, Art. "A Man with Humor" (syndicated column). (Charlestown, SC) *News and Courier,* November 28, 1963.

Chamberlain, John. "Books of the Times." *New York Times,* October 11, 1933.

Childs, Marquis. "Churchill Confident of Winning." *Miami News,* July 4, 1945.

Churchill, Randolph. "Ambassador Brings Vital Speech." *Evening Standard,* March 2, 1938.

———. "The Churchill Memoirs: Documents Discussing the Crisis." *New York Times,* October 17, 1948.

Churchill, Randolph S. "How I Mean to Win Success." *Daily Dispatch,* August 1, 1932.

———. "Letters from Evelyn Waugh." *Encounter,* July 1968.

———. "The Myth of Munich." *Time,* June 9, 1952.

Cooper, Lady Diana. "The Lion's Heart." *The Atlantic,* March 1965.

Cornell, Douglas B., and Associated Press. "Churchill Given U.S. Citizenship in Unique Honor." (Schenectady, NY) *Daily Gazette,* April 10, 1963.

Cullen, Kevin. "Finding Her Way in the Clan." *Boston Globe,* May 13, 2007.

Curtis, Charlotte. "Janet Jennings Auchincloss Presented in Newport." *New York Times,* August 18, 1963.

Dallek, Robert. "Untold Story of the Bay of Pigs." *Newsweek,* August 14, 2011.

Daniel, Raymond. "Son of Churchill Raps Beaverbrook." *New York Times,* November 20, 1952.

Douthat, Ross. "The Enduring Cult of Kennedy." *New York Times,* November 26, 2011.

Evans, Peter. "The Onassis Diamonds," *New York Social Diary,* June 25, 2008.

Geselbracht, Raymond H. "Harry Truman, Poker Player." *Prologue* 35, no. 1 (Spring 2003).

Gilmore, Eddy. "World Pauses to Honor Sir Winston Churchill At Momentous Funeral." Associated Press, *The Day,* January 30, 1965.

Gross, Michael. " 'Basically, I'm a Backroom Girl': Of Lovers, Husbands, Wealth and Power." *New York Times,* February 16, 1997.

———. "Mother of the Clinton Court." *New York,* January 18, 1993.

Grover, John, and Associated Press. "Lord Halifax Is Unusual." *Prescott Evening Courier,* January 13, 1941.

Halle, Kay. "Thrill of a Lifetime: White House Dinner." *Cleveland Plain Dealer*, November 18, 1961.

Hamill, Pete. "JFK: The Real Thing." *New York*, November 28, 1988.

Harris, Kenneth. "The Weight of Expectation." *New York Times*, August 31, 1997.

Hastings, Max. "Churchill Had Won the War." *Daily Mail*, August 27, 2009.

Irving, Clive. "The Shade of Churchill: Randolph in Retrospect." *Sunday Times*, June 1968.

Jones, Arthur. "Literary Scamp Evelyn Waugh." *Notre Dame* (Autumn 2003).

Kennedy, Jacqueline. "The Words JFK Loved Best." *Look*, November 17, 1964.

Kennedy, Joseph P. "The Churchill Memoirs." *New York Times*, September 26, 1948.

———. "The U.S. and the World." *Life*, March 18, 1946.

Kieran, James. "The 'Cabinet' Mr. Roosevelt Already Has." *New York Times*, November 20, 1932.

Koenig, Rhoda. "A Bathtub Odysseus." *New York*, June 16, 1986, p. 64.

Kuh, Frederick, and United Press. "Kennedy Winning British Hearts." *Bend-Bulletin* (OR), June 16, 1938.

Leary, David T. "Winston S. Churchill in California." *California History* (Winter 2001).

Lewis, Anthony. "British Shrine Honors Kennedy." *New York Times*, May 15, 1965.

Lyons, Leonard. "The Lyon's Den." *St. Petersburg Times*, September, 29, 1946.

Mahoney, Rosemary. "Powerful Attractions: Lady Jeanne Campbell." *New York Times Magazine*, December 30, 2007.

Mailer, Norman. "Superman Comes to the Supermarket." *Esquire*, November 1960.

Moynahan, Brian. "Guarding the Bulldog." *Sunday Times* (London), October 30, 2005.

Pearson, Drew. "Churchill Realizes an Old Dream in Conferences with Roosevelt." *St. Petersburg Times*, May 25, 1943.

————. "Merry-Go-Round: Tuesday Elections Barometer for JFK" (syndicated column). *St. Petersburg Times,* November 4, 1963.

Pegler, Westbrook. "American Jailed in Britain to Keep FDR Messages Secret." (Charleston, SC) *News and Courier,* April 18, 1955.

Picardie, Justine. "The Soames Saga." (London) *Telegraph,* June 6, 2010.

Prescott, Orville. "Books of the Times." *New York Times,* March 3, 1950.

Raidy, William A. "Richard Burton Returns to 'Camelot.'" *New York Times* News Service, June 27, 1980.

Reston, James. "Capital Impressed: Capital Is Moved by London Scenes." *New York Times,* January 31, 1965.

Schlesinger, Arthur M. Jr. "The First Close Portrait of John Kennedy." *Life,* July 16, 1965.

Sheppard, R. Z. "Books: An Establishment of One." *Time,* October 17, 1977.

Sidey, Hugh. "The President's Voracious Reading Habits." *Life,* March 17, 1961.

Stinnett, Jack. "Envoy Typical of 1941 Spirit." Associated Press, February 15, 1941.

Sullivan, Ed. "Little Old New York." *Pittsburgh Press,* September 25, 1953.

Thomas, Robert McG. Jr. "Kay Halle, 93, an Intimate of Century's Giants." *New York Times,* August 24, 1997.

Trumbull, Stephen, and David Kraslow. "Convicted Embassy Official Reported Smearing Kennedy." *Charlotte Observer,* April 9, 1961.

Vickers, Hugo. "Obituary: John Spencer Churchill." *Independent,* July 9, 1992.

Warrick, Pamela. "This Girl Just Wanted to Have Fun." *Los Angeles Times,* November 4, 1996.

Waugh, Evelyn. "Commando Raid on Bardia." *Life,* November 17, 1941.

White, William S. "Republicans Propose Churchill as Pearl Harbor Inquiry Witness." *New York Times,* January 18, 1946.

Wilson, Earl. "Burton, as 'Hamlet,' Had Churchill as Prompter." *Milwaukee Sentinel,* September 6, 1967.

Woodward, Kathleen. "The Incredible Mr. Winston Churchill." *New York Times,* April 5, 1931.

Wright, James L. "Joe Kennedy Sits in Inner Circle of Roosevelt Campaign Train." *Boston Globe*, September 25, 1932.

UNBYLINED MATERIAL

"At Sea: Angry Athenians." *Time*, September 28, 1939.

"B.M.T. Stockholders at Peace with Dahl." *New York Times*, July 16, 1932.

"Business: Four Men & One." *Time*, July 9, 1934.

"Business: Personnel." *Time*, August 1, 1932.

"A Chip Off the Old Block." *New York Times*, February 8, 1935.

"Churchill Discovers We Export Liquors." *New York Times*, August 5, 1932.

"Churchill Gives Time to Queries: Young Journalists Fire Barrage at Son of Statesman." *Spokesman-Review*, February 15, 1947.

"Churchill Hits Drys; Tells British Brewers That Prohibition Leads to Corruption." *New York Times*, March 16, 1926.

"Churchill on Lea." *Newburgh* (NY) *Evening News*, December 6, 1961.

"Churchill Rebukes His Son: Incident in House of Commons." *Indian Express*, June 14, 1945.

"Churchill's American Ancestors." *Life*, February 27, 1950.

"Churchill's Muse Pursued by Son." *New York Times*, November 27, 1966.

"Demand Facts on War Plans, Says Kennedy." INS, *Milwaukee News-Sentinel*, May 25, 1941.

"Democrats' Outlay Less Than a Million." *New York Times*, November 1, 1932.

"The Dublin Murder." *Quebec Saturday Budget*, May 13, 1882.

"Flood of Liquor from Abroad Seen." *New York Times*, July 21, 1933.

"Freedom of Communications: The Speeches, Remarks, Press Conferences, and Statements of Senator John F. Kennedy, Aug. 1 through Nov. 7, 1960." U.S. Government Printing Office, 1961.

"Germany: Herzogin von Windsor." *Time*, November 1, 1937.

"Hartington-Kennedy Union Stunned Society." *Boston Globe*, May 14, 1948.

"Honey Fitz." *Evening Standard*, June 24, 1938.

"How Lieut. Churchill Escaped from Boers." *New York Times*, December 13, 1900.

"International: The Old Adam." *Time*, July 24, 1944.

"Joseph Kennedy Buys Bradley Hialeah Stock, Plans 'Little Activity.'" United Press, *Miami News*, May 15, 1943.

"Joseph Kennedy Jr. Begins Navy Training." United Press, (Wilmington, DE) *Sunday Morning Star*, July 13, 1941.

"Kathleen Kennedy." *Washington News*, May 14, 1948.

"Kennedy Denies Son Jim Helped Secure Job." Associated Press, *Sarasota Herald-Tribune*, June 29, 1938.

"Kennedy Labels Article a 'Lie.'" Associated Press, *Ludington Daily News*, June 29, 1938.

"Kent Denies the Intent to Aid the Axis; Took Papers 'to Inform Senate.'" *New York Times*, December 5, 1945.

"The Londoner's Diary: Fifty Thousand Pounds from Play." *Evening Standard*, May 18, 1938.

"Long Friendship with Churchill Began at '19 Peace Conference." *New York Times*, June 21, 1965.

"L[or]d Hartington Killed in France." (London) *Evening News*, September 18, 1944.

"'Man of Mystery' Here Recognized: J. P. Kennedy, Roosevelt Adviser, Visits Boston." *Boston Globe*, November 3, 1932.

"May Allow Rise in Liquor Imports." *New York Times*, September 24, 1933.

"The Merits of Speculation." *Time*, September 22, 1967.

"M.P. Seat Sought by Churchill's Son." *New York Times*, January 20, 1935.

"Munich: Kennedy v. Churchill." *Time*, July 28, 1952.

"National Affairs: The World and Democracy." *Time*, March 24, 1947.

"A Nazi Drops In: Plane Narrowly Misses Kennedy's Home." United Press, *Milwaukee Journal*, October 1, 1940.

"The Nine Kennedy Kids Delight Great Britain." *Life*, April 11, 1938.

"Obituaries: Lady Sarah Spencer-Churchill." *Daily Telegraph*, October 19, 2000.

"Only A-Bomb Is Holding Reds at Bay, Churchill Tells Boston Audience." United Press, *St. Petersburg Times*, April 1, 1949.

"Oxford Union 'Regrets Domination' by U.S. in Vote after Fiery Debate." *New York Times*, June 2, 1950.

"Pamela Digby Wed to Churchill's Son." *New York Times,* September 26, 1939.

Parliamentary Debates: Official Report, Volume 367. London: H.M. Stationery Office, 1941.

"Pearson and Allen's Washington Merry-Go-Round." *Lodi News-Sentinel,* January 9, 1942.

"The Pen Is Mightier." *New York Times,* October 16, 1953.

"The Presidency: Dad's Gotten Sick." *Time,* December 29, 1961.

"The Presidency: No Cause for Alarm?" *Time,* March 25, 1946.

"President's Son Off to Travel in Europe." *New York Times,* September 27, 1933.

"Randolph Churchill Fined $50 by Court in New Canaan for 'Reckless Driving.'" *New York Times,* December 10, 1946.

"Remembering Katherine Murphy Halle" (privately published brochure for Halle memorial).

"Roosevelt Hailed by Throngs Here." *New York Times,* September 27, 1933.

"Roosevelt Son Answers Claim on His Income." International News Service, *Milwaukee Sentinel,* August 12, 1938.

"Sarah Churchill's Romance Not Yet Described as Such." Associated Press, September 22, 1936.

"Secrecy at Fore River." *Boston Transcript,* May 31, 1915.

"A Shadow Hung over Their Happiness." *Washington Times-Herald,* May 14, 1949.

"Sinclair, Day Silent When Liberty Denied." *Miami News,* September 1929, p. 6.

"Sinclair's Pal Enters Prison." Associated Press, *Youngstown Vindicator,* June 25, 1929.

"Society: The Big Weekend." *Time,* August 30, 1963.

"Son of Churchill Is Here to Lecture." *New York Times,* October 8, 1930.

"Stalin Pictured as Peace Power: Joseph P. Kennedy Urges Smaller Navy." Associated Press, *Toledo Blade,* May 23, 1944.

"State Department Explains Case of Tyler Kent, Jailed for Spying." *New York Times,* September 3, 1944.

"The Stormy Churchills: National Government Attacked." London dispatch in the *West Australian,* February 7, 1935.

"A Troubled Nation Weighs Its Future." *Life,* January 8, 1951.

"Winston Churchill: He Inspires an Empire in Its Hour of Need." *Life,* January 27, 1941.

"Young Churchill Impresses Oxford Union Using Father's Rhetoric in Maiden Speech." *New York Times,* February 21, 1930.

"Young Churchill Says War Will End in 2 More Years." Associated Press, July 22, 1942.

Index

THOMAS MAIER is an award-winning author and investigative journalist for *Newsday* in New York. His most recent book, *Masters of Sex*—about the lives of researchers William Masters and Virginia Johnson—is the basis for a Showtime television series starring Michael Sheen and Lizzy Caplan. His other books include *The Kennedys: America's Emerald Kings*, a multi-generational history of the Kennedy family and the impact of their Irish-Catholic background on their lives, and *Dr. Spock: An American Life*, named a "Notable Book of the Year" in 1998 by the *New York Times* and the subject of a BBC and A&E Biography documentary. His 1994 book, *Newhouse: All the Glitter, Power and Glory of America's Richest Media Empire and the Secretive Man Behind It*, won the Frank Luther Mott Award by the National Honor Society in Journalism and Mass Communication as best media book of the year.

Maier joined *Newsday* in 1984, after working at the *Chicago Sun-Times*. He's won several top honors, including the national Society of Professional Journalists' top reporting prize twice, the National Headliners Award, the Worth Bingham Award, and New York Deadline Club. In 2002, he won the International Consortium of Investigative Journalists' top prize for a series about immigrant workplace deaths. At the Columbia University Graduate School of Journalism, he won the John M. Patterson Prize for television documentary making and later received the John McCloy Journalism Fellowship to Europe. He lives on Long Island, New York, with his wife, Joyce, and has three adult sons, Andrew, Taylor, and Reade.